SCHOOL ADMINISTRATION AND MANAGEMENT

SCHOOL ADMINISTRATION AND MANAGEMENT

S.K. Kochhar

Revised by

Payal Bhola Jain

M.A. (Education), B.Ed.

STERLING

STERLING PUBLISHERS (P) LTD.
Regd. Office: A1/256 Safdarjung Enclave, New Delhi-110029.
CIN: U22110DL1964PTC211907
Phone: +91 82877 98380 / +91 120-6251823
E-mail: mail@sterlingpublishers.in
www.sterlingpublishers.in

School Administration and Management

ISBN 978 81 207 4788 3
First Edition : 1970
Revised and Enlarged Edition : 2011
Reprint : 2012, 2013, 2014, 2016, 2018, 2019, 2020, 2021, 2022, 2024

Printed and Published by

Sterling Publishers Pvt. Ltd.,
Plot No. 13, Ecotech-III, Greater Noida - 201306, U. P. India

Publisher's Note

The book *Secondary School Administration* has been in print for the last forty years and stood the test of time. It has served the students, teachers and administrators to execute their duties well.

Due to the developments in education in India, the universities have revised their syllabi, and, therefore, this book has been updated and thoroughly revised. With the revision of the matter of the book, the title of the book has now been changed to School Administration and Management. The following new topics have been added to this edition:

- Educational Management
- Educational Administration in Independent India.
- Communication in Educational Administration.
- Management of School and Approaches of Management.
- The Present Pattern of Education.
- Educational Administration and Management: New Challenge of the Twenty First Century.
- Major Components of School Management.
- Social Aspects of School.
- Health Education
- Yoga Education

We are grateful to Ms. Payal Bhola Jain, the educationist and author of books on education, who has thoroughly revised and updated the book, giving it a new format.

We welcome all suggestions for improvement of the book which will be taken care of and acknowledged in the subsequent editions.

February 1, 2011 *The Publisher*

Contents

Unit II Major Components of School Management

Unit III School Plants

Unit IV Internal Organisation

Unit V Social Aspects of School

Unit VI Health Education

Unit I

Administration and Management

1

Educational Administration

"Administration means the overall determination of policies, the setting up of major objectives, the laying out of broad programmes; while management is essentially the executive function involving actual direction of human efforts. The former is largely determinative while the latter is essentially executive."

— ***Herman***

"Administration is the organisation and the use of men and materials to accomplish a purpose."

— ***Nigro***

"Administration is the process and agency which is responsible for the determination of the aims for which an organisation and its management are to strive, which establishes the broad policies under which they are to operate. Management is the process and agency which directs and guides the operation of organisation in the realising of established aims."

— ***Oliver Tead***

"Administration is a determinative function. Management, on the other hand, is the executive function, that is primarily concerned with carrying out broad policies laid down by the administration."

— ***Spreigal***

"Administration means business management of public affairs, government, etc."

— ***Oxford Dictionary***

1.1 Meaning and Definitions of the term Administration

It is usually accepted that the concept of educational administration derives its meaning and scope to a great extent from the concept of 'administration'. Therefore, we may first look at the meaning of this term.

The words business, public affairs, and government are used here to indicate the forms of organisation or an institution. Thus, "administration" involves two concepts, i.e., the "management" and the "organisation."

The example of a business is shop.

The example of institutions are hospitals, post office, school, etc. (or for e.g. Public Affairs).

The example of a government is the Janata Government, Congress Government, etc. The term "administration" is closely related to education. In education the term administration is closely related to such words as superintendence, supervision, planning, guidance, direction, organisation, control, evaluation, decision-making, and regulation.

Administration deals with the human individual. So it is an art and not a science because it cannot deal with human beings ruthlessly or mechanically, but should handle them tactfully, cautiously and skillfully.

1.2 Meaning of Educational Administration

Administration has been defined by Ordway Tead as, "a comprehensive effort to direct, guide and integrate associating human strivings which are focused towards some specific ends or aims." Educational administration is also a comprehensive effort intended to achieve some specific educational objectives and it deals with educational practices, whereas educational philosophy sets the goal and educational psychology explains the principles, educational administration tells the do-how of educational objectives and principles. It is, in fact, the dynamic side of education. Educational administration deals with educational institutions - right from the schools and colleges to the secretariat. It is concerned with both human and material resources. The human elements include—

• Children • Parents • Teachers, and • Other employees in general - university or board of education at local, state, and national levels of government.

On the material side there are:

• Money • Buildings and grounds • Equipments and instructional supplies

Beyond these two elements are ideas, laws, and regulations, community needs and so on. All of these have a bearing on the educational process. The 'integration' of these 'parts' into a 'whole' is educational administration.

1.3 Definitions of Educational Administration

Educational Administration has been defined variously. Some important definitions explaining this concept are given below:

1. According to Samuel Mathai, "Educational Administration presumably means the combined operation of a large number of persons whereby the whole fabric of education in the country is maintained in good working condition. An administrator is the person who has a part to play in running an institution. He is a responsible servant whose duties include both giving orders and carrying out orders."
2. According to the Concise Dictionary of Education (1982) "Administration includes management, organisation, operation, and supervision of an educational institution. Usually includes all institutional functions other than teaching."
3. Stephen J. Knezevich (1969) describes educational administration as "a process concerned with creating, maintaining, stimulating, and unifying the energies within an educational institution towards the realisation of predetermined objectives."
4. The International Encyclopedia of Higher Education (1977) by Asa defines it as, "Educational Administration, in general, is concerned with the management of state and local school systems and with local school attendance units. Identified with the executive branch of government, educational administration is treated usually as a field of study in itself and not as a part of public administration."

1.4 Difference between General Administration and Educational Administration

S. no.	General Administration	Educational Administration
1	General administration is not a human process in all the aspects.	Educational administration is a human process. It is controlled by various factors i.e., philosophical, sociological, historical and political factors.
2	General administration is rigid and static. It is not free and dynamic. It does not allow changes.	Educational administration cannot be too rigid and static. It must be dynamic. It allows scope for changes.
3	General administration has no scope for experimentation to look for a better procedure.	Educational administration is dynamic and free. There is scope for experimentation, trial and error.
4	General administration totally ignores the inner personality of an individual.	Educational administration is mainly concerned with the inner development of human personality. It is not satisfied unless a person's inner personality is refined both, morally and culturally.
5	General administration is concerned with the production and profit motive.	Educational administration has no profit motive.

Dr. S.M. Diwakar says, "The striking difference between the administration and that of other business lies in the fact that the former is a human process very much influenced and controlled by various factors such as the philosophical, psychological, sociological, historical and the political."

Educational administration is different from other types of administration in the sense that it concerns itself with the development of human personality. As such administration of education has to take into account life as a whole, ranging from childhood to manhood. It is thus a difficult task which educational administration undertakes.

1.5 The Process of Educational Administration

Gulick and Urwick have utilised the word POSDCORB to outline the functions of an administrator. This is based on Henri Fayol's work, *Industrial and General Administration*. An organisation of duties under these major headings is apropos to the section under discussion.

POSDCORB refers to the functional elements of :

(i) Planning
(ii) Organising
(iii) Staffing
(iv) Directing
(v) Coordinating
(vi) Reporting
(vii) Budgeting

1. **Planning:** The plan should be flexible. There should be enough scope of change to cater to any unforeseen situation. There are many variables: the priorities may change due to unforeseen circumstances; equipment and grants may not become available as expected; personnel may be posted out or proceed on leave. All these variables contribute to the non-implementation of decisions. The very existence of variables and uncertainties, make decision-making and planning a necessity.

2. **Organisation or Organising:** Organisation is the combination of necessary human effort, material equipments brought together in systematic and effective correlation to accomplish the desired results. In education, we organise:

   a. Human beings into schools, classes, committees, groups, school staff, the inspecting staff.
   b. Materials into buildings, furniture and equipment, libraries, laboratories, workshops, museums, and art galleries.
   c. Ideas and principles into school systems, curricular and co-curricular activities, time schedules, norms of achievement and the like.

Organisation is the primary factor in efficient management. According to J.B. Sears – "The term organisation is used widely to refer to any collection of persons, materials, procedures, ideas or facts so arranged and ordered that in each case the combination of parts makes a meaningful whole."

3. **Staffing:** The administrative duty of staffing refers to the entire personnel function of selection, assignment, training and providing and maintaining favourable working conditions. The administrator must have a thorough knowledge of the staff. He or she must select with care and ensure that each sub-division in the organisation has a competent leader and that each employee is assigned to the job where he can be of greatest service. Personnel should exude energy, initiative and loyalty. The duties for each position must be clearly outlined. All members of an organisation must be encouraged to utilise their own initiative. They should be rewarded fairly for their services. The mistakes and blunders of employees must be brought to their attention and dealt with accordingly. Vested interests of individual

employees must not be allowed to endanger the general interests of all. The conditions of work should be made as pleasant and as ideal as possible. Both the physical and social factors should be provided for. Services rendered by the individual increase as the conditions under which he works also improve.

4. **Directing:** Directing is a responsibility which falls to the administration as the leader. He or she must direct the operations of the organisation. This means distinct and precise decisions must be made and embodied in instructions which will ensure their completion. The administration must direct the work in an impersonal manner, should avoid getting involved in too many details, and should see that the organisation's purpose is fulfilled according to established principles. Executives have a duty to see that the quantity and quality of performance of each employee is maintained.

   The administrator is a leader. His or her success is determined by the ability to guide others successfully towards established goals. Individuals with a weak sense of responsibility and limited capability cannot perform this function successfully. Good administrators must be superior in determination, persistence, endurance and courage. They must clearly understand their organisation's purposes and keep them in mind as he guides and leads the way. Through direction it is essential that faith be created in the cooperative enterprise, in success, in achievement of personal ambitions, in integrity of the leadership provided and in the superiority of associated efforts.

5. **Coordination:** It is the process of harmonising in a uniform programme of educational service all the elements - the persons, materials and ideas, knowledge and principles so as to interweave them to achieve a common objective and a single effect. To carry on the difficult task of co-ordination properly, the administrator should have the administrative competence to see clearly (i) the relations among people (ii) the allocation of tasks and (iii) division of labour necessary for organisational achievement.

6. **Reporting:** Reporting and recording are also essential elements of administration. The educational administrator is answerable to parents, higher authorities, societies, etc. for whatever is done in educational institutions. It is, therefore, very important that a faithful record of all the events is maintained and reports are sent to concerned persons.

7. **Budgeting:** As the word implies, budgeting refers to financial planning and accounting. It is the duty of the administrator to allocate to various sub-divisions the general funds allotted to the organisation. This must be done in a manner which is equitable and just. In carrying out this function, he must keep the organisation's purposes in mind and the apportionment of the available money to those areas or projects which will help most in achieving these purposes. It also means controls must be established to ensure that certain limits will be observed, so-called "budget padding" will be kept to a minimum and complete integrity in the handling of all the budgetary aspects of the organisation will be maintained.

1.6 Purposes of Educational Administration

The main purpose of educational administration is to educate the youth, children and adults in a country like India.

Kandel, while writing about the purpose of educational administration says, "Educational administration - fundamentally the purpose of administration is to bring pupils and teachers under such conditions as will more successfully promote the end of education."

K.G. Saiyidain's says, "Educational administration is not only concerned with files, procedures and techniques or even tackling of human relations, but should endeavour to become a living bridge between ideas and tested scientific knowledge on the one hand and practical problems and situations on the other hand."

Sampurnananda says, "Educational administration should be such that it must make the teacher believe in his work, bring out the best of which he is capable, stimulate him to bigger and bigger effort, come to his rescue when his courage begins to fail."

The main purpose of educational administration is:

i. To frame well-defined policies and programmes for better teaching and learning process.
ii. To make use of appropriate materials for effective development of human qualities.
iii. To execute dynamically the programme and activities of the organisation so that it must achieve its objects.
iv. To assume the growth not only of children but also of adults.
v. To achieve the growth of personnel involved in the management of the organisation.
vi. Fulfilling the aims of education, to make a good citizen bring about order and discipline in the organisation.
vii. Economy in expenditure, spending less money and good results.
viii. Efficiency in execution.

1.7 Characteristics of Successful School Administration

There are some essential features in a good school administration:

(a) **Flexibility:** One of the essential characteristics of successful school administration is its flexible character. The administration should be dynamic, not static; it should provide enough scope for additions and alterations. The rules and regulations should act as a means to an end and not an end in themselves. Dead uniformity and mechanical efficiency is the very antithesis of good administration. The framework of administration should provide enough scope to the administrator to help needy students, and needy teachers, to change the time schedule to suit the weather or to meet any emergency. A word of caution here. Flexibility does not mean that the administration should be in a fluid condition without any specific norm or standard rules and regulations, creating confusion and chaos at every step. What is meant is a proper balance between rigidity and elasticity.

(b) **Practicability**: The school administration must not be a bundle of theoretical principles, but must provide practical measures to achieve desired objectives. Whatever objective is decided upon must be achievable and practicable and avoid frustration.

(c) **Efficiency:** Successful administration is that which results in maximum efficiency. This will be possible only when human and material resources are properly utilised – right man at the right place; right work at the right time; and where every activity and project is well-planned and well-executed.

(d) **Successful achievement of desired objectives:** Successful administration is one which leads to the successful achievement of desired objectives of education in a particular community, for example, healthy social living, development of good physical, social, moral, intellectual, and aesthetic qualities and healthy democratic living.

School administration must facilitate education. It exists for the pupil and its efficiency has to be measured by the extent to which it contributes to teaching and learning.

1.8 Importance of Administration

The study of administration is important for all individuals. The important reasons for such a study are listed here:

(1) Administration is important in social, economic, political, religious and educational affairs. It affects every person. The manners in which organisations are administered determine the course for men's lives. It affects their way of living, their goals, ambitions, happiness and their achievements.

(2) Knowledge of administration will make it possible for the individual to recognise unsound practices in administration. Such knowledge will help in restricting the exploitation of human resources and further efficient management and organisation.

(3) Knowledge of administration will aid some individuals to decide whether or not to select this particular field as a career. It will aid them in evaluating their own qualifications for such work and will help them to predict their own possibilities for success.

(4) Administration is fundamental in achieving joint purposes. Individuals are imbued with ideas which they want to see come to fruition. These ideas do not materialise unless there is planning and cooperative action. Knowledge of administration facilitates the achievement of such aims.

(5) Knowledge of administration furthers good human relations. Good administration implies cooperating with one another, being able to overlook personal shortcomings, getting along with people in order to obtain utmost work output and efficiency, and possessing the ability to instill the feeling of "one big happy family."

Objective Type Questions

Multiple Choice Questions (Tick ✓ the right option)

(1) The human elements include
- (a) Children
- (b) Parents
- (c) Teachers
- (d) All the above

(2) The administrator is a
- (a) Leader
- (b) Teacher
- (c) Supervisor
- (d) None of the above

(3) The main purpose of educational administration is to educate the
- (a) Youth
- (b) Children
- (c) Adults
- (d) All above

(4) "Administration means business management of public affairs, government, etc." This definition is given by:
- (a) Oxford dictionary
- (b) Sprgal
- (c) Oiver Tead
- (d) Nigro

Fill in the blanks

(1) Administration involves two concepts i.e. the ______________ and, the ______________. [Management, organisation]

(2) Administrator deals with the ______________. [human individual]

(3) ____________ administration is dynamic and free. [Educational]

(4) ____________ is the primary factor in efficient management. [Organisation]

Important Questions

1. Define Administration and explain the meaning and concept of Educational Administration.
2. Explain briefly the main purposes of Educational Administration.
3. Explain the difference between Educational and General Administration.
4. Explain the importance of Educational Administration.

2

Educational Management

2.1 Meaning and Definitions of the term Management

Management is universal in the modern industrial world. Every individual organisation requires the making of decisions, the coordination of activities, the handling of people, and the evaluation of performances directed towards group activities. Numerous managerial activities have their own particular approach to specific types of problems and are discussed under such headings as farm management, hospital management, production management, and others. All have elements in common.

What is Management?

Experts agree that management is a distinct type of activity different from all other types of human activities and all true managers in any field of human efforts perform the typical managerial functions irrespective of what they are managing. In other words, managerial functions have universal application.

Definitions

"Management is management of people, not things. It emphasises personal management."

— ***James***

"Management is the art and science of organising and directing human efforts applied to control the forces and utilise the materials of nature for the benefit of man."

— ***American Society of Mechanical Engineers***

"Management is an activity involving responsibility for getting things done through other people."

— ***Cuthbert Ross***

"Management is the art of knowing exactly what you want to do and seeing that they do it in the best and cheapest way."

— ***F W Taylor***

"Management is a continuous process through which members of an organisation seek to coordinate their activities and utilise their resources in order to fulfil the various tasks of the organisation as efficiently as possible."

— ***Hoyle E***

We should modify the definitions to make it more comprehensive. A revised definition may be – "A manager is a leader who gets things done by working with people and other resources in an organised manner and achieving the pre-planned requests through effective communication, coordination and motivation." Management is getting the employee to want to do his prescribed work as planned, willingly and with enthusiastic co-operation.

2.2 Meaning of Educational Management

The origin of the concept of educational management as a field of study may be traced back to the 1880's with the publication of the "Practical Handbook of School Management by Teachers" authored by Harding (1872).

The development of educational management as a field of study began in the United States in the early part of the 20th century. In the UK, the concept of educational management found its place in educational literature in the 1960's.

Educational management is a field of study and practice with the operation of educational organisations. There is no single, generally accepted definition of educational management because its development has drawn heavily on several more firmly established disciplines like economics, political science and sociology. In the words of Tony Bush (1986), "Most of the definitions of educational management which have been offered by writers are partial because they reflect the particular stance of the author. Those which attempt a broader approach are often bland."

Educational management has been defined in *International Dictionary of Education* (1978) by G.Terry, Page and J.B. Thomas as, "Theory and practice of the organisation and administration is of existing educational establishments and system."

Educational management is concerned with spelling out the educational objectives, planning process, staffing pattern, organisational process, budgeting, financing, directing activities and evaluating performance.

2.3 Definitions of Educational Management

Educational management has been defined variously. Some important definitions explaining this concept are given below:

1) "Educational management is a distinct process consisting of planning, organising, actuating and controlling, performed to determine and accomplish stated objectives by the use of human beings and other resources."

   – George R. Terry

2) "The management process is concerned with helping the members of an organisation to attain individual as well as organisational objectives within the changing environment of the organisation."

   – Gray H. L.

2.4 Scope of Management

The school's management has to perform different kinds of activities to achieve its goal and for providing good education to the pupils. Those activities which a school manager performs come under the scope of management. They may be described as follows:

I. The management prepares the school budget and secures revenues for financing the school.

II. It ensures that all school money is economically spent and every expenditure is accounted for.

III. It selects and purchases school sites.

IV. It is concerned with the selection, supervision and inspection of the teachers and other employees. It also pays the teachers and other employee and promotes them.

V. It arranges for in-service education and refresher courses for the teaching staff.

VI. It ensures cooperation with the staff and promotes in them *esprit de corps*.

VII. It selects and arranges the supply of textbooks.

VIII. It provides assistance in curriculum construction.

IX. It provides health services and medical supervision.

X. It makes provision for extracurricular activities.

XI. It takes school census, organises and makes proper use of them.

XII. It ensures the regular attendance of the pupils in school.

XIII. It arranges for the guidance of pupils.

XIV. It maintains school records and accounts.

Besides these activities there are many other activities which are of special nature and occur at special occasions. The management has to pay full attention to them as well. For example, the training for air-raid precautions at the time of war also come under the scope of the school's management. Every day there occur one or more unique problems which are faced exclusively by others and may not have been faced by one so far. An efficient manager is always prepared to tackle them.

2.5 Scope of Educational Management

Input	Process	Output
Students, teachers, parents, community, school-management committee, etc.	Planning	Aesthetic development of students.
Money-funds	Organising	Cultural development of students.
Machines, workshops, etc.	Staffing	Intellectual development of students.
Materials – furniture, stationery and craftwork.	Directing	Moral development of students.
Methods – teaching management evaluation.	Coordinating	Physical development of students.
	Reporting	Social development of students.
	Budgeting	Spiritual development of students; Vocational development of students.

Here, the 'human elements' include: (i) children (ii) parents (iii) teachers and (iv) other employees in general, university or boards of education at local, state and national levels of the government.

On the material side, there are: (i) money (ii) buildings and grounds, and (iii) equipment and instructional supplies.

Beyond these two elements are ideas, laws and regulations, community needs and so on. All of these have a bearing on the educational system. The 'integration' of these 'parts' into a 'whole' is educational management.

Thus, educational management process is the 'coordination' of:

Planning	Organising	Motivating	Controlling
Fixing goals and forecasting	Division of work	Effective leadership	Laying down standards
Collecting and comparing data	Assignment of tasks – staffing and training	Effective communication	Evaluation of performance
Selection of best alternative and decision-making	Delegation of authority and responsibility	Providing incentives	Ascertaining reasons of deviation
Establishing policies, procedures and programmes	Fixing of responsibilities	Integration of people and tasks	Corrective measures

2.6 Principles of Educational Management

Henri Fayol's 14 principles of management (1916) are given below:

(a) Division of work
(b) Parity of authority and responsibility
(c) Discipline
(d) Unity of command
(e) Unity of direction
(f) Subordination of individual interest to general interest
(g) Fair remuneration
(h) Centralisation and decentralisation
(i) Scalar chain of employees in ranks
(j) Order
(k) Equity (fair treatment)
(l) Stability of tenure of personnel
(m) Initiate (eagerness to work)
(n) *Esprit de Corps* (team spirit)

Management may be compared to a lens that brings everything about the educational system into focus for the community, faculty and students. If it is a poor lens, the image is fuzzy, obscure and no one in the educational system or the community gets a clear picture of the educational system. If it is a good lens, the educational system becomes a clear-cut and vivid projection of the ideals and ideas whose existence have been envisaged.

To sum up, educational management implies a comprehensive effort to direct, guide and integrate associating human strivings, which are focused towards some specific ends or aims set for the society.

Objective Type Questions

Multiple Choice Questions (Tick ✓ the right option)

(1) "Management is management of people, not things. It emphasises personal management". This definition is given by
  (a) James
  (b) Ross
  (c) Taylor
  (d) Hoyle

(2) Educational management is a distinct process consisting of
  (a) Planning
  (b) Organising
  (c) Actuating and controlling
  (d) All the above

Fill in the blanks

(1) Management is ________ in the modern industrial world. [universal]
(2) School Management selects and purchases ________. [school sites]
(3) Management may be compared to a ________. [lens]
(4) Managerial functions have ________ applications [universal]

Important Questions

1. What is Management? Give some definitions of Management.
2. Explain the meaning of Educational Management?
3. Give some definitions of Educational Management?
4. Explain briefly the scope of Management.
5. Explain the scope of Educational Management.
6. Describe the 14 principles of Educational Management.

3

Educational Administration in Independent India

3.1 Historical Background of Educational Administration

The shape of educational administration which we see today was started as, public administration. Indeed educational administration is a part of public administration. In spite of being a part of public administration, it is different: because it is related to schools and the school in itself is a specific institution. On the one hand, it keeps the culture or society safe and on the other, it regulates a mind by purifying it. At the same time, an institution or school acts as a means or instrument of social change. In this way, education becomes a social process. Its administration becomes different from other kinds of administration.

The term "administration" has been used very little in Latin. But in Roman literature, it has been used very much. In the Roman Age, the term "administration" was used like it is used today. But the definite shape and meaning of this term was determined by "Camarial thought" (a school of thought) developed in Germany and Austria. This school of thought attached the activities of persons (government servants) working in public services with administration. To take this theory ahead the following three elements played an important role:

(a) Price defined administration in the form of "Policy"

(b) Zinky explained administration as "Management"

(c) Bonn Justy described administration as "Economy"

Camarial thought made administration sequential by providing a scientific base to it. But in the later half of the 18th century, Alexander Hamilton tried to define administration. At the same time he made clear his concept. Hamilton was of the opinion that the functions of the government in a broader sense are related to all those activities which have to be done by body politics. The body politics has to perform legislative, executive and judiciary activities. But administration is related to the activities of the executive only. In this way, the specific and delimited meaning of administration becomes clear. For the aforesaid functions of government; both the terms administration and management were used. On attaching administration with government activities, public administration got recognition. In the 19th century, the field of public administration became very popular. Consequently a special branch of the study of government activities emerged.

In 1887 A.D., Woodrow Wilson got a book published, titled "*The Study of Administration*." This book defined administration especially in the form of government activities. With the result, in 1906, the National Institute of Public Administration was established in the United States of America. Woodrow Wilson related administration to government activities, policies of states and plans, etc. Thereafter, Frank Goodnow distinguished administration and politics as different activities. The arena of politics is related to those functions of the government that are related to the expression of ambition and formulation of policies. In this way, Woodrow Wilson and Frank Goodnow have explained administration with a different meaning. Wilson expressed, "What kind administration ought to be" and Goodnow explained, "What it is". In this way the former explained it as "Normative" and latter made it clear as "Descriptive."

In post World War I, there were more developments in the study of administration. In this period, three schools of thought developed as follows:

1. Mary Parker Follett prepared the background of the social philosophy of administration. In the development of this philosophy, she took contents from industry, scientific management, political science and public administration and provided a new spindle to administration.
2. Morris L. Cooke, Peter Drucker, etc. supposed administration as such a process in which art, science, and ethical values, are coordinated.
3. About 1930, new things entered into administration. Consequently, functions of administration were attached with executive leadership. It was taken for granted that there should be qualities of a leader in an administrator.

The qualities of a leader, such as, taking initiative, presence of mind, the attitude to go ahead with a team, to create interest and commitment in workers towards their work, etc. were expected in an administrator.

Luther, Gulick and Urwick took sociological and psychological elements to be important in the development of scientific administration. On the basis of these elements; an administrator can be farsighted in providing a scientific base to administration, and the complementary variables to these are enumerated below.

1. Efficiency Method
2. Management Science
3. Quantitative Decision-making

These variables are affecting the process of administration in a progressively greater manner. Due to the effect of modern science mechanisation is affecting the variables, with the result that administration is becoming more and more objective-based, skilled and successful. Now an administrator is becoming capable in taking decisions with no risks involved. Controlling, planning and other administrative processes are running more easily. Today, the use of computers in the development of classroom programmes, computer time-tables, computer assisted time-tables, and the use of computers in controlling and planning due to the use of automatic apparatuses; administration is becoming more and more scientific.

3.2 Need of Educational Administration after 2000 AD

The educational managers of India must change and use style that fits into the socio-cultural and political change taking place in India. The traditional bureaucratic style may not work in the changed climate of the country. The educational managers in India are, in fact, facing a very critical situation today. They find that no style, neither bureaucratic nor democratic, is really working in most schools and university situations. Let us examine the kind of situation that exists in the field of education in which leadership has to be exercised.

The whole field of education has been inundated with political activism during the past twenty years. There are students' unions, teachers' associations, class III and IV employees' unions, citizens' councils, and parents' associations everywhere, which are becoming increasingly active day by day. They are bringing on all sorts of desirable and undesirable pressures on the educational managers to influence their decision-making process. In order to deal with them a new kind of insight and approach is required. It is not easy to say what kind of managerial style will be suitable in these situations, but a trained and insightful manager who is flexible enough can immediately identify which style will work.

Since the private sector in the field of education has been substantially cut down or made powerless, local control centres in the institutions have been abolished and the principals are finding it difficult to take work from teachers and other employees. Even the higher level managers are failing to help them. In this situation they are faced with the problems of maintaining the standards of teaching and effectiveness of the institutions. This calls for new skills and wisdom on the part of the administrators. An entirely new kind of leadership is required.

Insufficient grants and inadequate financial support caused by several factors have posed other problems for them. They are short of equipments and other teaching-learning facilities such as inadequate building, shortage of classrooms, staff rooms, sports ground, laboratories, etc. This has resulted in teachers' alienation from work and has also become a de-motivating factor for students' learning. How to manage this situation is another challenging problem for the present day educational manager.

Due to loss of control and misinterpretation of freedom and liberty, people in all educational organisations have become much more self-conscious and rights-oriented. They fight for even the smallest of things. The outcome is that the college and university are faced with many kinds of conflicts. The managers are required to possess skills and insight into management of these conflicts. Organisational conflicts are going to stay with educational institutions in future also. The educational administrators of tomorrow therefore, must learn strategies to manage these conflicts.

Today, decision-making has become more complex in the field of education with the advent of democracy in India. Democratic tradition as part of society's culture encourages the participation of more and more of those who are concerned with the task. This situation makes it imperative for the educational managers to possess the skills in participatory decision-making.

The emergence of the new concepts and approaches in the field of education such as non-formal education, vocationalisation of education, etc. require still additional cognitive background and specific skills on the part of educational managers.

3.3 Educational Administration – A New Chapter

With independence in 1947, a new chapter opened in educational administration in India. There could be no room for central administration in education. The roles outlined above became out of tune with the massive demand for education. It was realised that in a vast country like India, with its immense local-diversities, education should largely be a responsibility of state governments and local authorities. Entry 11 of list II of the seventh schedule of the Constitution accordingly, makes education a state subject. However, this provision is subject to the provisions of entries 63, 64, 65 and 66 of list I and entry 25 of list III. These entries are:

List I - Union List: Out of 97 items included in the Union List, the following entries pertain to education:

Entry 13: Educational and cultural relations with foreign countries.

Entry 62: Institutions of national importance like National Library, the Indian Museum, the Imperial War Museum, the Victoria Memorial and the Indian War Memorial—wholly or partly financed by the centre and legally declared as an institution of national importance.

Entry 63: The institutions known at the commencement of the Constitution as the Banaras Hindu University, the Aligarh Muslim University and the Delhi University, or any other institution declared by Parliament, by law, to be an institution of national importance.

Entry 64: Institutions for scientific or technical education financed by the Government of India—wholly or partially and declared by the Parliament, by law, to be an institution of national importance; partly or wholly financed by the Government and legally declared as institutions of national importance.

Entry 65: Union agencies and institutions for:

a) Professional, vocational or technical training including the training of police officers;
b) The promotion of special studies or research and;
c) Scientific or technical assistance in the investigation or detection of crime.

Entry 66: Coordination and determination of standards in the institutions of higher educational and research.

Entry 67: Ancient historical monuments and records; archaeological sites and remains legally declared to be of national importance.

List II: State List: Out of 66 items in this list, two pertain to education. These are:

Entry 11: Entry 11 of the state list lays down that "Education including universities, subject to the provision of 63, 64, 65 and 66 of Union List and entry 25 of the concurrent list should be state subjects."

Entry 12: Entry 12 of the state jurisdiction; the libraries, museums and other similar institutions controlled or financed by the state as well as recent historical monuments and records (other than those declared to be of national importance).

List III: Concurrent List: Out of 47 items in this list the following six relate to education directly or indirectly:

Entry 20: Economic and social planning

Entry 25: Vocational and technical training

Entry 26: Legal, medical and other professions

Entry 27: Charities and charitable institutions

Entry 39: Newspaper, books and printing presses

Entry 40: Archaeological sites and remains other than those declared by parliament, and law to be of national importance

There are certain provisions of the Directive Principles of State Policy included in the Constitution which have a bearing on education.

(1) Primary Education: Article 45 of the Constitution provides that the state shall endeavour to provide within a period of ten years from the commencement of this Constitution, for free and compulsory education for all children until they complete the age of 14 years. The expression 'state' includes the Government of India, the State Government, and all local or other authorities within the territory of India or under the control of the Government of India.

Economic and social planning (Entry 20 of List III) is a concurrent responsibility of the centre and the states. Educational planning being an essential element of economic and social planning, the Government of India and the State Governments have to work together in preparing and implementing national plans for the reconstruction of education.

Article 282 of the Constitution also enables the Government of India to give grants-in-aid to the states to develop their educational programmes.

The Constitutional provisions quoted above envisage:

(a) Education is the main state responsibility;
(b) The Government of India has an indirect but significant responsibility for education;
(c) There has to be a healthy partnership between the Central and the State Government in the national task of educational reconstruction.

For the purpose of implementation, the educational programme is divided into three categories:

(1) State Programmes: These programmes are eligible for financial assistance from the centre but the responsibility for executing them largely rests with the states.

(2) **Centrally Sponsored Programmes:** These are drawn up at the instance or suggestion of the Central Ministry, and have an all India applicability. These are also implemented through the state government like the schemes in the state sector.

(3) **Central Schemes:** These are entirely worked out and implemented by the Central Ministry.

The programmes in each of the three categories are so formulated that they reinforce and supplement the programmes in the other categories.

The Present Position

At present, schools are managed by three agencies: government, local authorities and voluntary organisations.

The government institutions form only one-fifth of the total. The institutions conducted by the local authorities are the largest in number, a little less than half of the total and most of them are primary schools. The institutions run by private enterprises form about one-third of the total, and dominate pre-primary and post-primary education.

As far as finances are concerned, the state supports not only its own institutions but also the local authorities and voluntary organisations to a substantial extent. In fact, it may be said that the bulk of the expenditure on school education comes from the state funds and fees and that only a small and relatively less significant contribution is made by local authorities or private sources.

3.4 Education on the Concurrent List

The forty-second amendment, 1976, brought about drastic changes in the Indian Constitution. It put education, hitherto a state subject, in the concurrent list.

The amendment makes Central and State governments equal partners in framing educational policies. The Union becomes supreme over states in e-law enactment regarding education. The executive power is given to the Union to give direction to the states. The states have the powers limited to the extent that these do not impede or prejudice the exercise of the executive powers of the Union. The centre can implement policies in any state. National institutions like UGC, NCERT and national bodies like CABE have higher power and strength to shape the education of the country.

It was the 42nd amendment of the Constitution which finally brought education in the concurrent list.

Advantages

1. The National Educational Policy can be implemented properly and satisfactorily—The constitutional obligations in respect of free and compulsory education and education for women and weaker sections of the community can be more effectively discharged if major decisions are taken by the centre and the administration is left to the state.
2. Education and planning can be put in one category—hence progress in education can be ensured.
3. States can be given financial help.
4. Centre can provide effective leadership.
5. Uniformity of educational objects, strategy and standards is ensured.
6. Equalisation of resources and opportunities can be ensured.
7. Ensures implementation of recommendations of committees and commissions.
8. Keeps vigilance over the educational activities of the states.
9. Supervises control over financial expenditure through central assistance.
10. Promotes experiment and research in education.

Disadvantages

1. Undesirable centralisation.
2. The local needs will not get proper attention.

3. Unwarranted interference in educational administration.
4. Uniformity will crush the elements of diversity in our cultural pattern.
5. Centralisation of education will affect the self-confidence, initiative, resourcefulness and competence of the state governments and encourage dictatorial tendencies which are harmful for the development of education.
6. Bureaucracy will delay the implementation of important decisions made for the improvement of education.

The Government of India has so far been practicing methods of goodwill and cooperation with the various state governments in matters of education. Examples can be quoted: adoption of a national scheme of basic education, locating the new primary teacher training institutions in rural areas only, introduction of the scheme of multipurpose schools and changing the first degree course in general education to three years.

The above practice can continue even with concurrent states of education. In special cases however, a central legislation can be passed either to expedite the process or to bring about uniformity all over the country.

Objective Type Questions

Multiple Choice Questions (Tick ✔ the right option)

(1) Price defined administration in the form of
- (a) Policy
- (b) Management
- (c) Work
- (d) Economy

(2) Mary Mark Parker Follett prepared the background of the ________ philosophy of administration.
- (a) Political
- (b) Social
- (c) Economical
- (d) None of the above

(3) At present, schools are managed by
- (a) Government
- (b) Local authorities
- (c) Voluntary organisations
- (d) All of the above

(4) Bureaucracy will delay the implementation of important decisions made for the
- (a) Improvement of education
- (b) Improvement of standard
- (c) Improvement of culture
- (d) None of the above

Fill in the blanks

(1) Bonn Justy described administration as ______. [Economy]

(2) Educational administration becomes ________ from other kinds of administration. [different]

(3) ________ has become more complex in the field of education. [Decision making]

Important Questions

1. Describe the historical background of Educational Administration.
2. Write a note on the "Need of Educational Administration after 2000 AD"
3. Educational Administration – A New Chapter. Explain.
4. What is the meaning of Primary Education?
5. Briefly explain the advantages of education being in the Concurrent List.

4

Nature, Objectives and Scope of Educational Administration

4.1 Nature of Educational Administration

Society is dynamic. It is subject to rapid changes—cultural, economical, philosophical, political, scientific, social and technological. It is therefore, very essential that educational administration must conform to the changing situation and an educational administrator must be very dynamic.

Educational administration is the embodiment of the ideal and a spirit. It must enable different limbs of education enterprise to function harmoniously in happy coordination; blending themselves into a composite personality like the different rivulets which join together.

Oliver Tead gives a definition which explains not only the administration but also leads towards an understanding of the good or bad administration. Tead says—".....administration is conceived as the necessary activities of those individuals (executives) in an organisation who are charged with ordering, forwarding and facilitating the associated efforts of a group of individuals brought together to realise certain defined purposes."

It may be quite clear from the above that good administration involves associated efforts in realising the defined goals. For the associated efforts to be successful, there must be certain principles put forward which ought to be followed. It is true that there are no perfect principles, which may lead to complete successful administration. On the basis of experience of the people in different directions in different types of organisations, certain ways of approach, adoption of attitudes and methods of attack have evolved. However, to apply them in specific situations, "comprises an art requiring great skill; discernment and moral fortitude." It is on account of the requirement of such skills in administration that Tead calls administration an art.

Administration involves creativity. A good administration is one which exhibits human creativity at its best. Good administration is the product of associated performance which continues towards perfection. Thus, the four main ingredients of good administration may be cited as (i) Associated performance - human beings work in close collaboration. Their responsibilities are organised and there is sharing of responsibilities and duties; (ii) Organised purpose - human beings have well-defined purposes before them and through mutual sharing of responsibilities try to achieve them; (iii) Creativity - the path towards the achievement of purposes is not present. It is through a dynamic approach that the group proceeds towards its goals. The group makes efforts to increasingly improve its methods of approach as it gets more and more insight into the problem; and (iv) Achievement - the feeling of achievement marks the culmination point of good administration. But achievement, good administration and a quest for perfection are interlinked. A good administrator is not only satisfied when he follows a particular pattern, he achieves perfection within the limitations imposed by the environment and thus allows his creativity to play fully.

4.2 Objectives of Educational Administration

Objectives of educational administration derive their inspiration from the philosophy as contained in the Constitution of a country.

The following ladder explains how our way of life, objectives of education, contents of education and educational administration derive their strength from our Constitution which serves as a beacon in our endeavours.

The foremost objective of educational administration is the fulfilment of the educational goals as envisaged in the Constitution of a country. As Kandel has observed, "Fundamentally the purpose of educational administration is to bring pupils and teachers together under such conditions as will more successfully promote the end of education."

While describing the educational needs of India, Secondary Education Commission (1952-53) says that, "India has recently achieved its political freedom and has after careful consideration decided to transform itself into a secular democratic republic. This means the educational system must make its contribution to the development of habits, attitudes and qualities of character which will enable its citizens to bear worthily the responsibilities of democratic citizenship and to counteract all those fissiparous tendencies which hinder the emergence of a broad, national and secular outlook." The Education Commission (1964-66) also emphasised, "In this context special emphasis has to be laid on the development of values such as temper of mind, tolerance, respect for the culture of their national groups, etc., which will enable to adopt democracy not only as a form of government but also as a way of life." The objectives of educational administration must broadly be seen in the development of democratic values. If this point is lost sight of, then the very purpose of educational administration goes into oblivion.

In operational terms, the objectives of educational administration are to enable the right pupils to receive the right education from the right teachers under conditions which enable the pupils to profit best by their learning.

4.3 Scope of Educational Administration

The term educational administration, due to variations in usages, indicate different levels and types of application of management to educational problems and situations. In its

Our Constitution

↓

Way of Life

↓

Objectives of Education

↓

Contents of Education

↓

Objectives of Educational Administration

↓

Processes of Educational Administration

broadest sense, it applies to the full range of administrative control in education ranging from classroom operations, school management, administration of educational institutions and programmes in a locality to the control of educational policy of a nation as a whole. Educational administration, in a narrower sense, refers to the operations of the administrative bodies set-up for providing various educational services or facilities with regard to "the direction, control and management of those aspects of administration such as teacher and pupil, personnel, programme of studies, programme of activities, curricula, methods, instructional aids and guidance."

In educational administration, various categories of personnel are employed at different levels—some of them at leadership and decision-making, some at technical, and some at office and clerical positions. Some employees are engaged in operations related to general management of the system such as personnel, finance and procurement while other employees are responsible for operations related to the educational process such as teacher-education, curriculum development, planning, educational evaluation and the like.

The scope of educational administration is very vast. In includes within its scope the building up of personnel, appointment of men, running the administrative machine, seeking cooperation of people, informing and educating the public and finally, organising a sound system of planning based as much on the participation of people at each level as on the best technical, economic and statistical information available.

Educational administration includes everything regarding the functioning of educational institutions - securing the greatest benefit to the greatest number through an adoption of practical measures. It interprets and clarifies the functions and activities of an educational programme in fruitful relationships and harmonises their mutual action. It ensures sound planning, good direction and efficient execution.

Objective Type Questions

Multiple Choice Questions (Tick ✓ the right option)

(1) Administration involves
- (a) creativity
- (b) flexibility
- (c) perfection
- (d) None of the above

(2) The scope of educational administration is very
- (a) slow
- (b) vast
- (c) All the above
- (d) None of the above

Important Questions

1. Explain the nature and scope of Educational Administration.
2. What are the objectives of Educational Administration?
3. Why does the nature of Educational Administration change?

5

Institutional Planning

> "I have a thesis about the manner in which a revolution in Indian education can come about. I have no hope of carrying; a revolution from Delhi to the thousands of schools. That is impossible; partly because no revolution can be born in Delhi and partly because even if such a revolution is born there, it will die by the time it reaches the remotest village. But there is every possibility of carrying out a revolution from the village school to Delhi. In other words, if we get some creative thought at the centre, the chances of this creative thought reaching the remote school and doing something useful there are rare. But if teachers are trying to face their problems creatively and originally, some new ideas might be born which might travel up to Delhi and fertilise the whole field of education. If this faith has some justification, I believe it has, we have to find a method wherein freedom can be given to teachers who want to do something so that they can become effective."
>
> — ***J.P. Naik***

New thoughts can enter social life only when the education system of that society is dynamic. A dynamic education system is capable of adapting to time and situations that makes progress possible. In this context the Education Commission (1964-66) quotes: "If the education system does not renovate itself continuously that goes out of time and situations and prevents the progress, because that creates a quantitative and qualitative ditch in between its working system and objectives, and new demands of development and requisitions."

Thus for the reconstruction of society and development, education has to be reorganised and developed. Education can be agreeable to the needs and demands of society only when its schools or institutes bring change in themselves; quantitative and qualitative for the progress and development of self by institutes whose programmes or plans are qualitative ultimately made only to provide help in reconstruction and development of education. Thus educational planning should not be kept limited to the centre, notwithstanding that it should also be carried to the institute which is supposed to be a unit. In other words, we can fulfil the need of organisation and reconstruction of education widely by bringing planning to schools and institutes which form the units.

5.1 Meaning of Institutional Planning

Institutional Planning is the description of programmes constructed by an institution. This is the detailed description of those programmes and activities which are to be performed by the school or institute throughout the session. Prof. M.B. Buch has defined institutional planning – "An institutional plan is a set of programmes prepared by an institution on the basis of its felt needs and the knowledge of its resources available and likely to be available with a view to improve the school standards and practices and with a view to provide for the future development of the institution." This plan can be short-term or long-term. It is based on the principle of maximum utility of resources available with the school and community.

By foregoing discussion, the following points are threshed out:

1. Institutional planning is a means of accomplishing widespread targets of education.

2. For the construction of institutional planning, knowledge is necessary of human and physical resources.
3. Maximum utilisation of available resources which are available with the institution and community.
4. This plan may be of long or short-term or both.

5.2 Need and Essence of Institutional Planning

An institutional plan is a programme of development and improvement prepared by an educational institution on the basis of its needs and available resources. It is based on the principle of optimum utilisation of the resources available to the school. The idea of an institutional plan was first conceived by the Education Commission (1964-66). The Commission felt that there were a large number of programmes which an institution can undertake on the basis of human efforts.

A tree simultaneously grows above and below the ground; while the roots penetrate deep into the soil, the branches spread out with the same zeal. So it should be the five-tier process of educational planning in India - Institutional, Block, District, State and National tiers. All these tiers are interdependent and they should be complementary to the total educational development—both quantitatively and qualitatively.

Every institution has to plan its growth and development keeping in view the resources for a period of one year in the beginning and long range plans after gaining a sound footing. These plans would constitute the block and district five-year plans. The district plans on the other hand, would form the basis of the state plans. These state plans are to be the ingredients of the national plans. Therefore, institutional plans are not opposed to the national plans; rather they form the basis of the national plan. This is the process of decentralisation in accordance with the main spirit of our Constitution.

Essence of Institutional Plan

An institutional plan is not the plan prepared by one individual. It is the plan of all sections of the institution. Human resources are the greatest resources and they are more important than the material resources. Whatever exists must be utilised fully. There is always scope for improvement. Tomorrow must be better than today.

5.3 Requisites of an Institutional Plan

The following are the requisites of a good institutional plan:

I. The plan should be prepared on the needs of the school as identified by the school staff.
II. It should be based on the principle of optimum utilisation of the resources available within the school and the community.
III. It should be a cooperative venture of the community, management, school staff and the students.
IV. It should be goal-oriented.
V. It should be tailor-made for an institution—there cannot be a plan for all institutions.
VI. It should result in the establishment of democratic procedures within the school.
VII. An important outcome of institutional planning should be the establishment of a better rapport with the community.
VIII. It should aim at school improvements as well as school development.
IX. It should be continuously developing. An institutional plan should not be rigid; it should admit changes.
X. It should result in improvement and motivation on the part of teachers, students, community and the management.

5.4 Objectives of an Institutional Plan

Shri J.P. Naik has listed the following objectives of an institutional plan:

1. It aims at imparting realism and concreteness to educational planning.
2. It aims at providing the local community with an opportunity to join hands and improve the school.
3. It aims at shifting the emphasis from expenditure-orientation to that of proper utilisation of resources.
4. It aims at encouraging the teachers to do something creative and thus provides job satisfaction to them.
5. It aims at involving every teacher in the formulation and implementation of plans.

5.5 Motto of Institutional Planning

Shri J.P. Naik has observed, for institutional planning our motto should be 'Not high aim but failure is a crime.' I do not mind how small a plan a teacher prepares. Let somebody say, 'I want to improve the handwriting of the children,' I will be quite happy; what we decide to do is immaterial. But once you decide to do something, I will not accept any excuse for a failure. This is what we have to insist upon; doing things with dignity, with pride in oneself and with success. If we can follow this up, the institutional plan is put successfully on the ground.

5.6 Steps in the Preparation of an Institution Plan

The major steps in preparing a plan of improvement and development for a school are:

1. **Survey** the felt needs of the school, and resources that are likely to be available in the school and the community.
2. **Prepare plans and projects;** experimental or developmental, or both, taking into consideration the school needs and available resources and local, district, state, and national plans.
3. **Execute** plans within resources and with maximum effort.
4. **Evaluate** improvement and development programmes in terms of needs and resources and find out if the plan is successful. If yes, institutionalise the principles and projects. If not, investigate the causes, remove defects and bottlenecks and evaluate.

Remember, in institutional administration no planning is a crime but failure is a worse crime; the best efforts are required to be successful.

5.7 Areas of Improvement and Development Programme

Institutional plans may be prepared to effect improvement in the following areas:

(a) **Administration:** A number of projects can be taken up to improve administration; for instance, developing procedures to increase the effectiveness of staff meetings; improving supervision; improving principal-faculty relations; improving staff relations; democratic organisation of school, giving main responsibility to pupils.

(b) **School-Community relations:** Utilising community resources for better learning in different subjects; arranging talks by community members, etc.

(c) **Academic:** Improving reading habits through a planned use of library; improving internal examinations; reducing wastage and stagnation; assistance to physically and mentally challenged students; education of the gifted; use of bulletin board for improved teaching.

(d) **Co-curricular Activities:** Trying out different ways of organising co-curricular activities; better use of leisure by teachers as well as students; trying out new programmes in the school assembly; promoting student interests in school activities; developing hobbies among students and so on.

This is a mere list of suggestions. It should not be difficult to think of other areas where we could do a great deal even within the existing resources, however limited they may be.

5.8 Scope of an Institutional Plan

Prof. J.P. Naik has spelt out the scope of an institutional plan as follows:

1. *Improving the School Plan –*

- **(a)** Provisions for more amenities to pupils – sanitary facilities, drinking water, transport, midday meals, medical aids, uniform, etc.
- **(b)** More and better equipments in the school – reading rooms, library, teaching aids, laboratory, etc.
- **(c)** Maintenance of school buildings – voluntary labour, contributions, etc.

2. *Improvement of Instruction –*

- **(a)** Supervised study and special tuition facilities.
- **(b)** Visiting teachers from the teaching fraternity as well as from outside.
- **(c)** Support to teacher improvement programmes like in-service training, refresher courses, summer schools, etc.

3. *Extra-curricular Activities for Pupils –*

- **(a)** Social service projects.
- **(b)** Work experience through participation in community projects.
- **(c)** Athletics and games.
- **(d)** Literary activities.

4. *Community Programmes for the Schools –*

- **(a)** Youth related activities and services.
- **(b)** Adult education programme.
- **(c)** Literacy programmes.

5.9 Basic Elements involved in the Preparation of an Institutional Plan

1. Where are we? (Existing situation.)
2. Where do we want to go? (objectives)
3. Which is the road to reach the destination or to achieve the objectives?
4. What are the means for the realisation of the objectives of the plans?
5. Whose help is needed to achieve these objectives?
6. How much time is involved?
7. What can be the problems in the implementation of the plans?
8. How can these problems be overcome?
9. How to evaluate the achievement regarding fulfilment of the objectives?

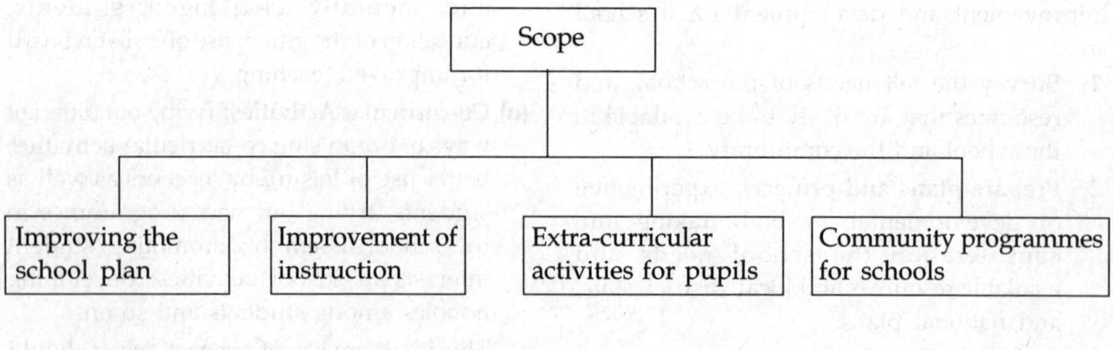

5.10 Institutional Planning and the Headmaster

It is the duty of the school headmaster to provide superior leadership to enable him to involve students, the faculty and the community in the preparation and implementation of an institutional plan. As planning is intended to introduce changes, he might have to face opposition by the teachers, who are threatened by the advent of changes. The headmaster must move cautiously.

He should look at the whole school as a system, assess the strengths and weaknesses of its staff members, and carefully create the feeling of readiness for change. His supervisory functions can be helpful in bringing about a sense of readiness among the teachers.

The headmaster should proceed in a planned step-wise manner for the preparation of an institutional plan.

The first step might be a series of individual conferences with the staff followed by group conferences. After this, there might be the staff meeting in which the headmaster and an outside expert like the D. E. O. or the extension worker may explain the whole purpose and the need for preparing an institutional plan. The headmaster should be very careful in evaluating the result of the first staff meeting.

The second step will be a discussion about the survey of the needs. Experts from outside, senior teachers and the headmaster himself will have to work with individual teachers and subject teacher groups to have a survey of the needs for improvement in various areas.

The third step will be survey of the resources available in the school and the community.

The fourth step will be the preparation of improvement programmes. Expert guidance and facilities should be provided to the teacher for the improvement programmes.

The fifth step will be the evaluation of the programmes after they have been implemented.

Special role of the Head of the school:

1. The head of the school should not expect the same performance from every teacher. He should appreciate limitations.
2. A school should not blindly follow the institutional plan of any other school. It should be clearly understood that every school has its own needs and resources.
3. The head should try to seek the maximum involvement of the school community.
4. The institutional plan should be prepared before the beginning of the school session.
5. In the preparation of the institutional plan, the head would seek the guidance of the officers of the education department/ department of public instructions.
6. It should be ensured that the institutional plan becomes an integral part of the overall planning.
7. The staff should be given adequate freedom.
8. The institutional plan should not be over ambitious. It must be based on feasibility.

5.11 Institutional Planning – A Challenge and an Opportunity

Shri J.P. Naik has observed, "The programme of institutional planning is both a challenge and an opportunity.

It is a challenge because of the several intricate and complex problems for which practical and realistic solutions will have to be found. It also requires that all the persons concerned – officers of the department, headmasters, parents and students – should be properly enthused. This is by no means, an easy task.

The programme is also an opportunity. It is probably the principal tool which will enable us to improve education in the present situation when financial resources are so scarce and the need to improve education is so urgent."

Institutional planning aims at placing the major responsibility of the improvement of the school on the school itself.

It reverses the normal trend followed today where the direction of planning is from top to bottom. Institutional planning will give the right direction to educational planning in the country, i.e., the upward direction from bottom to top.

Institutional planning introduces a scientific way for the improvement and development of education within the country.

5.12 Involvement of the Teachers

As a teacher is instrumental in any educational effort, his role is especially important in institutional planning. Education, they say, is essentially a stretching process. Naturally, teachers and students have to stretch themselves to their utmost, only then will good education be possible. It is good for the teacher to remember;

A poor teacher tells,
An average teacher explains,
A good teacher demonstrates,
And a great teacher inspires.

What is required to be planned at the teacher's level is the occupation of the students in a meaningful and challenging task. This is the challenge. How can it be met? We have to be committed persons, committed to knowledge, committed to social service, committed to hard work.

5.13 Role of the State Education Departments

They should not emphasise rigidity and uniformity, conversely, they should favour elasticity and dynamism and encourage creativity, freedom and experimentation on the part of institutions and teachers. It should be the responsibility of the departmental officers to guide the institutions in making and implementing their plans. The departmental officers will ensure that institutional plans of the educational institutions become a part and parcel of the state plans of education. Funds for the development and improvement of educational programmes of the school should be allocated on the basis of the institution's plans. Arbitrary decisions should be avoided. The needs and requirements of the institutions should be kept in view. The system of grant-in-aid should be reformed to encourage excellence. The state education departments should prepare guidelines for the formulation and implementation of institutional plans.

5.14 The Role of Management

In India, many institutions are under private management. They may be classified as:-

I. Religious organisations
II. The Registered trust boards
III. Private boards
IV. Certain individuals

A number of religious organisations like the Christian Missionary, the Arya Samaj, Ramakrishna Mission, Muslim *Wakfs* and the *Khalsa Diwan*, etc., are running private institutions. The atmosphere here is generally tinged with caste or religious prejudices but many of them are quite efficient and sound institutions. Even the institutions run by trust boards are meant to serve and promote the interest of certain sections of the society. This is all objectionable and against the directive and spirit of the Constitution. These institutions have their own managements - elected, selected or appointed. There are institutions like Jamia Milia Islamia in Delhi, Vanasthali in Rajasthan which are run by the teachers themselves. It may be noticed here that quite a number of institutions do not pay adequate salaries to the teachers and the institutions run by them are not well-equipped. This may be mostly for want of funds. The worst of it is some individuals are running these institutions for personal benefits.

Problems of Private Institutions

1. Financial problem; government aids are not adequate.
2. Difficulties in raising funds.

Remedies:

Nationalisation of schools or providing adequate funds.

Difficulties of the Government

(1) Popularity of good private institutions.

(2) Government's desire to involve the community in the educational enterprise.

(3) Faith of the people in religious and sectarian organisations and individuals.

(4) Limited resources of the government.

Recommendations of the Educational Commission

The Commission recommends that in spite of all deficiencies and limitations, the private institutions should be treated as an integral part of the common school system of public education. The good institutions should be developed as quality institutions by offering them more financial aid and granting them more freedom to manage their own affairs. The sub-standard schools should be given time and assistance to put their house in order. In case they fail to rise to the occasion they are to be dealt with firmly and either closed down or taken over by the government.

The Commission has recommended the abolition of stage up to standard 10th. It has also recommended that each private school should have managing committees consisting of the representatives of the management, the education department, and the teachers. It recommended staffing of the schools on the pattern of government or local authority schools.

5.15 Improvement of Granting Aids

The private institutions have done great service to the country. They have provided adequate number of schools at all stages of education. Reforms in their working are urgently needed and efforts should be directed towards them. Most of these recommendations have been accepted at the administrative level of the privately managed schools and colleges and they have improved comparatively.

In Karnataka, all the primary schools are taken over by the state government run by it. Except for these, the management is unwilling to hand over the institutions. In place of secondary schools and colleges, the state government has taken the responsibility of paying the staff all the schools, aided schools, and colleges.

Even in case of aided schools, there are other problems like building, playground, equipment, furniture, laboratory, etc. The Government is trying to look for solutions to these problems.

Objective Type Questions

Multiple Choice Questions (Tick ✓ the right option)

(1) The idea of an institutional plan was first conceived by the
- (a) Education commission 1964-66
- (b) Education commission 1986
- (c) Review committee 1992
- (d) None of the above

(2) The headmaster should proceed in a planned step wise manner for the preparation of an
- (a) Information
- (b) Institutional plan
- (c) All of the above
- (d) None of the above

Fill in the blanks

(1) In India, many institutions are under ________ Management. [Private]

(2) The educational commission has recommended the ______ of stage up to 10th standard. [abolition]

Important Questions

1. What is Institutional Planning? Why should the schools have Institutional Plans?
2. Explain the major steps involved in preparing Institutional Plans.
3. What are the problems faced by private managements in administering their schools?
4. Explain briefly the recommendations of the Education Commission for improving institutional administration.

6

The Educational Ladder

The educational structure ladder, as they call it, means the different stages of education connected with each other in an ascending order, each stage preparing for the next – higher level. There is a systematic order of the various stages. An ideal educational structure should have the following qualities:-

(i) There is no overlapping.

(ii) There are no gaps and lapses.

(iii) There is no duplication of effort.

(iv) It is uniform throughout the country to ensure smooth migration of the student community from one state to another.

6.1 History of Earlier Schools

The earlier schools in India were ungraded. The Brahmanic and Buddhistic schools and Maqtabs and Madrasas of the Muslims were supposed to accomplish limited-instruction. Any one who needed the instruction that these schools offered, attended them, no matter what his age might be. These were usually single teacher schools. The single teacher was every thing for the pupils in the school. Enrolments were usually small.

The education ladder in a systematic form was introduced in India by Wood's Despatch in 1854. This Despatch laid down the scheme of education from the elementary to the university stage. Before this Despatch, the structure of education presented a picture of a body without a head or a tail. The Great Despatch completed the picture by furnishing it with a head and a tail in the form of university education and the elementary education respectively. The entire educational programme constituted four stages – the primary, the middle, the high school, and the university. Although during the long years that followed, there have been changes here and there, but the main educational structure has remained almost the same.

6.2 Recommendations of Secondary Education Commission – 1955

The Secondary Education Commission, 1955 suggested some changes and adjustments. The recommendations were in brief as follows:-

(i) The first stage of the ladder should be 4 or 5 years or primary or junior basic stage;

(ii) The second stage will be middle or junior secondary/or senior basic stage- covering a period of 3 years;

(iii) The third – a higher secondary stage – which should cover a period of 4 years;

(iv) The fourth stage – the first degree of 3 year's duration.

In 1956, the Central Advisory Board urged speedy conversion of all the Secondary Schools to the new pattern.

In 1959, it recommended that high priority should be given to the conversion programme.

In 1962, in the Jaipur session, the Central Advisory Board considered the following memorandum of the Madras Government:

Elementary School	7 years
Secondary School	3 years
Junior College	1 year
First Degree Course	3 years
And total	15 years.

The board approved of the 15 years education scheme including 12 years of schooling. It laid emphasis on speeding up the Higher Secondary School pattern, and not making frequent changes in the number of years.

In 1963, the Central Advisory Board decided:

(i) Frequent changes in the educational pattern will be contrary to the aim of evolving a broadly uniform pattern.

(ii) It would be desirable to have 15 years of duration, including 12 years of schooling.

(iii) The states that can have 12 years of schooling instead of 11 years may do so. But in no case should the duration be 10 years for school education plus 3 years for college education.

In October 1963, the All India Council of Secondary Education outlined the desirable national pattern as under:

(i) A total schooling of 12 years to the students admitted at the age of 6;

(ii) At least 4 years of education at the higher secondary stage;

(iii) Two examinations during these 4 years – one after 2 years called higher secondary part I, and second at the end of 4 years, called part II.

(iv) The standard of higher secondary part II should approximate to the old intermediate standard, and make the student eligible for admission to the 3 year degree course, without undergoing pre-university course.

(v) The transition may take place in two stages. First stage addition of one year at the end of 10 year course. Second stage addition of another year at the end of 4 year course.

In 1963, the conference of State Education Ministers, Vice-Chancellors, and eminent educationists recommended:

(i) The 12 year plan of secondary education should continue;

(ii) The courses should be job-oriented;

(iii) The age of entry into university should be 17+;

(iv) The first degree course should be of 3 years duration.

The Sampurnanand Committee on Emotional Integration, 1962 mainly concerned as it was with the problem of emotional integration, laid due stress on evolving an effective uniform national policy to coordinate and maintain standards in the interest of emotional integration.

The Seventh Education Ministers Conference, 1964 noted the confusion in the educational pattern prevailing in the various states. It found a large variation in the pattern of school system of the country due to the non implementation of the reforms suggested from time to time by All India Bodies. The Conference made the following recommendations:-

(i) Schools in all states should confirm to a uniform school living standard;

(ii) The standard to be so achieved at the end of the secondary stage should be at least the Intermediate level of the former 4 year college with provision for appropriate diversified courses;

(iii) A 12 years course of schooling, before admission to the degree course, is the goal towards which a country must work, even though consideration of finance and man-power may not make it possible to implement such a scheme for all states in the immediate future;

(iv) The entire education at the secondary stage should be completed in the schools; classes such as the pre-university class started in the universities as a temporary measure, should be transferred to the schools as soon as possible in accordance with a phased programme;

(v) The new schools should be started in accordance with the accepted uniform pattern;

(vi) An appropriate machinery for determining the equivalence of standard at the school stage in order to facilitate the mobility of students from one state to another and for promoting uniformity in the school system, should be established by the Union Ministry of Education;

(vii) Every state should review the existing position and draw proposals for completing the proposed upgrading on the accepted lines by the end of the 4th plan as far as possible.

(viii) In order to reach the uniform school leaving standard, special assistance from the centre should be given to all states both for the programme of upgrading the schools and for the transfer of the pre-university class to the school stage.

6.3 Recommendations of the Indian Education Commissions – (1964-1966)

The Education Commission of India (1964-66) emphasised that there is a direct link between education, national development, and prosperity and stated that this can be possible only when the national system of education is properly organised both qualitatively and quantitatively. Realising that the total period of educational course and the duration of its different stages have a direct bearing on the quality of education imparted, it recommended a broadly uniform pattern of education and an extension in the total period of schooling to bring about a general rise in the standard of attainment. The Commission proposed the following educational structure:

One to three years of pre-school education.

(I) A primary stage of 7 to 8 years divided into–

(a) A lower primary stage of four or five years; and

(b) A higher primary stage of two or three years.

(II) A lower secondary stage of two or three years.

A higher secondary stage of two years of general or one to three years of vocational education.

A higher education stage having a course of three years or more for the first degree and followed by courses varying duration for the second or research degree. The Commission recommended that the age of admission to class I should ordinarily be not less than six years.

The first public examination should come at the end of first 10 years of schooling which would provide a course of general education without specialisation. The Commission recommended that no attempt should be made at specialisation until beyond class X.

The Commission visualised:

(i) The first ten years of schooling, covering a primary stage of seven or eight years and a lower secondary stage of three or two years, will provide a course of general education without specialisation.

(ii) The primary stage will be preceded, wherever possible, by pre-primary education of one to three years.

(iii) The age of admission to class I will ordinarily be not less than 6 years.

At the end of the primary stage, a proportion of students should step off the school system and enter working life (about 20%); some more should step off the stream of general education into different vocational courses whose duration may range from one to three years (20%); and the remaining should continue further in the stream of general education (60%).

The Commission also recommended that secondary school should be of two types–

(a) high school providing a 10 year course;

(b) higher secondary schools providing a course of 10 or 12 years.

Only the bigger and more efficient schools - about one fourth of the total - should be graded. The existing higher secondary schools should be downgraded if they do not deserve that status. A new higher secondary course, beginning in the class XI should be started. Classes XI and XII (and during the transition period class XI only) should provide specialised studies in different subjects. Where, however, existing higher secondary schools with integrated courses in classes IX, X and XI are running satisfactorily, the arrangements may continue until class XII is added.

There should be, as a rule, no integrated course of studies beginning with class IX. Classes IX and X should now form part of the first ten years of general education and classes XI and XII (and during transition period, class XI only) which should provide for specialised studies in different subjects at the higher secondary stage, should become an independent, self-contained unit like the sixth term in England.

The pre-university course should be transferred from universities and affiliated colleges to secondary schools by 1975-76 and the duration of the course should be increased to two years by 1985-86. The University Grants Commission should be responsible for effecting this change.

6.4 The Recommendations of the National Committee on 10+2+3, Educational Structure

The Government of India, Ministry of Education, and Social Welfare appointed a National Committee under the chairmanship of **Dr. P.D. Shukla**. The committee gave the following considerations for introducing a broadly uniform educational structure of 10+2+3 in all the states and Union Territories:

- **(i)** A broadly uniform pattern all over the country will strengthen national integration.
- **(ii)** The proposed structure will rationalise and strengthen school education.
- **(iii)** It will send more knowledgeable and mature students to the universities.
- **(iv)** It will reduce pressure for admission on universities and other centers of higher education.
- **(v)** It will provide an opportunity and a means to introduce appropriate vocationalisation at the higher secondary stage.
- **(vi)** It will provide an opportunity and a means to modernise and strengthen school and college curricula and to restructure them on mere scientific lines as well as to serve the social and economic needs of the adolescents and youth in a better manner.
- **(vii)** A broadly uniform pattern in all states and Union Territories will facilitate implementation of educational programmes, production of books and reading materials and teaching aids, training of teachers and their movements, reconstruction of syllabi, and improvement in examination practices.
- **(viii)** It will remove difficulties in the matters of education of children of the mobile population, which is continuously increasing in the country.
- **(ix)** It will help to solve educational problems of the minorities at least in two ways: (a) the minority language books produced in one area can be easily used in all other concerned areas, and (b) the schools adopting the minority languages as media of instruction in any state and Union Territories can be considered for affiliation to a Board of Secondary Education outside that State or Territory. The latter arrangement should reduce administrative costs and difficulties of some of the State Boards.
- **(x)** It will do away with the criticism that is generally levelled against the present higher secondary system that the students are required to take a decision at too early an age about the particular stream to be studied by them.
- **(xi)** It will contribute to raise the general standard and quality of education at all stages - school and university.

The Commission proposed a ten-year common undiversified lower secondary and a two-year higher secondary course, followed by a three-year degree course. It is argued that this merely combines the last year of the present secondary course and the existing Pre-University of First year. "This will have the startling effect" of lowering the standard of the general course equivalent to matriculation by one year, when the real need is for raising the standard. Secondly, as the upper secondary course examination is to be in the charge of another board, this will result in a needless multiplication of such bodies," says G.N. Acharya

6.5 Pre-Primary Education

Pre-primary education is of great significance to the physical, emotional, and intellectual development of children, especially those coming from unsatisfactorily home backgrounds. Modern researchers have shown that the years between three and ten are of the greatest importance for the healthy growth of the child.

James gave a public lecture and afterwards was accosted by an anxious mother with the question, "Dr. James, how soon can I begin the education of my child?"

"Madam", he asked, "How old is your child?"

"He is only a year old now", said the mother.

"Go home at once madam. Don't waste another minute!" said James.

Thus the modern trend is to emphasise pre-primary education to lay a healthy foundation for the future of the child.

Recommendations of the Indian Education for the Development of Pre-Primary Education

The Commission recommended that the pre-primary education should be developed on the following lines during the next twenty years:

(1) State level development centres for pre-primary education should be set up in each State Institute of Education; in addition, a district level centre should be set up in each district for the development, supervision, and guidance of pre-primary education in the area.

(2) Private enterprise should be made largely responsible for setting up and running pre-primary centers, the state assisting with grant-in-aid on the basis of equalisation.

(3) Experimentation in pre-primary education should be encouraged especially to devise less costly methods of expanding it. Children's play centers should be attached to as many primary schools as possible and should function as pre-school classes.

(4) The state should maintain State and District level play centers, train pre-primary teachers, look after research and preparation of literature on primary education, supervise and guide pre-primary schools and training institutions, assist private agencies with grant-in-aid and run model pre-primary schools.

(5) The programme of pre-primary schools should be flexible and consist of various types of play, manual, and learning activities accompanied by sensorial education.

6.6 Types of Nursery or Pre-Primary Schools

In India, there are a number of Nursery or Pre-Primary schools – the Kindergartens run by Convents or Missionary; Nursery schools; Montessori AMI schools affiliated to the Association Montessori International; Montessori schools that are strictly Montessorian; and the Pre-Basic schools.

1. **The Kindergartens run by Convents or Missionaries/Missions: -** These schools are essentially foreign in their culture and ways; and Christianity is of major importance to them. These are generally well-provided, spacious, and with healthy surroundings. Since their cost of education is rather high, only children of the upper socio-economic group usually join them. The medium of instruction is English. They do not necessarily use the Montessori or Froebelian apparatus.

2. **Nursery Schools: -** They cater mainly for the wealthier sections of the society. Being under the management of Indians, they are close to the students' own culture and ways. They serve a very useful purpose by

helping the total development of the child's personality.

3. **The AMI Montessori Schools: -** These schools are affiliated to the Association Montessori International and are a practical counterpart of the Montessori method as advocated by Montessori. There are about a dozen such schools in India. The full use of the Montessori apparatus – a complete set of which is required for every thirty children – is one of their main features. Only teachers trained under AMI are considered fully qualified.
4. **The Montessori School not Strictly Montessorian:-** These constitute the largest group among the pre-schools in India. Though called Montessori, they do not strictly adhere to the Montessori method; they freely make addition and alterations according to convenience and needs. Consequently, they are often biased towards one or the other of the K.G., the Nursery, or the Pre-Basic methods. Under competent and interested teachers, they seem highly efficient, presenting a happy adaptation of the Montessori method of varying Indian conditions.
5. **The Pre-Basic Schools: -** Though the Pre-Basic method is of Indian origin and is associated with the sanctity of Mahatma Gandhi's approval, purely Pre-Basic Schools are very few in India. These schools are inexpensive. In fact, the principle of inexpensiveness is carried to an extreme. Neither the necessary equipment and teaching-aids nor well-paid and fully satisfied teachers are there. The aims before these schools are lofty, namely child development and social regeneration. But how can anything substantial be done without proper and enough equipment?
6. **The Privately-sponsored, Single Teacher, Single Room Pre-Schools: -** These schools are generally started by an individual, usually a woman, in a room of her own house, or elsewhere, with a few children taught by herself.

There is sufficient impetus to start such schools on account of the popular acceptance of the results of researches on child development. It has been established that early environments exercise a great influence on the child's development. The child's intellectual potential, it is recognised, will be developed better if an early environment is favourable than if it is not. The early years of a child's life are impressionable, plastic, and educationally potent. What is lost in these early years cannot be made up even by improved conditions in later life. The cost of later life is set in the very early years. So, to be fair to the future citizens, the society will have to ensure that such conditions prevail as will make it possible for parents, schools, and communities to deal justly with the very young. For this reason, the nursery school becomes important in the educational ladder.

6.7 Primary Education

Our Constitution (Article 45) provides that the State should strive to provide free and compulsory education for all children up to the age of 14 years. This was to have been achieved by 1960 but due to so many factors as, (i) lack of adequate resources; (ii) tremendous increase in population; (iii) resistance to the education of the girls; (iv) large number of children of the backward classes; (v) general poverty of the people; (vi) the illiteracy and apathy of parents, it was not possible to make adequate progress in Primary education and the Constitutional Directive has remained unfulfilled.

The provision of free and universal education for every child is an educational objective of the highest priority for various reasons:

(a) Social justice and democracy;

(b) For raising the competence for the average worker; and

(c) For increasing national productivity.

The Education Commission suggested the following programmes:

(1) Five years of good and effective education should be provided to all children by 1975-76.

(2) Seven years of such education should be provided by 1985-86.

(3) Emphasis should be laid on the reduction of wastage and stagnation. The objective should be to ensure that not less than 80 percent of the children that enter class I reach class VII in a period of seven years.

(4) Children who are not yet fourteen-years-old at the end of class VII and who do not wish to study further should be reinstated in the educational system till they complete 14 years of age but should be provided with short vocational courses of their choice.

(5) Each state and district should be required to prepare a perspective plan for the development of primary education in its area in the light of the targets stated above and its local conditions. It should be given full assistance to move forward at its best face, and care should be taken to see that the progress is not held up for want of financial resources.

The Commission suggested a three-pronged attack on the problem: -

(i) Universal Provision of Schools: The expansion of primary schools should be so planned that a lower primary school is available within a distance of about a mile from the home of every child. A higher primary school should be available within one to three miles from the home of every child.

(ii) Universal Enrolment: A programme of universal enrolment should be organised simultaneously with the emphasis on the following:

(1) The present heterogeneity of age in class I should be reduced and the bulk of students in this class should consist of children in the age group 5-6 or 6-7;

(2) A system of pre-registration should be introduced;

(3) The transfer rate of students from the end of the lower primary stage to the higher primary (which is now about 80 percent) should be raised to 100 percent by the end of the fifth plan.

(iii) Universality of Retention: The most important programme to be implemented during the next ten years is to improve the quality of primary education and to reduce stagnation and wastage to the minimum. The target should be to reduce stagnation and wastage by about half by 1976 and to almost eliminate by 1986.

(1) Stagnation and wastage are very high in class I and their reduction should be a major programme. Of the various measures to be adopted for the purpose, three are very important:

(a) Treating class I and II (and wherever possible even classes I-IV) as one integrated unit;

(b) Introducing a year of pre-school; and

(c) Adopting play-way technique in class I.

(2) Stagnation and wastage in other classes should be reduced by providing various forms of part-time education, by implementing a nation-wide programme of school improvement, and by an extensive programme of parental education.

(3) All children in the age group 11-14 not attending schools and who have not completed the primary stage of education and become functionally literate should be required to attend literacy classes for a period of at least one year. These classes should be organised in primary schools in a flexible manner to suit the convenience of the pupils.

(4) Similar facilities for part-time education should be provided for children who have completed the lower primary stage and who desire to study further.

Expansion of facilities at the primary stage and programmes of universal enrolment and retention should be accompanied by qualitative improvement. Attempts should be made to take the primary schools as close to the home of the child as possible, even if this implies the establishment of smaller and costlier institutions.

6.8 Types of Primary Schools

Primary Schools: In the primary schools, children between 6-14 years without the distinction of caste, creed or colour, are gathered together to share a common experience which carries them beyond the family group, and introduces them under the sympathetic guidance of a teacher, to that larger group of life which they will always be a part. Most states have enforced some sort of act of compulsory education. The aim is to liquidate the colossal illiteracy of India. Efforts are being made to open a primary school in every village or within a radius of five miles.

There are two kinds of primary schools - single teacher school and multiple teacher school. These schools have 4 or 5 classes.

6.9 Administration of Primary Education

There are two important objectives of the administration of primary education in India. According to Article 45 of the Constitution of India, achievement of the objectives of the universal primary education and on the standard of the universal education, the basic education is to be implemented in the form of Ideal Excellence or Model of the National Education.

According to the Constitution, the state shall endeavour to provide free and compulsory education to all the children within the period of ten years from the commencement of this Constitution. This education will be provided to them until they attain the age of fourteen years. In this way, under the provisions of the Constitution, the arrangements for free and compulsory education for all the children till 1960 was the responsibility of the state but this objective could not be achieved till now. According to the Annual Report of 1960-61, this programme was not possible to be completed within the defined period due to several social and economic reasons. Therefore, the term of the educationist appointed by the Planning Commission, suggested in their meeting held at Poona that till 1965-66, the immediate efforts should be made to arrange the education for all the children of the age group of 6-11 years. The Government of India accepted the suggestions and took steps to achieve this goal. But the speed, in spite of the efforts made by the government too, remained slow. On this the Government of India appointed the Education Commission in 1964. The Education Commission suggested that till 1975-76, for all the children of the age group of 6-11 years and till 1985-86 for all the children from class 6-8 the objective of free and compulsory education should be attained definitely.

Through the Education Policy of 1986, it was declared that the objective of the education providing to all the children of the age group of 6-11 years could be achieved till 1990. Along with, the goal was fixed for providing education to all those children of the age group of 11-14 years. But this goal could not be attained till today. The slow progress of the primary education is being shown through the following table:

Enrolment in Primary Class according to Sex (in Lakhs)						
Year	Primary Classes from I to V			Upper Primary Classes from 6 to 8		
000000000	Boys	Girls	Total	Boys	Girls	Total
1950-51	138.0	54.0	192.0	26.0	5.0	31.0
1960-61	236.0	114.0	350.0	51.0	16.0	67.0
1970-71	357.0	231.0	570.0	94.0	39.0	133.0
1980-81	453.0	285.0	738.0	139.0	68.0	207.0
1990-91	580.1	410.0	990.1	209.0	124.0	333.0
1993-94	618.0	463.9	1081.9	242.1	157.0	399.2

Till 1990-91 there were 41.4% girls in primary classes and 37.4% in upper primary classes, out of the total enrolment. These facts tell us that we could not have provided 50% of free and compulsory education up to this level to the girls till today.

Under the 7th Five Year Plan, the accent was laid for achieving the goal of Universal Elementary Education till 1990. But that goal could not be attained. Thus, under 8th Five Year Plan, the following targets were fixed for elementary education:

(A) Enrolment: Under the 8th Five Year Plan, the accent has been laid down on the following points for attaining the above goals:

(1) For achieving the goal of elementary education, the expansion of formal system would be done. Along with it improvement would also be done.

(2) Open education system will be developed.

(3) Arrival of minimum learning level will be decentralised.

(4) School complexes will be developed.

(B) Reach:

(1) To make available primary school to all children at the distance of one kilometer around and to provide facility of non formal education to those who have left their studies in between such as boys who are working and girls who cannot go to school.

(2) At the level of upper primary to enhance the participation of girls in the present ratio from 1:4 to 1:2 in the form of pre-condition for additional opportunities from primary school to upper primary school.

(C) Retention for Continuing Studies:

(1) To reduce the present rate of the children who have left their studies in classes 1-5 and 6-8 to 20% and 40% from 45% and 60% respectively.

(2) Operation Blackboard is also to be increased to the level of upper primary and the school facilities are to be expanded.

LEVEL	Till 1997 Total Enrolment	Till 1997 Additional Enrolment	Till 1997 Additional Girls
Elementary Education	16.64 Crore	5.61 Crore 67%	3.76 Crore
(a) Primary (from 1 to 5)	10.53 Crore	2.02 Crore 82%	1.65 Crore
(b) Upper Primary (from 6 to 8)	6.11 Crore	3.59 Crore 59%	2.11 Crore

6.10 The Role of the Union Government in the Administration of Primary Education

The Union Government is a partner in the distinguished piece of work of making primary education universal and free. After achieving independence, a functional partnership was developed among the Union and State Governments in the reconstruction of education. For completing its liability in the field of primary education, the central government has made an All India Elementary Education Council under the Ministry of Education which advises the union government as an expert institution on the matter of expansion and development of primary or elementary education. In the present state of time in the Education Department, there are Joint Education Advisor and Director, etc.

The works done by the Central Government for extension of primary education can be divided in the following three categories: -

(i) **Programmes implemented by the Central Government:** - Programmes of these categories are planned and implemented entirely by the Union Government.

(ii) **Financing of the Programmes of State Governments by the Central Government:** - The state governments receive financial aids from the Central Government for their programmes which they formulate and implement.

(iii) **Programmes formulated by the Central Government and implemented by the State Government:** - Some of the programmes are formulated by the Central Government, but they are implemented through the agency of the state governments.

6.11 Secondary Education

The duration of the high school course is 3 years. The subjects taught at the middle stage are continued at high schools. There is a public examination S.S. L.C. at the end of the course in all states. It enables the students to have fundamental education necessary for choosing a career or entering the university. The examination is conducted by a special board established for the purpose in most of the states.

Objectives of Secondary Education

The following are the objectives of secondary education:

1) **To give the student such education as will make it possible for him to play the role of a useful citizen.** It gives him adequate alertness and capacity to further his own progress by the training that he has had.

2) **To provide a sufficiently comprehensive scope for those who finish successfully to further their education.** So there should be several avenues. It may lead to university education of the usual pattern or it may lead to technical and technological studies which will ultimately fit the candidates to various professions.

3) **To give an opportunity for students of diverse capacities and aptitudes to follow their logical inclinations after the compulsory stage of study.** Multipurpose schools should be set up to offer diverse courses of instruction. It can be concluded that Secondary Education does not primarily aim at fitting students to the universities. But this education has to be such that it gives a finishing touch at that stage so that the individual concerned may be a useful citizen of the society; gives him the wherewithal for a useful existence or gives an attitude for climbing up the ladder of education.

The Commission (1964-66) recommended the following enrolment policy:

1) The overall enrolments in secondary education should be broadly governed by the need for trained manpower.

2) It is essential to vocationalise secondary education and to work toward a target wherein about 20% of the enrolments at the lower secondary stage and about 50%

of those at higher secondary stage would be in vocational education.

3) There should be an emphasis on equalisation of opportunities in secondary education, and from this point of view, a large programme of scholarships should be developed at this stage. Efforts are also needed to reduce the large imbalances now seen in the expansion of secondary education in the different parts of this country and to spread secondary education among girls, scheduled castes, and scheduled tribes.

4) In identifying the children to be assisted in studying further at the secondary stage, 'ability' should not be understood in the narrow traditional sense to mean merely intellectual competence but the concept should be broadened to include all types of abilities.

Earnest efforts should be made to identify and develop talents.

The Commission suggested the following for the **expansion of Secondary Education:**

1) Enrolment in secondary education should be regulated during the next 20 years by (a) proper planning of the location of Secondary Schools; (b) maintaining adequate standards and to that end by determining the enrolment in terms of facilities available, and (c) selecting the best students.

2) A development plan for secondary education should be prepared for each district and implemented in a period of ten years. All new institutions should satisfy essential standards and existing institutions should be raised to the minimum level.

3) The best students should be selected for admission into Secondary schools, through a process of self selection at the lower secondary stage and on the basis of external examination results and school records at the higher secondary school stage.

Vocationalising Secondary Education

1. The Commission recommended that secondary education should be vocationalised in a large measure and enrolments in vocational courses raised to 20% of the total enrolment at the lower secondary stage and 50% of total enrolment at the higher secondary stage by 1986.

2. A variety of part time and full time facilities in vocational should be available at both these stages to meet the needs of boys and girls in urban and rural areas. Special sections should be set up in the Education Departments to help young people who drop out after class VII or VIII to obtain training on a full time or part time basis and to be in overall charge of the organisation of these courses.

3. The Central Government should provide special grants to State Governments in the centrally sponsored sector for the vocationalisation of secondary education.

6.12 Types of Secondary Schools

1) The Secondary School: The Secondary School comprises two stages-Junior and Senior. The former is also called the middle school or Lower Secondary School; or, if it adopts the Basic System, it shall be called the Senior Basic School. The junior stage extends in most states over 3 years, whereas in a few states, 4 years. The senior stage, known as high school stage is spread over 3 or 4 years. But in some cases, where the middle school goes up to the 8th grade or class, the high school consists of the last two classes - 9th and 10th. The middle school is generally attached to the high school so that the 6th and 7th years of the secondary stage form one course. Quite often the middle school classes form the apex of the elementary school.

After the introduction of the reorganised pattern of secondary education in 1955, two other types of senior secondary or high schools have been coming up, viz. the higher secondary school and the multipurpose schools. The higher secondary school adds two more years of study in order to upgrade the standard of attainment of the school leavers. The pre-university course is transferred to the school.

Besides the upgrading of high into higher secondary schools, efforts are being made to provide in higher secondary schools diversified courses of study such as Science, Technology, Commerce, Agriculture, and Fine Arts. The aim is to meet the varying aptitudes, interests, and talents of pupils. Such higher secondary schools are called multilateral or multipurpose schools. The diversification into different streams begins at the age of 14 plus. In some states diversified courses of instruction have been introduced in the high schools without the accompanying upgrading.

Secondary school leavers can proceed to colleges, polytechnics, or vocational institutions such as Trade schools and Industrial schools. Those who wish to join professional colleges in Engineering, Medicine, Agriculture, and Commerce have at present to pass the pre-university, the professional or the intermediate courses.

2) **Middle Schools and Senior Basic Schools:** These cater to pupils of the age group 10 to 13. Although both these types of schools are a continuation of the primary or junior basic stage and cover a similar educational programme, they adopt different methods of approach and teaching. The curriculum of this stage includes Language and Literature, Social Studies, General Science, Mathematics, Citizenship Training, Art and Craft, Music, and Physical Education. The languages taught include the mother tongue or the regional language, English in most states, and the national language Hindi or some other Indian Language in areas where Hindi is also the regional language. The aim of instruction at this stage is to introduce the pupil in a general way to significant departments of human knowledge and activity.

3) **High School, Higher Secondary, and Multipurpose Schools:** This stage covers the age group 14 to 18. Although the trend is to convert all high schools into higher secondary schools yet there are, for the present, functioning side by side both high schools and higher secondary schools. The high schools curriculum framed on the basis of abilities and interests which have taken shape in the middle schools, enlarges, and enriches the general courses already covered. In most states, the course subjects are the same as in the previous stage i.e., Languages, Science, Mathematics, Social Studies, (or History and Geography), Arts and Crafts, Physical Education and Citizenship Training. Some states have not yet made Science a compulsory subject to study. But several states have made provisions for special courses in Mathematics and Science as optional.

The higher secondary Craft provides **(a)** to all pupils a common curriculum consisting of languages, General Science including Mathematics, Social Studies and a Craft **(b)** diversified courses of study in one of the seven groups, namely Humanities, Sciences, Technology, Commerce, Agriculture, Fine Arts, and Home Science. The last year of the middle Craft is generally exploratory stage when teachers are expected to discover the particular programme most suited to the pupil's abilities and interests. Crafts includes hand spinning and weaving, wood-work, metal-work, gardening, tailoring, needle work, and embroidery, leather work, clay modeling, and paper mache, workshop practice and printing technology. Each diversified course includes several interrelated subjects, out of which the pupil elects his group according to his tastes and interests.

India is committed to a democratic socialistic pattern. "Training for democracy postulates a balanced education in which social virtues, intellectual development and practical skill, all receive due consideration and the pattern of such an education must be envisaged on an all-India basis." It is now the main responsibility of the schools to prepare citizens who would have the knowledge, skills, and the values essential for the creation and stabilisation of this social order.

4) **Public Schools:** There are a number of public schools on the lines of those in advanced European countries. In these schools, mostly boys and girls of rich people get their schooling. These impart education up to the Senior Cambridge Certificate. Most up-to-date progressive methods are followed in these schools and education is imparted on European lines. While discussing the role of the Indian public schools in the democratic set-up of our country, the Secondary Education Commission acknowledged their contribution in these words: "There are greater opportunities in these schools (public) than in the majority of Secondary Schools for developing certain essential traits of character, including the qualities of leadership."

5) **Military Schools and Academies:** Ambitious and suitable adolescents are picked up in the impressionable days and then are given training for careers in the Army, Navy, and Air Force. These cadet recruits are given training for 3 to 4 years in different branches of the three wings. They are later absorbed therein.

6.13 Agriculture Education

1) **Manjri Type School**: In such type of schools, a farm of at least 150 acres is attached to each school. The students do all the work, including cooking, laundry and cleaning. The object is to make each school self-supporting on the products of the farm. The programme of studies, which covers two years, includes agriculture, animal husbandry, dairying, animal disease, horticulture, marketing, and village industry. These schools are primarily organised to prepare students for village leadership. Those who have gone through a Basic school and had some secondary examination but have not necessarily passed the Matriculation Examination are admitted to the Manjri School.

2) **Rural Institutes**: The rural institutes have been functioning since 1956-57 under the direction and supervision of the National Council of Rural Higher Education. Four courses are offered in these institutes:
   (i) 3-year diploma course in rural education;
   (ii) 2-year certificate course in Rural and Civil Engineering:
   (iii) 2-year certificate course in Agriculture Sciences;
   (iv) Preparatory course for Matriculates for entry into the diploma course.

The diploma course follows on after the Higher Secondary Examination, and the diploma is regarded as equivalent in standard to an ordinary degree at a university. Core subjects such as rural problems, the history of civilisation and regional languages, are also taught in these institutes.

6.14 Technical Education

Technical Education includes vocational, technical, and professional training. The Ministry of Labour and Employment is in charge of industrial training institutes, while the Ministry of Education is seeking to expand the provision of technical courses in multipurpose schools, private industry is also being urged to launch technical training programmes.

1) **Industrial Training Institutes or Centres:-** The period of training in the vocational trades is 12 months. The period in the technical trades is 2 years, of which the first 18 months are spent in the institute and the remaining 6 months in a factory or in an industrial plant. Technical trade schools admit only high school students between the age group 16 to 25. But the vocational trade schools admit trainees of 14 years upwards, serving the same age group as the Secondary schools. Study up to the Matriculation stage is required for certain technical trades only. A certificate of proficiency is awarded to each trainee on the completion of the programme.

2) **Technical High School: -** Separate technical high schools have been established in Bombay State for teaching the elements of Mechanical and Electrical Engineering, and for providing a certain amount of workshop practice to students of the high school classes. Along with the technical subjects, the students also study certain core subjects such as regional languages, Hindi, Social Studies, and Science. In fact, these schools correspond to the technical streams of the multipurpose schools. They give a vocational bias but do not train the students for any specific vocation. Many of the students from these schools go on to a polytechnic or an Engineering College.

3) **Schools of Industry:-** Such schools provide craft training in weaving, carpentry, auto-mechanics, turning and printing. The programme is of 2 years duration. Students who have passed the middle school or its equivalent are admitted. The minimum age of admission is 15 years. Students who complete their training are considered semi-skilled. They can complete the training by apprenticing under a skilled worker.

4) **Junior Technical School: -** This is a scheme proposed by the Ministry of Scientific Research and Cultural Affairs. These schools are to be established in industrial centres and wherever possible attached to a polytechnic so as to share common instructional facilities. The course is of 3 years duration and is intended to provide vocational training opportunities in technical trades to secondary school-age boys of 14 to 17 years. The curriculum is to include a study of the Humanities and Languages, General Science and Mathematics, Elementary Mechanical Engineering, Drawing and Workshop training. Specific training is to be provided in turning, machining, fitting, smithing, tool-making, winding, sheet metal work, pattern-making, electrical work, motor mechanics, and other technical trades. Completion of the 3-year programme is expected to lead either to further vocational training at an industrial training centre or to further technical education in a polytechnic.

6.15 Commercial Education

1. **Commercial High School: -** These schools correspond to the commerce stream in the multipurpose school. The course includes Commerce and Bookkeeping, Type-writing and Shorthand, and prepares students for the Secondary School Certificate Examination. Then they will become eligible for entrance into a Commerce or Arts college.

2. **Government Commercial Diploma and Commercial Certificate Examination: -** Bombay State has established a Government Commercial Diploma and Government Commercial Certificate. They qualify for positions in government service. To be eligible for the Diploma examination,

a candidate should attend a recognised institution for 1 year if he is a Matriculate and for 2 years if he is a non-Matriculate. The examination covers English, Commercial Arithmetic, Elements of Book-keeping, Commercial Geography, Methods of Business and the subject elected from Shorthand, Accountancy, Typewriting, Indian Administration, Indian Banking, Insurance, Secretariat Practice, or Salesmanship. Commercial Certificate Examinations are usually taken by government servants and employees in commercial concerns.

6.16 Administration of Secondary Education

The development of secondary education in the country, in last two decades, has been rapid. The progress of this can be watched from the table given below:

Progress of the Secondary Education in Independent India
Enrolment according to Sex (in lakhs)

	Upper Primary (class 6-8)			High/Higher Secondary (class 9-12)		
Years	Boys	Girls	Total	Boys	Girls	Total
1950-51	26.0	5.0	31.0	13.0	2.0	15.0
1960-61	51.0	16.0	67.0	27.0	7.0	34.0
1970-71	94.0	39.0	133.0	57.0	19.0	76.0
1980-81	139.0	68.0	207.0	84.0	35.0	119.0
1990-91	209.0	124.0	333.0	140.0	69.0	209.0
1993-94	242.1	157.0	399.1	152.7	80.07	233.4

Situation of Secondary Schools and Teachers in Independent India

S.No.	Details	1950-51	1960-61	1970-71	1980-81	1993-94
1.	Upper Primary Schools	13,596	49,663	90,621	1,18,355	1,55,707
2.	High/Higher Secondary Inter College	7,416	17,329	37,051	51,624	88,411
3.	Teachers in Upper Primary School	86.0	345.0	638.0	851.0	1703.0
4.	Teachers in High/Higher Secondary Inter College	127.0	296.0	629.0	912.0	1405.0

6.17 University Education

The Government of India assumed responsibility for university education in 1855, and its association with the subject has continued unbroken to this date. The first universities were established under Acts of Central Legislature in 1897. Even when education was provincialised in 1870, the authority to legislate for universities continued to vest in the Centre. Under the Central Acts, the University of Punjab was established in 1882, and that of Allahabad in 1887. Between 1915 and 1922 Central Universities of Aligarh, Banaras, and Delhi were established. At this time, there are 94 universities in our country.

6.18 Objectives of the Universities

The objectives of the universities, as stated by the Indian Education Commission are:

1. To seek and cultivate new knowledge, to engage vigorously and fearlessly in the pursuit of truth, and to interpret old knowledge and beliefs in the light of new needs and discoveries.
2. To provide right kind of leadership in all walks of life, to identify gifted youth and help them develop their potential to the full by cultivating physical fitness, developing the powers of the mind and cultivating right-interests, attitudes, and moral and intellectual values.
3. To provide society with competent men and women trained in agriculture, arts, medicine, science, and technology and various other professions who will also be cultivated individuals, imbued with a sense of social purpose.
4. To strive to promote equality and social justice and to reduce social and cultural difference through diffusion of education.
5. To foster in the teachers and students and through them in society generally the attitudes and values needed for developing the 'good life' in individual and society.
6. In addition to these broad functions of the universities, Indian universities have to shoulder some special responsibilities in the present state of our social and educational development.
7. They must learn to serve as the conscience of the nation; and from this point of view they should encourage individuality, variety, and dissent, within a climate of tolerance.
8. They should develop programmes of adult education in a big way and to that end evolve a widespread network of part-time and correspondence courses.
9. They should assist the schools in their attempts at qualitative self-improvement.
10. They should shake off the heavy load of their early tradition which gives a prominent place to examinations and strive to improve standards all round by a symbolic development of teaching and research.
11. They should create at least a few centres which would be comparable to those of their types in any other part of the world and thus help to bring back the 'centre of gravity' of Indian academic life within the country itself.

The Commission recommended the following three programmes for the development of higher education: -

1) A radical improvement in the quality and standards of higher education and research.
2) Expansion of higher education to meet the manpower needs of national development and to some extent, the rising social ambitions, and expectations of the people.
3) Improvement of university organisation and administration.

6.19 Role of Universities and Colleges:

The Indian Education Commission suggested some programmes which can be undertaken:

1) Each college can be functionally related to a number of secondary schools in the neighbourhood and can provide extension service and guidance to them to improve their standards. A similar programme for the college themselves could be developed through the universities.
2) The universities can conduct experimental secondary or primary schools to evolve improved techniques of teaching and organisation.
3) The universities can conduct special diploma courses, either pre-service or in-service for improving the competence of secondary teachers. There can preferably be correspondence courses, requiring only short-term personal attendance.
4) The University and College teachers can take upon themselves the responsibility for improving school textbooks and providing better types of instructional materials.
5) The universities and colleges could select talented students from the schools in different subjects at an appropriate stage, say, in the age group 13-15, and help them to develop their knowledge in special fields through individual guidance, provisions of laboratory facilities, etc., over and above regular school work.

6.20 Expansion of Higher Education

The Indian Commission recommended that the expansion of facilities in higher education should be planned broadly in relation to manpower needs and employment opportunities. On the basis of the present trends the enrolments in undergraduate courses will have to be increased from about one million in 1965-66 to four million in 1985-86. Facilities in professional courses such as agriculture, engineering, or medicine and those at the post graduate stage have to be specially expanded.

6.21 Administration of University Education

By University Education is meant not only the education imparted directly by the universities, but also includes that education which is imparted in colleges connected or affiliated with universities. The university is an autonomous body, which manages its affairs according to the law viz. act, statutes, ordinances framed or approved by the Government. Before explaining its internal set-up, it is necessary to know the types of universities that exist in India. These can be classified as under:

1) **Central Universities: -** These universities are administered by the Central Government which bears their financial responsibility. There are 3 such universities in the country.
2) **State Universities: -** They are managed and financed by the state Governments.
3) **Institutions Deemed to be Universities: -** 34 institutions have been established under Article 3 of the University Grants Commission Statute.

The first and second type of universities can be classified in 3 categories according to their organisation:

1. **Affiliating University: -** This university provides recognition to the colleges located in its jurisdiction. It controls them, fixes syllabi for them, and organises examination for the students who study in them. In this way, we can put Agra, Faridabad, Reeva, Bangalore, and Jhansi universities etc. in this category.
2. **Unitary University: -** The teaching programme is conducted by this university through the teaching staff appointed by it. It has full command on its administration. This sort of universities are – Annamalai University, Annamalai Nagar; Jadhav Pur University, Calcutta; Jawahar Lal Nehru University, Delhi; Narender Deo Agriculture and Technological University, Faizabad; Jawahar Lal Nehru

Technological University, Hyderabad; and Rorkee University, Rorkee.

3. **Federal University:** -Under this university associated colleges impart education of university level. There are some universities in India – Cochin University, Cochin; Indore University, Indore; Mahatma Gandhi Agriculture Vidyapeeth, Rahuri; and Bombay University, Bombay(now Mumbai).

In 1950-51 in India, there were only 27 universities but now there are 200 institutes imparting higher education in which universities, deemed universities and the institutes of national importance are included, account of which has been given in appendix (2).

6.22 Internal Set-up of the Universities

The internal set-up of universities, barring slight disparity, generally conforms to a uniform pattern, leaving apart the central universities; the Chancellor of a university is the Governor of the state concerned. In addition, the Vice-Chancellor is a salaried whole time official, who conducts the day-to-day administration of the university. He enjoys a fixed tenure. It ranges between 3 to 5 years. The University Education Commission was of the view that the Vice-Chancellor should be a person who can win the confidence of both the faculty and the student community by virtue of his scholarship and personality. The Vice-Chancellor is supposed to be able to keep the university in a state of continuous animation. He should serve as liaison between the university and the community. Some universities have also a Pro-Vice-Chancellor or a Rector, who assists the Vice-Chancellor in his work. The Vice-Chancellor is selected by the Chancellor with the help of a Selection Committee.

Generally, a university has three administrative bodies:

1. **Senate or Court** – This body represents various interests such as those of principals, teachers, Nagarpalikas, vocations, industries and local affairs in addition to state legislature, donors and registered graduates. Some head of government departments are honorary members. Besides the Chancellor, the government also nominates some members. Policies touching on various functions of the university are formulated by this body. It also exercises authority on matters concerning budget. Of late the elected bodies also have started getting represented on this body. The Education Commission is of the view that students should also find representation on the body.
2. **Syndicate or Executive Council** – In the administration of the university, this council serves as a king-pin. It performs all the functions related to university administration and it carries on the day-to-day administration and manages the property and funds of the university. It is a small body on which the following persons are represented:
   - **(i)** Vice-Chancellor.
   - **(ii)** Director of Education of the State (Ex-officio member).
   - **(iii)** Representatives of the Senate or Court.
   - **(iv)** Members of the different faculties.
   - **(v)** Senior Principals of Colleges.
3. **Faculties** – They function through the agency of boards of studies. Actually, their function is to serve as a coordinating agency and take care of the common interests relating to different subjects. With the help of the academic council, they lay down the syllabi, teaching programmes, and procedural details of examinations. In some universities there are also boards of university teaching which control teaching in constituent colleges and bring about coordination between them. In many universities there is a statuary provision for creating a standing finance committee

and selection committees for teachers. In Uttar Pradesh, important changes have been affected in the administrative framework of the state universities through the University Act. Its details are described in the next chapter.

Autonomy of the University

The Kothari Commission is of the view that autonomy of the university is inherent:

(a) The selection of the students,

(b) The appointment and promotion of teachers, and

(c) Selection of different areas and problems for research in subjects of study and teaching methods.

Central Government and Universities

The University Grants Commission of India is a body of the central government that provides support to Aligarh, Banaras, Vishva-Bharati, Delhi, and Jawahar Lal Nehru universities with funds. It appoints the Vice-Chancellor and Pro Vice-Chancellor of these universities and their entire financial burden is borne by it.

Besides, the onus for maintaining exemplary levels of education in various universities and colleges falls on the central government. For keeping this objective in view, the central government established the University Grants Commission in 1953 on the recommendations of the University Education Commission. Since 1956, it has been functioning as an autonomous body. Through the agency of the University Grants Commission, the Union Government is doing work of great consequences in regard to the expansion and improvement of university education. This Commission offers grants for appointment of additional teachers, for augmenting library and laboratory facilities, research work, purchase of books, furniture and for student welfare schemes.

In addition to carrying out the responsibilities mentioned above, the central government offers grants-in-aid to state governments and voluntary organisations for propagation and development of higher education and also conducts various educational schemes and programmes with international collaboration towards the same end.

6.23 National Educational Policy, 1986 and Higher Education

Under the National Policy on Education, it has been envisaged that the higher education should be so dynamic which was never before. For providing essential speed to the system of higher education, the following points would be included in the main features of programmes and policies:

1) Integration and extension of institutes.

2) Development of autonomous colleges and departments.

3) Reorganisation of courses.

4) Training of teachers.

5) To strengthen researches.

6) Improvement in the working capacity.

7) At state and centre level, to prepare structures for coordination.

1) Integration and Extension of Institutes— Out of the many universities and 5000 colleges, many have not been provided establishment of minimum level for keeping their category and standard. For preventing downfall this system is inevitable to make available facilities. In the 7th Plan, there is a proposal to begin with the improvement in the facilities of these institutions which will continue in the 8th and later plans also. To achieve these goals, the following are the proposals:

(i) To prepare a programme for equipping of present institutes in the phases on the basis of fixed standards.

(ii) To prepare a scheme by U.G.C. for providing monetary help and other encouragements with model methods of development and progress of autonomous departments under the university.

(iii) To design guidelines for affiliating new colleges in which with other things, there should be facilities of audio-visual aids, V.C.R. and computers new teaching aids in each institute which are the minimum requirements.

(iv) On the basis of physical facilities, to control the admissions and develop entrance examination for the admission in the institutes of higher education.

2) **Development of Autonomous College and Departments**—To achieve this objective, the proposals being:

(i) The method of aids and guidelines should be prepared.

(ii) Liberty for preparing of teaching schedule, syllabus, and evaluation method of their own, should be given to the universities.

(iii) Special aid for selected colleges, for example, to establish the scheme of incentives.

(iv) For the programme of autonomous college, a full grant should be given by the central government.

3) **Reorganisation of Courses**—For the achievement of this target, the following are suggestions, that:

(i) Study circles should be reorganised in universities for making approachable the reconstruction of courses and for the development of subjects relating to employment.

(ii) Make sure the full participation of universities and faculties in reconstruction and re-establishment of courses of higher education.

(iii) Autonomous colleges and autonomous faculties would be the main resources in the development of reconstruction of courses.

4) **Training of Teaching**—Following are the proposals for achieving this goal:

(i) For newly appointed teachers, especially established programmes should be organised in science of teaching methods, education, and educational psychology etc.

(ii) For in-service teachers, a re-orientation course should be organised for each teacher, once at least in 5 years.

(iii) The teachers should be encouraged for participating in seminars and symposiums.

5) **Research Work in Universities**—Suggestions are as following:

(i) Establishments should be strengthened and budget for research work in university should be raised.

(ii) In the field of university co-research services should be established.

(iii) Relating education with research and starting such programmes which could be conducted under the framework of university contacted or the formal contacts could be developed with various research authorities.

(iv) At undergraduate and post-graduate levels schemes should be started for talent (geniuses)-search and pedagogy-stipend.

(v) All India Admission Examination should be organised for admission in Research Programmes.

6) **Improvement in Efficiency**—For achieving this goal, the following are the suggestions:

(i) In every university, there should be arrangement of computer that is in each university there should be computer for student record, accounts, and for administrative management and other data, upkeep of required files and papers.

(ii) Required information for research and to make sure approach for resource material.

7) **To Prepare Structures for Coordination at State and National Levels**—Suggestions for this are:

(i) To establish state councils of higher education in the form of legal institute.

(ii) For the guidance of state government, to keep models and rules, etc. prepared by the University Grants Commission (U.G.C.). In this there must be description of rights and organisation of state.

(iii) The chief functions of the Council will be the following:

(a) To prepare the integrated development programme of higher education in each state.

(b) Elementary protection of developmental programmes of universities and colleges (graduate and post-graduate).

(c) To give counsel and help or to give cooperation to U.G.C. for keeping the standard.

(d) To help the state governments in making sure of grants blocked.

(e) To encourage the programmes of autonomous colleges.

(f) To give pieces of advice to state governments in establishing new institutions.

(iv) An apex institute would be established at the national level to start integrated scheme for the settlement of the policy matters of higher education and for strengthening post-graduation education and inter-disciplinary research. The functions of this institute will be the following:

(a) To give control to the government regarding policy.

(b) To integrate the activities of other institutes in different areas.

(c) To encourage interdisciplineship and interdependence in different areas.

(d) To allocate the resources.

(e) To establish general organisations and institutes and manage them.

(f) To coordinate policy on external educational relations.

Mobility—For achieving this goal, states and universities will be desirous for providing admissions on the basis of knowledge of the students without considering their local domicile. For giving admission to the students of other states, plans would be prepared for providing necessary help and guidance to the institutes so that uniformity may be made everywhere in the country in the enrolment of students and capability of the staff of faculty. Priority will be given to the arrangements of hostels and construction of houses for students. Scholarship or stipend will also be given priority. Extension service and continuous education programme will be an inevitable part of the programmes and activities of all universities.

6.24 State Government and Universities

As we have already seen the university is an autonomous body. Although the government exercises no direct control over them yet, in reality, the government exercises adequate control over them in the following ways:

1. The Governor of the state is the Chancellor of the university.
2. The Chancellor appoints the Vice-Chancellor.
3. The rules and regulations as framed by the Senate do not become operative until and unless approved by the Chancellor. Only after receiving his assent, such rules and regulations get the authority of law.
4. The government has its nominees in the executive council and senate. Through them the state government influences the policies and decisions of the universities.

5. The government arranges the audit of the university accounts as the main source of their revenues is grants-in-aid given by the government.
6. State government provides grants to the state universities through the University Grants Committees.

6.25 Funds for University Education

The chief source of income of universities and their colleges are:

(i) Grants from State Governments.

(ii) Grants from the Central Government.

(iii) Fees.

(iv) Donations, etc.

Education is a joint responsibility of the central and state governments. The central government is playing a very important part in the sphere of education. The institutions which are playing important role in improvement and development of national education are the University Grants Commission, the National Council of Educational Research and Training and the National Institute of Educational Planning and Administration. They are involved in the implementation of the Policy. They have made important contribution towards development, improvement, and administration of education at all levels including pre-primary education, because it is at this level, that the foundation of the future of the child can be securely laid.

6.26 Multipurpose Experiment

The Secondary Education Commission recommended diversification of studies at the end of class VIII and the provision of a variety of courses in classes IX to XI. A number of multipurpose schools were opened offering different groups of elective subjects to students in the last three classes. Students were divided into streams according to their optional groups. But the experience of the last few years has shown that the experiment has not met with commendable success. Many administrators, heads, and teachers all over the country are seriously questioning not only whether the multipurpose experiment has been or will be a success, but whether it was ever necessary in the first place. At a recent convention on Secondary Education, organised by the All India Federation of Secondary Education, the consensus of opinion appeared to be that the scheme of Higher Secondary Education, which is an integral part of the multipurpose experiment, had failed and that it had been an obstacle rather than a help to the progress of Secondary Education, in the country.

Again, at a recent meeting of the Central Advisory Board of Education, a proposal was seriously mooted by the Madras Government, supported by some other State Governments that the existing Higher Secondary pattern of eleven years schooling on the Multipurpose pattern—followed by a Three-Year Degree Course—should be replaced by the old pattern of the Ten Year High School, a Two-Year Intermediate and a Two-Year Degree course.

6.27 Defects in the Scheme

(i) *Schools are not Multipurpose.* Most of the students who join these schools have only one purpose in view - to pursue their studies at a University. Consequently, streams like fine arts, and agriculture and even the technical stream, which do not lead to popular courses at the university stage, are taken up by a few students as the Science course is at a high premium.

(ii) *The Higher Secondary School Certificate is a College Entrance rather than a Life Entrance Certificate.* This puts it intellectually beyond the reach of a large percentage of the adolescents studying at the Multipurpose Schools who are, on leaving these schools, fit neither for college nor for a job.

(iii) *Even these diversified courses—Technical, Agricultural, Home Science and Commerce - which were specifically meant to be terminal, strongly vocationally biased courses have been made excessively academic and the vocational* *element in them has been considerably watered down.* With the result these courses not only requires as much intelligence as the mere academic courses—Humanities and Science—but also provide totally inadequate training for entry into vocation on leaving school.

(iv) *The Secondary Education Commission did not supply the details for organising and administrating the curricular in the multipurpose schools.* It was left open for the Centre as well as for the States to work out the details and carry out the scheme. By the end of 1965-66, many schools were upgraded to multipurpose schools. The policy of upgrading the old schools is like teaching the old dogs some new tricks. The old types of schools with the traditional outlook, the existing staff, and the usual administrative procedures failed to fulfill the objectives envisaged by the Commission. An adequate supply of trained teachers for vocational subjects, adequate teaching aids, proper textbooks, guidance programme and such other paraphernalia were not provided. At present, the position is not very different from what Dr. Harap remarked in his study about our Secondary Schools in 1959.

"The term multipurpose school stands for an idea rather than for a common practice, at least in the liberal sense of the word since I have not encountered a secondary school which offers more than two fields of specialisation, it would be more nearly correct to call the multipurpose school a dual purpose school, at least up to the present."

(v) *The comprehensive curriculum of multipurpose schools is so overloaded that apart from not providing an all round development even the study is not carried on right lines.* In the curriculum, there are nine subjects—three languages, three special subjects and three general subjects—Social Studies, General Science, and Craft. This leads to such a stress on the schools, time-table that no subject can be allotted adequate time. The cut is mostly applied to the study of general subjects—depth is lacking in the knowledge acquired by students. Dynamic methods have not acquired popularity due to inadequacy of time and fear of public examinations.

(vi) *Amongst the special subjects for which instruction is provided in schools only the Science group has gained popularity.* Study of other subjects is resorted to because of inability to seek admission to the Science Courses. Hence, the study of these subjects has recorded a fall in standards; the condition of humanities is pitiable to the extreme. The number of students offering humanities is so small in some schools that any expenditure on this item is unjustifiable.

(vii) *Arrangement for educational and vocational guidance in schools is not satisfactory.* Many a career has foundered on the rock of failure and frustration due to wrong choice of subjects. In the absence of standard tests, guidance has failed to inspire confidence in students and guardians alike.

What needs to be done?

1) *The multipurpose school for a start should not be regarded as a panacea for all the ills to which secondary education in India has been heir to in the past or is likely to suffer in the future,* nor should it be regarded as the only possible form of organisation for secondary education in our country. India needs multipurpose schools, but side by side, there also remains a need for separate specialised types of secondary schools. There should be Multipurpose, Bilateral, and Unilateral specialised high schools to meet the diverse educational needs and interests of the entire adolescent population.

2) The multipurpose experiment is only likely to succeed if it is carefully planned, supervised and nursed; if all those engaged in making it a success—administrators, heads and teachers and parents and the community at large are made fully aware of its many-sided implication, its strengths and weaknesses, and if they work together in fruitful partnership to capitalise on the former and to mitigate, if they cannot entirely eliminate, the latter.

"The greatest single obstacle to the successful working out of the Multipurpose School Experiment" wrote Austin A.D'Souza and K.P.Chaudhary, "are cynicism and deliberate obstruction on the one hand and complacency on the other."

(i) What is needed is its proper exposition, good implementation, coupled with experimentation. Educational reforms cannot function in a vacuum; a favourable climate of opinion has to be created to give it a fair trial. The multipurpose idea is fruition of a long period of the development of educational theory and practice. The theoretical basis of this idea needs a much fuller and more complete and convincing exposition than is provided in the Mudaliar Report, i.e., to convince the doubting Thomases about the feasibility of the idea.

(ii) *Enough coordination between State and State and enough give and take of experience needs to be provided.* Efforts should be made to bring about the necessary degree of basic uniformity, coordination, and cross-fertilisation of Multipurpose theory and practice throughout the country, to make the experiment a real and lasting thing.

(iii) Since the Multipurpose school is very much in a fluid and experimental stage, *a very real degree of autonomy be given to the State Governments by the Centre, and in turn, delegated by the State Governments to the multipurpose schools* themselves to work out the experiment in a manner best suited to local conditions—within broad limits so that they can experiment and break new grounds.

(iv) *A few schools in each state should be singled out for intensive study by teams of experts with a view to gleaning valuable information and experience as to the basic preconditions to be fulfilled if the multipurpose school is to function effectively.* A pilot scheme of this type should be put into effect immediately so that our infant multipurpose schools may be helped to grow into a healthy childhood, and gradually to reach full maturity.

(v) *In selecting high schools for upgrading into Higher Secondary Multipurpose schools, State Governments should make sure that certain basic minimum physical and material conditions are fulfilled.* The school should be well suited, it should have adequate grounds, it should have adequate class-rooms, and special room accommodation—and the school should have enough scope for expansion.

(vi) *Some schools are staging a stage back giving a signal that the experiment has failed. It should not be allowed by the Department.* If there are weak and ill-equipped multipurpose schools, the remedy in most cases is not to reconvert them to high schools, but to reinforce and strengthen them so that they are successful experiments. It is really a big tragedy if such a good idea is allowed to stagnate or die because of indifference or sheer inertia.

(vii) *The Central and State Governments should provide adequate funds in the shape of generous recurring and non-recurring grants,* especially in the form of teaching staff grants to enable all Multipurpose schools, Governments and non-Governments, to provide the staff, accommodation and equipment for the successful working of the Multipurpose schools.

(viii) *An effective school guidance service can do a lot to cater for the individual needs and problems of every child* at certain critical periods of his life and to build up a healthy staff-student relationship.

There is no fun in undertaking an experiment and doing that in a half-hearted way. We must carry it to the logical conclusion.

6.28 The Common School System and the Neighbourhood School

The Indian Education Commission gave a new concept of public-education—the concept of Common School System, the philosophy behind this concept is that such a system would provide "equality of access" to all children irrespective of their caste, creed, and community and social and economic status. All schools will cater to the needs of the "haves" and "have nots" alike and do away with the undesirable discrimination between school children coming from the different socio-economic brackets.

The Commission further stressed that the system will include all schools under the different management, viz. Government, local bodies, and private organisations (only recognised aided schools) in all parts of the country and thus allow for adequate co-ordination which is a *sine qua non* for the smooth functioning of the common school system. The Commission expressed a desire that such a system should be maintained at an adequate level of quality and efficiency so that no parent would ordinarily feel any need to send his child to the institution outside the system such as independent or unrecognised schools.

The Commission suggested some steps for the early realisation of the goal of Common School System:

1. Doing away with the discrimination between school teachers working under the different managements by providing uniform pay scales and other service conditions and by adopting the same method of recruitment in institutions of various categories.
2. Provisions of tuition-free education at the school stage.
3. Integration of the roles of the local bodies and the private managements in school education with those of the State Governments for the purpose of ensuring minimum conditions necessary for the successful functioning of educational institutions.
4. Neighbourhood school plan to realise this goal of the Common School System of public education. The Commission felt that this would provide an opportunity to all school children to share life with common people and that it would also make the privileged classes interested in the system of public education and thereby help in its improvement.

Some Practical Difficulties: - There are many practical difficulties which might arise in the implementation of these concepts.

(i) *Inter-State disparities and the disparities in schools run by the local bodies and the private managements within each State are very much pronounced.* Unless considerably larger outlays are provided for education in the overall development plans and the principle of equalisation (giving higher grants to poorer local bodies and private managements and lower grants to the richer ones) for the purpose of grants-in-aid adopted, the task of equalising the salary scales and other service conditions of teachers working in schools managed by the different agencies, may be difficult to accomplish.

(ii) *Provisions of minimum conditions for the successful functioning of educational institutions involves adequate finances* – thus the proposals may fall flat because of this limiting factors.

(iii) *There are a number of difficulties at the working of the neighbourhood school plan.* Children in all rural areas and in a large majority of urban areas are already

attending schools in the neighbourhood. The concept is thus only applicable to the metropolitan big cities which are small in number and where the heterogeneity among the population belonging to the different socio-economic groups is much wider. In these cities, parents from the higher stratum of society and also from the middle income groups vie with one another to send their children to independent public schools which are mainly residential in character and are generally located at places other than those where the children live. Thus, on the one hand, it is difficult to remove segregation between schools for the rich and those for the poor, on the other hand, the problem of effecting improvements through privileged and rich people will not get solved.

(iv) There might be indirect resistance from the privileged classes also. The political leaders may conspire with bureaucracy and the intellectual elites to maintain segregation between the privileged and the under-privileged classes.

Thus, it is obvious that the implementation of the recommendations of the Commission of the common schools system and the neighbourhood are fraught with practical difficulties.

6.29 Conclusion

When all has been said, what is needed the most is proper articulation between the different stages of education by making the educational institutions function in small groups instead of in isolation.

"One of the biggest problems at this time is there is little practical coordination between educational institutions functioning at different levels of education. The people at the university stage criticise those at the secondary stage for a fall in standards, and those at the secondary stage pass the blame on to the persons at the primary stage. This situation of mutual recrimination has to be changed into one of mutual help, and this can be done by making each higher stage of education take the responsibility for improving standards at the lower stages."

The Education Commission (1964-66) has suggested two ways in which this can be done:

1. The universities and colleges can assist the secondary schools in improving their efficiency.
2. The secondary schools can help the primary schools to improve their efficiency.

Objective Type Questions

Multiple Choice Questions (Tick ✓ the right option)

(1) Educational Ladder in a systematic form was introduced in India by Wood's Despatch in

(a) 1854
(b) 1852
(c) 1853
(d) 1856

(2) The entire educational programme constituted how many stages

(a) Three
(b) Five
(c) Four
(d) Eight

(3) Our Constitution (Article 45) provides that the state should strive to provide all children

(a) Free education
(b) Compulsory education
(c) both 'a' and 'b'
(d) None of the above

(4) The union Government is a partner in the distinguished piece of work of making primary education
 (a) Universal
 (b) Free
 (c) Both universal and free
 (d) None of the above

(5) The duration of the high school course is ____ years.
 (a) 3 Years
 (b) 4 Years
 (c) 5 Years
 (d) 2 Years

(6) Technical Education includes
 (a) Vocational training
 (b) Technical training
 (c) Professional training
 (d) All of the above

(7) Industry schools provide craft training in
 (a) Weaving
 (b) Carpentry
 (c) 'a' and 'b' both
 (d) None of the above

(8) At this time, there are how many universities in our country?
 (a) 92
 (b) 94
 (c) 93
 (d) 96

Fill in the blanks

(1) ________ university provides recognition to the colleges located in its jurisdiction. (Affiliating)

(2) In the administration of the university ______ council serves as a king pin. [executive]

(3) The ____________ of the state is the Chancellor of the university. [Governer]

(4) Education is a _________ responsibility of the central and state government. [joint]

Important Questions

1. Describe the history of earlier schools.
2. Compare and contrast the educational ladders as recommended by the Secondary Education Commission (1966). Which one do you prefer? Why?
3. Discuss the different types of Nursery Schools existing in India.
4. Discuss the concept of Common School System and Neighbourhood School in detail.
5. Discuss the arguments in favour and against on introduction of 10+2+3 pattern.

7

Inspection and Supervision

A dynamic system of supervision and inspection has been recognised as the cornerstone of a sound system of education. In a set up where all change tends to be initiated from the top and filter down through the administrative hierarchy to the schools and inspectorate forms an important link. With one foot in the administration and the other in the schools inspectorate forms a natural bridge between the policy framers and the teachers in the field. An educational system will not be able to rise above the level of its inspectorate; that is why supervision and inspection are today being considered as the backbone of educational improvement.

7.1 The Retrospect

(i) An inspection system on the British lines was set up in India on the recommendation of Wood's Despatch of 1854. A director of Public Instruction was appointed in each province: an education directorate and an inspectorate were set up. The authors of the Despatch stated: "An adequate system of inspection will also, for the future, become an essential part of our educational system and we desire that a sufficient number of qualified inspectors be appointed who will periodically report on the state of the colleges and schools which are managed by the Government, as well as such as will hereafter be brought under Government by the measures we propose to adopt. They will conduct or assist at the examination of the schools and these institutions." Thus from the very start, the inspector assumed the role of law-enforcer-cum-examiner.

(ii) In 1858, the Directors issued circulars specifying the conditions of grant-in-aid. The directors had inspectors to assist them and they not only inspected the schools but also recommended the amount of grant each school should get, thus the powers of the inspectors increased.

(iii) As a result of the Hunter Commission 1882, many changes were made by the East India Company in the educational organisation in this country. One of these changes was the appointment of inspectors for the purpose of checking the quality of instruction that was being offered and the manner in which the public money given in the shape of assistance and grants was being utilised.

(iv) After this, the inspectorate was given additional powers – the enforcement of discipline. Attempts were made by the British masters to curb the upsurge of Nationalism through this agency. In the wake of the Parliament Agitation of Bengal in 1908, the inspectorate of Bengal was given additional powers to suppress the national spirit of our schools. The condition of the aided schools deteriorated so much that national leaders tried to set up their own educational institutions which would be free of control.

Thus, by this time, the inspector had become a law-enforcer-cum-examiner-cum-disciplinarian. Discipline in the context had a new connotation, namely, a curb on the resurgent nationalism.

(v) The Sadler Commission of 1919 commented on the inspection practices.

"Inspection in most cases is hurried and lacking the friendly suggestions as to the methods of teaching and organisation which are most valuable functions of the school inspections."

(vi) In 1928, the Simon Commission appointed a sub-committee with Sir Philip Hartog as the Chairman to enquire into the growth of education in British India. The committee reported – "We have referred many times to the absence of an adequate number of well qualified and experienced inspectors and inspectresses and to the waste and ineffectiveness in the system of education which we believe to be due, in large part, to that inadequacy."

(vii) Commenting on the work of an inspector, the first Narendra Deo Report says, "The Education Code makes inspector's work too mechanical and too much occupied with routine. The office swallows the man."

(viii) The Secondary Education Commission 1952-53 remarked: "It was pointed out by several witnesses that inspections were 'perfunctory' that the time spent by the inspector at any particular place was insufficient that the greater part of his time was taken up with routine administration."

This Commission made the following significant recommendations–

1) Academic work of the school should be thoroughly inspected by a panel of experts with the inspector as chairman.
2) The inspector should have academic and administrative duties, i.e. annual inspection of records, office routine, etc. He should have a competent staff for administrative duties.
3) The Inspector should render help for the improvement of schools.

One Secondary Education Project Team was appointed by the Government of India in 1954 and funds to support the study of the Team were provided by Ford Foundation. In composition the team was of international character.

The team made the following recommendations:

1. The spirit of administration must undergo a change. The inspector should take his work as a matter of human relationship, rather than mechanical application of rules and regulations.
2. The inspector's function is to advise rather than to judge.
3. The Inspector should have specific training for the job.
4. Training courses should be organised for them.
5. Routine administrative work of the inspector should be delegated to an administrative assistance of Gazetted rank.

The school should be given more freedom. Each school should have the suitable organisation for effective teacher participation in planning and executing the school programme.

(ix) The Indian Education Commission 1964-66 also realised the importance of a dynamic inspectorate for accelerating educational reform. It outlined seven reasons for the weakness of the programme of supervision such as:

(a) Large expansion in the number of institutions which has not been accompanied by a corresponding increase in the number of inspecting officers;

(b) The combination of administration and supervisory functions in the same officer which affects supervision adversely because administrative work which has increased greatly in recent years always has a priority;

(c) The use of supervisory officers when they are members of the block development team, for non-educational work, leaving them very little for their own responsibilities;

(d) Continuance of old techniques of supervision, oriented-to control rather than to develop; and

(e) Lack of adequate competence in the inspecting staff.

The Commission recommended that one of the major programmes in the reform of school education should be to overcome difficulties and to create the new system of supervision.

7.2 Meaning of Inspection

The term inspection means static. It wants things to remain in the position in which they originally were. Educational institutions are ever growing-ever changing. Children grow every minute in mind, body, and emotions; teachers grow in knowledge and experiences every minute, and situations in the institutions also go on changing. It is therefore; wrong to expect things to remain static which the term inspection connotes. The educational inspection is altogether different from that of the term inspection used in other departments i.e. police, revenue, etc. Today, the word supervision is more popular than the word inspection.

According to the dictionary, meaning of inspection is to give test and test meant is to probe with easy and critical view. In the area of education also this sort of test is reflected from the inspection of school with activities related to education and conditions. The school inspector appointed by the government goes to various schools at times. There he tests some classes, laboratories and playgrounds. Besides, he receives some other information by asking questions from the principal/headmaster and teachers and by doing inspection of registers regarding office, financial matters with a view of critical appreciation. The information received in this way and on the basis of self-observation, the inspector prepares his report, and produces the report before his high officials. This report comes in the hands of various officers and each officer gives his remarks on it and passes it to the next one. In this way the remarks are entered on it. With the result, when it reaches the principal, a lot of the situation has changed which was criticised in the report. Thus, the result of inspection to a great extent automatically goes meaningless.

7.3 Meaning of Supervision

In the modern era, in the field of education new attitudes, movements and thoughts and tendencies have been born, with the result, revolutionary changes have taken place in the nature, objective, syllabus, and teaching methods of education, and with the changes the concept of inspection has also changed. The educationists have used a new word for expressing the new concept regarding inspection which is known as "Supervision." It is not merely change of words; notwithstanding, there is also difference of objective, field, method and viewpoint in these. For clarifying the concept of "Supervision" views of some learned persons are being expressed here:

(i) **According to Burton and Brueckner,** "Supervision is an expert technical service primarily aimed at studying and improving cooperatively all factors which affect child growth and development."

(ii) **In the words of Ayer**, "At its best, supervision is the most noble and dynamic of all educational endeavours. It is the most noble because it is the most considerate; it is the most dynamic because it is the most creative."

(iii) **Briggs and Justman Joseph writes**, "In general supervision means to coordinate, stimulate, and direct the growth of the teachers in the power to stimulate and direct the growth of every individual pupil through the exercise of his talents towards the richest and the most intelligent participation in the civilisation in which he lives."

(iv) **Adams and Dicky define** supervision as a "planned programme for improvement of institutions."

(v) **Moorar says,** "In modern education the term 'Supervision' is used to describe those activities which are primarily and directly concerned with studying and improving the conditions which surround the learning and growth of pupils and teachers."

(vi) **Wiles defines** modern supervision as "assistance in the development of a better teaching-learning situation."

(vii) **Another writer says,** "Supervision means essentially 'Superior Vision'. It is that phase of administration which undertakes the direct tasks assigned to individuals or small groups in order to assume correct and adequate performance."

An analysis of these definitions will show that there are certain distinct characteristics of supervision:

(a) Supervision's main purpose is improvement. It is a service activity.

(b) It is intended to stimulate, coordinate and guide and make the teachers self-directive.

(c) The concept of supervision is based upon the belief that the improvement of instruction is a cooperative enterprise.

7.4 The Modern Concept of Inspection and Supervision

The concept of inspection has undergone a vital change during the recent times. The following are noteworthy changes:

(i) ***The concept of inspection is being transformed to one of healthy supervision and guidance.*** Supervision is intended to cause improvement of teaching and learning by working with teachers who are working with pupils. It is now generally recognised that the School Inspector is primarily an educational advisor, charged with the duty not of finding fault but of giving practical help and guidance, it is democratic, not bureaucratic, or autocratic. Direction and regimentation have to be replaced by wise and constructive suggestions and expert guidance.

(ii) ***It is experimental in nature and scientific in method.*** This characteristic distinguishes it from the authoritative supervision of the past. One of the foundation stones of emerging philosophy and practice of supervision is the belief that current practices should always be questioned, examined, evaluated, and placed under the searching light of critical analysis and that such analysis should be applied to supervisory practice itself. Any aspect of learning situation is dropped or modified accordingly.

(iii) ***An attempt is being made to make the inspector powerful with the idea that the powers will be used to promote growth, responsibility, freedom, creativity, and initiative rather than conformity and obedience to orders.*** When the inspector is equipped with authority - present and obvious and is enlightened and creative - he can become a positive force for the improvement of educational activities in schools. He can help the schools to attain quality by bringing about significant improvements in the methods of teaching and learning, in the use of teaching aids, and in the school environment.

(iv) ***It is coming to be realised as a service activity intended to help teachers to grow professionally and do their jobs better.*** It is being rightly felt that teachers have greater potentiality than they use. Lack of vision, past experience, community pressure, lack of adjustment in human relations, poor personnel administration, inability to evaluate their work - all these factors prevent teachers from utilising all their skills and abilities. The inspector has to create congenial conditions where the best qualities, talents, and energies in teachers are realised for the benefit of the school. This is only possible when the inspector becomes a friend, philosopher, and guide.

(v) ***Supervision today is becoming a technical sort of thing. The inspector can become an effective guide only if he is trained for the job and continues to educate himself in the latest developments in education and techniques of supervision.*** Good supervision is not everybody's cup of tea and a miscellaneous gentleman will not be able to do the job. One should have innate as well as the acquired ability to deliver the goods.

(vi) ***It is participatory and cooperative.*** It offers the teacher rich opportunities to right the wrong, to commend the good and propagate the best. The supervision is a partner to teachers to help the teaching, not a detective to outwit him.

(vii) ***It is a planned programme for the improvement instruction.*** The inspector employs various activities like individual conferences, group meetings, visitation, use of instructional material, and exchange of ideas to direct teacher-learning and growth. As teachers learn, grow, and improve, pupils will also learn and grow. The pupils' growth in the last analysis is the ultimate goal of the total educative process. Supervision, therefore, is concerned with everything that furthers the development of teachers and pupils.

(viii) ***It focuses attention upon the whole range of elements effecting learning.*** Through supervision, emphasis is placed upon the teaching-learning situation and not upon a person or the techniques he uses. A cooperative formulation of aims and objectives, a study of the curriculum, the equipment and the materials of instructions and an evaluation of the results achieved are the conditions which affect teaching and learning, and, therefore, are the primary aspects of modern supervision.

(ix) ***It is a carefully planned technical service designed to improve the learning situation for children.*** Without planning, time and energy will be wasted or frittered away. Planning is both necessary and desirable because most supervisory activities stem from the needs of a situation in which many participate. Pupils, parents, teachers, citizens, administrators, and supervisors are all involved in some way or the other in a school situation. These are the persons who will determine cooperatively the functions and activities of the inspector.

(x) ***One of the major emphasis in modern supervision centers about the relationship between supervision and curriculum development.*** Although a variety of duties are performed by the inspector, the ultimate objective of each activity is the improvement of instruction and the curriculum. Because the programme of supervision cannot be developed fully when separated from the programme of curriculum development, every aspect of supervision should give attention to such curricular problems as the development of materials, the fullest utilisation of community resources, the capitalisation upon parental resources and the development curriculum planning procedures.

(xi) ***It inspires teachers, lifts them above themselves, and invigorates their flagging spirits.*** It does not furnish a detailed plan of action for the teacher and chart his every move but rather serves as a supplementary guide to assist him in working out his own plan of action. It is not expected of the supervisor that he can tell exactly what to do and furnish all the right answers. The teacher grows not by being "told" but by actually "doing" and "experiencing" through conferences, seminars, workshops, etc. He has to be exposed to practices and experiences to grow professionally.

(xii) ***It is harmonising.*** There is increased respect for human personality; there is a sense of purpose which overrides material self-interest; there is free and responsible participation; there is appreciation for leadership and respect for authority.

(xiii) ***Modern supervision is taken for coordination and integration of an educational effort.*** The sole aim is to effect improvement in the total educational programme. The inspector has to coordinate the school with the community, the school with the other schools and the school with the Education Department. Thus, the inspector is a key person in the community. Like an excellent doctor he not only diagnoses the disease but also offers a cure.

(xiv) ***The spirit of modern supervision stresses not merely teacher growth but teacher-participation in the study and improvement of the total teaching-learning situation.*** This necessitates a progressive movement away from the presumption of specific devices and towards the constant stimulation of the teacher to the understanding of principles and their use in guiding behaviour. The teacher of the future should be free, ingenious individual evolving his own everyday techniques by the intelligent use of principles. Supervision through minor suggesting techniques when necessary will always strive to develop in all workers the basic understandings underlying the various aspects of the entire educational organisation and process.

This changed attitude of inspecting officers and the general change in the character and sprit of inspection is an interesting feature of the educational systems in several countries of the world.

In Germany, for example: "The inspectors are the educational advisors who cooperate with the teachers: according to recent regulations, they must encourage good and promising teachers to use their opportunities and for the exercise of freedom and independence and must deal patiently with poor teachers."

A changed attitude is visible among Her Majesty's Inspector of Schools in Great Britain. The Report of the Advisory Council on education in Scotland says: "Increasingly in recent years, the Inspectorate has come to be looked on and have come, we believe, to look on themselves as, above all, consultants and collaborators, able to bring to the problems of any one school the experienced culled in many and to contribute to the solution of difficulties a judgement at once disinterested and well informed. To stimulate by discussion and suggestion, to spread ideas and be a link between school and school, to provoke the unreflective to thought and to awaken healthy doubts as to the sufficiency of familiar routines in such service lies the most valuable function of the Inspectorate and we would stress the very special value of its guidance and encouragement to the hundreds of small schools where teachers often inexperienced are working under conditions of difficulty and isolation."

To conclude we can say that supervision has emerged from the early emphasis upon *weeding out the deficient to the current challenge which seeks to help teachers become efficient.* The modern supervisor is a democratic leader, a coordinator, a resourceful person and is one in a strategic position to pool together the threads of evaluations.

7.5 Difference between Traditional Inspection and Modern Supervision

(i) The traditional inspection is limited to examine the shortcomings of current situations of schools and not responsible to remove them. According to modern tendency, supervision is related to the total agreement of school, their direction or running, day-to-day problems and their solution.

(ii) The traditional inspection is of short period, while supervision is related to looking after the day-to-day working and development of skill of the persons related to it; and there are provision for each individual to get educational suggestions and inspiration.

(iii) Current inspection is lawfully authorised or legalised, while supervision is democratic, cooperating and affecting (pathetical). According to some learned persons, the position-holders like, supervisor, school managers, headmasters, teachers and other persons appointed by the government, with the help of each other, do for the interest of the school respect reciprocally to each other's personality.

(iv) In traditional ways of inspection, mostly one man is held responsible for all arrangement for schools, but supervision is a process of cooperation in which efforts of all are jointly included, such as the headmaster, senior teachers, other teachers, manager and inspector (supervisor) appointed by the government.

(v) Current inspection is formal and unnatural. Besides, it is forced. The supervision is informal and natural, and it is originated from the real situations, that is, its demand originates according to the requirement.

(vi) In traditional ways of inspection, it lacks leadership. In these, the inspector does not motivate his subordinates for doing any work; notwithstanding, he compels them for doing that work. The supervision is based on creative-leadership. In this, supervisor forwards his colleagues for doing work by providing inspiration and guidance.

7.6 Need for Supervision and Inspection

There is a need for an agency of supervision and inspection in education for various reasons:

(i) ***Supervision as expert service on the consultancy basis needed in complex human undertakings like education.*** Supervision as expert service on the consultancy basis is the accepted principle in all difficult and complex human undertakings. Education particularly is complex and intricate and further more is carried on in minute divisions, classrooms scattered throughout a community and over the nation. In order that education is able to deliver the goods, it must continually change, modify, and sharpen. This is possible only when an expert service is made available right at the doors of the schools.

(ii) ***To ensure continuous growth, continuous evaluation is necessary.*** The Indian society in the post-independence period is making fantastic, yet exciting demands upon the schools. It is expected of the schools to lend vitality and vigour to society. To achieve national development in all its parameters, the obligations of the schools have increased manifold. "The destiny of India is now being shaped in her classrooms" – with this statement opens one of the greatest Reports on Education. This tremendous responsibility on the temples of learning necessitates that whatever is done is A-one. This will be possible if there is continuous growth. Continuous growth can be ensured through continuous evaluation. Hence, the need of supervision and inspection.

(iii) ***Supervision is necessary for effective coordination of the total programme.*** With increased demand for education at all levels, effective coordination of the total programme – pre-primary through high and higher secondary schools has become one of the pressing needs of education today. We can no longer afford to have the waste of human resources that is involved in overlapping courses, duplication of teaching effort and lack of continuity from one school to the next. Some careful research and experimentation by the external agency whose focus of work is

school is very much needed. An efficient inspectorate is the right answer.

(iv) ***Introduction of various programmes and services in the school programme requires the service of a team to coordinate and direct.*** The growth in enrolment of schools, due to social and economic factors in our nation, requires a vast expansion of services like, guidance programmes, remedial reading, health services, vocational training, and an understanding of the world's political problems. If these varied and important problems are to be met satisfactorily, an expert team, rather than an individual, is necessary to coordinate and to direct.

(v) ***Dispersal of good practice to improve the intellectual tone of the schools.*** Inspection is an opportunity for seeing good work done in schools by pupils, teachers, and parents. The Inspector can dispense the good practices and improve materially the intellectual tone of the schools.

(vi) ***To provide an opportunity for self-criticism, self-analysis and self-development.*** When expert guidance is readily available, teachers will grow and become self-directive.

(vii) ***To provide extraneous motivation to refresh and up-date the institution.*** It is said that all systems once established, tend to cease thinking except intermittently and operate by their own momentum. The machine, once started, functions as an end in itself, and self-content forgets the purpose for which it was created. Some agency is of utmost importance to provide extraneous motivation and to refresh and up-to-date the institution. In any scheme of educational improvement and expansion, it is the administrative machinery which can do the job. On this administrative framework, school inspection plays a very important role. Improvement of schools depends upon good teacher and efficient supervisory staff. To quote the Zakir Hussain Committee's recommendation:

"An efficient and sympathetic supervisory staff is almost as important as the new schools as well as well-trained teaching personnel."

(viii) ***Supervision and inspection is essential for untrained as well as for old teachers.*** There are still a large percentage of teachers who are untrained. There are a number of problems associated with beginning teachers that make good supervision essential. There is the problem of inexperience and the zeal to attempt too much.

There are a number of problems associated with the old teachers, who resist change. They lose professional ambition and thus cease to grow. They have to be brought around for accepting change.

(ix) ***For increasing the degree of perfection in schools, regular supervision and inspection are essential.*** No school is perfect nor has any attained perfection. If the process of training and learning were flawless, society could do away with an inspection. But, in a changing society, the kind of perfection we want has remained a myth; hence, the need for some kind of inspection of educational activities to ensure improvement.

7.7 Objectives of Supervision

1) Improve classroom teaching.
2) Evaluating the scholastic performance of the students.
3) Knowing the genuine difficulties of the teachers in teaching and organising various activities and suggesting ways and means for overcoming them.
4) Promoting the professional growth of the teachers by providing them in service education.
5) Discovering whether school is related to the community and if not suggesting ways and means to do so.

6) Acquainting the Department with the progress of the scheme of education and giving a factual account of the working of schools.
7) Demonstrating instructional, administrative, and supervisory techniques which are found effective.
8) Disseminating effective teaching methods and techniques in various schools.
9) Preventing misdirecting of resources and energies.
10) Helping administrators and teachers to deal successfully with the increasing complexity of the responsibilities of the profession.

The **Kothari Commission 1964-66** realised the importance of a dynamic inspectorate and stated, "A sympathetic and imaginative system of supervision and administration is essential for initiating and accelerating educational reforms."

7.8 Scope of Supervision

Supervision is a multifaceted technique. The area of supervision is quite varied:

1. **Supervision of Instructional Work:** The Supervisor or the Inspector supervises the effectiveness of the methods of teaching used in a particular institution, the audio-visual aids employed to make the teaching interesting and effective, the time-table enforced to carry out the instructional work, distribution of work among the members of the staff; distribution of the prescribed curriculum in suitable terms in the school year, written work done by the students and experiments conducted, etc. In fact, he is concerned with the entire planning of the institutional work. He inspects the teachers' diaries also.
2. **Supervision of Co-curricular Activities:** As the present education is not concerned with the mere teaching of three R's, the supervisors also supervise the work carried on in the co-curricular field. They are concerned with *scouting, games and sports, clubs, school government, school magazine, library service, hobbies, school museum, school exhibition,* and the like.
3. **Supervision of School Environment:** The supervisors are concerned with the discipline of the students, their personal habits, their general behaviour, etc. They look up into the cleanliness of the students, cleanliness of the school surroundings, beautification of the school, hygiene conditions of the school canteen, proper drinking water arrangements, cleanliness of urinals and latrines. They evaluate the steps taken by the school authorities for the welfare and the safety of the students.
4. **Supervision of the School Registers:** The inspecting staff examines all sorts of school records and registers. They scrutinise all accounts and boys funds. They see whether or not proper use of school funds is being made. They examine the school apparatus and equipment also.
5. **Supervision of Development Aspects:** The supervisors try to assess whether the school is justifying its existence or not. They examine the various steps taken by the school to serve the locality in which it is situated. They report about the school's participation in the social, cultural, and recreational programmes of the community.
6. **Supervision of Pupil's Growth:** The supervisors are also concerned with the many sided development of the children.

7.9 Changing Concepts of Supervision and Inspection

Today, supervision is greatly influenced by the increasing insight into the aims of education, the relation of the school to the society in which it exists, by the scientific method, and by the democratic philosophy. Supervision is becoming participatory and cooperative, that is, democratic; is increasingly oriented towards the fundamental aims of education and of society.

Beginning slowly in the twenties, developing rapidly in the thirties and forties, was the concept of cooperative supervision and democratic leadership. The supervisor being regarded as an individual who served to assist the staff, as consultant and friend, rather than as inspector and critic. Democratic supervision demands respect for personality. It makes ample provision for self-direction on the part of teachers, and participation to a great extent in their in-service growth.

7.10 Inspection Procedures

Important inspection procedures in vogue in our country are listed below:

(i) **School Visits: -** School visits can be of three types (a) *visits undertaken after giving due notice to the school,* (b) *surprise visits,* (c) *visits by invitation.* The inspectors visit each school in their areas at least once a year. Some problems may necessitate in more than one visit. It will be better if such a visit is undertaken after giving due notice to the school. In addition to the planned visit, there should be a surprise visit also to enable the Education Officer to check up the work of the teacher in actual classroom situation as well as the activities of the pupils inside and outside the classroom. The Education Officer can also be invited to the school for guidance or for showing some worthwhile practice or prospect, etc.

The Indian Education Commission recommends that every school should have two types of inspections - annual and triennial and two different forms should be used for the purpose, the former will be conducted by the D.S.B. for primary schools and State Education Department for the Secondary School. The Triennial inspection will be conducted by the D.E.O. for primary schools and the State Board of School Education for the Secondary School.

(ii) **Teachers' Meetings and Conferences:** Holding teachers' meetings and conferences is another inspection procedure. Conferences may be held as a result of the classroom visits and observation as will involve consideration of teachers' weak and strong points and opportunities for improvements. Difficulties and limitations of the teachers are also noted and efforts are made to remove them. The teachers' meetings may be held for consideration of common major instructional problems. The problems may be discussed and solutions suggested.

(iii) **Issuing Orders and Circulars:** Regular guidance is provided to teachers through circulars, containing suggestions for improved methods of teaching and for the study of books and journals containing the latest techniques of education. The circulars are sent to the schools for sending information on educational matters like change in syllabus, textbooks, examination system, decision of the Education Department and educational conferences, etc. Orders are also issued for various activities like contents, competitions, and tournaments.

(iv) **Demonstration Teaching:** Another inspection procedure of special value in certain situations is demonstration teaching. Its purpose is to illustrate a recommended method, teaching material or instructional approach. The demonstration teaching may be a work of the inspector himself, a classroom teacher or by some expert from outside. The Inspector sometimes teaches a lesson - taking over the teacher's class so that the teacher can observe his own students' response to a new procedure or approach. Often teachers are able to profit greatly from the experience of seeing another person teaching their class.

Demonstration teaching must be oriented to the needs and concerns of the teacher involved. The inspector and teacher identify specific problems and plans to use the technique of demonstration teaching to help resolve these difficulties.

Demonstration teaching, as an inspection procedure, requires careful planning and preparation. The objectives of the lesson, the content to be presented, the nature of the activities to be used and the evaluating measures to be employed – all must be carefully discussed.

The inspector and teacher should establish the nature of the demonstration. *The lesson may be suggestive, try out or experimental.* It may be a recommended procedure or model given for the benefit of an inexperienced teacher or it might simply show an experienced teacher meeting the normal instructional demands, in a fairly typical classroom. Each demonstration should be followed by a discussion session, as soon as possible, to compare impression, discuss the application of principles, evaluate the apparent success of procedures or materials used, explore applications or adaptations potentially useful to the observing teacher and clarifying misunderstandings.

(v) **Planned Intra-School and Inter-School Visits:** Visits within the school itself— intra-school visits, and visits among other schools— inter-school visits, may also be used as inspection techniques. In visits the problem of arranging a productive experience is vital. The Inspector must plan closely with the headmaster of the school or schools involved, must prepare teachers in advance of the observation, and must follow-up the experience, in order to ensure the most value from the activity.

The teachers need to prepare for the visit. They must have a worthwhile purpose in mind and they should have specific and significant things to observe. The teacher to be visited must be informed of the impending visit. He should also know the needs of the visitor. In this way, the Education Officer makes sure that his teacher has nothing to observe but a fun day of review, activity, work-book assignments, motion pictures and a unit examination.

The host teacher must have consented to the visit and be willing to discuss his instruction with the visiting teacher afterwards. This post-visit conference is essential, for it provides the opportunities to the demonstration teacher to explain his aim and procedures to be observed. It allows the visitor to ask questions, clarify impressions, and secure specific assistance. A follow-up discussion may be held in a committee, department, or faculty meeting in which the visiting teacher brings the results of his experience back to his own colleagues. In the case of intra-school visits, an inspector-teacher conference provides needed follow-up.

7.11 Types of Supervision and Inspection

1) **Authoritarian:** Authoritarian supervision is based upon practices like "I told you to do this." This kills the creative ability and initiative of the teachers and is a hindrance in improving instruction.

Authoritarian supervision forces and prescribes methods. An authoritarian thinks that because a method works well for him, it must be used by the teacher, and that it will succeed in the same way and to the same extent. Authoritarian supervision fails to take account of the fact that what produces results for one teacher in his particular situation with his individual personality may not produce same result in the case of the other.

Authoritarian supervision implies that the supervisor is a master, or super teacher, who can walk in, take over the class, and get the desired results. The teacher works in such a situation not by actually doing and experiencing but by being 'told.'

2) **Corrective:** This is also known as 'fault-finding' expedition. In this case, the Inspector visits a school to pick holes here and there and is always on the look out of bringing out inconsistencies and gaps to the notice of the head of the institution. Such an inspection does not serve any useful purpose. It simply makes the teachers unhappy. An inspector must remember that progress depends upon a judicious combination of encouragement to good work and removal of defects.

3) **Creative:** According to Fred C Ayer, "Creative supervision should encourage the discovery of all kinds of better ways of learning, teaching, and community improvement, not merely those who relate to self-expression and problem solving.

Barr, Burton, and Bruecknor think, "Creative leadership in the long run is vitally necessary to the success of democratic life."

Creativeness has been linked closely with such words as self-expression, initiative, originality, experimentation, and improvement.

Supervision seeks for latent talents. It provides opportunity for the exercise and originality and for the development of unique contributions.

4) **Humanistic:** This type of supervision aims at developing a healthy human relationship among all the partners of the educational enterprise, i.e., the pupils, the teachers, the parents, staff personnel, the managers, and the supervisor.

5) **Inspirational:** It inspires teachers, lifts them above themselves, and reinvigorates their flagging spirits. True inspirational supervision must strive to broaden the base of leadership by utilising the full potential of teachers. It will nurture qualities like initiative, originality, creativity, sincerity, and honesty. It will discourage rigidity and sameness in teaching. It will meet the needs of teachers sufficiently to serve as the foundation for a good programme of supervision. Inspirational supervision allows the freedom so necessary for real growth.

6) **Preventive:** This type of supervision helps the teachers to anticipate new situations and to find ways and means to remove them. It is obvious that this type of inspection is helpful to teachers.

7) **Democratic Supervision:** Democratic supervision eliminates the feeling that the supervisor is a superior being and the teacher an inferior worker. Democratic supervision tends to cooperative endeavour for the common good. Democratic supervision does not allow the supervisor to impose his will upon the teachers. It builds upon the power of the teacher to exercise self-direction through his participation in the formulation of methods and procedures for improving instruction. Democratic supervision seeks for the development of the highest potentialities in all. Democratic supervision recognises the dignity and worth of the individual.

Democratic leadership generates more leadership by providing opportunities to more and more persons to exercise leadership. It must be adapted to the levels of professional ability and to the differences in teachers – whether they are novices or veterans, weak or strong, poorly trained or professionally prepared.

Democratic supervision provides for group planning. It connotes a better organisation among both groups – teachers and children.

Democratic supervision is also concerned with coordinating the work groups in different schools and on various levels.

Democratic supervision encourages freedom while furnishing direction, advice, and suggestion.

7.12 Types of Inspection according to Supervisory Procedures

1. **Annual Inspection:** This is a detailed and comprehensive inspection of all aspects of the school; its staff, all subjects in all classes; its equipment and organisation.
2. **The Follow-up Inspection:** The follow-up inspection is conducted to ensure that the previous recommendations have been carried out.
3. **Partial Inspection:** This may constitute the inspection of the teaching of one subject only or some special aspect of the school life.
4. **Surprise or Unannounced Visits:** Supervisors visit schools without giving any prior notice. The idea behind such visits is to observe the working of the school under normal situation.

7.13 Duties of Educational Officers

1. **Administrative Duties:** An Education Officer is supposed to discharge various administrative duties. They are: executive, advisory, integrating, statistical, and departmental.

   Executive: He has to visit schools and see that the school laws and regulations are being followed. His executive duties pertain to correspondence, communication of Director's orders, disbursing of grants-in-aid, settlement of disputes between teachers and the management.

   Advisory: He has to give advice to his assistants and to the management of schools.

   Integrating: He has to attend meetings of various State Boards and establish relationship among the various educational elements within his jurisdiction.

   Statistical: He has to handle the collection and analysis of educational statistics of the schools under his jurisdiction.

   Departmental: He has to appoint government teachers and clerks. He has also to deal with the case of their transfers, leaves.
2. **Academic Duties:** On the academic side, the education officer is expected to guide the school in its entire programme of curricular and co-curricular activities. He will thus help to improve the standard of education in the State. Such guidance has become even more necessary now, with the introduction of work experience, varied courses, and integrated curriculum of core subjects at the secondary stage. But, as the Secondary Education Commission has pointed out, the multiplicity of the subjects taught in the school by specially qualified teachers now, makes it very difficult for any single officer, however qualified he may be, to inspect them thoroughly and to advice them on all their problems. The Commission has, therefore, recommended that the academic work of the school should be thoroughly inspected by a panel of experts with the Education Officer as their Chairman. Three experts, chosen from senior teachers or headmasters, should visit schools in the company of the Education Officer. They should spend two or three days with the staff. They should discuss with them all aspects of school life – the organisation of the curriculum; the crafts and other special subjects taught; the library and laboratory facilities; the programme of co-curricular activities; the use of holidays; and all other problems connected with school work. This should be done at least once in three years for every school.
3. **Establishing Contact between the Public and the Administration:** It is desirable to entrust the education officer with the task of establishing contact between the public and the administration on educational matters. A new programme of education can only be accepted by the people if they

realise its value and significance. Dissemination of information to the public and preparation of material for publication through the publicity organs of the State Government may well form part of the Civil Education Officer's Office. The Inspectorate should also keep in touch with the various training Colleges and Training Schools in the State, and give them all facilities for organising extension services for in-service teachers. The All India Council for Secondary Education has recommended that Boards of Secondary Education in the different states should have small research units to carry out investigations on examinations, school records, etc. The Secondary Education Commission has recommended that for improvement and assessment of textbooks. A high-powered committee should be appointed in every state. The Education Officer is in the best position to pose problems which have been brought to the forefront during discussions with teachers and Headmasters, to prepare a schedule of priorities, to get in touch with the various research units, and to find a solution or an answer to them. A problem may be big and complex and may have to be tackled from different angles by the various units concurrently. The Education Officer should serve as an important link, because, if research is to prove fruitful, the posing of problems in their order of priority and putting into practice the results of the work done, are as important as the solutions of a problem. The education officer is in a very good position to supply quantitative data to these workers about schools, teachers, etc. as he himself is a field worker.

7.14 Qualities of a Supervisor or Inspector

Brilly suggests that the motto of an Inspector should not be "Check your teachers, frighten your teachers, weaken your teachers, and examine them," but its variant, "Train your teachers, inspire your teachers, encourage your teachers, and trust them." Important qualities of such an Inspector are:

(i) **Man of Faith:** There is no use of being impatient, for growth and improvement always takes time. The inspector must have a far reaching programme, but putting through it, he should proceed item by item.

(ii) **Man of Planning:** The inspector should plan his work thoroughly and should not undertake it at random.

(iii) **Man of Educational Vision:** He should be aware of new trends in education, latest techniques in education, recent problems in the field and their solutions. He should not merely assess the academic achievements of the schools but also the all-round progress of the school should occupy his attention.

(iv) **Man of Experiments:** He must be an experimenter. An able inspector will select forward looking schools where the teachers and the headmasters have a progressive outlook on education and are imbued with the spirit of experimentation and will turn these schools nurseries wherein the seeds of educational reform and progress are sown, cared for and their progress carefully watched and the message carried to other schools.

(v) **Expert in Various Subjects:** An inspector should be a specialist in many languages and subjects. This is particularly important in our schools where different media of instructions are followed.

(vi) **Organising Capacity:** As he is to serve as "teacher of teachers", he should have the capacity to organise refresher courses, meetings, seminars, and discussions.

To sum up the qualities of an inspector, it may be stated that he should be a man of learning, faith, and imbued with a spirit of progress and experimentation and above prejudices of all sorts and petty personal affiliation.

7.15 Checklist for Evaluation and Supervision of Instruction

Teacher............ Date..............

Subject.............. Class.............

Note: Check on one of these three columns "A," "B," "C." If a given feature does not appear, check in the column "No."

Classroom Condition

S.N.	Classroom Management	NO.	A	B	C
1.	Was sufficient attention given to lighting and ventilation?				
2.	Was the equipment of the rooms (for example, desks, blackboards etc.) in order?				
3.	Were there sufficient, audio-visual aids? (for example, maps and charts.)				
4.	Were supplementary materials effectively arranged?				
5.	Was the teacher's voice pleasing and his enunciation, clear?				
6.	Was the teacher's dress suitable?				
7.	Were the teacher's manners suitable?				
8.	Did the teacher show evidence of possession of the following qualities? (a) Self-control (b) Tact (c) Resourcefulness (d) Sympathy (e) Fair-mindedness (f) Enthusiasm (g) Decisiveness				
9.	Did the lesson begin and in time?				
10.	Did the teacher handle laboratory material efficiently?				
11.	Were the students with defective sight or hearing seated on front desks?				
12.	Did students enter, leave and move about the room in an appropriate manner?				
13.	Were the postures of the students good?				
14.	Were pupil's responses well directed and expressed?				
15.	Was the attention of the entire class keen and continuous?				
16.	Was the group characterised by an attitude of courtesy and cooperation towards all its members?				

Arrangement of the Subject-matter

S.No.	Classroom Management	NO.	A	B	C
1.	Was the time effectively divided between (1) testing and drilling upon previous assignment (2) assignment and new material?				
2.	Did the assignment involve activity of the group?				

Teaching Devices

S.No.	Classroom Management	NO.	A	B	C
1.	Were all pupils kept busy throughout the entire period?				
2.	Was there proper balance between teacher activity and pupil activity?				
3.	Was emphasis placed upon the formation of good habits rather than the acquisition effects?				
4.	Were the questions suitable?				

Aims

S.No.	Classroom Management	NO.	A	B	C
1.	Did the teacher have a clear and worthy aim of the lesson?				
2.	Was the aim attained?				

7.16 Supervising Procedures and Guidance

A capable supervisor will not limit his supervisory procedures to the traditional classroom visits and the teacher's meeting. He will render assistance to teachers through such procedures as the following:

A. Guidance: - The supervisor or the inspector is expected to help the individual teacher or group of teachers to plan and carry forward the class projects which have a direct bearing on the improvement of learning conditions. These projects are:

- **(i)** Planning, testing programmes, and constructing tests.
- **(ii)** Analysing test results and planning remedial procedures.
- **(iii)** Collecting supplementary materials.
- **(iv)** Undertaking special projects in the use of audio-visual aids.
- **(v)** Planning and initiating instructional devices suiting individual students.
- **(vi)** Conducting workshops for the study of special problems.
- **(vii)** Utilising community resources for enriching classroom teaching.

B. School and Classroom Visits:- The procedure and techniques of visits are:

- **(i)** Observation of the work of teachers with a view to discovering opportunities for improvement.

(ii) Rating the teacher with some special device for diagnostic purposes.

(iii) Taking up demonstration lessons.

(iv) Making suggestions to teachers regarding new devices and methods, supplementary aids, economy of time, pupil control, adapting methods to pupil differences, and so on.

C. **Teacher's Meeting and Conferences:-** This point may be illustrated under two headings:

(i) **Holding Conferences with the Individual Teacher:** Such conferences will be held as a result of the classroom visits and observations and will involve consideration of teacher's weak and strong points and opportunities for improvement.

(ii) **Holding Teacher's Meeting for Consideration of Major Instructional Problems:** Points of common interests, some difficulties, and certain policies are discussed and suggestions made to improve school work.

Specific Guidance: Role of the Supervisor/Inspector

1) To provide professional leadership to educational institutions so as to improve their work and put them on the right direction and path.

2) To set suitable goals for the educational institutions.

3) To appraise the work of the educational institutions and to give suitable suggestions of work being carried on.

4) To help teachers to define and use the purpose of education as a dynamic force in their work with pupils.

To promote the professional growth of all teachers, by providing them 'in-service training'.

The main motto of the inspectors should not be, "Check your teachers, frighten your teachers, weaken your teachers, and examine them," but its variant, "Train your teachers, inspire your teachers, encourage your teachers, and trust them," writes an educationist.

7.17 Defects in the Present Supervision and Inspection

It is generally observed that the present type of supervision and inspection hardly serves the purpose for which it is designed. From time to time, this system has been examined by experts, measures suggested but without any substantial improvement. By and large, it is still the same as was the case before independence.

Here we can give the views of some experts on the state of supervision and inspection in India.

The Secondary Education Commission (1952-53) noticed the following defects:

(i) Inspections are perfunctory.

(ii) Time spent by the inspectors is insufficient and greater part of the same is taken up with routine work pertaining to checking of accounts, time-table, curriculum, etc.

(iii) Enough time is not devoted to the academic side.

(iv) Contacts between the teachers and inspectors are casual.

(v) The number of schools entrusted to the care of an inspector is too large and the range too wide for him to be able to acquaint himself with their work and appreciate their problems; nor is he in a position to advise and guide the teaching staff in improving the work of the school.

The inspector instead of being "the friend, philosopher and guide" of the school, behaves in such a critical and unsympathetic way that his visit is looked upon with some degree of apprehension, if not of resentment.

In the words of W.M. Ryburn, "The inspector holds an extremely autocratic position, where, if his will is not exactly law, it is so near to it that for all practical intents and purposes, the teacher and the headmaster regards it as such."

'Education in Eighteen years of Freedom' reads as, "Before 1947, inspection was a device to ensure that an institution receiving grant-in-aid from the Government utilised money correctly. Another function of the inspector was to extend recognition to privately managed schools on the basis of certain criteria. The concept of inspection has now changed, and inspection tends to promote the professional growth of teaching personnel. The role of inspector is that of a senior colleague to teachers. The re-designation of 'inspector' as 'education officer' in many states marks this shift in the emphasis of duties."

7.18 Suggestions for Improving Supervisory Practices

1) **Changes in the Techniques of Supervision:** Since environmental conditions vary from time to time, teacher to teacher, subject to subject, and group to group, supervisory techniques cannot be wedded to any set theory and practice, and, therefore, the Education Officer should have a plan ready in hands as to 'What', 'Where', 'When' and 'How' to observe and revise the plans periodically.
2) **Strengthening of the Supervisory Staff:** A major part of the time of the Education Officer is being spent on administrative activities with the result that adequate time is not left with him to discharge his supervisory activities. Keeping in view the present situation it is not advisable to separate the administrative and supervisory work. However, it is extremely important that the supervisory staff should be strengthened.
3) **More Clerical Staff is needed**: More clerical staff is needed to cope with the routine type of work of supervision and inspection. In many cases supervisory remarks (Reports) remain un-typed for months because of the shortage of typists and other clerical staff with the result that schools fail to derive immediate benefits from the supervisory remarks.
4) **Behaviour of the Supervisor:** The supervisor should greet the teacher in a friendly and courteous manner. Usually he should seat himself at the rear of the room. Generally speaking he should not interrupt the work of the class or take over any part of the instruction. He should record his observations as objectively as possible.
5) **Inter-school Visitation:** In many cases, teachers can offer valuable assistance or guidance to one another by mutually visiting their classes. For this it is very essential that a cooperative attitude may be developed among the teachers and the practice of inter visits of this type encouraged.
6) **Frequency of Inspections and Follow-up Work:** With regard to frequency of inspections, it is suggested that there should be at least two inspections in one year, one of them may be an informal visit and the other a regular annual visit. More visits are desirable especially in the case of those schools which in the view of the Education officer require special measure to become educationally sound. The needs of each school should be ascertained and remedial measure adopted.

   The remarks and suggestions of the Education Officer should be sent to schools within one week of the visit of the supervisor so that these may be considered by school personnel without delay.

   School inspections without any regular follow-up programme do not prove to be effective. Planning of follow-up programme is as essential as regular inspection.
7) **Encouraging Professional Growth:** Very little is done by the Education Officer for the professional growth of teachers.

   A number of teachers may be asked to demonstrate the techniques in which they are most successful. Discussion should always follow immediately after the demonstration. The observers should be given an opportunity to ask whatever questions they wish. All suggestions should be made and accepted like an ideal sportsman.

Motion pictures film strips may be used wherever possible.

The demonstrator should explain the application of principles in his procedure after the demonstration is over.

Adequate preparation should be made by the supervisor while giving demonstration lessons as this is likely to serve as a model for teachers. It should be well thought-out and well-planned and efficiently executed.

8) **In-service training for Teachers:** Refresher courses, seminars, workshops, study circles etc. should be organised for the benefit of principal and teachers. These will enable them to be in touch with day-to-day changes in the field of education.

9) **Dissemination of Educational Literature:** The supervisor may issue a bulletin at regular intervals for encouraging professional growth among teachers. The following types of material may be included in the bulletin:

(a) Abstracts or brief quotations from books, articles, or speeches.

(b) References to articles appearing in current educational periodicals to which the teachers have access.

(c) New items of what various schools or teachers are doing.

(d) Results of research, reports, etc. which have come to the attention of the supervisors.

(e) Brief review of the latest educational literature.

(f) Articles from teachers and other educationists on different aspects of education.

(g) Bibliographies of good references upon selected topics considered of immediate interests to teachers.

10) **Supervisor's Meeting with Teachers:** There are three chief types of teachers' meeting which should be held:

(a) Meeting for routine administrative purposes.

(b) Meeting for special purposes.

(c) Meetings that deal with the improvement of instruction.

These meetings should help in stimulating a desire to learn among school personnel for solving their own problems.

7.19 Conclusion

It must be remembered that when the teachers feel that the supervisor is one of them and is always there to help them as a true friend, philosopher, and guide, they will be able to discuss all their problems with the supervisors. All this requires that supervisors must be endowed both with the qualities of head and heart, i.e., keep themselves abreast with the growing and latest pedagogical literature as well as develop in themselves the behaviour pattern that would endear themselves to the teachers. This may appear to be a pious hope but the recent studies reveal that all people in the field of education right from the pupils up to the Department feel that the supervisor is an important link that can help in the growth of educational institutions in the proper direction. We may bear in mind that respect for personality is fundamental in democratic supervision for it recognises each individual as a person in his own right and as such entitled to growth along the lines of his own social choices.

Objective Type Questions

Multiple Choice Questions (Tick ✓ the right option)

(1) One secondary education project team was appointed by the Government of India in
   (a) 1954
   (b) 1956
   (c) 1955
   (d) 1952

(2) "Supervision is an expert technical service primarily aimed at studying and improving cooperatively all factors which affect child growth and development" This definition is given by
   (a) Ayer
   (b) Briggs
   (c) Burton and Bruecknor
   (d) Adams

(3) Supervision's main purpose is
   (a) Growth
   (b) Improvement
   (c) To guide
   (d) None of the above

Fill in the blanks

(1) ____________ is related to the total agreement of school. [Supervision]

(2) ____________ supervision forces and prescribes methods. [Authoritarian]

Important Questions

1) Write the meaning of Inspection?
2) What do you mean by Supervision?
3) "Good supervision is good teaching". Discuss.
4) Discuss the prevailing system of school inspection in your state. What suggestions would you give to make it more effective?
5) Point out the main defects of present supervision and inspection. Suggest measure for its improvements.

8

Communication in Educational Administration

Just as the previous centuries experienced their technological revolutions – the 'agriculture' and 'industrial' revolutions that radically changed the worldwide patterns of production and distribution – so the twenty-first century is said to have experienced a 'communication revolution' that is affecting the world scenario.

At the centre of the 'revolution' are communication technologies. Some are long established, like radio, television, and telephones. Others such as satellites, optical fibre, microcomputers, and video-recording on tape or video disc are quite new. Among the older ones, radio and television broadcasting have been improved, adapted, put to new uses, or linked with newer communication technologies. The result is wider distribution, greater accessibility, and more clarity, consumer control and economy. They have also been improved by techniques that enhance recording, text screening and printing, and the editing and manipulation of recordings.

8.1 Meaning of Communication

Communication means getting across ideas and information from one person to another. For communication to take place, it should originate from an individual and be transmitted to another who receives it and acknowledges it. Sending the message alone does not complete the process of communication. The sender might use language, signs, or actions to transmit a message. The receiver might use it by listening, reacting or by simply observing. In any case, the process of communication involves three things, a communicator (sender), a communicatee (receiver), and the contents of communication (message).

The word 'communication' originates from '*communis,*' a Greek word, meaning 'to make common.' Thus a concept, fact, idea, principle, or theory is passed from one individual to the other or others to affect communality.

According to Aristotle, communication is a means of persuasion to influence the other so that the desired effect is achieved.

Dewey defines communication as a process of sharing experiences till it becomes a common possession. It modifies the disposition of both the parties who partake it.

8.2 Process of Communication

D. Berlo thinks that communication is a process of interaction of ideas between the communicator and the receiver to arrive at a common understanding for mutual benefit.

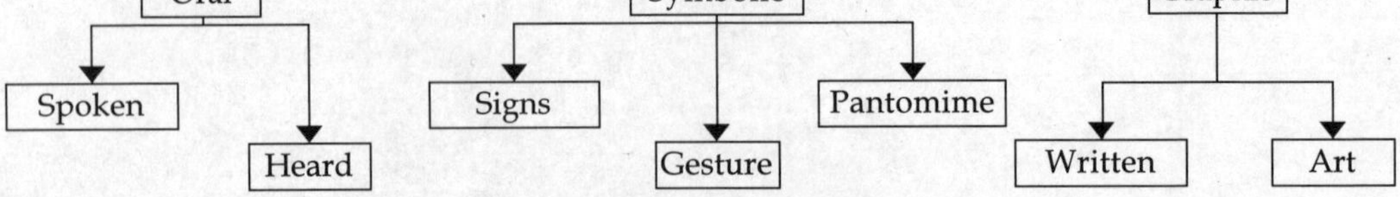

Fig. 1: Forms of Communication

Elements involved in the Communication Process

(a) **Sender:** Sender is the person who intends to send the information.

(b) **Message:** Message is the information in the form of an idea, feeling, attitude, opinion, thought, etc.

(c) **Receiver:** The person (staff) willing to share the message with the sender.

(d) **Feedback:** The reactions and responses of the receivers to the sender after receiving the message.

(e) **Noise:** The barriers of the message resulting in the distortion or black-out of communication.

Steps in the Process of Communication

Step 1: To have a clear perception of the idea or the problem by the sender.

Step 2: To secure the participation of other persons involved in the decision to communicate the message.

Step 3: To decide what to communicate, when to communicate, and how to communicate.

Step 4: To prepare the subject matter of communication in a suitable language.

Step 5: To select the forms or means of communication.

Step 6: To transmit the message to the receiver.

Step 7: To ensure the correct interpretation of the message.

Step 8: To evaluate the effectiveness of the message.

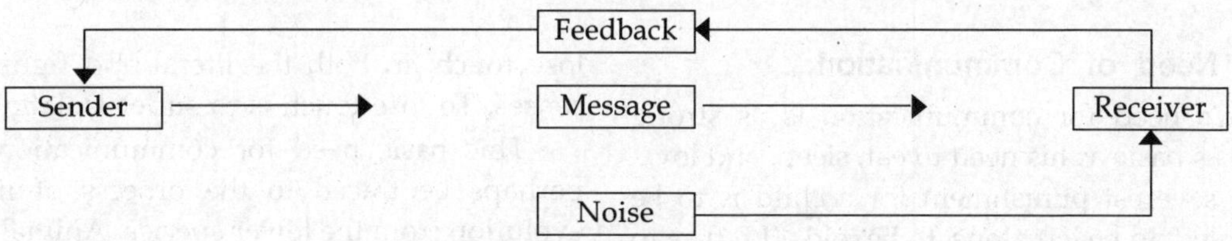

Fig. 2: Two-way Process of Communication

Forms of Communications

	Kind	Description	Examples
1.	Speaking-Listening	The sender speaks and the receiver listens.	Listening to a lecture. Listening to a lesson or talk on radio.
2.	Visualising-Observing	The sender uses visual symbols and the receiver observes.	Use of a diagram or an illustration.
3.	Speaking, Listening, Visualising, Observing.	The sender combines speaking and visual symbols while the receiver listens and observes simultaneously.	An educational T.V. programme. A video lesson. An educative movie.
4.	Writing-Reading kind.	The sender uses written words and symbols, while the receiver reads or feels those.	A hand out on a given topic. Silent reading from a textbook. Braille system for the blind.

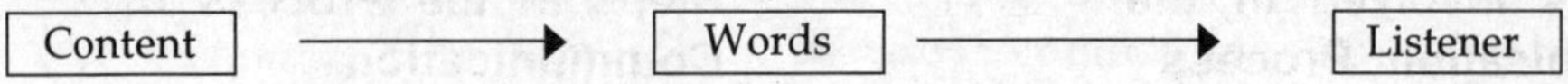

Importance of the Listener (Learner): The following diagram shows consideration to the learner. The earlier diagram can be amended.

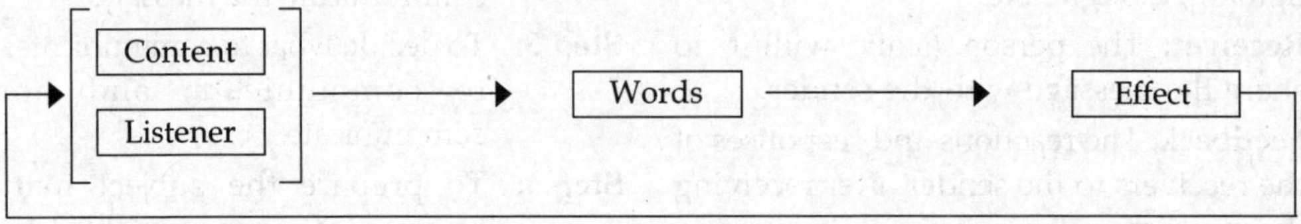

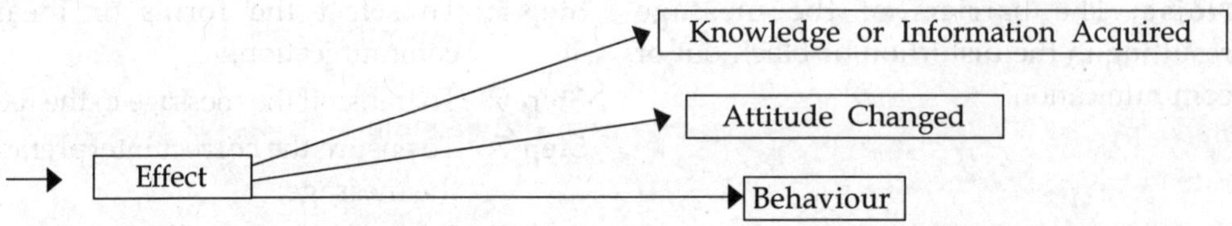

Fig. 3: Effects of Spoken Communication

8.3 Need of Communication

Man's need for communication is as strong and as basic as his need to eat, sleep, and love. The severest punishment for a child is to be isolated, to be left alone, to be told, "I refuse to talk to you." Grown-ups too, and especially the aged need company, to communicate. Society punishes criminals by locking them in solitary cells, thus starving that basic need to communicate. Only for a short time can man do without communication. For modern man it would be impossible to function without the mass media of communication, as they have become part of the fabric of modern civilisation – at least in the West.

Communication involves interaction with our environments – physical, biological, and social. Deprived of this interaction we would not be aware of whether we are safe or in danger, whether hated or loved, or satisfied or hungry. However, most of us take this interaction for granted, unless we experience some deprivation, when that happens we adapt ourselves, to the environment to state we don't lose touch, in both the literal and figurative senses. To lose touch is to suffer isolation.

This basic need for communication can perhaps be traced to the process of man's evolution from the lower species. Animals, for instance, 'have to be in sensory communication with their physical and biological surroundings to find food, protect themselves and to reproduce their species. A loss of sensation – the inability to hear a predator, for example – can mean loss of life. Similarly, to be lost from primitive social communication – from the pack, the herd, or the tribe – is to be condemned to death.' [Clark and Blankenburg: You and Media, 1973]

But sensory communication alone was not enough for man to survive. Hence, the invention of symbolic communication called language – from non-verbal gestures, grunts, and grimaces to the verbal, and then to the written and printed word. The acts have grown out of this same fundamental desire to express one and to reach out to others. Man adorned his caves with painting of animals and hunters. Modern man shows a preference for the abstract and 'pop', for the electronic and computer acts. But the human need to communicate has remained the same, only the forms have changed.

What happens to a person who is 'excommunicated' – cut off from communication by his group or society? Malcolm X, the Black Muslim leader, describes the experience as 'a state of emotional shock', when he was expelled by the Black Muslims from the group. Elaborating, he said that his state was like that of someone "who for 12 years had an inseparable, beautiful marriage - and then suddenly one morning at breakfast the marriage partner had thrust across the table some divorce papers. I felt as though something in nature had failed, like the sun or the stars. It was that incredible a phenomenon to me - something too stupendous to conceive."

Others who have been isolated for a period of time from human company are known to have experienced nightmarish hallucinations.

Lack of human communication can be as terrible an experience as too much of it as is the case today when we in the cities are bombarded by the mass media excessive information. The result very often is a mental and physical distress which Alvin Toffer calls 'future shock.'

Indeed, "The apparent effects of sensory deprivation and sensory overload are similar—anxiety, frequently impaired judgement, strange visions, and something akin to apathy, schizophrenia." [Source: - You and Media, page-42.]

8.4 Models of Communication

Here we give the models of communication.

(1) Shannon-Weaver model or Telephonic Model

Shannon and Weaver (1949) have given a mathematical theory of communication as shown in Fig. 4.

This model consists of five key components, via an information source, which involve:

(i) Message;

(ii) A transmitter for transmission;

(iii) A channel, which carries signal from transmitter to receiver;

(iv) The receiver, which reconstructs the signal into a message; and

(v) The destination, the final consumer of the message. A novel component is its noise source, i.e., the interference.

In this model, communication is an information source that creates a message, transmitted by an electronic device (telephone speaker) through an air channel with noise interference (such as telephone wire and sound waves) to the hearing mechanism of the person acting as a receiver (telephone receiver) that creates the message.

This model introduces the concept of noise. Noise in this model refers to disturbance in the channel that may interfere on the signal transmitted and produce different signals.

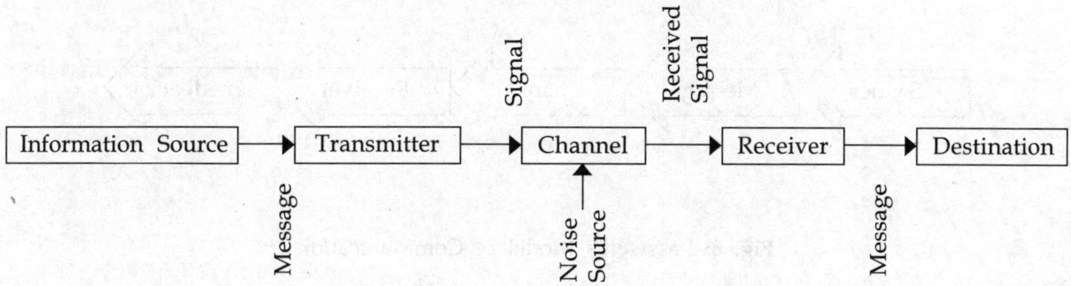

Fig. 4: Shannon—Weaver Model or Telephonic Model

(2) Schramm's Model

Schramm's (1963) gave another model in *"The Science of Human Communication: New Directions and New Findings in Communication Research,"* New York.

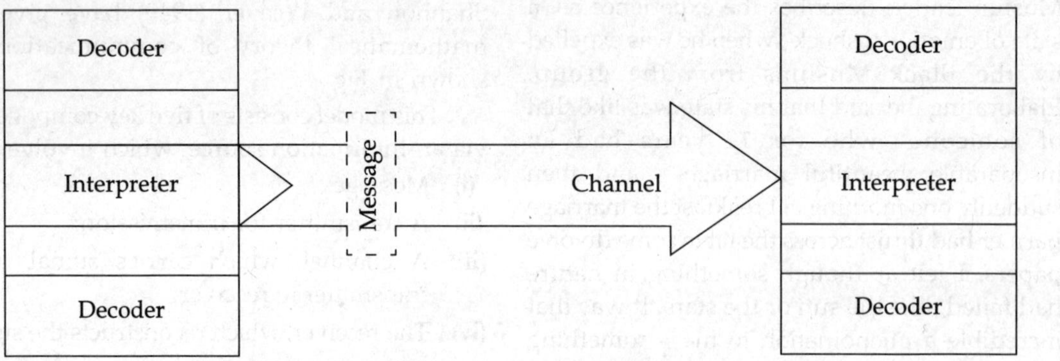

Fig. 5: Schramm's Model

(3) Lasswell's Model

Five essential elements in the communication process have been summarised as shown in fig. 6 by Harold D. Lasswell in an answer to this question, "Who says, what, in which channel, to whom with what effect?"

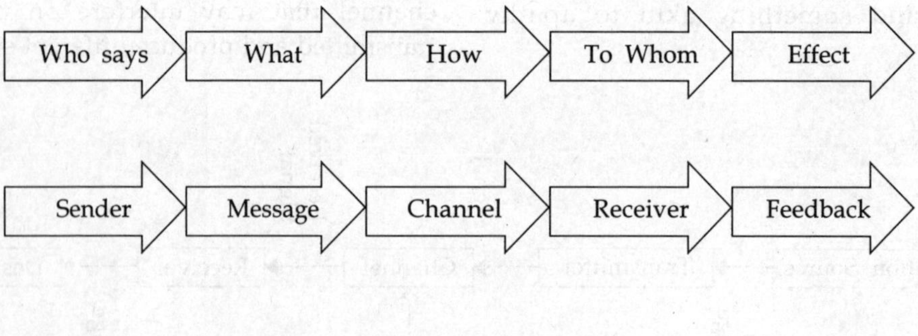

Fig. 6: Lasswell's Model of Communication

8.5 Communication Network

One of the ten wishes to reach out to more than one person. Then it is necessary to establish a network, i.e., a pattern of the relationship between the sender and the receivers. One may choose a network from a large number of possibilities, some of which are outlined as follows:

Chain Network—In a chain network, the sender communicates with one receiver, number 1, who then communicates with the next receiver 2 and so on until the last receiver *n* as shown in fig 7:

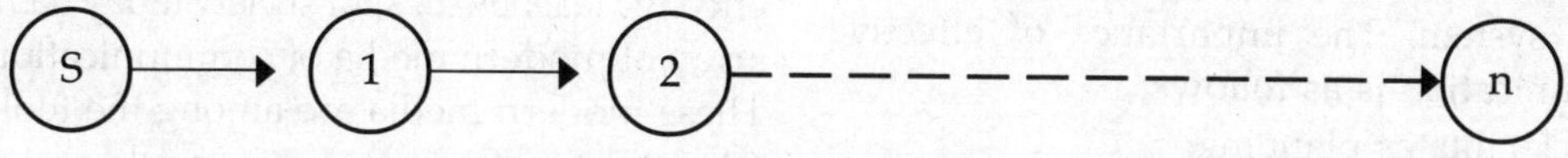

Fig. 7: Chain Network

A vertical chain for downward communication is often adopted in government bureaucracies and in the services.

Wheel Pattern—In a wheel pattern the sender assumes the central position and communicates directly with all the receivers, none of whom are able to communicate with one another as depicted in fig. 8. Such a centralized network operates with high efficiency in entrepreneurships and small establishments, particularly when a task must be done quickly.

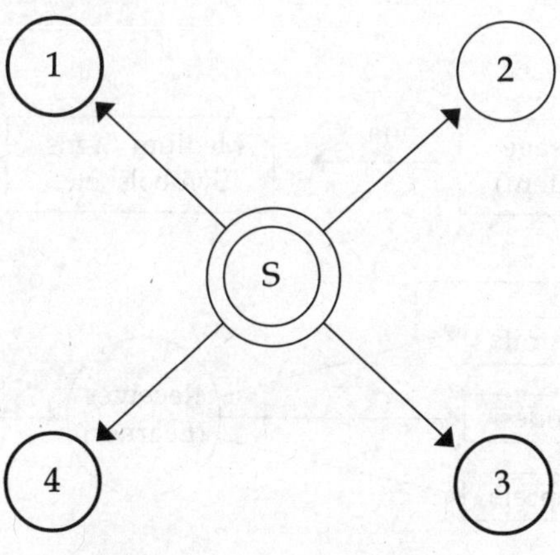

Fig. 8: Wheel-type pattern

There are some variations of the wheel pattern called Radial and Polygonal patterns. A radial pattern permits 2-way communication directly between the sender and each of his receivers. A polygonal pattern is an extension of the radial pattern where, in addition to 2-way communication between the sender and each of his receivers, there is some scope for adjacent receivers to communicate with each other.

Star Network— A star network permits all the persons to communicate mutually as shown in fig. 9. The 'sender' does not occupy a preferential position. Such a decentralised pattern is useful in dealing with the problems and innovations. Inter communication helps in reinforcing the messages and minimising distortions.

A manager, teacher, researcher, or an engineer may choose a network depending upon the purpose and his/her style of

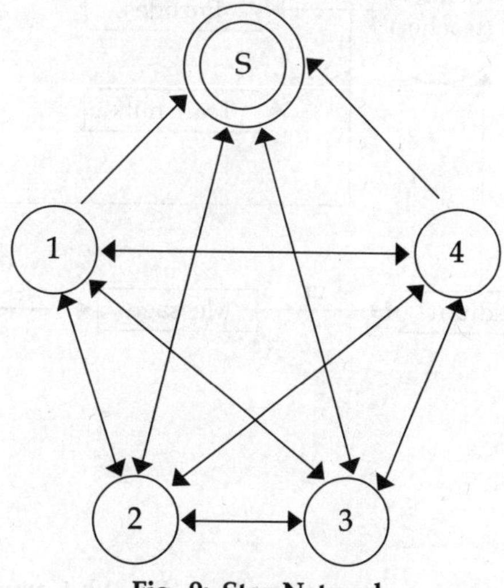

Fig. 9: Star Network

functioning. A general manager may choose a wheel-type network for the managers; a manager of R&D may adopt a star network to communicate with his research scientists/ engineers. In general, there is greater group satisfaction in decentralisation networks and greater short-term efficiency in centralised networks.

8.6 Role of Communication in Effective Management and Administration

Communication plays an important role in the working of an institution and especially the school system. The importance of effective communication is as follows:

1. It facilitates planning.
2. It helps in decision-making.
3. It facilitates coordination.
4. It improves relations.
5. It helps in the process of motivation and morale building.
6. It facilitates organising.
7. It helps to cope with the environment.
8. It brings efficiency in the system.

Communication assists the head and the teacher in performing the following roles in educational administration and management:

1. Administrative Roles
2. Managerial Roles
3. Supervisory Roles
4. Controlling Roles

8.7 Communication and Teaching

We may quote R. E. Kieffer and Lee W. Cochran, "Effective teaching and communications are synonymous, for good teachers are clear communicators and good communicators as effective teachers......Our society today has a vast array of modern media of communication .... These modern media are among the tools, the education profession uses to mould and shape human minds." Good teaching in fact is inter-communication. There must be reaction and interaction with constant feedback.

The message conveyed by the teacher and or the educational media may be verbal or visual and the receiver may listen, see or examine and react in other ways. The communication channel in the classroom should ideally carry both messages and counter messages.

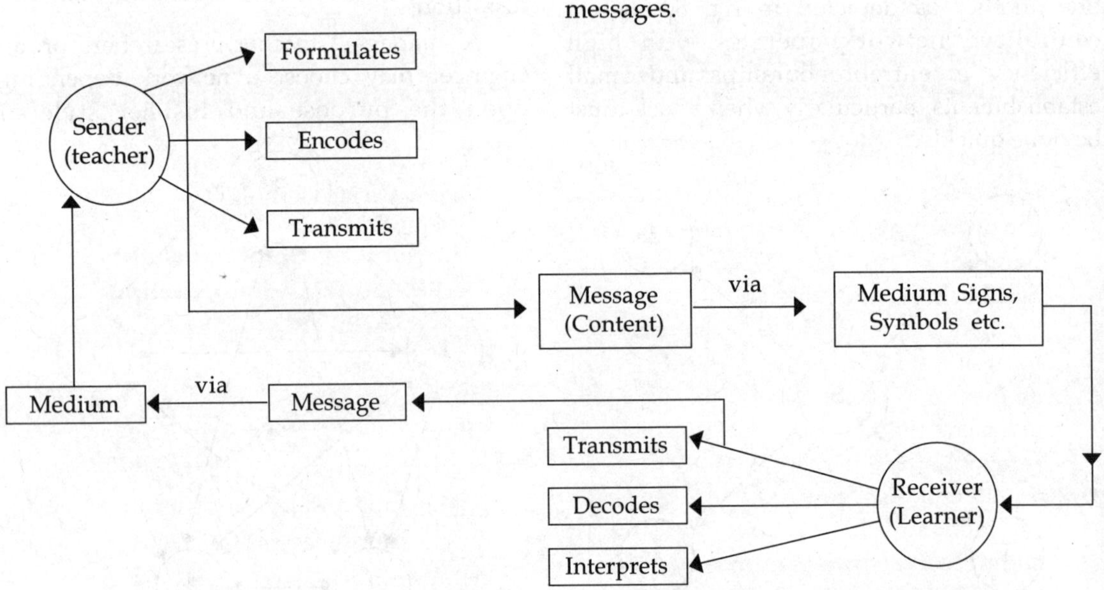

Fig. 10: Communication and Teaching

8.8 Communication in the Teaching-Learning Process

It is very important in teaching-learning as it is the chief means by which the teacher and the taught work together. It helps them to hold together by making it possible for them to influence and to react to each other. In fact communication is so fundamental that without it the organisation cannot exist.

A teacher might theoretically develop his plans, procedures, and the requisite organisational structure, but when it comes to implementation, he has to communicate this to his students. Unless the teacher has a communication skill, participation from the students may become difficult. The following factors may be considered in developing effective teaching-learning process:

1. **One-way versus Two-way Communication:** As the name suggests, it refers to the absence or presence of the facility to seek reactions, information, classification, etc. One way communication, i.e., telling or lecturing or demonstrating by the teacher denies the facility to the learners to seek clarification, confirmation, etc. the learners remain passive listeners. Two-way communication has a built-in-system to feedback. It ensures that further information, clarification, etc. are provided whenever possible. The receiver or the learners get opportunities to understand the message or the content.
2. **Feedback and Effective Teaching:** Feedback ensures that the message has reached the receiver. This can take the form of a nod, and acknowledgement or an execution of the behaviour suggested in the communication. Thus, the feedback provides a learning opportunity to the sender and the receiver because it mirrors the consequences of behaviour. In addition, if the behaviour has been found to be incongruous with the message it opens avenues to make corrections wherever necessary. Without feedback it would be difficult to ascertain whether communication has been received as intended or not. Positive and negative feedbacks may be used. When a learner does something commendable, a useful acknowledgement is made.
3. **Communication and Principle of Clarity:** A communication possesses clarity when it is expressed in language and transmitted in a way that can be comprehended by the receiver. Clarity requires a literature approach to language and familiarity with language patterns of the learners.
4. **Principle of Motivation:** The learners cannot listen or read with understanding unless they concentrate. Listening infits and starts, listening inattentively or ignoring or skimming out written words show slack in understanding. Adherence to the need for attention will gradually overcome certain barriers to communication, inattention, loss of transmission and poor attention. Motivation on the part of learners will increase the quality of learning and they will certainly feel encouraged for their efforts.
5. **Use of Audio-Visual Aids:** Teaching technology should be made use of in providing effective communication in classroom teaching.

8.9 Barriers of Communication in Educational Administration

There are certain elements in communication which create barriers in effective communication. These barriers may be grouped as under:

To overcome physical barriers

- Make appropriate seating arrangements.
- Ensure audibility and visibility.
- Minimize visual and aural distractions.
- Provide environmental comfort.

To overcome language barriers

- Use simple language and less verbalism.
- Explain and use graphic symbols.
- Prepare handouts and recommend books.
- Employ different methods of communication.
- Use audio-visual resources effectively.
- Take feedback as frequently as possible.

To overcome psychological barriers

- Call attention and motivate the listener.
- Use feedback processes.
- Provide assistance and show sympathy.
- Use interesting audio-visual resources.

To overcome background barriers

- Catch up with the individual's background.
- Explain the importance of the message.
- Employ different methods and resources.

8.10 Measures to Overcome the Barriers of Communication

Four types of measures for overcoming four types of barriers are:

I. Measures to Overcome the Physical Barriers

1. Making appropriate seating arrangement,
2. Ensuring audibility,
3. Minimising aural distractions,
4. Ensuring visibility,
5. Minimising visual distractions,
6. Providing comfort, and
7. Ensuring sound health.

II. Measures to Overcome the Language Barriers

1. Using simple language and symbols,
2. Using less verbalism,
3. Explaining with symbols and graphics,
4. Recommending specific books,
5. Using different methods of communication,
6. Using audio-visual aids, and
7. Providing frequent feedback.

III. Measures to Overcome the Background Barriers

1. Knowing the individual background,
2. Explaining importance of the message, and
3. Using different resources and methods.

IV. Measures to Overcome the Psychological Barriers

1. Sustaining the attention,
2. Providing motivation,
3. Providing assistance,
4. Providing multimedia resources,
5. Showing sympathy,
6. Providing regular feedbacks, and
7. Creating interesting situations and involving them to solve.

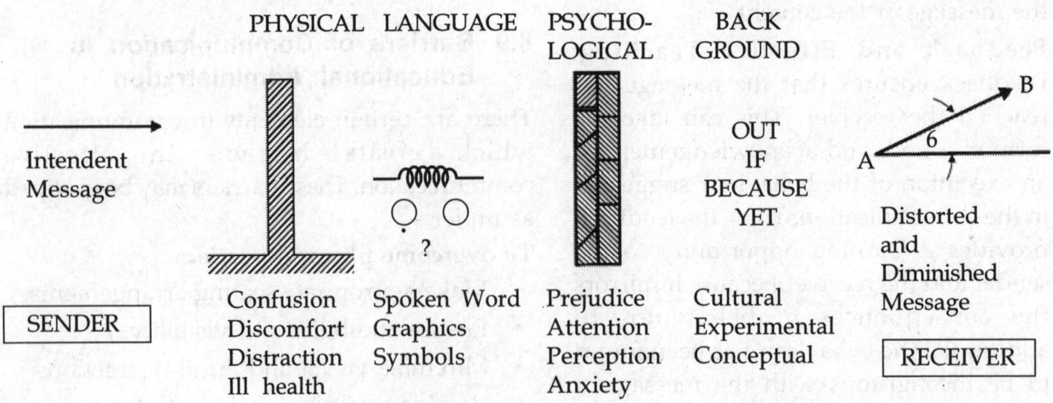

Fig. 11: Barriers to Communication: Distortion of Message

8.11 Principles of Effective Communication in Educational Administration: Making Communication Effective

1. Principle of clarity of language.
2. Principle of organisational facilities i.e. conferences, meetings, suggestions, etc.
3. Principle of priority.
4. Principle of formality, suitability combined with informality.
5. Principle of consistency.
6. Principle of adequacy.
7. Principle of two-way communication.
8. Principle of simplification.
9. Principle of selecting an effective communication channel.
10. Principle of feedback.
11. Principle of listening ability. This includes:
    - **(a)** Stop talking – you cannot listen if you are constantly talking.
    - **(b)** Put the listener at ease.
    - **(c)** Put the talker-listener at ease.
    - **(d)** Show the talker you are listening.
    - **(e)** Hold your temper.
    - **(f)** Be patient.
    - **(g)** Go easy on arguments and criticism.
    - **(h)** Ask questions.

Objective Type Questions

Multiple Choice Questions (Tick ✓ the right option)

(1) The word communication originates from
- (a) Communis
- (b) Common
- (c) Cominus
- (d) Comis

(2) Man's need for communication is as strong and as basic as his need to -
- (a) Eat
- (b) Sleep
- (c) Love
- (d) All the above

(3) Communication involves interaction with our environment
- (a) Physical
- (b) Biological
- (c) Social
- (d) All the above

(4) There are some variations of the wheel pattern called
- (a) Radial Pattern
- (b) Polygonal Pattern
- (c) Both 'a' and 'b'
- (d) None of the above

Fill in the blanks

(1) ________ plays an important role in the working of an institution and especially the school system. [Communication]

(2) Feedback ensures that the message has _______ the receiver. [reached]

(3) The _________ cannot listen, or read with understanding unless they concentrate. [Learners]

Important Questions

1) Define the meaning and concept of Communication.
2) Explain the need for Communication.
3) What are the Barriers to Communication? Explain how do you overcome these barriers.
4) Explain the Importance of Classroom Communication and the role of communication in the Teaching-learning process.

9

Management of School and Approaches of Management

School management implies systematic arrangement or framework of the school devoted to ensuring unity of effect, efficiency, goodwill and proper use of resources for the all round development of all the learners.

9.1 Changing Concepts of School Management

In view of the **new** challenges; the roles of the present day school have been radically changed and accordingly the concept of school management. Change is the order of the day and the school management must reflect a positive note in this regard. The old principles and practices of school management are now fading into insignificance in the dazzling light of the new ones.

[I] Traditional Concepts of School Management

A traditional school was considered to be a place where knowledge was manufactured and this used to be bookish, mechanical, and stereotyped. Education being uniform; no importance was attached to the individual needs of the children. Rote memory and memorisation played the dominant role. Children were regarded just like dumb driven cattle - Examination dominated the entire system of education. The rod was the chief weapon to educate the educand. 'The fear atmosphere' prevailed in the school. The teacher was called a policeman and drill sergeant. Co-curricular activities were almost unknown. No attempts were made to enlist the cooperation of the parents. The technology of teaching-learning was very simple.

[II] Modern Concepts of School Management

The functions of the present-day schools have undergone a great transformation in India, since the advent of Independence. Ours is a country wedded to the ideals of democracy. Democracy imposes many responsibilities on the citizens of a country. It is based upon love, cooperation, tolerance, open-mindedness, truthfulness, and fellow-feelings. If democracy is to survive, education must develop certain qualities needed for its survival. It must enable an individual to take part effectively and freely in the affairs of the group to which he belongs. Education is essentially a social affair. According to **Dr. S. Radhakrishnan,** all education is social. Education is the transmission of technical skills and cultural tradition from one generation to another. Education is literacy plus discipline – kind of an appreciation of the values of society of which we happen to be its members. Education is not worth the name, if it does not help an individual to live harmoniously and cooperatively in the society.

9.2 Characteristics of Modern School Management

Modern School Management must be based on the following characteristics:

1. Education in terms of traditional 3 R's has been replaced by the present 7 R's, i.e., Reading, Writing, Arithmetic, Recreation, Rights, Responsibility, and Relationship.

2. New activity methods such as Dalton Plan, the Project method, the Heuristic method, the Montessori method, etc., have brought about far-reaching changes in our methods of instruction.
3. Individual differences of children must be taken into account and diversified courses provided. The school curriculum is considered more in terms of activities and not in terms of subjects. Besides, subjects such as English, Mathematics, Hindi, etc., it is increasingly being realised that a variety of co-curricular activities must be considered as important as other school subjects. A well-organised system of guidance and counselling is also needed.
4. Let us look out the impact of the new pattern of education, i.e., 10+2. Far-reaching changes have taken place in the entire philosophy and practices of school management. The school curriculum and methods of teaching-learning have undergone important changes with the introduction of the new pattern of school education in 1975. All this had implications for principles and practices of school organisation management.
5. A present day school is expected to provide for a number of co-curricular activities which need an altogether new concept of school management.
6. The school of today is not only concerned with the intellectual development of the child but it is also to train him in the 'art of living together' which in itself is a complicated affair.
7. People are becoming increasingly education conscious. Today, we find a large number of students attending the school. They differ in tastes, needs, aptitudes and in various other ways. Family and social background of the students also vary. This has made the problem of educational management very complex.

9.3 Main Aspects of School Management

Management of a school has four main aspects—

1. **Management of School Plant:** Management of school plant includes the school building, laboratory, and playground, etc.
2. **Management of Human Resources:** This implies mobilisation of all people who are involved and interested in the educational activities of the school, i.e., pupils and their parents, school staff, experts, board of management, etc.
3. **Management of Material Equipment:** This includes material things, i.e., furniture and equipment, etc.
4. **Management of Ideas and Principles**: This means organisation of ideas and principles into the school system, curriculum, time schedule, norms of achievement, and cocurricular activities.

9.4 Features of a Well-Managed School

The Secondary school must be transformed into an "activity school," because activity has an irresistible appeal for every normal child and is his natural path to the goal of knowledge and culture.

The Commission observed, "We do not visualise" that these schools will have dull routine ridden formal lessons in the class plus a number of independent unrelated extra curricular activities which have no intrinsic relationship with them either in contents or methods. The entire programme of the school will be visualised as a unity and inspired by a psychologically congenial and stimulating approach, the so-called 'work' being characterised by the feeling of joy and self-expression usually associated with play and hobbies, and these having meaningful purposes which are normally considered a special feature of academic work. Thus by planning a coherent programme of these activities rich in stimuli, the school will not be frittering away either the time or the energy of the pupil but will be heightening their intellectual powers also side by side while training them in other fine qualities."

The good teacher, in the reorganised school, will endeavour to win the love and confidence of his children and establish his prestige on sincerity, integrity, hard work, and a sympathetic handling of their problems.

Another thing which will distinguish this school from most of the traditional schools is that it will be organised as a community.

We expect this school to devote special attention to craft and other productive work and thus redress the balance between theoretical and practical studies which have been upset for many years.

Every well-established and reasonably well-financed school will have workshops and craft rooms - where students will learn to handle tools and to fashion different kinds of material into form.

9.5 Approaches of Management

There are a number of approaches that can be used in the management of an institution. We will in this chapter confine our attention to the school management and will describe only those approaches that are relevant to the school management. The approaches that we are describing are—

[1] Manpower approach.
[2] Cost benefit approach.
[3] Social demand approach.
[4] Social justice approach.
[5] Decision-making approach.

[1] Manpower approach

This approach emphasises that we must plan for the future development of a country or nation. The development can largely take place through education. Hence, education for the people must be so planned that the educated generation will not only be gainfully employed but is also will be able to contribute its best to the society or nation.

The concept of management is derived from Economics. It has been observed that the human resources are much more vital in developing a nation as compared to the material resources. You may wastefully destroy your material resources if you have not learnt to make proper use of them. The manpower approach lays emphasis on the training and education of the human resources so that people are well equipped to put to the beneficial use of material resources.

Every society needs people in various fields of its activities. The education should be managed in such a way that there are available trained people for all its activities. If the people are well trained, are gainfully employed, are motivated, and efficient in performing their tasks the nation will prosper. It is an important obligation of education and school management to maintain constant supply of manpower for various activities of the society. The school education should be so managed that its product provides the required needs of the society of a trained manpower for various jobs.

Need of Manpower Approach

For linking educational management with manpower needs it is essential that the future projections for the need of human material in various occupations be carefully made. In advanced countries of the world there are efficient machineries to make such projections but in underdeveloped countries it becomes a very formidable task. It is essential that such machineries be developed in under-developed countries as well. The Ministry of Labour at the Centre with the close cooperation of the Ministry of Education and Industries can develop such efficient machinery. In India, attempts are being made to have manpower projections. What is urgently needed is to relate the manpower projections - with the educational expansion.

The Educational Commission (1964-66) has emphasised the relationship between educational enrolment and manpower requirements. It says, "If India is to achieve its targets of economic growth, it must have an adequate supply of educated specialists for each category of job to be performed. Conversely, if there is an excess of trained people in any category, it implies an imprudent use of scarce resources and also creates difficult problems of unemployment of the educated."

The estimation of manpower needs is helpful in planning for educational expansion in four ways:

(i) It helps in determining the total enrolments needed in secondary and higher education.

(ii) It helps in determining the enrolments needed in different types of courses.

(iii) It pinpoints attention towards shortages and surpluses in the manpower situation.

(iv) It focuses attention on priorities involved.

Machinery for Manpower Planning

The Kothari Commission feels that the following measures will have to be taken to relate the output of the educational system to manpower needs:

(a) **National Level:** Planning at the national level should be done by the Centre in consultation with the states and should cover all sectors crucial for national development. These should include engineering, agricultural, and medical education, and the preparation of teachers for higher education.

(b) **State Level:** The planning of remaining sectors should be done at the state level by state governments. The planning of facilities in secondary and higher education (excluding the sectors for which planning would be done at the central level) should be done at the state level.

Vocational education, both of school and college standard, will have to be expanded in all areas on a priority-basis in keeping with the manpower needs.

For enrolment in general education, however, which is under-developed in some areas and over-developed in others, a policy of equalisation will have to be adopted.

Manpower Planning, Employment and Education

All these three should be closely related. The education and employment should have direct link and there should be an indirect link between the output of the educational system and manpower needs of job or opportunities. Let us examine these relationships in some more detail:

(i) Manpower planning should be able to predict the number of jobs, the nature of jobs and the qualifications needed for various jobs. The educational system should be recognised in the light of the qualifications needed for the jobs available so far as its quality is concerned. From the quantitative point of view the output from the educational system should be related with the requirements in various areas of work.

(ii) Manpower estimates should be able to point out the need for the creation of more jobs. It should help in locating the areas where job opportunities are to be extended. The educational system must be so planned that there are people who can help in creating more jobs. For example, the projections for manpower planning may point out that in 2006 A.D. about 60,000, engineers will be needed. Comparison with advanced countries also points out that the industrial expansion is slow and its rapid expansion depends on individual entrepreneurship, particularly in manufacturing small parts of machines or as subsidiary to big industries. It may thus point out that engineering courses be so organised that a large number of engineers can set up their own manufacturing plants. In other words, the manpower planning should show the avenues of self-employment and give a direction to the educational planners in planning the content of courses.

(iii) Manpower planning should locate the areas of under-employment and the areas where a person with lower qualifications may work as efficiently as a person with higher qualifications. The enrolments in high education should then be made dependent on this aspect.

It may be clearly asserted that such a system of education is needed for this country that may have multiple terminal points and at each terminal point all those must get an offer of job who decide to enter the world of work. Such terminal points may be after the middle school education, the high school education, the higher secondary education, the graduation or the post-graduation courses. For this vocationalisation of education is very much needed. It is interesting to note that today at secondary stage 91% of students go for courses whose main objective is to prepare for the university. Our enrolment in vocational courses at the secondary stage are among the lowest in the world. This situation needs a change because otherwise educated unemployed will prove to be great threats to the stability of the nation, progress in the society and the economy of the country.

Limitations of Manpower Approach

1) The employment classification and manpower ratios used in most manpower studies in developing countries, as well as the assumed educational qualification corresponding to each category of jobs, are usually borrowed from industrialised economics and do not fit in the realities of less developed ones.
2) Manpower approach needs an interdisciplinary approach to educational planning. This needs an elaborate process and pooling of resources of various disciplines.
3) It is extremely difficult to make reliable forecasts of manpower requirements to be of significant value to educational planning.
4) It gives the educational planners only limited guidance. There is no doubt that there are uncertainties inherent in the tasks. Long term forecast of the growth of the economy has to be made and in order to provide guidance for educational planning it must be not only sufficiently detailed but also fairly authoritative. As new facts emerge and better methods of analysis are involved, fresh estimates will need to be made.

[II] Cost Benefit Approach

Maureen Woodhall explains this approach in these words, "A systematic comparison of the magnitude of the costs and benefits of some form of investment (in case of education it is investment in human capital) has to be made. All forms of investment involves a sacrifice of present consumption in order to secure future benefits in the form of higher level of output or income. Cost benefit analysis provides a means of appraising these future benefits in the light of the costs that must be incurred in the present."

This approach emphasises that the expenditure on any item or activity must give returns in tangible or intangible terms. The economists emphasise that if you spend Rs. 100 in any enterprise it must give a return of Rs. 101 at least; if not more. If this does not happen you lose your money and you are not able to recover your cost. Education was considered as an expenditure from which no returns in monetary terms were expected. But now this concept has changed. Education is also considered as an item of investment that gives returns not only in monetary terms but also in developing the quality of human resources. We will now expand this concept by emphasising how education is an item of investment rather than consumption and in providing education and managing the educational enterprise the benefit of the expenditure on it must accrue to the individual, society and nation.

In management, productivity is a very important requisite. That management is considered efficient which can enhance its productivity. In the management of an industry or business or in any other type of enterprise it is expected that the money spent leads to productivity not only in tangible terms but also in intangible terms. To assess to what extent the productivity is achieved the total profit or loss are calculated. Besides this it is also calculated as to what extent the cost has benefitted the organisation. The cost benefit may be calculated as a whole for the organisation or on an individual basis. When cost benefits to the organisation are determined it is called benefit analysis. For example, if we spend on education of our children twenty thousand rupees and they after education remain unemployed or underemployed the money on their education is wasted but if they are able to learn much more than that they would have earned in the management of education, we may also take into consideration the benefit of personal growth. But this cannot be numerically measured but only assumed.

Alfred Marshall refers to 'education as a national investment' in his 'Principles of Economics.' Marshall writes, "There are few practical problems in which the economist has a more direct interest than those relating to the principles on which the expenses of the education of the children should be divided between the state and the parents. But we must now consider the conditions that determine the power and the will of the parents to bear their share of the expense, whatever it may be."

John Vaizey has observed, "Education has become a major source of skills and trained talent. Higher the level of education an individual has, the higher his earning powers will be."

The rate of returns could be higher only when right types of skills are developed. This means appropriate educational reforms.

Education as Linked with the Development of a Country

In the table below taken from an UNESCO publication, the countries of the world divided in four categories show the relationship between Gross National Product per capita and the educational advancement.

TABLE 1

Stage of Development Measured by Selected Human Resource Indicators

Indicators	Under-developed	Partially developed	Semi-advanced	Advanced
GNP per capita (US dollars)	84	182	380	1100
First level enrolment ratio (Primary)	22	42	62	73
Second level enrolment ratio (Secondary)	2.7	32	27	59
Third level enrolment ratio (Higher)	0.15	1.6	5	11
Teachers (First and Second level)	17	38	53	80
Scientists and Engineers per 10,000 population	0.6	3	25	42
Physicians and Dentists per 13,000 population	0.5	3	8	15

It is clear from the above table that the per capita GNP in advanced countries is nearly 14 times that for underdeveloped countries and while first level enrolment is only four times in advanced countries the divergence is great at the second and third levels of enrolment.

It is being 22 times at the second level and nearly 73 times more while physicians and dentists are 30 times more. Thus, it is clear that for a higher rate of prosperity, education at all levels is a necessity.

Here is another table which gives per capita expenditure education and public expenditure on education as percentage of National Income.

From this table it is clear that the countries which are developed have a higher per capita expenditure on education than the underdeveloped countries. India, however, is making great efforts to increase its public expenditure on education. It was spending 3.7% (2.9% according to Education Commission Report) of its national income on education. However, it is a poor country and its resources are limited. So, per capita expenditure was only 1.3%. These figures are, however, rapidly changing and India's per capita expenditure is increasing. From the above tables it can be clearly realised that expenditure on education brings tangible returns. It is an investment which gives returns in the form of the development of the country. A country may have resources but it will fail to exploit them if it has people who are ignorant. Clark considers that, "The development of a widespread school system has been a major factor in pushing the income of the U.S. to a far higher level than it would have otherwise been."

Therefore, it is necessary that particularly in the early stages of a country's economic

TABLE 2

National Income and Public Expenditure on Education (1957-60)

Country	Per Capita–National Income in US Dollars	Public Expenditure on Education Per Capita in US $	Public Expenditure on Education as Percentage of National Income
Developed Countries			
(1) Japan.................	250.........................	14.6.........................	5.7,.........................
(2) U.S.A.	2,132	97.3	4.6
(3) France	960	32.5	3.0
Semi-developed Countries			
(4) Turkey..............	460.........................	10.0.........................	2.2.........................
(5) Chile	9.6	9.6	2.4
Underdeveloped Countries			
(6) India.................	66.........................	1.3.........................	3.7.........................
(7) Pakistan	51	0.6	3.2
(8) Burma	42	1.6	2.6

development education rather than consumer goods is instrumental in increasing output in all sectors of production and in creating a basis for continuing progress. It is the human element that is always the originator of everything that is created and is responsible for every development of himself, his family, and his country.

Limitations of Cost Benefit Approach

This approach when implied to education suffers from two handicaps–

(a) Availability and estimation of adequate cost data, and

(b) The calculation of future benefits.

This approach at its present experimental stage of development tells us more about the past than it does about the future.

In the end it may be said that none of these approaches provides an adequate basis by itself for educational planning. A synthesis of all these is needed.

Mark Blaugh and J.A. Lawvery point out in the Year Book of Education: "Each is only an index, a guide - certainly not an exclusive guide - to the formulation of educational policy. In one sense, they are not even indices of the same thing, but rather different views of the nature of education."

[III] Social Demand Approach

The prosperity of the Indian nation is greatly linked with the prosperity of her rural population. It is to the upliftment of the rural society that national efforts should be much more intensified. Till now the higher education has totally an urban bias. The villages have constantly been neglected with the result that the village community has remained at a very low level of subsistence. The fruits of modern technology, sciences, as well as the growth of knowledge in other field have not at all touched the village community. It is even today living in mud houses in the surroundings of dust, dirt, and filth. Hardly any village has any sanitary arrangements. The people are ignorant of personal hygiene and have no knowledge regarding the care of their children. A large number of villages have very meager means of communications. Hardly a few are connected by metalled road. The bullock-cart forms the only mode of travelling and the cow-dung as the only fuel. The backwardness of village community can better be described in the words of late Jawahar Lal Nehru who asserted that India is still living in the 'Cow-dung-Age.' It can easily be imagined that how gigantic is the task of raising the status of Indian Society from 'Cow-dung-Age' to the 'Moon and Mars Age' of seventies and to the space travel of eighties, electronic revolution of nineties and in telecommunication age of the first decade of the twenty-first century. But this is true that this task can be performed by an educational system which keeps village construction at the core of its programme. In this system not only the universal literacy, compulsory attendance but a higher education for the leader, reformer, and teacher and for creating general consciousness about modern advancement in sciences is necessary.

The village economy is in a very bad state of affairs. Till a few years after independence the zamindars were snatching the fruits of the toils of a farmer. They were growing rich while the farmer was left a destitute and a constant borrower of the money from the village money-lender. This was creating in him apathy towards more work and a loss of desire to produce more than what could serve his immediate needs. After abolition of the zamindari, this trend is still persisting since the village farmer is still exploited by the city businessman. He has no means of communication of his own to bring his produce to the open market in the city and has to remain content in whatever the city merchant offers him. Being mostly in debt he hurries up with the sale of his produce and is thus open to exploitation. This all is affecting the village economy very adversely.

Another factor responsible for low village economy is the fragmentation of the holding of the cultivated land by an average villager. The Indian peasant has less than five acres of land whereas his British counterpart owns 21 acres. This small holding of land by an Indian farmer limits greatly the possibilities of mechanized farming and of bringing other reforms in farming. This affects production to a great extent.

According to Planning Commission's estimates during the period 1987-88, 29.9 percent of the population of the country was living below the poverty line. Out of which 33.4 percent lived in rural areas and 20.1 percent in the urban areas. The average per capita income in 1991-92 was Rs. 5529 per annum. Agriculture is still the main source of livelihood for over 70 percent of the population in the country. A majority of the poor people live in rural areas without any property and land. These landless persons are earning their living by working on the farms of others or are taking up petty jobs for which they are paid very low wages.

In the fifth plan the concept of the Minimum Needs Programme (MNP) was introduced. It was realised that the benefits of planned development were not reaching to the weaker sections, of the society and the backward areas. Through the MNP this lacuna was sought to be overcome. The main features of the MNP were:

(i) To provide universal elementary education to the age group 6-14 years.

(ii) To make all the persons in the age group of 15-35 literate.

(iii) To provide one community health worker in each village to cover and make available services for sanitation, immunization, simple remedies, and referral services.

(iv) To assure supply of potable water to all villages.

(v) To connect villages with a population of 1000 or more with link roads.

(vi) To provide house sites and financial assistance for housing to all needy households.

(vii) To provide mid-day meals for children in the age group of 11-16 years and supplementary feeding programmes for undernourished children up to 6 years of age, pregnant women, and nursing mothers, and

(viii) To provide electrification of villages.

The MNP was primarily intended to provide infrastructure and social services to the weaker sections. Unfortunately its success was on a very limited scale. The Sixth Plan recognised this fact. It realised that the progress towards the development of the weaker sections had been both halting and slow.

In the Sixth Plan a new strategy for the upliftmeant of the weaker sections was introduced. It is known as Integrated Rural Development Programme (IRDP). Its main objective was to raise the weakest families in the rural areas above the poverty line on a lasting basis. It sought to do so by giving to these families income generating assets and access to credit facilities. The difficulties which this programme felt in its implementation were around a corrupt network which reduced the quantum of assistance to the needy and the failure of weaker sections to continue with the income-generating activities and relapsing back to poverty.

In the Seventh Plan it was sought to further strengthen IRDP. The defects in the implementation were removed through better planning, closer monitoring, and purging out of the corrupt elements. The policy in eighth and ninth plans was also directed towards raising the socio-economic conditions of ruralities.

In the later plans also rural upliftment was greatly emphasised.

The lot of landless labourers is very pitiable indeed. He gets work in the fields of the rich farmer and is paid very low wages. In a country where the cultivator himself is not fully engaged throughout the year, the work for landless labourer is still more difficult to find. It is the proverbial poverty of the landless that has motivated Acharya Vinoba Bhave's 'Bhoodan' movement.

The problem of unemployment in India is becoming grave due to the population growth at a rapid pace. In the western world there never was such a rapid growth so there the industrialisation led to full employment. In India, even industrialisation on the western pattern will perhaps not solve the problem. For example, in Great Britain in the middle of the nineteenth century the average growth of population was below 1.5 percent and there industrialisation plus migration of the population in large numbers to the New World that is USA, etc. resulted in better employment of its people. For India, today there is no such outlet for its surplus population. Added to this the modern technology is much more labour saving than was the advanced technology of the nineteenth century when western countries adopted it. Therefore, as Amlan Datta observes, "But however first the modern sector may be made to grow, it cannot under the condition mentioned above, absorb all or most of our large surplus labour force." According to him target of full employment in India cannot be achieved through industrialisation along conventional lines. For reducing unemployment, liberalisation of economy is necessary. But liberalisation may be misused by capitalists. Hence, liberalisation with social responsibility may be needed. Amlan Datta feels that the modern organised sector is going to stay with us and will expand. But it will be unrealistic to depend on that sector for removing poverty and unemployment. He considers that special attention should be paid to the other sector, comprising agriculture, handicrafts, and other 'informal' activities in our strategy of development. He emphasises the importance of traditional sector for solving our basic problems of poverty and unemployment. In the management of education and on establishing the modern set up of schools this fact may be kept in mind.

It may be pointed out that since 1968 India's production in food grains is speedily increasing. We have achieved Green Revolution. Let us see how a breakthrough in agriculture could be made possible.

There may be cited three-fold reasons for the breakthrough in agriculture. These are:

(i) The farmers took to mechanised farming. Through the community development programmes they learnt the value of using the chemical manures, good variety of seeds, and the use of tractors, etc.

(ii) The Agricultural Universities by conducting experiments on high yielding varieties of seeds, on modes of irrigation, and the chemical nature of soil were able, to supply much scientific data to the nation. Through their extension services they were able to inform the farmers in the simple language the use of farm technology in their farming.

(iii) The entry of educated personnel in the agricultural field helped in the use of scientific methods of cultivation. Many educated people in the last decade went back to their farms and started cultivation on scientific lines. For example, in Punjab the retired military personnel took to agriculture in a big way, thereby bringing a revolution in the pattern of raising crops.

There may be many other reasons but from the educational point of view the above three are outstanding. It may thus be seen that the proper arrangement of education greatly helps in building a better economic structure and since economy is the sub-system of social system, its impact on the over-all social system is clearly marked. Hence, there is a greater need for providing education, not only primary, but also higher to the rural population through crash programmes and the management of schools should take care of the social demands of the people.

Education through Space Satellite

The year of 1975 may be considered an important year for spreading literacy and social education in many states of India. In the beginning of the second half of this year education through space satellite was provided to a large number of village residents in five states of the country. The programmes of education fed to the satellite were relayed back to earth and were received by the television sets provided by the government to the village panchayats. Within a fortnight of the inauguration of the programme the T.V. programmes became very popular. The rural population rapidly learnt not only the three R's but also new methods of crop cultivation, sanitary habits, precaution from infectious diseases, etc. The programmes were providing education as well as entertainment to many such villages which had been completely neglected for centuries being in remote and inaccessible areas. This programme was for a limited period and had to be discontinued. But now the INSAT system is telecasting educational programmes.

By 1987, 70 percent of the population in India was covered by television. A large number of low power and high power transmitters had been installed all over the country to relay the television programmes from the satellite. The programmes from 90's are reaching to the urban areas as well as to the rural areas. Thus the satellite transmissions are being used for educating our people. Through INSAT system and micro-wave relay systems education is being taken to the doorsteps of the people.

The T.V. network is telecasting programmes through 36 high power transmitters of 10 Kilowatts (K.W.), 8 medium power transmitters (1 K.W.), and 37 low power transmitters (100 W). This number has increased in the seventh plan period. From 4 Doordarshan Kendras curriculum-based school T.V. programmes are being telecasted. Education television (ETV) programmes which are for general enrichment of knowledge for children in the age group 5-11 years are being telecasted in the regional languages through satellite six days a week, in the 6 INSAT states and relayed by all the transmitters in the 4 other Hindi speaking states. At the university stage the University Grants Commission (UGC) is telecasting programmes, one hour from 13.00 hours to 14.00 hours on all week days excepting holidays with repeat telecast from 16.00 hours to 17.00 hours under its scheme titled "Countrywide classroom." UGC has established Media Centres at different universities and institutions. It has established Education Media Research Centres (EMRC) and Audio-Visual Research Centres (AVRC). These centres are producing programmes for graduate students and are getting them telecasted at the hours mentioned above under the UGC scheme of countrywide classroom.

The development mentioned above show that steps are being taken rapidly for using the satellite technology for educational growth.

We may again assert in the end that in the present state of the world a nation needs skilled manpower, a populace which is educated in higher sciences, humanities, technology, and agriculture. A well-developed system of higher education brings these direct benefits to the people of nations. But education is equally needed for the indirect benefit which it brings. In the words of Alfred Marshall, "A good education confers great indirect benefit even on the ordinary workmen. It stimulates his mental activity, it fosters in him a habit of wise inquisitiveness, it makes him more intelligent, more ready, and more trustworthy in his ordinary work, it raises the tone of his life in working hours, it is thus an important means towards the production of material wealth, at the same time it is regarded as an end in itself, it is inferior to none of those which the production of material wealth can be made to subserve. Thus, education for prosperity to be organised both in terms of direct and indirect benefits."

Limitations of Social Demand Approach

This approach has been criticised on the under-mentioned three grounds:

(a) It does not take into consideration the larger national problem of resource allocation.

(b) It ignores the character and pattern of manpower needed by a country.

(c) It tends to overestimate popular demand and underestimates costs. This may result in their spreading of resources over too many students thereby reducing quality and effectiveness.

[IV] Social Justice Approach

A democratic, secular, and socialist state without social justice has no meaning. A welfare state without education is a contradiction in terms. The right to education is a fundamental right. It is needed for the optimum development of all individuals or citizens of a democratic state.

Appropriate type of education is considered a 'potent leveler' of all disparities.

Social justice approach demands that all should provide equality of opportunity in education.

The Preamble to the Constitution of India, 'Interalia' emphasises - Justice, Social, Economic, and Political.

Keeping in view the role of education in national development and social justice, the constitution makers made specific provisions for education in the Constitution.

Realising the importance of elementary education Article 45 provided for free and compulsory education to all children of age six to fourteen years. In 2002, this Article was amended and Article 21 A, Right to Education was added.

With a view to meet the demands and requirements of social justice, the Indian Constitution has provided special safeguard and special reservations in services, educational institutions and in Panchayati Raj Institutions for upliftment of the weaker sections like the SCs, STs, the OBCs, etc. Several concessions like fee concessions, free uniform, and stipends, etc., are given to the children belonging to these classes.

Direction in which efforts must be made to reorganise Educational System for providing Social Justice:

For achieving the target of social justice in India our efforts must be directed in many directions for reorganising the educational system. Some of these directions may be described below:

1) We must try to eradicate adult illiteracy as soon as possible so that everyone may be prepared to reap the fruits of education and also to remove the prejudices and biases concerning the social upliftment in general and exposure to education in particular.

2) We must make all efforts to increase the opportunities for education to all the weaker sections of the society like scheduled castes, scheduled tribes, backward communities, and women.

3) We must provide compulsory elementary education to all children at least 14 years of age so that no one may suffer because he has not got a chance for learning.

4) The higher education should be properly organised so that it may remain open for the talented irrespective of caste, creed, colour, or sex.

5) The Education Committee (1964-66) suggested that for equalisation of education opportunity, these measures may be adopted:

   (i) The country should work towards a stage when all education would be tuition free. From this point of view:

      (a) Tuition fees at the primary stage should be abolished in all the schools as early as possible and preferably before the end of the Fourth Plan.

      (b) Lower secondary education should be made tuition free in all schools preferably before the end of the Fifth Plan.

(c) For the next ten years, the main efforts with regard to fees in higher secondary and university education should be to extend provisions of tuition-free education to all needy and deserving students.

(ii) Free textbooks and writing materials should be provided at the primary stage.

(iii) Transport facilities should be provided imaginatively to reduce the cost of hostels and scholarships.

(iv) Facilities for students to earn and pay a part of their educational expenses should be developed.

(v) There should be liberal schemes for scholarships. At the level of higher education the Government of India should assume the bulk of such responsibility. At the school stage this responsibility should vest in the State Government.

(vi) There are wide differences in the educational development of different states. These become wider still at the district level. A reduction of the differences to the minimum is desirable.

The Commission has given many other suggestions regarding the education of Women, Backward classes and Tribal people. As we look towards the present situation we find that even after forty-five years the recommendations of the Commission have not been faithfully implemented.

[V] Decision-Making Approach

Modern writers on educational administration have greatly emphasised decision-making as a component of administrative process. It is considered as the core of administration. McCamy has gone to the extent to describe, "All other attributes of the administrative process being dependent or interwoven with and existent for making decision."

Culbertson, Jacobson, and Reller consider the decision-making process as lying close to the nerve centre of administration. They feel that, "It is administration what is switch-throwing mechanism is to an express train; it controls direction by selecting between and among alternative tracks or courses of action." In any administrative activity a choice has to be made or a course of action has to be chosen. The choosing of this course of action on the application of the rational thinking is the core of the decision-making. It does not mean that the decisions are not based on hunches or personal biases. But it does not mean that those decisions which are based on available adequate data and logical argument are superior to those made otherwise.

For making decisions the law, code, adopted policy, or prevailing practice are often valuable guides. In most of the educational decisions an appeal is made to them and an action is defined in accordance with them. There are, however, many circumstances, situations, and happenings in which a decision has to be taken without drawing upon the guidelines available from code, practice, etc. In such decisions the ingenuity, understanding, rationality, and capability of the administrator are taxed to the maximum extent.

The authors on educational administration point out that a rational decision is a conclusion reached from certain premises. Simon considers that these premises are of two kinds: *value premises and factual premises* which are roughly equivalent to purposes and means respectively. In the words of Simon, "Behaviour is purposive in so far as it is guided by general goals and objectives, it is rational in so far as it selects alternatives which are conducive to the achievement of the previously selected goals." The rational decisions thus depend on values and purposes. They also depend on the factual data available, the conditions existing and the stimulations provided.

Levels and Types of Decisions to be made

The decision-making can be done in a group, in an organisation or individually. In a group decision is taken through the interaction of the people in it who collectively arrive at a choice. Organisational decisions are taken through a process of the interaction with one another to arrive at a conclusion. The difference in organisational decision and group decision is that in organisational decisions direct and continuous involvement of a large proportion of membership is not necessarily needed. The individual decision making is done by the person and the process usually takes place in physical isolation of the other members of the organisation.

According to Culbertson, Jacobson and Reller there are three types of individual choices of administrators. They consider that "first there are those decisions that are relatively lacking in self-awareness, in the sense that they are repetitive and habitual." In this category they place the answering to a telephone call, coming to the office daily etc. In the second type they put the "executive choices that are made within the framework of clearly established policy." In this category they put decision regarding the preparation of a budget, employment of a new teacher, etc. Finally, they put in the third category "those decisions that are deliberate and are made in the absence of neatly prescribed policy." The examples of this type they cite are the decisions which occur during changes or re-orientation in policies or in the face of serious morale problems.

In India, the administrators at the school level are specifically concerned with only first type of choice-making. Many of them are concerned with the second type also but rarely they are required to make choice of the third type. If some such problems arise before them they simply refer them to the higher authorities who are concerned competent to deal with them. There is a clear cut hierarchy of officialdom in education and decision-making is also in the hierarchical order. A school principal is given limited power and it is usually expected that routine choices would simply be made by him. For budget, for selection of teachers, for re-orientation of policies, etc. he has to depend on the choices made by his superiors. Thus, in India more importance is attached to the decisions at the organisation level than those taken at the group level or individual level.

The decisions at the organisational level refer to the decisions at the directorate level. The group decisions refer to the decisions at the level of inspectorial staff where the policy decisions are put in the form of specific objectives to be achieved through the co-ordination of the efforts of the teachers, heads, and other personnel. The decisions at the level of the head of the institutions or teacher are of the third category.

How the decisions are made?

For making a decision certain steps are required to be taken. These steps are similar to that of problem solving since both are rational processes. In problem solving the first step is the comprehension of the problem. In decision-making the first step is to understand the purpose clearly. We may describe the various steps in the decision-making process as follows:

1. First Step: A clear comprehension of the goal to be served by the decision;
2. Second Step: Collection of data which means the obtaining of all the facts, opinions and ideas which are relevant for the purpose;
3. Third Step: Analysis and interpretation of the data collected in the light of sound judgement;
4. Fourth Step: Formulation of the alternatives which are available;
5. Fifth Step: Evaluation of each alternative in the light of its possible effectiveness in the achievement of the purpose or goal;
6. Sixth Step: Selecting the particular alternative which offers the most promise

when all possible consequences are considered.

In educational administration a large number of decisions have to be taken. The decisions regarding curriculum, textbooks, work experiences, vocational guidance, etc. are normally taken at the level of the directorate and also at the school level. At the directorate level they are more in the form of policy decisions and at the school level they are the decisions for execution of the policy decisions already taken. However, at both the levels the above six steps should be followed.

On what decisions depend: According to Culbertson, Jacobson, and Reller—"decision premises may be classified into three types: facts, values, and unsubstantiated information. They consider that as these premises impinge upon the administrator, they activate cognitive equipment, arouse emotions, and put violation to work." The administrator understands, feels, and wills and the decisions are taken. Thus, it can be said that the decisions depend on the values, facts as well as many a times upon information which is not substantiated.

The values which underlie decisions may be educational, economic, social, personal, or moral or a mixture of these. There may be many interrelated values involved in arriving at a decision regarding permitting girls to study side by side with boys.

An administrator finds many of the values involved in the school laws or educational policies. In cases where a decision is taken in the light of them the administrator's task is easy. But often he will find himself in difficulty when the decision has the implication of the involvement of less explicit values which are not embodied in the school laws or educational policies.

The decisions are also made on the basis of facts. According to Culbertson "a fact may be defined as a condition, object, or event that would be accepted as accurate by two or more observers." On the basis of funds available the decisions regarding the school budget are taken.

Decision-making may be based on simple guesses or complex mathematical analysis; we may divide decision-making bases between quantitative and non-quantitative. The prominent non-quantitative bases are:

(a) Institution;
(b) Facts;
(c) Experience; and
(d) Considered opinions.

The common quantitative means employed are:

(a) Operation research;
(b) Linear programming;
(c) Simulation;
(d) Monte Carlo;
(e) Queuing; and
(f) Gaming.

It is not advisable to put faith in any one approach. For effective planning a balanced and harmonious approach is needed.

Objective Type Questions

Multiple Choice Questions (Tick ✓ the right option)

(1) A traditional school was considered to be a place where knowledge was manufactured and this used to be

(a) Bookish
(b) Mechanical
(c) Stereotyped
(d) All of the above

(2) "All education is social". This definition is given by

(a) Dr. S. Radhakrishnan
(b) Plato
(c) Dewey
(d) Ross

(3) Management of school plant includes the
- (a) School building
- (b) Laboratory
- (c) Playground
- (d) All of the above

(4) The concept of management is driven from
- (a) English
- (b) Economics
- (c) Latin
- (d) Greek

Fill in the blanks

(1) The Educational Commission has emphasized the relationship between educational ________ and ________ requirements. [Enrolment, Manpower]

(2) In management ________ is a very important requisite. [Productivity]

(3) The ________ can be done in a group. [Decision-making]

Important Questions

1. Write a short note on the traditional concept of School Management.
2. Write a short note on the modern concept of School Management.
3. Write the characteristics of modern School Management.
4. What are the various approaches to Management?
5. Explain the manpower needs approach in the management of a secondary school.
6. What are the steps that must be taken in making decisions?
7. Why should we adopt manpower planning in our country?

10

Central and State Agencies of Education

10.1 Educational Administration at the National Level

The agencies at the national level concerned with the development of education are the Ministry of Education, the University Grants Commission and the National Council of Educational Research and Training.

10.2 National Level or Central Agencies

1. University Grants Commission (UGC).
2. National Council of Educational Research and Training (NCERT).
3. National Institute of Educational Planning and Administration (NIEPA).
4. Indian Council of Social Science Research (ICSSR).
5. Centre of Advanced Studies of Education (CASE).
6. National Council of Teacher Education (NCTE).

The Hon'ble Minister for Education controls the educational policy, directs it, executes, and ensures uniformity in the pattern of education in different states. He is assisted by one or two Deputy Ministers according to need.

The Educational Advisor is the administrative head of the Ministry. He is the Secretary to the Government of India and is the principle advisor to the Ministers on all matters of policy and administration. The Union Ministry at present functions mainly through five bureaus dealing with the heads:

1) School education;
2) Higher education;
3) Language, Literature and Fine Arts;
4) Scholarships; and
5) Planning and Ancillary Educational Services.

The Bureau of School Education deals with elementary, basic, and secondary education and the Central School Unit. The Bureau of Higher Education covers both university and technical education programmes.

The Bureau of Scholarships deals with all matters relating to scholarships, internal or external as well as general and cultural.

The Bureau of Planning and Ancillary Educational services includes the National Council for Educational Research and Training Unit, social education, planning, publications, statistics, and information.

The Bureau of Language, Literature, and Fine Arts looks after cultural matters and development of Indian languages and the three Academics.

The Scientific Research Division is allied to the Bureau of Scholarships.

Each bureau has been put in charge of a Joint Secretary or a Joint Educational Advisor to whom are attached divisional heads for the major subjects.

The Physical Education and Recreation Division and the External Relation Division are separated under the charge of a Joint Educational Advisor.

Advisory Bodies

The Ministry has set up a number of advisory bodies which function in different sectors of education. The oldest and the most important of these is the Central Advisory Board of Education. The Board is presided over by the Union Minister of Education and includes all State Education Ministers as members. Until 1949, it was the only body which considered the national problems in education and tendered advice to the central and state governments.

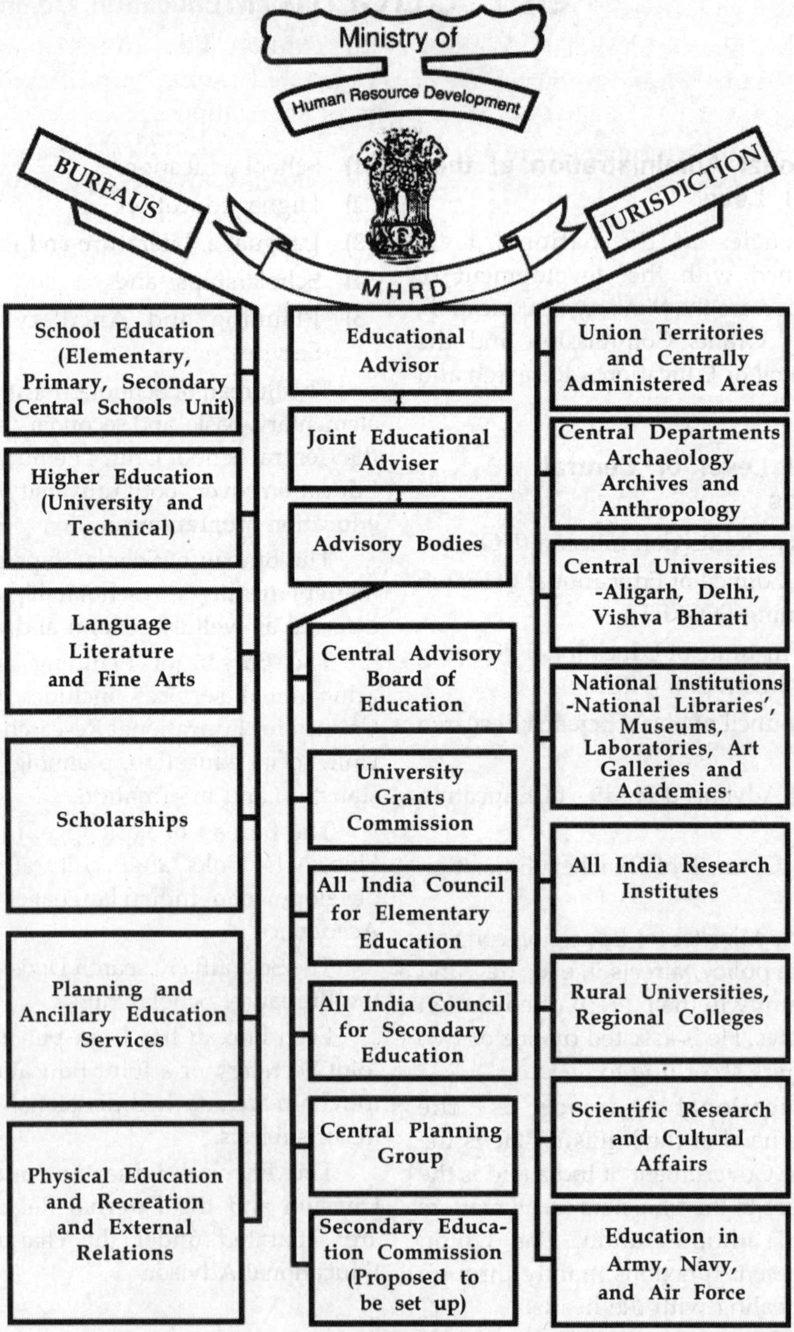

Fig. (1)

The volume of educational activities increased to such an extent that it was felt desirable to constitute a number of other advisory bodies to deal with special sectors of education. At present, there are 15 such bodies viz.:

1. Indian National Commission for Cooperation with UNESCO (1949);
2. Advisory Board for Social Welfare (constituted in 1951 and reconstituted in 1954);
3. Board of Scientific Terminology;
4. Central Board of Physical Education and Recreation (constituted in 1950 and reconstituted in 1956);
5. Hindi Shiksha Samiti (1951);
6. National Board of Audio-Visual Education (1953);
7. All India Council for the Sports (constituted in 1954 and reconstituted in 1959);
8. National Advisory Council for Education of the Handicapped (1952);
9. National Council for Rural Higher Education (1956);
10. All India Council for Secondary Education (1955);
11. Central Committee for Educational Research (1957);
12. All India Council for Elementary Education (1957);
13. Children's Literature Committee (1958);
14. National Council for Women's Education (1959);
15. Central Sanskrit Board (1959).

The institution for these advisory bodies has been found to be very helpful. They bring official and non-official workers together in the consideration of educational problems and tender advice to the Central and State Governments on issues, which are of importance in formulating educational policies and programmes. They also bring to bear an all India approach on the discussion of problems entrusted to them.

A practice of holding periodical conferences of State Education Ministers to discuss important educational matters is also growing.

10.3 Modifications Suggested by the Indian Education Commission

The Indian Education Commission has suggested some modifications in the recommendations of Secondary Education Commission and added new plans. It suggests the following advisory and executive bodies:-

1. *National Board of School Education* besides the Central Advisory Board of Education to coordinate the standards of education at the national level and help the States.
2. *Central Board of Secondary Education* to deal with all aspects of Secondary Education at the State level.
3. *National Staff College of Educational Administration* for training in educational administration and supervision.
4. *State Board of School Education* to deal with all the aspects of secondary education at the State level.
5. *State Institutes of Education* for providing in-service or regular training for supervisors and administrators and other programmes.
6. *State Board of Vocational Education* to look after vocational education in the State.
7. *State Higher Secondary Committee* to look after the Higher Secondary Education.
8. *State Evaluation Organisation* for prescribing standards, improving education techniques, prescribing textbooks, etc.
9. *District School Board* in each district, to administer elementary education in the district.
10. *Block School Committee* to look after the management of Government and local body schools in the area.

10.4 Functions of the Central Government

The Central Government has the following functions as far as education is concerned:-

1) **Planning:** It lays down the general policy regarding education to be followed by the states; determines targets and priorities and prepares a tentative plan-frame for the country as a whole. It appoints commissions, committees, and boards to study the various phases of education and suggests steps to improve the same.

2) **Organisation:** It appoints commissions and committees to organise special fields of educations like the mass education, professional education, employment of the educated, provision for backward classes, indiscipline among students, grants commissions for universities, research institutes and laboratories and the central universities. For these purposes, it has set up the All India Council for Technical Education, All-India Council for Secondary Education, the All India Council for Elementary Education, the National Council of Educational Research and Training, etc.

3) **Direction:** It directs and guides the state governments, local bodies, and individual enterprises so as to encourage education on right lines. Through the Central Advisory Board of Education; it tries to solve the baffling educational problems as medium of instruction, assessment, and evaluation, textbook nationalisation, teaching personnel, libraries, and laboratories.

4) **Control:** As the financial resources of most states are inadequate for supporting their educational programmes, they look to the Central Government for grants and subsidies for short as well as long-term projects. The Centre allocates suitable grants for the state, local bodies, private agencies, and individual scholars out of the Central Budget. It arranges student exchange programmes with foreign countries. It makes available certain fellowships and scholarships for outstanding scholars to go into advanced study of subjects. It arranges students training abroad and in-service training of teachers through the extension service departments.

5) **Equalising Educational Opportunities:** It provides financial assistance in such a way that the weaker or lesser states will be able to catch up with the forward states or at least reduce the large discrepancies that exists at present between them and the advanced states. It levels out the differences in respect of different types of education and tries to provide equality of educational opportunity to every child. The targets are fixed and weaker states are assisted to achieve the targets.

6) **Pilot Projects:** For showing new light for the people in the country, it undertakes certain pilot projects like Rural Universities, Education Extension Services, Regional Institutes, preparation of textbooks for different school subjects through the department of curriculum, methods, and textbooks. It can provide leadership for developing a programme of significant and fundamental research in education to assist state governments in improving the quality of education.

7) **Clearing House Function:** It serves as a repository and clearing house of information and ideas on education, research, training, and expansion for all the states. Educational statistics for the whole country are collected. The Government of India brings out three publications every year:-

   (i) Education in India (in two volumes);

   (ii) Education in the States; and

   (iii) Education in Indian Universities.

Besides, it also publishes a Directory of Institutions of Higher Education. It also publishes studies and surveys, reports of commissions and committees and such other educational documents and ideas. There is a special publications section and it has brought out about 530 publications. A number of magazines – Education Quarterly, Secondary Education, Youth, Indian Journal of Educational Administration and Research are published to disseminate improved techniques, practices, and latest ideas.

8) **Administration of Education in the Union Territories and Centrally Administered Area:** The Centre is directly responsible for education in the Union Territories of Delhi, Chandigarh, Himachal Pradesh, Manipur, Tripura, Andaman and Nicobar Islands, Laccadive, and the centrally administrated areas of Pondicherry, N.E.F.A., and N.H.T.A.

It may be pointed out here that the educational activities are not centralised in the Ministry of Education. Practically, every Ministry of the Government of India conducts some educational programmes.

10.5 Centre's Responsibilities in Education

1. Indian Education Commission (1964-66)

The Indian Education Commission made the following recommendations as the centre's responsibilities in education.

(i) The improvement of teacher status and teacher education;

(ii) Manpower planning in crucial sectors like agriculture, engineering, medicine, etc.

(iii) The development of a programme of scholarships;

(iv) The equalisation of educational opportunities with special reference to the reduction of inter-state differences and the advancement of weaker sections of the community;

(v) The provision of free and compulsory education directed by the Constitution;

(vi) The vocationalisation of secondary education and the improvement of standards at the school stage;

- (i) The development of higher education and research with special reference to the post-graduate stage;
- (ii) The development of professional education in agriculture and industry;
- (iii) The promotion of scientific research; and
- (iv) The promotion of educational research.

The University Grants Commission

On the recommendations of the University Education Commission, the University Grants Commission was established under an Act of Parliament in 1956 to look after the higher education.

The U.G.C. deals with about ninety universities and pays them development grants out of funds placed at its disposal by the Government of India. The U.G.C. arranges a visitation of the Universities every five years through visiting committees and grants-in-aid are sanctioned on the basis of their recommendations.

The Indian Education Commission (1964-66) is of the opinion that U.G.C. has a creditable record of work during the first ten years of its existence. The Commission has given the following suggestions to further strengthen the U.G.C.:

(i) The U.G.C. should represent the entire spectrum of higher education. It should be professionally concerned and adequately equipped to deal with all its problems. Agriculture, technology, medical sciences, and teaching will all be the richer for being part of this broad stream and by being concerned with the problems and needs of one another. All higher education including agriculture, engineering, and medicine should be regarded as an integrated whole and be brought within the purview of the U.G.C. This is the ultimate direction in which we should move.

(ii) For the time being, it would be more feasible to set up a separate U.G.C. - type organisations for agricultural, engineering, and medical education and to create machinery that would effectively coordinate with them. For immediate action the Commission has given the following proposals:

(1) It is not desirable that the Government should deal directly with the Universities. There should be a body-committee of persons between the Government and the universities selected for their knowledge and standing rather than for their political affiliation or official status.

(2) The U.G.C. type organisations, based on the above principles, should be set up for dealing with technical, agricultural, and medical education. They should be composed of teachers and scientists of eminence in their fields and should be small and compact bodies so that they can meet frequently and work expeditiously. They should function more or less like the U.G.C., i.e., lumpsum grants should be placed at their disposal by the ministries concerned and they should have the freedom to distribute them to the universities in relation to their needs, and programmes of development.

(3) For the purpose of coordination, there should be a certain overlapping membership between the U.G.C. and the U.G.C. type organisations.

(iii) The U.G.C. should consist of 12-15 members. Of these not more than one third should be officials of the Government. At least one-third should be from the universities. The remaining should be eminent educationists. To provide greater degree of rotation, the term of office of members may be reduced from the present six years to three with not more than one extension.

(iv) The U.G.C. should work through a number of standing committees set up to deal with important responsibilities. There may be standing committees on affiliated colleges, teacher education, preparation of university, textbooks, and development of literature in modern Indian languages, and students welfare.

(v) The inspections taken up by U.G.C. should be done in greater details and depth.

Activities of U.G.C.

During its short period of existence, the U.G.C. has been able to float a number of projects and schemes. Some of them are mentioned here:

1. Autonomous colleges.
2. Redesigning the undergraduate courses by making them more relevant and to link education with work/field/practical experience and productivity.
3. Consolidation of and expansion of facilities of the existing university departments and colleges.
4. Providing computer facilities to 93 universities and mini-computers to 200 colleges during the seventh plan period.
5. Setting up Academic Staff Colleges for the orientation of newly appointed university and college lecturers.
6. Special assistance for the promotion of research to individual teachers and colleges.
7. Setting up documentation centers like Nuclear Science Centers at JNU, Radio Astronomy Centre at Poona University, National Centre of Astronomy at Osmania University, Hyderabad.

8. Providing media and educational technology facilities. The UGC has provided coloured TV sets to 2000 selected colleges during the seventh plan period. The Commission is at present supporting four Educational Media Research Centres (EMRCs) at the University of Poona; Gujarat University, Ahmdabad; Central Institute of English and Foreign Languages, Hyderabad; and Jamia Millia Islamia, New Delhi. Seven Audio-Visual Research Centres (AVRCs) at the University of Roorkee; Osmania University; University of Jodhpur; Anna University, Madras; St. Xavier's College, Kolkata; Madurai Kamaraj University, Madurai; and Kashmir University, Srinagar, are being supported for the training of personnel of production of software. A proposal for establishment of a TV programme production centre at Bharatidasan University, Tiruchirapalli for production of model tele courses in fifteen chosen subjects for under-graduate students is under the Commission's consideration.
9. Adult, continuing, and extension programmes in 92 universities and 2,121 colleges;
10. Provides facilities to Scheduled Castes/ Scheduled Tribes;
11. Bilateral Exchange Programmes of college teachers;
12. Special assistance to universities to undertake well defined projects for research in women's studies; and
13. Selected university departments are recognised as Centres for Advanced Studies (CAS) and certain departments for financial assistance.

2. *National Council of Educational Research and Training (NCERT)*

In the Third Five Year Plan (1961-66) it was proposed to establish a training and research centre at the national level which should be an autonomous body and work for the promotion of research and training facilities in varied fields of educational activity. This led to the establishment of a National Council of Educational Research and Training in 1961 under the society Registration Act of XXI Statute of 1860.

The major objectives of the Council are to assist the Ministry of Human Resource Development in formulating and implementing policies and programmes in the field of school education.

It took over the Central Institute of Education (1947) (later on it was taken over by the Delhi University), the Central Bureau of Textbooks Research (1954), the Central Bureau of Educational and Vocational Guidance (1954), the All India Council for Secondary Education (1955), the Directorate of Extension Programme for Secondary Education, generally known as DEPSE (1955), the National Institute of Basic Education (1956), the National Fundamental Centre Education (1956), and the National Institute of Audio-Visual Education (1959). These organisations were set up in the year given in the brackets against each.

Structure and Administration

The Governing body is the policy-making body of the Council. It is headed by the Union Minister of Human Resource Development (formerly known as the Union Education Minister) and includes as its President (Ex-officio), Minister of State in the Ministry of Human Resource Development (as Ex-officio Vice-President), the Deputy Ministers, Education Minister of all the States and Union Territories as its members. In addition, it includes the Chairman of the University Grants Commission, the Secretary to the Ministry of Human Resource Development, four Vice-Chancellors of Universities (one from each region), Director of the Council, four educationists with known interests in school education (two of whom shall be school teachers), the Joint Director of the Council and three others.

Activities

For the realisation of the above objectives, NCERT undertakes the following programmes and activities:

- Conducts, aids, promotes and coordinates research in all branches of school education;
- Organises pre-service and in-service training of teachers mainly at an advanced level;
- Organises extension services for institutions, organisations, and agencies engaged in educational reconstruction;
- Develops and experiments with improved educational techniques, practices, and innovations
- Collects, compiles and disseminates educational information;
- Assists the States and the State-level institutions, organisations and agencies in developing and implementing programmes for qualitative improvement of school education;
- Collaborates with international organisations like UNESCO, UNICEF, etc. and with national-level educational institutions of other countries;
- Extends facilities for training and study of educational personnel from other countries;
- Serves as the academic secretariat of the National Council for Teacher Education (NCTE).

The National Council of Educational Research and Training runs the following:

1. The National Institute of Education (NIE).
2. Central Institute of Educational Technology.
3. Four Regional Institutions of Education formerly known as Regional Colleges of Education.
4. Seventeen Field Units.

Organisation of NCERT

At present the National Institute of Education consists of the following departments:

1) Psychological Foundation Department
2) Science Education
3) Teacher Education Department
4) Philosophical Foundation
5) Department of Field Services
6) Journal Cell and ERIC (Educational Research & Innovation Cell)
7) Department of Curriculum and Textbooks
8) Basic Education and Primary Education
9) Department of Audio-visual Education
10) Adult Education and Literacy
11) Central Science Workshop
12) Educational Survey Unit
13) Work-experience and Vocationalisation
14) Central Institute of Education Technology
15) Examination and Evaluation Unit
16) Education of the Handicapped, and
17) Guidance and Counselling.

Apart from the above, the Council has also established State Institutes of Educational Research and Training in each state and four regional colleges of education at Ajmer, Bhopal, Mysore, and Bhubaneswar catering to the need of the training of secondary school teachers and research works in this direction.

Objectives of NCERT

The Council works for achieving the following objectives:

1) To establish a National Institute of Education (NIE) and manage for the development of research and higher training for educational administrators and teachers.
2) To arrange for the establishment of training institutes for the professional and scientific enhancement of teaching.
3) To provide guidance and counselling services on a large scale.
4) To publish necessary textbooks, journals and other literature for achieving the objectives.

5) To organise extension centres in training institutions with the cooperation of the state governments and extend facilities pertaining to new methods and technologies among them.
6) To launch, organise and strengthen research works in various aspects of education.
7) To arrange pre-service and in-service training at the higher level.

Various Programmes of NCERT

The National Institute of Education, through its various departments deals with the following developmental works:

a) To investigate problems pertaining to in-service training, educational planning, and administration at different centres located in states.
b) To prepare charts, models, film-strips and audio-visual material for science and other subjects.
c) To investigate the problems of basic education and implement the programme of adult education.
d) To suggest suitable reforms in the curriculum and methods of teaching of science and mathematics and develop proper educational material, equipment and textbooks in this connection.
e) To expand the scheme of social studies and prepare its terminology.
f) To arrange for educational surveys in the field of group dynamics, direction and exchange of views on psychological basis.
g) To conduct research for bringing about economy in the construction of school building.
h) To launch areawise researches pertaining to the problems of teachers, curriculum methods of teaching and technology.
i) To arrange for providing fellowship for the encouragement of research works in different fields.
j) To conduct research works in collaboration with the health and welfare departments of USA.
k) To organise summer institutes in the field of social science and humanities for developing a suitable school curriculum.
l) To arrange summer institutes for science and mathematics teachers in collaboration with the University Grants Commission and International Technical Development Agency (USAID).
m) To provide summer school-cum-correspondence programmes for in-service teachers in the regional colleges of education located in different areas.

3. *National Institute of Educational Planning and Administration (NIEPA)*

Formerly known as the National Staff College for Educational Planners and Administrators, it began to function on 1st January, 1971 after it was registered under the Indian Societies Registration Act, 1860 on 31st December, 1970. With the expiry of agreement with UNESCO under which, the Asian Institute of Educational Planning and Administration was functioning, the Staff College from 31st March, 1973 moved to the new premises at the NCERT.

Thereafter it was renamed as National Institute of Educational Planning and Administration.

The institute has an important place in the national educational system of the country. It is the highest organisation of educational planning and administration. It has a important role in the area of educational planning, administration and training. It has the following functions in education:

1. It provides the training of educational planning and administration to develop the abilities and competencies in the educational administration as the in-service programme.
2. It integrates the educational studies and researches under the area of educational

planning and administration, and makes the coordination in these activities.

3. It also provides the training facilities in educational planning and administration at State level and regional level to develop efficiency at their level.
4. It has the extension programmes for new developments and innovations in the area of planning and administration.
5. It also encourages to the workers to solve the problems of educational planning and administration by organising seminars and workshops.
6. It provides the guidance at National and State levels in the area of planning and administration.
7. It establishes contact with other countries to understand the developments and innovations of the developed countries.

It has multi-dimensional activities in educational planning and administration. The educational planning and administration journal is published under extension programmes. The books and other booklets are published by the Institute of Education.

The educational research reports are published. The publication unit establishes the coordination between theory and practice. The review of studies of educational planning and administration of developed countries is also done by the institute. It is used to develop our education system and solve the educational problems. There are twelve books on different aspects of educational planning and administration which have been published by NIEPA. The seminars and workshops are organised and their discussions and results are published. It also evaluates the effectiveness or workability of new innovations. The orientation courses are organised for the educational administrators to provide the awareness of new developments in the area of planning and administration.

4. *Indian Council of Social Science Research (ICSSR)*

The Planning Commission realised the importance of social science research works. A committee was appointed by the Commission and it recommended establishing the Council at national level. This Council was established in August (1969) as an autonomous organisation. The main focus of the Council is to develop the social science researches and also establish coordination in them. The financial assistance and grants are provided by the Council. The Council has the following functions.

(i) To review the social science research studies and provide guidance for their applicability.

(ii) To provide grants and financial assistance to universities, colleges, and other institutes for social science research.

(iii) It also provides the financial assistance for individual research workers.

(iv) To provide the awareness about new emerging trends of society for conducting research studies in these areas.

(v) It encourages the interdisciplinary research studies and coordinates such studies.

(vi) To organise orientation courses, seminars, workshops for new methodology and new areas of studies.

(vii) To provide the financial assistance for conducting research studies and projects in social science subjects.

(viii) It provides the scholarships and fellowships for the full time research workers.

(ix) It provides the guidance for the social science research to the institute and research workers.

(x) It encourages the research workers to review the studies of developed countries to understand our own problems.

5. *Centre of Advanced Studies of Education (CASE)*

The teacher-education has been given great importance by the developed nations of the world. The teacher-education has to face new challenges. There are new changes in the education of India. The Centre of Advanced Studies of Education has been established in the university. The first CASE was established at M. S. University, Baroda (Gujarat). The U.G.C. has granted two centers of CASE in our state at University of Lucknow and Rohilkhand University, Bareilly. The CASE has been granted for the Kurukshetra University, Haryana. The centres function under the guidance of University Grants Commission. The CASE has the following main functions:

- **(i)** To encourage the cooperative research work in the discipline of education and teacher-education.
- **(ii)** To provide the valuable information to teacher-educators, planners, and administrators by publishing booklets and journals.
- **(iii)** To provide the scholarships and financial assistance to scholars and teachers.
- **(iv)** To encourage different types of programmes for the social development.
- **(v)** To encourage the teacher-education for the research work by providing teacher-fellowship and grants.
- **(vi)** To organise extension programmes with collaboration of NCERT, NCTE, and UGC.

The CASE Baroda had collected research studies conducted in Indian universities and other organisations. The Educational Research Survey was published by M.B. Buch for the first time in the country, for the use for research workers.

6. *National Council of Teacher-Education (NCTE)*

The Ministry of Education of the Government of India established the National Council of Teacher-Education (NCTE) in May 1973. It was formed with this view that it would provide guidance to the centre and states for solving problems and suggestions for the development. It had been given statutory statues and an Act was passed in 1993. Now it is an autonomous body for the development of teacher-education like NCERT. The head office of NCTE is at New Delhi in the campus of NCERT.

The NCTE has the following functions according to the Act of 1993:

1) Undertake survey and studies relating to various aspects of teacher-education and publish the results.
2) Make recommendations to the centre and state governments, universities, the UGC, and other institutions in the preparation of plans and programmes in the field of teacher-education.
3) Coordinating and monitoring teacher-education and its development in the country.
4) Prepare a guideline with regard to minimum qualifications for the candidates to be employed as teacher-education at different levels.
5) Develop norms for any specified category of courses or training in teacher-education, including minimum eligibility criteria for admission.
6) Prepare a guideline and specified requirements for starting new courses and programmes under teacher-education.
7) Develop guidelines for general teacher-education programme.
8) Promote innovations and research studies and organise them periodically or annually.

9) Supervise the teacher-education programmes and provide financial assistance.
10) Enforcing accountability of teacher-development programmes in the country.
11) Preventing commercialisation in teacher-education and maintain quality and standard of teacher-education to produce better teachers.
12) Entrust responsibility to other organisations, universities, and other institutes.
13) Prepare a programme for in-service teacher-education for orienting teachers for the latest development.
14) Establish international relations in the area of teacher-education.

Academic Programmes of NCTE

The following are the main academic programmes for NCTE:

1) Preventing B.Ed correspondence courses which are lowering the standard and quality of teacher-education. It has commercialised the teacher-education. K.L. Mali as Education Minister has also opposed this programme.
2) Code of Professional Ethics is to be maintained by orienting teachers in this context.
3) Development of curriculum of teacher-education pedagogical theory, working with community and teaching practice. The stagewise curriculum has been given in a separate chapter of NCTE.
4) Methodology of teaching and techniques evaluation procedures, continuing and non-formal education and administration structure has been given in the chapter of NCTE.
5) Role of teacher in social and vocational areas. The workshop was organised in Madras in 1987.

Future Programmes of NCTE

The following are the main future plans and programmes of NCTE:

1) Formulation of objectives of teacher-education general and stagewise.
2) Development of curriculum for different stages of teacher-education.
3) Development of four year programme content cure methodology teaching.
4) Organise National Seminars and Workshops.
5) Develop the criterion of admission.
6) Publish Teacher-Education bulletin.

The main **Central Agencies are the four** – NCERT, NCTE, UGC, and the Department of Education of the Ministry of Human Resource Development (MHRD). The proposed university will be the liaison between the NCERT and the State Government. As such it will be superfluous for the NCERT to maintain its field offices at State levels. It can also serve as the academic agent of the NCTE for the State, whenever the proposed university is established. It will not only carry on the accreditation work but will also take the NCTE's permission if a new institution is to be established. It is hoped that the UGC will extend to the proposed university all the benefits and facilities which it generally grants to a statutory university.

In the academic field, it will no doubt run the conventional Ph. D., M. Phil., M.Ed., B. Ed. courses, but will also introduce M.A./M.Sc. courses and the four-year degree course in Education as well. It can also organise post-graduate diploma courses in a number of fields. It will further fix a policy of recruiting the staff for training the teachers of higher secondary classes.

10.6 State-Level Agencies

1. State Board of Teacher Education (SBTE)
2. Universities Department Education (UDE)

3. Continuing Teacher Education Centre (CTEC)
4. Distance of Correspondence Teacher Education (DTE or DCTE)
5. Summer Institute of Education (SIE)
6. College of Teacher Education (CTE)
7. State Institutes of Education (SIE)

At the state level, there is a Directorate of Education, working under the direct control of the Ministry of Education. The Minister controls the educational policy and directs its execution. He is also responsible to the state legislative of which he is a member.

The Ministry of Education is not responsible for the entire education of the state. General education is his responsibility but other ministers and departments have under their control schools and colleges pertaining to their specialised branches like, medical education, technical education, agricultural education, industrial education, and the like.

The Minister administers his duties through the State Department of Education. The State Department of Education is organised at two focal points: policy making and coordination function in the Secretariat and the direction, regulation and inspection function at the directorate.

The Secretary is the administrative head of the Secretariat. He is directly responsible to the Ministry of Education. He is often a member of the Indian Administrative Service. He is assisted by a deputy and a few assistants or under-secretaries. The Secretary keeps liaison between Directorate of Education and the Government. The Directorate is an executive body. It executes the policy of the Government framed in the Secretariat. The Director is the executive head of the Education Department and is responsible for offering technical advice to the Minister and for carrying out the policy of the Department. He keeps the Government informed regarding the educational needs and actual progress of education in the state, people's reaction to a government policy of education, awards grants, conducts research, etc.

The Director contacts the Department through his staff at the Headquarter and Circle Education Officers. He is assisted by a number of Deputy Directors. Some states have the post of a Joint Director also to help the Director. In some states the Director is an I.A.S. officer.

A state is divided into circles. Each circle is in-charge of a Circle Education Officer. This officer looks after all the schools in the circle. The Circle Education Officers discharge their functions through a large number of District Education Officers. District Education Officers are assisted by Block Education Officers.

All states do not have identical administrative set-up but most of them practice a three-tier arrangement, namely the State Department of Education, the Regional or the Divisional or the Circle Officer and the District Officer. Though they differ somewhat from one another in the organisation of their departments of education, there is little variation in their organisation at the regional and district level. Some States, however, have only a two-tier arrangement - the State Department of Education and the District Office.

A decade ago, a single Directorate of Education used to control both general and technical education. Both these branches are now under two separate Directors of Education. Even general education is further sub-divided in some states into two parts - school and college education. Such a practice exists in Jammu and Kashmir, Kerala, Madhya Pradesh, Mysore, Tamil Nadu, and Andhra Pradesh. In short, Directorate of Education is tending to be concerned, in the main, with education at the school level. Administration of technical and higher education is moving towards independent forms.

Administrative Set-up

(As proposed by Indian Education Commission)

Ministry of Human Resource Development

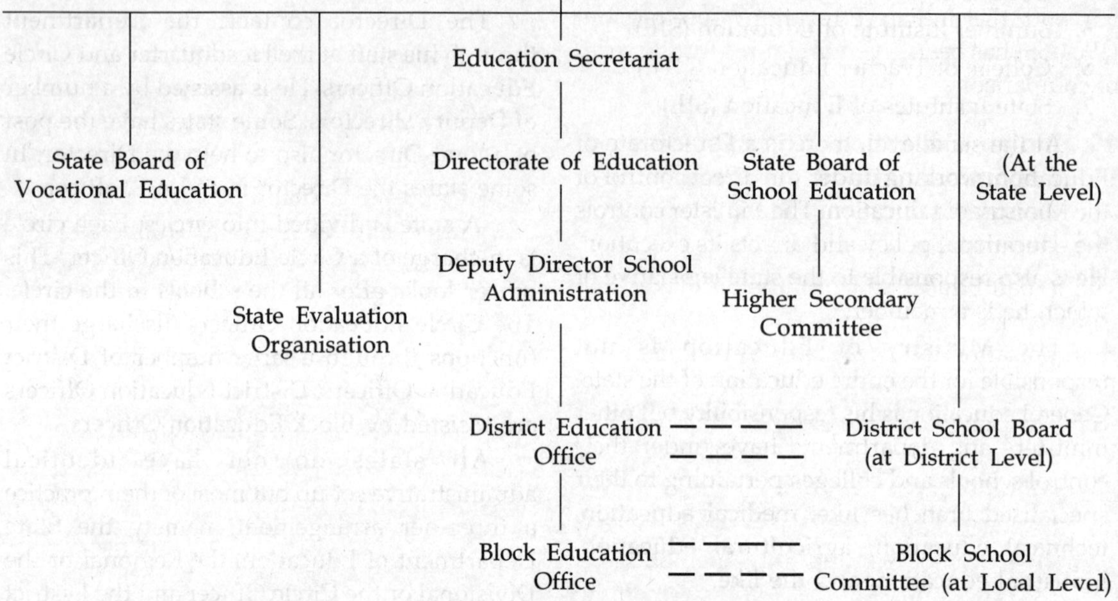

Administrative Set-up of the State Department of Education

(Proposed Pattern)

Ministry of Human Resource Development

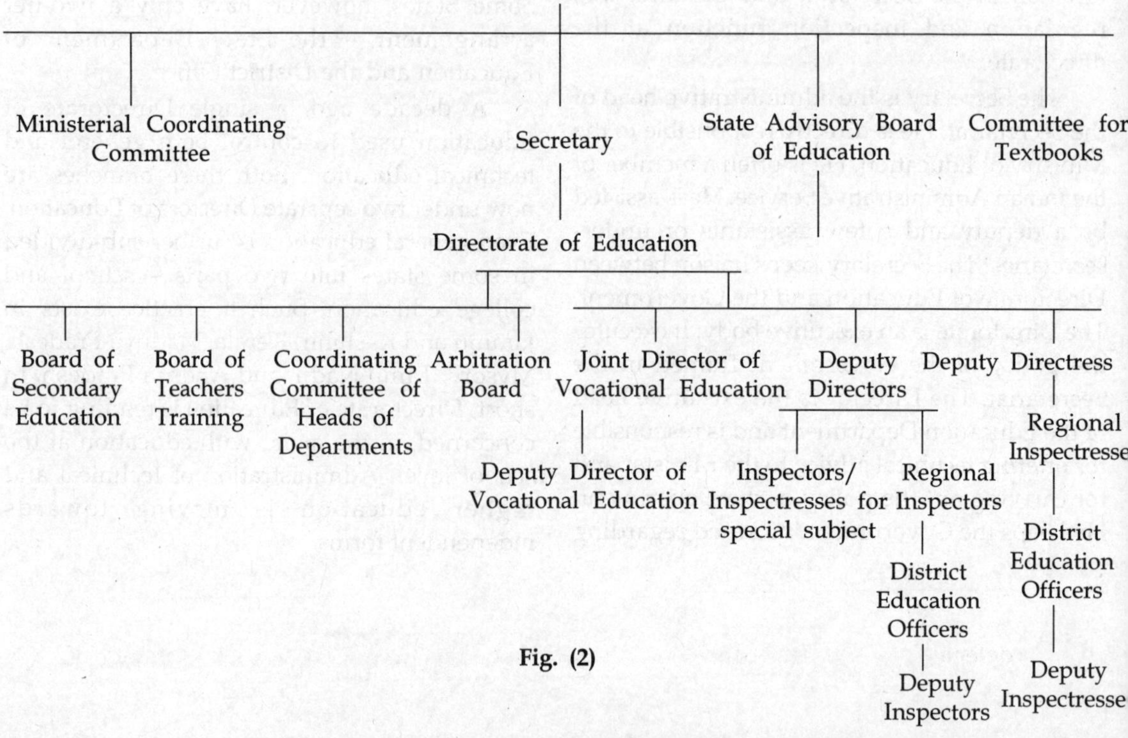

Fig. (2)

The Indian Education Commission (1964-66) recommended a different type of administrative machinery. The administrative set-up proposed by the Secondary Education Commission (1953-55) and the Indian Education Commission (1964-66) has been given in figures for the sake of comparison.

10.7 Indian Education Commission's Recommendations for the Reorganisation of State Department of Education

The Indian Education Commission makes the following recommendations for the reorganisation of the State Department of Education.

1. The State Education Department will be the principal agency to deal with educational matters and will, therefore, be responsible for
   i) Development and implementation of programme of school improvement;
   ii) The prescription and enforcement of standard;
   iii) The training and supply of teachers;
   iv) Inspection and supervision;
   v) Establishment and maintenance of a State Evaluation Organisation;
   vi) Maintenance of quality institutions and provision of extension services;
   vii) Establishment and maintenance of a State Institute of Education, and
   viii) Coordination and eventual assumption of responsibility for vocational and technical education at the school stage.
2. In view of the importance of strengthening the departmental organisation at the district level–
   (a) The District Education Officer should be given adequate status by including the post in the proposed Indian Educational Service;
   (b) Adequate authority should be delegated to the district level;
   (c) Scales of pay and qualifications of inspectorial staff at the district level should be upgraded;
   (d) The strength of the district staff should be increased with the addition of specialists and a statistical cell, and,
   (e) A fair proportion of the district staff should consist of women officers in order to encourage girls' education.
3. Headmasters should be selected carefully and should be specially trained. They should be vested with necessary authority and freedom.

10.8 Functions of the State Government

The State Governments have the following functions as far as education is concerned:

1. **Finance:** The most important function of the State Government is to find out all the resources needed for elementary and secondary education. This responsibility is subject only to two limitations-(1) Central grants that may be received from time to time, and (2) the contributions raised by local bodies and private agencies, if any.
2. **Legislation:** To pass laws for different types of education is the second major function of the state. To pass laws for compulsory attendance for elementary education, education for women, handicapped, etc. is the state's responsibility.
3. **Supervision and Inspection:** Since the state provides the vast bulk of the funds required for education and is responsible to account for it to the state legislature, it has to maintain an agency to supervise schools in all cases. Even when the authority over elementary and secondary education is transferred to local bodies, the state has to maintain a supervisory machinery of its own to watch over the manner the schools are being run by them. Where they fail to run the schools properly, the state takes over these schools.

4. **Recruitment of Teachers:** The states are responsible for recruitment for teachers, for prescribing the remuneration and other service conditions of teachers. The recruitment of teachers is sometimes done by the Public Service Commission and sometimes by authorities appointed by the state, for example, Subordinate Service Selection Boards. Even when it is transferred to local bodies, the state retains the right to frame recruitment rules and to lay down the procedures for recruitment.
5. **Prescription of Curricula:** The State prescribes the textbooks for the entire state or for different zones or regions in line with the curricula framed. The production and easy supply of textbooks is one of the major responsibilities of the state.

When the responsibility for education is transferred to local bodies, the state government has to take over to itself, in relation to the local bodies under its control, all those functions which the Centre has to perform in respect of the states viz.,

(a) It has to act as a *clearing house* and coordinating agency so as to bring about unity and coherence;
(b) It has to provide leadership through training of staff, supervision, research, and pilot projects;
(c) It has to equalise educational opportunities by providing special assistance to the poorer and more backward local bodies.

It is obvious that the state governments have supreme responsibility for education and that, even when local bodies are made to share the burden at times, the residual responsibilities of the state are still large and are of very great significance.

10.9 State and Secondary Education

Secondary Education is under direct and full control of the states. The state governments prepare their education plans in the light of their local conditions and needs and within the plan-frame prepared at the centre. State governments have been setting up Boards of Secondary Education especially after the recommendation of the Secondary Education Commission and now, Punjab, Haryana, Tripura, Assam, Himachal Pradesh, and Manipur almost all states have such boards. The boards are mainly advisory in character; they include secondary school teachers and headmasters, and representatives of universities. Through their syllabus committees, they frame and recommend curricula for approval by the Government and they also conduct the final school leaving examination. In the states which have yet to set up Secondary Education Boards, the university prescribes the courses of studies for the high school classes and conducts the external examination.

The state governments exercise control, partly direct and partly indirect, over all secondary schools irrespective of the type of management, through their power to accord aid and, or recognition. They give subsidies and grants-in-aid to other managements to meet a proportion of the total expenditure. This financial aid is subject to conditions of the recognition laid down by the Government. In this way, through the rules and regulations, supported by a system of supervision and inspection, the State Government exercises considerable sway over the whole field of secondary education in the state.

There are a few schools in each state not coming under state control: (a) Schools administered by other public authorities like, the Railway Ministry or the Defence Ministry which generally fall in line with the state system, and send up their pupils for final examination conducted by the State Board or the University; (b) The public schools, which do not fit into any state pattern but are residential institutions, catering to a select category of pupils, who generally take the Senior Cambridge Examination.

Finance – Sources of revenue at the state level are: (a) Government's funds (grants); (b) district board and municipal board funds; (c) private endowments; and (d) fees. Government grants and fees, accounts for more than four-fifths of the total income.

Grants-in-aid are made by the state to privately managed institutions for the following purposes:

(a) towards the salaries and allowances of the teachers;
(b) towards the rent and repair of the school building;
(c) towards the expenditure on furniture, equipment and teaching materials;
(d) for purchase, acquisition and extension of the school building or playgrounds;
(e) for meeting loss of income due to fee-concessions. For payments of these grants, the states lay down conditions from time to time.

10.10 State and Higher Education

States also control the activities of the university. They appoint commissions and committees to give suitable recommendations to improve universities. The state universities are dependent upon the state government. State disburses finances to help in the successful functioning of the university. State Government gets the things done through its education department.

A Recent Reaction

Eminent educationist and public men are having a strong feeling at the moment that education should be transferred from the state list to that of the centre and that if this radical change is not immediately acceptable to the states, the subject should be put on the concurrent list so that the Union Government is given more responsibility and authority for shaping national policies. They feel that the individualistic policies and plans followed in the different states have put the national system of education in a condition of virtual chaos. A uniform pattern of education and uniform pay scales and other conditions of service would be possible only when there is Parliament's control on the entire field of education. **Mr. Chagla**, the Ex-Union Education Minister said, **"Education should become a concurrent subject if we want to make real progress."** He very much emphasised the creation of an All India Educational Service as it felt that it would mean an "important beginning" to make education a "really national subject."

Though the states in general have not viewed with favour the idea of making education a concurrent subject, the recent conference in effect agreed that the Central Government should assume more responsibility and provide necessary funds. Block grants should be earmarked for the central projects. It has also recommended the creation of I.E.S. for streamlining the educational administration in the country.

The conference also agreed to the creation of the All India Educational Service. "All those steps" in the words of Mr. M.C. Chagla, "would take us a long way towards establishing a system of education which will be uniform and national."

10.11 Local Bodies

There is no uniformity regarding the role of local bodies in education in India. Even in the same State, there is lack of uniformity. In urban areas, the municipalities have been associated with education in Andhra Pradesh (Andhra area), Bihar, Gujarat (Mumbai area), Tamil Nadu (Tamil Nadu area), Maharashtra (Mumbai and Vidharbha areas), and Mysore (Mumbai and Chennai areas). In rural areas, the Panchayat Raj institutions have been introduced and placed in charge of education in all States, except Jammu and Kashmir, Kerala, Madhya Pradesh, Mysore, Nagaland, and Punjab. The method of association is also not uniform. The Municipalities are generally in-charge of primary education but they can also undertake other educational activities at their discretion. The Panchayat Raj institutions have been entrusted with lower primary education in some States (e.g. West Bengal); with the whole of primary education in some states (Tamil Nadu) and with both primary and secondary education in some states (Andhra Pradesh and Maharashtra). Authority of education has been delegated to the block level (in some states e.g. Rajasthan and Tamil Nadu); and to the district level in some others (Maharashtra). The system of administration and grants-in-aid also show similar variations.

The village Panchayat should elect a school committee consisting of some of its own members and some non-members interested in education. The committee should have its own Chairman and its Headmaster of the local school should work as its secretary. Where village Panchayats do not exist, their committee may be nominated by the Education Department. The following should be the duties and powers of these committees:

(1) To provide adequate accommodation and equipment to primary schools;

(2) To carry out current repairs of school buildings and if authorised, also to carry out special repairs and to construct new buildings;

(3) To exercise such supervision over the school as may be prescribed;

(4) To be responsible for the enforcement of compulsory attendance within its area;

(5) To provide and maintain playgrounds and school gardens;

(6) To make provisions for drinking water and necessary amenities required by school children;

(7) To provide wherever possible, mid-day meals;

(8) To provide school functions; and

(9) To celebrate school functions and to organise school excursions and other social and cultural programmes.

For meeting expenditure on account of these responsibilities, the school committee should receive:

1) a certain proportion of the income of the local village panchayat; and

2) a grant-in-aid fixed on the basis of equalisation, i.e., a larger grant being given to poorer areas and a smaller grant to richer areas.

The committee should supplement these receipts through voluntary contributions to the local community.

This proposal has great potentialities; and proper working of the proposal may show significant results.

The Balwant Rai Committee recommended devaluation of powers to a body which "will have the entire charge of development work within its jurisdiction." It is suggested that the jurisdiction of the proposed local body should be "neither so large as to defeat the very purpose for which it is created, nor so small as to initiate against efficiency and economy." Identified the community development block as such and recommended a local body at this, the *Panchayat Samiti*, which was indirectly elected by the village panchayat with some representation to municipalities and cooperation organisations located within its jurisdiction. The real operational authority is to vest in the *Panchayat Samiti*. Below it is the Panchayat, and at the district level is the Zila Parishad, mainly charged with the functions of coordination. Primary education was one of the subjects to be entrusted to these new local bodies.

10.12 Arguments against the Control of Primary Education by Local Bodies

Practical experience in various states has revealed certain drawbacks of local control in primary education.

1. Local bodies generally have limited financial resources. With the result, the conditions in the schools deteriorate to the disadvantages of both the pupils and the teacher.
2. The leadership available at the local levels is not sufficiently competent and experienced to deal satisfactorily with the

varied and difficult problems of primary education.

3. Teachers are the worst sufferers because (a) appointments are not judicious, (b) transfers are too frequent, (c) the provisions for remuneration in old age is inadequate, and (d) local politics interferes with the internal functioning of the schools.

The thinkers on education do not want to take primary education out of the hands of local bodies on these arguments alone. They say if proper leadership is not available at the local level through such experiments the leadership at the local level can be trained and built up. Also there are no short-cuts to the development of democracy and if we want to prepare the country as a democracy, we must be prepared to trust the local bodies and to give them the right to share in this social enterprise.

Some educationists are of the view that local bodies cannot function properly unless the people, as a whole are sufficiently educated. They, therefore, suggest that elementary education should be kept under government control and developed quickly through a phased programme till illiteracy is liquidated, and that elementary education may be handed over to local bodies only after fulfilling this task. They opine that the transfer of elementary education to the local control without this preparation will not be wise.

In opposition to this, there are educationists who point out that the bureaucratic administration of elementary education can never enthuse the people and achieve the desired results. Moreover, to argue that decentralisation of authority should follow the development of mass education is to beg the question and to put the cart before the horse. The best solution perhaps will be that the development of mass education and training in democratic citizenship should proceed side by side and the transfer of elementary education to local control will expedite this process.

The local bodies may be entrusted with certain duties as far as the elementary education is concerned, e.g., to provide adequate accommodation and equipment for primary schools, to carry out current repairs to school buildings and also to attend to emergency repairs, to construct new buildings; to be responsible for the enforcement of compulsory attendance within its area; to make provisions for ancillary facilities as mid-day meals, school uniforms and, to exercise supervision on the school.

10.13 How to make Success of Decentralisation Policy?

Certain safeguards are extremely necessary so that the policy of decentralisation of authority in respect of elementary education to district, block, or village level is successful.

(1) **Inspections:** - To supervise the working of local bodies and elementary schools, the state must maintain an inspectorate.

(2) **Recruitment of teachers:** - Definite rules should be framed by the state government for recruitment of teachers to see that local influences interfere the least with proper selection. The local bodies should have very few powers over the teachers. Whatever the powers are, these should be exercised through the executive staff and they should be subject to an appeal to a higher authority.

(3) **Administrative check-up by the staff officials:** - Officers of government – District Education Officers and Deputy District Education Officers should have the authority to supervise the work of local bodies, to call for their records and to inspect them if necessary, to suspend their resolutions or suspend or dissolve a local body and to take over its functions. Where the local bodies fail to discharge their duties efficiently, schools may be taken over by the state.

10.14 Arguments in favour of the control of Primary Education by Local Bodies

The main arguments which can be advanced in favour of the control of primary education by local bodies are:-

1) Association with the administration of primary education stimulates local interest in this enterprise and also assists in securing support for its maintenance.
2) Quicker and sufficient service in administrative functions like constructions or maintenance of school buildings, purchase, and upkeep of equipment, provision of mid-day meals, and supply of free books to poor and needy children can be possible through local bodies.
3) Enlightened local supervision can go a long way in improving standards in education.

Role of Voluntary Agencies

Voluntary agencies have made a very significant contribution in the development of Indian education. Approximately one-third of the educational institutions are conducted by them today.

Why should privately-managed primary schools be closed?

Various arguments are being given in support of the abolition of privately-managed schools: -

1) The elementary education is to be free. No fees are to be charged in any elementary school whether it is public or private, i.e., the entire cost of private elementary schools will ultimately have to be born by public funds through grants-in-aid. So they say why not spend money directly on public elementary schools alone which provide free education.
2) As the privately managed schools provide a higher standard of education the rich will send their children to these schools as they can pay for education but the children of the poor will be compelled to attend the government schools. In this way, class distinctions will be unnecessarily perpetuated.
3) Abolition of private schools may improve standards in public elementary schools. When there are no alternative facilities, the rich, it is agreed, might take greater interest in public schools and thus, the standards might improve.

But there are very sound arguments in favour of continuing private enterprise in education:-

i) The provision of free and compulsory education means that the state shall maintain an adequate number of free public elementary schools and take effective steps to provide free education for the child of every parent who demands it. It does not mean abolition of all fees.
ii) In a democracy, the parent has the basic right to choose school for his child and if he chooses a private school which charges fees, the state has hardly any justification to interfere in the matter.

So long as economic inequalities continue to exist in the society, social inequalities are inevitable. So, the solution does not lie in the abolition of private schools, but the improvement of public schools. Private enterprise is a valuable force in education in view of the increasing number of children to be taught in schools and the limited resources. It needs to be properly capitalised.

10.15 Indian Education Commission's Recommendations to improve the working of Private Schools

For the successful functioning of democracy, education is a basic necessity. For education to spread in the nook and corner of the country, an all out effort on all fronts - Centre, State, Local, and Private level is required. The task is quite big - every source must be tapped.

The Indian Education Commission (1964-66) has given the following suggestions to improve the working of the private schools-

1) The government should see that private aided institutions are satisfactorily managed through adequate support; those that are not so managed should be taken over or eliminated.
2) A discriminating policy needs to be adopted in respect of assistance to and control of private aided institutions. The better schools should be given more freedom and assistance so as to enable them to develop into the nucleus of the common school system.
3) Each private school should be assisted to strengthen its management in the following ways: -
   i) Each private school should have a Managing Committee consisting of representatives of the management, the Education Department and Teachers.
   ii) The staff of these schools should be broadly on the pattern of Government or local authority schools.
   iii) Grants-in-aid should be improved.
   iv) It should be an invariable rule that educational institutions must be conducted by non-profit making bodies in order to be eligible for assistance.

Grants-in-aid codes should be amended to authorise the State Education Departments to take over the management of private schools which do not satisfy requirements and which have failed persistently to come up to the prescribed standards.

10.16 Educational Administration at Various Levels

The Indian Educational Commission has recommended the following measures for strengthening educational administration at various levels:

i) **Common School System:** The Commission has advocated that only one system of public education, without any disparity should remain. It must include all Government, local body, and private schools. There should be no disparity from the point of view of fees charged, working conditions of teachers, status, or privileges.

ii) **Bifurcation of Administration and Supervision:** The Commission has recommended that supervision should be dealt with by D.E.O. while the administration should be handled by District Schools Board. But the two should work in close collaboration.

iii) **Double Inspection :** Primary schools should be inspected by-
   (a) District School Board annually, and
   (b) D.E.O. bi-annually.

The secondary schools should be inspected by-
   (a) Officer of the State Education Department annually, and
   (b) State Board School Education bi-annually.

iv) **The Neighbourhood School System:** All children in the neighbourhood should be required to attend the school in the neighbourhood. Ten percent elementary schools may be upgraded during the first 10 years so that the pupils get the opportunity of Secondary Education.

v) **The School Complex:** A number of elementary schools should work under a Central School in the area, preferably a Secondary School, so as to break the isolation of schools and help them to function, in small face to face cooperative groups and to make a delegation of authority from the Department possible.

vi) **District School Board:** The Indian Education Commission has recommended the following composition of the District School Board - a competent local education authority; an autonomous body in charge of all education in the district below the university level. The Zila Parishads, Municipalities, educationists, and concerned departments should be represented on it.

The Commission has recommended the following functions of the Board:

(a) Administration of all Government and local body schools within the districts.

(b) Giving grants-in-aid to all the private schools.

(c) Preparing plans for the development of school education within the districts.

(d) Providing guidance to all the schools.

(e) Maintaining an education fund for the upkeep of the schools, realised through various local sources, Zila Parishads or Municipalities.

(f) Recruiting and transferring teachers within the district, through a special committee consisting of the Chairman of the Board, the Secretary, and the D.E.O.

(g) The District School Board will create conditions of maximum cooperation and help from the local community so that the school and the local communities are intimately associated with the venture of educational process. Through this association of village Panchayats, Municipalities, and Zila Parishads, non-teacher costs of the school can be met.

Some remedies are:

1. Efficient and enlightened educational administrators.
2. Local leadership should be educated and associated.
3. Greater freedom to the teacher and the institutional administrator needs to be given.
4. Greater freedom to the individual institutions.
5. The decision-making power needs to be decentralised.
6. Men of inter-communication of experiences among the states needed.
7. More money for education in general and administration of education in particular needed.
8. Creation of D.E.S.
9. National Staff College for educational administrators.
10. Introducing elasticity and dynamism.
11. Education to be given statutory basis.
12. A system of priorities may be adopted at different levels.
13. Redefinition of the role of different agencies.

10.17 Some State Level Agencies (For Higher Education)

The main state agencies are seven – SBTE, UDTE, CTED, DTE, SIE, SIE, and CTE. The brief description of few agencies has been given in the following paragraphs:

1). State Board of Teacher-Education (SBTE)

The Kothari Commission (1966) recommended for the first time for establishing the *State Board of Teacher-Education.* The main function of the board is to develop teacher-education in the state and it should be administered by the board. The teacher-education of state was reviewed and state boards were established in M.P. (1967), Maharashtra, Jammu-Kashmir, and Tamil Nadu (1973).

The Ministry of Education had forced states to establishing state in the light of suggestions of NCERT. Almost in all the states such boards were established. The state board of teacher-education has the following functions:

i) Determine the standard of teacher-education institutions.

ii) Modify and improve the curriculum, textbooks, and the system of teacher-education of the state.

iii) Develop the criterion for the recognition of teacher-education institutions.

iv) Organise the guidance facility of teacher-education institutions.

v) Develop the criteria for admission in teacher-education and evaluate the teacher-efficiency of pupil teachers.

vi) Prepare the plan for qualitative and quantitative development of teacher-education.

vii) Provide guidance to the universities and state institutes for improving and modifying curriculum, textbooks, and examination system of teacher-education.

viii) Determine the educational and physical conditions for the teacher-education institutions for affiliations.

ix) Teacher-education facility should be organised for each level of teachers. The grants and financial assistance should be provided for these levels of teacher-education.

x) To develop the feeling of cooperations among university departments and other training institutions.

The main task of these state boards is to develop educational organisation and administration for all levels of teacher-education institutions. The state teacher-education should be given facilities and suggestions for their development.

2). *University Departments of Teacher-Education (UDTE)*

Education is now considered an independent field of study or discipline. Therefore, the UGC provides the grants to the university department of teacher-education. The higher level training is essential for teachers to their development and extension. The departments of education provide the training for educational administrators, curriculum specialists and improving evaluation procedures as well as the examination system. The university departments organise the M.Ed., B.Ed., and M.Phil classes as well as research work for Ph.D. and D.Litt. degree in Education. The first education department was started in (1917) at Calcutta University. There are departments of teacher-education in all Indian Universities for B.Ed., M.Ed., and Ph.D. degrees in Education.

The university departments of teacher-education have the following main functions:

(1) Develop the post-graduate studies and research work.

(2) Organise training for school teachers.

(3) Provide solid programmes for teacher-education and development research work.

(4) To start and organise some programmes for post-graduate teachers which are not organised in other centres.

(5) Develop language laboratory, prepare instructional material, and use new innovations and practices in teacher training.

(6) Organise and develop comprehensive college of education for training teachers for four years for duration-content-cum-methodology courses.

(7) Encourage the interdisciplinary courses and interdisciplinary research studies so that the requirements of other departments can be fulfilled.

(8) Organise extension lectures and programmes to encourage the teachers and research workers to contribute in the discipline of education.

(9) Provide the awareness of new methodology and technology to upgrade the standard of teacher-education.

(10) Develop the effective procedure of evaluation of theory and practicals in education.

We need a very strong academic and administrative machinery at the state level which should work in cooperation with central agencies. It should further aim at economy and integration of divergent elements, avoid duplication of efforts, consider and examine the needs of different types of institutions, give a proper turn to rising ideologies and tendencies and end corruption and exploitation.

Every state should have a university of Teacher Education of its own. It is to be unitary as well as entrusted with the power of affiliating all the teachers' colleges at graduate and post-graduate levels within the state.

3). *Centre of Continuing Education for Teachers (CCTE)*

There is isolation between teachers and teacher-education. There is rapid development in Education. The use of these developments is only possible when school teachers are continuously informed. The classroom can make proper use of these developments and innovations. There is need to have centres of continuing education for in-service teachers. The NCERT has established an extension service department for this purpose and it has set up centers in states. The summer institutes of education are organised to provide the knowledge of science subjects and new teaching methodology.

There is a great need for such centres for primary and secondary in-service teachers to make them up-to-date for the latest knowledge of the content and teaching techniques. There should be co-ordination between pre-service and in-service teacher-education programmes. The following points are to be taken into consideration:

1) The awareness of in-service programmes should be given for pre-service teachers along with the objectives.
2) There should be provision for encouraging in-service teachers to participate in such programmes.
3) Such programmes should be organised during summer and winter vacations and holidays so that school work does not suffer.
4) The programmes should be organised at regional level in view of local needs of the schools and the students.
5) These centres should provide the knowledge and practice by organising seminars and workshops of new methods and techniques of teaching.
6) The in-service teachers should be encouraged and they should not be forced for attending such programmes.

The follow-up programme should be organised by these centres for evaluating the workability of these programmes.

4). *Correspondence Courses or Distance Education for Teachers Education*

The correspondence courses for teachers were initially started for in-service teachers for clearing the backlog of untrained teachers. But they are now being used as big rackets for earning money. This has commercialised the teacher-education programme. Several universities have started B.Ed. and M.Ed. Correspondence courses or Distance Education – Himachal, Rohtak, Kota, Annamalai, Kashi Vidya Peeth and Lucknow in the form of modular course. The in-service B.Ed. correspondence has the following features:

1) Provide the awareness of pedagogy or theory of education and methodology of teaching.
2) Encourage the student for self-learning.
3) Orientation is given by the experts and specialists of the areas.
4) Contact programmes are organised to remove the difficulties and provide the guidance for the study.
5) Theory lessons are sent by post along with the assignments which are to be completed and sent to the study centres.
6) Study centres are established for the candidates.

A large number of teachers are admitted in such programmes and a heavy amount of fee is realised from them. The universities have the source of income to meet their financial requirements. It has adversely effected the standard teacher-education. The NCTE is taking some strong steps to close down such programmes.

Objective Type Questions

Multiple Choice Questions (Tick ✓ the right option)

(1) The agencies at the National level concerned with the development of education are the

(a) Ministry of Education.
(b) The University Grants Commission.
(c) The National Council of Educational Research and Training.
(d) All of the above.

(2) The Government of India brings out three publications every year

(a) Education in India
(b) Education in the states
(c) Education in Indian universities
(d) All of the above

(3) The U.G.C. consist of ____________

(a) 12-15 members.
(b) 14-16 members.
(c) 15-17 members.
(d) 16-18 members.

Fill in the blanks

(1) The Governing body is the ________ body of the Council. [Policy-making]
(2) The workshop of NCTE was organized in Madras in ____________. [1987]
(3) The Ministry of Education is not responsible for the entire ________ of the state. [Education]
(4) ____________ education is under direct and full control of the states. [Secondary]

Important Questions

1. Discuss the present organisation of the Ministry of Education.
2. Describe the Administrative Machinery of the Education Department of your state. Discuss its relationship with the local bodies and privately managed institutions.
3. For good planning, there should be choices available at all levels. Discuss what type of choices should be there.
4. Discuss the recommendations of the Indian Education Commission for improving the educational administration and planning in our country.
5. Write short notes on: -
   (a) University Grants Commission.
   (b) National Council of Educational Research and Training.

11

The Present Pattern of Education: 10+2+3

Attempts have been made from time to time to redesign and reset the educational structure to meet the country's needs and to bring it as per with those of the other countries of the world.

More than sixty years ago the Calcutta University Commission (1917-19) recommended replacement of the then prevailing 10+2+2 pattern by a 10+2+3 one. It had come to the conclusion that the two years intermediate course really belonged to schools. It also desired the increase in the duration of the under-graduate course to make it comparable to that in advanced countries. It did not suggest vocationalisation of education.

The Radhakrishan Commission (1948-49) accepted these premises but added to them vocational plans. Barring a few academic exercise on the subject, nothing concrete happened.

The Secondary Education Commission (1952-53) recommended school duration of 11 years followed by three years of the first degree course. Perhaps the decision was dictated by the compulsion of economy.

The Government of India's resolution on the National Policy on Education issued in 1968 stated that it would be advantageous to have a broadly uniform educational structure in all parts of the country; the ultimate objective should be to adopt the 10+2+3 pattern, the higher secondary stage of two years being followed in schools or college or both, according to the existing condition.

11.1 Structure of Educational System as Proposed by the Secondary Education Commission

After independence, it was considered imperative to bring about radical changes in the then prevalent educational system so as to make it an effective instrument for the achievement of new ideals and values in the changed circumstances. Keeping this in view,

<table>
<tr><td rowspan="2">Secondary Grade training 2 years</td><td colspan="3">Post Graduate Courses [2 Years]</td></tr>
<tr><td colspan="2">First Degree Course (3 years)</td><td>Vocational and techno-industrial Institutes [3-5 years]</td></tr>
<tr><td rowspan="2">Higher Secondary [4 or 3 Years]</td><td colspan="2">Post-University Courses [1 Years]</td><td rowspan="2">Higher Secondary and Multipurpose Schools (4 years)</td></tr>
<tr><td>High School</td><td>Technical High School</td></tr>
<tr><td>Lower Secondary Stage (3 years)</td><td colspan="2">Middle or Junior Secondary School, Senior Basic School</td><td>Industrial Centre
Trade School</td></tr>
<tr><td>Primary Stage (4 or 5 years)</td><td colspan="2">Primary or Junior Basic School</td><td>Trade School</td></tr>
<tr><td>Pre-primary Stage</td><td colspan="2">Kindergarten or Nursery School</td><td>Commencement of School Education</td></tr>
</table>

the Government of India appointed the Secondary Education Commission in 1952. Dr. A. L. Mudaliar was the Chairman of the Secondary Education Commission. So this commission is known as the "Mudaliar Commission." The Secondary Education Commission was appointed only with a view to examining and surveying the various aspects of the then prevailing systems of secondary education in the country, but as this level of education is naturally linked with the primary and university education, the Commission had to formulate its views on the pattern of education, in these areas of national life also. The new structure of education outlined by the Commission is as under:-

By this structure, it seems that the Commission suggested in the following manner for different stages—

1. Secondary education should cover a time span of 7 years.
2. This stage of education should commence after 4 or 5 years of primary and junior basic education.
3. The duration of secondary education should be divided in two parts:
   (a) 3 years of middle or senior basic stage or junior secondary, and
   (b) 4 years of higher secondary education.
4. Afterwards, there should be a provision for 3 years first degree course and thereafter post-graduate.

The Secondary Education Commission recommended a sound and uniform system of secondary education of 7 years for the entire country. But it was left to the discretion of the state government to accept or reject this recommendation of the Commission. The consequence of this policy was that the pattern of education got further differentiated. Some states had High School, others Higher Secondary Schools, and still others Intermediate Colleges. Also, the duration of the first degree course varied in different universities from 2 to 3 years. Because of this anomalous position, the children of those parents who left one state for another had to face great difficulty.

11.2 Educational Structure as proposed by the Indian Education Commission

1. Pre-primary education for 1-3 years should be provided prior to the commencement of general or school level education.
2. Duration of general education should be of 10 years and it should only consist of primary and lower secondary education. Age for admission to class I generally, should not be less than 6 years. First public external examination should be held after ten years of general education. Specialisation in subjects should not be allowed up to the tenth class.

TABLE 1

This Ladder of Education was Proposed by the Education Commission

Levels	Class	Age	Levels	Classes	Age
Lower Secondary	X XI VIII VII	16 15 14 13	First Degree Stage	III II	21 20
Higher Primary	VI V	12 11		I	19 18
Commencement of School Education	I	6			
Pre-primary Stage	I	6			

3. **Lower Secondary Level:** Two types of education –
   (i) General education for 3 years.
   (ii) Vocational education for 1-3 years.
4. **Higher Secondary Level:** The provision of two types of education at this level:
   (i) 2 years of general education.
   (ii) 1-3 years of vocational education.
5. **Secondary School:**
   (i) High Schools in which education should cover a time span of ten years, and
   (ii) Higher Secondary Schools in which duration of education should be of 12 years.
6. In classes XI and XII specialised education in different subjects can be imparted.
7. After Higher Secondary education, the first degree course should be of 3 years of duration.
8. The second degree course can be of 2 or 3 years' period, in universities, graduate schools may be established in which second degree or post-graduate course of 3 years' duration in some subject should be provided (see Table 1).

11.3 National Committee on 10+2+3 Education Structure

The Central Advisory Board of Education realised this in its 36th meeting that there should be a uniform structure of education in the entire country. With this view it (CABE) made the Education Ministry responsible for it. The Ministry of Education appointed a committee which is known as the National Committee on 10+2+3.

The Education and Social Welfare Ministry of the Government of India appointed the above mentioned committee in September, 1972 under the Chairmanship of Dr. P.D. Shukla. In this committee, the education-secretaries of U.P., Delhi, Tamilnadu, Gujarat, and Assam were its members. In addition to this, the Director of Education Planning Commission, Delhi was also its member. The Secretary, Central Board of Secondary Education of Delhi was Member-Secretary of this committee.

11.4 National Educational Conference (1977)

The National Review Committee was still considering the matter. In the meantime the Janata Government arranged for the National Educational Conference. This conference was held on 18, 19 and 20th December, 1977 in Delhi. The conference was headed by Dr. Shrimannarain, Chairperson of "Nai Talim Samiti" and "Kendriya Gandhi Smarak Nidhi." The Governor of Rajasthan, Shri Rashukul Tilak, Education Ministers of states, 30 Vice Chancellors of different universities of India, some members of Parliament and the educationists of various voluntary organisations participated in the conference. It was the speciality of this conference that in addition to high officials of the Education Ministry and the National Council of Educational Research and Training more than 100 workers of Basic Education also participated in it. The then Prime Minister of India, Mr. Morarji Desai inaugurated this conference and the closing of the conference was done by Dr. P.C. Chunder, Central Education Minister.

11.5 National Policy of Education (1986)

Whenever awakening is felt to be required, the education has always played an important role. We are going to step into the 21st century and the challenges of education are enforcing on searching out the knowledge so that, some light may be thrown on possible ways for making education arrangements according to modern requirements. Since independence there have been many changes in education. In bringing these changes, the National Education Policy of 1968 has marked a significant step. But the 1968 policy did not get translated into a detailed strategy of implementations. With the result, education could not reach the different classes of society. Along with expansion of education and improvement in level could not be done according to requirement. To find out the solutions of these problems is the first need of the hour.

11.6 National System of Education

The main points of this education system are the following:-

1. The concept of a National System of Education implies that up to a given level, all students irrespective of caste, creed, location or sex, have access to education of a comparable quality. To achieve this, the government will initiate appropriately funded programmes. Effective measures will be taken in the direction of the common school system recommended in the 1968 policy.
2. The National System envisages a common educational structure. The 10+2+3 structure has now been accepted in all parts of the country. Regarding the further break-up of the first ten years; efforts will be made to move towards an elementary system comprising 5 years of primary education and 3 years of upper primary, followed by 2 years of high school.
3. The National System of Education will be based on a national curriculum for the entire country in which there will be a common core and for other elements there will be flexibility which can be cast according to local environment and surrounding.

Plan of Action

In the Budget Session of 1986, the Parliament had deliberations and discussions on the "National Policy of Education (1986)" and gave its sanction to that. Then, Human Resource Development Minister gave an assurance that he would put up a plan of action in the Monsoon Session of the Parliament regarding implementation of the New Education Policy.

Education Structure in India[1]

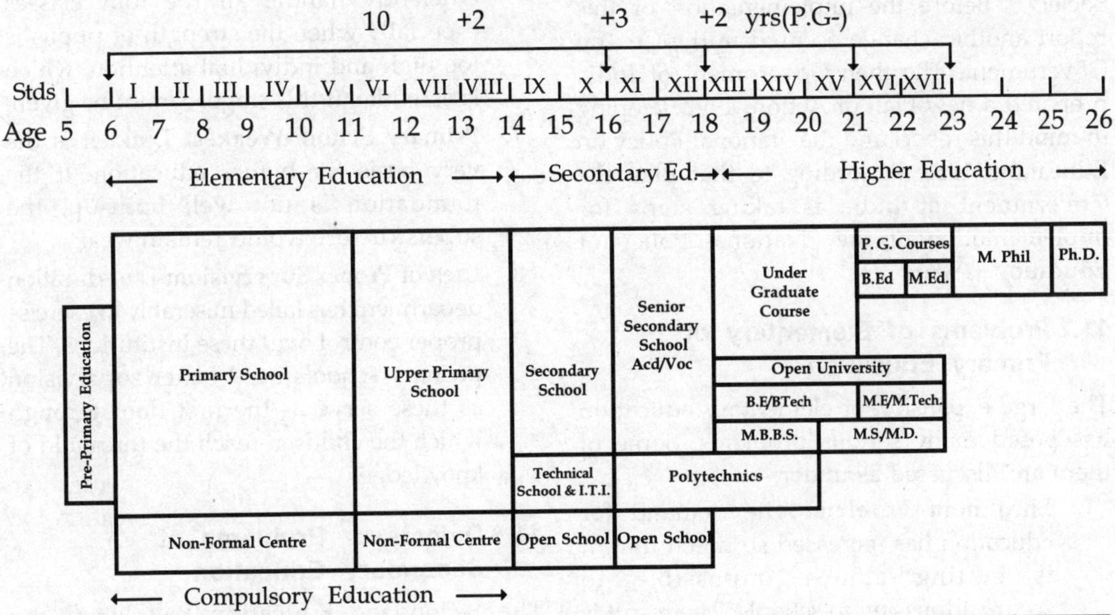

[1] *Development of Education in India : 1990-92, NIEPA and Department of Education, Ministry of Human Resource Development (MHRD),NewDelhi,p.4.*

Just after the Budget Session, the Ministry started work on the preparation of the Plan of Action abruptly. A conference was arranged on July 20, 1986, in which the Education Secretaries of the States and Union Territories participated. The suggestions received in this meeting were discussed vigilantly and carefully and keeping in mind the main topics (subjects) of the "National Policy of Education," the Plan of Action was prepared. In August, 1986 in the meeting of the Central Advisory Board of Education, this Plan of Action drafts was discussed and with some suggestions it was accepted. The Government of India got this document published in August, 1986.

As soon as the then Government of India enforced their Plan of Action, 1986 for implementation, a change took place in the Central Government , with the result of this change, a Review Committee was appointed under the Chairpersonship of Shriyut Acharya Ram Murthy for reviewing the "National Policy of Education (1986)." This committee submitted its report to the Government of India in December, 1990. This report was named as "Towards an Enlightened and Humane Society." Before the implementation of this report another change occured in the Central Government. The then Government of India prepared a new Plan of Action, 1992, keeping in mind this report and the National Policy on Education, 1986. According to that plan the Government of India is taking steps for implementation of the "National Policy of Education (1986)."

11.7 Problems of Elementary or Primary Education

The large expansion of elementary education has posed many serious problems. Some of them are discussed as under:-

1. **Enrolment Problem:** The demand for education has increased so much that, it is getting almost impossible to secure admission to schools. The result is that many un-recognised schools have cropped up which are charging very high fees.
2. **Element of Wastage:** Another problem arising out of rapid expansion is the resultant wastage. In India, about 40% of the total enrolment in classes is one to five (1 to 5) alone. The wastage in class I is more than half the wastage at the primary stage.
3. **Shortage of Trained Teachers:** In the third five year plan it was decided that the percentage of trained teachers will be raised by 75%. But unfortunately this target has not been touched.
4. **Elementary Education most Un-psychological:** Elementary Education is not based on the psychology of the child and method adopted are un-psychological.
5. **Absence of Model Primary Schools:** The working of the primary schools is rigid and formal. A few model schools in every important place needs to be opened so as to serve as role models.
6. **Single Teacher Schools:** These present great difficulties. A single teacher cannot efficiently handle all the four classes especially when the strength of pupils is too high and individual attention, which is essential at this stage, cannot be given.
7. **Primary School-Weakest Link:** It is the very basis for higher education. If the foundation is not well built-up, the superstructure would remain weak.
8. **Lack of Proper Supervision:** The education department has failed miserably to exercise proper control over these institutions. The primary schools need better supervision as these serve as the first door through which the children reach the threshold of knowledge.

11.8 Defects or Problems of Secondary Education

The Secondary Education has listed the following defects in the present system of secondary education:-

1. The education given in our schools is isolated from life.
2. It is narrow and one sided and fails to train the whole personality of the students.
3. Until recently, English was both the medium of instruction and compulsory subject of study.
4. The method of teaching generally failed to develop in the students any independent thought or initiative in action.
5. Increase in size of classes has considerably reduced personal contact between teachers and pupils.
6. The dead weight of curriculum has tended to curb the teacher's initiative , to stereotype the curriculum, to promote mechanical and lifeless methods of teaching, to discharge all spirits of experimentation and to place stress on wrong or important things in education.

The greatest point of criticism has been the high school curriculum. The commission has again pointed out the following defects in the secondary school curriculum:

1. The present curriculum is narrowly conceived.
2. It is bookish and theoretical.
3. It is over-crowded, without providing rich and significant contents.
4. It makes inadequate provision for practical and other kinds of activities.
5. It does not cater to the various needs and capacities of the adolescents.
6. It is dominated too much by the examinations.
7. It does not include technical and vocational subjects.

11.9 Major Defects in Higher Education

Some of these major defects are given below, as enumerated in the Education Commission's report:—

1. There is a general feeling in India that the average standard of higher education has been falling and that rapid expansion has resulted in lowering quality.
2. The content and quality are inadequate for our present needs and future requirements and these compare unfavourably with the average standards in other educationally advanced countries.
3. Only the stereo-type lecture method is followed by most of the teachers in universities and colleges and there is hardly any experimentation in the methodology of teaching.
4. There is little enthusiasm in teachers for teaching or finding out new truths because research is not considered as an integral part of traditions.
5. The majority of teachers suffer from financial worries especially in colleges where grades are low and thus are unable to buy books and journals of their own.
6. The physical working conditions of university and college teachers are far from being satisfactory.
7. The majority of the students come from comparatively uneducated homes and are, thus, ill equipped for higher education.
8. There are little discussions of intellectual matters between the students and the teachers. The main duty of the students is to attend interesting lectures, as usually given in a language which they do not understand adequately.
9. There is a dearth of standard textbooks and supplementary literature in Indian languages.
10. A large majority of students find full attention on academic work, very difficult.

Objective Type Questions

Multiple Choice Questions (Tick ✓ the right option)

(1) In which year the Janata Government arranged the National Educational Conference?

(a) 1977
(b) 1976
(c) 1972
(d) 1974

(2) The major defects of the secondary school curriculum were -

(a) It is bookish
(b) It is theoretical
(c) It is over crowded
(d) All the above

(3) Who was the Chairman of the secondary Education commission -

(a) Dr. A.L. Mudaliar
(b) Dr. S. Radhakrishnan
(c) Shri Rabhukul Tilak
(d) Dr. P.D. Shukla

Fill in the blanks

(1) The Government of India appointed the Secondary Education Commission in ________. [1952]

(2) The Secondary Education Commission recommended a sound and uniform system of secondary education of ________ for the entire country. [7 years]

Important Questions

1. Describe the structure of the educational system which is proposed by the Secondary Education Commission.
2. Write a short note on the National Committee on 10+2+3 educational structure.
3. Describe the structure of the National Committee on 10+2+3.
4. Describe the functions of the National Policy of Education- 1986.

12

Educational Administration and Management: New Challenges of the Twenty-first Century

In former times social life was very simple, the family provided the child with all the activities and experiences he needed for his inter-personal and inter-social relationships. Through the daily experiences of his life, the child became fully aware of the relationship that existed between him and his environment. Later, religious ceremonies connected with the temple or church began to serve the purpose. Then so long as occupations were centred around home or village, the family, the church and local community served as a school for life. The children learnt by imitating the work and life-pattern of their parents and neighbours. But with lapse of time, as society became large and complex, with the growth of civilisation and as human knowledge and experiences became accumulated in written form, home or family and other agencies of education were found inadequate for the efficient transmission of cultural heritage to the future generation. Thus, education of children became a specialised occupation of those persons who were highly learned and qualified for discharging this function efficiently. These persons began to be known as teachers or gurus.

12.1 Development of the School System

Thus, schools were established in all the ancient countries of the world, namely India, China, Egypt, Babylonia, Greece, and Rome. But schooling in those days was confined to the field of highest cultural knowledge only. It included the teaching of language, religion, philosophy, and mathematics and given only to the children of priestly class and noble families. The children of common people had no formal education. They continued to be educated through informal agencies, as before, "In fact, the idea that all children of all people should go to school, is a modern one."

There has, however, been a remarkable change in the role of the school, in recent times. As a result of discoveries and advances in the field of science and technology as well as the developed means of communication and changes in sociological conditions, modern civilisation has grown to such an extent that informal agencies of education have practically ceased to discharge their educational functions. So, the functions of the family and the community have also fallen on the school. Now, the school has to discharge not only its own educational function, but also to provide what home and community provided in the past. "It has to provide total education for background, for standards and values, for skills, for understanding, for culture, for making a contribution, for a sense of belonging, for attitudes, and for a proper orientation of the modern world." Moreover, with the coming in of democracy, universal education has not only become a necessity in the modern world but also an accepted social ideal. So, the school is required to discharge very important functions in modern society. Even then it should be clearly understood that the school must never be taken as the sole agency of education.

Education is and will always remain the joint responsibility of parents, teachers, and society. A school is only an active formal agency of education which stands in between the home and other informal active and passive agencies.

12.2 Challenging Tasks of Educational Administrators and Managers

The tasks facing educational managers and planners have become more challenging and complex over recent decades and their intensity is likely to increase further in the future. There are five important reasons for this:

(a) Phenomenal expansion of educational system to meet the needs of the growing population;

(b) Explosion of social expectations of the people for education;

(c) New requirement arising from socio-political, and cultural changes;

(d) Scientific and technical manpower requirements of growing economics;

(e) Use of technology in educational management and planning.

The task of an educational manager and planner is by no means an easy one. Though formal school system will continue to be a dominant structure within the educational system, its internal process has already began to change.

Open University, distance learning, schools of air, schools without walls, a variety of non-formal and non-instructional educational arrangements are reducing the domination of the formal school. According to many adjustments in educational structures process - planning and financing would be necessary in the future.

In recent times, expectations from the schools have increased enormously. In earlier decades what was expected from the schools was quite limited. We wanted them to teach the three 'R's and certain disciplines which were quite well demarcated and delimited. But today the schools are expected to prepare students for the 7 'R's i.e. traditional 3'R's of reading, writing, and arithmetic and the modern 4'R's of rights, responsibilities, relationships, and recreation. Achieving these objectives is indeed a very complex task and calls for a high order of planning and management skills.

The educational administrator and planner, while on the one hand will be required to keep his feet firmly on the ground, on the other hand, he will have to acquire some working knowledge of forecasting techniques to predict the future with reasonable accuracy to prepare the constituents of the educational system in the face of rapidly advancing scientific technology, socio-cultural, economic, and political demands on education.

Educational management and planning will have to be geared to the solutions of the problems of quality, quantity, equality, utility, and financial outlay in education. At the same time, management and planning styles will have to be relevant and responsive to indigenous conditions.

The National Policy on Education, 1986 observed under the caption "The Future" - concluding part of the document. "The future shape of education in India is too complex to envision with precision. Yet, given our tradition which has almost always put a high premium on intellectual and spiritual attainment, we are bound to succeed in achieving our objectives."

"The main task is to strengthen the base of pyramid, which might come close to a billion people at the turn of the century. Equally, it is important to ensure that those at the top of the pyramid are among the best in the world. Our cultural well-springs had taken good care of both ends in the past, the skew set in with foreign domination and influence. It should now be possible to further intensify the nation-wide effort in Human Resource Development, with education playing its multi-faceted role.

The National Policy on Education, 1986 has outlined the following measures for planning and managing the educational system so that it furthers our goals.

(a) It is obvious that these and many other new tasks of education cannot be performed in a state of disorder. Education needs to be managed in an atmosphere of utmost intellectual rigour, seriousness of purpose and, at the same time, of freedom essential for innovation and creating. With far-reaching changes, the process of introducing discipline into the system will have to be started, here and now, in what exists.

(b) The country has placed boundless trust in the educational system. The people have a right to expect concrete-results. The first task is to make it worth. All teachers should teach and all students study.

12.3 Programme of Action (POA) 1992 on – National Policy of Education

The Programme of Action (POA) prepared by the Department of Education, Ministry of Human Resource Development, Government of India, outlined the role of educational management in these words: "The task of ensuring effective implementation of the NPE rests on the education management system. Flexible and relevant management structures and organisation, processes and procedures are needed all along the line to secure the detailed planning and implementation of the Programme of Action (POA)."

It further demanded "A shift from inputs to performance and outcomes - consideration of cost effectiveness in all levels of educational administration and planning."

12.4 Shortcomings of the Present Management of Education

The POA pointed out the following shortcomings–

(a) There is absence of decentralisation.

(b) Performance at delivery point has not been an important criterion.

(c) It has failed to evolve priorities.

(d) It lacks objective oriented programmes.

(e) The personnel management is very weak.

(f) Educational Management System is budget-oriented system where efficiency is rated by the ability to "Consume" budget and not to demand more.

12.5 Suggestions for Reforming Educational Management

The reforms suggested in POA can broadly be studied under the following heads:-

(a) The concept of decentralisation has been envisaged as: "Decentralisation implies democratic participation by elected representatives of people in decision-making at the district, sub-district, and Panchayat level." According to the POA, the future course of decentralisation depends to a great extent on the Constitution Amendment (seventy-second) Bill, 1991.

(b) Necessary amendment may be made in the Constitution for carrying-out reforms in management.

(c) The NPE has envisaged the role and responsibility of the States and the Centre in regard to education as one of meaningful partnership. While the role and responsibilities of the states in regard to education will remain essentially unchanged, the Union Government should accept larger responsibility to reinforce the national and integrative character of education. The implementation of the NPE would require total involvement of both the states and the Centre and there has to be effective and positive interaction between these two partners for successful and effective implementation of the NPE.

(d) Recruitment is an important instrument of quality control as human input to the education system. Besides, the existing promotional practices for filling vacancies in management positions in education, provision should be made for direct recruitment to at least 25 percent of the district and block education officers as well as heads of secondary and senior secondary schools. The recruitment procedure for teachers and administrators should be modernized. The states should set-up their own mechanism on the same pattern.

(e) For streamlining the flow of information and development planning capacities at various levels of educational administration integrated education management information-system should be introduced. An effort will be made to integrate the existing separate system of collection of information for Planning, Statistics, Monitoring, Evaluation, Administration, etc. The system should be simple in its design, contents, and coverage. The coverage of information should be both qualitative and quantitative. The management information system in education should be coordinated with NIC network established at the district level.

Objective Type Questions

Multiple Choice Questions (Tick ✔ the right option)

(1) The children learnt by imitating the work and life pattern of their

(a) Parents

(b) Neighbours

(c) Parents and Neighbours

(d) None of the above.

(2) The Programme of Action was prepared by the

(a) Department of Education

(b) Ministry of Human Resources Development

(c) Government of India

(d) All of the above.

Fill in the blanks

(1) __________ is an important instrument of quality control as human input to the education system. [Recruitment]

(2) Through the daily experiences of his life, the child becomes fully aware of the relationship that existed between him and his ________. [Environment]

Important Questions

1. Write a note on the development of the school system.
2. Describe the challenging task of Educational Administration and Managers.
3. Discuss the Programme of Action (POA) 1992 on National Policy of Education.
4. Discuss the shortcomings of the present management of education.
5. Discuss the suggestions for reforming Educational Management.

Unit II

Major Components of School Management

13

School Management

A school is an educational institution and management is that means through which some organisation or institution is operated in a well-mannered way - may be it is an educational institution, administrative institution or community, religious or social service organisation. From this it becomes clear that management is related to groups of people and their activities, directly or indirectly.

Management is related to those people who work under some institution or organisation and the coordination of their activities. The relation of school management is mainly related to the managing committee of the school, the leaders of the school, i.e., the Headmaster and the teachers working under his leadership and other employees and along with it the physical material to run the educational process in a well mannered way. The head of the school is entrusted with the task of managing the work of the school and he performs the administrative duties of every day routine programmes and activities to be run smoothly and for the achievement of determined aims with the help of his colleagues. Democracy has faith that the leader of the school and the manager should have freedom in the management of the school so that they can take initiative actively in order to achieve the determined aims of education in an atmosphere of freedom. Since democratic system has been established in India, it becomes necessary that the leaders of the school and the Headmaster should have freedom in the determination of curriculum, textbooks, methods of teaching, etc. in the matter of their selection and executing the same. If the management has such type of freedom, it would adopt democratic attitude in the internal management of the school management.

13.1 Characteristics of Successful School Management

A school is the basal unit of the big hierarchy of educational administration. Today, as never before, India needs educational institutions not only to guard its past but also to advance its future. "The destiny of India is now being shaped in the classroom" this is the assessment of situation by the first ever comprehensive commission (1964-66) on Indian Education. Schools are to be the first class nurseries for the education of children in democratic citizenship which India needs to make its democracy permanently viable. Efficient school administration is crucial to the success of democracy. Some theory and philosophy will have to be evolved for guiding the educational administration process at all levels and to be clear about the objectives so that we do not miss the targets.

The characteristics of successful school management are given in the following points:-

- **(I)** Flexibility
- **(II)** Practicability
- **(III)** Conformity to the social and political philosophy of the country
- **(IV)** Efficiency
- **(V)** Successful achievement of desired objectives

The details of the characteristics of school management, have been given in the following paragraphs:-

(I) Flexibility: One of the essential characteristics of successful school management is its flexible character. The manager should be dynamic, not static. The management should provide enough scope for additions and alternations. The rules and regulations should act as a means to end and not an end in themselves. Dead uniformity and mechanical efficiency is the very antithesis of good administration. The framework of administration should provide enough scope to the administrators to help the needy students, and the needy teacher, to change the time schedule to suit the weather to meet any emergency. A word of caution here. Flexibility does not mean that the administration should be in a fluid condition without any specific norm or standard rules and regulations, creating confusion and chaos at every step. What is meant is a proper balance between rigidity and elasticity.

(II) **Practicability:** The school management must not be a bundle of theoretical principles, but must provide practical measures to achieve the desired objectives. Whatever objective is decided upon it must be achievable and practicable to avoid frustration.

(III) **Conformity to the Social and Political Philosophy of the Country:** There must be a close connection between school management and the social and political philosophy of a country. It must adjust itself to the impact of new ideas, new patterns, and new moves of the society. In an autocratic country, educational theory and practice will have to be different from that of a democratic country because education is one of the means to achieve social and political objectives. American education is decentralised and democratised whereas Chinese education is characterised by regimentation due to political philosophies of the respective countries. In India, school administration has to be democratic because of political democracy in the country.

(IV) **Efficiency:** Successful management is that which results in maximum efficiency. This will be possible only when human and material resources are properly utilised – right man at the right place; right work at the right time; every activity and project are well planned and well executed.

(V) **Successful Achievement of Desired Objectives:** Successful management is one which leads to the successful achievement of desired objectives of education in a particular community, e.g. healthy social living, development of good physical, social, moral, intellectual, and aesthetic qualities and healthy democratic living.

School management must facilitate education. It exists for the pupil and its efficiency has to be measured by the extent to which it contributes to teaching and learning.

13.2 Principles of School Management

India happens to be the largest democracy in the world. To make democracy successful, we have to revitalise and recharge our schools to the full. Schools will be able to add tempo to the struggling democracy if the following principles are taken into consideration while administering them.

Democratic Philosophy of Education: In his report on Indian Administration, Paul H. Appleby has emphasised the need for a philosophical but simple theory of administration for a country which is determined to create a welfare state. If a philosophy is necessary for general administration, it is all the more so for educational administration which is seeking to fashion a new pattern of education suited to the needs and aspirations of modern India. In an educational institution in a democracy, the administrator is a friend and a guide. He consults his colleagues, honours their opinions, confers with them in staff meetings, meets them informally in gatherings, and clubs. He is one among the quails. He recognises the worth of each individual child, finds out potentialities, and gives him help and guidance according to his requirements. Thus, the total management becomes a joint show of the headmaster, teachers, and pupils. Everybody has a clear consciousness and realisation of the purpose of democratic-philosophy with which the school is administered.

Our first and fundamental guiding principle in school management is that the management is based on a democratic philosophy. By democratic-management, we mean management which depends upon the good faith, tolerance, respect for others' opinion, justice, freedom of speech and action.

The other guiding principles which we are going to describe are the further elaboration of the first and fundamental principle cited above. All the principles being described here are, in fact, the principles of democratic-management. Once again we may repeat that since in our country the democratic ideal is accepted as the way of life, all our guiding principles of school management is those principles which ensure democratisation of our school.

Let us discuss the principles of school management:

1) **Principle of Sharing Responsibilities:** "The principle of sharing responsibilities signifies *the development of policies and the planning of educational programmes being undertaken jointly by teachers and managers with authority shared equally among those who participate in the process. In sharing of authority everyone who is sharing it is considered wholly responsible.*" The basic idea is that all those who have to participate in the process must share in planning, executing, and evaluating the process. The success and failure should also be equally shared and each should be held responsible for his part in the joint enterprises.

   The sharing of responsibility and authority is considered a sound principle since it is realised that more brains put together can work better than one brain alone. This principle is, however, opposed by the autocratic minds. They say that more brains, more muddle. In fact, this criticism is levelled against democracy as a principle of government. There is some truth in it especially when the minds involved are ignorant and untrained to work cooperatively. But the danger of muddle can be easily avoided *if the sharer of authority are well informed, know clearly the objectives, trained in group processes, and have a keen desire for improvement and for achieving success.* We have given above a quotation emphasising that democracy is learnt. The democratic processes take time to be ingrained in the human mind, so if there are any initial setbacks one should not loose heart or reject the democratic processes.

2) **Principle of Planning:** The democratic management believes in planning. It pins its faith in preparing a plan before embarking upon the process of execution. *But again plan is required to be drawn with the cooperation of those who are involved in the process.*

The principle of planning emphasises that "the planning should grow out of the recognised needs and interests of those who are affected by the plan and be based upon the carefully organised series of facts." The preparation of a plan depends upon a series of data which is pertinent in the process under planning. All the facts regarding that aspect which needs to be tackled must be obtained.

The reasons which are advanced in support of planning may be put as follows:

A Planning Programme:

1. *Secures a unification of effort by:*

(a) Continuous scrutiny and restatement of the aims of education.

(b) Evaluation of extent to which outcomes are being achieved.

(c) Continuous reorganisation and enrichment of the curriculum.

(d) Functional administration for carrying on the programme.

2. ***Secures better coordination among the teachers and managers and the other participants in the educational programme.***

1. Provides opportunities for the functioning of democratic leadership.
2. Ensures the participation of all concerned in the framing of policies.
3. Distributes responsibilities in keeping with the qualities of the participants.
4. Leads to an examination of the outcomes, and the resources available.
5. Informs the community about the plans, programmes, and the policies of school management.
6. Helps in choosing improved techniques of administration and management.
7. Promotes experimentation.
8. Provides good in-service training to the new recruits.

3. *Principle of Leadership*

In school management the leadership role has to be taken up by the managers. *This role they can perform either by dominating others and dictating their viewpoint or by adopting procedures where authority is shared and efforts are cooperative. In democratic management the defining of scope of action in making decisions is undertaken with mutual consultations*. The cooperation sought is not because the leader has an official status but because the participants feel that by joint efforts they will find more fruitful dimensions for success.

Leadership in management is considered a necessity because without it the work in the group and of the group cannot proceed. It is to bring harmony in the work, to keep the individuals in the group, to continue efforts in a coordinated manner, to prepare plan, programmes and procedures, to formulate objectives and to direct the efforts towards the achievement of these objectives that the leadership is necessarily required. In a democracy, educational leadership must be exercised in a democratic way. *The democratic leadership will have faith in individual's freedom of speech. It will have respect for individuality and will give supremacy to reason as against authority.* The democratic leader affords full opportunity for full and free discussion but remains all the time alert and channels the discussions in the right direction. He does not allow the controversies to develop so much as to engulf whole of the discussion and make it almost impossible for arriving at any decision. In the words of Briggs and Justman, *"The concept of democratic leadership assumes the ability to take the initiative in crystallising group thinking and in translating group decisions into action."*

When leadership operates democratically then the authority vanishes. There follows free discussions without fear or favour. Every member of staff is free to suggest or to put his argument. Any member may influence the discussion and direct them. Anyone may put a suggestion for an action or offer compromise to a controversy. When such becomes the atmosphere the 'emergent' or 'shared' leadership is bound to be in action.

In democratic management the will of one person is not superimposed over others. But many a times there may be shirkers or obstinate people who will not share the burden cooperatively with others. Such individuals make the functioning of democratic leadership very difficult. The shared leadership can be successful only in case those who participate are actively engaged in the solution of the problem. Thus to be successful, it is necessary that these shirkers take an interest in the problem or the programme. They should be motivated to shed off their lethargies and be persuaded to contribute their best.

4. *Principle of Flexibility*

The principle of flexibility is an important principle of democratic school management because it ensures that the manager will be prepared to change his programme or policy or attitude if such a change is in the interest of all concerned.

A democratic manager does not take a rigid attitude in his work. He is always amenable to change. His approach is that of constant modification in the light of past experiences. But this sort of flexibility on the part of the democratic manager does not mean that he does not have a set approach towards administrative problem. He is not a rudderless ship drifting in the winds without any inkling of any destination. The purpose of management is clear to him. He is fully aware of the goals he wants to achieve. He proceeds to achieve them in a methodical and systematic way but remains alive to incorporate any changes which the situation demands.

5. *Principle of Dynamism*

In a democratic state the *nature of society is dynamic.* It changes constantly. To keep pace with it *education should also be dynamic.* For dynamic education a dynamic administration is needed. By this we mean that in a democracy, management is not conventional. It is not that if in past a particular management policy has been followed then it should also be followed in the present and future also. The experience of the past is used as a convenient means of solving the existing problem but there is no slavery to the traditional or conventional modes of approach. To explain the situation let us consider the case of inspection in our country. The inspector owed his respect in the past due to his legalistic authority. Now, if any inspector uses it as an expression of his prestige he works against the principles of democracy. He has to win prestige on the basis of his scholarship and a humanistic approach towards the problems of teachers.

6. *Principle of Competency*

The democratic school management with its flexibility and dynamism is a difficult process. It requires efficient leaders who can understand the change in the social milieu and not only be guided by this change in their activities but also give a direction to the change. Thus, democratic management presupposes that the competent personnel are entrusted with the task of management.

The different individuals have different competencies to do a certain task. In educational management certain types of competencies are required in a person as different from others. Everyone cannot be an educational administrator or manager as everyone cannot be a good musician or artist or painter. One has to cultivate his faculties in a particular direction to become one of these. Over and above this one has to have some natural talent also. The democratic management thus, believes that the administrators or managers should only be those persons who possess the competency for this task.

7. *Principle of Individual Effort*

In a democratic society the individual effort has great importance. In communism, the significance of the individual is undermined, while in anarchy, group organisations are dissolved. But in a democracy neither the individual nor the group are ignored. Democracy believes that it is through the individual efforts that the new ideas are formulated and therefore, it should be encouraged to the utmost. Democracy also believes that the individual effort can find its fulfillment only in a social setting and so there must be a well knit social organisation. Thus, democracy values the individual personality but regards its development essentially in a social setting. In the words of Moehlman, "Democracy regards the individual in two ways, as a sovereign personality and as a member of sovereign group and its function is to establish and maintain a harmonious balance between these two views of sovereignty. The form of social organisation where the individual and the group are in relating balance or dynamic harmony is called democracy."

Much of good school administration and management is a consequence of the individual effort. This initiates, promotes, consolidates, and evaluates the desirable changes. It is, therefore, necessary that well trained and capable school managers are to be appointed. Above, we have discussed the competencies required in managers. The principle of individual effort is a corollary to that principle. If we identify the competencies and then entrust the task of administration to only those who hold these competencies, it will result in good management.

8. Principle of Human Relations

The concept of human relations has been a recent innovation. The authority in a group was legalistic some time back. Because of the status of the administrator his viewpoint was prevailing. It is now realised that it stifles the initiative of the subordinate persons. The school staff is forced to do that for which it might have contrary opinion. This results in half-hearted approach towards vital problems. The will to solve the problem in such a case is that of status leader and not of the subordinate worker. Now it is recognised that the functioning of a good school administration depends upon the better personal relations between the people engaged in administration. Hence, now we do not use the words 'school administrators'. These are replaced by 'school managers'.

9. Principle of Evaluation

This is an important principle in all types of management whether it may be democratic or autocratic. The success or the failure of a programme must be assessed so that the improvements in it can be brought about. Since in democracy a flexible approach in management is recommended, the evaluation of the managerial functioning is of great importance. The evaluation leads to the understanding of the defects in the programme and these are sought to be removed by bringing about the change in the management itself.

10. Principle of Maintenance of Standard of Efficiency

Democracy expects that the standards of efficiency in public and private services are kept at a high level. Often a charge is made against democracy that it is the government of the mediocrity. It is alleged that in democracy the higher intellect is replaced by the average intellect in administration. It may be true that sometimes the representatives elected to legislatures and parliaments are not of high intellectual calibre especially so in the backward countries. But this does not mean that the services are also of an average class. The efficiency of the services should rather compensate for the mediocrity of the elected representatives in the parliaments and assemblies.

In school management the maintenance of high standard of efficiency is very much needed. Without this the management becomes stereotyped and results in the failure of the educational system. Since for the preservation of democracy education is the most effective tool, any failure of the educational system will prove disastrous for it. It is for this reason why in a country which is backward, illiterate and with no well developed system of education autocracy or dictatorship replaces democracy.

For maintaining the standards of efficiency the work among the members of the staff should be distributed on the basis of qualifications, interests, and aptitudes of the teachers.

11. Principle of Professional Growth of the Staff

The school management must provide opportunities for the professional growth of the staff. Above we have emphasised that individual effort is needed to run an organisation efficiently. This effort will be of value only when the individuals are enlightened and have up-to-date knowledge.

The teachers should be encouraged to go for in-service training. The school management may organise refresher courses, conferences, seminars, etc. to keep its staff abreast with the latest trends in the field of education and the most modern methods of teaching. In fact, the management should use all available opportunities for the professional growth of its staff. It may give incentives in the form of increments, etc. to those members of staff who complete some refresher courses, etc.

12. *Principle of Student Participation*

The student participation in the planning of programmes and policies of the school should also be encouraged. Such participation ensures their interests in the work of the school and thus increases the chances of the success of the programme. The students resent any programme thrown over their heads by the teachers or their heads. On the other hand, if they participate in preparing that programme they very much like to see that it is successful.

The student participation does not mean that the students be associated with all aspects of management of school. There may be many aspects in which their participation may become a hindrance rather than an asset. A wise manager will pick and choose the situation where the student's participation will be of most worth and will involve them in that particular situation.

In the end it may be said that the school management should always remain alive to the needs of the school. It should from time to time assess the requirements of the institution. Its efforts must always be directed to provide for all these requirements.

Another most important factor on which the good school management depends is the atmosphere of the school. A good school is one in which there is cordiality, sincerity, sympathy, and work consciousness among the members of its staff. Such a school will always be successful in the achievement of the goals of education.

13.3 Scope of School Management

By scope, we mean the sphere within which the functioning of educational management takes place. The scope of educational management today is as vast as that of education itself. Any activity conductive to the achievement of educational goal is a part of educational management. Such activities could be at the school level, at the college level, at the university level or at the control level. Anything done to improve the quality of education at any stage may be ranging from the supply of material, human, and financial resources to the highest cultural or academic needs-comes under the scope of educational management and the following three heads:

1) Goal Development;
2) Programme Planning and Actualisation; and
3) Organisation.

1) **Goal Development:** The educational system is a sub-system of a society, and therefore, the society not only provides human and non-human resources but also certain expectations that the system of education will achieve certain goals. Since society is in a constant process of change, needs of the society change and so do the goal specifications. It is necessary for the educative process to be responsive to these changing expectations and it is through the educational management system that persons involved in the process of management can continuously examine, evaluate and change (if appropriate) the goals of education.

2) **Programme Planning and Actualisation:** According to the Oxford English Dictionary, planning is "to design some action to be done before hand." Phillips regards it as "the process of setting in advance a pattern of action to bring about overall national policies by the closest

possible means and ends." Thus, we can say that planning is the process of preparing a set of decisions for action in the future and directed towards realising some goals by the best possible means. The essence of planning is an appraisal of many operational alternatives as possible and then selecting the best for launching action. "Planning selects among alternatives, explores routes before travel begins and identifies possible or probable outcomes of action before the executive and the organisation is committed to any."

According to the *Education Commission* (1964-66), planning at the first two stages, i.e. national level and state levels alone suffers from some deficiencies such as (i) lack of emphasis on local issues in educational development; (ii) non-involvement of educational workers; and (iii) over emphasis on expenditure-oriented programmes. Planning at the local level, i.e. college level is only to offset these drawbacks. Planning at the college level does not mean that the principal or a few of the members of the faculty prepare the plan for various activities of the college. Instead it is a cooperative endeavour of all those who are involved in the implementation of the plans - not only members of the faculty, teaching and non-teaching, but even the students, the parents and the local communities must be associated while planning the programmes.

The goals that are developed by the management system become the rationale for programme planning and actualisation. Programmes represent the intended engagement opportunities for students who are to be educated. The responsibility for the planning and actualisation of programmes rest on the management system. It is, therefore, essential that the management system should provide technological support to the educative process in the form of consultations and services. The management system should initiate, coordinate, provide services and be part of these activities.

3) **Organisation:** Organisation has been a major problem in the field of education. The debate over the control of education has over and again raised the salient issue of how educational machinery should best be organised, politically, professionally, and administratively. Here too, as in several other vital areas, education is handicapped by tradition. If conventional biases and prejudices can be replaced by decisions made logically and scientifically, with the achievement of objectives as the only consideration, modern principles and techniques of organisation will provide the basis for effective distribution and coordination of functions.

13.4 Practical Measures for School Management

The practical measures for school management are given as follows (1) Staff Council, (2) Student's Council, (3) Staff Meetings, (4) Special Committee of Pupils, (5) Social Service Squads, and Practical Measures.

(1) **Staff Council:** The aim of the staff council is to plan all important matters of the school. The staff council may be further split up into committees to plan and execute specific tasks. Meetings of the staff council should be held frequently to discuss all important issues. Senior members of the staff should constitute the staff council.

(2) **Student's Council:** A student council consisting of Secretaries from different house, associations and clubs should form a student's council with the aim of giving the students training in self-government. The student councils can be guided and assisted by a staff advisor.

(3) **Staff Meetings:** Meetings of the staff should be called fortnightly to discuss the different matters and the staff should have the idea that whatever has been decided upon is mainly their work.

(4) **Special Committee of Pupils:** In addition to the student council, special committees should be formed, duly elected by the pupils to carry out specific duties and organise special activities for maintaining discipline, organising debates, dramatics, exhibitions, flower shows, literary societies, music concerts, etc.

(5) **Social Service Squads:** Such types of squads can render service in the form of laying roads, arranging committee functions, cleanliness campaigns in the neighbourhood, literary campaigns, helping the sick, looking after the families of the jawans, collection of national defence fund, etc.

(6) **Practical Measures:** Practical measures are to be adopted for democratic educational administration and staff council, student's council, staff meetings, special committees of pupils, social services squads, etc.

School Organisation

School organisation is a combination of two works, viz. school, and organisation. In order to understand the meaning of school organisation, it is essential to understand the meaning of school and organisation separately.

The purpose of school organisation and the administration is to raise the standard of education. Many factors have contributed to the decline in the standard of school education in India, but the main ones among them are the administrative difficulties of inspection or supervision and survey. Hence, the Education Commission has offered the following suggestions for improving the standard of education at the school level:

1) A common method of public education should be evolved.

2) School education be organised at the national level, with their distinct objectives – (a) bringing all institutions to a certain minimum standard, (b) giving each institution the opportunity to develop to the highest level which is capable, (c) taking each institution to the ideal point within the next ten years.

3) The officer of the district education officer should be made effective.

4) The state institute of education should be made more effective and powerful.

5) All kinds of programmes should be organised in the centrally administered territories.

The Education Commission has sought to solve educational administration problems on the basis of the principles outlined above.

13.5 Process of School Management

Scholars related to educational areas are of the opinion that the process of school management should be cooperative and democratic. Under it, the policy formulation and management process should also be in a democratic manner. So that freedom can be given to the workers of the human groups related to school to work according to their abilities. This process can be managed only by a skilled manager. It is very necessary for the manager to be endowed with the qualities of democratic leadership, efficiency, and power of taking decision. A manager would be more successful if he works by making the following principles as the basis

(1) Planning
(2) Organisation
(3) Direction
(4) Coordination
(5) Evaluation

(1) **Planning:** The general and the simple meaning of planning is that the efforts, the direction, the working system and the associate human groups and situations and the aid material - their broad and

meaningful outline must be prepared in order to accomplish the aims. No success can be achieved in any work without determining such type of outline. If no pre-determination is made of this type, we would go astray before reaching the goal. To prepare an educational plan is a progressive process. In it not only the present which is to be taken into account, but also the future is to be kept in mind. Along with it, the needs, principles, ideals, and its material resources of the child and society or specific community or any institution would also have to be taken into account.

While preparing a plan, there are certain compulsory things which cannot be ignored. These are like this–

1. The manager must have a clear idea of the goal of the plan, i.e. the aim for which the plan has been formulated should have stability and definiteness in it.
2. After determining the aims, broad outlines of the activities must be made and a list prepared for their accomplishment.
3. It should also be ensured as to what are the methods, systems, and technologies through which the different tasks can be accomplished.
4. After making decisions about the use of these systems there must be the selection of aid material and their classification for executing the same.

An able and skilled management while preparing a plan must take into account the above said important things. Even after doing all this, a serious thinking should also be given to the plan and its evaluation. If the evaluation is less than the goal or looks opposite to that and it looks that there must be change, in that case such flexibility must be kept in the plan that amendment, or change may be made in the plan due to the exigencies of the time.

(2) Organisation: Organisation is the basic function in all types of management. J.B. Seyers is of the opinion that "It is a machine of doing work which is built up by the individuals, things, thoughts, conceptions, symbols, forms, rules, principles, or the integration of all. Whether the machine can work itself or it is to be operated by human decisions and will."

There are two types of provisions under organisation – human and physical. The organisation of human resources can be done through class committees, teachers, and employees. Under the physical resources can be included building, furniture, libraries, and other material. Besides these two types of resources, the techniques of schools, curriculum, and time-table, etc. are also affected by thoughts, principles, and conceptions. In this way organisation integrates the different resources. So that the complete programme of the school may be implemented conveniently for the realisation of the aims.

(3) Direction: Guidance or leadership is the basis in the school management. The whole plan or organisation goes waste in the absence of successful leadership or guidance. Three things are very important under the direction or leadership – to make decisions, to declare those decisions, and to give a practical shape to the decisions. In this way direction is not an easy task. For this the manager is endowed with the qualities of abilities, knowledge, understanding, farsightedness, and wisdom. Besides, he should always be endowed with the qualities of patience, cooperation, tolerance, and sympathy. The capacity to form human relations is very essential for direction. If the leader lacks these qualities, he would not be successful in getting the work done from associates with the result that the direction of the plan would not be successful. For example, if the manager of the school or the leader of the school, who is also the Headmaster of the school, if he decides himself and gives an order—"This is my order and all have to act upon it. Let me see who does not obey the orders;" then by acting like this, he can neither win the confidence of his associates nor earn their goodwill. A skilled manager should take a decision only after consulting his associates by considering them to be an important part of human group. He should present his thoughts in such a manner which makes his associates feel that these thoughts are their own. To establish such type of mutual relations is the success of direction.

(4) **Coordination:** By coordination it is meant that all those elements which are related to the organisation, mutual relations should be established among them. To establish coordination among different elements is inherent in such a manner that the ends may be achieved by mutually working together. Wastage of both the labour and power can be checked through coordination. It makes the relations cordial and there is no struggle of differences.

(5) **Evaluation:** Evaluation is a very important element of school management. No function can be considered as complete till its results are evaluated appropriately. Through evaluation we come to know as to what extent we have achieved the determined aims. Management is a dynamic process. Therefore, there should be continuous progress in it for the success of different functions in it.

Difference between Organisation and Administration

It is very often seen that organisation and administration are considered to have the same meaning. But it is not so. As we have already discussed that organisation is a structure in which coordination occupies an important place. Administration is a process of management. Behaviour, operation, and better provisions are inherent in the administrative aspect. Under it if desirable objective is not being achieved through resolved organisation for reorganisation, in that case the management makes a series of efforts. In this way the head of the school should be a high quality administrator along with being a high quality organiser. It is because as a result of low quality of administration, the high quality organisation also becomes unsuccessful.

Organisation and administration are also closely related to each other. When we call a man as the administrator of a school, it does not mean that he is not responsible for the high quality organisation. Therefore, he is responsible for both, the administrative and organisational aspects. Organisation is a structure or plan, the creation of which is the important function of the administration. In this way both the aspects move side by side in the administration work. After studying the functions of administrators, Gullck has proved that both the organisation and functions related to administration are inherent in their functions. He has enumerated the functions of planning, organisation, appointment of teachers and other employees and managing their functions, operation, coordination, preparing a report and budget in the functions of an administrator. Therefore, it would be appropriate to say that both the organisation and administration depend upon one another.

13.6 Comparative Study of Management and Administration

There is often a discussion regarding the controversy in the words 'Management' and 'Administration'. There is no unanimity among the scholars related to it. Some scholars are of the opinion that there is some difference between management and administration. Some other scholars consider the two as synonymous, while according to some scholars administration is a part of management. We will discuss all the three viewpoints. Only then there can be a clarification about the difference in the meaning of the two.

I. **There is a difference between Management and Administration.** The scholars have taken resort to two basic things in order to clarify the difference between management and administration –

These two aspects are–

(1) Determination of policies.

(2) Execution of policies.

The difference between management and administration can be made clear in the following manner:

Administration is such a process or medium which determines various policies and aims. In this way, administration is a determining factor for setting of goals and functions of the policies and areas of an institution–it formulates different plans and provides safeguards to accomplish the same successfully. In fact, the structure of an institution is the main and highest concern of the administration and by administration it means those means which determines the aims which have to be achieved by the institution and its employees. Indirectly, the administration formulates those general principles which would be helpful in the operation of the functions of the institution in a regulated manner. These very general rules are called policies. Management is that function which is related to execute the policies and to make use of an organisation to achieve aims which are present before it by the administration. In this way management is an executive function which is mainly related to execute broad policies determined by the administration. The management function is executed by a medium level official like the head of the institution. In brief, it can be said that administration is a function which is related to the determination of general policies while the function of the management is to execute those policies determined by the administration.

II. **Administration and Management are Synonymous**. There are some scholars who do not accept any difference in the meaning of administration and management and consider them to be synonyms. They are of the opinion that there is no justification to differentiate in the meaning of the two. Their main argument is that it is not necessary that separate personnel should be responsible in the organisation for the two processes. Any manager or an administrator has to give his time for both the activities of management and administration. For example, any manager or an administrator of higher level of any institution has to look after the work of his subordinates along with the formulating of the policies and control of the work of others. In this way a manager has also to take part in the determination of the policies of the organisation in addition to the looking after the work of others. Even in practice, the use of two terms is used with the same meanings in all the types of institutions - may they be are governmental or non-governmental. The only difference is that the work done in government areas by the high officials and the work done by the management in non-government areas should have the minimum difference - the difference of only the name. Dr Kimball has clearly said, "To differentiate between management and administration is to increase the illusion. Both these words are synonyms." Henri Fayol also writes in this context, "In order to run any function in a well mannered way every institution (whether it is in the government area or in the private sector) needs planning, organisation, direction, coordination and control and all have to act upon the same principle. Therefore, it is futile to differentiate between the two words."

III. **Administration is a part of Management.** According to some management specialists, management is an etymological word. Therefore, it would be appropriate to look into it in the broad sense. In the broad sense are included planning, determination of policies, coordination in the activities, self-confidence, discipline, and control. According to this viewpoint administration gives information about some specific aspects of management tasks, i.e. administration is a part of management. According to specialists, management can be divided into two parts:-

(1) Administrative management

(2) Operative management

Administrative Management: Administrative management is related to the determination of policies for the achievement of determined aims, and to make amendments in these policies as are necessary, to plan them and to determine the standards of the works completed; and to evaluate the actual achievements along with the pre-determined objectives.

Operative Management: Such type of management is related to human resources, physical resources, and policies and plans to be given practical shape to them to operate the daily activities of the institution and make an appropriate use of power. It is also related to show the actual results of the progress of the work.

In brief, after studying the various aspects of management, we come to the conclusion that administration and management are the two sides of the same coin. The job of the administration is to give a thinking relating to policies and the job of the management is to execute the policies. Sometimes in non-government institutions the management works are given the name of management and while in government and public sector institutions, the same management works are given the name of administration. In fact, the executives at all the levels perform both types of tasks in different parts. There is virtually no dividing line between the formulation and execution tasks. According to another scholar there is no need of having two separate human groups of executives for performing administrative and management works. Every manager performs both types of tasks, i.e. he devotes some time for administration tasks and some for management tasks. Therefore, it is unnecessary to differentiate between the two.

Objective Type Questions

Multiple Choice Questions (Tick ✔ the right option)

(1) Headmaster should have freedom in the determination of
- (a) Curriculum
- (b) Textbooks
- (c) Methods of teaching.
- (d) All of the above.

(2) The Democratic Management believes in
- (a) Planning
- (b) Responsibility
- (c) Sharing
- (d) None of the above.

(3) In School Management the leadership role has to be taken up by the
- (a) Teacher
- (b) Headmaster
- (c) Manager
- (d) Pupils

Fill in the blanks

(1) In a democratic state the Nature of society is __________. [Dynamic]
(2) The concept _________ has been a recent innovation. [Human relation]
(3) _________ has been a major problem in the field of education. [Organization]
(4) Guidance or leadership is the ___________ of school management. [Basis]

Important Questions

(1) Give the characteristics of successful School Management.
(2) Describe the principles of School Management.
(3) Write the process of School Management and explain the practical measures for School Management.
(4) Give the difference between Organisation and Administration.

14

Role of the Headmaster

The headmaster, as educational leader, holds the key position in the school. As an important component of the school administration he has two important responsibilities, the administration of the school and the supervision of the personnel involved in teaching and learning. Everything in the school, the plant, the staff, the curriculum, methods, and techniques of teaching, co-curricular activities, etc. is organised by him. The efficiency of the school depends on the ability and skill, personality, and professional competence of the headmaster. He may be described as the sun around which educational plants revolve. He is the moon among lesser stars. In the words of P. C. Wren, "What the main spring is to the watch, the flywheel to the machine or the engine to the steamship, the headmaster is to the school. The character of the school reflects and proclaims the professional character of the Headmaster. He is the seal and the school is the wax. He is the organiser, leader, governor, business director, coordinator, superintendent, example teacher, guide, philosopher, and friend." Since the administration and supervision of a school requires a large number of specialised duties, the headmaster requires an adequate preparation.

14.1 The Headmaster

The Headmaster is that major component of school administration on whose ability and skill, personality and professional competence will largely depend the tone and efficiency of the school. "Schools are good or bad, in a healthy or unhealthy, mental, moral and physical condition, flourishing or perishing as the headmaster is capable, energetic and of high ideas or the reverse. Schools rise to the fame or sink to obscurity as greater or lesser headmasters have charge of them." Everything in the school, the plant, the staff, the curriculum, methods, and techniques of teaching, co-curricular activities, human relationships bear the impress of the personality of the institution. The school is as great as the headmaster is. It is rightly said that the school becomes great not because of the magnificent building but because of the "magnificent" headmaster. Harrow, Eton, and Rugby have been made famous by their great heads. In short, as is the headmaster so is the school.

14.2 Concept of Headmaster's Role

The headmaster is the keystone in the arch of school administration; he is the hub of the educational effort. The headmaster is a group leader who knows how to involve people, how to arrange conditions and initiate processes that will bring out the best in each participant. "No school can succeed," in the words of Mohiuddin, "if the teachers in it, work only as individuals and not as a group." The headmaster is the group leader to direct and stimulate group effort.

In the school administration, the headmaster occupies a unique position. He is in the strategic centre of a web of instructional relationships – teacher-pupil, teacher-teacher. It is he who arranges their coordinated efforts.

In the words of Jaswant Singh, "What the school is what it does, is determined largely by the intelligence, scholarship, imagination, initiative, personality, and social skills of the headmaster."

In the words of the Central Advisory Board of Education (CABE), "No scheme of educational reconstruction will produce the desired result unless it is administrated with vision and efficiency. The person who plans with vision, who executes with responsibility is an exact headmaster. The school is aptly called the lengthened shadow of the headmaster because the character of the school reflects or proclaims the character of the headmaster."

Secondary Education Commission (1953): "On the headmaster the proper working of the school ultimately depends. The reputation of the school and the position that it holds in the society depends in a large measure on the influence that he exercises over his colleagues, his pupils, and the general public. Similarly the discipline of the school and its *esprit de corps* are the special responsibilities of the headmaster. He holds an important place in the life of the community, where he can exercise a very healthy influence. By this contact with the parents and the general public he can help forge that link between the school and the large community which we have repeatedly stressed. He is also responsible for carrying out the policies and the programmes of the Department of Education and he acts as a liaison between it and the management of the general local community." In short, the headmaster is a constant factor in a school's leadership picture - his is the big role in the school play.

14.3 Nature of Demands made on the School Headmaster in a Democracy

1. **A New Type of Leadership:** Since ages, society has been making heavy demands on the school's headmaster – that he should be a man of character, an excellent organiser, a skilled administrator, a model teacher. Society today wants all these qualities in a headmaster plus something more. It wants that the headmaster should be a good leader to be able to inspire those who work under his direction. In a democracy, he cannot *drive* them. In the old authoritarian schools, where the headmaster was a dictator, a despot - his was perhaps an easier role. What he needed was the ability to inspire awe or fear among the staff and the students, and all went well. But now the emphasis is more on freedom of participation and reciprocal cooperation and less on dictatorship. "Leadership in a democracy is known by the personalities it enriches, not by those it dominates or captivates." Hence, the task of the headmaster has become rather taxing and challenging. The headmaster has to *earn* the leadership now. To make a success of assignment, he must come into close contact with teachers, pupils, and parents. He cannot afford to live in an ivory tower (Office) and command respect. He cannot afford to be a mere detective, critic or fault finder. His leadership should be constructive. The steering wheel is even now with the headmaster. His duty of direction and superintendence is still there. His job is to see that parts of the machinery work spontaneously and in harmony and unison - not under an artificial compulsion.

2. **The Headmaster - a Community Leader:** The Headmaster is a community leader. As such, he has to bring about a continuous long-range improvement programme. He has to exercise more initiative to meet the new needs than at any time in the past. As an educational leader, he has to keep a step or two ahead of their constituents. He has to be vigilant here because if he gets too far ahead, the public won't follow him. If he falls

behind, they will fire him. He would do well to study his community thoroughly, learn its resources of wealth, know the intricacies of political manoeuvring, and do his best so that the public is familiar with its schools.

3. **A Good Business Manager:** The rapid increase in school size and the changed conditions under which schools operate today have greatly increased the business responsibilities of the school headmaster. For efficient administration of school enterprise, it is necessary that the headmaster looks after the school plant and the school activities in a business-like manner.

14.4 Headmaster's Duties

The headmaster is supposed to discharge numerous duties which may be grouped under two heads – Specific duties and General duties.

(A) Specific Duties

1) Supervision
2) Teaching
3) Management
4) Special services

(B) General Duties

1) Duties before the session.
2) Duties throughout the year.
3) Duties at the close of the session.

Now, we shall discuss these duties in detail:

(A) Specific Duties

1) Supervision:

The headmaster as the leader of the school has to supervise various types of activities:

(I) Supervision of Instruction, Curriculum, Development and Improvement, and Evaluation Programme.
(II) Supervision of Co-curricular Programme.
(III) Supervision of Hostel.
(IV) Supervision of Registration Work and Accounts.
(V) General Supervision.

(I) **Supervision of Instruction, Curriculum, Development and Improvement, and Evaluation Programme:** Supervision of instruction, curriculum, development and improvement and evaluation programme is one of the most important responsibilities of the headmaster. The classroom is the heart of teaching. It is the centre of instruction. It is, therefore, natural for it to be a centre of supervisory attention. It is very important that the headmaster upgrades the quality of education through creative, cooperative, and constructive supervision.

And yet supervision of the teaching work is a very ticklish part of the job of the headmaster. It is not a simple matter of rushing into a classroom to make a correction or an adjustment or to apply a skill as an automechanic adjusts a faulty motor. Instead, it calls for deliberate and long-range planning. A motor is a thing within itself, but a classroom has many human ramifications, and its operation is tied into a multitude of connecting parts on the outside. Its supervision includes classroom visitation but also capitalises upon patient work with teachers in out-of-school study groups, extending over a period of time. Class visits, therefore, form an essential part of the duties of the headmaster. But that alone gives him no right either to snub or criticise a teacher in the presence of the class. If a headmaster feels that a teacher needs correction whether in the details of the subject-matter or in the technique of teaching adopted by him in the class he should send for the teacher for a post-visit conference. Then details may be freely discussed preferably over a cup of tea and advice given in as pleasant and friendly a manner as possible. The headmaster should prove himself an excellent guide in every possible way in the masterly suggestions about improved methods of teaching and the tactful way that he drives the suggestions home. The teacher should come out of the headmaster's office after a post visit conference as a better person, wiser and saner, and in a more pleasant mood than when he went to him.

There is need for flexibility, for willingness to recognise that there are many roads to Rome and that varied procedures can have a common goal. A headmaster must have the itching inclination to run everything smoothly and must avoid doing anything which hurts or is likely to hurt anybody's feeling, except where there is no other way out. The supervision should be comprehensive and creative.

(1) Curriculum Development and Improvement: The learning which takes place in the schools must be constantly adapted and improved so as to take account of the aspirations and changing needs of a nation. This requires constant revision of the curriculum of a school. Experimentation must be an accepted practice. In this respect, the headmaster can exercise his influence in a number of ways:

(a) He can understand and commend the good work that is already being done.

(b) He can encourage the attitude of inquiry. The headmaster can encourage the development of this attitude by being receptive to new ideas, by inviting from the members of his staff suggestions for improvements by consulting pupils and parents by conducting investigations of pupils progress, by promoting follow-up studies of drop-out and by posing questions of many kinds and setting the wheels in motion to find the answers.

(c) He can help his staff to understand better what the school should accomplish.

(d) He can provide security and recognition for those who attempt change. He can make it plain to those who undertake new assignments that all he expects is a "good try" that if a new programme does not work out successfully, there will be no recrimination, and that those who have made the attempt, will be commended for it.

(e) He can organise and administer the work so that it will be effective.

(f) He can provide time and facilities for curriculum work. He can keep work moving towards success.

(g) He can help to coordinate the work that affects other schools as well as his own.

(h) He can participate in curriculum programmes conducted by other agencies.

(2) Allied to Supervision of Instruction and Curriculum Development and Improvement is the Supervision of Evaluation: The introduction of internal assessment poses another challenge to the headmaster. This is a task which should be performed with great care. He should:

(a) Appoint a committee of teachers together and tabulate the marks in a proper manner.

(b) Periodically check the position of students and pull up those who are not faring well and encourage those who can obtain distinctions.

(c) Pick up the talented and weak and ensure adequate attention to them.

(d) Send the awards to the Board after thoroughly checking in time.

(II) Supervision of Co-curricular Programmes: As a comprehensive co-curricular programme is a very important part of today's educational programme, the headmaster has to see that all the activities are efficiently planned, carefully carried on and result into student development. The patronage of the headmaster and his keen supervision of the various societies and clubs is important for improving the standard of activities. One of the main things to be checked in this connection is to see that the teacher entrusted with the job not only knows it thoroughly but, his interest in it is genuine. He should also pay attention to the smartness and alertness of the group. He himself might give occasional demonstrations of minor games by taking active part in them. He should:

(a) *Distribute the activities according to the interests and aptitude of the teachers.* If possible, training facilities for some specific activities like Athletics, Scouting, N.C.C., First Aid, Home Defence, may be provided or the teachers deputed for such special training.

(b) *Encourage voluntary participation of students and give guidance to them for proper selection.*

(c) Keep a proper record of the participation of students and ensure sound evaluation.

(d) *Make adequate budget allotment for activities.* A sense for proper use of money should be developed in the students and all wastages and unnecessary expenditures should be checked.

(e) Recognise creditable participation.

(III) **Supervision of Hostel:** The headmaster is also responsible for the careful supervision of the hostel, if there is one. He should see that the atmosphere of the home rather than that of the hostel prevail therein. Every now and then the headmaster should taste the food supplied to the boarders and examine the cooking arrangements, the kitchens, the dining rooms, the arrangements for washing dishes, and so on. He should go into the question of diet with the superintendent and see that it is the best that can be supplied for the money that is being paid. Occasional visits must also be paid to the hostel to see its management.

(IV) **Supervision of Registration Work and Accounts:** It is also the function of the headmaster to supervise the various registers and accounts. In this way, he will know his teachers and will know whose work needs special attention and supervision. The headmaster office is said to be "the heart around which and through which the life of the school operates." It is generally recognised that the competence of the headmaster is measured by the manner in which the office is run. The headmaster, therefore, should see that the office procedure are systematised and duties are properly assigned to the teachers, so that office work may not take too much of his time and energy. All registers should be carefully checked occasionally. He should also see to the accounts because it is he who ultimately is responsible to the managing committee or to the department for these sums.

(V) **General Supervision:** The headmaster is responsible for the all-round progress, development, and upkeep of the school. High standard of school administration can be the result of constant vigilance on the part of the headmaster. Everybody in his place, everything done in a systematic manner - will only be possible if the headmaster keeps his eyes wide open and is well-informed. There are so many problems which can be solved right from the time they raise their heads, if the headmaster knows the situation and tackles them well in time. "Prevention is better than cure."

2) *Teaching:*

Despite the frustrations of administration and demands on his time, improvement of instruction is one of the most important responsibilities of the headmaster.

He has to be an effective instructional leader who perceives the right moment to initiate action, to lend encouragement, to inject new zest, to give due recognition, to evaluate and to culminate the activities. The headmastership and leadership are synonymous in education. He is the key person, charged with the responsibilities of improving instruction.

No one expects him to be an expert in all instructional areas but he must be an expert at least in one or two subjects. He should take two or three periods per day and teach one or two subjects in which he has specialised. He should be a first rate teacher and should be well conversant with the latest methods as well as content of a number of subjects. This will give him a number of advantages - he will come into contact with his pupils and establish relationship with them. He will also be able to understand the difficulties of teachers as well as pupils.

The headmaster should take both the lower and the upper classes. One period a day in the lower classes ensures a strong foundation and creates love in the youngest pupils for the school and the headmaster.

It is also expected of the headmaster to be an expert in coordinating, organising, stimulating, activating, encouraging, planning, and evaluating techniques, directed towards improvement of instruction in all areas and on all levels.

3) *Management:*

The headmaster has got to discharge various management duties, viz.

(A) School Plant Management
(B) Equipment and Supply Management
(C) School Business Management
(D) School Office Management

(A) *School Plant Management:* The headmaster has important responsibilities in planning plant facilities, in managing the utilisation of these facilities, in equipping the facilities and in administering the maintenance and operation of these facilities.

Using the plant for educational purposes requires careful direction or much of its effectiveness can be lost. Effective utilisation is all the more a great problem when the headmaster has to work in outmoded or poorly planned buildings.

Utilisation includes several factors:

(a) There is the *quantitative problem* of assuring that each room of the building is used somewhere near its capacity. It is his function to ensure that some spaces are not overcrowded while others remain idle.

(b) Coupled with this quantitative problem is the question of the *educational effectiveness* of the use of school plant facilities. Here again, the headmaster must ensure that space is well used and that space assignments reflect careful consideration of the best educational use of each available space.

(c) The headmaster is responsible for seeing that the space assigned to him for the school programme is utilised quantitatively to a degree that is defensible. Teachers sometimes develop an ownership complex towards their assigned spaces. The headmaster should ensure that such a complex does not lead to a waste of space. On the other hand, the headmaster himself should not develop a utilisation complex in which he loses sight of unassigned space. Although *100 percent utilisation is not a desirable goal, 100 percent educational efficiency* in the use of available space is both desirable and defensible.

(d) The headmaster should *periodically review the use of special rooms,* e.g. fine arts room, music room, laboratories, etc. to ensure that they are being used in terms of their planned purposes as they are specially arranged and equipped to meet the needs of specific subject areas.

(e) In addition to the effective use of special rooms the headmaster must be concerned with the *effective utilization of academic classrooms*. The headmaster should see that they are used properly.

In fact, all school facilities should be designed to serve educational or other school purposes and the headmaster needs to evaluate regularly the degree to which such facilities are effectively used to meet the purposes.

Equipping the school plant also requires care and caution on the part of the headmaster. Here are some ways in which the headmaster can take care of the school plant:

(a) The headmaster and his staff need to consider educational specification for equipment in order to determine the educational purposes it is to serve and to determine the amount of equipment of any given kind necessary to serve the enrolment expected.

(b) It is a rare school indeed that has all the equipment it needs. The headmaster and his staff need, then, to develop procedures for anticipating equipment requirement and for assigning priorities to various needs. If, as often happens, the headmaster has Rs. 2,000/- for all the equipment for a given year and his need is for Rs. 5,000/- worth of equipment, what should he do? The success of what he does depends to a large extent upon the degree to which he has established a long-range plan for purchasing new equipment and replacing old equipment. The faculty needs to be involved in this planning, and a teacher should know when his turn can be expected.

(c) If it is a rare school that has all the equipment it needs, it is an almost equally rare school that does not have unused, antiquated equipment hidden in various corners and closets. This equipment is usually using needed space and often has a cash value that can be used in purchasing new equipment. The headmaster needs to assure himself that equipment is being used. If it is not, he should either determine ways that it can be used or recommend that it can be disposed of in the most profitable manner.

The headmaster is responsible for the proper *maintenance and operation of the school plant*. *Maintenance* refers to those cyclic but intermittent services intended to keep the plant near its original state of preservation, in other words, repairs and replacement; while *operation* refers to the normal routine daily services required to keep the school open and usable for its intended purposes. In the former category, are included such thing as painting, roof repairs, repairs to furniture and the like. In the latter category are such activities as keeping the building warm or cool, daily sweeping, and dusting, care of the grounds and the like. The headmaster has to see that the school is ready for use each day and that sufficient care is taken of the plant so that it does not deteriorate as a useful school faculty. The headmaster should see to it that a major part of the responsibility for the maintenance and operation of a school is borne by those who use the school.

The headmaster should attend to the following to keep the plant tidy:

(a) Ample containers for waste-paper and other miscellaneous trash should be provided.

(b) As an attractive building is generally treated with more respect than a shabby building, every positive step should be taken to brighten up the school. Halls should be attractively painted and decorated. Rooms should be kept neat and clean and should be well-decorated with pictures, charts, etc. The general outlook should be pleasant enough to elicit respect.

(c) The headmaster staff personnel and pupil personnel procedures should lead a healthy school spirit to a high morale to help solve the maintenance and operational problems.

(d) The headmaster should prepare regular schedule for painting, inspection of equipments, and other preventive maintenance measures. Teachers, whose work involves the use of equipment, should be encouraged to follow regular preventive maintenance schedules. The headmaster needs to know when equipment will be available for inspection and upkeep. The vacation period during the school year should be used for maintenance purposes. A school plant should be useful for fifty years or more but such a period of usefulness cannot be realised without wise maintenance procedures.

(e) The headmaster should solicit regularly the opinions of his staff regarding ways in which plant and equipment are helping or hindering the programme of the school. These opinions should be organised so that interpretation is possible. Then these organised opinions can become the basis for future expenditure and space and equipment assignments.

(f) In administrating the school plant, it will be desirable if the headmaster makes use of certain records and reports. For instance,

(i) Scale drawing of each floor of the school plant, indicating room numbers and type.

(ii) Inventory of equipment, including current assignment and room number.

Senior Model School
Classroom Inventory Card

Class: VII **Room No. 19**
Date: 1.4.2009

Items	Quantity	Remarks
Desk.....Teacher	1	
Desk.....Students	40	
Chair.....Teacher	1	
Chair.....Students	40	
Blackboard	1	
Stand.....Blackboard	1	

Fig. 14.1 Classroom Inventory Card

Senior Model School
Inventory Card

Items: - Chairs-Students
Accounting Unit: - Each

Date	Received From	Quantity	Unit rate	Issued to	Present Location Remarks
31.7.09	Garg & Co. Chandigarh	50	Rs. 24.50	— –-	Store Room
05.8.09	— — —	—	— —	Class V	Room No. 16
17.8.09	Bhatia & Co. Ludhiana	70 22.50	Rs. — —-	— 40 Store Room	
22.8.09	— — —	–-	— —	Class VI 25	Room No. 18
24.8.09	— — —	–-	— —-	Class VIII 35	Room No. 22
24.8.09	— — —	–-	— —-	Class IX 20	Room No. 23

Fig. 14.2 Inventory Card

(iii) Enrolment date for a room and subject for each period of the day.

(iv) Maintenance schedule.

(v) School policy relating to community use of school facilities and other school plant matters.

(vi) Calendar of use of school facilities by both school and non-school groups outside of regular school hours, or for example, in the case of an auditorium and examination hall, during school hours.

(vii) File of instruction manuals relating to various pieces of equipment in the building. This file should include guarantees, etc.

(viii) List of equipment servicing agencies approved by the department to make necessary inspections or repairs of the equipment in the building.

(B) ***Equipment and Supply Management:*** A headmaster has vital responsibilities for procuring, protecting, and using the school supplies. This involves careful planning. Estimates have to be prepared regarding the quantity and quality, to be purchased and how to be purchased. Specifications for each item have to be laid down, quotations have to be invited, goods have to be ordered, inspected and checked on arrival, properly stored to obviate any chance of damage or loss through insects, rain, etc. and finally these have to be issued as and when required.

To manage the supplies efficiently the headmaster should make the following arrangements:

(a) ***Appoint a Selection Committee for Purchase and Maintenance of Equipment*** – This Committee will prepare the list of items of purchase, which are needed and prepare the budget. The Committee should invite quotations from the leading firms. The lowest quotation is to be approved by the headmaster. Economy should be ensured without sacrificing quality.

(b) ***Start School Cooperative Department***: This department may procure, store, supply, and sell petty items of daily use like stationery, etc.

(c) ***Ensure Protection to the School Equipment and prevent Damage***: This can be achieved with the cooperation of the students, staff, and the menials. He should bring home to the students the necessity of keeping the equipment spick and span.

(d) ***Ensure Proper Record of the Equipment***: He should see that a proper record of the equipment is maintained, every year a physical verification of the items of equipment is made, unserviceable and consumed items are written off, damaged articles are auctioned, and lists of new requirements prepared. He should keep an accurate and up-to-date inventory which should indicate both the quantity of equipment within a building and its location. Another inventory card for rooms may be used for determining the exact equipment within a single room. Room inventories should be taken yearly and the room figures checked with the item cards.

(e) ***Know the Latest Trends in Equipments***: He may go in for modern scientific equipment such as epidiascope, tape recorder, loud speaker, fluorescent lights, if the funds permit.

(f) ***Ensure Effective use of the Supplies***: Regardless of the nature of the supply, ineffective use of it is hardly excusable. Equipment and materials that are allowed to remain in storage have little value.

(C) ***Business Management:*** Business management encompasses those jobs that relate to the efficient and effective handling of money and materials within the school. This task area is an important part of the headmaster's job and one that needs to be performed with care.

(i) *Internal accounting*: Whether the school is managed by Government or by private management bodies, it does involve a great deal of money. Students clubs, class groups, athletics, dramatics, and musical programmes, each of these and many more spend and receive money. The responsibility for these internal funds or non-appropriated money almost always rests squarely with the headmaster. This means the headmaster needs to be responsible for the development of a system that provides for the following:

(a) Preparing budgets.

(b) Recording receipts.

(c) Crediting receipts to the proper funds.

(d) Banking receipts.

(e) Authorising expenditures.

(f) Receiving invoices or statements.

(g) Making payments for expenditures.

(h) Billing expenditures to the proper fund.

(i) Issuing regular financial reports.

(j) Providing for periodic outside audits.

(ii) *Budgeting and Finance*: The headmaster should have the understanding of the roles of the various levels of government in financing education, of the source of income which are both fiscally adequate and socially equitable of the various types of grants-in-aid and of the interrelation of education and economic growth. For good administration, it is necessary that the best possible use is made of available funds. For this there should be long-term planning educationally and financially, with close coordination between the two.

(D) School Office Management: The headmaster has great responsibilities as far as the management of the school office is concerned. The office is the contact point between the school and the public. The impression that people receive from the office is often the impression they have of the entire school. Thus, it is very important that the office is well-managed.

The headmaster, however, must avoid making himself an office manager. He is an educational leader. Office management is only one part – and a small part of his job. He should not become enmeshed in official details, as although this may result in an efficient office, it can lead to a most inefficient use of the headmaster's time. All of the different office tasks must be provided for, but the headmaster is not meeting his challenge, if he provides for these tasks himself.

The headmaster should attend to the following for the proper management of the school office:

(a) Be aware of the office work necessary for the efficient operation of the school.

(b) Staff the school office with sufficient personnel to make it possible for the necessary office work to be done.

(c) Delegate the management of the office to responsible clerical assistant.

(d) Periodically evaluate the effectiveness of the school office, check irregularities, remove inefficiency, and ensure regular and prompt work.

(e) Know his varied type of duties:

- **i)** Legal duties, i.e. the duties for which he is legally responsible;
- **ii)** Duties prescribed by the Education Department or the Managing Committee or both;
- **iii)** Compliance of the rules and regulations prescribed by the University or the Board to which the school is affiliated;
- **iv)** Routine duties such as admission, classification, checking class register, cash book, acquittance roll, attendance registers, register of accounts of various fees and funds, etc.

Much of the school office work can be made routine. Whenever possible, forms should be developed to facilitate the work of the school. Not only do forms make work go faster, they also eliminate errors that occur from the random recording of information.

4) Special Services:

In a modern secondary school so many special services have been introduced for the proper development of the pupils – school health services, school guidance services, free supply of mid-day meals, school uniforms, textbooks, etc. It is obligatory on the headmaster that these ancillary services are administered well so that maximum numbers of pupils are benefitted.

(B) General Duties

1) ***Headmaster's duties before the commencement of the academic year: -*** The headmaster has to do so many things before the commencement of the academic year. The following items demand a careful attention on his part:
   - (i) Preparation of the school calendar showing details of different courses, co-curricular activities, rates of tuition fees, school timings, duration of the class-period or recesses, a list of holidays, the practice for the collection of tuition fees;
   - (ii) Completion of teaching, clerical and menial staff;
   - (iii) Distribution of work – teaching and administrative;
   - (iv) The school time-table;
   - (v) Purchase of necessary equipment, books, and supplies;
   - (vi) Completion of the admission of as many new pupils as possible; and
   - (vii) Formation of new classes showing the names of pupils of each class.

For the convenience of teachers, a school administration bulletin may be prepared. It should show the distribution of work of different teachers, the co-curricular duties, different committees of the schools, clubs, and associations, dates of staff meetings, the procedure of taking casual leave, etc. Every teacher should be supplied with a copy of the bulletin. It proves very helpful to a new teacher, acts as a reminder to the old teachers, and is an aid to the headmaster to plan for the coming year.

The opening day of the school must be planned with great care. The classrooms, the library, the lavatories, the laboratories – all should be spick and span to receive the new comers. Two or three days before the school is to reopen, a staff meeting for facing the new problems with confidence, is a must. Let every one be familiar with the work he or she is supposed to do.

On the first day, the headmaster meets the students, clarifies the day's arrangements of work to the pupils.

During the first week, so many problems need immediate solution, e.g. arrangement of optional subjects, balancing class sizes, adjustments of classrooms and equipments, etc.

2) ***Duties throughout the year***: One or two week's preliminary work should settle the major issues. After that the headmaster has to do so many things – planning the supervisory programme, organising the guidance service, arranging medical examination of children, checking the evaluation programmes, sending internal assessment marks, informing parents regarding the deficiencies of their children.

   The headmaster has to administer the entire programme of the school through his personnel supervision and direction. He is the person who reaches the school before the regular work begins, inspects the sanitary arrangements of the campus, attends the school assembly, does office work, supervises curricular and co-curricular activities, meets visitors and parents and is the last to leave the school.

3) ***Closing the school year***: Before the close of the year, the headmaster should be ready with:

(i) Arrangements of the final examination programme setting and printing of question papers, evaluation of answer-books, preparation of result sheets, and declaration of results;

(ii) Completion of pupil's cumulative records, and the date on which they are to be submitted to parents for information;

(iii) Announcement of the next year's textbooks to pupils;

(iv) The issue of school leaving certificates to pupils, desiring to leave the school before close of the year;

(v) The annual report of the school.

14.5 Headmaster's Relationships

(I) ***Headmasters and Teachers***: It is true that upon the headmaster of the school rests the chief responsibility of organisation and administration, and that the tone and efficiency of a school depend largely on his personality and professional competence. But living as we do in a climate of radically democratic opinion, it is important for the administration to realise and to act upon the realisation that headmasters are 'head teachers', *Primus inter pares*, that many teachers are as well-qualified, as experienced and as capable as their headmaster are and hence, they must be given a positive say in matters of school policy. The headmaster should remember the wise statement of **Ronald Gould**: "No quality education is possible without good personal relationships. When teachers are treated as allies and colleagues are consulted, and given responsibility, they respond with better teaching results." If, on the other hand, teachers are given no effective power, the truth of Adlai Stevenson's axiom becomes apparent, "Power corrupts, but lack of power corrupts absolutely!"

The headmaster must *establish democratic relationships*. The attitude – here is not to reason why, here it is but to carry out orders, good, bad or indifferent – will create deep frustration among teachers. The relationship must be democratic. Teachers need to be given a much bigger share in the actual day-to-day administration of the school and the headmaster should strive to establish true rapport within the staff through informal and formal, individual and group consultations and conferences. There should be frequent staff meetings of the whole staff or sections of the staff, at which there is full and frank discussion and two-way traffic of ideas on all matters pertaining to the welfare of the school. Headmaster and teachers can educate each other about new developments in educational theory and practice – these are essential means of promoting healthy and creative teamwork.

The headmaster should remember the commandments laid down by **Sir Ronald Gould** in an address to World Confederation of Organisations of the Teaching Profession:

"Thou shalt educate thy teachers well,

Thou shalt encourage thy teachers to teach

Thou shalt trust thy teachers

Thou shalt treat thy teachers not as bandsmen but as partners."

To get the best cooperation the staff should be his major concern. He must be skilful in assisting staff members to improve their competence in making their individual contribution as well as to gain competence in working together with others on specific assignments.

(II) ***Headmaster and Pupils***: Contact with pupils of the school is one of the important secrets of the success of a headmaster. The headmaster, who sees the pupils only through the eyes of his assistants, lacks in the essential quality of responsibility. He must be helpful to the pupils. He must try

to know as large a number of children in his school as possible. He can achieve this end by taking some periods in the lowest class. This will also make the problem of discipline easier because the pupil will come to know their headmaster earlier than usual. Students must be associated with the school administration through Students' Council, Students' Panchayat, and Students' Parliament. They must be entrusted with the organising and running of co-curricular activities. Wherever possible, they should be entrusted with positions of responsibility. There are problem cases in every school. They should be reclaimed tactfully.

The headmaster should have easy access but certainly not one to be trifled with. He should be able to maintain the prestige dignity of his office without, however, giving the impression that he is harsh, indifferent, or callous to his students. He should see that he is respected but not feared.

(III) Headmaster's Relation with Public: The school, if it is to serve the community, must enlist the cooperation of the parents of the pupils. No headmaster can be really successful, if he does not look beyond the four walls of his school and is contended with organising and directing its internal activities only. He should take every opportunity which presents itself of getting into touch and keeping in touch with the parents of pupils. This will add to the effectiveness of the work of the school, make its scope more comprehensive, and enable the parents and teachers to pull in the same direction. The Headmaster's relation with the public must be cordial but he must not take sides so far as political parties are concerned.

At the same time, the headmaster should be adept in handling the delicate inter-personal relationships. He will be well-advised to remember the advice Polonius gave to his son Laertes, 'to lend his ear to everyone but none his tongue'. Patient listening will tell the headmaster what the speaker is trying to communicate. A mother coming and complaining of the education in the school or against a teacher might just be ventilating on the low achievement of her son, not willing to admit to herself that her child is mentally backward and no amount of expensive dose of teaching can enable her son to become a genius. A father storming the office of the headmaster and enumerating his acquaintances may just be trying to say, "Look I am a very important person and, therefore, my son ought not to be judged by the standard fixed for other boys." The headmaster should be patient when parents put up such a front, because they are his customers and a customer can never be wrong. Secondly, the parent can get away with whatever he may say or do. The headmaster is to play a delicate role of balancing the demands of the parents, the opinion of the public, perception of the teacher and the biological needs and aspirations of the students.

(IV) Relations with the State Department of Education: As far as the State Department of Education is concerned, the headmaster of a high school should know fully well the rules and regulations fixed by the Department from time to time for the administration of secondary education particularly regarding admissions, withdrawals, attendance, school timing, promotion rules, time-tables, size of classes, medical examination, physical education, leave rules, etc.; courses of study and textbooks prescribed for different classes; regulations regarding schools and hostel buildings, equipment and furniture; rules regarding recognition of schools and finance, rules regarding grants-in-aid, accounts, tuition fees, scholarships; and procedure for the maintenance of records.

The headmaster of a private high school should further know every detail about recognition of schools and about the advantages it can get through recognition.

It is very necessary that the headmaster should know what he has to do, what he may do and what he must not do.

(V) ***Relations with the University or School Education Board***: In certain states, it is the University which conducts the school leaving certificate examination; in others School Education Board does so. Certain rules and regulations concerning the examination are fixed, curriculum is drawn, and textbooks are prescribed. The headmaster should know all these details.

(VI) ***The Headmaster and the Managing Committee***: Private institutions are run by the Managing Committee. For achieving the best results in education, it is necessary that the headmaster of the school is the Secretary of the Managing Committee. The Committee may correspond directly with the department in all matters pertaining to external management of the school, but in all matters of internal administration, it is the headmaster who should correspond directly with the department.

14.6 Problems of Staff Cooperation

Efficient running of a school is a cooperative endeavour in which the staff, students, and the community all make their contributions. Without active co-operation and teamwork no school can be efficiently or successfully run. The headmaster must have dispassionate approach and must not allow his personal prejudices, likes, and dislikes to cloud his judgement. He can enlist the active cooperation of both teachers and students, if he succeeds in democratising administration and involving them in taking decisions. Even so-called problem teachers should be associated with the running of administration. Probable causes of friction with the staff are:

(a) *Inefficiency of some teachers*: - Inefficient teachers get on war path when they are admonished for slipshod work or general tardiness.

(b) *Private tuitions:* - There are general bickering over tuitions. If the headmaster is just not impartial to all and takes sides, he is likely to find himself in trouble.

(c) *Political wire pulling:* - Some teachers do depend on political strings and this leads to a very awkward situation.

(d) *Authoritarian attitude of the headmaster*: - Staff is generally alienated if the headmaster acts like a dictator, and tries to run the administration through ordinances.

(e) *Dishonesty or partiality of the headmaster*: - If the headmaster is not honest or impartial, it is difficult to secure the staff co-operation.

(f) *Tactless or un-psychological approach*: - If the headmaster is not tactful or psychological in approach, he bungles and alienates the staff.

Suggested hints for securing cooperation:

(a) If the headmaster sincerely believes in democracy, he can associate the staff with the administration and thus, steer clear of all chances of conflict.

(b) He must repose full confidence in them and by his adroit handling make them feel that they are running the school.

(c) If the headmaster has real qualities of an educational leader, he will experience no difficulty. He will be sympathetic so far as the limitation of the colleagues are concerned, will be objective in his outlook, and will involve them in taking decisions.

(d) Each teacher should be made to feel: "I have been consulted. This is my job now and I must do it and do it well."

(e) Problem-teachers must be reclaimed.

14.7 Faculty Meetings

For democratic administration of school it is necessary that members of staff occasionally meet for sharing responsibilities as well as experiences. Such a meeting is called Faculty Meeting. Faculty meetings should be occasionally held and there should be at least one meeting every fortnight. Now when the programmes of education have to be built around projects, workshops, discussion groups, laboratory techniques, etc. such meetings should be a regular feature of the school programme. The faculty meeting can provide opportunities for cooperative thinking, staff planning for presentation of worthwhile demonstrations of talks by consultants for interchange of ideas and "know-how" and the feeling of *camaraderie* that exists in any group dedicated to an important task.

(1) ***Planning the faculty meeting*: -** Faculty meetings called, conducted, and convened by the headmaster are as outmoded as the birch rod. Although it smacks of redundancy, faculty meetings are for the faculty. In order to be successful, they must be based on problems which teachers can easily recognise as their own.

The faculty meetings, to be really effective, need to be carefully planned. The following suggestions may prove useful:

(a) The physical climate of a meeting is important as well as the emotional climate:- It should suggest unity. Comfortable chairs, arranged in circular fashion, provide face-to-face contact and eliminate possible "blind spots." The most important determinant on the meeting's emotional climate is the headmaster. He should create an informality tempered with seriousness of purpose. He may or may not act as the chairman.

(b) The meetings to be effective should be informal, where the members of the staff feel free to express themselves.

(c) The headmaster should see to as wide a participation of the different members as possible. He should see that the more vocal or more aggressive members do not monopolise the discussion. The faculty meeting should not break with the impression that it was a show of two or three persons.

(d) In order to introduce the right type of atmosphere, the headmaster would do well not to start with serious business straightaway, but have a friendly chat for two or three minutes to put the members of the staff at their ease.

(e) The headmaster should honestly respect the opinions of the staff and their decisions. Otherwise, if the members of the faculty feel that these meetings are just a formality or a machinery to impose the views of the headmaster on them, they will not only prove futile but also engender attitudes which may vitiate the atmosphere of the institutions. The headmaster should not ordinarily override the decisions of the staff.

(f) The headmaster should not dominate these meetings but let the staff do most of the talking. His skill as a leader would lie in proper summing up of the discussion and then guiding them to a correct decision through careful analysis of the implications of the decisions.

(g) Whatever is decided by common consent must be implemented with all sincerity and earnestness.

(h) Agenda of the meeting should be well-circulated. Minutes of the meetings should be carefully recorded by a member of the staff.

(i) Time of the meeting should be such that most of the staff may be in a position to attend it conveniently. Headmaster must recognise that after-school meetings are handicapped by fatigue, anxiety of married teachers who have home responsibilities. Moreover, the after-school staff meeting does not permit coaches and supervisors of activities to attend.

(2) *Characteristics of good faculty meetings*:

(a) The subject discussed should be of interest to all present.

(b) The faculty should be advised of the specific phase of the subject to be discussed in order to avoid hasty judgements and irrelevant discussions.

(c) All discussions should be above the personal level.

(d) Faculty meetings should be economical in the matter of time. They should start in time with something important; discussion should not go off the track. Talking by individuals in between should be discouraged. The meeting should finish in time.

(e) All matters for discussion should be listed and given time allotment.

(f) There should be a definite policy adapted to the degree to which the discussion should be kept secret.

(g) Faculty meetings should be a part of the professional growth of the institution.

(3) *A few "musts" for the faculty meetings*: Whatever may be the custom or administrative set-up of faculty meetings, there are 'musts' for their success. They are:

(a) They must be teacher-centred, not headmaster centred.

(b) They must deal with problems or topics that are pupil-centred.

(c) They must be continually appraised as to their worth.

(d) They must become a functional activity of prime importance.

14.8 Staff Club

For smooth administration of the school, it is not enough that the administrative policy is formulated jointly by the headmaster and the staff. It is also desirable that members of staff come in close contact with each other in an informal atmosphere. Staff Club can be organised to meet the social and emotional needs of the teachers. Staff Clubs provide every teacher an opportunity to understand others in a natural setting. This can prove helpful in removing personal misunderstandings which are generally the cause of quarrels and are responsible for loss of mental equilibrium.

Staff Club is organised on voluntary basis but such traditions need to be evolved that every member participates in the activities organised by it. In faculty meetings, head of the institution controls deliberations. Staff Club is organised by the staff and its secretary should be elected every year so that everyone gets a chance of leading others. Contributions – monthly or annuals – may be decided by the staff.

Staff Club can arrange the following types of activities: -

(a) Some refreshment may be arranged during recess and some informal discussion can take place over a cup of tea.

(b) Welcome and farewell functions for newly appointed and outgoing teachers may be arranged. Through the club, new members can be introduced to the rest of the staff.

(c) Picnics and excursions may be arranged during holidays.

The headmaster should take an active part in the activities of Staff Club. Through this valuable medium, he can gather valuable information about temperamental, educational, social, cultural, and political background of teachers under him and thus utilise the services of the most suitable teachers for the welfare of the school, when necessary.

Thus, faculty meetings and Staff Clubs can go a long way in establishing democratic atmosphere in the school.

14.9 Some hints for the Headmaster to build Morale in his team and secure Cooperation

Below are given, some hints for building morale in the team:

1. ***Establish fair policies and administrative regulations-*** The headmaster should establish fair policies and administrative regulations and be sure staff members understand why they are fair. Apply policies and regulations fairly. Be as fair as possible to individuals and staff, as a whole, with respect to assignments and promotions, and make deliberate efforts to create an awareness of that intention. Work to develop a reputation for fairness. It will create effectiveness of his work and that of staff members.
2. ***Encourage staff members to discuss troubles and discontents-*** Listen sympathetically. Almost everyone has, or thinks he has, troubles which to him are real. Let staff members know you are concerned about them and desire to be helpful.
3. ***Help staff members guard against a sense of failure-*** Encourage partially successful efforts with appreciation and aid. When a person or group fails in spite of sincere effort, smile, and say, "We hit a foul ball. Let's try again."
4. ***Protect teachers against unfair criticism-*** Let them know you support then sincere effort to work well.
5. ***Help your staff build a sense of purposeful group solidarity-*** By means of committees, staff meetings, announcements and conversations, help the staff set and value group goals. Demonstrate your appreciations of group effort and arrange public recognition such as acknowledgements in annual reports.
6. ***Be friendly-*** Most staff members are more loyal to a friendly leader than to an austere one. Even in large systems where personal contacts are few and brief, feelings of friendliness can be conveyed. Commendations at staff meetings, smiles, and informal language in appropriate situations help. Most of the members generally respond with an enlarged sense of appreciation and responsibility.
7. ***Recognise moral implications of reassignments and dismissals-*** Obviously an administrator cannot condone incompetence or genuinely irresponsible action that lowers the quality of schooling and undermines morale. To maintain quality school service, it is occasionally necessary to reassign some staff members to duties which correspond with their abilities and temperament. At times, incompetent persons must be suspended or dismissed according to law and department policy. But the possible effect of such actions on capable and sincere staff members should be carefully appraised.

   It is extremely important that staff members know that reassignment and dismissal policies are fair and fairly administered. A staff council should help set policy and all the members of the staff should be informed about what the policy is. In some cases, specific assignments and dismissals should be discussed with members of the staff council, who in turn can convey the fairness of the actions to other staff members.
8. ***Define realistic standards of competency-*** All rational decisions to praise or criticise, to reassign, or dismiss personnel should be based on some concept of reasonable competence. Both ideals and practicalities are involved. Good-quality schooling depends on capable personnel; beyond a point, incompetence cannot be accepted. But the average capabilities of even well-trained groups are limited. No staff member is completely competent; few are totally incompetent, the administrator should develop and integrate the capacities staff members possess. If he

does so, he can stimulate amazing improvements and increase staff confidence in his leadership.

Thus, an administrator must formulate a standard of competence and group relationship which can be achieved by a large majority of staff members and commit himself to efforts which help members reach and surpass that standard. Involve staff members in policy formulation and administrative decision. Individuals like to be consulted and they have better understanding of policies and decisions that they have helped think through. Research shows that much staff participation in formulating policies and action plans is practical and pays large moral dividends. A well-organised system of staff committees and thorough staff discussion of committee proposals are common and effective means of facilitating participation.

Committees should not be so numerous that their functions overlap or that they require inordinate amounts of staff time.

Participation can also be encouraged by other less formal means in casual conversation at parties, etc.

Naturally, in large school systems not all administrative acts can be discussed with all staff members and to keep a system running, an administration must make the decisions necessary to execute policy. The staff should have the confidence that the administrator can make decisions. For example, in case of an untoward happening he must issue "No school today" notices; he must make decisions which settle prolonged disputes. He should inform staff members of the action he takes and the reasons for it. This will indicate his respect for them, increase their willingness to support his decisions, and help to maintain their confidence in him.

14.10 Qualities needed in an Ideal Headmaster

To perform the difficult and manifold duties, the headmaster should possess so many qualities. We discuss below some of them.

1) ***Sound Educational Philosophy***: - The headmaster should have a clear understanding of the philosophy of life and the values on which society is based. He should have a clear conception of the functions and objectives of school education as also the correct methods and practices through which the objectives can be effectively realised. This philosophy must be constantly examined and received in the light of new problems and new insights.

2) ***High Scholarship***: - The headmaster primarily is an educational expert. Only then can he win and hold the real respect of his staff as well as the community. "It must not only be known by his staff and scholars that he is their headmaster by appointment but felt that he is their headmaster by superior ability, energy, and character." The headmaster should be able to take intelligent interest in the work of all teachers and be able to give valuable suggestions.

3) ***Adequate Professional Training***: - Educational administration, as discussed in earlier pages, is a specialised job. Without specialised training in the line, proper leadership is not possible. The headmaster should have adequate professional training to make him conversant with the administration technique.

4) ***Proficiency in Human Relations***: -The headmaster must be an expert in human relations. He should be able to enter understandingly and sympathetically into the thoughts, the aspirations, and the motives of teachers, pupils, and parents. He must know how to win the goodwill and respect of others and how to motivate them to put in their best efforts for the success of the school. He must keep the channels of communication open from the top to the bottom and *vice versa.* It is better to anticipate the demands and requirements before they become vocal

through organised effort. The headmaster should have sympathetic attitude. He should not be partial to anyone. His colleagues should get the impression that they are running the whole show.

5) ***Good Physical, Mental, and Emotional Health***: - To discharge the multifarious and heavy responsibilities of his office the headmaster should have sound physical, mental, and emotional health. He should keep himself young, fit, active, healthy, and physically energetic as possible.

6) ***Qualities of Personality***: -The headmaster should have qualities of personality like sound judgement, self-control, and integrity, general purity of character, firmness, initiative, resourcefulness, and common sense. If he is not a high power dynamo, there will be inertia and listless apathy all round. He must be progressive.

14.11 Role of the Headmaster in Evaluation

This is one of the important duties of a headmaster that he should evaluate his total arrangements from time to time. He has implemented, the policies, which have been formulated for running school. To what an extent they are successful. To know this fact evaluation is essential. "To improve the level of teacher and for making it high and principles and processes which have been used those, and co-curricular activities, organisation, and direction, in getting the objectives of education, how far or till what extent have been successful or helpful? Discipline of the school and its general tone, how far have they been helpful in developing social and moral qualities in children. To know all these things also, he requires conducting evaluation necessarily. "For the knowledge of all these things, the headmaster should use various methods, like observation, probing, interview, questionnaire and record, *etc*.

The headmaster should pay attention on the following points for knowing about progress, promotion, their capacities, and difficulties etc., of his students:

1) It should be watched whether *"Question Papers"* of examination are not too easy or too hard.

2) Weekly and monthly tests should be arranged and upkeep of record of these tests should be maintained.

3) *Cumulative Record* of children should be prepared. In these records, a detailed description of test of various aptitudes and qualities should be given, for instance, general knowledge, acquiring knowledge practical capability, social and citizen activities, expression, service motive, co-operation, health progress, traits, of personality, character, firmness, leadership, industriousness, self-confidence, self-control, sociability and presence of mind. These qualities of students should be recorded and maintained in the office of the headmaster. It is very essential for him to know the opinions and ideas of teachers and guardians as well in this matter.

The headmaster has not to do evaluation only of his policies, processes and activities of children (students) notwithstanding it is essential for him to examine his associates and actions of other functionaries of school also. At the time of evaluating the activities of these officials, the headmaster should keep in mind the following points:

(i) He should tell clearly the merits and demerits of his colleagues.

(ii) He should conduct evaluation for bringing about improvement in their working.

(iii) He should develop feelings of self-evaluation and self-development in his workers.

(iv) For making human relations appropriate, he should have sympathetic and helpful attitude towards his subordinates. He should not conduct the evaluation with the viewpoint of destruction.

Establishment of Human Relations

The most essential condition of success of headmaster is this that he should establish appropriate human relations with his colleagues, subordinates, students and their guardians and the other members of the society. For this, he should keep the following points in mind:

1. The headmaster should recognise his colleagues personally. Along with this, he should know about the personality of each of them. Only by doing so, he would establish appropriate human relations with them, and he could get willing cooperation of them also.
2. The headmaster should endeavour to seek maximum participation from all the persons. For this, he should involve his colleagues in decision-making and by doing so they would not only come in his, contact only but they would realise their responsibility also in each matter and perform that in a suitable manner.
3. The headmaster should do development of policies and processes of school on the co-operative basis. By this, he could establish proper human relations with his associates and students, etc.
4. The headmaster should develop faith, affection, and feeling of respect in his associates and subordinates, students and guardians.
5. The headmaster should strive continuously for the development of self and his colleagues.

14.12 Role of Headmaster in Guidance and Motivation

Guidance as a function of a headmaster is of recent origin. He is expected to provide educational and vocational guidance. Here are some of them:

1) The students in the selection of the subjects at the secondary stage, leading to suitable vocations after the school leaving stage.
2) The students in their day-to-day activities and instructional work.
3) The teacher in organising, teaching and other activities, in making a deeper study of their subjects, and in solving specific problems of discipline, backwardness, teaching, etc.
4) The parents in supervising the education of their wards, in planning their education according to their abilities and aptitudes.
5) The higher authorities in matters of curriculum, textbooks, school organising, framing of educational policies and other educational problems.

Out of all these tasks, educational and vocational guidance is of the utmost necessity, although it is neglected so far. The headmaster must reconvene meetings of the staff for purposes of planning, educational guidance, and organising a full-fledged guidance programme. He should start a guidance unit in the school and appoint the necessary staff for guidance.

The guidance unit must provide not only curricular and vocational guidance but also personal guidance to those young children who lack adjustment. For this purpose he may have to seek help from psychologists and other organisations. The headmaster shall have to act as a liaison between the School Guidance Unit and the State Guidance Bureau, employment officers and other organisations.

Every headmaster has to extract work from his colleagues, this he cannot do smoothly and effectively through an autocratic attitude. He has to motivate his subordinates to work conscientiously and enthusiastically. The headmaster has to create motivating situations prompting others to accomplish the task for attainment of the full goal. For this purpose, he is expected to use human skill, besides technical skills. The human skill will mean ability to motivate others to work, judgement to evaluate their work, understanding of the sources of behaviour of others and patience to deal with difficult situations.

Objective Type Questions

Multiple Choice Questions (Tick ✓ the right option)

(1) The efficiency of the school depends on the ability and skill, personality and professional competence of the
(a) Teacher
(b) Headmaster
(c) Pupils
(d) Staff

(2) Private institutions are run by
(a) Managing Committee
(b) Administrators
(c) Both 'a' and 'b'
(d) None of the above

Fill in the blanks

(1) The headmaster must be an expert in __________. [Human Relations]
(2) ____________ function of a headmaster is of recent origin. [Guidance]

Important Questions

1. "A good headmaster is not merely a good administrator." Discuss and explain what additional qualifications the head of a school should possess?
2. What would you regard to be the headmaster's responsibilities of the head of a school? Why?
3. What are the functions of the head of a school? Select any one function and describe how it can be performed effectively?
4. "In a democratic organisation, the head of the institutions should realise the importance of democratic practices." In the light of this statement, outline the relationship between the head of the institution and his colleagues.
5. "In an ideal democratic school, there should be no headmaster." Discuss giving reasons, in support of your answer.
6. You are the head of a Secondary School. How would you organise an effective staff study club? State the objectives of the club, give details of its organisations and suggest a useful programme of activities for an academic year.
7. Give some hints for the Head to build morale in his team.
8. A young headmaster has developed strained relations with his assistants. Enumerate the probable reasons for this situation. Give suggestions for improving this situation.

15

Role of the Teacher

In the human resources of the school, the first place goes to the headmaster. But, it can be possible only when he gets cooperation from all his teachers from time to time according to the needs. A headmaster, howsoever he may be a scholar and an able individual, would not be able to run his school smoothly without the cooperation of his able teachers. If his able teachers do not march forward with him he cannot be successful in his work. Headmaster and teachers are two big powers in human resources which act as a foundation stone for any school. The physical resources can be used properly and in the right manner only when the headmaster and teachers unite together dedicatedly towards their duties. Therefore, it would be appropriate to say that the teacher is the second human power after the headmaster which brings elegance to the future of the child and makes him conscious and a dedicated citizen of the country. This statement is correct and complete in itself that the building of the future of the country is through the medium of the classes of the schools of that country.

It is the teacher who is the real dynamic power of the school and educational technique. It is true that school building, curricular activities, instruction programmes, and textbooks, etc. have all important places in the educational programmes, but till vitality is not infused in them by good teachers, these would remain meaningless. Teacher is that power which leaves its impact on the coming generations directly or indirectly. It is only the teacher who crosses the national and geographical frontiers and marches forward towards world establishment and progress of the human race. Therefore, it can be said that the progress of human society and country depends upon teachers.

15.1 Definitions of the Teacher

It needs no description that the teacher is the pivot of any educational system of the younger students. On him rests the failure or the success of the system. If the teachers are well educated and if they are intellectually alive and take keen interest in their job, then only, success is ensured. But, if on the other hand, they lack training in education and if they cannot give their heart to their profession, the system is destined to fail. Hence, the teacher is another vital component of the school.

The teacher is the yardstick that measures the achievements and aspirations of the nation. The worth and potentialities of a country get evaluated in and through the work of the teacher, "The people of a country are the enlarged replica of their teacher." They are the real nation builders.

The role of the teacher is best explained by the following prominent thinkers of education.

1) **Manu:** "A teacher is the image of Brahma."
2) **S. Radhakrishnan:** "The teachers place in society is of vital importance. He acts as the pivot for transmission of intellectual traditions and technical skills, from generation to generation and helps to keep the lamp of civilization burning."
3) **Swami Vivekananda:** "The true teacher is he who can immediately come down to the level of the student, transfer his soul to the student's soul and see through and understand through his mind. Such a teacher can really teach and none else."

4) **Indian Prayer:** "The teacher is Brahma, the creator, he is God Vishnu, and he is God Maheshwara. He is the entire Universe, salutations to him."

5) **R. N. Tagore:** "A teacher can never truly teach unless he is still learning himself. A lamp can never light another lamp unless it continues to burn its own flame. The teacher who has come to the end of his subject, who has no living traffic with his knowledge, but merely repeats his lessons to his students can only load their minds, he cannot quicken them."

6) **Humayun Kabir**: "The success of educational system depends upon the abilities of the teachers. In the absence of good teachers, even the best educational system would prove to be a failure. Even most of the defects of educational system can be removed through good teachers."

In this way the importance of teacher is clear in both the society and educational system. A teacher builds up those future citizens on which depends the rise and fall of the nation.

15.2 The Role of the Teacher

An ideal teacher has been accepted the builder of man; nation builder, foundation stone of educational system and provider of dynamism to the society, etc. Ordinarily it is considered that such teachers are imbibed with the qualities of having the power of understanding the nature of children, capacity to work with them in an appropriate manner, teaching abilities, will power to work and cooperation, etc. Such qualities are neither generally found in every teacher nor the quality of good teaching is found in every teacher. Good teaching is not everybody's cup of tea. In fact, this work can be done by only those individuals who are endowed with certain specific physical, intellectual, social, moral, and emotional qualities. Teaching is a spiritual process which establishes relationship between one brain and other. The appropriateness or inappropriateness of this relationship largely depends upon the personality of the teacher. Some studies from time to time have been made related to it. A study was conducted in U.S.A. in 1913 by Dr. F. L. Clap on the basis of which he mentioned ten qualities of a good teacher. These qualities are as follows:

(a) Pronunciation or addressing;
(b) Physical appearance;
(c) Optimism;
(d) Patience;
(e) Zeal;
(f) Mental impartiality;
(g) Auspicious;
(h) Sympathy;
(i) Good vitality;
(j) Scholarship.

As a result of the studies conducted by Bagel and Keith, these qualities of teachers have further been added-

(a) Skill;
(b) Capacity of leadership;
(c) Good level.

In order to prepare these lists, these scholars had taken the acceptance of the headmaster, inspectors, and superintendents of the schools. While formulating them they did not make use of the opinions of the students. But Bossing made the opinions of the students as the subject of his studies and on the basis of these, he added two more qualities of the teachers in his lists - humorous disposition and an attitude of friendliness with the students.

On the basis of the above discussion, the following are the main role of teachers in the school:

1) ***Teacher is the most vital single factor in the system of education*:** - It is the teacher who matters most as far as the quality of education is concerned. "A significant change", in the words of Prem Kirpal, "in the educational process is governed by the extent of his receptivity and initiative." The well-equipped teacher is a supreme factor in education. The framers of the

Second Five-Year Plan observed, "At all times, the teacher is the pivot in the system of education. this is especially the case in a period of basic change and reorientation." The Secondary Education Commission 1952-53 also points out, "Every teacher and educationist of experience knows that even the best curriculum and the most perfect syllabus remain dead unless quickened into life by the right methods of teaching and right kind of teachers."

2) ***A teacher affects eternity*: -** Henry Adams stated so well, "A parent gives life but, as parent he gives no more. A murderer takes life, but his deed stops there. A teacher affects eternity, he can never tell when his influence stops." The teacher plays an important role in shaping and moulding the habits, tastes, manners and above all the character of the students. That is how he affects the young for all times. For imparting good education, not brick and mortar, aids and equipments, however, important they may be, but good teacher is needed. Only he can affect eternity.

3) ***Teacher is the backbone of society*: -**The teacher, the national integrator as he is, is the backbone of society, particularly so in the remote villages. He stands as an outstanding figure among the illiterate and semi-literate families. He is their friend, philosopher, and guide.

4) ***Teacher works as the social engineer and the useful social worker*: -** The teacher actively shares the responsibility for reconstructing a social order, the values and traditional beliefs of which are being eroded by the surge of new ideals and practices. He has to be a social engineer.

In most Indian school system, teachers are even assuming the role of counselors to the community, mediating not merely between pupil and pupil but between pupil and parents, and even in the domestic affairs of the families. The indication is that teacher is fast becoming a useful social worker.

5) ***Teacher works as a superior guide*: -** At the back of every great man, not often, a good teacher is there who kindled enthusiasm, fostered confidence and guided him to the way of progress. A conqueror of the stature of Alexander the Great said, "I owe my birth to my father but life to my teacher." And the poet Kabirdas, out of Guru and Govinda, preferred to bow to the Guru since it was he who had shown him the way to "see" Govinda.

6) ***Teacher works as the nation builder*: -** The teacher is always concerned with the children who are potential leaders of tomorrow. Tomorrow's nation will depend upon the type of citizens trained and educated today in the temples of learning. On the teacher devolves the responsibility of building the nation. Humayun Kabir said so well, "Teachers are literally the arbiters of a nation's destiny."

15.3 Duties of the Teachers

A teacher is supposed to discharge numerous duties. For the sake of convenience, we shall group them under the following heads: -

1) Planning the curricular and co-curricular programme.
2) Educating.
3) Organising the programme.
4) Supervising and guiding the pupils.
5) Maintenance of cumulative records, etc.
6) Evaluating the achievement of the pupils.
7) Reporting.
8) Maintaining relations with pupils, colleagues, headmaster, parents, and community for effective education.

1) ***Planning the curricular and co-curricular programme*:** Every teacher is supposed to be in charge of some curricular and co-curricular programme. For effectively carrying on this programme, he should plan it well and in advance, divide the

syllabus into weekly and monthly units and plan it according to the time available, fix dates and time for the co-curricular activities, decide about the students who will take part, the person who will preside, etc.

2) *Educating*: Teaching is his first and foremost duty. It is his duty to have a thorough knowledge of the subject, he teaches to study and practice the latest techniques of teaching, select the learning materials, manage the daily routines and procedures of teaching, and motivate the students to learn. He should give sufficient and adequate home-task and make regular correction of written work. He has to direct co-curricular activities and look to the all-round development of pupils.

3) *Organising the programme*: A teacher has to organise the various activities and programmes for which he is responsible. He has to make the proper seating arrangement, arrange the audio-visual aids, organise the instructional work, prepare the home-work assignment, and arrange their effective checking.

4) *Supervising and guiding the pupils*: The teacher has to ensure regular attendance and regular work, detect irregular and truant pupils. He has to check the practical and written work; and supervised study of the pupils and guide the pupils according to their needs. He has to supervise the co-curricular activities and help them in proper selection. He has also to supervise the boarders.

5) *Maintenance of cumulative records, etc.*: The teacher has to maintain the cumulative records of his wards and keep them up-to-date with all sorts of needed information.

He has to keep record of the work of the pupils and of their day-to-day participation in activities. He has to record 'their admission attendance', realisation of fee and other matters. He has to help the office in maintaining certain school records such as stock of furniture, issue of furniture, supply of equipment, university results, and scholarships awarded to pupils.

6) *Evaluating the achievement of the pupils*: After all sorts of curricular and co-curricular programmes have been carried on he must evaluate the achievement of the pupils, diagnose weaknesses, spotlight brightness, and offer guidance in the light of achievements. For this purpose, he has to conduct weekly, fortnightly, monthly, and terminal tests, score papers, tabulate results, help in the determination of policies of promotion, and prepare results. The teacher must be fully conversant with the latest techniques of evaluation.

7) *Reporting*: When the achievement of the pupils has been assessed and the position of the child ascertained, the parents must be kept informed.

8) *Maintaining relations with others*: The teacher has to maintain good relations with the pupils, colleagues, principal, parents, and community for effective education of the children.

15.4 Teacher's Relations with Others

(1) Teacher's relation with Pupils: The following points should guide the teacher's relations with his pupils:

(i) He must know the child fully well; discover his abilities, aptitudes, likes, dislikes, and limitations.

(ii) He must respect the child, sympathise with his fundamental needs, and take genuine interest in him. The pupil should have faith and confidence that the teacher is sympathetic to his demands.

(iii) He should be serious yet approachable. He should be able to elicit genuine and willing respect from the pupils.

(iv) He must not suffer from a false sense of dignity. He should be able to come down to the level of the pupils.

(v) His behaviour should be above board. He must act as a model for the pupils and must not do anything that he forbids the pupils to do. He must avoid such unworthy action as smoking, drinking, gambling, etc.

(vi) He must be able to inspire the pupils to learn more and more. It is well said, there are no dull and hard subjects, and there are only dull and hard teachers.

(vii) Teachers should be a firm believer in fair dealings. Any display of favoritism will cut at the root of good relations between the teacher and the pupils. He should be a guide, philosopher, and friend to all pupils.

(viii) The teacher should be tactful in his dealings with the pupils. He should be able to handle the best and the weakest student so tactfully as to elicit the best efforts.

(ix) He should neither flatter nor be amenable to flattery.

(2) Teacher's relations with his Colleagues: If the school teaching is a co-operative enterprise, a teacher must be able to pull on well with the members of the staff. Readiness to join with teachers in other departments and work out common programme is an important need. He must be able to work like a team with the other members of the staff and must be a ready worker to fall in line with the policy of the school.

He should avoid the following:

(i) Backbiting.

(ii) Unnecessary interference in the tasks assigned to others.

(iii) Criticism of the teaching ability of others.

(iv) A desire for self-aggrandisement.

(v) Lust for gold and money.

(vi) Work against the administration.

(vii) Untoward behaviour towards colleagues in the presence of the pupils.

Individuals differ in abilities and achievements. Differences can also arise among the colleagues due to differences of opinions, likes, and dislikes and yet we can agree on the basic need of a pleasant atmosphere in the school for the welfare of all. That is why, it is important that teachers should develop a friendly, cooperative attitude. A well-knit friendly faculty is a sure means of developing loyalty among the pupils and will provide an effective check to student indiscipline.

(3) Teacher's relations with the Principal: The teacher should try to have perfect understanding with the principal. He may have difference of opinion on the same point but once the decisions have been arrived at, it is obligatory on him to carry out these decisions in the interest of smooth functioning of the administration.

There must exist happy friendly relations between the teacher and the principal – any form of hostility and ill-feelings is bound to affect adversely the tone of administration.

(4) Teacher's relation with the Parents: In the interest of pupils, a teacher should have intimate relationship with the parents. He may know the pupil better if he knows his parents and his family background. Hence, the teacher should take all the measures of contacting the parents such as – visit to homes, sending progress reports, inviting parents to school functions, and finally by organising parent-teacher association.

It is the duty of the teacher to educate the parents also. For this purpose, he should arrange special lectures, cinema shows, exhibitions, etc. in the school, and the parents should be invited.

The parents may have their own special problems which they want to communicate to the teachers. It is only when there is a free and frequent connection between the parents and the teacher that all the problems concerning the education of the child can be solved. Teachers need to get co-operation from the parents in the discharge of their duties. Parents can adopt philanthropic attitude and give material help.

It has been observed that the parents are some time unnecessarily critical of the teachers. The teacher should use his restraint and show toleration. It is better to convince the parent through reasoning and other modes of persuasion, than to pay him back in the same coin. The teacher also should not be unmindful of the financial, professional, and other problems of the parents. For instance, he can help the parents in the solution of the following problems:

(a) Mid-day meals.

(b) Procuring stationery and books at concessional rates.

(c) Arranging conveyance for coming and going to the school.

(d) Providing medical aid.

(e) Bestowing stipends and scholarships to the needy.

(f) Providing special coaching.

(5) **Teacher and Community:** The school springs from the community and works for the enrichment of the community. The teacher should re-establish this forgotten relationship between the two. The community, if invited to take interest in all that the school strives to achieve, is sure to look to the needs and requirements of the school. The teachers should not entertain the wrong notion that community has nothing to contribute to the school substantially. If the teacher is resourceful, he can approach the local doctor, the local engineer, the local postmaster, the local carpenter, or local weaver and tap resources of such society members for the benefit of the school. The teacher should, therefore, establish fullest contact with the community. He should himself be an active member of non-political organisations, which have a cultural and social aim. Often the teacher's social relations are confined to their own professional group, and this isolates them from other professions. In the present day democratic setup, social cohesion is necessary for mutual understanding and mutual welfare. Hence, a teacher should join not only a professional organisation but also should take as much interest in the welfare of the community as a doctor or an engineer or a businessman takes. It is only through social interaction that he will be able to find for himself a status and a respected place. Isolation will turn him into an outcaste.

15.5 Teacher versus Class-Teacher System

A problem which generally taxes the brain of every principal is whether to have "class-teacher" or "subject-teacher." Each of these has its own merits and demerits. Let us first consider the arguments in favour of the subject-teacher system:

1) A teacher who is given the subject with which he is best acquainted and in which he is most interested, gives a *fresh, broad and original treatment* to his subject and stimulates his pupils an *interest* in and *enthusiasm* for that subject. A special room may be allotted to the subject which will have the atmosphere of that subject.

2) This system ensures an equal distribution of interest. It is not possible for a class-teacher, teaching all the subjects, to be equally interested in all the subjects. But a specialist is interested in his subject. With the result, in every subject the class will get interesting teaching.

3) The specialist knows more about his subject, but a class-teacher who has to teach many subjects, cannot know all the subjects fully well. He cannot hope to keep up-to-date knowledge in all subjects but a specialist can. So, naturally the methods of teaching are bound to be better under a specialist teacher system.

4) Contact with a number of teachers, which the subject-teacher system involves, broadens the pupil's outlook and provides better opportunities for finding their own natural bent.

5) Subject-teacher having to teach the same subject or subjects is able to plan a well coordinated course of study and to relate the various stages of instructions in that subject to one another. He can also bring about a better adjustment of the material of instruction to the mental level of the pupils of different grades.

But this is only one side of this picture; There are arguments in favour of the class-teacher system also. They are as follows:

1) It is said that the subject-teacher is interested in the subject but the class-teacher is interested in the class. In the words of Percival Wren, "There can be little real training , little discipline, little personal influence, little anything but poor paltry knowledge from the system that subordinates the boy to the subject and substitutes for the teacher personally interested in boys, the lecturer personally interested in his subject! The senior boys can benefit by the help and guidance of a cycle of subject-teacher but children need the teacher – the man who studies them and knows them and who in the light of that knowledge and of his skill as a practical psychologists, can train and mould them and make them what no mere subject-teacher can ever make, men and stout fellows!"

2) The special subject-teacher leaves his pupils and they leave him and he goes his way entirely regardless of their fate, only concerned with having performed with credit to him. He is clear-cut, logical, precise, beautifully connected, yet avoiding all close laborious exactness. He does the work and goes, but the class-teacher makes the pupil work and stands and falls by what they do and disregards all precise plans, provided that a close, laborious and exact exercise of mind is the result.

3) A class-teacher has a better chance of balancing the work of a class and gauging their progress, knowing their weaknesses and where to put stress. He can adjust the total demands of the work and the strain involved to the pupil's capacity and with a fuller insight into personalities of his pupil's, assists their development on right lines.

4) One-sidedness, undue emphasis on any particular subject and water-tight compartmentalism of subjects are avoided.

5) The teacher himself has scope for variety in the work of the teaching when he passes from one subject to the other and thus sustains his interest in an undiminished measure.

6) In subject-teacher system, there is a danger of the subject-teacher considering only his own subject as important and ignoring the others, requiring too much home-work for his subject and generally putting too much stress on it. Such dangers are more easily avoided in the class-teacher system.

7) In a class-teacher system, time-table framing does not present problems. The class can have teaching of different subjects at the proper time. For instance, it is generally thought that subjects which are difficult should be taught when the brain of the child is quite fresh, i.e. in the second or third period. This can be easily achieved in the class-teacher system but is not so easy under the subject-teacher system.

Conclusion: - Both the systems have their own merits and demerits but the best results can be secured by the compromise of the two systems. In the lower classes, the class-teacher system may be adopted but in higher classes, subject-teacher system will do good and even here, given the permanent teacher in sole control of the class and responsible for its mental, moral and physical education, the visiting teacher of a special subject may be useful. In this way, the advantages of both the systems can be secured.

As far as a big high school, a higher secondary, or a multi-purpose school is concerned, it is desirable to organise the school on departmental lines. A senior teacher may be made the head of the department with four or five teachers as his assistants. This department can be left entirely in charge of the teaching of that particular subject. The departmental head can conduct meetings, plan courses of study, select textbooks, and evaluate achievement, budget supplies, and instructional material.

15.6 Qualities of a Teacher

As the teacher is to guide the pupils by his example as well as by his precept, he must posses certain definite qualities. The best teachers are those who have certain natural qualifications for the job. What are those 'natural qualifications', we shall now proceed to discuss.

(1) *Personality of the Teachers*

(i) *The teacher must be good-looking.* The young children are attracted by the outer charm and repelled by the shabby look of the teacher. The teacher must be extra-careful about cleanliness, and smartness of his dress. This will help him in his job. The dress should be decent and sober.

(ii) *The teacher should have calm nature, sweet looks, charming face, and pleasant demeanour, so as to exert a good influence on both the public and the pupils.*

(iii) *His character should be above reproach.* A teacher is a public man. He is being watched and held up as a model by scores of children who look up to him for guidance. He must possess all those moral qualities which constitute integrity of character. He must be frank, sincere, and honest in all dealings. These qualities will win him respect of his pupils and of the general public.

(iv) *Good mental and physical health is another essential to be a good* teacher. Children have a right to expect a teacher who is strong both physically and mentally. The teacher must have alertness, cheerfulness, and emotional stability. A person who is given to temper tantrum or the person who displays fear of and consequent retreat from decision demanding situation, will not be able to do justice to his job. A teacher must be a happy, cheerful, good-humoured, contended and above all an optimistic fellow. He should be able to take every disappointment in stride. He should know the secret of using frustrations as aids to his own spiritual development. He should be able to bear the cross because he knows how to make it serve higher purposes. He knows how to make the bitter tree of his cross bear sweet fruit. He should possess a philosophy of life that enables him, when he is powerless to change his environment, to change his soul; he should possess an inner strength that may enable him even with a wound to attend to the wound of others.

(v) *Sociability is another essential trait for a teacher.* Motivated by a sound social philosophy, he must also make his best contribution to the society. He must have the qualities of leadership – leadership that depends for its force and effectiveness upon character and upon the respect which one commands from others. He must be sociable enough to be popular amongst his students and colleagues.

(vi) *The teacher must have a sense of humour.* Pent-up feelings and over-wrought nerves can be easily relaxed if the teacher can take advantage of the humour of the situation. A good laugh during a tense moment is the best means of bringing a group into co-operative and harmonious relationships. The classroom has no room for the confirmed pessimist and long-faced humourless grouch. The classroom needs to be a happy place and it cannot be that without a good-natured teacher in-charge.

A teacher should be a person with whom children can have normal, friendly human relationships.

In short, the teacher must possess a well-rounded chiseled personality. He should be particularly careful about the following:

(a) He must be punctual to the minute.

(b) He must be just, fair, and impartial in all his dealings and should be known as such.

(c) He must have pleasing manners and should be courteous to all.

(d) He must respect pupil's opinion and should invite free discussion in the class.

(e) He must be able to earn respect.

(f) He must be reasonable in his talk and in his behaviour.

(g) He must not be too rigid, too strict – yet should be prompt and business-like.

(h) He must be kind and sympathetic.

(i) He must be extremely honest.

(j) He must be self-reliant and self-directive.

(k) He must be an enthusiast – an enthusiast in child-study, an enthusiast in his subject, and an enthusiast in the matter of method.

(l) Last but not the least important, he should know himself.

(2) *Professional Efficiency*

(i) *The teacher must be dedicated to his job.* Teaching is not everybody's cup of tea. It is not a soft option. It requires hard labour, sweat, and tears. Only those who have got a genuine love for this calling will be able to do the job well. Jesus Christ said to his disciples: "He that loseth his life shall find it." There are joys in teaching that can only be attained by those who are sincere and steadfast.

(ii) *A teacher, if he is to be worthy of his calling, must continue to be a student all the days of his life.* He must keep alive the flame of his own mind if he expects to kindle the minds of his students. "Only a burning lamp will burn another lamp."

(iii) *The teacher must be a good experimenter* because it is only through experiment that an advance can come. He must experiment with new methods and techniques and provide enough opportunities to the pupils for creative work.

(iv) *The teacher must be equipped with the weapons of originality and creative power.* He must not be a blind follower of textbooks or course of study. These are just guides and should be treated as such. There are certain classroom situations which call for adapting subject-matter to the level and interest of pupils. The individual who lacks initiative and originality will find himself hopelessly at sea in many class-room situations and the tragic of it is that the pupils will realise it before he does. Creative power is what he needs: that sense of security and confidence that comes from being master of the situation and being able to control and direct activities constructively.

(v) *The teacher must possess a fair knowledge of current affairs.* He should be a voracious reader of books in his own subjects and other allied subjects. Today knowledge is expanding its frontiers – it is extremely important that he knows a lot about his own subject and other subjects, about his own community and other communities, about his own country and other countries of the world. He must possess enough information to satisfy the hungry souls.

(vi) *Not only the new matter but also the new methods the teacher must know*. There is no machine more complicated or difficult to manipulate than man's physical organisation and the mind of man is infinitely more intricate. The teacher has to deal with both - the physical and the mental health of the child. The right type of education can never be given if this matter of method of teaching is neglected. Neglect of method in teaching is as fatal to the lives and development of our pupils as behaviour of a motor driver - who does not know how to apply his brakes or regulate his petrol. The petrol may be good, the car may be excellent, the driver - a man of fine character, but if he does not know how to manipulate the car, he is a positive danger to the lives of the passengers. So the efficiency in teaching can only be ensured if the teacher is fully conversant with the most progressive and up-to-date methods of teaching.

(vii) *A teacher must be the most committed student* who should treat the facts as raw material for understanding basic relationships and the whole job of teaching as if weaving a fabric of relationship to attach this to so many points in the students life that it becomes a part of him.

(viii) *Teacher should have a sense of calling to the profession*. "There is nothing more inspiring than having a mind unfold before you. Let people teach who have a calling. It is never just a job." All students irrespective of their own endowments recognise and revere good teachers for they have seen the 'undying fire' sparkle.

(ix) *The teacher should not only have a legal authority to teach - he must also have a moral authority to do so*. For a real teacher, teaching is not merely a money-earning device. To him it is a struggle, a life mission. He loves to teach as a musician loves to play, as a singer loves to sing, as a strong man rejoices to run a race. The deep satisfaction that comes from a life well lived, duties faithfully performed, and torches lighted in the hearts and mind of young ones, are more precious to him than anything that external recognitions can give.

(x) *A teacher must boast of having his own code of work and ethics and behaviour as the architect of the nation*. Unless he tears himself apart and raises himself from the common level, he will naturally get lost in the crowd and be treated as an ordinary employee in a 'profession.'

Few, if any, states are unwilling to right the wrong done to the teacher if the means can be provided. But who is to provide the means?

It can be done. The sources exist, the know-how exists. The money cost, though large would be trivial compared with what the Government are spending on meeting the agitations of students and teachers and on those "frill" schemes which are being introduced to fill up the lacuna left by an unsatisfied teacher.

It will be done, but only if public opinion adds its plea to government efforts.

To ignore the upsurge of discontent among the teachers and leave the things as they are is not to risk disaster but to make it certain. This is a writing on the wall - will those who matter heed it.

15.7 Indian Education Commission 1964-66 and the Teacher

The Indian Education Commission rightly said that "Of all the different factors which influence the quality of education and its contribution to national development the quality, competence, and character of teachers are undoubtedly the most significant. Nothing is more important than securing a sufficient supply of high quality recruits to the teaching profession, providing them with the best possible professional preparations and creating satisfactory conditions of work in which they can be fully effective. In view of the rapid expansion of educational facilities expected during the next three plans, and specially in view of the urgent need to raise standard to the highest level and to keep them continually improving, these problems have now acquired unprecedented importance and urgency."

"A programme of high priority in the proposed educational reconstruction, therefore, is to feed back a significant proportion of the talented men and women from schools and colleges into the educational system. For this purpose, it is necessary to make an intensive and continuous effort to raise the economic, social, and professional status of teachers in order to attract young men and women of ability to the profession and to retain them in it as dedicated enthusiastic and contended workers."

The Commission rightly sensed the problem and recommended certain positive measures for the improvement of general conditions of teachers.

	Teachers	Remunerations
1.	Teachers who have completed the secondary school courses and have received two years of professional training.	Minimum for trained teachers .....Rs. 150 Maximum salary to be Rs. 250 reached in a period of 20 years. Selection grade (Rs. 250-300) for about 15 p.c. of the cadre.
2.	Graduates who have received one year's training.	Minimum for trained graduates Rs. 220, Maximum salary (to be Rs. 400 reached in a period of 20 years) selection grade (for about 15 p.c. of cadre), (Rs. 400-500)
3.	Teachers working in secondary schools and having post graduate qualifications.	Rs. 300-600
4.	Heads of secondary schools.	Depending upon the size and quality of school and the qualifications. The principal should have one or the other of the scales of pay for affiliated colleagues recommended below:
5.	Teachers in affiliated colleges.	Lecturer: Junior scale: Rs. 300-25-600 Senior scale: Rs. 400-30-640 40-800 Senior Lecturer: Rs. 700-40-1100 Principal: I 700-40-1100 II 800-50-1250 III 1000-50-1500
6.	Teachers in university departments.	Lecturer: Rs. 400-40-800-50-950 Reader: Rs. 700-50-1250 Professor: Rs. 1100-50-1300-60-1600.

(*a*) *Improvement in the scale of pay*: - The Indian Education Commission suggested higher scales of pay for teachers of all categories. The Commission suggested that a teacher in a secondary school should get more than what a graduate gets in other professions. Also, the differences in the pay at different levels (primary, secondary, etc.) should be reduced. Teachers may work at the primary or secondary level, but they should be paid on the basis of qualifications and not on the level of school.

N.B. The proportion of teachers in the senior scale to those in the junior scale should be progressively improved. By the end of the 5th plan, this proportion should be raised to about 75% on an average.

(a) House rent allowance, and other allowances are extra.

(b) The scales apply uniformly to all teachers, government, local authority, or private.

***Improving Conditions of Service and Work*:** For improving conditions of work in educational institutions and conditions of service otherwise to enable teachers to function at the highest level of efficiency, the Commission gave some recommendations.

1. ***For Improving General Conditions of Work*:** The Commission suggested the following:
   (i) The hours of work should be similar to those of other public servants.
   (ii) Work load should not be high. Account should be taken of non-teaching work also, such as curricular activities, tutorials, etc.
   (iii) Facilities should be provided for professional growth such as grants for purchase of books, grants for research, deputation to seminars and summer institutes.
   (iv) Terms and conditions of service in private institutions should be the same as in Government institutions.
   (v) New conduct and discipline rules should be framed.
   (vi) Arbitration Boards or Committees should be established to look into the appeals and grievances of teachers and to consider matters relating to suspension, dismissal, etc.
2. ***Additional Source of Income*:** A teacher has few additional source of income. Private tuitions are most common, but they lower the morale, status, and efficiency of the teacher. The Indian Education Commission, therefore, recommended that private tuitions should be disallowed and controlled. Special coaching for children who need may be arranged on an institutional basis. Teachers doing extra coaching to such gifted or backward children may be paid adequate remuneration. The Commission recommended that examinership may be permitted though care should be exercised to see that the concession is not abused and that teaching work does not suffer.
3. ***Security of Service*:** Full security of tenure should be guaranteed. Services should not be terminated; transfers should not be stopped without adequate grounds.
4. ***Retirement Benefits*:** The Indian Education Commission recommended that the normal retirement age for the teacher should be 60 years, with a provision for extension up to 65 years on condition of physical fitness. In some cases, it may be extended even up to 70 years. As per Provident Fund, higher rate of interest should be given to teachers, and for this purpose a better system of investing these funds should be devised. All teachers should be required to contribute to the provident fund. The teacher should be entitled to employer's contribution even with less than five year's service. Provident fund may be invested in Post Office Savings Bank or in enterprises which gave 6 p.c. interests.
5. ***Triple Benefit for Teachers*:** The Indian Education Commission recommended that Triple Benefit Scheme, i.e. pension-cum-

provident fund-cum-insurances should be instituted for all teachers.

6. *Residential Accommodation*: The Commission recommended that every effort should be made to increase residential accommodation for teachers in rural areas and state subsidies should be made available for the purpose. A programme of building, construction, and grant of adequate house rent allowance should be adopted in big cities. Co-operative housing scheme for teachers should be encouraged and loans on favourable terms should be made available for construction of houses.
7. *Welfare Services*: The Commission suggested the strengthening of the welfare services already started by Government of India. It recommended that all teachers should contribute one and a half p.c. of their salaries and the State should pay an equal amount. The fund should be administered by joint committees of representatives of teachers and government.
8. *Other Free Services*: (i) The children of teachers should be given free education throughout the school stage. (ii) Teachers should get a concessional railway pass to any part of India once in five years on payment of a reasonable contribution to his salary. (iii) Teachers wishing to go to health resorts or holiday camps or to attend educational conferences, seminars, etc. should be given travel concessions and leave facilities. (iv) They should be given free medical attention and treatment in hospitals and dispensaries.
9. *Facilities for Women Teachers*: Special facilities should be given to women teachers. Part-time teachership, in the case of married women, should be allowed.
10. *Library and Research Facilities* should be granted to teachers.

(b) Improving Social Status: - For improving the social status of the teacher, the Commission gave many suggestions:

1. *Invitations to Functions:* The teacher should be invited to all important public and state functions.
2. *Representation in Higher Bodies:* The teacher should be given representation in State Advisory Board of Education, Legislative Council, and Senate of the University, Examination Bodies, Municipalities, and other public organisations. The Commission recommended that teachers should be free to exercise all civil rights enjoyed by citizens and should be eligible for public offices at the local, district, state or national level. No legal restrictions should be placed on their participation in elections, but while doing so, they are to be expected to proceed on leave.
3. *Educational Consultations:* The Commission recommended that consultations should be held with the teachers on matters relating to school education, general and professional education of teachers and their salaries and conditions of work.
4. *Constituting Joint Teacher's Councils:* The Commission recommended the constitution of joint teachers' councils in each state and Union Territory to discuss all matters relating to teachers' salaries, conditions of work and service and welfare service.
5. *National Awards:* The Commission recommended that the scheme of giving national and state awards should be made more effective by :
   - **(i)** Increasing the number of national awards to 500, so that 200 awards are distributed to secondary teachers and the remaining to primary teachers.
   - **(ii)** Strengthening the selection committee.
   - **(iii)** Giving travelling allowance to the awardees similar to that sanctioned for Class I Officer of the Government of India.

In addition to these incentives, the following devices can also help in improving the status of the teachers;

6. Honours and Distinction: Teachers should be given public recognition through merit certificates, medals, and other honours.

The Commission also suggested that teachers' training programme should be made more effective by removing the isolation of teacher training, improving the quality of professional training and making the teacher grow professionally continuously through short-term courses, refresher courses, workshops, seminars, conferences, study circles, and clubs, etc.

The time has come to improve the lot of the teacher for the nation's children. The Commission gave the right direction. Improvement of the lot of teachers is the basis of progress and is the best guarantee for attracting the reasonable percentage of top grade youth to this noble profession and saving the country from a headlong catastrophe. Conditions must be created, where a Young man 'chooses' teaching and stays in teaching. If this is not done, it means that there continually will be an erosion of the cultural life of our country. If persons of inadequate ability enter into the teaching profession, the next generation will be deficient to a great extent. The Commission gave a rousing call for immediate action. Action must be taken here and now by those who possess the power to bind and loose before it is too late. We must save the teacher for there lies the safety of the nation!

15.8 Teacher: A Good Counsellor

The following can be the roles of the teacher in the guidance and counseling programme:-

1. To collect information concerning the pupils and to prepare the cumulative record.
2. To identify the adjustment related problems.
3. To prepare the case history of the problem history.
4. To observe the pupils in various situations.
5. To send reports to the parents of the pupils, their guardians and to the headmaster.
6. To participate actively in the parent-teacher association.
7. To help the pupils in evaluating their progress.
8. To provide various opportunities to the pupils for their maximum development.
9. To seek expert opinion just to study the pupils.
10. To help the pupils in their adjustment in educational, vocational, and social areas.
11. To create best environment in the class.
12. To provide cooperation to other guidance workers.
13. To provide personal counseling to the pupils.

15.9 Problems of Teacher

The teachers in schools face a number of problems. Those teachers, who aim at perfection and try to attain it, get only disappointed and frustration. The following are some of the usual problems that our teachers face in schools.

1. **Feeling of Frustration:** There are trained graduate teachers with post-graduate and sometimes with research degrees. They have been in the department or in an aided school for years but have failed to get better jobs. They develop a sense of frustration and fail to perform their duties with devotion.
2. **Feeling of Rejection:** This is the feeling of highly qualified and experienced teachers who apply for better jobs but do not get them. This is very common in aided schools where the principal is not selected from amongst the staff members. Senior teachers, though not all, get a sense of rejection, and are not able to give their best to the school.
3. **Feeling of Rivalry and Jealousy:** Amongst the staff members there is healthy but sometimes unhealthy rivalry and even jealousy. Partisanship, favouritism, and

nepotism are attributed to minor assignments and offers of remuneratory jobs like the work of investigation.

4. **Feeling of Insecurity:** Some teachers on transfer might have some sad experience of other principal(s). They abhor every action of the principal and try to trace evil intentions behind every move.
5. **Group System:** Sometimes there is a tussle for leadership between two or more teachers. This results in the formation of groups which view all the actions of the principal from the angle of their group without caring for the larger interest of the school and the students.
6. **Right-minded rather than Duty-minded:** The good old days of 'duty before right' are over. The teachers like all other employees now bow after rights. The principals who sermonize duty are 'in' for trouble.
7. **The Problem Teachers:** There may be some 'foot draggers' who may like to criticise and even condemn the headmaster right or wrong. Wiles has given the following types of problem teachers:
   - **(i)** The lazy teachers are alienated from teaching.
   - **(ii)** The colourless teachers.
   - **(iii)** The older teachers.
   - **(iv)** The undemocratic teachers.
   - **(v)** The disagreeing teachers.

Objective Type Questions

Multiple Choice Questions (Tick ✓ the right option)

(1) "A teacher is the image of Brahma". This definition is given by
   - (a) S. Radha Krishnan
   - (b) Manu
   - (c) Swami Vivekananda
   - (d) Pt. Jawaharlal Nehru

(2) Teacher is the backbone of
   - (a) Society
   - (b) School
   - (c) Community
   - (d) None of the above

Fill in the blanks

(1) A teacher is a __________ man. [Public]

(2) The teacher must possess a ______________ knowledge of current affairs. [Fair]

(3) The teacher must be _____________ to his job. [Dedicated]

(4) ___________ and _____________ are two big powers in human resources which act as a foundation stone for any school. [Headmaster, Teachers]

Important Questions

1. From your personal study of some successful teachers, list some essential qualities which contributed to their success.
2. Write a short essay on "The teacher we need in India today."
3. "The way to child-centred education can only be through teacher-centred school." Discuss.
4. "No system of education can rise higher than its teachers." What role can be played by teachers to make democracy a success in our country?

5. Analyse the roles of a teacher under the following heads:
   (a) Teaching and guiding children. *(b)* Contact with the local community. *(c)* Relationship with the principal and colleagues. *(d)* Administrative duties.
6. Discuss in detail the recommendations of the Indian Education Commission, 1964-66 regarding the working conditions and the status of the teacher.

16

The Pupils

The pupils are the legitimate occupants of the school – it is for them that all educational efforts are organised. It is they who occupy the focus of the limelight – the pivot, the centre of educational administration. It is for their all round wholesome development that curricula are designed and planned, plant is set, qualified teachers and principals are appointed, auxiliary services are arranged. In fact, pupil is the measure of all these endeavours and is all important. In fact, he is the common denominator in the arithmetic of educational administration. In this chapter, we shall discuss some very important problems regarding pupils – their admission, attendance, classification, and promotion. As there are different types of secondary schools in our country, the mode of dealing with all these problems differ from school to school and from state to state.

16.1 Admission of Pupils

There are three major points where problem of admission is very important, the beginning of primary school, i.e. in class I, the beginning of class VI, and the beginning of high school, i.e. in class IX. Some states hold departmental examinations for all pupils completing primary and middle school education. In others, departmental examination is held at the completion of middle school education only. The marks secured in these examinations serves as the criteria for admission to the next class. In states, where there are no such public examinations, the high school principal can hold an admission test for admitting pupils in VI and X classes. The admission to other classes is done in two ways – the pupil should produce a certificate from the school last attended, failing which the pupil is given a test and is then admitted to the class for which he may be found fit.

Admissions are generally made within the first term of the school year only. Under special circumstances, the transfer of the parents etc., admissions may be made in the course of the academic year.

The Indian Education Commission recommended that the first public examination should come at the end of the first 10 years of school.

16.2 Pupil Attendance

For teaching-learning process to go on smoothly and satisfactorily, the pupil's attendance for the maximum of working days is essential. Without regular attendance, learning will be interrupted – the breaks in between will lead to so many problems. For good learning to take place, pupils must be punctual and regular.

Poor attendance and consequent wastage and stagnation are one of the biggest taxing problems of school administration. It is the mother of all pupil problems. Let us study the causes of poor attendance.

16.3 Causes of Drop-out Behaviour

The causes of drop-out behaviour have been found to be complex. Usually more than one factor is responsible for making a student drop out of school. The commonly reported causes are:

1. ***Low achievement:*** - With the usual exceptions, drop-outs get poorer grades, score low on standardised tests, show invariably a record of subject or grade

failure, and are usually retarded by one or two years.

2. *Low socio-economic status:* - The majority of drop outs come from families of low socio-economic status. This has important implications for education. As is well-known, such families usually do not value education greatly, and are often actively resentful in sending their children to school. There is no pressure on a person coming from such a family to continue in school. On the contrary, there is sometimes a pressure on such a person to withdraw from school.
3. *Size of the school and its classes:* - The rate at which children leave before completing high school has direct bearing on the size of the schools and its classes. Schools with larger enrollment and large classes tend to have a higher percentage of drop-outs than smaller schools.
4. *Lack of a sense of belonging:* - Most children leave school because they lack a sense of belonging to the school. They are dissatisfied with the school; they are unable to get along with teaching. Finding no source of attraction, they leave the school at the first opportunity.
5. *Inadequate curriculum:* - At times, curriculum offerings are too poor to hold the pupils in the school. Thus, they leave the school.
6. *Non-participation in school activities:* - Existence of few co-curricular activities in school and lesser participation by the pupils also contribute to the drop-out behaviour. A pupil does not find anything interesting, challenging and exciting to keep him occupied – thus he leaves school. Researches have shown that those who leave school early are not significantly involved in co-curricular activities. They are usually the "left outs" who feel out of place.

In a democratic setup the school is responsible for the maximum development of all students. It has a definite responsibility towards those who, for one reason or another, are not able to complete the secondary school programme. What can the school do for such students so that they are retained in school? We have found ways and means to keep these children in school for their own good and for the good of the country. Some suggestions are listed below:

Suggestions:

1. *Rich and Diversified Curriculum:* - Rich and diversified curriculum can help the schools increase their holding power. Every child who comes to the school should find something to satisfy his need and aptitudes.
2. *Educating Parents:* - To counteract the influence of the parents for non-attendance, the school should try to reach such families and try to educate them regarding the advisability of keeping their child in school.
3. *Provision of Guidance Service:* -Guidance services have an important role to play in preventing drop-outs. Apart from identifying the potential drop-out, guidance services can make his school experiences more meaningful for him by helping him to plan his programme in accordance with his interests and abilities, by diagnosing his special difficulties and providing remedial help where necessary. Through counseling, he can be helped to understand the current outlook for the employment of drop-outs and the need for finishing high school.

16.4 Classification of Pupils

Sound Classification Necessary

The fact that "The nucleus of school organisation is sound-classification" cannot be denied. A good class is not a mere aggregation of children, arbitrarily grouped, as a matter of mechanical administrative convenience, but the members of a class are related by common interests, equal or almost equal attainments, similar aptitudes and common aims. *A class is a homogeneous group of pupils - homogeneity existing in the various spheres of human attainment - intellectual, physical, social, and emotional.*

Classification is a necessary and at the same time an embarrassing problem of school administration. This is so because it is very difficult to group the complex individuals into homogeneous units called classes. Particularly in the world of today when education has been psychologised, when the individual has come to the forefront in the arena of education, it is said that the class system is going to meet its death. But it should be remembered that although the patient is in a bad way, the corpse is hardly yet available for the postmortem! The class, as a *unit of teaching,* may disappear; but as a *unit of organisation,* it will certainly stay until we have a better method of organisation to replace it.

Advantages of Class-system

(i) ***Class makes the child socially conscious:-*** The class as has been said above is not a mere aggregation or conglomeration of children, but they are related by common interests. The very fact that interests are common provides them with incentives of work. Each individual is enabled to measure his own ability against those of others. A strong stimulus to activity is furnished through emulation and cooperation. We are in entire agreement with L.P. Jacks when he says that the most precious art in the world is that by which crowds can be turned into communities. School is undoubtedly the first and foremost agency which can perform this duty most efficiently. With a community life of its own, it is an excellent training ground for children and the class is an organisation in this society. When the child cannot live in this small organisation on a cooperative basis, how can we expect that he will pull on well in a very complex world where co-operation is a necessity? So as opposed to individual treatment the child will become socially conscious through class. He will learn to sacrifice his own interests for the interests of his class and this may form the very basis of his later sacrifices for his community, nation, and country.

(ii) **Again,** ***the advantages of collective teaching lie in the discovery and removal of misunderstandings which have arisen during individual and group work.*** It is also very useful in clearing up of general difficulties which arise in individual and group work.

(iii) ***Time and money are also saved by class methods: -*** If individual methods are followed, the cost of education will certainly go up manifold. This fact alone may result in reducing the scope and extent of the most humanitarian and essential service. In class methods we see that one teacher can teach a class of 30 pupils or so at one time and thus the cost thereof is within manageable limits.

(iv) ***There are some subjects especially inspirational subjects which can be taught better to a class than to an individual: -*** History, music, and religious instruction are examples of such subjects. The "sympathy of numbers" in these cases is extremely helpful to the quality of instruction.

(v) ***The class-system is based on the principles of equality and cooperation and these are necessary, if we are to save ourselves from class-distinctions: -*** If we provide education to a few only instead of giving general education to the masses, we shall be on the high road to creating a new class of intellectual aristocracy. This will be against the very foundations of democracy.

(vi) **Lastly:** - *It should be carefully borne in mind that pupils learn not only from teachers but from each other also.* The class system, which permits free mixing of pupils, helps in that direction and provides facility for the same.

Disadvantages of Class-system

As opposed to a few advantages of class-system, there are some disadvantages also:

(i) ***Individuality is ignored in class teaching:-*** The class-teaching is based on the assumptions that the differences between individual children are not enough significance to be considered in the organisation of class-room procedure, that all pupils will react in a similar manner to similar situations and will progress at the same rate. But this is not the case in reality. Nothing in the world presents a greater range of variety within the type than a class of boys. There is the mathematician, the linguist, the scientist, the artist, the clever-handed, the subtle, the dull, the keen, the lazy, the weak, the amenable, the slow, the thorough, the superficial, and there are the knave, the fool, and the righteous! There are as many types as there are boys. *Individuality is generally ignored by the class-teaching.* As opposed to this, individual instruction makes for the development on initiative and individuality. Mass teaching so often tends to exercise memory and memory alone. Individual methods teach pupils to think, feel, and act for themselves and not subordinate themselves to the majority without rhyme and reason. The very attitude of the pupil to school and school work undergoes a fundamental change from being passive recipients of knowledge to becoming active partners in the work.

(ii) ***In a class, the teacher adjusts his teaching to the average child, but an all-round average pupil is a statistical myth: -*** However homogeneous the class may be, there is no average boy in it. In fact, no two boys are identical in ability, energy, tastes, aptitudes, and the desire to learn. No doubt, children have exactly the same gifts and potentialities of body and soul. So the uniform intellectual diet that the teacher offers to the class often suits none completely. There is a danger of holding back the bright and over-pushing the dullards. If the teacher directs his attention to the bright section, the dull are dragged along hurriedly beyond the natural pace of their mental process and suffer a severe strain physically and mentally. If the teacher directs his attention to the weak, there is a danger of making the bright also weak and thus turning them into backward children. But this is not the case under the individual work system. In this case, each pupil works according to his own ability and aptitude.

(iii) ***In a class system, individuals cannot derive equal benefit from the teacher's efforts which are considerably wasted through lack of adjustment to individual needs:-*** In the words of Sultan Mohiyuddin: "It is like pouring water from a bucket into bottles with necks of different sizes; some bottles get more and some less and a great part is spilt." But under an individual work system, the teacher gets far more real satisfaction from his work. When dealing with his pupils individually, he is able to understand and meet their difficulties. He is also able to make sure that his pupils understand his explanations. He is able to vary his way of dealing with a view to suit different individuals. In this way, he is being of real help to his pupils and, in point of fact, he is being of far more help to large numbers of them than he can possibly be under a system of class-teaching. He can put in more time with those who need it, and he is able to teach them how to think and work for themselves. In everyway, the teacher realises that he is doing the job for which he is in the school much more efficiently and this naturally gives him satisfaction. Working in such a scheme may and does mean harder work for the teacher, but the extra work entailed is certainly well worthwhile.

(iv) ***Class organisation takes no care of the individual rates of progress:*** **-** All pupils have to devote a fixed time to a fixed subject. But some students need less time for History and more for Geography, while with others the reverse is the case. In the case of class-teaching, however, all have to work uniformly.

16.5 Factors for Determining the Size of a Class

The size of a class can be determined by a number of factors. They are as follows:

It is evident from the above that neither class-teaching nor individual instructions are unmixed blessings in themselves. Class-teaching, therefore, is not the order of the day only because it costs less but it is necessary and inevitable because of its utility. The best method consequently would be a combination of both the methods. Individual work should be judiciously interspersed with class-teaching; or the classes should be made so small that it should be possible for every teacher to study each pupil individually, have personal contact with him and discover his likes and dislikes, tastes, and aptitudes. We, therefore, advocate *the intermingling of opposites so that evils of both may be avoided and their good points incorporated and made use of.*

(i) ***The grade:*** **-** The size of class would depend on the grade of the school – whether it is a part of the primary, middle, or high school. If it is primary, the number should be less than in the middle or high school, because individual attention is more necessary in the initial stages. In the primary class, the number should not be above twenty-five, but in middle and high school classes, the number may go up to thirty and in exceptional cases up to thirty-five. Some writers are of the opinion that forty-five is the optimum of the size of group.

(ii) ***Subjects taught:*** - The size of the class would depend on the subjects taught. As mentioned already in the foregoing pages, there are some subjects, which need emotional appeal such as music, religious instructions, poetry, etc. In the case of these subjects, therefore, classes can be made bigger. In case of practical subjects, however, individual treatment is necessary and here smaller classes are inevitable.

(iii) ***Personality of the teacher:*** - The personality of the teacher is also one of the greatest single factors in education. It is operative as much in class-teaching and management as in the social aspects of school life. Large classes, therefore, should not be given to an untrained teacher; they should be put under the charge of gifted teachers with special qualities of head and heart.

(iv) ***Size of the classroom:*** **-** In every case, the size of the classroom is also to be considered. If it is not big enough to accommodate 35 pupils, how can that class be made of 35 pupils. Although this sort of a consideration does not, as a rule, arises yet when it does, it is decisive.

The Indian Education Commission recommended the following maximum number for the different stages of school education:

Lower Primary	50
Higher Primary	45
Lower Secondary	40
Higher Secondary	40

The special purpose for which a class is formed is another consideration in the determination of the number of a class. If the class is a *teaching unit,* the number will necessarily be small; but if the class is only an *organising unit*, the number might be large.

These are some of the factors determining the size of the class. But the real problem before us is the problem of sound classification. The question before us is, "Is it the business of the school to teach and train every boy or is it enough to offer knowledge which only the clever and hard working boys can take and digest?" The answer to this question involves the gravest differences in organisation in schools. We are not concerned with inanimate matter in schools but "the eternal problem of education" as Mazzini says, "is the eternal problem of human nature." Classification of children is not an easy matter. It is a vexed, embarrassing, and intricate problem which at times baffles the ingenuity of even the most successful principals.

16.6 Basis of Classification

(i) ***Chronological age:*** **-** It is considered by some as the basis of classification, but there are backward and retarded children as well as bright and gifted ones. In view of this, the chronological age may only be taken as a starting point for an investigation in regard to the mental and scholastic standing of a pupil. It, by itself, does not indicate what the pupil has already done in regard to school work or can do in future. These are the main hindrances in the way of adopting chronological age as the basis of classification and they are formidable indeed.

(ii) ***Mental age:*** **-** It is another basis of classification commonly adopted now-a-days. It is especially useful in classification of pupils on entry into school, and particularly on admission to a primary school where past achievement in school subjects is comparatively of less account, as compared to other classes of school. It is so because the intelligence tests test largely the innate ability and not acquired knowledge. But for grades of education beyond primary, intelligence tests alone do not furnish an adequate basis for classification. Experience points to the desirability of classifying pupils in primary school mainly by general intelligence rather than by *attainment* and in higher grades by *both attainment and general intelligence.*

(iii) ***Biotypological examination:*** **-** An examination of each child, embracing all the aspects of his personality - *anthropometric, sexological, chemical and urinary, physiological, psychological, general, medical and psychiatric* – is now suggested as a basis for classification. Although each individual is in a way unique and classification into types is not supported by modern psychology yet a classification of biological types is not considered impracticable. Therefore, it is quite desirable to keep complete biotypological record of every pupil in every school. It might contain a full account of his personality including the teacher's observation regarding his social behaviour, powers of leadership, and the emotional and other side of his character which cannot be easily assessed by objective techniques. This record certainly proves very useful for guidance regarding the selection of the course of study, vocation, or preparation and even for reorganisation of the system of education.

(iv) ***Attainment in school subjects may also provide another basis for classification:*** **-** The students might be examined in important subjects and thus they might be classified and promoted. This would be much better if scholastic tests are supplemented by "intelligence tests."

(v) ***Elasticity in classification required:*** **-** It has already been said that no two pupils work at the same rate. Flexibility in classification is absolutely necessary. There are two courses open for this – one is by

having two or more courses of study differing in the amount of work to be done, but with the same minimum amount for work expected of all; the other is by having a single course of study for all and accelerating the pace of the bright pupils and slackening that of the slower ones. The first course has been more widely adopted in England. In that country pupils are divided into three categories at the age of 11 then admitted into different schools, depending upon their achievements and capacity. The triple-track that is provided has varying bias in each case. In the case of superior pupils, emphasis is on academic work, whereas in the case pupils below the average, the course is less ambitious and emphasis is laid on practical work. Provision is made for the average as transfer from one track to another, according to the progress made. This plan of differentiation tends to avoid a heavy incidence of failure and other undesirable results of a uniform standard for all children in the class. It is, however, argued in some cases that such type of argument is defective. The segregation of backward pupils from the superior and the gifted children deprives the stimulus of the former and incentive of the latter. But in our opinion *a child below average does not get much incentive from a pupil much above him. He emulates rather a boy who is only a little ahead of him and whom he can overtake if he wills.* This method, therefore, can and should be adopted but provision and arrangements must be made for a periodic re-test and re-classification.

16.7 The Ungraded School

The latest research findings in child rearing and education have pointed out the unsuitability of graded schools for the normal development of the child. The graded pattern is compared with Procrustean standard. In the words of Goodland and Anderson, "Certain time-honoured practices of pupils' classification, while perhaps not lethal, trap school age travellers in much the same fashion as Procrustes has trapped the unwary. Then, the content of the work is laid out within the grade to be 'covered' and to a degree, 'mastered.' The slow are pulled and stretched to fit the grade. Sometimes because their God-given limbs lack enough elasticity – they are non-promoted or left behind, when perhaps another year of stretching will do the trick. The quick are compressed and contracted to fit the grade. In time, they learn to adept to a pace that is slower than their natural one."

Planned flexibility is a key to maximum growth.

The Education Commission also recommended that it would be desirable to treat the lower primary stage covering classes I to IV as an ungraded unit, because this would help the children coming from different backgrounds to advance at their own pace. As the conditions in most primary schools, however, are not favourable to the general adoption of this procedure, the Commission recommended that the experiment should be tried out in the beginning in classes I and II which should be regarded as a single ungraded unit. This will put an end to the existing practice of detentions in class I and the drop-outs and wastage resulting therefrom, and will also provide continuity and flexibility in the educational programme of the first two classes. The two year block may be divided into two groups, one for the slow learners and other for the fast learners to enable different pupils to proceed at the level of their ability and move from one unit to another. If the experiment regarding the ungraded unit succeeds in classes I and II, it may be extended to the remaining classes of the lower primary stage.

16.8 Promotion of Pupils

The last issue naturally raises the issue of the promotion of pupils. The promotion of the pupils is one of the most important problems confronting teachers and administrators. The effects of promotion upon the child and home are lasting and may be for good or evil. A failure may be the turning point in a pupil's life. It may cause him to put forth more effort and better school work, or it may cause him to take the opposite attitude. The philosophy the administrators have, affects their thinking on the question of promotions. Promotional practices are directly dependent upon the organisation, the administration and the curriculum carried on in a school system.

16.9 Principles of Promotion

One of the things that are often neglected by the administration of a school system is a positive promotion policy. It is the duty of the administrator to see that each school unit cooperatively works out definite promotion policies which may be followed by all teachers throughout the school system. These policies should be made known to all pupils and patrons of the school, so that there will be no misunderstanding by anyone concerned. There are certain principles which should be borne in mind. We now proceed to consider them.

(i) *Promotion should be decided on the basis of the individual pupils.*

(ii) *Promotion should be on the basis of many factors.* The final decision as to whether a particular pupil should be promoted should rest not merely on academic accomplishments, but also on what results in the greatest good to the all-round development of the individual.

(iii) *In order that promotion procedures may be more or less uniform throughout a particular school system, a definite set of factors should be agreed upon which each teacher will take into consideration in forming his judgement as to whether or not a particular pupil should be promoted.*

(iv) *Criteria for promotion must take into consideration the curriculum offerings of the next higher grade or units and the flexibility of its organisation, its courses of study and its methods.*

(v) *It is the duty of the next higher grade or unit to accept pupils who are properly promoted to it* – from the lower grade or unit and to adopt its work to fit the needs of those pupils.

(vi) *Promotion procedures demand continuous analysis and study of cumulative pupil case history record* in order that refinement of procedure may result and guess work and conjecture be reduced to a minimum.

(vii) *Promotion should not be dependent on any purely quantitative mathematical grade or combination of grades.* It should not be based on a single sort of measurement or on a set of tests given at a single time. But it should be a gradual process – beginning when the year's work begins and based on every task, that is done during that period.

(viii) *It should be a cooperative process in which the child is consciously participating.* Define standards of efficiency by which the child can daily judge his own work, should be kept before him. He should be required to criticise constantly his own attainments, discover his own deficiencies, and record his own standing.

(ix) *The reports to parents should be such as to keep them fully aware of the probability of advancement and means of avoiding demotion.* No friction should ever arise from questions of promotion. Such should be the spirit of the school and of its relations to parents that promotion would never be thought as a matter of favouritism. Neither teacher nor pupil should regard promoting a child as favouring him or retarding him or as a point on which there could be a difference of desire between them.

(x) *It is not the teacher's business to criticise and reject but to detect and demonstrate to the pupil his deficiencies and to guide him in remedying them.* A teacher who cannot locate the pupil's difficulty early in the year and plan with him remedial work or who does not know until the term is over that the child's work is sufficient for the promotion, should not be entrusted with the decision of the matter.

Keeping the pupils in suspense as to their promotion is an objectionable sort of incentive. It induces cramming and spasmodic efforts rather than sustained work. Reward for efforts, like punishment for wrong doing, should be so sure, so prompt and so obviously self-acting that just as soon as a child has done his duty well, he should know that so far as that task is concerned, he is already promoted. In a word, the rigid and arbitrary rule must give way to the flexible, sympathetic rule in matters of grading and organisation.

16.10 Examination as a Basis of Promotion

The formal examination, despite its educative usefulness, has been thoroughly discredited as a sole basis of promotion, because of the following reasons:

(i) It is not a reliable measure of attainment. Three sources of chance enter into its use - child's physical and mental condition at the time of examination, scope of the particular question asked, and different standards among teachers or of the same teacher at different times.

(ii) So far as formal examination tests anything, it tests appearances rather than real attainments, verbal memory rather than more useful abilities, the crammed knowledge of the examination day rather than the abilities which will be available in later life.

(iii) It has a pernicious effect on the pupil's study and habits of study. It puts a premium on neglecting work through the term and on cramming just before the examination. It rewards skill in "spotting, the teacher," "bluffing," memorising, and other temporary make-shifts rather than a true love of knowledge and desire for permanent growth. It is the devil's own device for leading pupils into temptation.

(iv) As an incentive to work, it fails to stimulate those who are most in need of being aroused while the over-sensitive and too ambitious are affected beyond reason or profit.

(v) The physical strain arising from examination promotion has brought nervous breakdown and even death in some cases to the most ambitious and deserving children.

16.11 Kinds of Promotion

(i) ***Annual Promotion:*** - The grading of school work on the annual basis and promotion of pupils at the end of each year has been the traditional form of promotions. These are not only economical but also easy to administer. There is no need of big class-rooms and a larger number of members on the staff. Subject matter of instruction can be organised and developed in large convenient units in annual system of promotions. This also gives scope for variation in the rate of progress, according to the difficulty of the matter dealt. The teacher has the same batch of pupils for a longer time and can know their needs better and thus can adopt the methods of work more effectively to their needs.

The main defect of the annual promotions is that a pupil who fails in one subject has unnecessarily to repeat the work of the whole year, even in the subjects in which he has attained a good standard. Repetition generally leads to dullness and an ultimate dislike for work. Moreover, definition of pupils does not give them sufficient chances to speed up their steps if they have missed somewhere.

(ii) ***Combined Annual and Terminal Promotions:*** - This is a compromise of the annual and terminal promotions. Average pupils might be promoted annually while superior ones might be promoted after short intervals. The main advantage of such a plan is that the average pupil is not over pushed while the superior one is

not pushed back. Each can go on his own pace. Under such type of promotion, the child of average ability has an opportunity for recapitulation and revision. The more intelligent and more industrious boy, promoted from lower class, has a chance to make good the ground lost in the first term.

(iii) ***One Hundred Percent Plan:*** - There are some schools in America which follows what is known as the one hundred percent promotion plan. This provides for so many years of school experience, during which all children move along with their age group without regard to subject-matter achievements. *Social maturity is the criterion for grouping*. Grade level is abandoned, and groups are designated as the "first year group", "fifth year group," or "twelfth year group," and so forth. *This plan of promotion really considers the development of the whole child not merely subject achievement as the major concern of the school*. When administrators, teachers and parents realise that children grow in all ways each day and each year, and that the total growth is the important problem of the school, the one hundred percent promotion plan will be considered and probably will be adopted on a much wider scale.

(iv) ***Trial Promotions:*** - Trial promotion is an administrative scheme of giving those pupils who fail or those who are known as "border line" cases a chance in the next higher grade or subject. Experiments show that a large percentage of those pupils who are given trial promotions do about as well in the next grade as they did in the past year and better than some who are regularly promoted. The success of the pupil who has been promoted on trial depends upon his attitude and maturity and upon the ability of the teacher to make the necessary adjustments that will help the child to succeed. There are administrators and teachers who are very much opposed to trial promotions. They feel that the effect of demotion, if found necessary, will be far more harmful to the pupil than outright failure.

(v) ***Semi-annual Promotions:*** -It is argued that promoting twice a year would reduce the amount of retardation and at the same time accelerate the brighter pupils. But this plan appears to be much more expensive to operate. It also fails to make the necessary changes in the school to meet the need of the individuals. It makes two entrance dates for the first grade children all right but this often proves to be a disadvantage in those cases where children enter the first grade in the middle of the year and move to a school which do not have semi-annual promotions.

(vi) ***Special or Double Promotions:*** - In some school, there is a fad among school people to give certain pupils who have high achievement in subject-matter a double promotion. The entire basis for such promotion is social maturity, health, and age. The argument advanced in favour of special or double promotion is that it gives the superior child a chance to work at his own level of ability. But this type of promotion often puts very young immature children into older group of pupils with whom they are socially maladjusted. It causes teachers additional problems because of the immaturity of children and the diversity of interests. Special or double promotion is not advisable except when pupil is overage or more mature than his classmates, as well as more advanced in subject-matter achievement. So, many factors must be considered before a child is denied a year's experience in the school.

(vii) ***Subject Promotions:***- Subject promotion has never been followed to a great extent in the lower elementary grades but has been used extensively in junior and senior high schools. If a pupil carries four subjects in the high school and fails in one, he repeats only the subject in which he failed. This is a sort of school adjustment which can be of great help to the individual. However, if a pupil fails in a subject he will have to make up the deficiency in some manner before he can graduate in time. The common methods used for making up such failures are by having private tuitions or attending some academies. But this practice is not sound because if a child cannot do satisfactory work with a normal load, he certainly will not do satisfactorily work with a greater than normal load.

16.12 Solution of Promotion Problems

It is generally seen that most schemes for securing better promotional practices have not been entirely satisfactory, especially to the individual pupil. For this very reason, the solution of the promotion problems lies in better classification practices and better adaptation of the subject matter to the needs of the individual pupil. The schools must devote more time to studying individuals and to a consideration of changes in the curriculum and in the methods of instruction to meet the needs of all pupils. A better teacher-pupil understanding will solve many promotion problems.

If the pupil understands his interests, abilities, and capacities, if he is assisted in making a wise choice of a programme of work, and if the methods of instruction are adapted to the individual, there is little reason for pupil failure. If the pupil has put in his best efforts the school should accept his work as satisfactory. In most cases, it is not the student who fails; it is the school that fails. The school that is serving "all the children of all the people" cannot hold them to identical standards of subject matter achievement. *"The achievement of each pupil must be evaluated in terms of his ability and not in terms of a mythical grade standard."*

The Effects of Non-promotion:- After all that has been written and said concerning promotion practices, one still finds a great number of children, approximately 10 percent of all pupils going to school, failing each year. In some school system, certain teachers are responsible for most failures, while in other schools, teachers of the same grades or subjects are responsible for few failures.

The effects of non-promotion upon the pupils, the school, and the community are numerous. The greatest loss is to the pupil. He becomes a retarded pupil and must repeat the grade or subject. He loses his self-respect and may become maladjusted in every way. His friends, his parents and the members of the community look upon him as an incompetent person. He will develop an inferiority complex, and leave school as soon as possible with a very bitter feeling. There is no way to measure the actual damage done to society by the failures in our schools. This problem is so great that teachers, administrators, and citizens should work cooperatively to make the schools more meaningful in the lives of all pupils.

The dropping out is the result of the feeling of a lack of confidence, interest or satisfaction in the pupils. A majority of those pupils, who drop-out of school, do not feel they are getting a desirable type of education. The education imparted in the school should be made meaningful to the pupils so that they might take full interest in it and chances for failures be lessened.

16.13 Special Classes for the Exceptional Children

We have discussed in the foregoing pages the methods of classification for the normal children. But in every country there are children who are sub-normal or super-normal. The nation owes a special duty towards these children – as it is in the interest of the nation itself to increase the level of intelligence to as high a degree as possible.

Education of the Exceptional Child

In 1859, Darwin brought out his "Origin of Species." This book formed the basis of

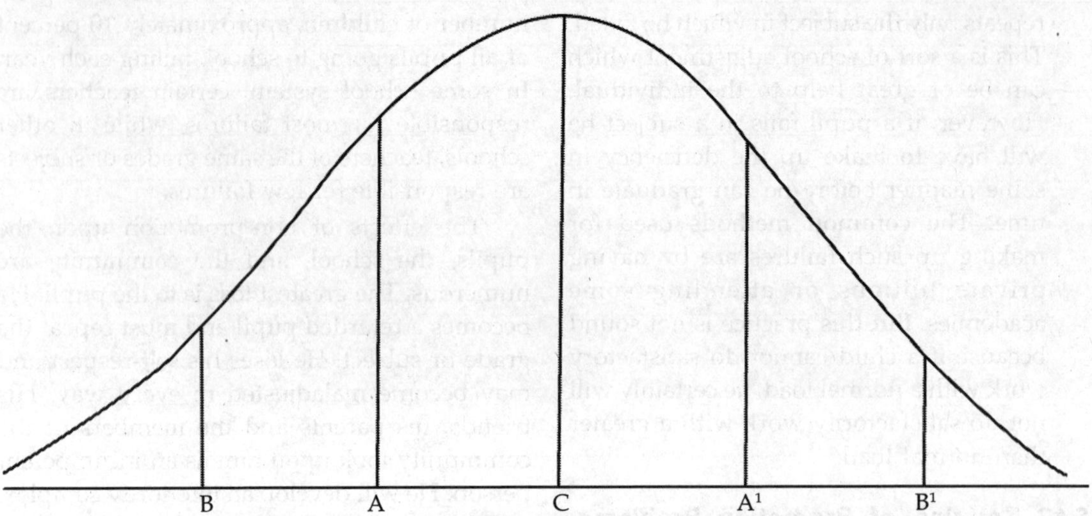

Fig. 1

recognition of individual differences. Sir Francis Galton followed Darwin's work and stimulated further study towards this aspect of human life by publishing his work 'Hereditary Genius.' Terman believed that this was the beginning of an era of strong interest in individual differences. The study of individual differences, however, required better statistical tools and Karl Person developed the techniques for analysing and describing the patterns of individual differences.

Psychological studies have definitely concluded that individuals differ not only in physical characteristics but also in mental, emotional, and social traits. Almost any trait, if objectively measured for a large unselected group, will be distributed somewhat like the curve shown below. In statistical terminology, this curve is known as the normal probability curve. The vertical height at any point shows the number of cases that lie at that point. Thus, many cases pile up round a central point but go on decreasing and decreasing as we move in either direction from the central point. In the figure, 'C' is the central position. About two-thirds of the total number of cases lie between A and A′ and about 95 percent of cases lie between B and B′.

The usually accepted definition of 'exceptional child' is that exceptional child is he who differs markedly in physical, mental, emotional, or social traits from an average child. On account of this marked difference, the exceptional child needs special educational services. However, children who deviate to the point that they require special medical or psychological treatment are not included in the class of exceptional children as defined above. They are abnormal cases and cannot be taken care of in ordinary classroom situation.

Two types of exceptional pupils are discussed here – (1) the gifted children, and (2) the feeble-minded or retarded children. This classification is based on mental characteristics rather than physical, emotional, or social traits. According to the various studies made by psychologists, the Intelligent Quotients (the ratio of the mental age is determined by the intelligence tests to the chronological age multiplied by 100) are classified as follows:

Classification of Intelligence Quotients

	Classification	Intelligence Quotient
1.	Near Genius or Genius	140 or more
2.	Very Superior	130-139
3.	Superior	120-129
4.	Above Average	110-119
5.	Average or Normal	90-109
6.	Below Average	80-89
7.	Dull	70-79
8.	Feeble-minded	50-69
9.	Idiot	49 or less.

In a very large number of children, about two and a half percent will be found to have an I.Q. of 120 and above and approximately the same percentage having an I.Q. of 80 or less. About one percent of the total number of children in a group can be classified as very superior and about the same number as feeble-minded. Thus, in a school population of a thousand children, it may be expected that ten children would have I.Q.'s of 130 or higher and five I.Q.'s of 140 or better. Similarly, ten children or near about, would have I.Q.'s of 170 or less and about five I.Q.'s of 60 or less. *Children with I.Q.'s of 130 and above and 70 or below are extreme cases. They are exceptional children. The former are 'gifted children' and the latter are known as 'feeble-minded or retarded children.'*

Contrary to the common belief, studies have proved that both the gifted and feeble-minded come from all racial stocks and economic level. Both sexes are included in the two categories. However, majority of the gifted children belong to the favourable socio-economic status, and a very substantial majority among the retarded come from the lower levels of social and economic strata. Furthermore, studies made by psychologists reveal that traits of the gifted are inherited. Training can only develop these traits but cannot create them. Similarly, the incomplete maturation among the feeble-minded children is apparent from birth or begins to show from very early age.

Exceptional children are basically like other children. They have all the needs, desires, and physical energy of children in general. However, specific exceptional conditions in them require special services in their educational programme. These children need emphasis on the individualisation of classroom work. Success should always be defined in terms of the goals that each individual sets for himself. These goals, in turn, should be selected in the light of the abilities that an individual possesses. If the goals are too high, the individual will meet frustration and thereby create more problems for himself. *It is laudable for an intellectually superior child to work for high honours; it is tragic if a very dull child makes a similar attempt. It is praiseworthy for the gifted track athlete to attempt to run hundred yards dash in less than ten seconds; it would be ridiculous for an average college student to try to do so.*

Education of the Retarded Pupils

(1) Different types of retarded children: Retardation, like superiority in a child, may be physical, emotional, social, or moral, but generally the psychologists use the term 'retarded children' for children with I. Q.'s lower than 90, i.e. children who are intellectually retarded. There are various names and classifications of the children with lower I.Q.'s as given in the table above. The lowest group is called 'idiots.' They have the most severe degree of mental deficiency. Even as adults, idiots cannot take care of themselves and are unfit for any occupational task. Their mental development never exceeds that of the child of five or six. Feeble-minded are the next category. Under favourable conditions, feeble-minded children can be taught to take care of themselves and their daily needs. They can be taught to master the rudiments of school learning. They can learn some simple skill in some of the simpler occupations. They reach their mental maturity by the age of fifteen, but their mental age ranges from six to twelve years. Both these categories require special type of schooling. The idiots are usually institutionalised, i.e. they are sent to mental hospitals, where environments are shaped to fit the needs of such children.

Contrary to the common belief, studies have proved that both the gifted and the feeble-minded come from all racial stocks and economic levels. Both sexes are included in the two categories.

Children with I.Q.'s of 70 or more are to be found in usual schools. They can be divided into two groups: (1) Below average with I.Q.'s ranging between 80 and 89, (2) Dull with I.Q.'s ranging between 70 and 79. Large proportions of children in these two groups are 'trouble makers' in the school. The 'troublesomeness' of such children does not arise, however, because they have low I.Q.'s and hence, have a special bent of mind to get into trouble. The trouble lies in the fact that too high demands are put on them and they cannot come up to these demands. They are required to keep pace with the average children, to learn the same thing at the same rate. The speed is too fast for them, and therefore, they cannot enjoy the satisfaction that comes with achievement. They soon realise that others are much better and that they are no good. This creates feelings of frustration in them. *They have to be changed into normal children and educated to become useful members of the society.*

Psychologists believe that intelligence is native. Every person is born with a fixed amount of intelligence. It appears when the child is a month or two old and develops in spurts, followed by periods of consolidation up to the age of 16. At that age it reaches the maximum and thereafter, it begins to decline. The retarded child is born with the same type of mind as a normal child, but for some reasons, it stops growing very early, or grows very slowly. Such a child fails to learn at the rate and in the manner as the brilliant child does. There are two reasons for failure to learn. In the first place, failure to learn is due to both psychological and physiological conditions which are inherent in the pupil's constitution. Secondly, there are the environmental reasons. There is lack of opportunities for overcoming the remedial handicaps.

In order to provide educational facilities for the dull children, they could be put in a special class of an ordinary school attended by other normal children. Dull children are likely to have smaller gap between ability and achievement than the children of average intelligence. Care in imparting them instruction at their rate of learning, will help them to realise their potentialities. It is advisable to reduce the level of expectation for these children and give them work better suited to their abilities and needs. A change in the curriculum or a reduction in the number of subjects taught will help. Studies have shown that there is relatively little correlation between mental and motor abilities. Those, who achieve high positions in mental abilities, do not necessarily achieve the same high positions in motor abilities. Nor do the low achievers in mental abilities remain low in motor abilities. There are, therefore, many everyday skills, that do not require any amount of inventiveness and problem solving that could be taught to the less intelligent children. In ordinary subjects also remedial help could be given to the dull children. Methods could certainly be followed that arouse their interests rather than embarrass them. Of course, this requires an understanding and friendly teachers.

Although good traits tend to be positively correlated, they are by no means perfectly correlated. A child, who is less bright, has potentialities for acquiring good social relationships with others. Proper attention to the moral and emotional education of the retarded children would yield fruitful results in making them useful members of the society. They should be taught to live and mix freely and happily with their own kind and with normal children and adults. This would help them to make social adjustment and develop attitudes necessary for community living. Opportunities should be provided to them for the full expression of their interests and aptitudes. They would then acquire self-confidence, consistency, and emotional stability. Their moral sense should be developed by teaching them to differentiate between right and wrong. They should be made amenable to the uplifting influence of religious education and practices.

(2) Role of parents and teachers: In educating retarded children, the relationship between child, his parents, and his teachers is very important. On the nature of these relationships depends the success or failure of educating the retarded. Since, they need love and security more than the normal children need, both teachers and parents should show sympathy and continued kindness. They should infuse in them confidence and not scare them. Right atmosphere, specially trained teachers and suitable methods and materials are sure to promote the all-round development of the retarded children. They will certainly make progress commensurate with their limited abilities and aptitudes. In the tasks that lie ahead, those of us who are working with exceptional children have a very significant role to play. If the teachers have the insight, ability, and energy to give the pupils timely assistance, we shall have the children well-poised physically and also mentally. This assistance should comprise guidance and understanding, sympathetic but realistic building of morals which will help each person to adjust, and exerting extraordinary efforts in properly placing and following up each of the exceptional children.

(3) Early identification is necessary: It is desirable that the exceptional children should be identified clearly in order that a long term programme of education may be planned. Every year a survey should be made in each school. Many fields of diagnosis are necessary. It is essential that the child's I.Q., his sensory powers, his interests and his emotional characteristics, attitudes, anxieties and conflicts, his interests and aptitudes, and his personal and family history must be studied. Treatment, curricula, and methods should be formulated after recording these findings. Unless a careful diagnosis is made, the programme for exceptional children cannot function and exceptional children are lost in their hopeless competition with children of regular grades.

The soundest policy is that education must fit every boy and girl according to his or her unique nature and needs. It is time to consolidate efforts for all types of children - normal as well as exceptional - support for the crippled is worthy, but it is no more worthy than for the child with a reading disability, with a feeble-minded set-up. *The conscience of democracy requires that efforts must be directed towards an educational programme for all – the genius, the normal, and the retarded. It is then that we shall have a generation with the desire and ability for work and activity suitable for their abilities and aptitudes.*

16.14 Education of the Gifted Pupils in Secondary Schools

A perpetual and compelling challenge to the earnest teacher is posed by talented (gifted) pupils in whichever class they may be. In the sixth grade, Ravi displays unusual ability in science and mathematics. Pawan is extraordinarily adept in verbal comprehension and vocabulary. In the seventh grade, the teacher discerns that Dickey has persistent curiosity and deep interest in science, and Rajan is always "off the beaten track." In the eighth grade, Gagan has caught his eyes by his ability to analyse, reason, and organise. The teacher of ninth grade is happy to have Deepak in his class on account of his proficiency in all subjects. Then there is Raman who has set up a new university record in the Matriculation Examination.

It is obvious that *talented pupils are different from one another as each child is different from every other child.* This individuality in talents creates many problems for the teacher. They have to devise ways to keep these pupils profitably engaged while most of their time and energies are consumed by average and below-average pupils. It is a well-known fact that average and below-average students constitute a large majority in every class. It is also a hard fact that teaching in most schools is beamed to the "mythical average." No teacher worth his salt has found the final answer to running a classroom where everybody learns to his maximum.

High creative children have got their own problems. They are generally in a fix – they must either repress their creativity or learn to cope with the tensions which arise from being in a minority. Repression of creative needs may result in personality breakdown. Loneliness, conflicts, and other problems of adjustment come in the wake of this breakdown. A small proportion of the talented show serious maladjustment – they find it difficult to adjust with those whose abilities and interests differ greatly from their own - they find the textbooks and instruction dull and boring. Researches have revealed that average individuals, who are either over-ambitious or 'grade-conscious' will do tiresome and boring things. On the other hand, the talented will persevere with a zeal comparable to Edison's if they are given genuine motivation, whether it is for pure creativeness or for learning an ordinary skill. To teach such a group is not at all easy. To direct the spontaneity and talent of the bright is admittedly delightful, stimulating, and satisfying, but it must be pointedly stressed that the task is exacting, if not exhausting. The needs of the talented have to be studied by educators who come into contact with them.

Researches have shown that talented children maintain their lead throughout life. If proper guidance is given to them, they are able to adjust themselves in life. Their great inner resources enable them to succeed in human relationships and make a mark in life.

Education of the gifted essential: - Today, the group of academically talented pupils is more neglected than any other group of exceptional children. It must be conceded that superior intellectual endowment is significant both for the individual possessing it and the society that needs them. It is thus for the teachers to be imaginative enough to develop the talents so that they can ultimately be beneficial to the society. *Superiority needs nurture to maximise nature.* Harvey Zorbough has rightly said, "Superior children are the accident of birth, superior adults are the result of the training." Education must, therefore, aim at the maximum possible development of every boy and girl according to his or her own unique nature and needs. Special amenities must be provided to facilitate learning and expedite educational and social adjustments. Remember, the talented child in India is asking for a right guaranteed by the Constitution – equality of opportunity for obtaining a full education which will help him acquire the social pattern necessary to live well with his fellowmen. There is nothing undemocratic in providing a superior education for any student who is able to profit by such education. Mass education must not be taken to mean, 'reduction of the best to the level of the average.' For the pupil who has special abilities or interests and also ample energy – there is no reason why he should not be encouraged to be himself. If a talented person does not fit into the standard "round" mould, he should be allowed to have a few sharp edges. There should not be any attempt to round them off.

All able youth will not be the same. There are many kinds of abilities. It is the job of the educator to identify and appreciate individual differences, encourage and develop the special talent possessed by the pupils under his charge. The potential leaders, discoverers, scientists, inventors, thinkers, educators, must not be neglected. They must not be driven to develop their own skills in their own way and in terms of personal initiative alone. Superior talent calls for special attention and opportunities. Under the present circumstances the demand for trained manpower is increasing day by day. Any loss of talent must be viewed with alarm. No effort should be spared to enlarge the talent pool and to minimise waste consequent upon oversight. More adequate programmes will have to be evolved in secondary schools for developing the potentialities of the talented.

Identification of the talented, determination of characteristics, and the development of necessary services present difficulties to the teacher. Discussions about the talented are usually about the following points: -

How to discover them? Where to discover them, within or outside school? How to treat them after they have been discovered?

Interest in the first point is caused by the worry that, since many of the talented pupils never gets to college; something should be done about them at the earliest.

Teachers, normally, do not bother about discovery and cultivation of "genius." Genius is too rare, too mysterious, and too unmanageable for a school system to adapt itself to even if it knew how. The problems of the teacher are "what should be done for the student who does the same kind of work as his fellow students do but does it faster, more accurately, in larger volume, or better than they? How is a particular child able to undertake and complete task after task? It should be borne in mind by the teacher that a student, who has persistence coupled with high energy, can produce better results than another who is able but less interested and energetic. The following factors have to be considered: -

The background to which the individual has been subjected, the way in which he is superior to others in his complex mental organisation; the depth and nature of his interest; his energy level; the strength and persistence of his motivation. The task of properly identifying all of these academically talented students (who if given the chance, will become the educated, trainer thinkers of tomorrow) is no small one. It is one of the primary duties of the secondary school to so organise its educational programme that the talented may be fully involved, more fully developed.

16.15 The Programme for Educating the Talented

Educating the academically talented involves total educational planning - curriculum, instruction, administration, guidance, resources, teacher preparation and community relationships. Improving provisions for the academically talented is not simply a matter of changing a course of study or a class; it rather involves broader study and planning. Where good programmes are operating, there is evidence of an attempt to coordinate all aspects of the educational process.

No single pattern for educating the talented pupils can be recommended for the diverse secondary schools. Although every school must discharge its responsibilities and development of academic talent, no structural mould can be expected to apply equally to all secondary schools. The problems of an appropriate programme for able students are too complex to yield to a quick and easy formula which will apply equally to all secondary schools. For the talented, *the school administration can make special arrangements for acceleration, grouping and enrichment, extension of experiences in and out of school, 'use of community resources' and 'guidance and counseling.'* No single adaption is guaranteed to fit all kinds and degrees of academic talent. Each calls for considerable study, to be followed by testing in local situation.

It has been established by research that talented pupils prefer occupations that are intellectually demanding. They profit most if they are allowed to progress at a rapid pace and when they are given more freedom in specialised subjects. An unquenchable curiosity enables many to concentrate for a long period of time and to work for remote goals not contemplated by average children. For this very reason, the *principle of enrichment in regular classes* is gaining increasing support. Stress can be laid on such activities and experiences as *creative pursuits, differentiated assignments, discussions, independent study, unit work, workshops, experiments, special projects, directed reading programmes, etc.*

(i) *A programme of intensive work in specific subject-matter is worthy, educationally sound and indeed necessary for the proper education of talented students.* Intensive work of a high level in different subjects may be undertaken. The aim should not be to accelerate the pace of learning and not to give extra-coaching. They should not be even tutored to jump through high hoops. So, the aim should be to provide such a kind of teaching work as shall, by its depth and breadth, truly challenge the mind and character of the students on the one hand and resourcefulness and imagination of the teachers on the other hand. Every conceivable effort should be made to provide experiences for increasing or improving their interests, for developing their skills and for stimulating their creative abilities. Tedium such pupils cannot stand. *They will persevere with a zeal comparable to Edison's if they are genuinely motivated.* Motivation may be for pure creativity or for learning an ordinary skill. There should be special activity rooms where talented pupils can work together on advanced projects. Their abilities can be directed into constructive channels by such projects as afford opportunities for rich literary experiences, extensive use of the library, scientific investigation, varied speech activities, creative expression in writing practical application of knowledge and meaningful social activities.

There is, *these days, a trend to pay special attention to gifted children.* But it is not a good educational practice to single them out and give them a label. On the one hand, it is to be assured that no child is denied free association with other children; on the other hand, special classes may be started for the talented.

An effective use of personnel resources in school and community should be made. Ways should be found for bringing enthusiastic young minds into contact with imaginative and mature minds in formal or informal encounters. For example, there may be arranged evening seminars, involving research scientists. Mature high school students should be free to spend time with persons who can serve as "models."

(ii) *Some teachers say that double promotion is a good expedient to effect adjustment of the school programme to the special needs of the talented.* Their plea is that double promotion or grade skipping provides an incentive for learning; it maintains interest and prevents boredom. Holding back talented pupils may result in loss or interest. Consequently, they are likely to become slack or careless in work. Such students should be helped to move at their normal pace which will naturally be faster than the others. This device may be termed as *Acceleration*. It is one of the means of providing for the special needs of this group. The tradition that every student should spend three years in a secondary school disregards the capacity of the academically talented to surpass others and go ahead rapidly. It also does not take into account the resultant delay in completing college work. Such delay is quite avoidable in the case of academically talented student.

In terms of career readiness, it may be stated that rapid learners not only prepare for their careers more fully through "accelerating" but also have more years ahead for creative work and leadership. *Failure to accelerate these boys and girls in harmony with their potentialities may be a disservice to them.* They may waste their time in school, may be insufficiently motivated, and may be delayed in getting into suitable vocations. Further, a judicious amount of acceleration may result in a greater development of the individual's capacities, may motivate them towards higher achievements, and may instill a greater sense of responsibility.

One of the chief arguments advanced against double promotion, acceleration of grade skipping is that it places the child in competition with older pupils and thus adds to his problems of social adjustment. There is as much danger of social and emotional imbalance from retardation as from acceleration. Research studies prove that the disadvantages of acceleration have been exaggerated. Academically talented boys and girls who enter college early achieve, in the main, well-rounded growth and satisfactory personal adjustment; they tend to lead their classes scholastically and to participate fully in college life. Terman's work with gifted children shows that children who enter college early achieve in the main, well-rounded growth and satisfactory personal adjustment; they tend to lend their classes scholastically and to participate fully in college life. Terman's work with gifted children has shown that their interests are a useful index to their general social adjustment. Other things being equal, the child who has wholesome interests in the things about him, in his companions, in reading, in school, is probably happier and better adjusted than the child who has no such interests. Moreover, girls do not seem to encounter the social problems that some boys do. Girls also do not mind being among the younger members of a class. Apparently, their earlier maturing enables them to adjust faster to new groups. So, more girls than boys may be accelerated. But no hard and fast rule can be laid down with regard to amount of acceleration.

(iii) Under ordinary circumstances, the average teacher is agitated over the problem of genuine enrichment of the educational programme. He has to meet the requirement of talented pupils. *Separation from the rest* of the pupils is another way of paying special attention to the talented. It is assumed that special classes with special teachers would lead to greater utilisation of the abilities of the pupils. Moreover, there is nothing unreasonable in the expectation that non-graded, homogenous grouping would have a desirable effect on the social and emotional adjustment of some children. The average works nearer the limit of their capacities. They learn the fundamentals better and they get an opportunity for shouldering social and civic responsibilities and privileges not usually enjoyed by other pupils of their abilities. They are able to complete successfully. They gain fresh confidence and joy in being elected class representatives and office bearers in various pupil service organisations. The slow child would seem to have a better chance to develop a sense of personal adequacy, since he is no longer inevitably the low man on the *totem pole* as far as his classmates are concerned. The fast child would seldom feel rejected by his immediate classmates because he is a "brain." Moreover, the talented will enjoy the privilege of being together. They may achieve greater depth on their studies, more technical skill, broader background, richer experience and more companionship with their peers than those in regular class-groups. In May, 1952 the Bureau of Educational Research, Division of Tests and Measurement, New York reported on the performances of intellectually talented children in special classes. The children had been matched on the basis of the school attended, grade placement, sex, mental age, chronological age, and other factors. These matched pairs were tested, and after 14 months were retested for academic achievement, for personal and social adjustment, and for interests and attitudes. The evidence showed that talented children in special progress classes make significantly superior gains in their achievement in comparison with their peers in normal progress classes. It is clear, therefore, that *if disciplines and subjects needed by a talented child can be taught better through homogeneous grouping, there should be no hesitation in forming such groups. The talented should constitute a separate section.*

While having special groups of the talented, the following precautions should be taken: -

(i) One criterion for special grouping should be ability in individual subject; it should not be "across the board" grouping in all subjects. The "track plan" on which a student is assigned to a special group, even though he may not be talented in all of the areas is not to be adopted.

(ii) The number of special groups into which a student may be placed may in some instances be limited to two or three, regardless of his ability; or some students may be in special groups in all subjects.

(iii) The flow both into and out of the special groups should be free. The 'late bloomer' concept justifies this view. There are other sound reasons for keeping the identification a perpetual process. Children do not develop in a smooth, orderly way; they sometimes develop by spurts.

(iv) There should be at least 300 students before such grouping is undertaken.

Screening of students for classification, and formation of special groups are specific problems. They require to be solved.

Enrichment of Curriculum

Special classes may or may not be formed but the curriculum must be enriched for the talented. Instruction must be tailored to meet their requirements. There can be enrichments without acceleration; but such acceleration does not provide enrichment in school studies is of doubtful value. The education of a boy of superior intellect should emphasise experiences and activities that effectively challenge his ability, provide opportunity for initiative and originality, offer a number of activities for the learning and development of interests, and form the basis for socially significant values. Their education should be rich, stimulating, and dramatic. The talented pupils must be provided multifarious experiences, in art and music, with machines and things, with people and groups, as well as with ideas, symbols, and relationships. They should be given a sound general education in the humanities, the social sciences, and the natural sciences. Such a general education should consist, however, of something more than exposure to some of the knowledge of particular disciplines. There should be opportunities for creative exploration in various areas of living and learning. The curriculum must have meaning and purpose for them otherwise they may tend to place a premium upon school marks and competitions.

Scholarships, honour societies, science fairs, and mathematical teams are motivating influences for many boys and girls. Special science projects release the creative energy of students and spur them to seek, 'postures new and to extend frontiers on their own.' They are powerful motivating factors. Opportunities for independent study should be there. Constructive summer time projects, extensive use of the libraries and laboratories and museums should be encouraged. Community resources should be constantly explored for appropriate activities to enrich the education of able students. In many instances community leaders would be found willing to serve as speakers and leaders for student groups. They would enlighten the students about recent industrial and scientific development.

Perhaps, the best way to serve talented pupils is 'keep out of their way.' Genuine distinction should be allowed to emerge unhindered. The rigidity and number of requirements, the inflexibility of transfer work between school and departments, the demand that things be studied in formalised sequence are major repressions to spontaneity and to superior work. No matter how one rationalises it, the interferences of institutional management are a major impediment to individual student treatment. And yet within even these limitations there are many things which the teacher, and even more the student, can do to make school career distinctively rich.

16.16 Need of Articulation among Elementary, Secondary and College Stages

There is an urgent need of articulation among elementary, secondary, and college stages for the benefit of the talented. The problem of articulation is largely concerned with communication. The problems of articulation and closer relationship among teachers in elementary, secondary schools and colleges should be understood clearly. Schools have a responsibility in identifying the talented, helping them to determine their objectives, and tailoring the instruction to meet the requirements. Colleges should establish an agency to discover what advanced work has been done. Such advanced work is given credit. Everything possible should be done to provide for the advanced placement of academically talented pupils. Articulation between elementary and secondary schools may be facilitated by such devices as:

(i) System-wide organisations built around feeder schools with membership made up largely of teachers from kindergarten through senior high school.

(ii) System-wide meetings between subject area teachers in the middle and high schools.

Here are a few suggestions for improving articulation between high and higher secondary schools and colleges:

(i) There should be organised state-level inter-visitation conferences composed of high school and college faculties, which include visitation at the universities and in the high and higher secondary schools.

(ii) The development of a plan which would (a) involve inviting high school teachers to teach for a period of time in the universities, and (b) provide an opportunity to university professors to teach in the high school.

Articulation between schools and colleges will be improved if all academically talented pupils take a programme of fundamental subjects vital to both the college and the non-college pupil. Their subjects should contribute to education for citizenship. Languages, mathematics, foreign languages, science, and history should be studied intensively.

Certain economic barriers, if removed, would enable the talented to make more of his opportunities. Special fees, charges for extra-curricular activities or the need to go to work at the earliest possible moment, force many talented students to give up their studies. Take the student who is driven by poverty to expend his time and energy in un-academic employment and the equally talented student who is free to devote himself to his studies; the latter has a great advantage over the former: one cannot pull a rickshaw and read a book at the same time. *Adequate financial support to the talented in every form is necessary so that no valuable talent is wasted for lack of financial support.*

16.17 Role of Parents and Teachers

Studies show that talented pupils are most likely to develop in accord with their promise if they have the good fortune to have parents who offer them appropriate stimulation and encouragement. It is a tragic fact that many talented pupils are unfortunate in this respect. So the school must seek to identify and encourage them. Moreover, even if a talented pupil comes from a stimulating home environment, he needs the help of the teachers in exploring and enriching his interests and in developing skills and attitudes. Thus the teacher should first discover or identify that talent and then make sure that no talent is wasted. Mentally superior children are anything but mediocre. The teacher should realise that their bright, inquiring minds and excessive energy are likely to produce problems for teachers. Teachers must be keen observers so that the potential of the talented is invariably discovered; they must capture their desires and remould them into goals. Teachers should promote the urge, locate the potential, formulate the appropriate challenge, kindle the light in eyes, and produce the thrill of knowing! If a talented student has any interests, these must be encouraged. If he shows a special talent, it must be sharpened. The teacher, with warmth and sensitivity, must help the students define his personal goals and self-concepts.

The talented youth has a wide variety to choose from. He needs help in understanding the alternatives, in estimating his own potentialities and in seeking the possible consequences of decisions. Indeed, *guidance must be comprehensive, continually available, and realistic in terms of desirable educational objectives.* For this very reason, the importance of the teacher as a model, inspire-guide, and provider of challenge is generally recognised. The teacher of the academically talented should have an exceptional degree, some of the qualifications expected of all teachers, e.g. a good mind, broad intellectual curiosity, creativeness, energy, experience, enthusiasm, emotional balance, personality, and a deep interest in students as individuals.

For handling the talented, more than anything else, *inspirational teaching* is required. It depends on the drive from within the teacher to make a difference in someone else. Superior teaching of superior students requires superior teachers. This does not mean that the teachers should have an I.Q. comparable to that of their pupils. They should be emotionally balanced and be able to work with pupils brighter than themselves. The greater the training and skill a teacher has in recognising individual differences among pupils, the better he can meet the needs of the academically talented. Talent of pupils can be exposed only in the influence of experienced teachers.

Greater cooperation between teachers of the same subjects at different levels is urgently needed. Special courses, workshops, and institutes designed to bring together academic scholars and able high school teachers concerned with deep understanding of their subjects as well as the most effective teaching of these should be available in increasing numbers. Teachers may be encouraged to undertake more research. For this purpose, they should be given relief in work.

In the case of many talented pupils, inspiration from books, audio-visual aids also accelerate learning. Teachers should, therefore, build up their own libraries and constantly improve their interests and skills.

16.18 Role of Counsellors

Counsellors can also play a great part in guiding the talented. They can identify able boys and girls through careful study of cumulative records as well as by the interview with students and their parents. They can often pass on to teachers' information and suggestions that will be helpful in understanding and motivating the student.

16.19 Conclusion

The problems of guiding the talented are too complex to yield wholesome and definite results. Much research is needed in such areas as critical thinking, creativity, attitudes, interests, motivation, high ability-low achievers, classroom methods and materials, subject matter content, supply of teachers, the quality of teaching, and the dimensions of a successful programme for the academically talented.

On the secondary schools fall the big responsibility of training the nation's brain-power to the highest potential. No effort should be spared to offer guidance and stimulation, education and training to the talented in the school. There must be a special curriculum, special classes, and special funds. Let teachers and schools be adequately equipped to make creative scientists, engineers, philosophers, historians, economists, psychologists, educators, writers, out of the rough and raw but promising material.

Objective Type Questions

Multiple Choice Questions (Tick ✓ the right option)

(1) The pupils are the legitimate occupants of the
- (a) Society
- (b) School
- (c) Community
- (d) None of the above

(2) The size of class would depend on the grade of the
- (a) School
- (b) Atmosphere
- (c) Both 'a' and 'b'
- (d) None of the above

Fill in the blanks

(1) The __________ of the pupils is one of the most important problems confronting teachers and administrators. [Promotion]

(2) _________ have a severe degree of mental deficiency. [Idiots]

Important Questions

1. Study the Admission Procedures in your state. Suggest improvements.
2. Discuss the causes of Drop-out Behaviour. What measures will you suggest to increase the holding power of the schools?
3. How are children classified in the schools you are familiar with? Suggest improvements in the classification process.
4. If the teachers fail to ensure regular attendance of pupils in the classes, all teaching will become haphazard. Comment and suggest measures for ensuring regular attendance of pupils.
5. What disadvantages do you find in allowing the class to continue as a teaching unit? What methods would you suggest to make the class more elastic?
6. What criteria should form the basis for classification of pupils in schools? How does the present unsatisfactory system of classification create problems of indiscipline?
7. Discuss the factors for determining the size of a class. What are the administrative objections to (a) small classes, (b) large classes?
8. Study the promotional practices of your state. Suggest improvements.

9. Discuss the reasons for and against special classes for the exceptional children.
10. What arrangements would you make in a secondary school for the education of the (a) Retarded children, (b) Gifted children?

Unit III

School Plants

17

School Building and Furniture

The school plant is a factor of tremendous importance in education. The more the emphasis on speeding up the learning process, the more will be the emphasis on good learning environment. Non-functional, meagerly equipped, and unattractively decorated school plants have given place to plants with superior lighting, attractive decoration, comfortable seating, useful service facilities such as library, multipurpose room, functional playgrounds, and classrooms with chalk and bulletin boards, sinks, work areas, filing and storage facilities, and pupil's lockers. Although because of financial handicaps, all these requirements may not be met, this is the ideal. It is necessary that our school plants become the learning laboratories. They should provide opportunities for the child to do his own study, a group to study real problems, to think together, to arrive at conclusions, and to plan constructive programmes; and a community meeting place for the year-round educational, recreational programmes.

17.1 Meaning of School Plant

The school plant is now a very broad concept. It includes classroom, library, laboratory, playground, furniture, apparatus, teaching aids, supporting devices which are used in school functioning.

There is rapid expansion of schools and colleges to meet the requirements of our society. It is a serious problem of our education system. The school infrastructure requires funds in the very beginning to start with. There is continuous increase of educational institutions from primary stage to university level. This problem had the adverse effect on the student's performance as well as quality of education.

Every one realises the need and importance of school infrastructure. It is the second home of students during daytime. The Kothari Commission (1964-66) has very rightly stated in its opening sentence that, "The destiny of India is being shaped in her classroom." The classroom is the basic unit of a school and schools are units of our education system of the country. The schools and educational institutions have a great importance for our society, community, and national development. The quality and standard of an educational institution is assessed by its physical infrastructure which has all types of facilities available for the students in a school.

Now, there is a rapid growth of schools and colleges in private sectors as to earn money by establishing attractive infrastructures of institutions but quality of education is not being paid due attention in the self-financing institutions.

The physical infrastructure is the aspect of school management. The lack of facilities of classroom has introduced the two shift system in our schools mainly in aided institutions. Everyone cannot afford to send their wards to private CBSE Board affiliated schools. They charge very high fees from the students. In urban areas this is a great problem before the parents.

17.2 The Site

A school cannot be put up anywhere and everywhere. Its sitting has a great importance and significance. There are some very definite considerations which a proposed site must fulfill before it can be declared suitable for building a school on.

(i) *Good location, not the low cost, should be the deciding factor* as the expense involved may be such a heavy drain on the resources of the school that the essential services may have to be curtailed to the detriment of the education function. Thus the cheapest site in the long run may actually prove more expensive.

(ii) *As far as possible, the site should be outside the town.* Adequacy and suitability should be the primary consideration. Particular attention should be given to the relationship of site to the existing or the future traffic routes, with a view to minimising the danger to children on their way to school. W.M. Ryburn says, "The site should be near a road, yet back from the road as far as can be arranged to escape as much dust as possible."

(iii) *The direction in which the town is growing and extending should also be borne in mind, so that it may not be within the reach of the town in a short time.* Crowded streets, heavy traffic, stagnant drains, and rubbish heaps should serve as a challenge to the school authorities.

(iv) *The school should be located in correct relationship to the other physical facilities of a community such as parks, health centres, libraries.*

(v) *The site for the school should be located near the present and probable future centre of the school population to be served.* The educational authorities are generally of the view that elementary school pupils should not be asked to walk more than three-fourths of a mile and secondary pupils more than a mile and a half.

(vi) *The site should have pleasing surroundings which soothe the eye and please the soul.*

(vii) *The school should be constructed in places which are open and spacious enough.* The child requires above all space to be active. The conception of education as a process in which the child was immobile and receptive, while the teacher was active and energetic, has been replaced by one of the child learning through his own activity, while the teacher is observantly and unobtrusively controlling the direction of the activity. For this new conception of education, space within the school and the ground is essential. The School Building Committee of the Central Advisory Board of Education, Delhi has recommended the following minimum area:

No. of Children	Area of the Building	Area for Playgrounds
For 160 children	2/3 acre	2.3 acres
For 320 children	1 acre	4.5 acres
For 480 children	1 1/3 acre	6.7 acres

Fig. 1

(viii) *The site should be a little raised if possible and at any rate should be dry.* There should be no ponds or low lying water-logged ground near at hand.

(ix) *The proposed site should be such as to permit a direct play of sunlight in even the remotest corner of the school building for quite a good part of the day.*

(x) *The site of the plant should be fairly level with the building located near the high point, so that the ground can be sloped away from the building.*

(xi) *Care should be taken to avoid land which is low lying, made-up, damp, subject to floods.*

(xii) *The site should be sufficiently removed from the noise, dust, smoke, and physical dangers of factories, railroads.* A stagnant pool, a swamp, a stable or other source of disagreeable odours or breeding place for insects and germs are the disgraceful environment for a school.

(xiii) *The site should permit proper gardening and landscaping.*

(xiv) The site should provide sufficient space for future expansion.

17.3 School Building

There are no two opinions on the idea that a school building must be excellent – planned spaciously, functionally and with pleasing architectural features. **"Buildings are to education as body is to mind." "A sound mind can only be there in a sound body."** It is very well expressed in the statement: **"A fine building makes a fine school and a poor building a poor one."** *Schools should be housed in beautiful buildings, which are not only stimulating centres of education for children but are also vital centres of community life.*

A school infrastructure should have the following buildings for its organisation: -

(a) Main building for teaching subjects in classrooms. It should have subject wise department rooms.

(b) The library building and reading room.

(c) The laboratories and museum.

(d) The student hostel.

(e) The playground for the students games and sports.

(f) Agriculture farm, lawn, and garden.

(g) Principal and teacher's quarters.

(h) Staff quarters and other modern facilities.

The American Association of School Administration has suggested the following seven principles for planning a school plant building:

(i) ***Curriculum adequacy:*** **-** The plant must be planned to provide the facilities necessary for the efficient and effective accommodation of all the phases of the curricular, cocurricular, and community activities for which the plant is intended.

(ii) ***Safety and well-being:*** **-** The school plant should be so planned as to protect the comfort, health and safety of pupils, teachers, and all who will use its facilities. Lighting, heating, and ventilating should be in accordance with the best practices.

(iii) ***Inter-functional coordination:*** - Each unit or portion of a plant may be well-planned for its specific purpose, yet if the units are not put together with respect to their mutual relationships, the plant, as a whole, will be unsatisfactory.

(iv) ***Efficiency and unity:*** **-** The school plant should be planned and assembled in a manner that will promote efficient school management and convenience of pupils and the public in its use.

(v) ***Beauty:*** **-** The entire school plant should be cheerful, attractive, and pleasing.

(vi) ***Adaptability:*** **-** A school plant should be planned for economical future adaptations to changing requirements.

(vii) ***Economy:*** - A school plant should be economical in its original cost, upkeep, and operation.

The school building may be made of any material - metal, glass, or *kaccha* material - all should be universally adapted to the uses of young life growing up in sunlight and cherishing the ground as its native birthright. Low initial cost, functionality, durability, appearance, acoustical properties, case of maintenance and low operational costs should decide the type of building we construct for our children.

17.4 Master Planning

The campus of the future school should have a master site plan that reflects the thoughts of many and conforms to the general purpose of the instruction. If we are going to organise the education to catch up with the future, such organisation had best be done before we master plan. No master planning or building has even the remotest chance of being any better than the intelligent thought that went into it. Changes in main direction play havoc with the finances. Hence, a master plan or 'blue print' of the building before the construction of the building!

It is necessary that a careful master-plan is drawn up for the sight as a whole. In doing this, it should be remembered that *schools are neither built for the past nor for the present. They have to be planned and built for the future.* The anticipated enrollment and the future developments and requirements of the schools must be taken into consideration. Studies must be made of the trend in the expansion of industries, construction of roads and railways and development of community projects. To guarantee the future, plant adaptation, flexibility in functional layout should be provided to the fullest extent possible. Dr. Olson in his book on 'Child Development' points the new way we should think as we plan the learning environment of the child. He makes it clear that the layout is to provide opportunities for *child growth.* He lists six essentials for child growth: (1) food, (2) exercise, (3) shelter, (4) clothing, (5) health protection, and (6) opportunities for learning. With the exception of clothing, the modern school now attempts to provide for these essentials.

(i) All of these needs then must be *fully* met in the ideally planned school building. But that is not the entire problem.

(ii) Most of the writers agree that the school plant should be designed in terms of the changes likely to take place in the social purposes of education.

(iii) The school building should be planned in anticipation of better methods and materials for teaching, of course, in terms of new development in architecture, both as to methods and materials.

(iv) *The school plant should be adaptable to change.* The programme, scheduling, and methodology should be able to change as fast or as slowly as the principal and the faculty feels to be necessary. The building actually can move, flexing and bending to suit programme needs. The flexibility would permit a gradual change-over from current educational practices to those envisioned for the future and provide a high educational return for the rupee spent.

(v) *While planning, the concept of individual differences should also be taken into consideration.* A school planned along these lines will accommodate any student, whether gifted, slow learning or "average." Remedial rooms, advanced laboratories, and workshops, special spaces for individual study should be included.

(vi) *Self instruction is another valuable concept to be considered.* Man has always been able to teach himself new skills but Indian education has never fully capitalised on this concept beyond at the most providing a library. Now, the new technology encourages school planners and designers to create spaces that will exploit self-instruction. New schools should provide extensive student resource centres and individual study circles.

(vii) *Grouping very large and very small numbers of students also merits the attention of planners.* A very large group means all students enrolled in particular section. They might meet together for 40, 50, or even 60 percent of their instruction. Very small group would be 15 or 20 students, working with a teacher for more individualised instruction. Depending on the subject, pupils should be able to work in small groups in direct contact with the teacher for 40 to 60 percent of time devoted to that subject.

When a school is planned according to these concepts, it will accommodate today's practices and be adaptable to tomorrow's requirements.

17.5 Classrooms

In the secondary school it is desirable that each section of students' should have a room, though in teaching, two sections or more can be accommodated in one big room designed to seat about 70 pupils. It is desirable that some rooms should accommodate as many as 70 and others 30 – 40 students. About one-fourth to one-fifth of the rooms should be larger and smaller than the average.

All classrooms should have workshops or learning laboratories and as far as possible each room should have its individual character. The new tendency is to have a larger period, a portion of which is to be utilised for direct study. There is also a tendency towards more informal small group activities and therefore, more space is needed for books, reference books, etc. Twenty-five to thirty-five sq. ft. of space per pupil is a desirable objective. The classrooms should be further provided with adequate storage cabinets, shelves, and filing cases for teaching supplies, materials and books. Sufficient tack-board at eye level and black-board should be provided for the teaching programmes.

The classroom should present a pleasant and inviting look. The walls should be tastefully decorated. Rooms with northern and eastern light should have warm colours such as red, yellow, orange, etc. and rooms with southern and western light should have cool colours such as green, blue, and certain compositions of grey. In dark coloured wall-rooms, ceiling should be white, in others, it should be cream coloured.

The walls of the room should be utilised to the fullest advantage. One wall should have writing surface throughout its length, and green is preferable to black because the latter causes glare. One wall should have wooden surface covered with flannel for pinning notices, new sheets, charts, maps, etc. The other walls should have built-in cupboards for keeping books, equipment, and other teaching aids. It is desirable that the classroom should have one door opening outside.

The classroom should have not only space for good study but adequate space for using maps, charts, pictures, specimens, models, exhibits, reference books, tools, craft materials, experiment apparatus, and the like. Every instructional room should provide a healthful living and working environment for pupils and teachers.

In addition to the classrooms, the following special rooms are needed in a good school:

1. Library.
2. A Multi-purpose room with a Stage and Folding Seats – Auditorium.
3. Science Lab-cum-Lecture Room.
4. Craft Room.
5. Art Room.
6. Home Economics Lab-Lecture Room for co-educational or girls school.
7. Music Room.
8. Staff Room.
9. Principal's Room.
10. School Office.
11. Museum.
12. Cafeteria.
13. Storage and Supply Rooms.

These rooms are not absolutely essential but they do facilitate and improve instruction when available and used efficiently. Where it is difficult to offer a *pucca* school, *kaccha* walls covered with thatched roof can serve the purpose. It should not be necessary to spend all the funds on a few *pucca* rooms and starve the school in the matter of more important facilities like furniture, equipment, apparatus, etc.

1. Library

The library is the hub of the academic life of a school. With new techniques of teaching, the library should be the centre of the school educational programme. When resources permit, reading room should be separate from the library hall, otherwise the square hall preferably 24×80 sq. ft. can serve both the needs. The secondary school library should be located so as to make it easily accessible to all the classrooms and near those departments that use it most, but remote from centres of noisy activities, such as the street or athletic field.

Objectives of a School Library

A school library should function for the following objectives:

1. To introduce the students with proper use of books, handle the library catalogue and the reference books.
2. To guide the student through various library activities and make them interested in various fields of knowledge.
3. To assist the teaching staff in their higher studies and research.
4. To provide the recreational reading of the students and teachers. As a result the students and the teachers will not idle away their time. They will use their leisure – for self study and self-culture.

The library should be centrally located with respect to classrooms. It should be large enough to serve the needs of the schools. The library room should have adequate natural light with sufficient windows for proper ventilation. It should be "attractive, colourful, and inviting."

Functions of School Library

The opening hours of the school library should cover the whole period of the week, when there is demand. It should have a full time librarian. Where an assistance teacher is in charge, he should open the library regularly. However, government should appoint a trained and full time librarian in each secondary school. The school library is to perform the following functions:

1. The library should prepare cards, catalogue, and arrange them properly.
2. It should exhibit new books that are purchased from library grants to attract the students.
3. It should create a conducive reading atmosphere to encourage students to read general books.
4. It should provide useful social experiences.
5. It should promote inter-library cooperation by contact and visit to other school libraries.
6. It should organise an orientation programme by arranging lectures to explain the importance of library in school life.

The students pass the valuable time of their life in school. Therefore, the school should have a library with a full time librarian to stimulate learning. Let us conclude with the words of the **Education Commission** (1964) that, "A collection of books, even a collection of good books does not constitute a library. Given enthusiastic teachers who teach with books and librarian who can cooperate with them in converting the library into an intellectual workshop, even a comparatively small collection of sensible chosen books may work wonders in the life of students. Without such staff the most luxurious building or extensive book collection may have no effect at all." So the library should be an intellectual hub in the school with a qualified librarian.

2. Assembly Hall

The assembly hall is an important general-use facility of the secondary school plant because it is here that general meetings, dramatics, lectures, exhibits, declamation contests, and many activities are arranged. Its size will be determined by the local needs, but the hall should have a suitable stage of not less than 20 by 30 feet with green rooms and other equipment and furnishings.

The hall should be located on the ground floor and possibly in a wing isolated from the quieter areas to ensure safety of crowds, easy access for both pupils and the public, reduced sound interference and accessibility to parking.

The hall should have good acoustics. A speaker should be audible in every part without undue strain on the speaker or the listener.

The hall can be used as a multi-purpose room, as an auditorium with a combination of functions such as gymnasium and refreshment room, or as the audio-visual room.

3. Science Laboratories

The school must possess well-planned and equipped science room and laboratories to aid instruction and stimulate greater interest in science courses. The old practice of having separate lecture and practical rooms is now giving place to multiple-use room – a good size for an average school room is 24 feet by 42 feet. If service connection for gas, electricity, and water are provided in the wall, it will be easy to use the movable tables in one position for class work and in another for laboratory. Built-in cupboards for storing chemicals and apparatus should be provided. They will save space and also assure a better look.

Science rooms, as in many other classrooms, should include various types of instructional aids, such as projectors, screens, and suitable electrical outfits for various visual educations. They also need growing beds for plants; cages for small animals; and cases for insects. Storage space should be provided for class-instructional material for each group and for individual pupils using the room. Delicate instruments and dangerous chemicals should be stored in separate compartments equipped with metal shelves.

Meaning of Laboratory

The word 'Laboratory' is used for a large room where practical classes are conducted and a group of students carry out practicals. 'Science laboratory' provides instruments, apparatus, chemicals, and other materials safe and secure and ready for use. Various types of apparatus and material are placed in shelves or almirah under lock and key. The environment and the setting of the laboratory encourage student's participation. Laboratories help in the development of a sense of cooperation and a spirit of competition.

Objectives of Laboratory

1. To develop scientific attitude among children through practical work in the laboratory.
2. To develop the skill in handling scientific apparatus, instruments and equipments.
3. To provide opportunity for the training in scientific method.
4. To help students in developing the co-operation of resourcefulness, initiative, self-dependence, self-confidence, cohesion, sociability, self-reliance, and self-discipline.
5. To provide real and stable knowledge of science.
6. To provide opportunities to think, observe apply reason to arrive at a decision/ conclusion independently.
7. To encourage students to save the time, resources as well as energy.
8. To arrange an atmosphere conducive to learning science.
9. To enable the students to interpret and verify the various scientific principles.

Quantity and Quality of Laboratory Apparatus

The quantity and quality of the apparatus depends upon the following factors:

1) **Scheme of Work:** - The apparatus and material should be adequate to provide demonstrations and class practical work for the students. The quantity of chemicals consumed and the sets of apparatus required are roughly proportional to the time spent on practicals.

2) **Level of Students:** - The level and number of students should be considered while equipping a laboratory. So the apparatus in the laboratory should be planned according to the level and number of students.

3) **Finance:** - It controls the quantity and quality of equipment of a laboratory.

4) **Storage Space:** - It is important that there should be enough storage space for the equipment ordered.

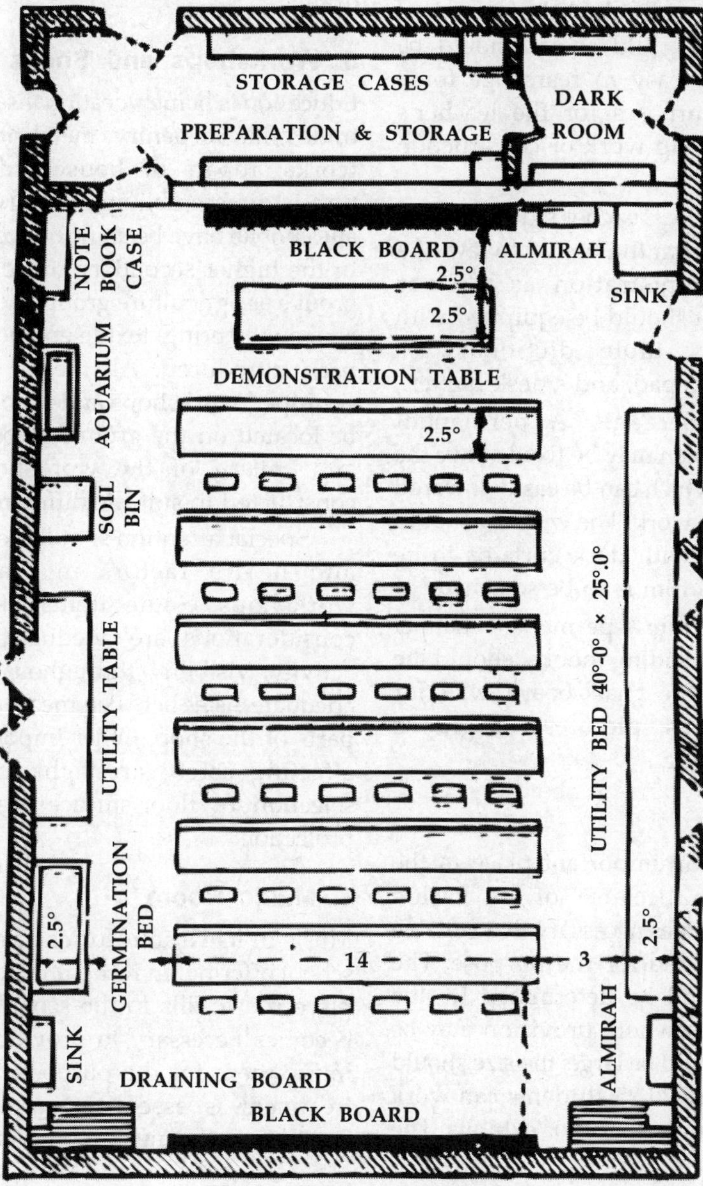

Fig. 2 All Purpose Laboratory

Necessary Furniture

The necessary items of furniture in a social studies laboratory are tables, chairs, shelves, stands, map-racks, almirahs, and blackboards. The tables should be small and flat which can be easily rearranged for group work. The general arrangement of the room should be determined by the teacher and students, for discussion, forums, group work, or viewing a film.

(i) **Seating Arrangement:** It should make for comfort, health, and efficiency of the pupils. Seats, individual desks or dual desks or tables and chairs should be movable and easy to rearrange for a variety of purposes for the teacher's lessons or group work or construction of all kinds.

(ii) **Teacher's Desk:** Teacher's desk should be movable from the point of view of a general administration as well as instruction. It should be equipped with an atlas, a table dictionary, a memorandum pad, and a desk-blotter.

(iii) **Projection Screen:** A permanent projection screen may be fixed above the blackboard which can be easily lowered for projection work. The window should be provided with dark curtains to be used when a film is to be screened.

(iv) **Channel Railing:** A permanent channel railing with sliding hooks should be fixed along the chalk-board wall for hanging maps, pictures, or graphs during teaching.

4. Art Room

Art is being given an important place in the school curriculum because of its varied potentialities. It becomes necessary that suitable art rooms are provided for the purpose. The size of the room will be determined by the number of pupils for whom provision may be made. The room should be large; the size should be such as groups of 20-25 students can work at a time leaving ample space for exhibits. The room should be airy and well ventilated. It should be lit from one side, i.e. the North and should additional light be necessary, it may be got by roof-lights facing North. Built-in cup-boards should be very handy for storing supplies, products, tools, etc. A minimum of 30 square feet of floor space per student is considered desirable.

There should be a water tap and a sink so that the pupils may wash their hands after completing a model and before beginning to draw.

5. Workshops and Sheds

Education is being vocationalised. A number of trades like carpentry, metal fittings, electrical works, repair of household gadgets and transistor assembling, masonry, and repair of automobile have been introduced in the Syllabi. In the higher secondary schools, a number of groups as agriculture group, mechanical group, civil engineering, textile engineering, etc. have been introduced. All these necessitate well-equipped workshops and sheds. These should be located on the ground floor. Floors, walls, and ceiling of the workshops should be constructed to suit the different activities.

Special attention should be given to safety and health factors in planning school workshops. Some items needing special considerations are adequate area for each activity, visibility throughout the shops and adequate aisles between mechanics and various parts of the shop. Other important conditions effecting safety are light and ventilation, selection of floor-surface material and fire protection.

6. Music Room

Music in its various forms has become a basic school offering. In recognition of the significant place music fills in the school programme, it becomes necessary to provide well-equipped music-room for the purpose. Special acoustic treatment is essential for all music-rooms. Sound from the music room should not interfere with the work in quite areas of the building.

Special attention should be given to built-in-wall cases and adequate storage for instruments. A small music library may also be provided.

7. Medical Examination Room

Every secondary school should have a room set aside for medical and dental services. It should be equipped with running water and electric power outlets.

8. Office for the School Counsellor and the Career Master

In a secondary school, provision of guidance service is essential. A room should be given to the school counsellor and the career master where the pupils may see him or he may see the pupils when needed.

9. Cafeteria

A cafeteria will be a valuable adjunct of a secondary school, if it is in efficient hands. The size of the cafeteria and the equipment needed will vary with the size of the high school and the number of students who patronise it. The best location for the cafeteria, if space allows, is probably a separate wing of the main building.

10. The Administrative Suite

The necessary administrative space for the principal and his staff is important in the planning of a modern secondary school. *Since administration is emerging into a leadership and service function, the administrative suite should be planned to feature hospitality, pleasant and attractive design, and ease of access for pupils, teachers, and the public.* The principal's office should be large enough to accommodate small conferences, should open into the general office, the public space, and a corridor. Privacy should be possible without the area being inaccessible or uninviting. It should be tastefully decorated and the furniture provided should be comfortable.

11. Office Equipment

For efficient functioning, the school office should be equipped with modern equipment. A well-organised office should have time-saving device as the computer, etc. duplicating machine, desk calendar, and rubber stamps, clock for the bell system, storage space for instruction and office supplies. If a school can afford to have telephone, book-keeping machine, sorting equipment and computing machines, etc. much of manual labour can be saved. A fire proof vault or safe is a 'must' in every office for the safe keeping of cash and confidential records.

12. Staff Room

A room should be made available to teachers where they can meet each other, may work together or individually. This room should have cupboards in the walls or lockers may be provided where the teachers may keep their things.

13. Storage and Supply Rooms

Some rooms should be there for storing the tools, unused furniture, laboratory, workshop, and office equipment, athletic supplies, etc. These stores should be at a fairly safe place.

14. The Hostel

With the rapid increase in the number of schools, the need for hostels is decreasing. Anyhow, where the hostel is attached to a school, it should be housed in a proper building with good sanitary arrangements.

The hostel should be constructed in the school compound and should be in a quite corner, away from the main road. It is desirable to have a single storeyed building, quadrangular in shape with a courtyard at the centre. On the three sides of the quadrangle, dormitories of the pupils can be constructed; the kitchen and the dining hall may be located on the fourth side. At the back of this wing, the bathrooms may be located.

Latrines may be provided at a little distance from the main building.

The quadrangle should have a main gate which may be closed at night.

Every dormitory should be long enough to accommodate 10 or 12 pupils. Every inmate should be provided with a wall-shelf, a chair, a table, and a cot.

The superintendent's quarter should be located at a little distance from the main gate.

15. Teacher's Quarters

The teacher's quarter should be considered as an integral part of the school plant. In the words of the late Prime Minister Jawaharlal Nehru, "It seems to me more important to have a proper house for the teacher than to put up a building for the school. The teacher could keep the equipment and teach outside. The school revolves round the teacher and not round the building........" Moreover, the provision of such quarters will enable teachers to stay in the villages where they are posted and will greatly assist in improving the standard of instruction in the schools. Desirable as they generally are, such quarters become a must in the case of women teachers in rural areas and of both men and women teachers in tribal areas. With the increasing emphasis on the public side of education, community activities and crafts and science, it has become necessary that teachers spend more and more time in the school. The Secondary Education Commission Report says, "We feel that the presence of the Headmaster and of the staff in or near a school, particularly if there are hostels attached or where the schools are residential, will be of the greatest benefit to the school going population......." The community life of the teaching staff to be encouraged by the provision of quarters in the area would go a long way to promote their sustained interest in school and their united effort for the better running of the institution. A minimum of three-roomed quarters with some open space should be provided to every teacher on the campus.

16. School Farm and Agriculture Shop

Agriculture and gardening as an activity is being introduced in higher secondary curriculum as a major subject. For the proper teaching of the subject farm is indispensable. 'Farm is to agriculture as a laboratory is to science.' Farming is directly concerned with the 'lie' and 'layout' of the land, water supply, soil management, labour, farm equipment, seeds manure, and marketing of the products. We have to take account of all these before we decide to have a farm.

It is necessary that 10 acres of land are attached with every Higher Secondary school and this land is fully utilised.

In order to accommodate the department's great number and variety of activities, its equipment and work-area requirements, the agriculture shop needs much more space than a regular classroom. We shall discuss this in greater detail in a later chapter.

17. Museum

One room in the school may be kept apart for a museum as it can go a long way in making teaching of science, social studies, agriculture, etc. effective. It should be a place which may mirror the life of the school. The material in the school museum may represent the flora and fauna of the locality, the geography, and history of the province, the art, and painting of young artists and the cultural traditions, etc. of the locality. As a valuable adjunct to the school, museum can be a supplement to classroom teaching, by way of providing correctly specific background in historical and geographical background of the community. Various discoveries of science, technology and geography, etc. can be best shown through specimens and models, etc. placed in the museum.

If the museum is considered more or less a fixed part of the school, an accurate record of each exhibit – names of teacher and pupil responsible, date, purpose, utilisation, expense, and any other necessary information about it should be made and kept in a record book or in some other permanent form. If the list of exhibits is very extensive, an appropriate catalogue should be printed and made available to all the teachers.

The museum should be given as important a place in the school as the library.

Importance of Museum in the School

In the words of the Secondary Education Commission, "Museums play a great part in the education of school children as they bring home to them much more vividly than any prosaic lectures, the discoveries of the past and the various developments, that have taken place in many fields of science and technology. Museum as an agency of education and recreation is invaluable." "For the scholar they represent repositories of the objects for study and research; for the educationist and the teacher they are a storehouse of concrete and vivid adjuncts which lend colour and reality to all forms of teaching; for the child the spark which can ignite wonder and curiosity, for the ordinary citizens they are a source of pleasure, delight and knowledge."

Every school can have a museum. Children like to collect objects. Many of them have collections of their own. They will react more favourably toward the idea of a school museum and cooperate more enthusiastically in developing it. Planning, accepting, and discharging individual responsibility, doing the necessary research in obtaining, understanding, classifying, mounting, and labelling exhibits, and working together for the common good may provide educational benefits for all concerned. Such a project can capitalise on almost any kind of collecting interest, guaranteeing variety in the final exhibits. "No environment is so poor as to afford no materials of such value, and none so rich as to require no supplementation."

Advantages of Social Science Museum

It has the following advantages:

1. Instruments of Education.
2. Teaching History.
3. Teaching Geography, and
4. Teaching Civics.

1. **Instruments of Education:** - Importance through visits to museums is becoming increasingly popular in all progressive countries because museums, especially those which preserve historical and cultural objects, impart wholesome education at all levels. They give new impetus to teaching methods. They are instruments of public education with vast potentialities. In Canada, a well-organised modern museum is considered essential to the educational system of the community. In Sweden, visits to museums are connected with the curriculum. Museum collections are a valuable aid to teachers in giving life and reality to school courses, at every stage of formal education. Visits to the museum have been the accepted practice in most countries of Europe and America for several years. Guided tours, walk talks, and illustrated lectures at the museum supplement book-bound curriculum of schools.
2. **Teaching History:** - Every school should have a museum with a separate section for each subject. The social studies museum can be gradually built. Efforts should be made to find real objects, authentic but not valuable. There should also be models, photographs, diagrams, charts, paintings, etc. There should be a social studies museum in each school to invest this area of school curriculum with a sense of reality. History will come to life when the children see the relics of the past. The picture of old monuments, ruins, sculpture, etc. will impress upon them that history deals with real people, real places and real things.
3. **Teaching Geography:** - The specimens of the rocks, seeds, soils, etc. are very useful. Similarly, various types of maps, models, etc. will create interest in the subject.

4. **Teaching Civics:** - The preamble to our Constitution, Bills of Rights, Declaration of American Independence, etc. will enable pupils to know something about the efforts of man for independence and a better way of life.

Sections of Museums

The materials in a museum should be well-classified so that the pupils could get a fair idea of different events and developments. There can be three sections in the museum: local, national, and international.

1. **Local Section:** It may be built with local relics, local specimens, models, charts, etc. Images of gods and goddesses, carvings in bricks or stones, pottery pieces, ancient books, ancient coins, costumes, etc. stimulate the interest of the pupils in the local history and geography and invest the study with a sense of reality.
2. **National Section:** It can be built up with the help of models as it may not be possible for each school to get original relics. Some commercial agencies in the country also supply educational models. Models may be prepared by the pupils with the help of social studies teacher, and art master on civilisation, sculptures of Gupta Age, Dams, and Projects, etc.
3. **International Section:** In it can be kept curios from different countries, stamps, coins, flags, dolls, etc.

Organisation of the Museum

In a museum an elaborate account of each exhibit - name of teacher and pupils responsible for the collection of the item, date, purpose, utilisation, expense and any other necessary information about it should be kept in a record book or in some other permanent form. The relics collected should be presented in chronological order with proper titles and annotations. The exhibits should be neatly displayed. The relics, not immediately required, should be kept stocked in boxes and exhibited on appropriate occasions.

18. The School Playground

The playground and few other smaller areas for different games must be considered at least as important for educational purposes as school building with their classrooms and other paraphernalia. A school which has no playground has no right to exist, for the playground is said to be the cradle of democracy. If play is to be accepted as the natural agency for the education of the child up to the age of puberty, then the lower half or more of our school will have to think and act not in terms of rooms, seats or desks but rather in terms of activities, games or projects which can be conducted only in the open. Hence, schools will have to adopt sensible, sound, and satisfactory means for providing open spaces, garden plots, play areas, sufficient ground spaces under shady trees and so on for different types of school work.

"Playgrounds and open space students' recreation are essential. It may not always be easy to secure enough playground and open spaces in a crowded city, but such open spaces as are available must be conserved to be utilised by groups of schools, if necessary. It is desirable that all cities, more particularly in the big cities, a committee representative of the school management, headmaster, city authorities, and others interested in the physical welfare of the students together with representative of the state should be organised to promote 'play centre movement' and from time to time see that the playgrounds available in the city are effectively used by the school-going population."

Importance of Playground

The school campus is not complete without a playground. A school with no playground is no school! Wellington said, "Waterloo was won on the playing-fields of Eton." Hence, it is very important to realise the value of playground for the proper development of the personality of the students. Due priority should be given to the provision of the playground while planning any school building. There is need of playground for games like hockey, cricket, basketball, volleyball, football, kabaddi, etc. Maximum number of games should be provided by the school. Every school should find ways and means of providing playfields to their pupils. Open places and public parks in cities, must be utilised for this purpose through special permission from the municipal authorities.

Necessary Elements of Playground

It should have the following elements:

(i) **Boundary wall:** A boundary wall is constructed around the playground.

(ii) **Shady trees:** Lovely and shady trees add to the charm and glory of the playground.

(iii) **Flower beds:** Grassy lawns and flower beds should be developed.

(iv) **Allocation and Demarcation of area:** Permanent allocation and demarcation of area should be made for different games like cricket, hockey, football, volleyball, and basketball.

19. Sanitation

There should be one urinal and bowl for 60 students. These should be regularly inspected to assure proper cleanliness and working condition. Obscene pictures and writings, if any, should be immediately removed. Toilet rooms should have moisture-proof concrete floors which can be easily washed.

So far as drinking water is concerned, in urban areas the supply of water can be obtained from the main line of the town. In rural areas, underground water may be pumped by means of section lift pump to a reservoir. Water should be checked up before use.

20. Lighting

The increase of short-sightedness among children of school age imposes an additional responsibility on the educationist for proper means of lighting the rooms. The light arrangements should be as much approximate as possible to creating conditions in the classroom with reference to light in it as one finds in the open air on a dull day. The light in the room should seem to come from no particular source but should be well diffused about the room and should cast no shadows. The light should come in only from the left so that no shadow is cast by the pen or the pencil when the child is working at his desk. The desks, therefore, should be arranged in such a manner as to take full advantage of the light coming from the left. If this consideration is disregarded, the light will either shine in the teacher's face or dazzle the children.

The arrangement of seats and desks with reference to the doors and windows, the position of the blackboard with reference to the class, the fitting, and furniture inside the rooms should also be guided by hygienic considerations. Suitable curtains and screens should be provided to alter the intensity of light according to need. When artificial lighting is necessary, it should be so arranged that the room is uniformly lighted and there are no shadows.

17.6 Planning and Designing School Building

The need for school building is tremendous. The Working Group on General Education for the Fourth Plan calculated that the India School system is short of nearly 53 crore sq. ft. of space. Fifty percent of its elementary schools are in rented or extremely unsatisfactory buildings. At Rs. 10 per sq. ft. which is a modest sum, the cost of clearing the backlog would be Rs. 530 crores. Thus, the problem of providing building for our schools is a big one. What needs to be done?

17.7 Planning for Elementary Schools

A number of suggestions have been given to meet the problem of shortage of accommodation at the elementary stage:

(i) ***Open-Air School System:*** - Our late Prime Minister Pt. Nehru suggested opening elementary schools under simple sheds, while the actual class teaching is done under the trees. He felt that "Our climate helps and it is better to sit outside under a tree or in a grove except during the rainy season. Also our old traditions fit in with this open-air teaching." He was of the opinion that we should stop buildings in rural areas and devote the money thus saved to a better class of teachers as well as to some equipment. The idea of open air school system is not bad but it has certain limitations.

Limitations of the Open-Air System: The open-air system has certain limitations.

(a) In many regions of the country, there are rigours of climate which make open air schooling difficult in certain parts of the year.

(b) Some covered space is needed not only for sheltering school apparatus, books, and furniture but also for organised craft work.

Shri Saiyidain is of the opinion that we should strike a balance between these various considerations, and in view of our resources, we must per force strike the balance in favour of economy. He suggests the idea of a nucleus school.

(ii) ***Kaccha Building with some Essential Accommodation:-*** A good idea was given by the late Maulana Abul Kalam Azad in his Presidential Address to the 25th meeting of the Central Advisory Board of Education when he said, "Our climate is such that for a large part of the year classes can be held in the open. If school holidays synchronise with the monsoon, we can to a large extent reduce the need for full scale school buildings. We can also economise by using simpler methods of construction for school purposes." This proposition is non-acceptable under the present circumstances. We should not go after *pucca* buildings with full accommodation. We can have *kaccha* buildings with some essential accommodation i.e. a few classrooms, a storeroom, and the teacher's room if his residential quarter is not provided elsewhere. We can also appeal to the villagers to take responsibility of maintaining and repairing these.

(iii) ***Nucleus First Scheme:-*** Shri K.G. Saiyidain has suggested Nucleus First Scheme, i.e. starting the building with a nucleus and then proceeding by stages for expansion according to the needs. According to this scheme, a functionally designed school room will provide sheltered space for storage, etc. while the classes will be generally held outside.

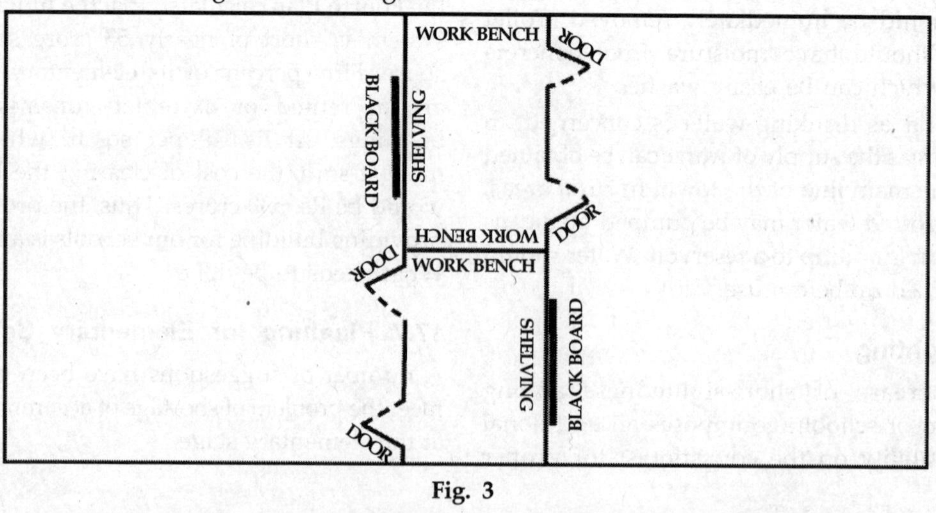

Fig. 3

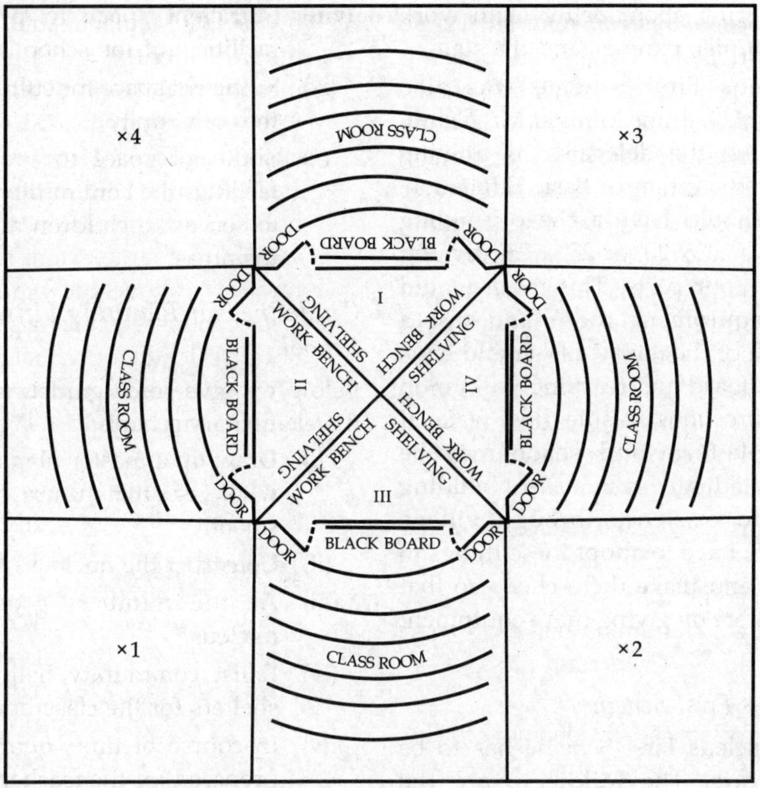

Fig. 4

Shri Saiyidain has suggested two plans under this scheme.

Nucleus First Type School for Two Teachers

In this plan, we can build a *pucca* room of suitable size and partition into two equal rectangular parts.

Nucleus First Type School for Four Teachers

This plan consists of constructing a square room of suitable size and partitioning it diagonally into four equal isosceles triangles. Each triangular room so formed will have two openings on the outside with a chalk board between them fitted to the wall. The triangular room will give storage space for equipment, craft tools, and material and various other teaching aids...The classes will sit in the open making use of the chalk boards. Space x 1, x 2, x 3, between the classes will be used by the classes for activities like gardening, planting and other craft work. The nucleus can thus provide excellent facilities for four grades in an elementary school.

Shri Saiyidain mentions the following advantages of the Nucleus First Scheme:

1. It would enable us to get a well-equipped school functioning quickly with a minimum of expenditure.
2. It would provide a flexible long range plan within the means of every community.
3. It would provide the teachers with better tools than are available in present school buildings.
4. It would induce and inspire local effort.
5. It would give local effort a simple plan of action.
6. It would shift financial responsibility from the state to local effort.

7. It would bring about better team work between pupils, parents, and the state.

The Nucleus First Scheme was also approved by our late Prime Minister Mr. Nehru. While addressing the delegates to training course on Administration of Basic Education, he said, "We should have a cheap building with a room say 20′ x 20′ or 25′ x 25′ divided diagonally into four parts. This room would serve as an equipment room and not a classroom. Each of the four walls should have outside a blackboard and teaching will go on in all the four directions outside those walls. If necessary, a platform and shade may be provided and gradually even a *pucca* building may come into existence through village cooperation. We have to adopt these things to our conditions and make them cheap so that we can concentrate on giving more equipment and wages."

Site for Nucleus First Scheme

Site for the Nucleus First Scheme has to be chosen with care. The following are the requirements of the site:

(i) Sufficient building space for future expansions.

(ii) Sufficient outdoor instructional space as may be demanded by new methods of teaching with particular reference to New Education.

(iii) Sufficient play space.

(iv) Sufficient space to provide for community recreational activities.

(v) Sufficient space to have community facilities on school grounds (clinics, reading-room, etc.).

(vi) Sufficient space to construct houses for teachers.

(vii) Sufficient space to provide garden plot for teachers.

(viii) Sufficient space to provide feeding facilities for the school.

(ix) Sufficient space for cultural activities of the community.

(x) Sufficient space to provide whatever facilities the community desires to add to serve the children and the adult of the areas.

Guidelines for Planning Future Elementary School

Below we give some guidelines for planning the elementary schools:

(i) Draw up a master plan for the site as a whole, so that future development is smooth.

(ii) Construct the nucleus.

(iii) As the numbers grow, repeat the nucleus.

(iv) Enlist community help for providing shelters for the classrooms.

(v) In course of time, quarters should be prepared for the teachers. Prepare plan for capital outlay in advance.

(vi) To cope with the increasing numbers, two shifts should be introduced in the same school building.

17.8 Different Types of Designs for Secondary Schools

There are a number of types of designs in vogue for secondary schools in our country:

(i) The I type – consisting of a row of classrooms.

(ii) The L type – I type with an extension on one side.

(iii) The T type – I type with extension on one side both ways.

(iv) The U type – two I's joined on one side.

(v) The E type, and

(vi) The H type.

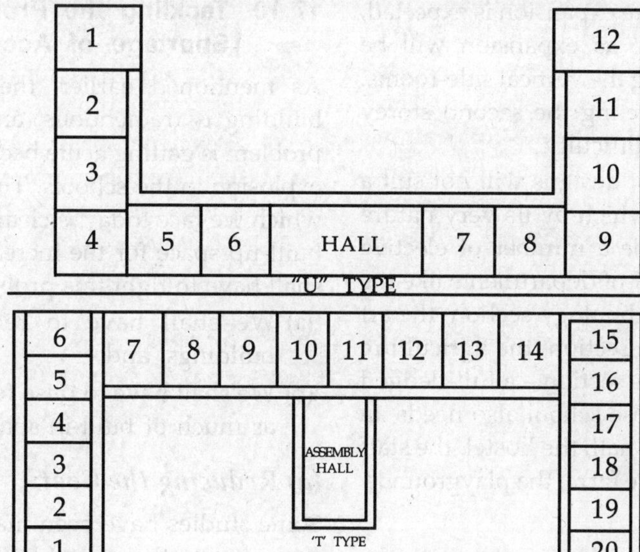

Fig. 5

Any one of the above six types can be selected for a Middle or High school which does not need more than 25 rooms. The selection depends upon several factors such as:

(a) The size and shape of the site.

(b) The number of rooms needed; and

(c) The possibility of future expansion.

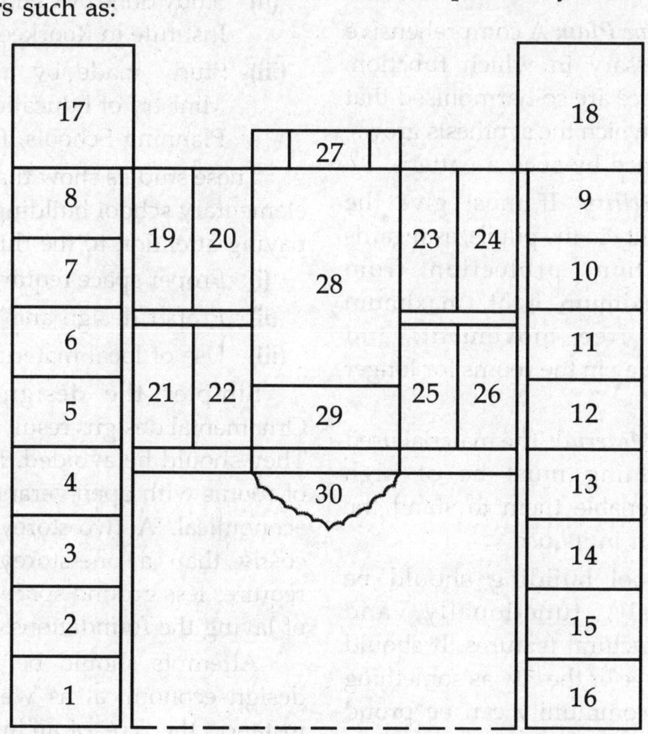

Fig. 6

For instance, if more expansion is expected, we can select H type as expansion will be possible by lengthening the vertical side-rooms. At the same time, erecting the second storey will not entail much difficulty.

The above types of designs will not suit a multipurpose school which by its very nature is supposed to provide a number of elective groups - and a number of departments like the science section, the technology section, the art section, the commerce section, the agriculture section, the humanities section - a full-fledged residential multipurpose school also needs an extension campus, the hall, the hostel, the staff quarters, the agriculture farm, the playgrounds, etc.

17.9 Essential Qualities of School Architecture

School architecture should have the following essential qualities:

(i) *Simple but elegant and beautiful design.*

(ii) *Low cost.*

(iii) ***Comprehensive Plan:*** A comprehensive plan is necessary in which function, farm, and space are so harmonised that the soil from which the synthesis grows, will be enriched by such a pattern.

(iv) ***Maximum Utility:*** It must give the maximum utility to the pupils, as regards accommodation, protection from weather, maximum light, maximum ventilation, free movement, and comfortable stay in the rooms for longer hours.

(v) ***Use of Good Material:*** The material used for the building must be of high standard to enable them to stand the great load put in its use.

Any ideal school building should be planned spaciously, functionally, and with pleasing architectural features. It should stand out in the village or the city as something of which the local community can be proud of.

17.10 Tackling the Problem of Shortage of Accommodation

As mentioned earlier, the need for school building is tremendous, and day-by-day the problem is getting acute because of population explosion in the schools. The biggest problem which we face today is clearing the backlog of built-up space for the increasing millions. We shall have to fight this problem on two fronts.

(a) We shall have to reduce the cost of buildings; and

(b) We shall have to raise funds for providing as much of built-in space as possible.

(a) Reducing the Cost:

Some studies have been made in our country for reducing the cost of buildings.

(i) Studies made by the Committee on Plan Projects in Delhi. The conclusions of this study are found in Reports on Delhi School Buildings, 1960 and Reports on Primary School Buildings in Delhi, 1963.

(ii) Study done by Central Building Research Institute in Roorkee University.

(iii) Study made by a committee of the Ministry of Education in their brochure, Planning Schools, for India, 1959.

These studies show that the total cost of an elementary school building can be reduced by paying attention to the three aspects viz.

(i) Proper space requirements.

(ii) Proper design and specifications.

(iii) Use of local material.

Simpler the design, lesser the cost. Ornamental designs result in unnecessary cost. They should be avoided. Rectangular designs of rooms with open verandah on one side are economical. A two-storeyed building is less costly than a one-storeyed building, as it requires less ground space and there is no cost of laying the foundations.

Attempts should be made to make the design economical as well as beautiful. For instance, the type of architecture designed by La Corbusier who designed Chandigarh combines the essential qualities of maximum beauty with minimum labour and cost. The designs of primary and secondary schools at Chandigarh are worth copying.

Some new designs have been invented by architects in some tropical countries, like Egypt, Iraq, Iran, New South Wales, etc. In one design there are pivoted doors that can be adjusted to weather, the building may not be facing east, so that it avoids the sun inside the rooms. If the building faces north-east or north-west, we can avoid and a good number of windows can be let open, reducing thus the material to be used for the construction of walls.

We can affect an economy by using the local material which is readily available. We can have slate roofs, where less slates are available locally, stone walls where stone is available. In rural areas we can have thatched roofs, where plenty of grass is available. In mountain regions, where timber is cheap, most of the material used for the building - walls, floors, roof, etc. may be timber. In areas of low rainfall, un-burnt earthen bricks - so cheap as compared to burnt bricks and tiles can be used. If the walls are made of stone or good bricks, plastering can also be avoided. Hedges may be planted to serve the purpose of boundary walls. Lift pumps may be provided for drinking water. Portions of the walls may be painted black, so as to be used as blackboard.

We can economise on labour also by getting help from the local community, like student population, teachers, etc.

These methods can bring down the cost of constructing five class-rooms from Rs. 2000/- to Rs. 1000/-. It will be still better if the entire cost of constructing the buildings and their repairs may be entrusted to State Building Corporation in every state.

(b) Raising Funds:

Funds shall have to be raised for providing the minimum essential of built-up space. The three methods which can be suggested for this purpose are:

(i) Taking loans;

(ii) Getting donations; and

(iii) Creation of a non-lapsable fund.

All these methods have been tried in our country with good results.

The loan system has been tried with success in Mumbai. The Government of Mumbai took over the responsibility of maintaining the provident fund accounts of all the elementary teachers, and advanced loans to local authorities for the building purposes out of provident fund amounts. The total deduction of G.P. fund amounted to Rs. 80 lakhs per annum. The loans were given through District School Building Committees. The success of the scheme can be very well estimated by finding that between 1952 and 1961, Rs. 250 lakhs were advanced as loans, and 10,000 new class-rooms were built, and special repairs were done to 1,200 classrooms. This system can be followed by other states also.

The philanthropists from the local areas can be approached to lend a helping hand in constructing school buildings. They can be approached for giving rent free accommodation, accommodation on nominal rent for school purposes. The community can be approached for helping cash, kind, and labour.

The third method of raising a non-lapsable fund was tried by Mumbai state. A primary school building's fund was created in each district. All the grants and loans and public donations were credited into it. The fund remained permanently, and there was no usual risk of annual grants being lapsed. This system can be tried in other states also.

17.11 Recommendations of the Indian Education Commission – 1964-66

The Commission has recommended the following:

1. In view of the present unsatisfactory position regarding school buildings, it is necessary to take steps to clear the backlog of unconstructed school

buildings as well as to provide additional buildings for new enrollment.

2. Allocation for construction of school building should be increased in the Central and State budgets, and community resources mobilised on the basis of equalisation. Loans and grants-in-aid should be given on a liberal basis to private schools for the construction of buildings.
3. *Reduction of Costs:* The norm and guidance available as a result of the work of a number of committees appointed by the Central and State Governments and on behalf of the Ministry of Education, the Ministry of Works and the Planning Commission, U.G.C. and Central Building Research Institute at Roorkee and the Indian Standards Institute, for spacing and planning of school building should be put into practice.
4. In view of the shortage of traditional building material and the cost involved, well-designed and *kaccha* constructed structures should be accepted as a part of the school system.
5. In rural areas, efforts should be made to encourage local initiative and contribution in putting up school buildings. The "nucleus" approach suggested by the Ministry of Education is recommended for general adoption.
6. *Buildings in Urban Areas:* Economy in these buildings should be effected by using locally available materials, omissions of certain finishes, and acceptance of a lower standard of construction. Temporary structures may be used wherever possible and improved techniques of construction may be adopted in putting up *pucca* buildings.
7. *Expeditious Construction:* In order to accelerate provision of school buildings, constructions in rural areas may be entrusted to local communities or village Panchayats, and in urban areas, municipalities and corporations may be utilised for the purpose.
8. In order to supervise and guide the programme of construction of school buildings and introduce improved techniques, an Educational Building Development Group should be set up in each state within the Public Works Department and working in close association with the Education Department. These groups will standardise details of construction in the region so as to make possible the mass production of the components on a factory scale. A similar Building Development Group should be set up at the centre to coordinate the work of the state groups.
9. To avoid delays in the construction of government buildings, a separate unit of the P.W.D. should be set up for the execution of educational building programmes. At a later stage an Education Building Consortia may be set up to exploit the advantages of industrialised buildings.
10. The economy measures worked out by the Educational Building Development Group should be made known to private institutions and grants-in-aid given on the basis of upper cost limits.

17.12 Furniture

If the school plant is to function efficiently suitable furniture and equipment has to be provided.

Furniture plays an extremely important part in the physical, moral, and mental welfare of the scholars. Great care should be taken in providing the same – for "education is the cultivation of a first and legitimate familiarity between the mind and the things" – as is said by Bacon. Each and everything in the school affixes its stamp upon the individuality of the child and "the whole efforts of a school ought to be directed making boys manly, earnest and true by everything around them, all they do and all that is done to them, being the best stamp." We can only have the best workman if we accomplish him with the best tools. It is, of course, true that fine teaching can be done with little furniture (the example of Santiniketan of Tagore), and very bad instruction can be given with a wealth of appliances. But this is also true that sufficient furniture, good apparatus, and useful appliances in the hands of a first class teacher can produce results which cannot be obtained under any other circumstances.

Old furniture was the symbol of immobility and conformity. Long desks, each sitting ten or twelve children, all of the same height, inevitably suggested exactly similar children, seated immobile in a minimum of space, working in the same way or at a similar pace.

Proper furniture and equipment are the essentials for the successful working of a school. Improper seating arrangements lead to physical deformities and thus endanger the health of the pupils. If the desks are of the wrong kind or if benches are used instead of desks, curvature of the spine, contraction of the chest, roundness of the shoulders and a confirmed stoop may result as *physical injury*; bad discipline, irritation, discontent and discomfort may result as *moral injury* and inability to sustain attention and concentration owing to lack of bodily ease may result as *mental injury*.

The fact that furniture may need to be shifted frequently in today's secondary class-room implies that it may be *movable* besides being *flexible, adaptable, and durable.*

(a) An Ideal Desk

The best school desk is one which is designed to afford comfort to the child and to allow effective school work at the same time. It should not be needlessly cumbersome or heavy and should be easily movable to allow the room being cleaned without much inconvenience.

There are three things about a desk which must conform to the conditions required before a desk can be declared as the best – (a) The height of the desk, (b) The seat, (c) The writing surface. The height of the seat above the ground floor should be such that while sitting, it permits the upper part of the legs to be *horizontal* and the lower part of the leg, to be either resting on the ground or on a suitable footrest. The height from the seat to the writing surface should be such as to allow the child when writing to sit upright in an easy position. The seat should be so designed as to afford comfort to a child when either he stands up or is working on his seat. Arm-rests may be provided as they allow the child to sit with the chest thrown out. The writing surface should be plain board at an angle of 15° to the horizontal. With reference to the seat, the writing surface may have three positions as plus, minus, and zero. In plus position, there is some space between the edge of the desk and the edge of the seat. In zero position, the two are on a line and in minus position, the edge of the seat is under the writing surface. In order that the desk may be capable of being adjusted to these positions, the top of the desk should be movable.

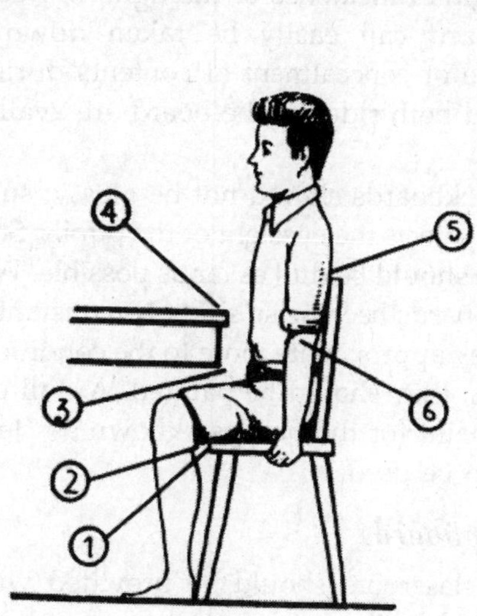

Fig. 7

1. No pressure under the knees.
2. Free space back of inside angle of knee.
3. Room above the thighs.
4. Back edge of table overlaps front edge of chair.
5. Low back, open at bottom, support for hollow of back only.
6. Table top higher than elbow when arm is straight.

(b) Blackboards

A blackboard is a necessary equipment of a classroom and a handy apparatus at the hands of a teacher. A teacher who does not use his black-board is not a teacher. He is either a lecturer or nothing at all that has a name and place in the educational scheme. Blackboards are many and various and include painted areas of the wall, framed wall boards, swing slates and board rising and falling, wall-boards and the blackboard and the easel. Of all these, blackboard with easel is the best for the reasons that it can be moved to any part of the class-room, that it can be raised as the teacher works downwards on it and its angle can be instantaneously changed to meet a change of the angle of incidence of the light. Moreover, the board can easily be taken down for purpose of concealment of contents during a test and both sides of the board are available for use.

Blackboards should not be glossy; such a surface affects the eyesight of the pupils. So the surface should be dull as far as possible. When black-boards become so shiny by constant use that they approximate more to the condition of mirrors, they should be painted. A dull dead black paint for the purpose known as "Jersey Jet" can be used.

(c) Cupboards

Every classroom should be provided with a cupboard for the accommodation of such stock as is issued daily in the class and for the safe keeping of models, specimen, apparatus, etc. If this be a glass-fronted cupboard and part of it can be turned into a museum of specimen provided by the pupils, so much the better.

17.13 The Campus

A beautiful, neat, and attractive school campus can motivate both the teachers and the pupils to work best. It is said, "The campus is to the school what dress is to a woman." A campus can be made beautiful without much expense. With the help of the Persian Wheel or the electric motor, the problem of water supply can be solved. Trees and ornamental bushes or climbers once planted, need only regularly watering and occasional pruning. A few evergreen shady trees in the campus, if well planted according to good planning, can provide good effect. Flowering trees can make the campus beautiful. Some wall climbers are very prolific in a variety of richly coloured flowers which blossom for many weeks and give a gay look to the building. In this connection, bougainvillea is very rich in possibilities. These can be easily trained into arches and bushes and in themselves are enough to lend a positive appearance to the campus.

Hibiscus, oleander, poinsettia are other ornamental plants with extensive possibilities. These give flower for many weeks.

Green hedges if properly pruned and trained can be very valuable in isolating different areas. With well-groomed hedges and a few coloured flowers, the school can be made to look happy if not exactly pretty. In this connection, Gardenia with white flowers, Hibiscus with scarlet flowers may be tried.

If flower growing is introduced as a regular hobby in every school, if agriculture is introduced as a craft, there will not be any difficulty in making the school campus neat and attractive. All students have wonderful potentialities – the only condition is – let us give them the opportunities.

17.14 Plant Maintenance and Plant Utilisation

1. Plant Maintenance

All facilities and equipment in the school must be regularly and frequently inspected in order to assure its proper working at all times. The headmaster should be very vigilant to protect the school plant from defacement and damage. Any defacement marks and obscene writing should be removed immediately. Both teachers and students should be made to imbibe the virtues of good house-keeping. No wastepapers, pieces of chalks should be lying about. The cooperation of the faculty is essential in building up attitudes on the part of the pupils against carelessly dropping wastepaper, etc. in the halls or on the classroom floors or on the grounds. Such cooperation results in desirable training for citizenship in addition to improving the appearance of the school. The rooms should be free from dirt accumulation on walls, tables, equipments, etc. School plants should be regularly and periodically inspected for detecting the needs of repair. General repairs might be undertaken during vacations while the emergency repairs should be immediately attended to.

2. Plant Utilisation

It is a matter of common knowledge that school plant, on which so much is spent, is utilised only 5 or 6 hours a day and about 6 months in a year. Rooms in the schools, particularly the library, science rooms, drawing rooms, craft rooms, auditoriums and halls are put to 50 to 70 percent use and may be even less in some cases. In many schools, halls are used only for examination or for holding three or four meetings in a year, while science laboratories are used only for a few periods every day. Similarly, the school building and other facilities remain unused during the summer vacations and long breaks. This under-use of education resources cannot be justified. Ways must be found out through proper planning and scheduling for greater utilisation of the plant. Some suggestions are given below:

1. School day may be lengthened.
2. Double sessions can increase build utilisation.
3. Scheduling the regular use of library by groups or classes.
4. Laboratories may be used for general purposes.
5. Playground may be utilised by carefully scheduling classes in physical education throughout the day and by consciously using playgrounds both for sports programme whenever weather conditions permit and for those games that can be played out of doors. The careful scheduling of intra-mural sports after school will also help utilise the playgrounds to maximum advantage. Games that require much space but provide opportunity for a few to participate should not be permitted.
6. Auditorium can be more fully utilised if proper provision and scheduling is made for cultural activities. It can also be used to hold workshops, seminars, and other projects.
7. A school plant can be so used that the full life of the community can centre in it. It can be used as a social centre, as a polling station during elections and as a meeting place for civic societies, welfare associations, as well as parent-teacher-associations. It can serve as a recreation centre where the children, youth, and adults of neighbourhood use the playground, the gymnasium etc., during out of school hours.

Objective Type Questions

Multiple Choice Questions (Tick ✓ the right option)

(1) The schools and educational institutions have a great importance for our
- (a) Society
- (b) Community
- (c) National Development
- (d) All of the above

(2) The library is the hub of the academic life of
- (a) Class
- (b) School
- (c) Site
- (d) None of the above

Fill in the blanks

(1) The library should be __________ located with respect to classroom. [Centrally]

(2) The word __________ is used for a large room where practical classes are conducted and a group of students carry out practicals. [Laboratory]

Important Questions

1. Explain the main considerations to be kept in view while planning a new building for a school. In what respects should a rural building differ from the one in an urban area.
2. "It is said that school buildings should be less costly and more functional." What principles would you follow in planning and designing building and equipment for schools in our country?
3. How is it possible to provide effective education in tents and sheds? Under the present stress of economy what minimum building and equipment requirements would you suggest for primary school in cities?
4. Discuss the principles that should guide in determining the needs of the school building.
5. Discuss the requirements of a secondary school so far as school plant is concerned.
6. "Schools are neither built for the past nor for the present. They have to be planned and built for the future." Discuss.
7. Discuss the main features of ideal furniture in a school.
8. Suggest some means for effective utilisation and maintenance of school plant.

18

The School Farm and the Workshop

Agriculture, woodwork, metalwork, spinning and weaving, needlework, etc. are the significant activities considered educationally useful in education. The positive influence of all these on the development of the brain has become an educational truism. They furnish a direct appeal to the child's desire to make things; they vitalise school work by bringing it into close contact with everyday interests and afford capital training not only of the hands but also of the brain. It is not a mere metaphor to speak of the hand as the 'thinking hand', for all manual work involves some intellectual activity. These activities develop the creative powers of the pupils. They reduce the gulf between the life and learning. *Deeds, and words, in fact, are the language of the complete man.*

These activities cannot be properly carried on in the classroom. These need well-organised farms, suitably equipped workshops, and specially qualified teachers. Farm is to agriculture as a laboratory is to science. Workshops for woodwork and metalwork are equally essential. Productivity is an important concomitant of a sound programme of craft education and of good craftsmanship. All this presupposes that every type of work undertaken in an educational institution is done scientifically and properly so that the amount of time and money spent is well-justified. Some obvious gains must accrue from these.

Just as a classroom needs to be well-organised for effective teaching and learning, similarly a farm and a workshop need to be well-organised. In a farm and a workshop, the teacher has to be vigilant about a good teaching-learning situation – he has to make the maximum of gain within the minimum of time. So his efforts are to be well-planned and organised so that the pupils are in an optimum mood for learning.

18.1 Principles of Farm Management

"It is a fundamental error to suppose that farming is neither a business nor a profession. It is a business which requires the highest business talent; it is a profession which requires the best technical skill. No other profession requires such a variety of learning, such an insight into nature, and such a skill of technical kind in order to be successful as the profession of farming."

If this is so, the work must be given a good start in the school time. The work of the farm demands system. First, a specific decision must be made by the teacher about economic organisation and operation of the farm. He must decide about the kinds and amount of resources to use and the products to produce. He must know how to get the work done; sequence of operation; how much time to devote to each job and the method of doing the same. Farming is concerned directly with 'lie' and 'layout' of the land, water-supply, soil management, farm equipment, seeds, manure, and marketing of the products, etc. In farming, the major factor which matters is 'nature.' Nature will neither be forced nor driven, and is very often very hard to be led, but will do wonders when properly assisted. It is for this reason, scientific planning, and management are important. Good management can ensure continuous profits consistent with the welfare of the school.

It is necessary that 10 acres of land are attached with every school and this farm is easily accessible.

18.2 Planning the Farm Layout

In planning the farm layout, the location of the buildings and farmstead and their size and arrangements need a good deal of consideration. Initial errors committed in this direction will result in a heavy loss in the long run. Poor arrangement may mean a serious annual drain on the working forces or expenses for correcting faults. A shed for a pair of bullocks and two rooms 18′ x 24′ will be sufficient for the school farm. Implements and tools can be kept in the shed as well as in the room. These rooms should be at the centre of the farm if the farm is situated at a distance from the school; otherwise a room adjacent to the school building facing the farm can be used for the purpose. A slope in the bullock shed can be had to keep it clean. The urine of the bullocks should be stored in a pit near the cattle shed.

18.3 Planning the Field Layout

The layout of fields on a farm reflects the judgement of the manager and illustrates his efforts to overcome the handicaps of nature. Planning the field layout involves two things:

(i) The consideration of the rotation to be followed; and

(ii) The consideration of the soil.

Most crop production systems require growing a crop on different fields year after year. The bigger the field, the better is the result. Irregular fields demand far more time to manage than rectangular ones of similar size. The ideal layout for level land would be rectangular fields of the same size. In rectangular fields, the ploughing and cultivating is done in less time because fewer turns are needed. Triangular field take more time because of so many more short rows.

Slope and drainage must be kept with great care. Excess water of the rainfall should go through the drains without doing any loss to the fields. Washing of the fields should not take place at the time of the rainfall. The boundaries of the fields should be such as to retain required quantity of water. They should not be too low or too high. Water channel should feed each and every *kiari* economically. The loss of water through seepage must be minimised. Proper roads should be there for approaching the fields.

Fences are intended to confine stock. They must be kept clean. They should not become the breeding place for weeds and insects. Square fields take fewer fences per acre than oblong or irregular fields.

18.4 Soil Management

"Success or failure in farming starts with the soil. The soil will make or break you.'

With good soil and poor soil management, one may fail. But failure is certain if both soil and its management is poor. Soil may not be the best but with good management the chances of success can be better than a mere gamble.

In India, there is more poor soil than good soil. A teacher should know what he can do to enhance his profits by proper soil management. The teacher has to work hard, plan wisely and execute smartly. Success or failure starts with the soil. Thus, good farm management must start with considerations of the soil. Husbandry of soil is the very essence of agriculture.

Soil erosion should be prevented as far as possible. Soil fertility should be kept by proper layout, proper drainage, proper manuring, proper rotation, and proper fallow. Water the soils and crops at proper time. Water-logging should be avoided. Proper drainage system must be adopted along the farm – otherwise water will become a foe instead of a friend.

"Work with your soil not against it."

18.5 Selecting and using Farm Equipment

"Tools can keep you in the black or dump you in the red."

Good tools save time and money. The student will take much more interest if the tools are modern and good than otherwise. The first selection of adequate tools is very important. But good management not only means adequate tools for a kind of crop and size of operation but also means getting savings and profits by finding greater utilisation of tools.

The two major considerations in equipment arrangement are:

(i) Multiplication of human labour in terms production; and

(ii) Saving in production costs.

Increase in farming depends much upon using land equipment and labour in the right proportion. Often land and labour are wasted because of inadequate equipment. It is needless to say that with poor equipment, the field work is heavy and irksome; so it is poorly done and the crops are inferior. With sufficient and efficient tools, a man can do his work easily and well. Human labour is valuable, and the wise teacher gives much attention to saving time and energy. Work done with poor tools is not only costly but also done poorly.

18.6 Efficient Use of Labour

"Your labour is worth what it produces."

Healthy growing children are an important farm resource. Plans should be carefully chalked out for using this valuable resource wisely. A reasonable amount of work under pleasant surroundings is enjoyed by school boys and girls. The teacher has every opportunity to keep his pupils busy at farm under his own direction and at things that are worthwhile and educational. Strong boys and girls like to do some of the bigger things like using the team. They want to plough, to cultivate, to help harvest. Youngsters are also good at hoeing, chopping, and weeding, picking fruit and many other hand jobs.

The students should not be overworked in any case. Too long periods should be avoided. Occasional days off for themselves should be a part of the plans and strictly adhered to.

The work programme should be so arranged that in spite of variation in weather, each crop and livestock will get proper and timely attention.

During slack season, the fixing of fencing, repairing and clearing of buildings, water channels, farm sheds, etc. should be done.

Hired labour should be employed in rush seasons.

To labour efficiently does not mean to 'work harder', it means 'to work more effectively', with greater accomplishment per hour and per year. Planning use of time is the very essence of good farm management. The teacher should have a clear idea of the work to be done tonight, tomorrow, the day after and even the next week. Success with crops and livestock depends to a very great extent on doing the right things at the right time and in the right way.

A work calendar should be prepared. It should include work plans for the boys and the hired labour. These work calendars should be the result of year's experience with a lot of common sense thrown in.

18.7 Efficient Use of Water

Water is blood for the farm crops. Without adequate supply of water, farming cannot be successful. So, first of all the teacher should think of the water supply. Water must be suitable for the crops. Saltish water is not good for the crops. It makes the soil alkaline or acidic according to the base of the salt. Water must be tested by the agricultural chemist of the locality. Adequate supply of water should be there for the farm. The supply of water should be available throughout the year.

It is advisable to have *pucca* water channel though it is expensive at first, yet it pays in the long run. Water should not be wasted by seepage. The loss through seepage is much more than the cost of making the channel *pucca*. The location of the channels should be fixed and should not be changed after every six months or a year. The field should be irrigated by making adequate sized *kiaries*. The flood system should be avoided as far as possible. To facilitate distribution of, and to economise water, each acre should be divided into a number of compartments or *kiaries*.

18.8 Proper Care and Feeding of Bullocks

There is an old saying, "The eyes of the master follow his cattle." Watchful care of the bullocks is very important. Major field operation is done by the bullocks. Sowing and carting require the services of the bullocks. The role of the bullocks in the Indian agriculture is very important. The old saying seems to be true: "The earth rests on the horns of the bullocks." The bullock occupies an eminent place in the economy of Indian farmers.

In the proper care and feeding of the bullocks the *shed* is very important.

There should be at least a 150 sq. ft. open enclosure for a pair of bullocks - out of which 30 sq. ft. should be covered, so that the bullocks may sit in the shade in hot weather. The pair requires 16′ x 16′ space for housing. There should be one window and two ventilators. The feeding trough should be cleaned before and after the feed. There should be two bars at the gate. A *kaccha* building is more useful in summer. It remains cool and comfortable. The floor should be *pucca* or cemented having grooves so that the cattle might not slip. Just behind the tending place of the bullocks, there should be *pucca* drainage for passing the urine away in the *pucca* pit outside the shed. The urine should be collected there. The urine from pit should be emptied and carried in buckets to the manure pit.

18.9 Proper Use of Farm Waste and Green Manure

Land without manure does not give good returns. It becomes uneconomic if proper manuring is not done. Most lands in India are made to starve. Manure, in sufficient quantities, is not given to them. Their yield of crops is diminishing. Manures are the concentrates for the land.

The waste at the farm should be properly collected and conserved in a pit. The farm waste includes, rubbish collected near the steading, cattle dropping, waste straw, ashes from the fire, dry leaves and stubbles. This waste can be converted into good compost. The teacher should see that all such waste is carried to the manure pit which should be dug away from the cattle shed, in the corner of the farm. No waste whether it is cotton stalks, sugarcane, trash, uneaten fodder residue, should remain unconverted into farmyard manure. All such things are organic matter. The benefits which organic matter confers on the soil are indeed very great. The making of compost of all these things is, therefore, very beneficial for the farmers.

The pit should be protected from the sun. It should not be at the low level of the farm; otherwise it will be a pond of water during the rainy season. But adequate amount of moisture should be there for the decomposition of organic matter.

18.10 Green Manuring

Farmyard manure is not available in sufficient quantity for the crops. The method of green manuring can be used beneficially if the water supply is adequate. It is good manure, having all the important elements of plant food. Green manuring involves growing a green crop, preferably and generally a legume and ploughing it in the field, when in flower. The crops most commonly used are *san, hemp, and guara*. The former is preferred in submontane tracts as guara does not grow well there. A heavy 'sohaga' is run over the crop in the direction along which ploughing is to be done. When the crop is thus laid flat, a furrow turning plough is used to bury the crop. The field may then be left after going over it with the sohaga until the green manure has decayed to some extent. It is advisable to water the field a few days before ploughing in the crop. Four to five weeks after the burying of the crop, the cultivation required for the succeeding rabi may be begun.

Green manuring has been found to be very useful in sandy soils, as it has a binding effect on such soils.

18.11 Growing of Crops in the Field

Growing of several kinds of crops which ripen at different seasons is a key to successful farming. In a locality, those crops should be grown which thrive well there. More area should be devoted to the major crop or cash crop of that area. From the point of view of management, it is best to plant crops in a manner that will distribute both labour and income as evenly throughout the year as possible. A cultivator can use his time, oxen, and equipment more economically.

In growing the crops, proper rotation should be carried on. By following such a plan, the fertility of the soil is improved. The yields are increased from year to year. Soil can rest and is revitalised by its being fallow. It recoups its fertility in taking rest and by accumulating some nitrogen from the air. This becomes, therefore, partly a substitution for manuring. Such a scheme eliminates weeds and prevents some of the diseases and the soil also remains fertile. The main points about planning a rotation are: -

(i) Crops of the same natural order should not follow each other.

(ii) Crops of the same type of root system (shallow or deep) should not follow each other.

(iii) Leguminous crops should be included in the rotation.

(iv) Green manuring and forage crops should be given a place in the rotation at regular intervals.

(v) Crops such as potatoes requiring more thorough cultivation than others should be included in the rotation as their cultivation means a good preparation for the following crops.

18.12 Disposal of the Farm Products

The farm products must be sold at a proper margin of profit. In the sale of products, attention should be given to grading and quality. People are willing to pay 20 to 25 percent more for clear, pure, and fresh things. In the sale of produce, it is well to remember that good quality service and businesslike methods will be amply rewarded. The best price of the crop is not just got after the harvest. At that time, the market is glutted with the crops. So try to withhold the produce for some other time in order to get a better price.

Bhusa should be stored either in small stacks thatched with straw, in low circular stacks roofed with mud, or in low peaked heaps covered with mud. These are respectively known as *Kup, Palla,* and *Dhar*.

The disposal of the vegetables and the fruits should be done soon after their picking.

18.13 Farm Records

Careful accounting is the first step to successful farm management. With proper records the manager can come to know where undue expense and loss have occurred, and where profits have been made. Accounts of the various field crops should be kept wherever possible. Such accounts are simple to keep, and at the end of a year, they will reveal useful information.

At the school farm, a simple method of book keeping is necessary for the efficient conduct and physical development of a farm. The simpler the accounts kept by the beginner, the greater the choice of their proving useful.

In the school farm, the ledger, the cash book, balance sheet, daily labour sheets etc. are some of the records which can prove useful.

The following are a few specimens of necessary and important items of book keeping for the school farm:

1) ***The Ledger:*** **It is the principal book of accounts kept in a business. It is the book that contains a classified and summarised record of all transactions**

The Ledger is ruled as under

Date	Particular	Folio	Amount in Crore Rs. P.	Date	Particular	Folio	Amount in Crore Rs. P.

Fig. 1

of the business transferred or posted to it from the other books of original entry.

2) **The Cash Book: -** The cash book facilitates references. A separate register is maintained to record all the transactions involving cash receipts and cash payments.

3) **Balance Sheet: -** It is made up of the assets and liabilities and may be defined as a statement setting forth the various assets, liabilities and the capital of business of any given date. All assets and liabilities are set out in the Balance Sheets in a classified form, so as to show clearly the financial position of the concern on the date balance is reckoned.

4) **Daily Labour Sheet: -** It is meant for recording the daily occupation of labour employed on the farm whether hired or unpaid 'student labour.' It is usually designed to contain a daily record of manual, bullock, and machine labour with details of the work done on each operation or crop, field by field or on other enterprises.

Daily Labour Sheet of Work: People at.......................

Farm on..........

Name of Crop of No. of Plot	Nature of work in detail	Manual Labour			Bullock Pair	Machine Persian Wheel	Other	Area	Remarks
		Men	Women	Boys					

Fig. 2

18.14 Workshop Maintenance

Maintenance of the school workshop must be carried out methodically and intelligently as a continued activity. However, efficient and up-to-date a piece of machinery or equipment may be, or however well organised a particular process, optimum output cannot be secured unless proper working conditions are maintained and service activities are properly taken care of. Lack of maintenance can lead to bottlenecks resulting in reduced output or high rate of scrap work leading to low student morale. Workshop maintenance is also essential to reduce service expenses.

Workshop maintenance can be of five types:-

(i) ***Capital Replacement:*** - Use the equipment till it completely wears out its useful life and then replace it by a new one.

(ii) ***Break-down Maintenance:*** - The equipment is to be attended only when it fails due to some reason or prevents the desired rate of output.

(iii) ***Scheduled Maintenance:***- It consists of the preparation of a list of major items of equipment in the workshop and suggests to the workshop superintendent the items likely to require attention during the calendar year. A tentative or annual schedule is drawn and sanctions obtained for the purpose.

(iv) ***Planned Maintenance:*** - Planned maintenance endeavours to answer what maintenance is to be carried out and by whom.

(v) ***Preventive Maintenance:*** - In this type of maintenance the work of inspection, maintenance, replacement, or modification nature is broken down in elements and are studied to improve methods and to obtain more accurate work contents.

A good maintenance system would include the following:

(a) A log or record sheet for each equipment or machine.

(b) A daily work programme.

(c) The list of persons responsible for maintenance.

(d) A chart showing expenditure or money and time and quantity of production.

(e) Charts of different types of equipment and process for serving visual aids.

(f) Number of students attending the workshop in the different periods.

For optimum utilisation of the equipment, and for maximum output in terms of material production and human development, through equipment and production, every part of the workshop must be kept spick and span.

18.15 Principles of Workshop Encouragement

Workshops are necessary for certain crafts like woodwork and metalwork, but these workshops in an educational institution have to be different from workshops in a factory and business premises. It is rather difficult, nay impossible, for the young children bubbling with enthusiasm to work with the hammer and chisel or to work on lathe mechanically. Children detest routine type of work; they never want to work in response to specifications given by the instructor. Even when they do, they are not at their best. If the teacher wants that children should love to work in a workshop, he should bear in mind the principles listed below:

1. *Physical conditions in the workshops should be excellent.* The arrangement of light should be proper. If necessary, artificial light may be provided. Adequate and good material should be provided in the workshop to avoid irritation. The size of tools should be suitable to those who are to use them. Tools should be in good condition.

2. *Craftwork in a workshop must provide a high degree of imaginative activity leading to the creation of original forms.* Routine activity, with little or no accent on creativity, kills the interest of the pupils. When all the

pupils in a woodwork class are engaged in the production of the same type of article the specifications of which have been given by the teacher and when creative imagination of the pupils is not given any outlet, pupils will not be interested. Expression of individuality is one of the most important functions of craft.

3. *A large measure of freedom should be given to children to choose, plan and execute the kinds of craft projects on which they would like to work.* There is no justification for pupils in all basic schools to manufacture the same articles. Dull uniformity, regarding the preparation of objects, should be avoided. Students should be encouraged to make all kinds of articles, including toys. The guiding principle should be the promotion of originality and creativity.

4. *Emphasis should not be laid on the quantity of goods produced but on quality, not on the number of hours per week spent on craftwork but on good craft teaching and on the acquisition of skill and artistry by the pupils.* Stress should be laid on good craftsmanship so that children learn to take pride and to find satisfaction in a piece of work skillfully executed. Students should be helped to conceive and perform good designs in an art class and create things of artistic appeal in a workshop. Craftwork which is devoid of artistic appeal may succeed in developing some mechanical skill, but it cannot touch, much less affect, the source of some of the greatest joys in life – the aesthetic emotions.

Thus, if we want that crafts like Agriculture, Woodwork, Metalwork, etc. yield intended results, the problem of their proper planning and arrangement must occupy our immediate attention. If any activity is worth doing, it needs doing well. Let us worry about the process – the product will definitely take care of itself.

Objective Type Questions

Multiple Choice Questions (Tick ✓ the right option)

(1) Manures are the concentrates for the
(a) Soil
(b) Land
(c) Farm
(d) None of the above

(2) Workshops are necessary for certain crafts like
(a) Woodwork
(b) Metalwork
(c) Both 'a' and 'b'
(d) None of the above

Fill in the blanks

(1) ________ is blood for the farm crops. [Water]
(2) Land without ________ does not give good returns. [Manure]

Important Questions

1. Discuss the importance of a School Farm in a higher secondary school. Describe briefly the essentials of farm management.

2. Suggest an ideal scheme of farm and field layout for a high school farm.
3. What principles can guide us in managing the School Farm?
4. Why is it necessary to keep proper accounts of the products in a School Farm? What type of records would you suggest?
5. What steps can you take to ensure continuous interest in workshop work in a school?
6. How would you manage a School Farm?

19

The School Office

The school office is, truly speaking, the nerve centre of the school - controlling its life in various branches. It is a place where various records, reports, and registers are stored, where the important matters of administrative policy are discussed, where the visitors are received. Thus, the school office serves as a 'home-base' for the principal, 'professional centre' for the school staff, and the 'service centre' for the entire school. No wonder the school office is said to be the fulcrum around which the whole of the school rotates. On the efficient organisation and management of the school office, will depend the efficient administration of the entire school.

19.1 Functions of the School Office

The school office can help the smooth running of a school in a number of ways:

(i) *The office can keep an up-to-date file of data about the children in the school.* Teachers should be free from the onerous task of book-keeping wherever possible. The clerk should be mainly responsible for book-keeping, so that the teacher's energies may be released for the creative job of guiding the development of children.

(ii) *The school office can take the responsibility of setting up the actual schedules.* Every school has to establish certain rules for the control of such materials and spaces as the Assembly Hall, Music Room, Laboratories, Workshops, Visual Education Equipment, Textbooks, Supplies, etc. After the teachers have determined the ways by which they desire these to be handled, the office can take the responsibility of setting up the actual schedules. The office can circulate the blank schedules for the use of different faculties, get the teachers' comments, get the principal's final approval, prepare a master copy of the schedule, duplicate it or type it so that each teacher could have a copy for constant reference. Thus, the office can act as a *service agency*.

(iii) *The school office can assume the responsibility for the clerical task of making up supply order and doing the actual purchasing.* Let each teacher determine his own needs, all of which may be sent to office and compiled as a total list of needs for the school. This compilation may be examined by the staff to determine whether the total is within the limits set for such expenditures. Any cuts in amounts or kinds of materials may be cooperatively agreed upon by all teachers. Thus, the approved revised list may be sent to the office for ordering. It is the responsibility of the office to order the goods, and deliver the goods to the individual teachers. Thus, the office can also act as a *central collecting and distributing agency*.

(iv) *The school office can help teachers in survey tests.* After the teachers have agreed upon the kind of testing programme they desire and have selected the tests appropriate to their purposes, the actual task of ordering and distributing the tests can be handled by the office. The office can help the teacher perform his or her tasks with a minimum of clerical labour.

(v) *The school office can help on duplication or typing of teacher-made materials.* Modern school techniques include the use of teacher-made materials, materials that are made especially for an actual group of children, based on their present needs. The office can prove useful here as well. New materials, assignments, etc. can be duplicated by the school office. In this way, office can help in good teaching practices as well.

(vi) *The school office can help in acquainting the community with the work of the school through desirable publicity programmes.* Copy of newspaper releases, brochures depicting the work of the school, notices sent home with children announcing school functions, invitations to parents and patrons to visit the school - are some of the ways by which the office can lighten the burden of the teacher. Whenever the school needs to communicate with the outside world, the school office should supply the technical facilities.

19.2 The School Clerk

The school clerk is an indispensable assistant of the school principal. Without him, the principal is generally burdened with office work. As the supervision duties of the principal have multiplied, a clerk for handling office work, correspondence, records, stores, registers, etc. is a valuable aid.

19.3 Duties of the Clerk

The school clerk can be assigned the following duties:

1. Office work.
2. Correspondence.
3. Maintenance of records.
4. Typing and duplicating.
5. Banking and accounts.
6. Stores.
7. School Meals.
8. First Aid.

It is absolutely necessary that the clerk is trained in these jobs.

19.4 Filing and Filing Systems

Proper filing of necessary documents is one of the main principles of good office work. The different letters, papers, and reports have to be filed in such a careful manner that the documents when required for reference are available at a moment's notice.

The following are the chief filing systems in use in schools today:

1. The Flat File System.
2. The Vertical File System.

1. The Flat File System

This system is very useful for some schools. In this system, the files are kept in a wooden-box with a number of drawers - one drawer is used for two or three alphabets. The names of files in each drawer are pasted on one side of the box.

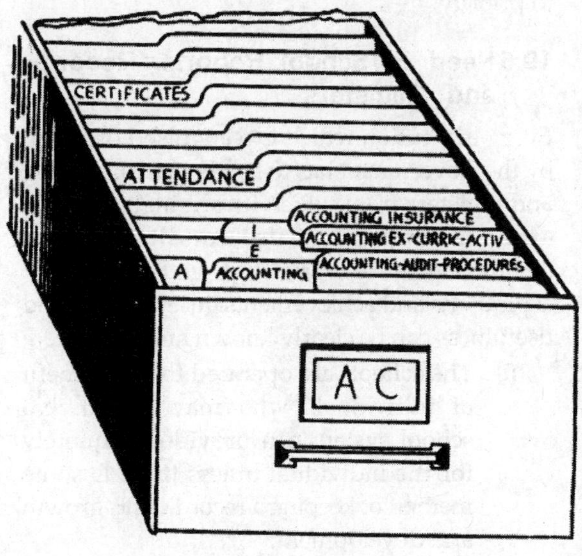

Fig. 1

2. *The Vertical File System*

This system is generally adopted in schools. In this system, all materials pertaining to a subject are filed together. The files are arranged in an alphabetical order. As such, there is an alphabetic index.

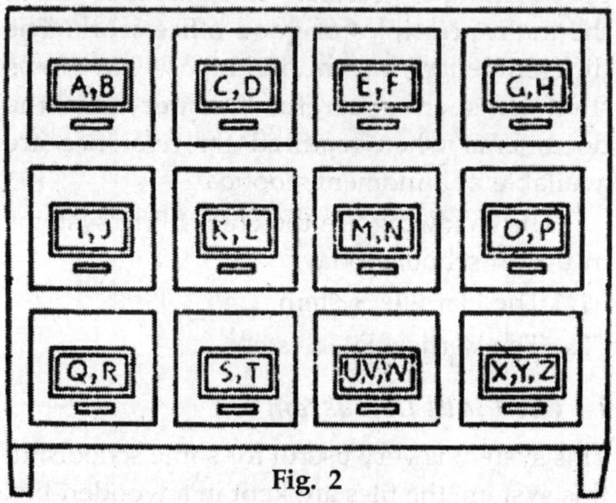

Fig. 2

A number of compartments in the office rack may be labelled according to the nature of the problem, e.g. "Urgent," "Deferred," "Immediate", "Reports from Teachers" and so on. This will facilitate handling cases according to priority.

19.5 Need of School Reports, Records and Registers

Every institution which is recognised or is run by the Government has to keep records, reports, and registers from which its origin, its growth and development, its conditions and circumstances of various periods, its aims, aspirations and achievements, its efficiency and usefulness can be clearly known and estimated.

(i) The schools are operated for the benefit of individuals who may attend. No school system can provide adequately for the individual unless there is some method of keeping a record of his growth and development.

(ii) The state laws under which the schools operate make it mandatory for the administration to keep records of the school age of children.

(iii) The progress of institutions depends upon research. Complete information on the pupil's progress, instructional materials, standardised tests, physical development, promotion practices, marks and so forth, must be secured through a system of pupil personnel records.

(iv) The development of good home-school relationship is essential for the maximum development of the individual child. Reports on pupil's progress issued to parents at stated intervals will help develop such desirable home-school relationship. The progress reports require a system of records which will enable the teacher to make an accurate and complete evaluation of the pupil's growth and development.

(v) From these records, the educational progress and needs of particular localities, and even of the state as a whole, can be judged.

The great problem for the organiser is therefore, to keep the records and reports so that they will be of most benefit to all persons who deal with the individual child. To develop such a system, there is need for some realistic planning. There are certain fundamental principles which must be considered in selecting, maintaining, using, and storing pupil's personnel records and reports if the school system is to render the maximum service to all individuals of the community. The recognition of some basic principles should give impetus to the establishment of a good record system.

19.6 Kinds of Records, Reports and Registers

There are many kinds of records – those relating to middle and high schools that can be classified under the following heads:-

(a) General: - 1. Calendar 2. Log Book 3. Visitor's Book 4. Service Registers 5. Admission Registers 6. Transfer of

Certificate File 7. File of Enrolment Cards 8. Teachers Personnel Record 9. Record Register having record of all Registers.

(b) ***Financial:*** - 1. Acquittance Roll 2. Contingent Order Book 3. Contingency Register 4. Register of Fee Collections 5. Register of Receipts and Expenditure 6. Bill Register 7. Register of Donations 8. Register of Scholarships 9. Practical Instruction Order Book 10. Funds Register 11. Trunk Call Register 12. T.A. Check Register 13. Cash Book 14. Stipend Register, etc.

(c) ***Educational:*** - 1. Pupil's Attendance Register 2. Teacher's Attendance Register 3. Class timetables 4. Teachers' Timetables 5. General Timetables 6. Teachers' Monthly Programme of Work 7. Monthly Progress Register 8. Terminal Examination Result Register 9. Register of Corporal Punishments 10. Private Tuition Register 11. Teacher's Diary 12. File of Transfer Cards 13. File of Elementary School Report Cards 14. File of Promotion and Failure Report 15. Project Register, etc.

(d) ***Equipments:*** - 1. Stock Book of Furniture and School Appliances 2. Library Catalogue 3. Accession Register 4. Library Issue Book 5. Stationery Issue Book 6. Stock and Issue of Sports Material 7. Stationery Register.

(e) ***Correspondence:*** - 1. 'From' and 'To' Registers 2. File of Departmental Orders and Circulars 3. Public Examination File 4. Register of Casual Leave Granted 5. D. O. Letter Register 6. Pending Cases Register.

A few of the important school records, reports, and registers are described below.

19.7 Mode of Keeping Records

(i) In every institution, a stock list of registers should be prepared.

(ii) On the outer cover of each register, the following particulars should be written:

(a) The name of the school (b) The serial No. of the register (c) The name of the register (d) Number of the volume (e) The number of pages in the volume and dates on which the volume was opened and closed.

(iii) When a register is opened, the pages should be numbered consecutively, either in red ink or with a numbering machine.

(iv) Registration should be kept tidy. Writing and figuring should be such as will give a neat appearance of the entries. Figures must not be joined. Registers should not be folded or the pages crumpled. Over-writing should not be permitted.

(v) Entries should be countersigned by the principal. A new volume of a register should not be opened every year, if the previous volume contains some blank pages. Whenever a fresh book is put into use, a remark on the flysheet of the book that the previous volume has been fully used and lodged in the records should be recorded and the date from which the new register is used and the number of pages it contains should also be noted therein.

These are some of the suggestions for keeping the records and registers up to the mark that they may serve the purpose for which they are kept.

19.8 Some Important School Records and Registers

(1) School Calendar

A school calendar is a useful record which a school should keep. It can help in the systematic organisation of the school activities. The calendar should contain the following items of information and such others as may concern the work of the institution from time to time:

(i) General, partial, and local holidays.

(ii) Dates for the submission of monthly, quarterly, half yearly and annual reports and returns.

- **(iii)** Dates of public and school examinations.
- **(iv)** Dates of sending up applications for public examinations.
- **(v)** Dates of meetings of School Committees, Teachers Associations, different clubs and societies, school tournaments, school excursions and educational tours.
- **(vi)** The dates of periodic and terminal tests in different subjects.

The school calendar, in short, can give us a clear picture of the various activities to be conducted throughout the academic year. It is helpful to the administrator, teachers, and pupils.

(2) Log Book

It is necessary that every school should keep a log book. At present only the inspecting officers are entitled to put down their remarks in it. But we feel that it should contain a complete record of events and as such it should furnish material for a history of the school. It should contain mention of special events, the introduction of new textbooks, apparatus or courses of instructions, any plan of lessons approved by the inspector, the visits of the inspecting officers and other distinguished persons interested in education, absence, and illness of any of the school staff and any failure in duty on their part, changes in the working hours of school, some special circumstances affecting the school that may deserve to be recorded for future references or for any other reason.

(3) Admission Register

The admission register is a record of all the pupils who are admitted to the school. In it are entered that date of admission, the serial number of the pupil, the age and name of the pupil, the father's name, caste, occupation and address, the class to which the pupil is admitted and the date on which he leaves the school. According to the departmental rules, admission register has to be preserved permanently. Special care should be taken in keeping the register so that there are no mistakes whatsoever, especially in the column of the date of birth of the pupil when he is admitted to the school. This is so because this register is often required by some superior authority in a court of law as evidence for the date of a pupil. Fresh entries have to be made when pupils move from one department to another in the school.

(4) Pupil's Attendance Register

This is another register which is absolutely necessary. As far as possible, only one attendance register should be kept by one teacher. Exceptions may be made, however, in those cases where classes are small. The attendance registers in our country provide a separate column for each session of the school day. So the attendance has to be marked for both the morning and the afternoon sessions. Attendance should be marked as soon as the class assembles at the prescribed time. Holidays and their nature should be shown in the attendance register. It should show the absences, tardiness, entrances, withdrawals, promotions, failures and other information which may be desired by the administrators.

These registers should be preserved for five years.

(5) Cash Book

A cash book is another important record to be carefully maintained in a school. All financial transactions occurring from day to day are to be entered in a cash book. It should be a bound volume and should contain pages numbered in print.

All transactions to which a principal is a party in his official capacity must be brought in the school cash book and all sorts of amounts received on a particular date should be deposited in full into a Government Treasury or the Bank, as the case may be.

Cash Book------------------for the---------------------of-----------------------2010

Cr.

Month & Date	Receipts	Ledger Folio	Amount Rs.	Amount P.	Total Rs.	Total P.	Month & Date	Payments	Ledger Folio	Amount Rs.	Amount P.	Total Rs.	Total P.

Fig. 3

All transactions relating to the school, such as salary, fees, and fines, should be entered in this register. The cash book must be kept up-to-date. There must be agreement between entries in the cash book and the corresponding entries in the other registers. For instance, Contingent Register, Union Account Register, Admission Fee Register, Medical Register, Games Account Register, etc. as also with the remittances and withdrawal in the pass-book and the copies of the challans.

(6) Stock Register of School Equipment

This is the register of all the movable property in the school. Whenever any equipment or furniture, which is of a more or less permanent nature, is bought and placed in the school, it must be duly entered in the property register. Along with the name of the article should appear the date of receipt of the article in the school, its price, and authority who ordered the purchase. The stock of equipment should be checked by the principal at least once a year and verification should be recorded in the stock register, with an explanation for discrepancy if any and action taken for its regularisation. Checking is much simplified if room-wise property inventories are prepared.

Kind or Location of Property	School Invoice Number	Value beginning of School Year	Increase During Year			Decrease During Year			Value at end of School Year
			Capital Outlay	Mainte-nance	Total	Depre-ciation	Loss or Sale	Total	
1									
2									
3									

Fig. 4

(7) Teacher's Attendance Register

A register for the purpose of recording the daily attendance of the teachers in a school is another necessary record. This should show the time of arrival of the teacher and the time of departure each day. This should be regularly filled in and signed by all teachers, morning and afternoon, every day. Latecomers should indicate the time at which they arrive. The principal should also mark his own attendance and check the attendance of his assistants at the commencement of each school session. Holidays and their nature should also be indicated in it. Leave and nature of the leave should be shown and all applications for leave should be filed in the school office. The number of days of casual leave or other leave taken by each teacher during the month should be noted in the register by the principal at the end of the month.

(8) Personnel Record

It is generally seen that the head of the schools change positions rather frequently. A principal going into a new position encounters many situations with which he must be acquainted. One important factor that demands his attention is the teaching force. Whether it is a small or large school, there should be a complete personnel record of all the employees. This record is not only valuable in helping the principal to study and become acquainted with the teaching personnel, but is also essential for the teachers' welfare. Fig.5 is an example of a teacher's personnel record which brings together much information about the individual.

Teacher's Personnel Record

Name.. Sex M.. F........................

Home Address..

Birthplace...

Date Employed in.. Kind of Work..

Date Left Employment of School.. Reason of Leaving................................

Training before being employed				Experience before being employed		
Schools Attended	Dates	Qualifications	Experience	Schools	Date	Position

Fig. 5

(9) Enrollment Record

Upon entering school for the first time, all pupils should be required to furnish certain general information. A form showing the information to be collected is given in fig.6. The enrolment card should be made in duplicate, one for the superintendent's office and one for the principal's office. This record may be used as a continuous enrolment card and should be kept up-to-date at all times. Some schools have found it advisable to print the enrolment card in different colours, one colour for the superintendent's office, and another colour for the principal's office.

(10) Pupil's Progress Reports

It has been a traditional practice in schools to appraise the accomplishment of each child, particularly with regard to his mastery of subject-matter and report this judgement to the home on a form popularly known as the progress report. Even now this practice is quite popular. This report card establishes a link between the parents and the teacher. Parents should be given an honest and complete evaluation of the child's growth and development. The method of reporting should be developed cooperatively by all concerned. Reports should stress the kinds of behaviour in a democracy. It should provide for individual differences. It should be constructive, diagnostic, and complete in all phases of child growth and development. The reporting system should be consistent with the educational philosophy of the whole school. The report card plays an important part in building goodwill in the home towards the school. This is a very important factor and should never be overlooked. The schools need the support of the homes if the greatest good is to be done for the largest number of children.

YADAVINDRA PUBLIC SCHOOL

PATIALA

Name .... Report for the .... term 2010
Class.. Age.. Average Age of Class........................
Absent .... days. No. of Boys in Class ....
Position in Class at the end of last term ....

TERMINAL RESULT

Subject	Max. Marks	Marks Obtained	Position	Quality of Work
English..........................				
Mathematics................				
History..........................				
Geography..................				
Hindi............................				
Punjabi.........................				
Sanskrit........................				
Science.........................				
Hygiene and Physical Education...				
Art...............................				
General Knowledge...				
Total.............................				

Fig. 6

(11) Promotion and Failure Report

Some schools make out a promotion and failure report at the end of each year. Figure 7 shows the form to be used. If such a table is worked out at the close of each year, it may show the principal certain danger points which deserves his attention. It will also give the teacher a chance to see his situation in relation to the whole school. Should a grade or a subject have unusually high percentage of failures, further investigations should be made to find out the reasons. It is through such studies as these that the principal of a school can locate pupil promotion problems that should be solved.

Promotion and Failure Report

School .... Date...

Grades or Subjects	Number Enrolled	Number Appeared	Number Promoted	Percentage Promoted	Number Failed	Percentage Failed
1.						
2.						
Maths						
History						
Language						

Fig. 7

Objective Type Questions

Multiple Choice Questions (Tick ✓ the right option)

(1) The progress of institutions depends upon
  (a) Research
  (b) Materials
  (c) Standard
  (d) None of the above

(2) It is necessary that every school should keep
  (a) Registers
  (b) Log Book
  (c) Cheque Book
  (d) None of the above

Fill in the blanks

(1) The _______________ system is very useful for some schools. [Flat life]

(2) The _______________ is a record of all the pupils who are admitted to the school. [Admission Register]

Important Questions

1) What are the various registers and other documentary records needed in the organisation of a school? How are they to be maintained?
2) Why is the School Office considered the nerve centre of the school?
3) Discuss different types of filing equipment.
4) Why is it important that secondary school office be organised efficiently?

20

The School Library

There is an extract in the foreword addressed to the Reader in Eastman's Books that have shaped the world:

"Books are not mere paper, ink, or cloth, they are persons. For the most part, they are a company of the immortals who have weathered the centuries and are now marching toward eternity. They told me of their adventures, their romances, their meditations, and their exploration of the inner world. They lifted my horizons. They made me laugh and cry and rejoice living in the same world. They invite you too."

20.1 Unique Place of Library in a Modern School

There is no denying the fact that a library occupies a very prominent place in the educational set-up at present. The changing patterns of education demands that the learning must be accelerated and broadened by the use of many and varied devices and materials. In a dynamic approach to teaching, the library is an essential part of the school. It not only supplies enriched materials in all fields of study but also supplies materials in all levels of difficulty. "All good methods of education postulate the existence of a well-stocked, efficiently organised library." The teaching in the new set-up cannot be classroom centered but has to be child-centered and library-centered. The child's learning has to be self-directed and he has to acquire reading skills and do reading activities through the agency of the school library.

Whereas a curriculum and textbook aim at providing the least common multiple of all students in a class, the library aims not only in bringing out the individual differences but also developing special interests and aptitudes to their best advantage. Civilisation has progressed by virtue of specialisation, and specialisation is fed by out of the rut studies. Library habit creates specialists.

All children need an environment of attractive books from the beginning and it is one of the duties of the school to provide this environment. If a child's early experiences with books are pleasant, a sound foundation is laid for their use in his future development because once the child has been taught to read and brought to love books, he can explore. Carlyle has also aptly said, "The ultimate aim of education is to teach boys how to read. Once they learn to read, education will take care of itself."

Recent discussions about the part of library in the life of the school have led to the following conclusions:

(a) The library is a collection of a "background material" which can be drawn upon to enrich the work of the curriculum.

(b) It is a place where the use of books as sources of information may be taught and practiced.

(c) It provides material to inspire and develop a pupil's extra-mural interests and pursuits.

(d) It is a place where various valuable responsibilities may be exercised.

Hence, the school library can play an important role in all aspects of education. As all education does not take place at home or school, its service makes a substantial contribution to children's education during school life and also helps in their future search for knowledge. No wonder, therefore,

H. G. Wells was forced to remark, "A school without an easily accessible library of at least a thousand volumes is really scarcely a school at all, - it is a dispensary without bottles, a kitchen without a pantry."

Frances Henne writes, "Good schools, very good schools, and excellent schools, all need excellent libraries. Inferior schools need excellent libraries too, to overcome the omissions of the curriculum and to compensate for the poor instructional programme."

20.2 Functions of the School Library

The more varied are the curricula in the school, the heavier are the demands on the library. The functions of a school library are:

1. *To facilitate the instructional programme for the teacher*. With a wide variety of text and reference books related to various school subjects, it facilitates the instructional programme. Also it provides reading materials to the pupil for answering questions, doing assignments, and solving problems.
2. To teach a skillful use of books for self-education.
3. To create an atmosphere conducive to the growth of reading habits.
4. To stimulate literary appreciation.
5. To demonstrate the desirability of books and libraries as companions in one's leisure.
6. To provide fruitful social experiences.
7. To make the library an agency for:
   - (a) Curriculum enrichment;
   - (b) Pupil exploration; and
   - (c) The dissemination of good literature.

20.3 Important Library Resources

(a) Book Resources

Books are essential for presenting different points of view, for providing adequate background, for understanding the people, the processes, and the places. In book resources we can include:

(i) ***Textbooks:-*** The library should contain a variety of most up-to-date textbooks in various subjects.

(ii) ***Unit Booklets:*** - The booklets on a variety of topics ranging from family life and neighbourhood to people of other lands and places should also be available in the school library.

(iii) ***Literary Materials:*** - Inspirational and imaginative literature, particularly tales of adventure, should appear prominently along side books of information on children's hobbies - which may be anything from boats and balloons to kites or from doll-houses to dress-designs. Easy biographies, historical series, animal stories are favourites with children. Travel books are really magic carpets to those who cannot leave their homes. These will help make curriculum lively and interesting.

(iv) ***Reference Materials***:- The school library should be fairly well-equipped with reference materials. Reference materials may be divided into two categories viz.

1. Standard or Conventional Reference Books, and
2. Non-conventional Reference Books.

Conventional reference books include Dictionaries, Encyclopaedias, Directories, Year Books, Atlases, Maps, Charts, Pamphlets, Handbooks, and Manuals. The Dictionary and the Encyclopaedia are basic reference works which help form the look-it-up habit. The Oxford Illustrated Dictionary and a set of Oxford Junior Children's Encylopaedia or a Book of Knowledge must be provided in the school library even if they are costly books. There should be some picture collections which should only include reproduction of well-known masterpieces and everything to which teachers and children are attracted, e.g. animals, insects, flowers, portraits, seasons, holidays, places of interests and events. These prove most valuable to teachers especially for classroom use.

The non-conventional reference material consists of all other library books that may be employed for reference service of any other kind. They include books on miscellaneous information and books on special subjects.

(b) Non-Book Resources

The curriculum is concerned with happiness in the local community, the state, the nation, and the world. Naturally, therefore, it becomes essential that books are supplemented by periodicals, pamphlets, newspapers, and other such materials which may help vitalize the teaching of subject. The following are the important non-book resources which should be available in the school library:

(i) ***Periodicals:*** - These include current events, periodicals and magazines, telling us about the current events and various aspects of life showing art, literature, music, dance, etc. These aspects mirror the social trends of the period.

(ii) ***Pamphlets***: - Pamphlets published by various Government agencies and bureaus for specialised services are also very important sources of information about different walks of our social, economic, and political life. They are generally low priced. Every school library should subscribe for these.

(iii) ***Newspapers:*** - It is desirable for each school to provide local newspaper, one or two other daily newspapers of all-India circulation. It is essential that the teachers and pupils keep well-informed of events of national and international importance and newspaper is a wonderful agency for that.

(iv) ***Special Documents and Publications:*** - Brochures, yearly calendar, date-books, published by the state Governments, folders containing rich information about various places, regions, and towns published by tourist bureaus, and important business concerns should also form important part of library materials.

(v) ***Audio-Visual or Non-reading Materials:*** The library that does not have magazines, newspaper pamphlets, etc. is poor. It is a second rate library if there is not an extensive picture file. So a library should have maps, globes, charts, graphs, models, films, film strips, slides. Among the auditory materials may be included radio, tape-recording, television, and sound films. Audio-visual equipment such as projectors, recorders, radio and television receivers, etc. may, also be housed in the library for use by the entire school.

20.4 Requisite of an Ideal Library

(i) ***Library Rooms:*** - The first essential for a school library to work efficiently is that it must have a separate room. The room should be large enough not only for the present enrolment of the school but also for any subsequent increase in the enrolment. The minimum size should not be less than the size of an ordinary classroom. It should be centrally located and within easy access from any point in the school building. The library should have good natural light; artificial light should also be provided by means of semi-direct fluorescent light which should reach all the dark corners of the room. The floor should be sound proof as far as possible or a matting of soothing colour should be spread out. The library should also have a storage room which may store books that need binding and other essential audio-visual materials. There should also be a work-room consisting of a big table for purposes of mending books, mounting pictures, and preparing books for the shelves.

(ii) ***Furniture:*** - The library should be well furnished with reading tables and chairs. The chairs should be light but strong, and preferably without arms. The library should have a magazine stand or a rack, a desk for the librarian, card catalogue case, a clock, and a bulletin board. The almirahs should be arranged all round the walls. The shelves should preferably be open and not very high.

There should be an interesting display of new books on the New Arrival display rack. There should also be a "Show Window" in which some Forgotten Books and books by eminent authors are attractively displayed. The Library Display Board should have attractive books, jackets, and pictures of real educational value to the students and teachers.

(iii) ***Scheme of Organisation:*** **-** The resources of the library should be classified, catalogued, and filed. The scheme of organisation should be simple enough to the understood easily. According to Dr. Ranganathan, the proper arrangement can satisfy the following basic law of library science:

(a) Books are for use.

(b) Save the time for the reader.

It will help in increasing the efficiency of service to pupils and teachers.

(iv) ***Resources:*** - The library must possess adequate books appropriate to age, taste, and standard of the children in the school. The books chosen should deal in the main with human action and with motives which can easily be understood. The story element should dominate in the junior classes. In the senior classes, books of a more serious nature such as tales of travel and exploration, biographies and playlists may also be included. History and biographies are not only informative but also transportive to other times and lives. Fairy tales, legends, and myths, stories of animals, as well as of stirring incidents in the lives of great men and women, adventures and experiences of boys and girls all these furnish suitable material abundantly. In short, library should spread such literary fare as tickles the palate of the young reader.

The general and class libraries should not consist exclusively of story books. There should be plenty of practical books dealing with subjects pertaining to the environment of the pupil, the everyday world around him such as plants and animals, steam engine and railways, ship, motor, the aeroplane, the radio, cinematography, the television, architecture and fine arts, games and scouting, etc.

The library should subscribe to a number of periodicals, and magazines. Newspapers form an indispensable part of any library. Pamphlets and clippings have been called the *short-cuts for the busy*. These are invaluable reference aids.

(v) ***A Code of Rules:*** **-** For efficient service, a code of rules to regulate the use of library is to be evolved. The rules should be clear and simple and should place the fewest possible obstacles in the way of the use of the library. The librarian must compile and maintain a shelf register, accession record, catalogue and issue statistics, and decide upon circulation methods and other routines. He must arrange for the withdrawal, binding, replacement of torn out or damaged books.

(vi) ***Decoration:*** - The library should be decorated with beautiful and meaningful pictures. These should be on all possible topics. These should illustrate and supplement class work. One or two distinct works of art, a few vases for flowers, coloured maps, hung low and bright posters preferably made by pupils themselves, would add a lot of colour and cheer to the library and make it a pleasant place to browse in.

(vii) ***Atmosphere:*** - Last but not the least important, the atmosphere in the library should breathe a sense of a general

seeking of knowledge and a love of "the true, good and beautiful." It should provide relief from the daily routine of the timetable programme and classroom discipline and provide inspiration when one needs an idea. The library should really become the intellectual 'hub' of the school where readers come to refresh themselves and recreate themselves and can thus become 'the pride' of the institution.

20.5 The School Librarian

Dr. Johnson has said, "Knowledge is of two kinds. We know a subject ourselves or know where we can find information upon it." It very well shows the important role which a librarian can play in facilitating the spread of information. As an engine cannot work unless and until there is somebody who could control and put life into it, similar is the case with the library. When the readers come in the library, there should be someone to receive them with a smiling face as well as ready to help them. Dr. K. L. Shrimali rightly emphasises in his book "Problems of Education in India" as "in libraries as in other human institutions the human factor is the most important." Similarly Mc Colvin says, "Books themselves are nothing. They have no meaning than the white paper on which they are published, unless they are made serviceable by demand." Books are artificial entities and there must be something to put life into them.

Each school must have a trained and qualified librarian or enthusiastic teacher who has undergone in-service training in library technique. The librarian has a special part to play in making library service popular. He should enjoy books, enjoy library work, and enjoy the library. His fundamental aim should be getting "as many books into as many hands and their contents into as many heads as possible." The smallest proportion of the books in the library should remain on its shelves. Only then the library deserves to be called in the words of Dr. S.R. Ranganathan, 'a live workshop.'

The librarian must be capable of discharging the functions with success and ability, preparing and circulating book lists suitable for different grades, conducting study projects and study circles, giving due publicity to books old and new. In the words of the Report of the Secondary Education Commission, "He will have to act as the pivot, and inspiration of the intellectual and library firmament."

Whenever children come with a specific question to answer, the librarian must guide them not only to the correct cupboard but also to the likely books. The librarian should ensure that individual reading is progressive in quality. The method he uses should be persuasive rather than imperative, indirect rather than direct. He should possess a tactful, sympathetic approach. He should have a cheerful and easy-going disposition that would encourage the shyest of children to approach him for advice on every conceivable problem. Upon him devolves, in fact, the supreme responsibility of training the children in the use of libraries.

20.6 The Teacher

The teacher's part in library service, is in a sense, passive. The wise teacher must know how to keep himself in the background while he is actively engaged in providing reading material suited to the grade. The classroom teacher should stimulate pupils to use the library, to find and organise materials on selected or class projects, encourage pupils to use the library for recreational leisure reading, borrow books for use in the classroom, and encourage pupils to select books for this purpose and keep the librarian informed of prospective classroom demands on the library and enjoy reading and sharing good books with the students. The teacher should make the library a functional part of the child's everyday experience. He may also prepare and administer comprehensive tests.

The teacher should prepare his class for the visit during the library period, take a note of the librarian's suggestions, and ask questions, should be alert and interested and make suggestions and comments.

Children readily acquire the habit of obtaining their information at the proper source, if so guided by the teacher as well as the librarian. For every strange word encountered in the course of reading, for every question left in suspense, the appropriate book of reference may be recommended, the atlas for the exact position of a town, the dictionary for a term in current use. They should be encouraged to go for their information to the best source available in the library so that they may develop in them a sense of objectivity.

20.7 Library Service and its Function

Our age is witnessing the change-over from being an age of libraries to one of "library service." The nature and scope of library service is an index to the character and quality of curricula and instruction being followed in a particular school.

Library service not only includes the material contents, e.g. books, periodicals, but also their circulation. Without library material, there can be no library service. But the converse is not true, i.e. there can be library without library service.

By quality the library service is meant not only the kind of books in a school but also provision of the library room, furniture, library periods, circulation of books, and inculcation of reading habits. If the library is to be the centre of intellectual life of the school, a centre of supervised study, a source of disseminating knowledge, it must have a very well-planned and systematically organised library service. For this purpose, it is necessary that library should contain a well-balanced collection of books not just stored but stored to advantage. Every pupil should be reached by the programme. Library reading experiences should be pleasant and inviting.

20.8 Motivating Pupils to Utilise Library Resources

The following devices may be used to motivate the pupils to utilise the library resources:

(i) ***Create a link between the child and the book:*** - The library should not be regarded simply as an additional classroom in which purely curricular activities are carried on. One of its most important objectives is to develop in the child a love for books and reading. This cannot be achieved by formal instruction. It is, therefore, necessary to create a link between the child and the book - a link which is to be personal and informal - a link which should have nothing to do with school or organised education. This can only be done by encouraging the child to read for pleasure. The pupil may be encouraged for the pure love of reading. It must be remembered that pupils cannot be *bribed to read.* So the beginnings have to be made on lines which are attractive. In the beginning, pupils may be allowed to choose a book of their own sweet will. Efforts should be made later to lead him from these, by gradual and imperceptible stage, to better literature. Let us "enter in through the pupil's door and lead him out through our own."

Story-telling is very effective in rousing interest in books. For small children, single stories should be told; for older ones; a cycle story *tour* should be fixed; the latter may consist of a series of six to eight tales from literature and mythology.

Brief comments, informal reading, and talks with individual children often help to rouse interest in books.

(ii) ***Assignments:*** - Pupils may be given assignments which require research work in the library. Before any work is assigned to the child, the teacher must

make sure that necessary material is available in the library.

(iii) ***Reading groups:*** - Reading groups may be organised. Pupils may be asked to keep diaries of what they have read. The record should not be just of titles. They should write synopsis of stories. They may be invited to give brief resumes of the books they have read, or to suggest titles of subjects for addition to the library.

(iv) ***Proper record of the books read by the pupils:*** - The principal and the teacher should keep their finger as it were on the pulse of their students' general reading. Proper records of the books read by pupils should be maintained. Where ordinary issue registers – rather than issue cards – are maintained, each student must be allotted a few pages of the registers in which all books studied by him are entered date-wise. Through this, the class teachers and principal can see at a glance what each individual has been reading and can give him necessary advice and encouragement. Frequent opportunities should be provided to the children to have a free and heart-to-heart discussion about the books with the teacher.

(v) ***Minimum library reading to be prescribed:*** - While there is to be no limit to the maximum reading to be done by the pupils, minimum limit should be fixed for each pupil. It may be different for different classes, according to their standard. Lists of different types of books, both fiction and non-fiction, should be prepared by the teacher in consultation with the librarian. These lists should be provided to all pupils and they may be asked to read the required number of books.

(vi) ***Celebration of days:*** - Birthdays of great men and days of national importance may be observed, and the students may be urged to write articles and draw illustrations for these occasions. Good articles and illustrations may be displayed on Bulletin Boards or on the board for the wall-magazines.

(vii) ***Book competition:*** - Book competition can prove very helpful in stimulating children to read. Questions on titles, authors, and subject matters may be set. It will make the pupils anxious to improve their knowledge of books.

(viii) ***Honour roll lists:*** - Honour roll lists of the books read can be kept. If the pupils are rewarded for reading books – they will surely like to read. Certificates of various types may be awarded.

(ix) ***Teacher's use of library resources:*** - The teacher should pay frequent visits to the library, sit, and read there so that students may emulate them. While teaching a certain unit, he should bring with him such books as contain interesting accounts particularly relevant to that unit and read out a few paragraphs in the class from those books. He should, then, give to his pupils the name of the books, the name of authors, and those of their publishers and ask them to collect material from them, related to the unit under study. He may check up later to find out whether the pupils have actually read the books or not.

(x) ***Open shelf-system:*** - The open shelf-system may also be introduced. This will enable the pupils to have access not only to the books they want but also many other relevant materials. This will give them freedom to look for many interesting reading items. There may be a few casualties – some books may be spoiled or lost, but that will be a small price for the great benefit the student is likely to gain from the free use of the library.

(xi) ***Teacher-librarian cooperation:*** - The teaching staff should cooperate with the librarian by letting him know in advance the work to be covered by various classes during the month. The librarian should display books, pictures, and other relevant material. He should ensure proper circulation of books. The availability of books also helps in maintaining the interest.

The teaching staff can cooperate with the librarian by marking magazine articles and by collecting pictures for the librarian to file. Teachers know their syllabi much better than he can, and that can help him to file really useful articles. This will help the pupils very much as they will be able to read current literature on a particular subject from the set of magazines in the file.

20.9 Conclusion

The library is today, considered to be the "Intellectual Laboratory of the School." Library and school are taken as inseparable life forces. Teachers appreciate that textbooks are no longer "Educational Bibles" to be used alone. The library is the treasure vault of ideas, the storehouse of knowledge, and the flowing streams of living thought. As such, it must become an integral part of the school programme.

Objective Type Questions

Multiple Choice Questions (Tick ✓ the right option)

(1) The library is a collection of
- (a) Background material
- (b) Books
- (c) Journals
- (d) None of the above

(2) The curriculum is concerned with happiness in the local community
- (a) The State
- (b) The Nation
- (c) The World
- (d) All of the Above

Fill in the blanks

(1) The general and class libraries should not consist __________ of story books. [Exclusively]

(2) ______________ is very effective in rousing interest in books. [Story–telling]

Important Questions

1. 'The school library has a pivotal place in the modern instructional programme.' How will you use the library for effective teaching?
2. What are the important functions of a School Library?
3. What is the function of a class library? How can a class library be organised and utilised effectively?
4. How should a school library be organised and used to the best advantage of students and teachers?

5. What are the various library resources which can prove useful in the teaching of different subjects?
6. Why is it essential for Secondary School to have a whole time librarian?
7. What are the essential requisites of an ideal School Library?
8. How can a teacher encourage his pupils to read?

21

The School Exhibition and Museum

21.1 Museum as an Educative Agency

Museum – the temple of the Muse, as the word implies, is intended to be a place for study. Since ages, the museum was conceived as the reference file of real objects by which to verify and amplify knowledge, acquired, and preserved in other forms. It is a place where one learns by seeing what is of interest. It is also a centre of recreation where one learns pleasantly but principally one enjoys seeing beautiful and strange things.

Instruction by museum is becoming increasingly popular in all progressive countries: their collections are being more and more utilised for mass education. It is being generally recognised that museums, especially those, which cater for historical and cultural objects impart wholesome education at all levels. The museums which contain collections of natural archaeology, history, traditions, and culture impart education to general public and function as instruments of teaching, on as wide a scale as possible.

In most progressive countries, the museum is recognised to be a living thing; as an instrument with vast potentialities for public service. In Canada, a well-organised modern museum is recognised to be essential to the educational system as a free public library. In Sweden, visits to the museum are connected with school curriculum. Lessons are given by museum lecture. Museum collections are a valuable aid to teachers in giving life and reality to school courses at every stage of formal education. The organised class visit to the museum has been the accepted practice in most countries of Europe and America for several years. Close cooperation between the educators and museums has been notably successful in giving impetus to mass education, guided tours, talks and illustrated lectures, supplement book-bound curriculum of the schools. Museum, in fact, is an important link of the new environment with the older world in which its own institutions, thought, pattern and mode of life has their origins. In the words of the Secondary Education Commission, "Museums play a great part in the education of school children as they bring home to them much more vividly than any prosaic lectures, the discoveries of the past and the various developments, that have taken place in many fields of science and technology. Museum as an agency of education and recreation is invaluable. For the scholar they represent repositories of the objects for study and research; for the educationist and the teacher they are a storehouse of concrete and vivid adjuncts which lend colour and reality to all forms of teaching; for the child the spark which can ignite wonder and curiosity; for the ordinary citizen they are a source of pleasure, delight, and knowledge."

21.2 Importance of Museum in Schools

Not only should every school have a museum – but every school can have a museum. It is well known that children like to collect and that many of them have collections of their own. If it is appropriately suggested to them, they will doubtless react more favourably toward the idea of a school museum and cooperate more enthusiastically in developing it. Such a project is intriguing and it is educative. Planning, accepting, and discharging individual responsibility, doing the necessary research in obtaining, understanding, classifying, mounting, and labelling exhibits and working together for the common good certainly means educational benefits for all concerned. Such a project is not so difficult. It can capitalise on almost any kind of collecting interest, thus guaranteeing variety in the final exhibits. "No environment is so poor as to afford no materials of such value, and none so rich as to require no supplementation."

21.3 What Type of Exhibits in a School Museum?

A good school museum is not merely a collection of items but is a useful collection of useful items. A great proportion of the exhibits should be immediately functional that is, directly related to regular classroom activities rather than an end in itself. Making a relief map, a natural habitat or a picture scrap book or collecting minerals, leaves, nests will bring a natural approach to the curriculum, motivate the necessary research and when completed, will represent a neatly tied up summary of the unit. The school museum should be a repository of educative material.

21.4 Contents of the Museum

A school museum should be divided into various sections. The number of sections will depend upon the subjects taught and the specimens collected in the school. The most important sections may be:

1. Art and Painting
2. Crafts
3. Photographs
4. Posters
5. Teaching Aids
6. Home Industry
7. Geology
8. Zoology
9. Botany
10. Physics
11. Social Studies
12. Home Science
13. Statistical

21.5 Value of School Exhibition

One of the excellent aids to learning is the exhibition of learning materials or of samples of the pupil's work. Exhibits of the pupil's work in the field of art, home science, social studies, and related subjects are always sources of great pride to the young people and are of great value to many.

If such exhibits are arranged systematically in the form of exhibitions, they can serve to acquaint the public with the work of the school and also apprise the student's body of the important activities of the community. Educational exhibitions can play a significant role in the task of educational reconstruction. They can demonstrate to us the progress made by students in the various educational projects undertaken by them from time to time.

What Type of Exhibits?

In a school exhibition the following type of exhibits may be displayed:

(i) Models prepared by the students.

(ii) Actual products prepared by the students – embroidered work, cloth work, durries, towels, etc. tables, chairs, paintings, dolls and other imaginary production, etc.

(iii) Albums containing collection of postage stamps, photographs, leaves, flowers, insects, drawings, portraits, pictures showing life in other lands in sequence, etc.

(iv) Charts throwing light on the problems of general interest.

(v) Charts showing the activities of the school.

(vi) Tools, equipments, etc.

Types of Exhibitions

We can have different types of exhibitions on specific occasions: (i) Exhibitions specially arranged for different subjects, e.g. Science Exhibition, Agriculture Exhibition, Home Science Exhibition, Geographical Exhibition, Art and Craft Exhibition. (ii) Exhibitions to give publicity to some school programmes – Book Exhibition, Photographic Exhibition, Defence Exhibition.

Guidelines for arranging an Exhibition

As exhibition is to be an educative agency, we must arrange and plan it in a very serious manner. Below we list some guidelines for the purpose: -

- **(i)** The exhibits should be as varied as possible.
- **(ii)** Every exhibit should be properly classified and labelled.
- **(iii)** The exhibits should be made out of durable material to stand the wear and tear of time and save rough handling on the part of the visitors.
- **(iv)** The exhibits should be kept in the cases or display cabinets to keep them free from dust. They should be cleaned at regular intervals.
- **(v)** The organisation of an exhibition should be undertaken as a cooperative enterprise between the members of the staff and the students. A committee of teachers should be appointed to guide the students to organise an exhibition.
- **(vi)** Each department of the exhibition should have a student guide who should be conversant with the various details of the exhibits – the process involved, time and money spent, number and names of the persons responsible for the production to guide the visitors.
- **(vii)** Special exhibitions should be organised at suitable intervals.
- **(viii)** Due publicity should be given about the exhibitions. The time and duration, when the exhibition remains open may be specified. To avoid rush of visitors different periods for different groups can be kept.
- **(ix)** Parents and guardians of the students should be specially invited.
- **(x)** Exhibitions should be considered only as a means to good learning; they should not be considered as ends. No exhibition should be arranged at the cost of classroom instruction.
- **(xi)** Whatever is displayed – a painting, a model, a chart, should have a pleasing appearance.
- **(xii)** A record of each exhibit should be maintained. Each exhibit should be given its number. The record should contain the name of the maker of an exhibit, time taken for its preparation, cost incurred, sales price, etc.
- **(xiii)** A visitor's book should be maintained. The visitors should be asked to give their comments on the exhibits, they see. Their constructive suggestions should be welcome and attempts made to incorporate these in the preparation of the articles to be produced later on.
- **(xiv)** Exhibitions can prove a source of income too. Prices should be fixed and pasted on the slips attached to the products. The student guide should be able to advise buyers on the utility of the various products.
- **(xv)** To raise the quality of exhibits prepared by the students some incentive in the form of prizes, may be kept. Judges may be appointed to select the best exhibits and prizes may be awarded.

Objective Type Questions

Multiple Choice Questions (Tick ✓ the right option)

(1) Instruction by museum is becoming increasingly popular in all progressive
(a) City
(b) Country
(c) World
(d) None of the above

(2) Museum collections are a valuable aid to teachers in giving life and reality to school course at every stage of
(a) Informal education
(b) Non-formal education
(c) Formal education
(d) None of the above

Fill in the blanks

(1) Museum as an agency of __________ and recreation is invaluable. [Education]
(2) __________ exhibitions should be organized at suitable intervals. [Special]

Important Questions

1. **What suggestions can you offer for setting up of a museum in a Secondary School?**
2. **Discuss briefly the educational value of school exhibition. How would you organise an exhibition of your children's work?**
3. **How will you organise any one of the following exhibitions:**
   (i) Science Exhibition
   (ii) Book Exhibition
   (iii) Home Science Exhibition
   (iv) Agriculture Exhibition
4. **How far and in what way can School Museum assist in the school as an effective agency in education? What measures would you suggest to improve school museum?**

22

The School Hostel

In India, after the proposal of free, universal, and compulsory primary education, it is quite natural that there should be expansion of secondary education also abruptly, but secondary and higher secondary schools cannot be opened on each place or in all the villages and towns like primary schools. Thus, it is necessary that a high school or higher secondary school, wherever it is located, should fulfill the requirements of students of its surrounding. If secondary school is far from some village or town, the children of those places would feel, difficulty in daily up-down from home to school. Therefore, school management should arrange properly for their lodging and boarding. This sort of arrangement may be done only in a school hostel. Besides, the students who do not find a healthy and appropriate atmosphere at home, can have a pleasant, healthy and appropriate atmosphere in a hostel. A school hostel is essential for those students also whose guardians are often transferred from one place to another. By frequent transfers, they find difficulty in their studies. In the arrangement of hostel, these difficulties may also be done away with. Thus, hostel is an important and essential institution.

It would not be inappropriate to say that a good hostel plays an important role in education. In a hostel, the children avail those facilities for the development of mental, physical, and moral aspects, which are generally not found in homes. For physical development of students, there is appropriate arrangement of nutritious food, clean drinking water, physical, exercise and games and sports. For mental development, proper arrangement is done through library, reading room and studies. For moral or ethical development they get opportunities for leading a regular life and development of good habits. In hostel, self-reliance and self-confidence like qualities also develop, and children learn to lead a disciplined and self-controlled life easily.

Rousseau wrote about the utility of hostel life, *"The lessons that boys can get from each other in the playing fields and the hostel are a hundred times useful to them than lessons given in schools."*

22.1 Need for a School Hostel

The demand for secondary education is growing day-by-day. The people are realising that if a child's education ends at the age of 13-14, it will be like laying the foundations of a house and stopping there, for there is no guarantee that a child is prepared for life in the complex and ever changing world if his formal education ends at 14 – the most critical and dangerous period of his life. Secondary education for all is a natural corollary of the elementary education for all. This will mean more secondary schools. But it is also felt that a secondary school should be well-equipped and as comprehensive as possible. Such type of schools, it must be remembered, cannot be opened anywhere and everywhere. Such type of schools will have to be established at some central places to cater to the needs of a number of villages. It is obvious that the distance from the home to the school in many cases will be quite considerable to allow daily coming and going between home and school. Some suitable arrangement for boarding and lodging in the form of a hostel will have to be made by the school to facilitate the proper education of the children.

Again, there is a need for hostel for those children whose home environment is unhealthy and unhappy.

Also, there are pupils whose parents are frequently transferred from one place to another leading to a serious disruption of their studies. For such children, hostel is very necessary.

Schools having hostel facilities are of great value to the parents who do not find good schools in the neighbourhood and are anxious that their children should get good education.

22.2 Site of the Hostel

The hostel should be constructed at a small distance from the school, neither too far, nor too close. It should have nice sanitary and hygienic conditions.

22.3 Building and Equipment

It is desirable to have a single storey building, quadrangular in shape, with a courtyard at the centre. If the number of inmates is small, we can have I or L shaped hostel building, otherwise quadrangular type of building is ideal for a school hostel for two reasons (i) for effective control and supervision (ii) for safety purposes as it can be enclosed at night.

In a school hostel, big dormitories are preferable to cubicles or even two-seated and three-seated rooms so that effective supervision is possible. The dormitories should be constructed on the three sides of the quadrangle, and the kitchen and the dining hall on the fourth side. In addition to the dormitories, a good school hostel should provide the following rooms:

(i) Common room to provide for indoor games like Carrom Board, Cards, Chess, Table Tennis, etc. A radio-set should also be provided for every common room.

(ii) Reading room for providing reading material for leisure time. A good hostel should subscribe to a number of dailies, weeklies, and monthlies, depending upon the number of boarders.

(iii) Guest room to accommodate parents of the boarders or other essential guests.

(iv) Visitors room to provide place for meeting relations and friends of the boarders.

(v) Sick room – for boarders who fall sick and who have to be segregated.

(vi) Dispensary for providing first aid and small scale medical aid to hostelers.

(vii) Superintendent's quarter.

In addition to these rooms, the hostel building also contains kitchens, dining halls, storerooms, fuel go-downs, servants' rooms, sweeper's quarters, latrines, bathrooms, in accordance with the number for hostelers.

Every boarder should be provided with a cot, a table, a chair, a book rack, and an almirah. Lighting and ventilation arrangements should be perfect. The main objective is to make the student as comfortable as possible.

Care should be taken to make the boarding house as attractive as possible. The courtyard should be made beautiful with trees and flower beds and no effort should be spared to make the rooms as cheerful as possible.

22.4 Cottage System and Dormitories System

These are the two systems of managing the hostels. In the cottage system, small houses are built more or less close together. Each house or cottage accommodates 8 to 12 students. A teacher's cottage is attached to each cottage. The teacher and the pupil live together as one family. A much closer contact between the teacher and the taught is established. Every cottage is a self-sufficient unit with dining room, kitchen, common room, etc.

This is an ideal system of hostel management if our pockets permit the heavy expenditure which it involves.

Dormitories system is much more economical than the cottage system. A number of students share the dormitory. Students learn to live together; effective supervision is possible and, at the top of it all, it is economical. Care should be taken to provide a floor area of not less than 50 to 55 sq. ft. for each student and the distance between beds should not be less than 3 ft.

22.5 The Hostel Superintendent

The Hostel Superintendent is the pivot of the whole residential system. The success of the hostel, as an instrument of education will depend to a great extent on the personality, status, and qualifications of the hostel superintendent. It is he who determines the character of the hostels – good or bad. It is he who will turn young raw students into a disciplined community. As far as possible, the superintendent should be a whole-time employee. The superintendent, therefore, should possess the following essential qualities:

(i) He should be a man of imagination and clear ideas.

(ii) He should be a man with amiable personality.

(iii) His treatment and attitude towards the boarders should be fatherly.

(iv) He should be democratic in outlook.

(v) He should be academically and professionally well-qualified to be able to guide boarders in studies, etc.

(vi) Above all, he should be able to command respect, elicit obedience from the boarders because of the qualities of head and heart. The boarders notice his sincerity, approachability, his unobtrusive fairness, his temper, in fact, everything. So he must be above board.

22.6 Duties of the Hostel Superintendent

The Hostel Superintendent is supposed to discharge a number of duties connected with hostel management. Some of the duties are listed below:

(i) ***Supervision of Living Conditions in the Hostel:*** The superintendent is responsible for providing living conditions in the hostel which are conducive to the all-round growth of the boarders. He should see that every inmate is provided with essential piece of furniture and equipment. He should create a pleasant and congenial atmosphere which may help in the development of desirable habits of punctuality, obedience, tolerance of differences, obedience to rules and regulations, shouldering responsibility, cooperation with others, etc. He should see that every common place like latrines, bathrooms, kitchens, etc. are kept spick and span, and every servant discharges his duty well.

(ii) ***Supervision of Mess Arrangement:*** - The superintendent should supervise the quality of food and service. He should see that wholesome balanced diet is provided to the boarders at a reasonable cost. Food should be hygienically cooked and well served.

(iii) ***Supervision of Accounts:*** - The superintendent should supervise the maintenance of the accounts of mess and other contingency expenditure so that no doubt is left about the proper use of money.

(iv) ***General Supervision:*** - The superintendent has to see to the various general aspects of hostel life:

(a) He should see that every activity is planned according to a scheduled programme and is well-conducted.

(b) He should create a family atmosphere by providing maximum opportunities for practicing the qualities that help in building a social life.

(c) He should introduce democratic practices; help the students share the hostel administration. He should associate the students with the food committee, the sanitation committee, the literary committee, the cultural committee, the games committee, the discipline committee, etc. This participation will help in creating a homely atmosphere on the one hand and reduced burden of the superintendent on the other.

(d) He should enrich the hostel life with varied co-curricular activities.

(e) He should keep in touch with the parents and keep them well-informed about the progress of the child.

(f) He should regulate the whole life of the boarders by preparing a proper schedule of the daily work. He should fix up the various times – time for getting up and going to bed, meal times, study hours, etc.

(g) He should also see that the life of the boarder is not so completely routinised that he is left with no free time to spend it as he likes, for if his life is too fully organised to give the boy no room to train himself to organise his own leisure, he would be sent out as a helpless being into the world or to a university, caring only to respond to the bells, but not knowing how to occupy himself usefully during the spare time. So, the superintendent should plan some out-of-school activities for which every member should have the opportunity and still some others in which he would expect only a few to be interested.

22.7 Records and Registers for the Hostel

There are certain records and registers which must be maintained in the hostel for efficient administration of the hostel. Some of the registers are:

1. The Property Register
2. Admission Register
3. Attendance Register
4. Security Register
5. Mess Accounts Register
6. Cash Book
7. Committee Register
8. Correspondence Register
9. Reading Room Register
10. Common Room Register
11. Visitor's Register

The warden has to maintain many records regarding the arrangement of hostel. He should supply these different records and registers properly, and should check that these registers are regularly maintained by the various committees. The following are the main features in the hostel records:

1. **Property Register:** It is like the school property register. All movable property of the hostel is entered in this register. A complete detail of things purchased for the hostel or received from other sources are maintained in it – date of purchase or receipt, cost and other specific details. Unusable and old material can be disposed off or sold with the due permission of the principal. It is also recorded in this register.
2. **Admission Register:** The names of all students who sought admission in the hostel are entered with parentage and full addresses in this register.
3. **Attendance Register:** The daily attendance of students is entered in this register who live in the hostel. It would be better, if attendance is taken two times a day, i.e. in the morning and evening (night).
4. **Security Register:** That amount is recorded in this register which is taken from students at the time of admission as security.
5. **Mess Register:** All kinds of income and expenditure accounts are kept in this register relating to the mess. The mess

secretary, who is elected by the students, keeps its full details. The warden should inspect it with great care. He should see from where the vegetables and other commodities were purchased and the expenditure incurred on them was genuine or not. It is also essential to see whether the amount received from children has been deposited or not.

6. **Cash Book:** It should be maintained like the cash book of a school. Every day income and expenditure are entered in it.
7. **Registers of Various Committees:** In these registers, names of members of committees, proceedings of meetings, and details of works done are recorded,
8. **Reading Room Register:** In this register, those newspapers, magazines, and books are recorded which come in the reading room.
9. **Guest Register:** In this register, the account of guests is maintained. These guests may be friends and other relatives of the students who come to see them. The day, date, time, and purpose of visit are recorded in this register in detail. Various other guests and parents of children who come in the hostel, their arrival and stay in hostel are also recorded in this register.

22.8 The Boons and the Banes of Hostel Life

The hostel life has its boons and banes.

The Boons

(i) ***Community life:*** The hostel is a community in itself 'in a full and real sense with a corporate spirit, corporate activities, a corporate pride, and a common will.' The number of hours spent in a classroom by a day scholar and a boarder is identical. But out of the total number of 168 hours in a week, every boy spends not more than one-fifth in a classroom. Thus while a day scholar spends only one fifth of his time in a week actually learning, in the case of a boarder all the 168 hours in a week are at the disposal of school authorities to do what they like with the boy. The total responsibility is a very serious one for the hostel authorities; it is not only a responsibility but an excellent opportunity because in the case of a day scholar, only the class work and a few extra activities become the responsibility of the principal, in the case of a boarder, he has to plan for all the twenty-four hours. This helps in building a community life as the principal has at his disposal more of the actual areas of the student life, he has also more facts of their lives for which he can make arrangements for their development.

(ii) ***The community of all ages:*** - Another important boon of the hostel life is that the hostel community contains a variety of persons of different ages, activities and backgrounds, which is not found in a family. There are persons of the boy's own age, those who are few years older and younger, and right up to the maximum age of 18 years, if it is a full-fledged higher secondary school. There are a number of youngsters of his own age with whom he studies, plays games, forms friendships, eats, sleeps, and listens to the radio. He will be judged by the public opinion of his contemporaries and seniors, however, just or unjust that judgement may be. He also comes to understand the hierarchy that stretches above him in gradation up to the principal himself. This large community exerts a tremendous influence over the new youngster either for good or for evil, to be judged on his own merits, and either accepted or not accepted by this new society. Thus, a youngster has to be on his own, self-dependent, self-reliant, to be successful in the hostel community.

(iii) ***Good training ground for democratic citizenship:*** - The prefectorial system in the hostels and the various offices in the houses to which the boys are allotted gives opportunities for increased responsibility. There are varieties of situations which provide opportunities for developing the capacity, for assuming responsibility for leadership and for handling people – for instance duties in the dormitory, games, sports, cleanliness, mess arrangements, etc. This process of finding one's place in such a complex society is not an easy one. It demands intellectual ability, emotional resistance, as well as emotional stability, physical prowess, social response – all these help the boy to grow and to respond to all these opportunities.

In such a community, there are opportunities for a boy to grow to his full stature. Such a background and the facilities provided in the hostel ensure that the boy or girl develops the qualities of honesty, loyalty, resourcefulness, integrity, courage, sociability, self-confidence, poise, cooperation, strength of character and body, and capacity to shoulder responsibility and to assume leadership.

(iv) ***Inculcating esprit de corps:*** - The hostel life goes a long way in inculcating *esprit de corps* as it provides opportunities for living, eating, and playing together. The so called distinctions of caste, creed, or colour are eliminated and brotherly feelings are created.

(v) ***Opportunities are provided for a well-organised life leading to the strengthening of the academic side of the students:*** - In a well-managed hostel, there is time for work, and there is time for play, students who are serious can get ample time for studies. They can have good companions also.

(vi) ***Opportunities of social service:*** -In a corporate hostel life, so many situations arise which give ample chances for social services, like helping a roommate when sick, helping a poor companion. These opportunities remove the kinks in the boy, his corners are rounded off. He becomes a 'social individual.'

Thus, the hostel can be an effective instrument for the development of physical, mental, and social aspects of the personality of the students. The only condition is that hostels are well-managed and well-supervised. If there is any laxity on this score, the boon may turn into *bane*. Let us see against what banes the principal and the superintendent should guard.

The Banes

(i) ***Wastage of time in idle gossips:*** - The students are immature when they come to the hostel. They are likely to waste their precious time idling away in gossips, and they are likely to be let away by mischievous senior students. Such students, instead of taking advantage of the time in the hostel, may deteriorate in studies and thus waste the hard-earned money of their parents. The superintendent's keen watch over the activities of these students can save students from being misled.

(ii) ***Developing bad habits:*** - The hosteler may form bad habits as he might feel there is none from home to observe his behaviour. He may waste his time in undesirable pursuits – visiting cinema houses, gambling, drinking, etc. Proper supervision of the inmates of the hostel can check these evils.

(iii) ***Hostels may become the centres of political parties and thus become the cause of indiscipline in the institutions:*** - Students may also form their parties leading to quarrels and bickerings. Constant vigilance on the part of the principal and the superintendent is needed to keep the hostel atmosphere good. No mischief should be made so that the very tone of the hostel should condition the children in good ways of life.

22.9 Some Important Points Related With Girl's Hostel

When girls seek admission in secondary school, their age becomes a little more than 11 years. Generally, in this age they are imparted training at home regarding household work. So there should be proper arrangement of such training for them here also when they seek admission in hostel, so that they may get practical training of household activities as far as possible.

The most important problem of girls in hostel is their security. For this, it is essential that their hostel should be in a safe place and it would be still better if there is a boundary around it. Besides, there should be a sentinel at the main gate so that no person may enter the hostel without permission.

One more important problem of girl's hostel is the persons who come to see them. For this, the warden of girl's hostel should talk to the parents of girls at the time of admission in the hostel and take a list of relatives and local guardian to whom the girl may visit and they may visit the girl in the hostel if she wants. In vacations, she may be allowed to go to her parents or relatives. The details of visitors should be recorded in the visitors register with date, time, and purpose and duration of stay in the hostel. The male visitors cannot be allowed to stay in the hostel. If mothers or sisters of the girls come from other cities, arrangement of separate room, if possible, may be done for their stay.

It does not seem proper to allow girls alone for purchasing things from the market. For this, the lady warden herself should go with them or they should be allowed under the care and custody of some lady teacher.

When girls go to their homes in long vacations it would be better to go in someones care. The parents of each girl should be informed regarding the date of long leaves in due time prior to occasion, so that parents would manage accordingly to take them to their homes.

In girl's hostels, there is an important problem of employing servants. For this, as far as possible women servants should be employed. But, there are some duties, for instance, to carry goods from outside, or a night watch, for these duties only male servants have to be employed. Their appointment should be done with great care or on the verification of police authority.

Possibly the girl student may feel boredom in hostel due to these restrictions. Therefore, it is necessary for making the hostel life attractive and useful. For this, some recreational activities should be arranged for them. Arrangement of regular games and sports seems to be the best. Sometimes educational movie shows should be arranged. It is essential for making the hostel useful and attractive. For this a rich and interesting programme of co-curricular activities should be executed, so that the girl students may lead a busy and a happy hostel life by selecting activities of their choice. And they may acquire proper education for future life.

Objective Type Questions

Multiple Choice Questions (Tick ✓ the right option)

(1) Type of building is ideal for school hostel
- (a) 'I' Shaped
- (b) 'L' Shaped
- (c) Quadrangular shaped
- (d) All of the above

(2) Every day income and expenditure are entered in
- (a) Cash Book
- (b) Cheque Book
- (c) Guest Register
- (d) Mess Register

Fill in the blanks

(1) The most important problem of girls in hostel is their ____________ [Security]

(2) Proper ____________ of the inmates of the hostel cam check the bad habits. [Supervisor]

Important Questions

1. Discuss the role of a school hostel in providing training for democratic citizenship.
2. What is the need of having hostels? Discuss how you would regulate the life of a student in the hostel to make it most profitable for him.
3. What educational goals should hostel life aim at? Discuss the place of prefect system in this context.
4. What are the boons and banes of hostel life?
5. How will you organise hostel life to promote emotional integration?
6. Discuss the role of the hostel superintendent in the organisation of corporate life in the hostel. Illustrate your answer with specific examples.
7. What major qualities a hostel superintendent should possess? What are his duties?

Unit IV

Internal Organisation

23

Curriculum Construction

The various studies, organised activities, both curricular and extracurricular activities and the entire social life and atmosphere of the school, find their respective places in the curriculum. Each is designed to make its contribution toward the attainment of the ultimate goals of education. It becomes clear with this statement that the curriculum contributes in the attainment of goal of each activity of education. It is also apart from its literal meaning.

23.1 Meaning and Definition of Curriculum

The genesis of the word "curriculum" is from the word "currere" of Latin language, which means - Race Course. This is a race course, on which a person runs for getting his goals. In recent years, definitions of curriculum have altogether changed. According to the old concept, the meaning of curriculum - is supposed to be a list of reading material. Reading material was generally called as study subject. In fact, reading material was delimited to school subjects. Mostly, knowledge or experiences acquired by a child from outside the classroom, was not granted the part of curriculum. At that time, schools used to attach more importance to the subject instead of the requirements of the child. But, in modern times, definitions of curriculum have become widespread. These definitions in themselves are not only school subjects, but they also unite all other activities and experience of a child for which the school guides. Now, all these activities come in their fields which were familiar with the name of extra-curricular activities. In this way, in modern times the curriculum is viewed in a very widespread form. The above mentioned views can be seconded by the following definitions:

"Curriculum includes all the learners experience in or outside school that are included in a programme which has been devised to help him to develop mentally."

— ***Crow and Crow***

"The curriculum may be defined as all the experiences that pupils have while under the direction of the school, it includes both classroom and extra-curricular activities, work as well as play."

— ***Watter C.***

"Curriculum consists of all the experiences of the learner under the control of school. It is more than the textbook, more than subject-matter, more even than a course of study. It is the total situation or group of situations available to the teacher and school administrator through which to make behaviour changes in the endless stream of children and youth who pass through the doors of the school."

— ***Brubacher***

"Curriculum does not mean only academic subject traditionally taught in the school, but it includes the totality of experiences that pupil receives through the manifold activities that go on in the school, in the classroom, library, workshop, playground, and in the numerous informal contacts between teachers and pupils. In the sense the whole life of the school becomes the curriculum, which can touch the life of the students at all points and help in the evaluation of a balanced personality."

— ***Secondary Education Commission***

23.2 Principles of Construction of Curriculum

For getting rid of defects of current curriculum, the Secondary Education Commission has propounded the following principles, keeping in mind the curriculum that should be formulated:

1) For reorganisation of curriculum, the elementary point should be that, through which the gulf between school subjects and those rich and various activities should be finished which prepare the warp and weft of life.
2) The base of curriculum should be the whole life of the school. In the works of the Secondary Education Commission, it should be clearly understood that according to the latest educational thinking, the meaning of curriculum is not taken from classical subjects only which are taught in traditional ways in the school, notwithstanding the totality of experiences is included in it which the child receives through manifold activities. These activities are continuously going on in the school, classroom, library, laboratory, workshop, playing-field, and in many informal contacts amongst teachers and students. With this view, the whole life of school becomes a curriculum, which touches all aspects of life of children and it may help in the development of a balanced individual.
3) There should be sufficient diversity and flexibility in the curriculum, by which individual disagreements, interests, and requirements may be accomplished or fulfilled.
4) The curriculum should be related with the community life so that it may explain its main and important things to the child and it may bring him in contact with its important activities.
5) The curriculum should be helpful in the supply of local requirements.
6) The curriculum should be planned in this way that it should not train students for work only, notwithstanding it should impart training for holidays also. For this, various activities of the school, social games and sports, aesthetic works, etc. should be organised and they should be taken as a part of the curriculum.
7) Its educational importance should not be destroyed by dividing curriculum in many separate and unrelated subjects, notwithstanding the principle of co-incidence should be acquired in the curriculum so that, union may be established with life in the best form of subject-matter.

According to the latest educational thinking we should make the base of the curriculum capability of the child, interest, and need, etc. but it does not mean that its social base should outright be neglected. Thus, determination of curriculum should be done with both points of view - child and society. Today, our country is facing the problem of national integration. So, at the time of determining the curriculum, it is also essential to keep in mind how we can achieve national goals through it. Thus, the curriculum should be formulated keeping in mind the condition and demands of all—that is of individual, society, and nation.

Anderson and Gruhn have put emphasis on the following principles for the organisation of curriculum—

1. Organisation of curriculum should be done in such a way, so that students feel facilitated in understating relations between different subjects of school and experiences regarding tendencies.
2. For attaining the needs of individuals, the curriculum should be experimental and diversified.
3. Organisation of curriculum should be based on problems so that students may get help in development of required attitudes and skills. Along with, they may

be able in understanding democratic society.

4. Organisation of curriculum should be done in such a manner so that appropriate adaptation may be established among the experience of learning of various levels.

23.3 Types of Curriculum

1. **Child-Centred Curriculum:** In modern age, it has become the most important change that the child-centred education has occupied the place of subject-centred education. Now organisation of curriculum has begun by making child a centre. Its (curriculum) is based on the philosophy of experimentalism. The principal propagator of this thinking, Flaum is of the opinion that "*the experience is not static like atmosphere of some man.*" Due to this cause, in curriculum, interests and needs of the student should be made centre, not the previous determined curriculum a base. In curriculum of this type changed needs, intentions, emotions, etc. of student are made a base. Education Kingdom, for curriculum of this type is indebted to John Dewy's "Laboratory school" also. This curriculum is functional which provides purposeful learning. Through it, liability of learning is fixed on the students themselves.

2. **Activity-Centred Curriculum:** It makes base to work or activity. For this curriculum also, Education Kingdom is indebted to John Dewy. Dewy assumes knowledge is the result of activity. According to him, experience, knowledge, or learning is the result of activity. Due to this reason, this curriculum is also called as "Experience Centred Curriculum."

3. **Core Curriculum:** It developed due to reaction against "subject-centred curriculum" and "child-centred curriculum." It very much prevails in the schools of America. The main cause is that it is the social order of modern age. This curriculum puts emphasis on this matter that school should bear more social liabilities and build socially skilled individuals. This curriculum is centred on the general development of pupils. In personal and social problems of student, it is vested.

23.4 Bases of Curriculum

1. **Philosophical Bases:** One principal base of curriculum is philosophy. Construction of curriculum is done for achieving objectives of education. Objectives of education, we get from philosophy. Thus, the problem of curriculum is the philosophical problem. According to various schools of philosophy, the curriculum is determined in different forms:

   (i) Idealism: This school of thought stresses on eternal values and ideals. Therefore, this main base of curriculum assumes thoughts and ideals of man. Due to this cause, idealism provides a principal place to literature, art, music, history, and language, etc. in the curriculum.

   (ii) Naturalism: This emphasises on the individuality of the child. According to this, free development of the individuality of child is supposed to be the aim of education. Due to this reason, naturalists are supporters of providing unlimited liberty to child for self-expression. Thus, the naturalists want to add those activities in curriculum through which possible tendencies of a child may develop. So, the naturalism provides an important place to exercise, games, and sport, swimming, geography, natural sciences, etc. in the curriculum.

   (iii) Pragmatism: This school of thought also provides an important place to the child. This thinking along with assuming the child as the centre point of education, places accent on the principle of utility. Construction of pragmatically made curriculum is done according to the interests of the child. They build curriculum of elementary classes on the basis of curiosity, practical interests, sophisticated expression (artful), interest of mutual exchange of thoughts. Along with, they also make the base to principle of utility so that he may settle successfully in his future life. Due to this reason, they include art, language, mathematics, woodcraft, spinning and weaving, social activities, vocations, etc. in the curriculum.

(iv) **Realism:** This thinking provides an important base for curriculum. Through it emphasis is laid on the practicability of life. Realism includes those activities in curriculum through which knowledge can be obtained of real situations of life.

2. **Sociological Base:** According to this base, those subjects and activities are included in the curriculum, which provide assistance in developing appreciation of sociability. From this point of view, place is given to Language, History, Literature, Sociology, Geography, Ethics, etc. in the curriculum.
3. **Psychological Base:** According to this base, formulation of curriculum is done according to the interest of the child, natural tendencies, requirements, the capabilities, and abilities of the child. In the other words, we can say that this determines curriculum by assuming the child as the centre point.
4. **Scientific Base:** All round progress of science has provided one more base for constructing curriculum of education. According to this base, more importance is given to scientific subjects in curriculum.

23.5 Purpose of Curriculum

1. **Character:** To lay foundation for rich, useful, and moral life so that they may do work for social welfare.
2. **National Heritage:** To make children capable of understanding their national heritage and having faith in it. Along with it to evoke feeling for honour of an individual.
3. **Health:** To build healthy children and to develop appropriate mental and emotional points of views and habits.
4. **Clear Thinking and Observation:** To develop conscientious power based on appropriate hypotheses, so that they may differentiate right and wrong, or truth and untruth. In addition to it, to develop interest and ability in the children.
5. **Knowledge and Skill:** To develop knowledge and various skills in children according to their ability.
6. **Aesthetic Feeling and Expression:** To develop aesthetic-appreciation and creative expression in children for the use of beauty.
7. **Social and Economic Relations:** To develop appropriate social and economic relations, so that they may lead life in family, school, and society with appropriate manners. Besides, to develop vocational skill in them and to provide them the knowledge of economic relations of human society.
8. **Citizenship:** To create faith in them for the Indian Republic and a feeling of pride. In addition to this, to make them aware with citizens rights and liabilities, but this citizenship would not be limited to our country only, notwithstanding, its field would be international for developing goodwill and sympathy.

23.6 Views of Education Commission about School Curriculum

The Commission is of the opinion that school curriculum is in the condition of transition (changing). It faces criticism in developed countries also. Generally, it is said against it that school curriculum is opposite, inappropriate and insufficient in prevailing conditions and it does not fulfill the needs of present times. In the United States of America which is developed educationally, traditional curriculum has been changed due to influence of progressive education. But, again today, many learned men and teachers of eminence of universities have started movements for bringing improvement in the curriculum of school education. There are many reasons of this dissatisfaction related with curriculum. Out of them some main reasons are the following:

1. In recent years, many defects have come in current curriculum due to the development of knowledge, and reconstruction of basic concepts of physical, biological, and social sciences.
2. Due to various new thoughts in Education Kingdom, this demand has been raised that the period of education imparted in general secondary schools should be increased. Besides, nature of education should be made as per needs.
3. For the last few years, a tendency was going on to include some other important facts in much heavy curriculum. Due to this tendency, the curriculum became heavier. So, this meaningless burden should be ousted from the curriculum and dynamic and inspiring facts should be included in place of it.

In view of the above mentioned points, it has become necessary to improve the school curriculum.

23.7 Curriculum Prescribed by the Kothari Commission

(A) Curriculum of Lower Primary Level (Classes 1-4)

The Education Commission has determined the following teaching subjects for classes 1 to 4:

1. One Language – the Mother Tongue or the Regional Language.
2. Mathematics.
3. Study of Environment in classes 3 and 4, Science and Social Studies should be taught.
4. Creative Activities.
5. Mark experience and Social Service.
6. Health Education.

(B) Upper Primary Level Curriculum (Classes 5-7)

1. Two Languages – (i) Mother Tongue or Regional Language, (ii) Hindi or English.
   N.B. - One third language (English or Regional Language) optional studies may be offered.
2. Mathematics.
3. Science.
4. Art.
5. Work Experience and Social Service.
6. Social Study (or History, Geography, and Civics).
7. Physical Education.
8. Education in Moral and Spiritual Values.

(C) Curriculum of Lower Secondary Level (Classes 8-10)

1. **Three Language:** Generally, in Non-Hindi speaking areas, following should be the languages:
   (i) Mother Tongue or Regional Language.
   (ii) Advanced or Elementary Hindi.
   (iii) Advanced or Elementary English.

   Generally, in Hindi speaking areas, there should be the following Languages:
   (i) Mother Tongue or Regional language.
   (ii) English or Hindi, if English has been offered as the mother tongue.
   (iii) Besides Hindi one other modern Indian language.

N.B. Study of classical language may be done on optional basis, in addition to the above mentioned.

2. Mathematics.
3. Science.

4. History, Geography, and Civics.
5. Art.
6. Work Experience and Social Service.
7. Physical Education.
8. Education in Moral and Spiritual Values.

(D) Curriculum of Higher Secondary Level (Classes 11-12)

The Commission is of the opinion that at this level; arrangement should be made for providing vocational curriculum for 50% of the children. For the remaining children, general education should be arranged. The Commission has prescribed the following teaching-subjects in the curriculum of general education:

1. Any two languages in which any modern Indian language, any modern foreign language, and classical language should be included.
2. Any three subjects from the following:
   - (i) One additional language,
   - (ii) History,
   - (iii) Geography,
   - (iv) Economics,
   - (v) Logic,
   - (vi) Psychology,
   - (vii) Sociology,
   - (viii) Art,
   - (ix) Physics,
   - (x) Chemistry,
   - (xi) Mathematics,
   - (xii) Biology,
   - (xiii) Geology, and
   - (xiv) Home Science.
3. Work Experience and Social Service.
4. Physical Education.
5. Art and Craft.
6. Education in Moral and Spiritual Values.

23.8 Curriculum Prescribed by the Review Committee, 1997

The recommendations of the Education Commission (1964-66) and according to the proposal related with the National Policy of Education in 1968, the Central Advisory Board of Education decided to enforce the educational structure 10+2+3 in November 1974 in the Fifth Five Year Plan. The National Council for Educational Research and Training constructed curriculum and textbooks on the basis of outlines proposed by the Education Commission for the 10+2 school education. Till the end of the year 1976-77, the Council enforced this structure with curriculum in 19 States and Union Territories. Towards this education structure and curriculum, both kind of reactions, were noticed. Letters from different areas came to Dr. P. C. Chunder, Union Minister for Education of Janata Government, in which opinions were expressed regarding proposal and execution of educational structure of 10+2+3. The Central Education Minister appointed a Review Committee in July 1977, keeping the views expressed in these letters in mind. The Chairman of this committee was Dr. Ishwar Bhai Patel, Vice Chancellor, Gujarat University, Ahmadabad. This committee was entrusted the work of "Review" of curriculum of 12 years School Education, constructed by the National Council for Educational Research and Training. Counseling with various specialists of different areas, the committee submitted its report to the Union Government in November, 1977. Its main recommendations were as below:

1) Accepting the principles of Basic Education propounded by Mahatma Gandhi, the present system of education should be made. According to Gandhiji Work Education should be made the centre point of education system.
2) Component elements of school education – literary (Anthropology) and scientific work, etc. should be the component parts of the school education. On the basis of these elements, there should be construction of curriculum of school education-by making this the base.

23.9 Curriculum of School Education

Curriculum of Classes 1-4

(1) Language.
(2) Mathematics.
(3) Study of Atmosphere (Social Studies, Study of Nature, and Health Education).
(4) Socially useful productive work.
(5) Games and Sports and Creative Activities.

N. B. – Socially useful productive work is purposeful and meaningful physical work, with the result that there may be production of (some) thing to community which may be served in any form.

Curriculum of Classes 5-8

1. Languages.
2. Mathematics.
3. Integrated Curriculum of Science.
4. History, Civics and Geography.
5. Arts (Music, Dance, Painting).
6. Socially useful productive work and community work/service.
7. Games and Sports, Physical Education and Supervised Study.

Curriculum of Classes 9-10

1. Languages.
2. Mathematics or optional subject.
3. Science or optional subject.
4. History, Civics, and Integrated Curriculum of Geography.
5. One subject from the following:
   (i) Music, Dance, Painting.
   (ii) Home Science.
   (iii) Agriculture.
   (iv) Commerce.
   (v) Economics.
   (vi) Social Reconstruction.
6. Socially useful productive work and community work/service.
7. Games and Sports, Physical Education and Supervised Study.

23.10 Curriculum Prescribed by the National Review Committee 10+2 Committee

In October, 1977 the Union Minister for Education, Dr. P. C. Chunder appointed a National Review Committee under the chairmanship of Dr. Malcolm S. Adiseshiah, Vice Chancellor, Madras University, Madras. The Committee was entrusted the work of review of curriculum of school education 10+2+3 educational structure. Only for this reason the committee is known as the "Plus Two Committee." The committee did its work in the context of "Vocationalisation of Education." The Committee submitted its report to the Union Education Minister, on 28 February, 1978. This report was titled as "Learning to Do – Towards a Learning and Working Society."

The Committee divided +2 or higher secondary education in two streams, as:

(A) General Education.

(B) Vocational Education.

(A) Outlines of Curriculum of General Education

1. Languages.
2. Socially useful productive work.
3. Three subjects from the following of your choice:
   (i) Languages (other languages besides compulsory one).
   (ii) Mathematics.
   (iii) Economics.
   (iv) Chemistry.
   (v) Political Science.
   (vi) Biology.
   (vii) Geography.
   (viii) Physics.
   (ix) Sociology.
   (x) Psychology.
   (xi) Philosophy.
   (xii) Home Science.
   (xiii) History.
   (xiv) Commerce and Accountancy.

(xv) Fine Arts.
(xvi) Physical Education.

(B) Outlines of Curriculum of Vocational Education

1. Language.
2. General Foundation Course – This course would be taught up to two years, and 4-5 periods would be allotted for it. The Committee has divided this course in two parts, as-
   (1) **"Part A"** – The course of this part would be equal to all vocations. The Committee has given place to the following in it:
      (i) Gandhian concept of Education.
      (ii) Agriculture in the National Economy.
      (iii) Rural Development.
      (iv) Problem of Urban Slums.
      (v) Health, Hygiene, and Sanitation.
   (2) **"Part B"** – Nine sections have been given in this part. The student has to select one section according to his vocation out of these. These sections are as under:
      (i) Small Scale and Cottage Industries.
      (ii) Entrepreneurship.
      (iii) Cooperation and Credit Facilities.
      (iv) Marketing.
      (v) Sales Promotion.
      (vi) Unemployment, Under-employment, and manpower utilisation in India.
      (vii) Human Relations.
      (viii) General Exposure to World Trends and Changes.
      (ix) Environment Protection and Development.

(3) Any three subjects from amongst the following-
   (a) Agriculture and Agriculture-based Vocations:
      (i) Agriculture.
      (ii) Soil and Water Conservation.
      (iii) Repairing and Maintenance of Farm Machinery.
      (iv) Agri-based and Agro-based Industries.
      (v) Agricultural Chemicals.
      (vi) Rural Reconstruction Technology.
   (b) Business and Office Management:
      (i) Banking.
      (ii) Office Management and Secretarial Practice.
      (iii) Stenography and Typewriting.
      (iv) Office Machine Operator.
      (v) Accounting and Auditing.
      (vi) Telex and Telephone Operator, etc.

(4) Para-Medical-
   (i) Multipurpose Health Worker.
   (ii) Laboratory Technician.
   (iii) Ophthalmic Technician.
   (iv) Orthopedic Technician.
   (v) X-ray Technician.
   (vi) Radiology Technician.
   (vii) Dental Technician.
   (viii) E. C. G. and E. E. G. Technician.
   (ix) Health Extension Worker, etc.

(5) Educational Services-
   (i) Audio-visual Technician.
   (ii) Maker of playthings regarding Education.
   (iii) Primary and Balwadi Teacher.
   (iv) Music and Dance Teacher.
   (v) Workers of Library and Museum, etc.

(6) Local Body and Other Services-
   (i) Village Level Worker.
   (ii) Development Worker.
   (iii) Extension Worker.
   (iv) Block Extension Educator.
   (v) Furniture Making.
   (vi) Editing Work.
   (vii) Newspaper reporting, etc.

(7) Vocations Relating with Home Science-
- (i) Textile Design.
- (ii) Laundry.
- (iii) Interior Decoration.
- (iv) Food Processing and Preservation.

(8) Other General Services-
- (i) Commercial Art.
- (ii) Pottery.
- (iii) Printing and Lithography.

23.11 Outlines of Curriculum Prescribed for 8+4+3 Educational Structure

The National Education Assembly prescribed for 8+4+3 educational structure along with the outline proposed of the curriculum for 8+4. This outline is as the following:

(A) Outline of Curriculum of Primary Education

Under primary education come classes from 1 to 8. Its curriculum has been divided into two parts, e.g.

(1) Curriculum of Primary Classes (classes 1-5):
- (i) One language.
- (ii) Mathematics.
- (iii) Study of Atmosphere.
- (iv) Socially useful productive work.
- (v) Games and Sports and Creative Activities (Music, Dance, Painting, etc.).

(2) Outline of curriculum of classes from 6 to 8-
- (a) Languages.
- (b) Mathematics.
- (c) Integrated Curriculum of Science.
- (d) Social Sciences (History, Geography, and Civics).
- (e) Socially useful productive work (co-curricular activities should be included in it).
- (f) Games and Sports and Physical Education.
- (g) Supervised Study.
- (h) Library and Reading Room study work.

(B) Outline of Curriculum of Higher Secondary Education or + 4.

With a view of curriculum the classes of this stage have been divided into two parts - class 9 and 10, and 11 and 12. Curriculum of these is being given below separately:

1. Classes 9th and 10th

(A) Compulsory Subjects.
- (i) Languages.
- (ii) **Social Reconstruction:** This is for those students who would not offer History, Geography, and Civics. It means no subject from the above three.

Or

General Science: This is for those students who would not offer science.
- (iii) Socially useful productive work and community service.
- (iv) Games and Sports and Physical Education.
- (v) Supervised Study and Library and Reading room study work.

(B) Any three subjects from amongst the following:
- (i) Physics.
- (ii) Chemistry.
- (iii) Biology.
- (iv) Mathematics.
- (v) Geometrical and Mechanical Drawing.
- (vi) Home Science.
- (vii) Commerce.
- (viii) Agriculture.

(ix) History.
(x) Geography.
(xi) Economics.
(xii) Political Science.
(xiii) Physical Education.
(xiv) Classical Language.
(xv) Music.
(xvi) Dance.
(xvii) Painting.

2. *Class 11 and 12*

(i) Languages
(ii) Supervised Study or Library and Reading Room study work.
(iii) Games, Sports, Physical Education, Curricular Activities.
(iv) Selected vocation from the following topics related with vocations:
1. Agriculture and Agri-based Business or Vocation.
2. Business and Office Management.
3. Health and Office Management.
4. Education Service.
5. Vocation related with Home Science.
6. Engineering and Technical Vocation.
7. Diversified.

23.12 Work Experience

The most important thing of curriculum determined by the Education Commission is the proposal of "Work Experience." The Commission has prescribed it from 1 to 10th class and with vocational subjects for classes 11 and 12. But here the question arises is: "What is work experience?" The Education Commission has written explaining the work experience, *"Work experience is to participate in production work in school, home, workshop, field, and factory or in any producing unit or situation."*

Purpose of Work Experience

The purpose of work experience was published in "10+2+3", "A Major Change in School Education" by the Central Education Ministry. The objective of Work Experience have been determined as under:

1. By acquainting with various fields of work, students may assess their interest, capacity, and ability.
2. To make production units of students through training of production works.
3. Economic saving plan by doing essential work of home, school, or community.
4. To develop scientific and technical aptitude during performing various productive activities in home, farm and factory.
5. To make students agreeable for bearing their social liabilities in the framework of human liberty and equality.
6. To provide knowledge of human and physical relations, involved in some organised production work.
7. To develop inclination for accomplishing some work jointly.
8. To bring school and community nearer.

23.13 Work Experience at Different Stages of School

At the time of selection of activities of work experience for various stages, it is essential to keep in mind the daily needs, folk arts, and national culture in the background of economic and social conditions of the country. In the above magazine published by the Union Education Ministry, 49 activities have been enlisted under the schedule of work experience. But, keeping in mind appropriateness and condition of Indian schools, a chart of different activities and stages is being given ahead.

WORK EXPERIENCE FOR VARIOUS STAGES

Level of School and Classes	*Industry Based Work Experience*	*Agriculture-Based Work Experience*	*Science Based Work Experience*
Primary Level (Classes 1-5)	Paper and cardboard work, earth and plastic work		Manufacturing of ink, polish, soap, vinegar and phenol (for class 5th)
Lower Secondary Level (Classes 6-8)	Leather work, printing, binding paper mache work, model making sewing and embroidery, mason work, internal decoration, dyeing work, nursery work, candle making, basket making, etc.	Flower and seed production, horticulture, crop growing, poultry keeping, goat and sheep keeping	Paint and varnish making, hair dyes, production of cosmetics, mirror coating
Higher Secondary Level (Classes 9-12)	Printing, leather work, photography, plastic work, model making, ceramics, spinning and weaving, sewing (tailoring) and embroidery, commercial painting, denting and spray dying, textile printing, gardening cane work, production of goods of games and sports, watch repairing, repair of musical instruments.	Animal husbandry, production of forage, preservation of vegetables, and fruits, seed production, production of milk commodities, bee-keeping, fishery.	Cosmetics, hair dye making, lime production of chemicals, battery repair and upkeep, electroplating, radio-repair and upkeep.

23.14 National Curriculum

In the National Education Policy 1966, a national educational system has been envisaged based on other flexible variables with a common core on the framework of the national curriculum. In the National Education Policy/ Working Plan, it has been envisaged of accepting child-centred viewpoint for education. In this background efforts would be done for bringing sufficient improvement in the category of education for encouraging enrollment of all children and to retain them in schools upto 14 years. In Working Plan, 1992 the emphasis has been laid for taking the following steps:

1. Accent would be laid on lessening quantum of curriculum.
2. The steps would be taken for developing textbooks methodically, revision in curriculum and school system.

3. The following steps would be taken up for establishing Minimum Level of Learning (M.L.L.):
   - **(i)** Main attention would be given on development of total teaching based on education in "Minimum Level of Learning" Working Policy.
   - **(ii)** For knowing present level elementary evaluation of teaching attainments would be done.
   - **(iii)** If it was necessary, revision would be done in Minimum Level of Learning for making local achievements favourable.
   - **(iv)** For teaching-based Minimum Level of Learning, teachers training books would be prepared.
   - **(v)** To prepare unit tests and other evaluation materials.
   - **(vi)** For making teaching process activity-based and interesting provision would be made of capacity-based teaching material.

The stage of Secondary Education has been divided into two separate substages. Secondary Education up to classes 10th , which is general education stage and higher secondary, class 11 and 12 which is separate due to its diversity and speciality. In the National Education System, as it has been mentioned in the National Education Policy, a National Curriculum Framework is required. It has already been prepared for secondary education, though its execution is not similar. For secondary stage, the task of revision of curriculum, near about in all States and Union Territories was started. The National Council for Educational Research and Training also prepared guidelines, curriculum, and textbooks for all stages of school education. Moreover, no curriculum has been released yet for higher secondary stage. In 1988, the National Council for Educational Research and Training prepared a draft but due to new facts coming in the light, it requires revision. The Work Plan, 1992 proposes that:

(i) In 8th Five Year Plan, in the entire country, school education that is 10 (5+3+2) +2, was adopted for educational structure the following steps were envisaged to be taken:

(i) As an immediate step, the States and Union Territories which have not yet adopted national uniform educational structure, would be asked to ensure 10 (5+3+2) +2 structure in each new school expected to be opened. The States and Union Territories have already started the process to bring +2 in the school system. A working committee would be built for speeding up the efforts in this context.

(ii) For removing problems and difficulties coming in the way in adopting a uniform structure, a working committee would be formed with the consultation of educational authorities of the States and Union Territories concerned.

The National Council for Educational Research and Training published a revised edition 1988, keeping in mind the objectives and recommendations with the main areas of curriculum of the National Education Policy, namely, **"National Curriculum for Elementary and Secondary Education – A Framework."** In it, it has been mentioned in total the subject-matter of education and different variables of process and of various areas of subjects upto the secondary level. This framework is the base of guidelines of various subjects, curricula, and textbooks and other educational materials prepared by N.C.E.R.T. According to this framework, secondary education which is the last phase of general education, subject-matter of that would be prepared keeping in mind the following fields of curriculum:

1. Language (Mother Tongue, Hindi, English)
2. Mathematics.
3. Science.
4. Social Sciences (History, Geography, Civics, Economics).

5. Work Experience.
6. Art Education.
7. Health and Physical Education.
8. Value-based Education.
9. Population Education.

The Higher Secondary (+2) stage is an important phase of school education because after this stage, the student acquires eligibility for becoming an engineer, technologist, doctor, or teacher or keeping continued educational activities on third phase. A lot of students from amongst them attach with Work Kingdom also. Thus, at this stage only, the students should be introduced with the structure of separate subjects, for instance, Physics, Chemistry, Biology, Mathematics, Geology, History, Geography, Political Science, Economics, Sociology, Philosophy, Psychology, Language, and Art, etc.

In the subject-matter of each subject, that much quantity of up-to-date development should be given which is relevant for +2 stage, and essential bases of each subject also should be given so that needs of other areas of further education and various vocational curricula of these subjects may be accomplished.

For higher secondary education, the framework of National Curriculum would be finalised at the earliest time possible. N.C.E.R.T. was asked for completing this work till end of March, 1993. An important thing of this framework would be the semesterwise system of higher secondary education. In different fields of subjects this framework would indicate increasing importance of knowledge base and the availability of essential skill in all subjects. Keeping in view the framework of curriculum N.C.E.R.T. would develop guidelines, routine of teaching educational package in series. Before the end of the 8th Five Year Plan, execution of a new frame of the educational authorities of the States and Union Territories would be given advice.

23.15 Defects of Present Curriculum

The Secondary Education Commission has pointed out the following defects in the current curriculum:

1. Present curriculum is of narrow vision. It has been experienced as the supply of requirement for seeking admission mainly in educational institutions. This condition is still in force, while various efforts have been made to get away with its defects at times.
2. This puts emphasis on bookish knowledge because at all levels of education, there are classical and theoretical teaching subjects to a great extent and mainly related with micro-thoughts and generalisation.
3. There is a tendency of loading with much more facts and micro-thoughts to subject-matter of each discipline or subject. Mostly these facts are of little importance which put unnecessary burden on the memory.
4. Our curriculum makers have borne mostly loss caused by accepting the views of "Specialists." With the result of this point of view, they tried to keep more and more matter in their textbooks and curriculum, and did not pay heed to requirements, psychology, and interests of learners rather they paid attention on logical and scientific facts of subjects.
5. It does not tally with individual differences. In adolescent age, there develops various individual interests, attitudes, and specific points of view in students. But the present curriculum hardly pays any attention towards these individual differences.
6. The present curriculum is authorised by examinations – this is the subject of daily experience. For this, teacher, parents, and child all may produce proof because they all are laden with it.

7. In present curriculum, it lacks establishment of technical and vocational subjects.
8. In the end, the curriculum is not related with real life. Only for this reason, it has been a failure in preparing children for life. It does not provide presence of mind to children in understanding the external world in which they have to enter after school life.

Objective Type Questions

Multiple Choice Questions (Tick ✓ the right option)

(1) The genesis of the world "Curriculum" is from the world

(a) Curie
(b) Currere
(c) Currie
(d) Curiclum

(2) The main types of curriculum are

(a) Child Centred curriculum
(b) Activity Centred Curriculum
(c) Core Curriculum
(d) All above

Fill in the blanks

(1) Present curriculum is of ____________ vision. [Narrow]

(2) Curriculum means the ____________ [Race Course]

Important Questions

1. What do you understand by curriculum? Explain.
2. "Wholeness of experiences lies in curriculum." Discuss this statement.
3. What should the objectives be of curriculum?
4. Which defects have the Secondary Education Commission indicated in current curriculum?
5. Which principles would you keep in mind at the time of construction of curriculum?
6. Which defects have the Education Commission indicated about the school curriculum?
7. Describe in brief the various types of curriculum.
8. Which new points have been included in the proposed curriculum by the Education Commission?

24

Co-curricular Activities

Some time ago, games and sports, debates, drama and music, etc. activities were supposed to be out of the curriculum and they were called as "Extra-curricular Activities." At that time the school authorities did not take any interest in these activities and sometimes they took them as sheer wastage of time and strength. The controversy that has flickered for years as to the proper place of the student activity programme has been resolved rather effectively through the justification of student activities on the basis of educational, social, and personal contributions to student learning.

H.C. Mckown has categorised three stages of development of extra-curricular activities. First is the stage, when teachers and administrators overlooked it. Second stage was in which these were opposed openly. And the third stage is the modern age in which they are supposed to be essential for attaining educational objectives.

In modern times educationists have agreed on this matter that if these activities are demonstrated properly, they would prove to be of great educational importance. Today these are viewed as "Co-curricular Activities," and are supposed to be an integral part of the curriculum. Whichever experience or activity has educational importance that is one part of the curriculum. So, these activities in fact are co-curricular activities.

India is the largest democracy in the present world. Democracies, as we know, are nourished by democratic methods adopted in the various institutions of a country. It depends more on the quality of its school than on the educational contribution of any other single social institution with the possible exceptions of the home. The quality of the schools will depend upon the educational experiences provided to the pupils. Co-curricular activities form a vital link in the pattern of blended educational experiences so necessary for all boys and girls in the modern Indian School. A great variety of educative experiences is to be provided in the school programme which may contribute to a long, happy, and normal life. Only well-adjusted citizens will be able to ensure national development in all its parameters.

These educative experiences comprise experiences inside as well as outside the classroom, curricular as well as extra-curricular, curricular as well as co-curricular to cover all facets of growth pattern and ensure balanced development of the child and good citizenship for the country. In fact, the distinction between the curricular and extra-curricular must cease to exist. The Education Commission also stressed: "We conceive of the school curriculum as the totality of learning experiences that the school provides for the pupils through all the manifold activities, in the school or outside, that are carried on under its supervision."

24.1 Advantages of Co-curricular Activities

Co-curricular activities are useful to the students; they help in the curriculum improvement and are significant factors in promoting school-community relations;

(a) The co-curricular activities are useful to the students in a number of ways:

(i) *They provide opportunities for the pursuit of established interests and the development of new interests.* No one can deny that the pursuit of desirable interests gives zest to life, broadens horizons, provides an excellent background for the profitable use of leisure time, and not infrequently, materially affects vocational choices. School clubs potentially contribute more to the achievement of this objective than do any other types of activity. Athletics, music, and school publications are other kinds of activities that make substantial contributions to this function.

(ii) *They educate for citizenship through experiences and insights that stress leadership, fellowship, cooperation, and independent action.* By reason of the social appeal of student activities, their cooperative methods, their spontaneity and their intrinsic interest, they are a significant social medium for the civic training of the young. Student council and school assemblies, etc. can make the greatest impact on the development of citizenship among the students of the school.

(iii) *They develop school spirit and morale.* This is the universal testimony of the teachers, the principals, and the administrators. It is, in fact, self-evident from the psychology of the dictum "whom one serves, one also loves." This applies to institutions as well as persons. If students can be persuaded to make sacrifices for the school, they will learn to love it and take pride in its success. The need for enforcing discipline will cease when there will be an army of lovers of the school. Moreover, when the student and the faculty alike are proud of their school and enjoy working together the school is likely to have a strong instructional programme and a good staff of teachers. The activities programme may make its contribution to the objective of creating a distinct school spirit and morale through inter-scholastic activities, student council and many other activities.

(iv) *They provide opportunities for satisfying the gregarious urge of children and youths.* These activities provide social conduct laboratory of vital significance. They give practice in the right social conduct in actual social situations. Training for effective service comes to fulfillment when opportunities for service are presented in the school. They make for like-mindedness and give opportunities for the exercise and development of *esprit de corps*. The individual identifies himself with the group of his own choice - a debating or a dramatic club, etc. He is no longer an individual but is a member of the group. His gregarious urge is satisfied. The activities like student council, clubs, and societies, dramatics, etc. serve this particular need the best.

(v) *They encourage moral and spiritual development*. No one can deny that the development of moral and spiritual values is basic to all other educational objectives. Education uninspired by moral and spiritual values is directionless. Values unapplied in human endeavour are empty. And the best method of imparting moral training to the youths is to get him to take in the actual life about him. "For every ounce of moral experience is worth a pound of ethical teaching." There is only one lamp which can guide the feet of children and that is the lamp of experience, co-curricular activities furnish innumerable opportunities for the inculcation of moral standards. Moral qualities such as honesty, truth, justice, and purity are put to test, and therefore, forced into functioning. Through these, the pupils find opportunities to decide and choose the right and to learn the great value of self-control and moderation. The child is brought gradually from the place where he is unable to control himself to the point where he is the master. The child learns through the free community life of games, excursions, and the school societies an inner discipline which abides with the child as a directing and restraining influence when he is away from the school and even after he has ceased to be a pupil.

(vi) *They strengthen the mental and physical health of students.* Well-conceived and supervised sports activities can and do make for better physical health. Good mental health must be promoted through provisions for a wide variety of activities in which the student has a chance to be at least moderately successful in something, be it learning to dance, writing a poem, or serving as a member of a committee, etc.

(vii) *They provide for a well-rounded social development of students.* The pupils can be taught how to act properly in a wide variety of social settings. For instance, they can be instructed about the accepted procedure at a dance, they may be instructed how to participate effectively in a group discussion, they may be instructed how to use approved table etiquettes. All these can make for well-rounded social development of students.

(viii) *They widen student contacts.* As individuals move toward maturity their horizons become more comprehensive. They broaden their contacts with people and they learn new ideas and ways of doing things. They become concerned about new issues and problems. The co-curricular activities can help in this process of maturing through sports, trips, excursion, etc.

(ix) *They provide opportunities for students to exercise their creative capacities more fully.* These activities provide with opportunities for novel pupil expressions. Writing an editorial for the school, magazines, painting a mural, developing plans in the student council to improve the functioning of the school – all these are illustrations of typical experiences which demand the utilisation of creative power. These activities provide the children with a chance to develop their creative abilities.

(b) The co-curricular activities contribute a lot to improvement of curriculum:

(i) *They supplement and enrich classroom experiences.* Pupils are frequently stimulated by certain classroom experiences and may wish to explore certain areas still further and may form clubs for the purpose. Dramatics, music, and citizenship activities often stem from stimulating classroom experiences and can return to them to enrich them.

(ii) *They help in exploring new learning experiences which may ultimately be incorporated into the curriculum.* Learning experiences stemming from classroom activities, if found valuable in co-curriculum, can be made a part of the curriculum. We have got a number of recognised classroom experiences, e.g. music, intra-mural sports, etc. which served their apprenticeship in the activities programme.

(iii) *They provide additional opportunity for the individual and group guidance.* With the help of the varied activities, the latest potentialities of the pupils can come to the surface. In the light of these revelations, educational and vocational guidance can be given. In fact, guidance is inherent in all the co-curricular activities.

(iv) *They motivate classroom instruction.* Theoretically, we admit, the classroom should generate its own motivating forces. But practically it seems safe to assume that many times external stimulation is needed to insure that a student is learning best at his level of capability. Many a boy has been kept in school because of his interest in sports; many pupils have become better oriented through school assembly; interest in club activities has frequently generated greater interest in class-work; and so on.

(c) *The co-curricular activities contribute a lot to more effective school administration:*

(i) *They foster more effective work between students, faculty, administrative and supervisory personnel.* Teamwork, we know, is essential for the smooth functioning of the various organs of the school. Teachers expect cooperation in the classroom and the student in turn expects his teachers to be interested in the things which interest him such as sports, plays, and other similar activities. These activities provide opportunities for more personal and friendly relations between the student and the faculty. Through the student council, students help in the determination of school policies and help in seeking the solutions to some of the perplexing problems facing the school.

(ii) *They provide opportunities to the youth in the worthwhile utilisation of their spare time.* Many students have one or more hours of leisure time at the end of the school day. Informal intra-mural activities, marching band rehearsals, and play practices during these periods will help in the proper utilisation of the spare time. Thus, leisure can be converted from a curse into a blessing, from a burden into an opportunity for a fuller, richer, and noble life.

(iii) *They enable teachers to understand the pupils better.* The teacher can get a more complete idea of his students by studying their behaviour in play and other school activities of their own choosing. He may see the boy who is a "dud" in his History class, having the thrill of his life as he plays a match or runs a race; he may see some of his shy pupils behaving in an unrestrained manner in groups of their associates; and he may learn what students really think about their school experiences and teachers by merely standing around and listening, by going on trips with groups of students, or by becoming a fellow worker in any of these shared experiences.

(d) *Co-curricular activities contribute a lot to the community:*

(i) *They promote better school and community relations.* The school and the community can be drawn closer together when the pupils go out on excursions and camps, when the schools arrange debates, declamation and music concerts, where citizens may be invited; when the schools hold hobby fairs in which students, faculty, and town people participate.

(ii) *They encourage greater community interest in the school.* When parents and other members of a community are well-informed about their school and have participated in some of its activities, there is a tendency for interest and cooperation to increase. They may be motivated to improve their schools with the facilities at their disposal. A clearer understanding and appreciation of the potential contributions of the co-curricular activities, translated into practice, will result in better programmes for youth.

24.2 Some Principles Essential to a Good Co-curricular Programme

Below we list some principles which may be considered as essential to a good co-curricular programme:

(i) *Democracy of opportunity must be ensured.* An opportunity for all to think and act without fear of ridicule, is to be provided with the belief that every individual, if given the chance, can make at least some contribution to the common welfare and to his own happiness.

(ii) *The number of such activities should be the maximum that a school can afford, and they should be as varied as possible.* This will help satisfying the diverse needs of a large number of students in a school.

(iii) *Few, if any, restrictions should be placed on participation.* All interested students should be permitted to participate in different activities to the extent to which they are capable of participating with some measure of satisfaction and success. The nature of the activity may make some restrictions necessary, but they should be held to a minimum.

(iv) *We should ensure distribution of participation as widely as possible without compulsion.* This will be possible through personal conference and group discussions.

(v) *The programme should take into account the special or unique needs of a particular school.* No two schools are ever exactly alike. The programme of each must be adjusted to the particular need of its own students. The needs of young people in a rural community will differ from those who live in a wealthy urban area. Even though such activities as clubs and assemblies are common place, the learning experiences made available through these activities can and should vary from school to school and the degree of variance should be reflected in the programme.

(vi) *Co-curricular activities should furnish a rich source of motivation for class instruction.* Learning to do percentage problems in a mathematics class may be strongly motivated for some pupils by using problems involving pitching averages in baseball or foul shooting in basketball.

24.3 Aims of Co-curricular Activities

It is a strong demand of democratic society that its youths should avail laboratory of social experiences in which they may utilise democratic theories taught in the classroom. Thus the stress may be put on group activities, opportunities of contact between teacher and child and those activities in which the child may get democratic experience by participating. The objectives of these activities are as under:

(1) To make the moral feeling high of the total educational programmes of school and its personnel.

(2) To provide self-government to students, and valuable experiences in the use of democratic process so that they may have skilled democratic citizenship.

(3) To develop the feeling of cooperation and co-existence in the children coming from various atmospheres, and to make them one emotionally, so that the path of national integration may be made wide.

(4) To improve relations of school and society together and to encourage society for taking interest in programmes of schools.

(5) To help children for their all-round development.

(6) To prepare children for proper utilisation of their leisure time.

24.4 Guiding Principles for Organising Activities

French *et al.* have suggested the following principles for organising and administering co-curricular activities:

1. The justification for each activity must lie in the contribution it can make to the learning and development of youth. They should not be used to publicise the school or glorify the principal.
2. The activity programme for each school should grow out of the life of that school and be adapted to the local situation.
3. To be vital, the student activity programme must be dynamic. When interest in any activity shows signs of waning, it should be discontinued.
4. Participation in student activities should be equally available to all students with restrictions related only to competency and interest in the given activity.
5. Student activities should be a recognised responsibility of the school and as such should be planned and supervised.
6. There should be a continuous interpretation to the public of the activity programme. Many a time such activities are adversely criticised and therefore, the community should know the significance and importance of various activities in the programme of education.

24.5 Some Important Co-curricular Activities

1. The Student Council

Why should there be a School Council? The following reasons can be given:

(i) A feeling of urgency to make democracy function as it should in view of the increasing world tension;

(ii) A realisation of the fact that intelligent participation in democratic action must be learned;

(iii) An increasing faith in the contributions that young people can make to democratic thought and action.

Specific Objectives

The following are the specific objectives of having a school council: -

(i) To allow pupils to participate in or manage co-curricular affairs.

(ii) To develop student responsibility, initiative, leadership, and school pride.

(iii) To promote the welfare of the school through proper student faculty relationships.

(iv) To promote citizenship training.

(v) To promote general welfare.

(vi) To aid in the internal administration of the school.

(vii) To provide for pupil expression.

(viii) To furnish a working model of government.

Guiding Principles underlying Effective Council Activity

(a) *The Council must be desired by the school:* - The students, teachers, and administrators should believe in a Council and what it can achieve before a Council is organised. If the Council idea is not understood and accepted by potential participants, then the chances of the Council becoming a success are very dim indeed. To inaugurate a Council, it is desirable to move slowly. At no time should the organisation of the Council be hurried. It should be introduced in response to a felt-need of the school citizens.

(b) *The entire school should be represented on the Council.*

(c) *The work of the school council should be so conducted that each member of the school community will feel that he is represented.* Each individual should have the opportunity to suggest problems and projects for the Council's consideration, to assist with determination of policies and activities, to vote for certain council officers, and to otherwise participate in the work of the Council.

(d) *A Council should be begun gradually.* Even after there is an evident desire for a Council, the succeeding steps should be taken slowly to insure that everybody understands and approves of them. It is better to sacrifice speed for firmness of foundation; particularly at a time when a new council is in the process of being born.

(e) *The organisation of the Council should be kept simple.* The organisational plan should be adapted to the conditions existing in a particular school. Plans borrowed from other schools seldom fit local needs.

(f) *The duties and responsibilities of the Council must be clear, specific, and understood by all.* A clearly written statement should be developed about the obligations and policies of the Council to leave no scope for any estrangement on any side.

(g) *Sufficient authority should be granted to the Council to permit it to formulate rules and regulations governing the chartering and supervision of other co-curricular activities.* One of the major responsibilities of the Council should be that of general supervision and coordination of the entire co-curricular programme. Such a responsibility would include: (1) forming clubs, (2) recommending the elimination of activities that have outlived their usefulness, suggesting modification of any activities that seem to be ineffective, assisting with the establishment and co-ordination of the financial structure of the curricular activities and helping to determine and administer school policies for the co-curricular field.

(h) *A constructive programme of activities is essential.* The Council should concentrate on construction projects designed to improve the school. It is essential that council programmes be challenging to students and result in successful achievement.

(i) *Council activities must be supervised.* The co-curricular programme is in reality a part of the total instructional programme of the school. The Council is primarily an organisation in which learning takes place through the planning and completion of projects. It is as important that an advisor be present at all Council meetings as it is that a teacher be in his room for every class period. The chief function of the advisor is to serve as a consultant or guide.

The Organisation

School councils are frequently composed of members elected by different houses - classes and clubs. It is very important that the council should be representative in scope and thoroughly democratic in its methods of election. The Council should be the voice of all the people. It should be the legislative branch of the total school government in which all school citizens participate actively - organisers, teachers, and students. The Council should have powers and privileges and its checks and emotions should be defined as clearly as its powers and privileges. Each school should evolve the constitution of its own council and separate types of committees should be set up for the purpose. Limitations of jurisdictions may be necessary but should be carefully stated in the constitution and not continually used as a threat by faculty.

The veto power should be seldom used but never emphasised.

Regular and adequate time should be provided, during the school days for elections, discussions, reporting, and evaluation. The organisation plan should be simple and workable. It should be developed and conducted on a basis of clearly defined constitutional areas of responsibility.

The school council member can be chosen in a variety of ways:

(a) In some schools, there is the practice of representation by clubs, in others grade level of school class is the basis. There are the automatic, the ex-officio council plans under which the class officers or the school administrative officers or the honorary society, are constituted as the school's student council.

If the schools are to move in the direction of a true all-school council, the organisational plan should reflect such a goal. Provision should, therefore, be made for representation of the faculty and the other adult citizens of the schools.

Activities of the Council

School councils can take up the following activities:

(1) Co-curricular regulatory activities.

(2) Assembly activities.

(3) Orientation of new students.

(4) Recreational activities.

(5) Welfare activities.

(6) Income producing activities.

The number of activities in which students can participate effectively can vary from school and one administrative system to another. It also depends upon the morale of the institution.

2. *The School Assembly*

The school assembly can serve as the focusing centre of all forms of co-curricular life of a school.

Objectives

The following objectives can be achieved through school assemblies:

(i) *To unify school.* The assembly can afford an opportunity for the entire school personnel to work, think, and even plan together as a unit. Just as members of a family need to get together from time to time to share experiences and problems and to socialise, so do the members of the school family need to learn to know, understand and appreciate those with whom they come in contact in the school. By working together as a unit, each feels that there is a common bond.

(ii) *To interpret work of the school.* One of the most important talks of the assembly programme is to share what is going on in the school both in and out of the classroom. Every department or subject-matter field and every major school activity should be urged to assume responsibility for at least one assembly each year. Such assemblies might well stimulate new interests, suggest vocational choices and tend to improve the activities themselves by spotlighting them on assembly programme.

(iii) *To develop desirable attitudes and appreciations.* Through assemblies such desirable attitudes as respect for property, consideration for people of all religions and races, responsibility for one's actions, obedience to constituted authority and a willingness and ability to cooperate may be strengthened. Appreciations are best developed by frequent exposure to activities in a setting to which the learner reacts with some favourable emotional responses. Students can be stimulated to do their best in studies also.

(iv) *To assist in the selection of a vocation.* Assembly programmes can be designed to be of material assistance to the student as he chooses a vocation and as he strives to become competent in the vocation of his choice. Activities such as lectures by successful individuals, a dramatic description by the commercial department of the vocational requirements of workers in the field, carefully selected motion pictures, etc. can prove quite useful.

(v) *To develop better understanding of critical issues and problems in our contemporary*

culture. The youth of today is surrounded by tension all round and he is losing his bearing. In order to enable him to adjust to the mores of his environment, he must be informed about religion and politics, social and economic set-up, and service in the armed forces. School assembly is a very good forum for the purpose.

(vi) *To furnish opportunities to appear before an audience.* The school assembly may well serve as a laboratory for learning how to become an effective leader. Appearing in plays, reciting a song, making a speech all help to "break the ice" and give assurance and competence to the participants.

(vii) *To learn more about the community and how it functions.* Through assemblies, members of the community can be invited to participate in the life of the school. The school can emerge from its "ivory tower."

(viii) *To recognise superior achievement.* The assembly can be utilised to give public recognition of superior achievement – athletic prowess, special music talent, high scholastic attainment, superior citizenship, commendable honesty.

(ix) *To encourage the development of good audience behaviour.* Good audience behaviour is one of the essentials of good citizenship and yet how difficult it is to obtain it. A lot of time and intelligent supervision will enable us to achieve the goal.

(x) *To furnish wholesome entertainment as well as to educate.* We can have assembly programmes which have entertainment as well as educational value.

Guidelines For Making Assembly Programme

Some guidelines for making assembly programmes are listed below:

(i) Every pupil and teacher should actively participate in at least one assembly programme each year.

(ii) Assemblies should include a wide variety of activities.

(iii) Important speakers and entertainers should be invited to participate in the assembly programme.

(iv) The programmes should be well-planned. The programmes should be conducted by teachers and students, both cooperating in the planning and in carrying out its programmes. Assembly committee composed of several students and two or three members may well be made responsible for the assembly exercises.

(v) Careful preparation should be done. If the problem of the Assembly is to be the "Clearing House" of the school corporate life, careful preparation is very necessary. Programmes should be reviewed and rehearsed before they are actually staged.

(vi) Reasonable order must be maintained.

(vii) Assembly programmes must be supervised.

(viii) Programmes should be evaluated.

(ix) Seldom should class assemblies take more time than that allotted to a regular class period.

(x) Assembly programmes should be regularly scheduled at the same time of day and on the same day of each week.

(xi) Meetings of the assembly should be held frequently, say, once a week. One good programme a week is better than daily routine affairs consisting of formal talks and necessary announcements.

(xii) School assemblies should be open to all students.

(xiii) Reprimanding or pious sermonising and heavy subjects should be avoided. Talks in the assemblies should be interesting, instructive and inspiring.

The School Principal and School Assemblies

The principal is responsible for all the assembly activities by virtue of his position as the administrative head of his school. It is not his duty to "run" all assemblies. It is better for him to stay in the background. He should restrain the tendency to occupy the centre of the stage too long or too frequently realising that when he needs to speak, his words will be all the more effective.

There are, however, some very necessary things he can do both directly and indirectly:

(i) Firstly, he must understand what specific contributions the school assembly can make to the total educational programme of his school. He should see to it that effective student and faculty leadership are selected.

(ii) He should assist in the determination of policies governing school assemblies and should approve all those policies that are consistent with the general policies of the school system.

(iii) He should delegate authority commensurate with responsibility to those selected to implement all approved policies and should back up those in charge.

(iv) He should see to it that sufficient time for school assemblies is allocated within the school day.

(v) He should do everything within his powers to guarantee that the maximum potential of school assemblies is reached in his school.

(vi) The principal should not point out the faults and shortcomings of the pupils frequently at the school assemblies.

3. Excursion

The school excursion is any group experience not had in the classroom. It may be as simple as the first trip of a five-year old to explore the school plant or as ambitious as the week's visit to the nation's capital taken by the senior high school class. The purpose is to supplement the curricular experiences.

It is felt by the modern teacher that those things which can be learnt best in school should be learnt there. Those things which can be learnt best outdoors should be learnt there. Many things to be learnt best out of doors range from the discovery of the smallest forms of life that students can observe to the study of heavenly bodies; from an enjoyment of constructive purposeful work to interest in natural beauty; from having fun to learning how to work together.

The Objectives

(i) *To capitalise educationally the migratory instinct of the child.* Man is a migratory animal by nature. He wants to wander, explore, and "be on the go." He wants to sense new things, have new experiences, meet new associates, and live temporarily at least, in the new surroundings. The school excursion properly initiated, organised, and conducted, completed and evaluated represents excellent capitalisation of his migratory urge.

(ii) *To acquaint the pupil with his environment.* When the pupil in a purposeful and definitely planned trip visits a fire department, court or council in session, post office, historical monuments, he acquires information that is complete, accurate because it is correlated with some idea or relationship that is being presented in his school work.

(iii) *To interpret, supplement, and enrich curricular experiences.* A great deal of the usual curricular work of the school is formal and academic and hence, lacks vitality. The average bookish description of a water works plant, the publication of a newspaper, the significance of a great memorial is not appealing to the average student because they are more or less remote from reality. Of course,

> these book accounts are necessary but how much more interesting and meaningful they become when they are supplemented by actual first-hand experience with the items in their functional relationships or settings – when the pupil sees, how water is obtained, purified, and distributed, when he follows a cheque through the bank, when he witnesses the getting out of the newspaper, when he stands in reverence before some memorial.

Excursions may be undertaken for securing information, changing attitudes, awakening interest, developing appreciations, promoting ideals, enjoying new experiences. They can initiate a unit of study; they can be part of the core of it or they can give it the finishing touch. They are a very good means of getting knowledge first hand, of confirming and supplementing second-hand knowledge.

Types

Excursions may be of many types. Some are complex undertakings requiring elaborate transportation, full day planning, and additional adult helpers. These longer journeys/trips to historical sites and special events beyond the local community not only have exciting destinations to be explored for problem solving and project executing but also offer valuable opportunities for observation of the environment along the way. Some trips are shorter and more easily planned as visits to factories, radio stations, newspaper plants, wholesale and retail establishments, libraries and the like. Still others are simple to undertake, and may be embarked on almost at the moment of conceiving the idea – the walk around the block to see nature, and man getting ready for winter, the journey to the neighbouring farm, the walk through the park to gather some needed specimens.

Planning

A successful school excursion does not happen. It must be wisely conceived, democratically planned, properly organised, ably conducted, and profitably capitalised. Permitting our pupils an immediate reconciliation with "life in the round," it admits the maximum of romance which may, unless you are alert, be little more than romance. Thus, it requires a preface and follow-up. It ought to be connected with and extended to classroom study. It may also initiate it. It should be much more than "going to places and seeing things."

Before an excursion is actually taken up, it is important that every pupil as well as the teacher, becomes fully aware of why this particular trip is being planned and if it is related to his own classroom experiences and activities. Appropriate audio-visual aids may also be used both for initial motivation and for general orientation to what will be seen in the trip itself. The atmosphere must be one of anticipation and not merely of suspense waiting for whatever may happen to surprise them next. It will be better if the teacher suggests guide questions which the pupils might put while approaching community leaders from whom they want useful information about the various aspects of community life. Major purposes should be clarified and made specific. In no task is cleverness more essential than in preparation for excursion, demonstrations, and other forms of instructions which involve unaccustomed situations, otherwise unusual irrelevant elements yielding only incidental value consume the entire pupil's energy.

Children also need to be directed while they are observing. The most interesting matter is not necessarily the most important, nothing is easier than to *look at* something and yet not *see* what is essential. Moreover, it is extremely difficult to correct a misconception growing out of careless observation. Hence, it is always advisable to test the success of the observations while they are still being made.

Now the question that naturally arises is who should be responsible for the arrangement? In this connection, there are three possibilities:

(a) The teacher may do all the planning and executing.

(b) The pupils may do these.

(c) The teacher and pupils may together work out the details and handle the event.

Although the first possibility may result in desirable efficiency, it robs the pupils of educative opportunities. The second plan is not feasible. The third plan is the best of the three because it capitalises both pupil and the teacher's interest and experience and in this way helps to make the event attractive and successful in its direct effects, in connection with the class work and in its indirect effects through the very real and natural experience that the pupils receive in helping to plan, organise and execute.

A committee may be formed which should gather material, formulate questions, and in other ways increase the interest of the group, not merely in seeing, but seeing the 'how' and 'why' of the thing. The teacher should only be a guide. A few sub-committees may be appointed by the teacher or selected by the pupils - the committee of arrangements with the individuals in charge of the place or institution to be visited, planning the time, etc., in such a way as to cause as little inconvenience as possible. There should be definite periods for serious work, during the excursion if maximum results are to be secured. It would be worse than useless to plan a trip carefully and then allow anything to interfere. It is poor practice to make plans and then abandon them. The teacher or the student committee should definitely take care of some important matters, i.e. the number of students taking trips, time, place, object, results, used in class-work, expense per student, name of officer or guide to whom thanks are due, remarks regarding food, conveyance, accommodation, etc. Definite follow-up activities also form an integral part of any well-arranged trip. The follow-up may take the form of reading books on the places observed, writing reports, or descriptive accounts, preparing scrap books, holding of panel or forum discussion.

Last but not the least important, excursions should be evaluated in terms of the originally established purposes, mistakes and difficulties should be diagnosed, conduct of the group should be discussed, letter of thanks should be written to the persons concerned and highlights of the trip should be recorded in some permanent form for future use.

4. School Publications

School publications present a field of activity which almost invariably fascinates pupils. The result can be of enormous importance to the community, the school, and the individual pupils. It is therefore, the business of the principal, teachers and pupils to accept or formulate a constructive policy for the proper conduct of this activity.

Aims and Values. School publications unify the school spirit. They mould and influence school opinion; they encourage desirable school activities and enterprise; they give authentic information regarding the school to students, parents, patrons, old students and other schools. They serve as a medium of expression of student opinion. They provide opportunity for creative work and self-expression. Qualities of co-operation, tact, accuracy, tolerance, responsibility, initiative, and leadership development and cordial relations among different schools are fostered. Moreover, they record the history of the school and help to advertise the institutions.

Through the editorials of the school papers, total school support for projects and activities can be mobilised. Through articles and letters to the editor, the real voice of the student body can be heard and evaluated. It is difficult to imagine how a school without a newspaper of its own can develop genuine school unity and "togetherness." This is likely to be true even in small schools but it is especially important in large schools where such total school communication is difficult. Pride in the school depends in the last analysis, upon the degree of identification which students come to feel with the school as an institution. If it is to become *our* school, *our* council, *our* teams, *our* assemblies, *our* clubs, there must be avenues of prompt and effective communication among students. By supplying a democratic medium of public opinion, school publications can play a significant role in unifying the school.

They are an effective agency for interpreting the school to the public. School publications offer an immediate incentive by furnishing the writer with an audience. It is a socialised cooperative learning experience through which students can learn the skills of democratic participation. These considerations are weighty enough to encourage an average school to have its own paper.

The School Magazine

Aims and Values: - The school magazine can serve as an avenue of socialisation by distributing news, building up school spirit, creating popular support for school enterprises and providing a literary medium for the constructive criticism of school life. It offers excellent training to a few, both in writing and leadership and is not without value to the many. Art and literature are its concerns. Consequently, there are more opportunities for students of widely differing abilities and interests to produce the type of material in which they are interested.

Magazine production is a laboratory experience in creative journalism. The very existence of a good magazine in the school will prove a spur to creative efforts of students in all fields.

The magazine should reflect the best work, students can produce; but what is "best" should be subject to constant scrutiny in terms of the interests of the readers. This means continuous exploration of the interests of the reader and planning of future issues in accordance with the findings of such evaluation.

Selection of the Editorial Board: The editorial board should be carefully elected on the basis of merit by some combination of the staff and the student choice. Editorial work calls for specialised and technical ability and hence can, never in so heterogeneous a group as the ordinary high school, be trusted to popular election.

Some Possible Limitations: It is feared that the magazine is likely to attempt to carry more news than it should. Usually its contents fail to grip the interest of students and its humour may be largely borrowed, its literature not worth publishing, its editorials, and moralising of no particular value, and too few students may participate in the production of the magazine. Moreover, there may be the likelihood of its being expensive. But these are minor difficulties and can be overcome. One danger must be guarded against that if the magazine is to prove successful, it must be *a publication of the school and not merely of the staff*. It must secure variety and omit material likely to be uninteresting to students. No particular group or interest should be allowed to monopolise its pages.

Conclusion: To conclude, we can say that the school through this agency expands its sphere into the wider world. The number of educational opportunities will be multiplied. The interest of students will be increased. The magazine will convey a monthly message home. In this way, it can prove very helpful to the pupils, parents, and the school.

5. Handbook

Every high and higher secondary school must have a handbook which may orientate the newcomer about the school. It can give all sorts of important information about the schools and can act as the best informer. The following may be included in the school handbook:

1. A picture of the school.
2. Brief history of the school.
3. Location of the school and how to reach it.

4. Plan of the building showing various facilities.
5. Names and assignments of the staff.
6. School mottos, emblems, and songs.
7. Subject offerings.
8. Rules of attendance, classification, promotion, etc.
9. Calendar of the school year.
10. Examinations.
11. Progress reports.
12. Timetable.
13. School celebrations.
14. Clubs and society with rules and regulations.
15. Medical and health services.
16. School guidance service.
17. School uniform.
18. Stipend and scholarships.
19. Alumni association.
20. Homework.
21. School canteen.
22. Manners and courtesy.
23. P.T.A.
24. Fees and other costs.
25. School publications.
26. Student council.
27. Awards and prizes.

Careful planning and intelligent editing are as important for the handbook as for the other publications of the school. It may be produced as a part of an upper class project to foster the orientation of incoming classes. Or it may become the responsibility of a student council committee or a member of the staff representing the entire student body. In any case, it should reflect the students interests and judgements and should be written and produced by students. And in this way, it can be a very useful educational experience for all concerned.

6. Clubs and Societies

Aims and Values: Clubs and societies are also very useful. The interests of the pupils can best be improved through school clubs which offer opportunities for exploring, developing, and widening the interests of the students. They will develop the quality of leadership. They will train the pupil in definite forms of good parliamentary usage. Club activities train students – the citizens of the school – to perform better those desirable activities that are likely to be performed *carelessly*. The best way, perhaps the only way, of giving pupils the idea of how to become the chairman or to write properly secretary's minutes is by direct instruction coupled with experience. Club work also develops *initiative, spontaneity, cooperation,* and *respect for law*. It affords opportunities for the development of leadership and the formation and cultivation of friendship based on mutual interest in things that are worthwhile.

The activities of literary and debating societies, dramatic clubs, and other school organisations afford sources of excellent inspiration for the regular work of the school. Students attracted to any subject or phase of a subject may have through clubs, and their programmes, opportunities for further work in it.

Through clubs the schools can serve both the present and the future needs in recreation. Like other phases of the activity programme, the active clubs provide a wholesome outlet for the adolescent energy and satisfy the normal school desire of the pupils. They also may develop tastes and interests which will deepen with experience. The amateur photographer, musician, or dramatist will find the horizon of his hobby expanding as the years go on.

Clubs afford opportunity for the practice of group planning and decision. In the activities of the clubs pupils may learn how to work together to develop plans, how to make wise choice of leaders, how to adjust differences and disagreements, and how to appraise their progress towards the goal they have set.

Organisation: A simple constitution defining the purpose, organisation, and activities of the club and stating the time, place, and frequency of meetings and the duties of the different officers, is also needed. Children should be taught the need for system, rules, and regulations and the teacher may act and be accepted as a safe adviser.

Need of Variety: There is the need of a variety of clubs - dramatic clubs, historical/ geographical associations, literary societies, walking or travel clubs, boating and swimming clubs, fine arts clubs, science clubs, and so on.

7. Athletics and Games

Aims and Values: Games are said to be man's common heritage along with hunger and thirst. Young people in their adolescence possess an exuberance of energy which, if not properly utilised often leads to their over-stepping the bounds of reason and control. Physical exercise provides a healthy outlet for surplus energy. It further secures organic development to the limit of inherited possibilities and makes for feeling of well-being. It also promotes the development of that control of the muscular system which gives skill, resourcefulness, and fundamental basis for a broad manual, industrial, and artistic training. It provides an opportunity for securing mental and moral discipline - the alertness, precision, determination, self-control, courage, team-work, self-denial, loyalty, leadership, and sportsman-like magnanimity. The playground is said to be the *cradle of democracy.* In fact, as has been observed, "The battle of Waterloo was won on the playground of Eton." It means that the activities on the playground go a long way in the development of the personality of the individual. They represent a welcome and, on the whole, a healthy diversion from school routine. We can say that these activities have a great physical, social, recreational, and educational values.

Organisation and Supervision: If the benefits of the games are to be secured and evils eliminated, the advice of the teachers is quite necessary. The teaching staff should be represented in the management. It should control such things as time and place for training, competitive games with outside teams, the method of raising and spending money and the making of such rules as will prohibit those who are negligent in their school from playing in the several teams. But this guidance should not be over-done.

The school should aim at giving all the pupils a chance to participate on equal terms and under careful control, in a widely varied range of games and sports. A desirable motto for the school might well be "A sport for every pupil and every pupil in a sport."

Competitive athletics limit participation but the best way to develop school loyalty is to hold a contest with another school. But when inter-school competitions are given undue prominence, the benefits of physical training are limited. The importance attached to victory not only leads to the adoption of unethical practices but also to wrong educational procedure. To quote Shri Krishanaya : "What our students of today should strive for is neither to be victorious athletes, prize gymnasts, nor champion strong men but to have some of the *alertness and endurance of the athlete and some of the grace and skill of the gymnast, all combined with the poise and dignity of a gentleman."*

In order to make the athletic programme very effective and useful, we should bear in mind the following points:

1. The athletic programme should be a well coordinated part of the secondary school curriculum.
2. Opportunities should be provided for many students to participate in a wide variety of sports in every sport season.
3. Training in conduct, game ethics, and sportsmanship should be given for participants.
4. The programmes should include a well-balanced programme of intra-mural sports.
5. All athletic competitions should grow out of and form an integral part of the physical and health education programme of the school.

Proper facilities for the girls should also be provided.

Needs of a Competent Instructor: A competent physical instructor can give good and useful physical education to young boys and girls. The instructor must be endowed with sympathetic insight, educational ideals, and social leadership so that he may recognise individual capacities, needs and tastes and give sympathetic encouragement and stimulus especially to the less fortunate and keep games and sports running with the school.

8. Boy Scouting

Aims and Values: Scouting is also very important among the co-curricular activities. It is said that the best way to teach youth to be *good* is to give them lessons in *doing good*. To talk about the beauty of unselfishness while gratifying every wish is to render the teaching useless. To teach about generosity is not to teach generosity itself. Practice and preaching should go together or better still practice should precede precept. This is the aim of this movement. It aims to give boys a useful and enjoyable time in the open air, outside school hours; to train them in habits of self-control, self-help, self-reliance, and self-sacrifice; to help them towards character-building, with a view to making better men and citizens, not only of their motherland but of the whole world. It creates a healthy environment through clubs, camps, and sports where boys learn to play the games for the team, where they are trained in social service and civic sense and are definitely encouraged to live *purer, nobler*, and *healthier* lives. It develops in boys' *honour, loyalty, obedience, resourcefulness, and a desire to serve.* It trains them to accept responsibility not only for the *assigned tasks* but also for the *unexpected emergency.* It emphasises the spirit of the good turn - for a scout must do 'a good turn daily.' The scout method is eminently practical - "Do" rather than "read about" is its characteristics. In the words of Dr. L.D. Coffman, "Scouting gives no long lectures on vocational guidance and yet it teaches the meaning , the importance and dignity of work; it operates no bank and yet it teaches the meaning of thrift; it contains no jails and yet it teaches the meaning of self-control; it does no preaching and yet it teaches devotion to a cause and loyalty to a purpose; it is founded upon no religious creed or sectarian doctrine and yet it emphasises above all things the importance of religion. It is universal in appeal, natural in its outlines, strengthened and cemented by the bonds of fellowship and the idealism of the movement." Scouting has marvellous potency for converting the restless, irresponsible, self-centered boy into a straight-forward, dependable, helpful young citizen.

The Scouting and the School: One hour each week or more should be found for all these activities. It is desirable to use scouts for guiding, first aid and other purposes whenever possible, making them feel privileged to be of service. Although scouting is not a subject for examination, it must receive adequate encouragement. The scout-master should be a real leader, with plenty of energy and cheerfulness, ripe knowledge and wide experiences of the world, and capacity to organise, instruct, and inspire the young people placed in his charge. He should be able to give practical training in scout games and handicrafts that are appealing and useful to pupils. He should be able, above all, to live up to the scout law himself. Not only by instruction but by example, he should be able to guide and inspire his followers. It is he who can do away with the wastage which we meet in scouting in schools. The training must be extended to two or three years and it should not be a mere show for some days when an Education Officer is to visit the school.

9. Girl Guides

Aims and Values: The Girl Guide Movement has a purpose no less practical than that of scouting. It occupies the mind and time of adolescent girls by teaching her through play the elements of home making, of building a strong body and of becoming a good citizen. The girl guide activities including the study of nature, nursing, country dancing, cooking, laying games, singing., etc are calculated to train healthy, cheerful, serviceable, and good women. This movement opens up great opportunities for the development of character and the encouragement of social service. Proper use of leisure is promoted.

This movement has three branches; The Blue-Bird Flock for girls below 11, Girl Guides Company for those from 11 to 16, and Ranger Company for girls 16-year-old or above.

All the above mentioned activities lead to the cultivation of the School Spirit.

It includes more than either "Corporate feeling," "School loyalty" or *esprit de corps.* It may perhaps best be described as attitude of 'our schoolness' plus a sense of belonging to the school, plus a 'we feeling.' All the activities mentioned heretofore contribute to the promotion of school spirit and its tone. Such an attitude of 'we feeling' is a valuable asset to the school. *School sentiment is the junior edition of public sentiment and public sentiment is the strongest force in human society.* It makes a *cooperative effort easy and natural.* In fact, so powerful is the influence of the established school customs, forms and standard that there comes to be an expectancy and a mental adjustment on the part of the children even before they actually become members of the school, and after they have joined the school. Its ways, its customs and its standards grip them and begin to fashion them. The individual is made to feel the compelling power of the group standard towards the right kind of conduct. The stirring up of group loyalty and the arousing of collective pride is bound to have a 'tonic' effect upon the future conduct of pupils. This 'we feeling' towards the members of the schools means respect for authority in the classroom, in the assembly hall and on the playing fields. It ensures the minimising of class, communal and sectarian distinctions. Social coherence helps to isolate an institution from the contagion of undesirable influence and movement outside.

Pupils also gain invaluable training through the subordination of petty and selfish considerations to the common good. They acquire the habit of cooperation, team work, and "pulling together." Each one feels his personal responsibility for the whole and meets it by doing his part.

It also benefits the society. The cultivation and exercise of school loyalty and *esprit de corps* lead to a keener civic sense and public-mindedness.

10. Speech Activities

Speech activities like debates, declamations, dramatization, etc., have also a great educational value.

(a) *Debates:* Debates have important educational values. They emphasise clear, forceful and persuasive delivery, the ability to analyse the facts which bear upon an issue and to organise those facts into a well-organised and convincing whole. The topics for debates should be chosen from the present real life of the students, problems of national and international importance. Opportunities for public speaking should be given to as many students as possible.

(b) *Dramatization:* Dramatization has universal appeal to old and young alike. The fascination is of universal human appeal, whether it be playing a part oneself or seeing some phase of life made real as the characters materialise before our eyes. This characteristic attitude of youth has not been sufficiently capitalised for educational purposes in most schools. As a method of teaching, it has an important use in the classroom as well as for club meetings and assembly programmes. The fields of literature and history naturally lend themselves to this type of activity. But dramatization may be used effectively in any subject, a science class re-enacting

circumstances of some famous scientific discovery; a mathematics group showing the application of mathematics in daily life. The opportunities are varied and many. It all depends upon how the teacher utilises them. The alert teacher will think of many adaptations which can be made in his own teaching field.

The school library should include several volumes dealing with the various problems involved in dramatic production – play selection, direction, costuming, make-up, and construction of scenery.

The actual choice of play should be a cooperative activity of director and club.

Dramatic work is valuable in that at its best it can train the imagination and develop initiative, originality, and ingenuity. It can give scope to many different talents – every member of the class can help in some way as actor, scene-shifter, property maker, prompter. It may open an entirely new environment to the child, enabling him to project himself into the character he is acting and thus to express himself more fully perhaps than in any other way. Speech activities are valuable in making us richer personalities. The experience of self-expression through speech has a therapeutic effect on the personality development and can help us to develop insight into our own problems and potentials and into those of others with whom we associate. In business ventures, speech ability can be crucial. In all lines of earning a living, it is important to be able to get and hold a job. Good speech can be helpful in winning friends and influencing people. The power to express one's thoughts clearly and engagingly, together with the corollary power to listen graciously to others, is a real lead to social success.

11. Music

So universal is music that it appears to satisfy a basic need in human experience. J.L. Mursell says: "Music is one of the most universal human needs. The impulse to create and enjoy it exists among men everywhere, and has existed always........while men remain the beings they are; they will continue to need music."

Thus, the case for "music for all" is to be built on a basic love for this means of expression, the enhancement of appreciation through maximum participation. Modern psychology has demolished the older notion that music talent is born not made. The impulse to produce or to listen to music is universal. Human beings, from childhood on, are sensitive to music as a natural means of expression and pleasure, although their sensitivity may not be highly cultivated.

The singing school will surely be a happy school. Tasks and problems do not loom so large or life so vexing, after a lively session of song with one's fellow.

24.6 Weaknesses in the Administration of Student Activities

(i) In certain schools, *various activities have been introduced simply on the ground that those very activities have been very successful in certain other schools.* There is no real understanding by teachers and pupils of the function it should perform with the result such type of ventures have to be abandoned as hastily as they had been introduced. They leave bitter experiences behind.

(ii) *Persons in authority have no good faith in the ability of the pupils* to make intelligent decision and accept and shoulder responsibility. It is often seen that student councils are staff dominated, other activities being entirely staff directed. At places responsibilities have been thrown on the untrained, unprepared, and weak shoulders. No wonder the results are not commendable. We want to have good citizens of democracy who should neither be slaves nor rebels. In a world where democracy is the watch-word, an autocratic set-up will not succeed. Pupils and teachers must play the proper roles.

(iii) *It is generally seen that participation in the activity programme is limited to too few pupils.* It is because of two causes. There are regulations which deny opportunity to pupils scholastically unsuccessful. The management fails to provide for appropriate distribution. There are pupils for whom the less formal activities of the extra curriculum represent the only phase of school experience in which they may achieve success and satisfaction. To deny them this opportunity is to refuse them the only real education the school affords them.

In some institutions, a group of capable or prominent pupils monopolise the opportunities available.

This is quite undesirable. Fair distribution of activities is very necessary.

(iv) *In some school, competitive aspects of the programme have been over-emphasised.* Winning of contests becomes the sole aim. Often the effort to equip competitors and to finance their attendance at state and national contests has taxed school resources and diverted funds which should have been available for extensions of opportunities within the school. For promoting the democratic spirit, spirit of cooperation should be promoted. To win the game should not be our sole aim.

(v) *In certain institutions, organisations which are representative of special groups in the community or engaged in promoting one point of view on controversial issues on which public is divided, are permitted to function as school organisations.* The school is there to serve all the people of the community. So organisations which deepen class lines or foster discrimination should have no place in the school which aims to promote democracy.

(vi) *The activity programme has not been related to the curriculum.* Activities are considered to be an extra burden. Only when they take their place as vital parts of the total educational experience will their full value be achieved. "Wherever possible, extra curricular activities should grow out of curricular activities and return to them to enrich them." Activities should not be recognised as a means of keeping young people "out of mischief" but as an important idea of adolescent education.

(vii) As has already been pointed out, *there has been no consistent effort to evaluate activities in terms of fundamental objectives.* When introducing activities, we have no set objects before us. Activities continue somehow or the other. When we do away with the activities, we have no system or principle to evaluate them.

(viii) *Teacher-training institutions provide the academic training all right, but they have failed to provide appropriate experiences for prospective teachers to prepare them for responsibilities in relation to student activities.* Like other practical training, the training to shoulder the future responsibilities, should also be one of the parts of the course.

(ix) *These activities are considered to be an unnecessary burden by teachers for the simple reason that they have to do such jobs in addition to their already heavy load.* Burden is increased but the recognition of the burden does not increase. The appropriate "teaching-load" should be determined in the light of a realistic consideration of the teacher's total contribution to the school. Administrators should be alive to this fact that some shoulders are not taxed too much at the cost of others.

(x) *Activities take place in season and out of season.* There is no fixed and well-prepared programme. Sometimes it is seen, the annual sports day is fixed when the annual examinations are just at hand. In some institutions, so many activities take place just near the end of the year. This is not desirable. In some schools, a period of a week or two is devoted for the various functions. In this period, there is no academic work. This practice is good in so far as regular school work does not suffer much.

Objective Type Questions

Multiple Choice Questions (Tick ✓ the right option)

(1) Co-Curricular activities are useful to the
(a) Parents
(b) Students
(c) Teachers
(d) All of the above

(2) Learning experiences stemming from
(a) Classroom activity
(b) Classroom atmosphere
(c) 'a' and 'b' both
(d) None of the above

Fill in the blanks

(1) School ______________ are frequently composed of members elected by different houses, classes and clubs [councils]

(2) The School ________________ is any group experience not had in the classroom [Excursion]

Important Questions

1. Co-curricular activities add to the appeal of the school and realise the creative talents and social aptitude of students. Discuss.
2. What children most require is an abundance of opportunities for wholesome activities wisely directed. If these can be made sufficiently stimulating, varied and regardful, educative growth is inevitable. Discuss and suggest ways to derive the proper results.
3. 'Co-curricular activities as organised in our schools at present fail to achieve the desired aims.' What suggestions will you offer to organise the activities properly?
4. "The playground is an open-air school." Discuss.
5. Discuss the importance and place of co-curricular activities in a Secondary School. Enumerate some of the activities you would introduce.
6. Mention any three co-curricular activities which you would like to organise in a rural high school. What objectives will you keep in view in respect of each of these activities? How will you ascertain that the objectives have been achieved?

25

The School Timetable

Have you ever been to a school where the bells do not ring, where there is no allotment of periods for various subjects, where specifications are not given to teachers or students for different activities or work. This may appear utopian, but in some parts of the world you may be able to find a few such institutions. In India Nai Talim Sangh of Mahatma Gandhi started some such schools, without any fixed timetable in the form and name of ideal Basic Schools. But these are only exceptions. Timetable is an essential part of all traditional, special, progressive and public schools. So it is useful to discuss various elements of a school timetable.

25.1 Meaning of School Timetable

The plan or the chart in a school showing the daily allotment of time among the several subjects, activities and classes is known as the school timetable. What a school stands for and how it functions can be assessed from the school timetable. It is, in fact, a mirror that reflects with some accuracy the entire educational programme followed in the school. It is said to be the 'spark plug' of the school which sets into motion its various activities and programmes. It determines how the time and other facilities of the school will be allocated among different uses to secure the objectives of education. A timetable is a medium through which is reflected the philosophy of the school as well as the professional competence of the principal.

A timetable is a necessary tool for the efficient working of a school. Its primary objective is to provide time for suitable and varied learning experiences for all the children. It prevents waste of time and energy by directing the teacher's attention to one thing at a time and saving him from digression, confusion, and unnecessary repetition. It gives each subject and activity the place, attention and emphasis that it deserves. Again, it ensures the most effective use of time at the disposal of the school by regulating the distribution of the work. It also makes it possible to fix courses wanted by each pupil. Finally, timetable secures the adjustment of the school work to the pupils with regard to the demands it makes on their energy and their capacity to meet them. Thus, it is a very important element in the internal economy of the school and is indispensable from the pupils', teachers', and principals' point of view. No wonder, it is so well styled as the "second school clock."

Definitions of a Timetable

(1) In the words of H.G. Stead: "It is the timetable that supplies the framework within which the work of the school proceeds. It is the instrument through which the purpose of the school is to function."

(2) In the words of Edmonson: "The timetable is an outline of the day's work which indicates (i) Time of beginning and ending of school day; (ii) Time of beginning and ending of each class period, activities period, and homework period; (iii) Subjects and activities offered; (iv) Room in which class or activity is held; and (v) Time, length and number of intermissions."

25.2 Importance of the Timetable

If the work of the school is to be conducted efficiently, there must be a detailed plan of action of all the works in which there should be division of time for various subjects and activities of each day of the school. Such plan or timetable is very much an essential element for internal arrangement of the school, through which every day time has been divided among different subjects and activities. In want of it, there is a possibility of disturbance in school-work. In the construction of a timetable the school authorities should be very much alert, because on the construction of a good timetable can school work run efficiently. Along with this a good timetable prevents misuse of strength, time, and money and provides opportunity to the children for development of their personality. So far the attainment of school objectives, all elements of school – physical and human – for converting in action, timetable, or programme planning is the most essential, so that work is done in a better way for achieving all its objectives. Construction of time-table is essential with both points of view of children and teachers.

The place of a timetable is important in a school because it is a mirror in which all educational programmes of school reflect, that manages the work of teachers and helps them in keeping their balance. Alongwith this, time-table utilises time by the management of programmes of a school nicely. The maximum utility of school time is assured by allotting time for different subjects and activities, etc. according to their importance and requirement. If there is want of timetable in a school or it is not well constructed, it is very natural to have mis-utilisation of time and strength.

Ethically, the importance of timetable is also great. By going according to it the children develop various good habits and qualities in them. For example, power to understand the importance of time, regularity, right vision, dutifulness, etc. It is also important for teachers. It helps them in creating points of view in accordance with law towards work.

It has also got importance in view of psychology because its construction is done keeping in mind the needs and interests of children. A good timetable plays an important role in simplifying the process of learning in which proper time is given to children for developing their various aspects, interests of eating and drinking and for planning various activities.

A timetable is a good source of establishing discipline, through it the whole life of school is run properly. By going according to it, one feels busy in their work. Alongwith this, the school is provided skill and definiteness by a time-table.

25.3 Types of Timetables

Generally, five types of timetables are used in a school: (1) Class timetable, (2) The Master timetable, (3) Individual teacher's timetable, (4) The check list, and (5) Special timetable.

(1) ***Class Timetable:*** - Every class should have its own timetable which should indicate the distribution of subjects with teachers and assignment of classrooms for each period. Every class should have its homework timetable. For even distribution of the amount of homework to be given to the students, the class teacher should prepare such a programme in consultation with subject-teachers. It is desirable that a copy of this timetable be displayed along with the general class timetable in the classroom.

(2) ***The Master Timetable:*** - It gives a complete picture of the entire programme of the school per day. It indicates the details of the work of individual teachers. Different sheets may be used for the days in a week, or there may be prepared a comprehensive chart showing the programme of all the working days.

(3) ***Individual Teacher's Timetable:*** - Every teacher should have a copy of his own

programme of work. It should show the details of his academic and non-academic work.

(4) *Vacant Period Timetable:* - A special timetable showing the vacant periods of all the teachers should also be prepared. This will be helpful in allotting work when some teacher is on leave. This type of timetable will show the teachers vacant in a particular period and thus these teachers may be requested to keep the vacant class occupied when needed.

(5) *Games Timetable:* - This timetable shows which particular group or house is engaged in a particular time, the games being played, and the playground being utilised.

(6) *Co-curricular Activities Timetable:* - A timetable of all co-curricular activities should be prepared in the beginning of each session showing the different types of activities, the place where they are to be held, and the time when they are to be undertaken. Such a time schedule will facilitate a lot of duplication, and overlapping and facilitate in the formation of groups of pupils, participating in the activities of their own choice.

(7) *Homework Timetable:* - Homework constitutes an important part of the school programme. To see that homework does not become a mental strain on the average pupil, a timetable should be prepared beforehand by each section and class. It should show the amount of homework to be given by each teacher for the class or classes in his or her own subject, during a week. In this way, homework can be adjusted among the various teachers teaching the class and thus no teacher can unnecessarily overburden the pupils with work in his own subject, without caring for other teachers. A copy of this timetable should be put in each class or section for the guidance of the teachers. It is also advisable to send a copy of the homework timetable to parents to secure their cooperation. In some schools, a homework handbook is introduced. In this book, the homework assigned by different teachers in different subjects is written daily and the pupil is required to get his parent's or guardian's signature with date after completing the homework assigned to them on the particular day. Such a practice inculcates in the pupils the good habits of regularity, revision, and independent work, even after school hours. It also establishes good parent-teacher relations as through this device, the parents come to know what is being done by the school and thus can cooperate.

25.4 Framing an Ideal School Timetable

The organisation of the instructional programme in a school is closely related to the aims and objectives of the school, the relationship of different school activities to these objectives and the methods of teaching adapted to the psychology of learning. The problem of supervision and programme of work differs according to the extent and character of curricula, range of activities, and plan of teaching organisation. Consequently, no single programme can ever meet the requirements of all types and grades of school. A timetable is generally prepared by dividing the minutes of the school-day by the total number of periods prescribed for each subject, and thus determining the length of each period.

A good timetable satisfies the following criteria:

(i) *It should provide the most appropriate work for each teacher.* In allotting work to teachers, care should be taken that each teacher is assigned those subjects whom he is best qualified to teach. Teaching load should be almost evenly distributed so that there may be no bickering on that score.

(ii) *It should look to the needs of every pupil.* A good timetable should make it convenient for every pupil to take the optional subjects he desires.

(iii) *It should provide variety.* Change of work is the best form of rest. This applies to both pupils and teachers. Children should not be kept at the same subject or type of subjects which are high in fatigue-causing power for too long at a stretch. So it will be better not to have the same subject for two consecutive periods excepting, however, the practical subjects as science, handwork, art, etc.; easy and difficult lessons should alternate. For example, physical exercises or music can be introduced between Mathematics and Literature, singing or writing work should not follow physical exercises. This provision should apply to teachers also. For instance, a teacher of English or mother tongue should not , as far as possible, have a run of oral lessons one after the other; writing and composition lesson should alternate with oral lessons.

(iv) *It should provide the best room and equipment utilisation.* The number and size of classes and classrooms also affect the school timetable. For example, in a school where two classes are held in the same room, the timetable should be drawn up in such a way that one class may do silent work and other may, at that time, be engaged in vocal work such as reading. The fitting and furniture available in the school also determine the timetable to some extent. Drawing and manual instruction, for instance, require specially furnished rooms. Further, all the classes cannot have those subjects simultaneously, even though a particular time in the school day may be the most suitable for them.

(v) *Incidence of fatigue.* Children get fatigued at certain school hours or certain days in a week. The symptoms of fatigue are (a) weakening of attention and perception, (b) a diminished power of insight and initiative, (c) a diminishing work-rate. Given below are some measures that tend to minimise fatigue:

(a) The length of the period should decrease with the monotony and increase with the variety of the activity required in the lesson.

(b) There should be alternations of intense and of easier talks, of mental and of physical applications, of study and of recreation. Singing, marching, or games, which flush out the lungs and invigorate the circulation, should interrupt sedentary work about once an hour in primary classes and almost as frequently among older children.

(c) The "hard" subjects should claim the best part of the day. It has been observed that the best work is never done during the opening periods, but only after a certain momentum has been gained. It is said that the curve of power on a school day, reaches its highest point only during the second and third periods, and then declines rapidly. The same principle is true in the case of the working days of the week. One is at best on Tuesdays and Wednesdays, but lethargic on Mondays and Saturdays. Mondays, in the case of many resident students, are days of recollections, and Saturdays are full of expectations, since on a Monday following a visit home on Sunday, their mind is full of recollections; on a Saturday, they think of visiting their homes the next day.

(d) Age, physical condition, and season are important factors to be considered while fixing the duration of periods. Pupils, in lower classes, need frequent

changes of occupation, with short periods to prevent incidence of fatigue. Pupils in higher classes can have longer periods of forty-five minutes' duration each. Unhygienic surroundings are not conducive to studies. During summer, pupils are tired very soon; hence shorter school periods and shorter school day.

(vi) *The size of the classes should be almost equal.* Secondary school has generally several sections of the same class. There are also groups for optional subjects. These sections and groups should be of uniform size. Too many large and small classes are not desirable in the interests of the school.

(vii) *The timetable should provide variations to suit local conditions.* The needs of the particular locality should be taken into consideration while adjusting the working hours, and the duration of summer vacation, spring recess, and winter recess. The needs of a rural school are different from those of the urban school. Similarly, the needs of the school in a hilly area is different from those of the school in the plains. For example, it is not inconvenient or impracticable for a school in the plains to start work at 9.30 AM., whereas, for a school in a hilly area, it is very inconvenient and not feasible to start work before 10 AM.

(viii) *Provision of shorter as well as longer class periods.* Some subjects require shorter periods while others longer. There should be the provision of this facility in the school timetable.

(ix) *Provision for time for teachers' conferences.* Some time should be provided in the school timetable for teachers' conferences for joint planning in the interests of pupil needs.

(x) *Provision for an opportunity for cooperative teaching in the integrated programme should be made available if and when teachers want it.* Cooperative teaching implies that two or more teachers and their classes during the lengthened period may work together for one or for several days. It includes interchange of work and is based upon joint planning for the work of the classes. A good timetable should provide this.

(xi) *There should be the provision for shortened period for conferences.* Conferences and nothing but conferences should be scheduled in this period. The conference period should be during the day and not at its close. In this period, students can have access to teachers, teachers to students, and teachers to teachers.

(xii) *Timetable should be fluid and dynamic.* It should be fluid enough to allow variations within a broad frame whenever desired. So there should be periods of various lengths ranging from 30 minutes to three hours. Shorter periods can prove quite useful for sectional meetings and assemblies, school recess, or even for revision lessons. Supervised study, cooperative planning and discussion of co-curricular activities, audio-visual instruction, field trips, etc. should be assigned longer periods.

For instance, the pupils of the same class can be engaged in a combined course of two subjects, such as social studies and mother tongue for a unit of three or four periods. To start with, the different teachers should lead the class to plan out the particular units which can be combined and integrated. They can then divide the class into different groups, each group entrusted with a definite unit. The groups work under the guidance of teachers. The learning experiences of the different groups are to be finally pooled together. Final discussion is to take place when the whole class assembles.

Obviously, such type of work requires adjustment of work among subject teachers, classes, and rooms. Only a flexible timetable facilitates such adjustment.

Yet flexibility, however desirable, should never be interpreted as a licence to teach anything without regard for the total instructional programme. It is wrong to spend a disproportionate amount of time on any particular subject or area. Flexibility, if it is to contribute to the quality of instruction, must be interpreted as a responsibility as well as an opportunity for each teacher to tailor the daily programme to the particular needs of the children.

(xiii) *Timetable should be continually revised.* It should never be accepted as a fact for all times. It should be examined critically in the light of the particular factors operating in the school.

25.5 Basic Facts of Timetable Construction

A timetable is called the second watch of the school. This presents the account of those periods through which school work is done. Along with it, it is also demonstrated by it that in some specific period of time and class, what work is done, and which teacher would guide that work. Its supremacy can improve more and more in progress of the school and its inappropriateness can impede the efficient working of the school. So, it is the duty of the headmaster of each school that he himself or his some colleague should prepare a good timetable. Though there is no definite rule for building a good timetable, but, even then, there are some such facts in the following, keeping which in mind a satisfactory timetable may be built.

(1) Facts Relating to the Interest of Children – The important objective of the school is to develop the personality of children. Thus its total programme is determined for attaining this objective. Therefore, the construction of time-table also should be done keeping in mind their interest, ability, and needs. This is the construction of the timetable:

(i) Children should avail the opportunity of selecting subjects according to their interests and ability.

(ii) So far as possible, children should be given a chance to fulfill their personal needs.

(iii) Determination of period for timetables should be done according to the age of children. Psychological researches have proved this fact that the children of 6-9 age groups can study any subject from 10 to 15 minutes only with concentration. The children of 9-12 and 12-14 years of age group can concentrate their minds 20-25 minutes and 30-35 minutes respectively.

(iv) The sequence of periods should be kept in mind. In view of work the first and last periods are not supposed to be good, because in the first period a child comes from home by walking, therefore he is fatigued. In the last period they are at off end by the whole day's work. In these periods interesting and easy subjects should be managed for study.

(v) Attention should also be kept for sequence of subjects. According to this, two difficult subjects should not be set in continuation because the child would possibly feel tired due to two difficult subjects in continuation. For this such arrangement should be made in the timetable that easy one after a difficult subject should be put or after theoretical work, second round should be fixed for practical work.

(vi) For getting rid of fatigue of children it would be better to arrange two recesses in the timetable. The recess should be after the third and fifth periods.

(vii) Place should be given in the timetable for the activities related with other aspects of development of the personality of children. For example, they should be given opportunity for participating in games, sports, exercise, prayer, and co-curricular activities, etc. through timetable for the development of physical, ethical, civil, and social aspects, i.e. there should be definite time for activities in the school timetable.

(viii) Sequence of days should also be kept in mind. In a week, only six days are available for doing work. In these days, Monday and Saturday are not supposed to be more appropriate because they are suffix and prefix holidays, i.e. they come first and after Sundays. In both days difficult subjects should not be taught to the boys and girls as they are in a holiday mood, they won't like to work hard on these two days.

(2) Facts relating to the Interest of Teachers – At the time of construction of a timetable, the needs of teachers should be kept in mind. For example, its construction should be done in such a manner that they should not have to do similar work continuously and they must have some time for rest or study. In this regard, the following points should be kept in mind necessarily:

(i) Each teacher should be entrusted the same work in which he has interest and ability.

(ii) So far as possible, each teacher should be given equal quantum of work.

(iii) Limits and inclinations of teachers should be kept in mind.

(3) Facts regarding School-material – At the time of building of timetable, it is essential to keep in mind about the available resources of school. For example, the number of teachers, arrangement and their material of special and general classrooms, furniture, library, playing ground, material for conducting co-curricular activities, and educational material, etc. so that child may use them easily.

(4) Rules of Education Department – Generally, school session, and period of school days, and determination of a number of periods of each subject is done by the Education Department. So it becomes necessary that in a time-table each subject should be given time according to its importance and suitability keeping in mind the rules framed by the Education Department.

(5) Other Things – At the time of construction of a timetable, it should be kept in mind that through it children and teachers could more and more be brought in contact. By doing so, not only the high level of teaching, notwithstanding, common moral feeling could also be made high. Besides, more and more contact of these, would enable teachers in knowing children individually and that knowledge would prove worthy for guidance of children.

Manley is of the opinion that in the timetable of a secondary school, time should be fixed essentially for the guidance of the children. It should be must. Besides, there should be arrangement also for integrated education in them.

Keeping the above mentioned facts in the mind, the timetable of a secondary school, according to Findlay may be on the following outlines:

9.00 A.M. – 9.45 A.M.	Attendance, Prayer Assembly, and Religious Teachings or Discourses
9.45 A.M. – 10.15 A.M.	Mathematics or Science
10.15 A.M. – 11.00 A.M.	Language
11.00 A.M. – 11.15 A.M.	Interval
11.15 A.M. – 11.30 A.M.	Music or Recreation
2.00 P.M. – 3.00 P.M.	History, Geography, or Literature
3.00 P.M. – 3.15 P.M.	Recreation or Physical Education or Exercise
3.15 P.M. – 4.30 P.M.	Craft, Nursery Work, Needle Work, or House Craft.

25.6 Defects in the Traditional Timetable

The traditional timetable, rigid as it is, has got so many defects:

(i) *The school day is broken up into uniform chunks of 35 to 50 minutes, allocating certain hours per week to the study of individual subjects.* The non-academic programme of education usually finds no place in the daily timetable. Such type of rigid timetable, a timetable which is designed to accommodate an educational programme consisting mainly of classroom teaching and testing of small, daily fragments of knowledge is being denounced as out of date.

(ii) *The timetable with fixed provision of time and place puts teachers and students in a kind of lock up; it tends to fix the nature of learning experience in a relatively straightjacket manner.* Thus instead of serving as a good servant, it becomes a ruthless master; instead of being the means, it becomes the end.

(iii) *A rigid timetable does not contribute to the total growth of the pupil's learning experiences.* It militates against the integration of various subjects. It does not permit students to work continuously for two or more consecutive periods. It presupposes that a pupil can be a Mathematics learner at 11 A.M. and Social Studies learner at 11.45 A.M. Educational activity has to stop abruptly because of the sound of the bell. At times, the activity is made to cease when interest is right at the peak – the peon counting the minutes on the clock determines the fate of an educational experience, so to say. When any educational activity has to stop abruptly because of the sound of bell, it is conducive to neither physical nor mental health.

(iv) *The conventional timetable does not permit adequate coordination of the efforts of teachers.* No time is provided for conferences and cooperative planning. Hence, there is an inadequate provision for the in-service training of teachers in the new techniques and procedures. If there is cooperative planning, two or more teachers and their classes may work together for a period of longer duration. The new methods such as Project Method, Dalton Plan and audio-visual education cannot be easily adopted if the timetable is rigid.

(v) *The conventional timetable hampers attempts to make guidance and instruction an integral part of the total learning activity.* In this set-up, teachers, as a rule, are primarily concerned with instruction in subject-matter. Teachers have little opportunity for conferences with other teachers to discuss pupil interests and needs and ways and means of meeting them.

(vi) *The conventional timetable does not reflect the aims or philosophy of the school attempting to develop a programme of education that promotes integration.* It divides the school day and the educational offerings into piecemeal bits which are the outgrowth of the philosophy on which the subject-curriculum is built.

(vii) *Most of the time for the sake of so called uniformity, the Department of Education, the University, or the Board lays down the details – the number of periods to be given to each subject, the duration of period, the length of the school day and so on.* This again leads to rigidity in the practice followed in every school. It should not be the business of any external agency to tell the school about the periods or the length of the periods to be devoted to the different subjects and so on. These are administrative details and should

be the responsibility of the principal. The provisions, if any, regarding the timetable should be only in the nature of recommendations. The principals should be left to themselves to devise the time schedule according to the requirements of their school system.

In view of the above mentioned practical difficulties and intricacies, modern educators plead that the conventional timetable should be dispensed with. They want to emancipate the child from its cramping limitations. They should allow him freedom to adjust his time in the school to the various subjects according to his own needs and capacities, likes and dislikes. The Dalton Plan and the Project Method are proposed as alternative plans to remove the rigidity of the timetable. Dewey goes further and, instead of regarding curriculum as composed of different subjects, he regards it as a "continuing stream of child activities, unbroken by systematic subjects, and springing from the interests and personally felt-needs of the child." If this concept of the curriculum is accepted, we cannot spilt the school day into smaller units and allot them to different subjects to be taught. 'Centres of interest' will have to be provided for. Whatever schemes are followed, one thing is clear that some sort of time arrangement is required where teachers, pupils, subjects, equipments, and schools are involved. We have to find ways and means to remove the shortcomings mentioned above.

25.7 Timetable in Double-Shift School

Double-shift system has been introduced in a number of high and higher secondary schools due to over-crowding of pupils and non-availability of enough school buildings. The following four types of double-shifts have been introduced:

(i) *Ladder-wise shift:* - In this type, high and higher secondary classes attend the school in the morning shift and middle classes in the afternoon.

(ii) *Section-wise shift:* - In this type, half the sections of each class attend the school in the morning shift and the remaining half in the afternoon.

(iii) *Sex-wise shift:* - In this type, girls attend the school in the morning shift and the boys in the afternoon.

(iv) *Overlapping double-shift:* - In this type, some classes attend the schools in the morning shift, some in the afternoon and some in both the shifts for certain special subjects like music, drawing, science, sanskrit, home science, art and crafts. In this case the same teacher teaches these subjects in both the shifts,

In all types of double-shift schools, there will be some special factors which are to be considered while following the timetable.

(i) Duration of each teaching period has to be shorter as compared to that of a normal high and higher secondary school as the time available is short.

(ii) Students who attend the morning shift have to be in school quite early. Similarly, those who attend the afternoon shift will have to keep quite late.

(iii) Because of the shortage of school time and the inclemency of weather conditions, the provision of all types of psychological and social needs into consideration is hardly possible. We shall have to do the things 'any how.'

The Check-list: The check-list is required to detect and remove any conflicts in respect of assignments of teachers, classrooms, subjects, or classes. In this chart, the distribution of work for each day for different periods is shown. To economise time and space, different types of symbols are used for the class, the subject, room number, and teacher's name.

25.8 Role of a Teacher in the School Timetable

The basic purpose of preparing a school timetable is to assign duties and responsibilities for teachers. It is a guideline for teacher's working. A teacher has to perform some roles in a school timetable:

1. Generally a senior teacher of a school or an expert teacher of timetable is the in-charge of timetable. He has to prepare the timetable and try to satisfy all the teachers as far as possible.
2. Every teacher also has to note down his own timetable as well as the class timetable, as he is also the classteacher.
3. A teacher has to note down the courses of his teaching to different classes in his diary.
4. A teacher can assess his teaching workload and can compare with other teachers.
5. Timetable in-charge has to make an arrangement for teachers who are on leave or absent from the school.
6. If a class is vacant, a teacher has to engage the class.
7. Timetable indicates the role, duties, and responsibilities of teachers in the school.
8. Timetable helps the teacher for his class management.
9. A class is an unit of school. If class management or teachers are good it means school management is also good.
10. A teacher has to follow the schedule of the timetable for completing his courses which has been assigned to him before the examination.

Objective Type Questions

Multiple Choice Questions (Tick ✓ the right option)

(1) How many types of timetable are used in a school

- (a) 5
- (b) 6
- (c) 7
- (d) 4

(2) The check list requires to detect and remove any conflicts in respect of assignment of

- (a) Teachers
- (b) Classrooms
- (c) Subjects or classes
- (d) All of the above

Fill in the blanks

(1) A________________ as an unit of school. [class]

(2) A________________ is a good source of establishing discipline. [Timetable]

Important Questions

1. Outline the importance of the school timetable in realising the true goals of instruction. What are the general principles of timetable construction? Mention different types of timetables maintained in schools.
2. If you are framing a class timetable for the eighth class of a Secondary School, what general principles would you keep in mind? In particular, what considerations would guide you in scheduling time for (i) Mathematics, (ii) Physical Education, (iii) Craft Work, and (iv) Co-curricular activities?

3. As the principal of a school, what points will you bear in mind while drawing up the timetable in a school? Explain.
4. How can the defects in the conventional timetable be removed?
5. How many types of timetables should be maintained in a school? Give reasons.
6. Discuss the pros and cons of extending the daily working hours and reducing the long summer break of secondary schools in your state.
7. "The conventional daily schedule does not reflect the aims or philosophy of the school attempting to develop a programme of education that promotes integration. It divides the schoolday and the educational offerings into piece-meal lists which are the out growth of the philosophy on which the subject curriculum is built." Discuss.
8. A good timetable is a good reflection of the smooth work in a school. Explain the statement and briefly indicate the fundamental principles to be borne in mind while planning a balanced timetable.

26

Homework

Writers hold diametrically opposite views on the value of homework. There are writers like Bray who say that "under normal conditions, a reasonable day's work for a child has been done at the close of the afternoon session and homework, as it is generally organised, does more harm than good as a rule in this country, except, perhaps from the point of view of examination success," and if a boy has been kept well at work for five or six hours, he has been reading, writing, and thinking, the evening should be devoted to games, recreation or a hobby. But there are others who hold that "home lessons render material assistance in the direction of private effort without which self-reliance is impossibility." "Plenty of occupation is the one secret of a good and healthy moral life," says Thring.

26.1 Homework Necessary?

But homework is necessary for its great educational benefits. Homework properly understood, skillfully planned, intelligently assigned, and sympathetically checked is indispensable and invaluable. It gives opportunity to the pupils to plan and perform their work, independent of the guidance and help of the teacher. It is a valuable means of study without the restrictions of classwork and supplements the teaching work done in the class. The pupils' ability in the better use of books and resources outside school improves. It involves much repetition that is essential for fixing up the lesson that has been taught in the class. It develops the moral and intellectual qualities of self-reliance, self-direction, and initiative in grappling unaided with the problems arising from the work. It stimulates in the pupil voluntary effort to follow up the study of subjects that appeal to his interests and accustoms him to revise and consolidate the work done in the school. Moreover, the syllabus for different subjects is so heavy that it will be impossible to cover it without the aid of homework. It is also with the help of this device that the parents are able to examine and inspect from time to time the work of their children and to suggest further improvements with the cooperation of the teacher. So homework serves as a link in the teacher-parent cooperation. Further, homework establishes a habit of reading regularly – a habit which goes a long way in the pursuit of knowledge.

But unless proper care and thought are bestowed on the problem, there is the risk of homework becoming oppressive and inflicting incalculable moral, intellectual, and physical injury on the pupils and thus defeating the end, we want to achieve.

26.2 Amount of Homework

Many teachers use homework as a means of punishing the children. About this attitude one educationist says indignantly: "Any teacher who assigns homework, as a disciplinary measure, exacting quantities of drill and meaningless busy work penetrates an outrage on the teaching profession. This is not teaching but exploitation."

When teachers boast that they give four or five hours a day of homework, a good thing, unfortunately, is being carried too far.

The major criticism on the problem of homework is directed, not on assigning homework but on the amount of homework generally assigned to children. This is not a problem in any one country alone. Recently The Times of London Educational Supplement carried this excerpt from a mother's letter to a grammar school principal:

"Once more a note to ask you to excuse Richard's unfinished homework but it has been dragged on all this evening from 5 P.M. to 9 P.M. and I've now called it to a halt. I am not certain whether he has not got the ability to assimilate or to applicate himself to the work but if he's not exhausted by it, I am, so please excuse him once again."

This is an eye-opener for the teachers. There is something definitely wrong when parents have to supervise their children's serious work and all that teachers do in school is to make sure that it has been done. There is no justification in expecting pupils to do most of their study out of school hours.

Most of the times, each teacher fancies that his subject is important and is jealous of his pupils' time demanded by others. Between the masters, the pupils suffer.

One remedy for this annoying situation is mutual understanding and concerted action on the part of the staff. A homework timetable not only clarifies the atmosphere but is the only way of curbing the enthusiasm of the professional egotist who is immune to all considerations except the divine right of his particular subject. The other way is to set as little work as is absolutely necessary. It must be added, however, that where children are encouraged to utilise their spare time on the subjects and activities they enjoy, be they mental or manual, when they follow their bent and pursue their inclinations under the guidance and inspiration of their teachers, the total amount of time available will assume elastic dimensions.

26.3 Reasons for Less Amount of Homework

There are various reasons why we should call a halt to the excessive homework assignments:

1. Conditions for study are unsatisfactory in most homes.

(a) In very few homes, adequate light, quiet and privacy are available. The discomforts and distractions with which children have to put up in some homes make study more harmful than profitable. Home duties, reasonable and unreasonable, interfere in the case of some boys and girls.

(b) In the case of better homes, there is often much of "helping" of the misguided sort, which is worse than none at all, upsetting the teacher's plans and deceiving the teachers utterly as to the child's effort and capacity.

(c) Home conditions introduce disparity between pupil and pupil, for, some get no help, others get too much, and others yet get help of the wrong sort.

2. *Too much work is injurious to the health of the child.* There is danger to the health of the pupil who works hard through the school hours and late in the evening. There is no use studying when nature wants the child to sleep. Keeping fit and ready for next day's work should be considered a definite requirement.

3. *Long hours of work are conducive to habits of dawdling.*

4. *Assignment of too much work develops a general attitude of indifference on the part of the pupils.* "To set too much homework is to give pupils something they may neglect, and it is the worst possible thing, when something which a teacher wishes to be carried out, is not done. This risk should not be taken,"

5. *At times play, hobbies, and social activities may have more educative value than some school duties.* Too much homework leaves little scope for these activities.

What amount of homework should be given to the children in school? There should be a sliding scale, as it were, for homework. Children below ten, in the primary school, should have no work of an academic character, prescribed for performance at home. If they have been kept well at work at school for three or four hours, that should be enough normally. For the rest, let them play and carry on their hobbies. In the Middle School, for children aged 11-13, about one or two hours' work might be considered adequate. In the High School, two to three hours, should be regarded as the limit, the work increasing from year to year. Of course, much will depend on the nature of the work and its attractiveness. It must be added also that though trying to conform to a graded scheme may mean ignoring differences in capacity among pupils, it is still worthwhile to be able to consult some sort of a regulator.

26.4 Types of Work

It is not merely the quantity of work that is often to blame but also the quality. Wrong types of work are just as dangerous and wasteful as burdensome ones. Therefore, a few principles are suggested here for guidance in the choice of suitable tasks.

1. *Homework should be of a type that pupils can undertake without assistance from parents or a private tutor.* The teacher who expects pupils to secure assistance from parents or tutors is inviting trouble because:

   (a) Most parents are not competent to give the needed help.

   (b) Those who can may not have the time.

   (c) Those who can and have the time may not know the approved technique and may, therefore, cause confusion in the child's mind.

   (d) At homes, lasting disrespect for the teachers is sometimes created by an egotistic parent or tutor.

   So, it is necessary that the child is prepared for the type of problems that are set for home, although they may be challenging and simulative of effort. New laws, principles, and generalisations should never be left for children to learn at home. Even the first applications of a newly encountered principle or method are usually a source of considerable difficulty for the pupil and needs close attention of an instructor. So, most of the work would have to be deductive – the applications should be typical, fool-proof, if possible. The opportunity of doing the work unaided and yet successfully, will develop self-reliance and make possible greater confidence for the higher tasks.

2. *Homework should be actually beneficial to mind and body, not simply a weary round resulting only in physical injury and mental disgust.* Unmitigated grinding routine work such as transcription of pages of matter, cramming verses, neither understood nor appreciated, or "mugging" multiplication tables without realising their significance so often and so easily prescribed as homework, must not be prescribed. On the other hand, the spelling of the word met with, the writing out of lines which have been already studied, memorising of selections done in the class, the reading of passages containing familiar vocabulary, are examples of the right type.

3. *Homework should not always be in the form of writing as the only mode of expression. Diversification of work is essential if we want to keep homework from becoming synonymous with what is uninteresting, unintelligent, and unintelligible.* Verbal expression must have a place in the system and weekly debates among the members of the class is a useful way of promoting this. Homework may be given as revision of previous work and the preparation for a coming lesson. It may be in the form of problems that will challenge the pupil's powers and furnish motives for the work. It should be for individuality and self-teaching, not for examination cramming.

4. *Hobbies, if encouraged and properly guided, can prove as absorbing homework.* Given a fairly good library, any teacher should be able to fix types of valuable voluntary

homework, which, if not of immediate examinability, must widen the boy's outlook, deepen his interest, heighten his ideals, and lengthen his hours of real intellectual life.

5. *Homework should be used to enable a pupil to leave the school with the ability to use books as a means of gleaning knowledge.* The actual study to be done at home should be planned to guide the children into an abiding interest in the recalling of such history, travel, and literature as is contributing to the lives of culture and refinement.

6. *Schools can foster a taste for art, music, and drama, and encourage its pupils to take advantage of the finer opportunities for recreation.* If this is done and if teachers in selecting the tasks for the evening and for the holidays, would look for those things into which the whole family might enter, it is likely that family circle, and its interests might begin to be built around the fascinating lessons of the school. In this way home life can be enriched and beautified. Homework, instead of being a nightmare, will become a blessing.

With these changes, homework will be done better, the amount will be reduced considerably, and the character itself will be modified, becoming less formal, less boring, and less discouraging. Homework will thus become interesting work begun at school and finished at home - and no longer a headache to pupils, parents, and teachers.

Objective Type Questions

Multiple Choice Questions (Tick ✓ the right option)

(1) School can foster a taste for

(a) Art
(b) Music
(c) Drama
(d) All of the above

Fill in the blanks

(1) Too much work is ______________ to the health of the child [Injurious]

(2) Homework should not always be in the form of __________ as the only mode of expression [Writing]

Important Questions

1. Discuss the reasons for and against giving homework to the pupils.
2. Suggest the amount and types of homework which may be given to Secondary School students.

27

Discipline in School

Discipline is the most vital aspect of the secondary school administration. The type of discipline obtained in a particular institution will depend upon the philosophy behind its educational programme. The democratic philosophy will have its impact on the discipline techniques and so will the autocratic philosophy shape the discipline structures.

27.1 Meaning of Discipline

The word discipline is derived from the Latin word "Discipulus" which means to *learn.* It is the same root from which the word disciple is derived. From Indian history, we know that the *disciple* used to submit himself voluntarily to the "Guru" thus curtailing his liberty and freedom voluntarily in order to achieve his objective under the direction and orders of the preceptor.

Sir Percy Nunn has defined the word discipline in a very apt way:

"Discipline consists in the submission of one's impulses and powers to a regulation which imposes form upon chaos and brings efficiency and economy where there would otherwise be ineffectiveness and waste. Though part of our nature may resist this control, its acceptance must on the whole be willing acceptance, the spontaneous movement of a nature in which there is an inborn impulse towards greater perfection."

An analysis of the above viewpoint to certain basic ideas regarding discipline:

(i) It is a process of education.

(ii) It is the control of behaviour to attain a goal and purpose, the subjugation of emotions and actions under the direction of a leader in fulfillment of the aim.

(iii) It implies a good understanding of right conduct, the formation of desirable habits and attitudes and an adherence to such standards as are just and necessary.

(iv) It implies the subordination of individual interests to group interests to bring efficiency and economy.

(v) It implies the willing acceptance of the controls, i.e. the individual must do either what he is required to do or must not do what he is forbidden to do.

27.2 Concept of School Discipline in the Past

Only a few decades back, school discipline was that of the rod. With the help of rod, order was maintained. The principal was absolute monarch of the school, his word was final. He exercised the powers of a despot in obtaining unqualified and humble submission of the pupils to his authority. The Birch and the Book were the twin instruments with which the teacher worked. "Spare the rod and spoil the child" was literally practiced. The first law of the school was order, the first task of the teacher was to compel order, and the first duty of the pupil was to obey and behave. In fact, it were the greatest floggers who were regarded as the best school masters.

This type of discipline was based on fear: it was superimposed, it was negative, prescriptive, and destructive, and its main aim was to keep order. No wonder, this discipline crushed all initiative in the child. He felt himself helpless in situations where there was no preceptor to guide his activities.

27.3 The Modern Concept of Discipline

Authoritarian discipline began to crumble at the beginning of the 18th century. There was a considerable reaction against this type of discipline. Initiated by Rousseau and followed by Pestalozzi Froebel, Montessori, the modern reaction against this concept of discipline reached its climax and found its most persuasive exponent in the American philosopher-educationist John Dewey. Also with the adoption of democracy both as a political creed and as a way of life in modern times, need was felt of educating him, anticipating the future needs.

Today, we teach children to obey, but we want this obedience to be a thinking obedience, not merely a reliance upon authority. Children are led gradually to discipline themselves. They are taught that there is a time to keep quiet and a time for activity, a time to converse and a time to listen, time to work, and a time to relax. Teachers today realise that it is not possible to teach by coercion; the goodwill of the pupil is always essential.

Freedom is the watchword of the new school. All kinds of superimposed and unnecessary restrictions have been wiped. The teacher, instead of working as a hard task master, is a friend and a guide. The pupils have gained such boons as the right to move about the new classroom at will, to form natural groups, to talk, to choose their subjects, to handle objects, to have a voice in the student disciplinary matters and to take a large and active part in a general way, in class and social affairs. Modern discipline satisfies the needs of self-respect, security, and activity. It creates an earnest desire in the child to do the right thing – the child becomes a true co-partner in the educational process. Discipline emphasised is of positive and creative type. The teacher, who is a skilled disciplinarian, integrates character and education into every learning situation. Right attitudes and desirable habits are formed in the pupils.

The modern educator believes in self-discipline. The source of control is to be largely within the individual, not external to him or imposed from without by force. The capacity for self-control and self-direction is developed. The child makes decisions and assumes responsibility for his actions without always requiring a vigilant watch over him. In short, *the modern discipline helps the pupil to become self-propelled, self-controlled, and self-guiding person.*

27.4 Importance of Discipline

Discipline is very much important in one's life. In want of it man cannot utilise powers properly given by nature (God). Through discipline only, man can attain better power, and by this power he becomes capable of developing his natural tendencies. With personal viewpoint, discipline is very important. Along with it, the discipline is also very important with social viewpoint. The great philosopher Aristotle said, "A nation is not built by mountains and trees, notwithstanding it is built by character of its citizens." This statement is completely true. When the citizens of some country would be disciplined, they would be capable to take their country on the path of progress. A disciplined person is of good character and pious by mind, words, and actions. In this way, it is clear that for the nation or for the entire society discipline is very important. This fact can be made clear with the help of history also. History is witness that, when some country became prey of indiscipline; it had to accept slavery of external powers. Through discipline a man and entire society or nations have created alertness among them. In want of it, this power perishes which results severely, i.e. its consequences are very terrible. In this way, what a man, what a nation, and what a society – personality of all are made the great by discipline.

The statement of P.C. Wren is very true, "As in the army, the navy, or the state, so in the school, the prerequisite, the very condition of existence is discipline." In the absence of it, entire working of school cannot be run properly. In the want of it, there would be reign of anarchy in it. Thus, discipline is that power through which person, society, nation, and school are taken on the path of progress and their personality is made splendid.

27.5 Need for Discipline in a School

Discipline is essential for helping the child in the growth of individual personality, for giving him the feeling of security, a sense of confidence, and the knowledge of the boundaries of his freedom.

Discipline is essential for the teacher also. Before he can teach the children, there must be proper conditions to do so. For good teaching, good conditions are as necessary as good ideas and good teachers.

Discipline is a necessary condition of good administration. If the administration is interpreted as all those things administrators do for the purpose of creating a situation favourable to learning, it becomes evident that maintaining discipline is one of his major tasks.

Discipline in a school is also the requirement of society. Without constructive and proper discipline, aims, and aspirations of society cannot be realised.

27.6 Principles of Discipline

Some of the principles of discipline discussed below are:

(i) Disciplinary procedures should be in harmony with the total goals of education.

(ii) *Discipline should be based on and controlled by love and not by fear.* Seldom, if ever, it should sink to the bottom level - the level of compulsion. Discipline based only on love will be able to bring about "the renovation of heart and will."

(iii) *The discipline should be mainly positive and constructive.* The procedures used within as well as outside the classroom should be *positive* and not *negative*. The teacher's general attitude should be manifested in a challenge, "Let us do this" not in frequent prohibitions, "Don't do that," remembering always that the youth can be *led*, they cannot be *driven*.

(iv) *Discipline should ensure equal justice for all, respect for the rights and dignity of the individual and humanitarian treatment for all.*

(v) *Discipline is not an end. It is just a means for the successful functioning of the school programme.* In the words of the Secondary Education Commission, "Discipline is the fruit, the valuable byproduct of cooperative work willingly and efficiently undertaken."

(vi) *Discipline cannot be a uniform standardised thing to be administered impartially.* It is more like a skein of elastic threads stretching from the teacher to each child. It is for the teacher to assess how much each thread can be slackened and how much stretched.

(vii) *Disciplinary policies and procedures should be primarily preventive, secondarily corrective, and never retributive.*

(viii) *School discipline should be designed to place upon the child more and more responsibility in respect of his own choices, purposes and behaviour as he grows in the ability to shoulder such responsibility.*

(ix) *Discipline is something which the teacher helps children to attain - not something that a teacher maintains.* The dictum of Mill - the best government is one that governs the least, applies with equal force to the school discipline.

27.7 Good Classroom Discipline – How to Obtain it?

Teachers are responsible for classroom discipline. They should be able to obtain it without outside help. Discipline in the classroom is not an entity in itself; it is a product of good teaching. Though all discipline problems cannot be prevented, yet most of them will not arise in the classroom of intelligent, hardworking teachers who plan their work efficiently, motivate their students skillfully, and provide a friendly climate. Undoubtedly, problems of classroom discipline will disappear if there are efficient and strong teachers. In the words of Cunningham, "Only strong personalities survive this test of maintaining discipline."

The pupils expect the teacher to generate enthusiasm. They want his classes to be alive. They expect him to be skilful, understanding, patient, and demanding. They want him to respect them for what they are and most of all, what they can become. In short, he must be a fine teacher. In order to be successful in obtaining discipline, the teacher should bear in mind these points:

(i) ***Be familiar with curriculum:*** The teacher must plan his programme of work well. His planning starts with the entire school life of the students. He should be reasonably familiar with the curriculum content of his field at each level. Curriculum and discipline are closely inter-related. A student, who fails to see the relevance of what he is learning, is not ready to learn. Moreover, too much material crammed into one school year also causes frustration, which, in turn, may lead to discipline troubles. The teacher, if he knows what his pupils have been exposed to in previous grade, can balance the curriculum and remove the cause of the trouble.

(ii) ***Plan the lessons well:*** The starting point for all preventive discipline is a good lesson, carefully prepared and skillfully executed. The first rule in preparing a lesson plan should be to err in the direction of too much material rather than too little. Too much, i.e. in the *plan* not in the *actual presentation*. When a teacher has run out of material with still fifteen minutes to go and resorts to a hasty device such as "start reading the next chapter," the actual trouble starts. A good lesson plan is somewhat detailed but need not be lengthy.

(iii) ***Conduct the lessons well:*** While teaching, the steps – Motivation, Orientation, Presentation, Participation, Application, and Evaluation – should be properly taken care of.

(a) ***Motivation:*** Unless the student realises that their course, their unit, and the lesson are important to them, little or no learning can take place. To avoid the situation where the teacher is pitted against the pupils, motivation must be done properly.

(b) ***Orientation:*** The unfamiliar should, as far as possible, be related to the familiar. Students should be shown the forest before they are asked to examine the bark of the trees. They should be shown how each unit and each lesson proceeds from the last and meshes with the next.

(c) ***Presentation:*** The choice of methods should be based on a judgment of the best way to teach a particular material to a particular group at a particular time. Excessive use of lecture method often gives rise to problems of classroom control.

(d) ***Participation:*** Students should be involved somehow in the lesson. They should do something, even if it is only to answer a question now and then. Every minute in which some or all students are doing nothing is an invitation to disciplinary problems.

(e) ***Application:*** Immediate reinforcement is necessary to retention in learning. The successful learner likes his subject matter. Retention must be obtained before any progress can be made.

(f) *Evaluation:* Presentation should be properly evaluated by the teacher. Nothing can contribute so quickly to poor morale as an unfair test. Many students consider this a form of cheating on the part of the teacher and may then turn to cheating in response.

(iv) ***Know each pupil by name:*** Every child has got a fascination for his own name. Familiarity of name can reduce problems of discipline. It will help the teacher to call only when the pupil is involved in the case.

(v) ***Do not get nervous:*** The teacher must never lose temper. He must keep nerves, words, and activities under control. Undisciplined teachers cannot expect to have disciplined pupils.

(vi) ***Be a good disciplinarian and the pupils should know it:*** If the teacher finds it necessary, he should remove a pupil from the class for some time, or give him suitable punishment.

(vii) ***Handle classroom discipline problems yourself:*** Only rarely should a disciplinary case be reported to the head. If too many cases are referred to the head, it will undermine the standing of the teacher in the eyes of the pupils and the parents.

(viii) ***If necessary, utilise the seating arrangement as a preventive measure:*** Like the chairman of a meeting who is well-acquainted with the participants, the teacher can prevent a great deal of annoyance by a judicious seating arrangement.

(ix) ***Work with the child's uniqueness:*** The teacher should find out individual differences in respect of temperament, reaction time, and size of coordination control. The range of potentialities is as large as the population. Consequently the variability in achievement in any field is tremendous. The teacher can obtain effective results by working with the child's uniqueness.

(x) ***Establish habits of independent study:*** Blessed are the teachers who have brought their class to the stage where they say, "Whether I am present or not, the class carries on. The group has achieved independence."

27.8 Good Discipline in a School – How to Ensure it?

Good discipline is a *prior* condition for the efficient working of a school. It is both a cause and a consequence of the successful functioning of a school. It can be ensured in the following ways:

(i) ***Effective teamwork:*** Effective teamwork in the wake of intelligent professional leadership is the key to sound disciplinary policies. There must be teamwork between the principal and the staff; teachers and teachers; teachers and pupils; pupils and pupils; principal, teacher and pupils. All must pool their resources and put their heads together to achieve a desired end. Let responsibility be divided among different persons and departments. Let definite duties be assigned to them so that the principal is free from disciplinary difficulties.

(ii) ***Good school traditions:*** School discipline is not a matter like a written constitution. Conventions and traditions of the school go a long way in maintaining discipline. A school without conventions and traditions may be as unruly as a mob knowing no law. Healthy traditions will reduce the incidence of indiscipline. The pupils staying in the school for a number of years get used to its ways of life – the new ones will not feel uneasy in the flowing stream. Traditions are not established in days.... they take years. So the problem of discipline is to be taken as a continuous challenge.

(iii) ***Well-planned school work:*** Before the session starts, the work plan must be got ready in order to avoid all confusion and delay in execution of the work. Classwork by no means should be allowed to substitute teachers or stop-gap arrangements.

(iv) ***Unified discipline policy:*** There should be a unified discipline policy evolved through joint deliberations with the staff. Everyone in the school must be made fully conversant with objectives and techniques of discipline.

(v) ***A suitable programme of co-curricular activities:*** The corporate life of the school should be so organised as to provide ample and varied opportunities for the expression of the pupil's impulses and the flow of their vital energy into worthy, fruitful and satisfying channels. Co-curricular activities give the pupils a sense of social cooperation, make them self-directing, developing the insight for law and order, heighten the respect of the authority and give fine training in leadership. Apart from these moral values, these activities develop the tastes and temperaments of all the students and help them discharge a portion of surplus energy in the playground or club instead of mischiefs in the classroom.

(vi) ***Well-conducted school assemblies:*** It will be very useful if the school day starts with a general assembly where the whole of school population meets. School assemblies tone up the general atmosphere of the school. It can serve as a common meeting ground. It can be the family altar of the school to which each can bring his offerings. It can help the cultivation of group consciousness and *esprit de corps*. It promotes school loyalty. The school daily programme can start with a prayer or a short address of an inspiring nature by the principal or teacher or some resource personnel. Announcements can be made. It can make for a common knowledge of rules, customs, and traditions. Appeals for better conduct on school functions and participation in the religious and cultural life of the school can be made there. Thus there will be good opportunities to control and direct the efforts of the pupil body as a whole.

(vii) ***Personal contact:*** Classes should not be very large. The teacher can then develop personal contacts. The skilled teacher, with a ready wit and tact, can turn a tantrum into a purposeful activity, mischief into useful assistance and prevent a display of indiscipline. As the bond of love between teacher and the child is the basis of school discipline, this bond must be strengthened.

(viii) ***Good school premises and sufficient library and specialised rooms:*** Physical facilities contribute a lot to the general atmosphere of the school. Healthy surroundings, good sanitary arrangements leave little scope for irritations. Adequate library and reading room facilities, special room for the different subjects, common rooms, etc. will keep the children profitably busy and away from indiscipline.

27.9 Need of Positive and Negative Techniques of Discipline

In the previous pages, we discussed certain essentials to obtain and ensure good discipline in the classroom as well as in the whole school. We discussed – the content of instruction should be proportioned to the capacities and related to the present aptitudes and needs of pupils; teaching should be made vital and dynamic by appealing to their innate impulses; impulses should be harmonised with themselves and with the needs of society; their understanding, judgement, faith and devotion should be awakened and properly directed; the corporate life of the school should be so organised as to provide ample and varied opportunities for the expression of the pupils' impulses and the flow of their vital energy into worth, fruitful and satisfying channels. Placed as we are with all types of limitations of increasing number and limited facilities, perfect ideal conditions are difficult to obtain. Moreover, human beings as we are we cannot be reduced to formulas. There might be certain individuals going off the ideal track. Self motivation, as a means of conduct, may fail to obtain good ideal social conduct involving welfare of all. This situation might necessitate a positive incentive or some disciplinary action or even a penal measure. As long as human organisations are imperfect, there will always remain a need for positive as well as negative motivations for purposes of 'welfare of all'. Moreover, children differ markedly in their emotional and intellectual dispositions and they differ in their response to different types of techniques and processes. Apart from these variations, there are a number of age and socio-cultural variations also.

With these limitations in mind, certain measures and techniques are suggested which may prove useful in creating motivation and conditions for good learning. These may be used with discrimination.

27.10 Rewards as a Discipline Technique

Rewards sometimes are used as a discipline device to make the right conduct and hard work. They assure a condition of satisfaction and pleasure. It is thought that this condition strengthens the effectiveness of any action or conduct.

Rewards are symbolic of approval from the authority. They seem to be important for learners who have a strong desire to win self-respect or approval from superiors. Rewards by giving status often impel pupils to greater activity.

Many psychologists and educators frown on rewards because they too frequently become ends in themselves. It is argued that in many cases, receipt of the reward becomes a signal for termination of effort. Witness a student who thoroughly enjoys a course but who sells his textbooks as soon as he has done his duty in the final examination. Hobbies that have no definite reward are often pursued far more persistently. Rewards, so to say, have a demoralising effect on the pupil because these tempt him to work not for duty's sake but for the sake of winning a prize. There are educationists who argue that the institution of reward is a *must* for every school to provide the necessary incentive and inducement for making consistent efforts to achieve success, satisfaction, and pleasure.

27.11 Types of Rewards

Two types of rewards can be given to the pupils:

(i) Material Rewards in the shape of prizes – medals, cups, trophies, money, etc. These rewards are extrinsic rewards given on the *result* rather than the *efforts* made by the winner.

(ii) Non-material Rewards – praise, commendations or appreciation, position of honour or distinction, granting of more freedom and responsibility. These are intrinsic rewards and give incentives to further growth.

27.12 Criteria of Sound Educational Rewards

Sound educational rewards are those:

(i) (a) which are given in recognition for the encouragement of sustained effort. They should not be given for a startling performance which may be the result of chance or luck.

(b) which have no value in themselves.

(ii) which are given to a group as will help pupils become socio-centric rather than ego-centric. Such rewards will help promote teamwork and the school spirit;

(iii) which are of intrinsic value, few in number and difficult to attain.

(iv) which are granted to all who reach the standard previously set.

27.13 Administration of Rewards

Below we list some principles for the administration of rewards to achieve maximum results:

(i) The rewards should be devised and administered as to the higher motives of pupils in seeking rewards.

(ii) Rewards should generally be given for efforts rather than for attainments.

(iii) While giving a reward, the educator should determine what appreciation will motivate him to conform to conduct approved in the school. Since individuals react differently, the same reward may not be effective with all. What may inspire or stimulate one, may leave another cold. Some pupils may need impressive trophies or praise, of which they can boast; others may feel contended with public prizes, commendation, or appreciation; still others may vie for the approval of their peers. A few may comfort themselves to win a good name for their parents, the school, the community, state or country while a small fraction will act in the light of their conscience.

27.14 Punishment as a Support for Discipline

Children are dynamic, effervescent and, therefore, heedless. They need checks to prevent excesses, restrictions to keep them within the paths that lead upwards, and determinants to halt their impulses to exceed the 'speed limit' of propriety. That means, situation do arise in schools where some penal measure becomes imperative. Punishment, in the form of blame or reproof, sarcasm, detention, moral punishments, repetition, fine, suspension, expulsion, corporal punishment, etc. are tried according to the nature of the offence. Punishment that follows any misconduct is a painful or annoying experience and tends to weaken the bond of connection between the stimulus and response. It reduces the chance of recurrence of that form of misbehaviour. As offences can be of all kinds, from relatively minor ones, like persistent late coming to serious offences against moral code like thrashing and bullying, so the corrections will vary in severity and be according to the purpose to be served.

But the teacher and the principal must make sure that they are not making a mountain out of a molehill, and that they have satisfied themselves that they are not the cause of the problem.

27.15 Principles of Punishments

1. Punishment should never be mechanically exercised. It should fit not only the crime but the criminal also. Every human situation is a unique event. Identical punishment may in actually work out differently. Uniform rule are socially and educationally undesirable.
2. Teachers should be very careful in deciding the punishment; but once a particular punishment is decided upon, he should be firm about it.
3. Punishment should not be administered in anger, or have any tinge of retaliation.
4. Punishment should never result in degrading the child before his peers; such action is an offence against the pupils' personality, and is likely to result in resentment which will effectively prevent any good future influence of the teacher or the principal.
5. Punishment should be corrective and therapeutic, rather than punitive.

6. Punishment should be very rare, and it should be inflicted only after all other avenues have been explored.

27.16 Theories of Punishment

Some of the well-known theories of punishment are discussed below:

1. *Retributive Theory:* - The purpose of the punishment according to this theory is to avenge the wrong done by the individual in violating the law. If one does evil he must suffer befitting consequences. "An eye for an eye and a tooth for a tooth" – so to say, it cannot be justified, for in the heat of the moment the punishment inflicted might overweigh the crime.
2. *Vindication of Law:* It points out that persons breaking the law must be punished. Revenge is the motif, 'punishment is administered until the punisher is satisfied.' Such vindictive motive should not find a place in our schools because the degree of offence cannot be measured by any means. Also the child has to be convinced not only about the supremacy of law but also about its justice and reasonableness.
3. *Exemplary Theory:* Punishment is given so that it should act as a deterrent to the rest of the class. As a practical expedient this is often quite effective in the case of routine misdemeanors, such as unpunctuality and disobedience which clearly violates law and order of the classes. If this punishment has the sanction of the rest of the class and if it is not unreasonable in the eyes of the pupils, it will probably have a salutary effect and be generally beneficial. If the particular pupil has, moreover, been duly warned with the rest of his classmates, he himself has no reason to feel that he has been unjustly treated. If, however, he has been "picked upon" among a number of other offenders and selected for special treatment, the effect upon him and others is likely to be negative. Even if the deterrent acts, they are but negative in character, in as much as they keep pupils from committing wrongs and do not reform them by developing positive and socially helpful conduct.
4. *Reformatory Theory:* It aims at reforming the criminal. Punishment is inflicted for its reformative value. It aims at making the offender realise that he has committed something wrong and should not have done it. The child is convinced of the wrong act. He is made to feel that he should reform himself. Punishment inflicted deters him from the repetition of the offences as much as from similar offences. The aim of this theory is to restore the individual to socially acceptable behaviour patterns.
5. *Preventive Theory:* This theory is the natural outgrowth of the social thinking and research of the modern age. Its aim is to prevent the situations which call for remedial measure. It is believed that an enormous amount of anti-social behaviour would never occur if we could remove its causes and provide a desirable environment for the children to grow. An effective curriculum adapted to individual difference, well-trained, and competent teachers, adequate materials and desirable physical facilities are regarded as essential in securing good discipline.

27.17 Forms of Punishment

1. *Reproof:-* The tongue is said to be the most powerful weapon with the teachers. Its use may vary from a mild reproof to the bitterest sarcasm and vulgar abuse. A mild form of rebuke may prove very effective whereas scolding, ridicule, abuse, and sarcastic remarks may produce very adverse effect on account of the emotional disturbances they cause in the child's mind. During the lesson the teacher may pull up an erring child just by calling his name or casting a directed look upon him. Sometimes, the teacher's taking the pupil into confidence

and having a heart to heart talk with him proves very effective in reforming him. Reprimand, rebuke, or mild scolding may be resorted to only when the fault of the child is of serious or persistent nature. But such cases will be rare and, therefore, these weapons should be used very sparingly.

2. *Keeping the pupils out of the class:* - No matter how good the educational programme may be, there are likely to be times when it is desirable to remove a pupil from the classroom for misbehaviour, with the remark "Now you will miss what we are doing until you can behave sensibly again." The decision as to the length of time he is to stay out, must be determined by the effect of the banishment on the pupil. The culprit is usually in a suitable frame of mind to have a short talk and return reformed.
3. *Detention:* - Detention, that is making the boys stay after the school hours is usually resorted to for punishing late coming, laziness and disorderliness. Detention should be resorted to carefully, lest the pupil should associate the school with an unpleasant experience and work done during that time may become dreadful. Detention is likely to be effective only when the pupil is not given the opportunity of joining his fellows in games or other interesting activities or detained during recess or after school hours. But detention of pupil demands detention of the teacher also and entails wastage of the precious time of the teacher. This sort of punishment should be tried on troublesome and disorderly children.
4. *Fines:* - Just as fines are regarded as appropriate for certain adult offences, they are sometimes used in schools also. For example, the librarian finds them essential for maintaining control of the equitable use of books. Damaged school property must be repaired or replaced. It is but proper that the offenders should pay if they cannot repair the damage. But certain points need to be taken notice of. The parents should not be penalised for the faults of children. Steps, therefore, should be taken to see that the student does not simply obtain this money from his parents. The child should work for the money either at school or at home.
5. *Moral punishment:* - Great care must be taken in inflicting punishment like obtaining apologies, public or private; degrading pupils from their position, putting into disgrace with the group, etc. Common sense and good judgement would not permit hasty and arbitrary withdrawal of privileges for petty reasons. It hurts their self-respect and disturbs their emotional balance. Demotion of pupils, whether permanent or temporary, is outdated, being both unjust and un-psychological.
6. *Deprivation of privilege:* - It is a useful and efficient form of punishment; loss of school privilege like fee concession, stipend, loss due to removal from magazine editorship or leadership in school teams, etc. can go a long way in improving the wrongdoer when he lacks sense of responsibility and duty. However, there should be provision for the restoration of the position and privilege when the teacher feels the culprit has repented and improved to the desired standard.
7. *Repetition:* - The setting of the ordinary "hundred lines" is a form of punishment usually resorted to when the pupil has not done his homework. But generally such form of punishment does no good. It rather spoils the handwriting of the students. Setting a poem to be learnt by heart may prove useful.
8. *Suspension:* - It is to be rarely used, and that too on those individuals who persist in disrupting the school order seriously. The purpose is only to protect other students. Its effectiveness depends on whether the pupil cares for the school or

not. It causes the student to fall behind the schedule of work. To disinterested students it may serve as a reward rather than a punishment. Any case of suspension must, however, be notified to the parent or guardian of the pupil immediately. Suspension should be regarded as a fairly drastic punishment since it involves a definite academic penalty. It is an extreme measure which is resorted to in chronic cases where all hopes of improvement have failed and where the individual proves to be a source of contamination or a cancer in the scholastic body. Persistent disobedience, impertinence, and moral depravity warrant this form of extreme punishment. After expulsion, the student is deprived of all chances of reformation. It also exposes the weakness of the teacher. According to Percival Wren, "Resort to expulsion is a public confession of weakness, a proclamation of the victory of the bad boy and our acknowledgement of the failure of the school to train." Expulsion must be resorted to for the good of the student. It may be resorted to after other devices have failed, and when it is realised that the continued presence of the pupil in the school is a menace to its moral values.

27.18 Corporal Punishment

It is the oldest form of punishment. The Old Testament states:

"He that spareth his rod hateth his son, but he that loveth him, chasteneth him diligently."

Luella Cole and Joan J.B. Morgan comment in a well-known textbook:

"Up till sixty years ago, children were slapped, struck, or flogged both at home and in school. The extreme methods formerly used are certainly to be condemned but milder punishment of this type has its values."

There are some writers even in the modern age who favour corporal punishment. Father Flanagan of Boys' Town fame advises:

"No form of punishment is more disputed than spanking....it is better to spank the boy (before the age of reason) than to let him risk getting hit by a speeding car......No deep humiliation is felt when punishment is for the act."

Dr. David Goodman writes:

"The school kids of today are a lot of hoodlums. What they must need is discipline, occasional whacks with a heavy ruler would help."

Peter Granfield in his book "Disciplining Your Child" says:

"In our era, the beneficial psychological effects of corporal punishment have been overlooked."

27.19 Views Disfavouring Corporal Punishment

The views disfavouring the use of corporal punishment can be traced back to the first century when Quantilian, the Roman Educator, condemned the practice in no uncertain terms.

"First......it is a disgrace, and a punishment for slaves, and in reality an affront; secondly, because if a boy's disposition be so abject as not to be amended by reproof, he will be hardened, like the worst of slaves even to strips, and lastly, because, if one who regularly exacts his tasks be with him, there will not be the least need for any chastisement......It does not provide any permanent motivation to study and sometimes it causes such shame as depresses mind and makes children shun people's sight and feel a constant uneasiness."

The modern educationists believe that in an effective plan of discipline, there is no place for corporal punishment. They believe that a child hardly gets clue from this punishment as to how wrong his behaviour has been.

The Encyclopaedia of Child Care states:

"The plain statistical truth is that most delinquent are children who have been brought up under harsh discipline usually with corporal punishment."

Keneth H. Hoover comments about corporal punishment:

"That not only is this a dangerous technique for the teachers (the student may strike back) but it can be physically and pathologically damaging to the student."

According to Zipf, punishment arouses resistance to the teacher and dislike for the activity, and the effect continues even after the threat has been removed.

27.20 The Present Position of Corporal Punishment

Except Denmark, Switzerland, and Eire, corporal punishment has been completely abolished in all European countries according to a recent memorandum of the Educational Institutes of Scotland on punishment in schools. In India, too, it has been banned.

27.21 Arguments against Corporal Punishment

1. It is both inhuman and brutal. It degrades both persons – the one who inflicts and the other who receives it.
2. It is negative in its results. It causes hatred. It ends in sullenness, lack of confidence in the teacher, a feeling of injustice or unwillingness to cooperate. It will not help the child to become an intellectual person. The very aim of education will thus be defeated. The pupil may start hating the subject and begin to scorn the school.
3. It may lead to external obedience and internal rebellion. Researches have shown that most delinquents are children, who have been brought up under harsh discipline usually with corporal punishment.
4. It is not educative. If education means the act of leading out, the act of unfolding, the act of developing, corporal punishment can never be educative. It very seldom enables the child to adjust himself to his environments. He may become rather more undisciplined, quarrelsome and anti-social. He may develop the tendency to produce social chaos, out of hatred directed to against the teacher who is *loco parentis* to him.
5. The key to successful punishment is that it should not only 'fit the crime' but also the 'criminal.' This consideration is usually lost sight of while a teacher inflicts corporal punishment. He may make criminals while trying to cure them.
6. A successful punishment is that which meets the approval of the punished. According to Adams, "Corporal punishment can be inflicted only with the consent of the culprit, and unless he consents, it is a fight." Corporal punishment is seldom given with the consent of the pupil - hence, it is wrong. It leads to disintegration of class morale.

On these grounds, it is generally argued that it should be dismissed as a weapon in the secondary school teacher's arsenal.

Gurudev Tagore, while condemning the use of corporal punishment says, "When we see a living enthusiasm lacking in those who act as guides to their pupils, who are ready to raise to them ruling rods from a distance but not extend to them the helping hand by their side as is too often the case, they should be reminded that they have chosen a wrong vocation and should, for the sake of humanity, change it without delay for that of a jail warden." Low, a modern educationist - denounces corporal punishment. "Delinquency is only an outward sign of a disease, the causes of which must be ascertained before any remedy is provided. It is unwise to mete out corporal punishment to the offender. Such external measures leave the inner life of the delinquent child untouched."

At present some controversy is going on over this issue and a trend is being witnessed throughout the country to regard a return to its use in our system as a partial answer to the problems of delinquency. It is argued that, some students with emotional or behavioural problems, do not respond to the counseling of the school or to less severe types of punishment. They do show a favourable change in their overt behaviour after corporal punishment is administered. In a comprehensive survey carried out in 1949-50 by the National Foundation for Educational Research, High Field, and Pinsent (1952), it was found that 89.2% of the representative sample of teachers in State Schools in England and Wales thought that corporal punishment as a last resort should be retained.

One warning here! The decision to resort to corporal punishment is an administrative one. Before the decision is made, many facts must be considered. Decision should not be made without considerable knowledge of the student as well as of his offence.

These then are some of the techniques of obtaining discipline in school. Many teachers and administrators feel that they work. When they do work, it is usually because they are administered with mature judgement, and a good deal of commonsense.

27.22 Student Indiscipline

Student indiscipline has today assumed alarming dimensions. Ever-increasing incidence of defiance of authority, even by pupils at the secondary stage, has made educators and the public sceptical about the efficacy of education in making better human beings. Hardly a day passes without the student of one or the other institution threatening strike or leaving classes on the slightest provocation. Surplus energy of the students, not finding a legitimate outlet results in idleness, misadventure, misconduct, and mischief. Both inside and outside the educational institutions, students indulge in rowdysim – take the law in their own hands and dictate their terms to authorities under the threat of strike and picketing. No wonder, then, that this student unrest has become an acute national problem and has tended to throw the educational machinery out of gear...... "Leaders are worried, the parents are harried, and the teachers are in a fix because the country needs a trained and discipline youth and not a rabble of irresponsible heads." This problem must be properly analysed and an effective solution found, before it is too late.

27.23 What is meant by Indiscipline?

Breach of social order, good moral behaviour, self-accepted and self-maintained social values of life, is termed as indiscipline.

The simplest and also the most fundamental meaning of discipline as stated earlier, is willingness on the part of an individual to put forth all effort that is required to achieve an object deliberately chosen. Indiscipline, therefore, consists in an unwillingness to put forth such effort, an unwillingness which consequently results in the failure to achieve the objective chosen.

Indiscipline may be negative or positive. Negative indiscipline is indicated by mere unwillingness. It becomes positive when the student is unwilling, and is also engaged in such pursuits as not only having nothing to do with the objective deliberately chosen but also are harmful in a number of ways. Instead of attending classes, students may spend most of their time in play, in seeing pictures, etc. But indiscipline becomes dangerously positive when they indulge in acts of defiance of authority of teachers, administrators, and parents.

27.24 Types of Indiscipline

Educational institutions are usually faced with two types:

(1) Individual indiscipline.

(2) Collective or mass indiscipline.

Not individual indiscipline, but mass or collective indiscipline is agitating the minds of all sane people. All schools, colleges, and universities are afflicted by this. Failures of a few students in a class to do their work and defiance by a few of the authority of teachers, are not uncommon phenomena. No one gets worried over these, because various effective methods have been suggested by educationists to deal with these. The mass indiscipline of today is rather formidable. An effective remedy to cure it is yet to be found out. It is highly organised; it has behind it a regular machinery, interested in keeping it alive and making it a normal feature of student life. This machinery is of two kinds. One is within educational institutions consisting of students' unions, their managing committees and office bearers, and has relatively rich managing committees and office bearers, and has relatively rich finances. The other is outside educational institutions and consists of Youth Congress, leagues and federations affiliated to political parties. This machinery has succeeded in creating a new set of authorities rival to teachers and educational managements and claiming and securing the loyalties of students.

Such undisciplined elements can look to "new type politicians" for support in their unruly acts. Most of these politicians are without education and culture. Power-hungry as they are, they lose no opportunity to exploit students. Not only this, they incite the students. Under pressure of these influential people, standards are lowered in regard to admissions and promotions. As a matter of fact, corruption is let loose in the temple of learning. They even hold a brief for such students. They exercise their influence over the authorities. Consequently, the students either are let off or are lightly punished.

Students stay away from school on very flimsy grounds such as the refusal of the administration to grant a holiday or to change the dates of examinations. Some of them even go on a hunger-strike on the appointment or removal of certain teachers, or on the nomination of a Vice-Chancellor. News appears of acts of hooliganism against lady students, teachers in the classroom and outside, invigilators in Examination Halls and outside. Sometimes this hooliganism is directed against proprietors of cinema houses or organisers of some cultural shows who refuse to give a concession on tickets. Students' scuffles and clashes with the police also are not uncommon. We hear of colleges and even universities being closed for an indefinite period due to the rowdyism of the students.

These are the dangerous spots; these alarming outbursts of indiscipline are a cause of great concern – these call for some speedy and effective action.

27.25 Causes of Indiscipline and its Remedies

Why have students become so undisciplined? Why do they behave like hooligans? Why are so many anti-social acts committed by them?

Various answers are being given to these questions. No one answer is wholly satisfactory, though each seems to have some element of truth in it. It has been rightly remarked that indiscipline is a consequence and not a cause. The probable causes responsible for this 'consequence' are given below:

1) ***Student unrest is a part of the wider unrest of the contemporary world:*** In the words of Humayun Kabir: "There has in recent years been a great deal of discussion about the problem of student unrest in India. Such discussion at times overlook that the unrest is part of the wider unrest of the contemporary world." None around the students – parents, leaders, and teachers – behave in the way in which they ought to behave. People have lost faith in traditional values and standards of morality.
2) ***The system and policies of education are defective:*** Students have a general feeling that education which they receive does not really help them in later life, and that it does not enable them to get a good employment. They tend to attach no significance to their education. In the absence of any motive, they do not strive to get themselves educated.

The problem is rather aggravated when a teacher does not "speak the language of the students." The teacher verbalises too much. He does not reach the students; that education cannot satisfy the students for long which provides no guidance to conduct, no spur to action, and no inspiration to high endeavour. Bored with futile and barren teaching, students break out into undesirable forms of action. They get interested in what goes on outside the classroom rather than inside the classroom. They detest impositions and abstractions.

Again, all types of students join secondary schools and colleges. Owing to lack of proper educational and vocational guidance, they make wrong choices, they fumble and flounder. Feeling frustrated, they pin their faith in their ringleaders. These ringleaders, at times, not achieving their personal interests, drag the fellow students into undisciplined acts.

Certain demoralising and corrupt practices have also crept into almost every educational institution. Dishonest methods of marking attendance, encouraging, and condoning malpractices in examination, influencing the examiners in so many undesirable ways, political pressures in the selection and removal of teachers, interference of politicians in examination results, are a few of the instances in point. Standards are lowered to save "Pass percentages." Since all students, fit or unfit, are sent for public examinations, mass failures are but a natural consequence.

Rules regarding promotion from one class to another are also lax. This fact has resulted in poor achievement of those who are supposed to enter colleges. The result is that those students who have no aptitude and ability for college education are not weeded out earlier. Students are not able to fare well in their studies and become troublemakers.

To remove 'trouble,' certain positive steps ought to be taken in this direction. Educational planning should be better and sounder. Admissions to educational institutions must be regulated. The matter of right type of training at the appropriate stage of life must receive immediate attention. Education should provide a harmonious development of the physical, mental, moral, and social aspects of the student's life. Activities must be provided for the best utilisation of the leisure time of the students. Why give them so many "off hours" to spend in non-academic activities which constitute the core of indiscipline?

Not all and sundry should be allowed to enter colleges; only those who are fit by ability and aptitude should be admitted in colleges. There should be a clear and consistent policy with regard to English in the educational system.

3) ***Examinations:*** Poor children always dread the examiner and feel he is out to catch them in what they do not know. They never have the feeling that the trend of the examiner is to find out "what they know and how much."

The examination system in vogue in India is another cause of student indiscipline. Lack of preparation for the examination, resulting in nervousness in the examination hall, adds fuel to the fire. So rowdyism starts, teachers and superintendents are manhandled, furniture and windows of the hall are smashed. In certain cases, injuries prove fatal.

It is of utmost importance that the examination system is changed and made rational, scientific, and objective.

4) ***Loss of leadership of the teacher:*** In ancient times, the teacher was highly respected in society. But now the teacher has lost that leadership. Teacher's leadership is challenged and guidance is doubted because teachers are not highly qualified. Teachers do not keep their knowledge up-to-date. With their eyes on examinations, they fail to create a hunger for knowledge among students,

There are also many bickering among teachers themselves. As Dr. Shrimali said:

"Teachers themselves have been found to instigate students to start agitation." No wonder, students do not accept the leadership and guidance of teachers.

Quite often teachers have been found to be a party to malpractices in the examinations. How can the students be expected to respect such teachers?

Again, personal contact between the teacher and the taught is conspicuous by its absence. So teachers fail to discharge their responsibilities towards students.

Teachers must command prestige by virtue of their merits. They must take a broader view of their duties; develop stronger will and greater capacity to rouse the students to take greater interest in their studies. They should have a high standard of personal conduct and moral integrity. In teachers lie the constructive remedy for indiscipline. If they fail, every remedy fails.

5) ***Lack of teacher-parent cooperation:*** Parents have aggravated in their own way student indiscipline. Parents do not frequently cooperate with teachers and managements in enforcing disciplinary measures. They are indifferent to what goes on in educational institutions. This is one of the gloomiest features of the present situation. Lack of cooperation between teachers and parents encourages undisciplined students.

   Parents must lend a helping hand to teachers. They should attend college and school functions and take a keen interest in the activities of the young. In this connection the formation of Parent-Teacher Associations should prove beneficial.

6) ***Role of political parties and professional politicians:*** On no aspect of student indiscipline is there so much unanimity of view as in regard to the role of political parties and immature politicians in fomenting them. These immature politicians take the lead in diverting the attention of the students from academic work into fields which have nothing to do with education. They achieve this object through Youth Congress, Leagues, and Federations. They thrive on agitation based on grievances whether genuine or manufactured. They are behind all acts of hooliganism of students. It is they who are responsible for the presence in educational institution of a large number of unfit children.

   Political parties are also responsible for this indiscipline. Most of the political parties open their respective branches right into the unions in the educational institutions. They are generally at the back of the unruly elements. Shri C.D. Deshmukh also observed that political parties - and especially those who had no hopes of coming into power in the near future - were responsible for most of the troubles.

   What can be done under the circumstances? The remedy suggested for this source of trouble is: 'Let there be a gentleman's agreement among all political parties not to exploit the students for political ends. Let politics not vitiate the atmosphere in the temples of learning! Education should be exclusively controlled by educationists and not by political leaders.

7) ***Wrong values given to certain things:*** Wrong values have been given to certain things. In the words of Dr. L. Mukherji, "We have lionised our cinema stars rather too much recently. Once upon a time, the actors and actresses were not accepted in the society. They were virtual outcasts..... But today the pendulum has swung to the other extreme. We display our film stars in the cricket fields. We expect them to grace and popularise our social and political functions. Even our Congress session is no exception to it.....All political leaders right from the top are eager to pay all attention to them and be photographed with them..... Perhaps this excessive devotion to the film songs has generated and fostered our Roadside Romeos who feel that life is all a

film land and their attitude is a cheap imitator of the behaviour displayed by their favourite elders."

8) *Spirit of youth:* In the words of Shri G. D. Sondhi: "Youth is the critical period between puberty and adolescence. The sap of life is rising strongly in young bosoms and demands action. Newly come on the stage of life, they want to display and assert themselves. They want to do things their own way and resent direction and control." It is because of the extra energy that they join hands with their fellow beings and lacking maturity of thought and action easily fall a prey to those who preach strikes or walkouts.

9) *Dearth of leisure time activities:* Lack of proper facilities for play, absence of reading room in the school, lack of encouragement and facilities for individual hobbies or such organised activities - are all potent cause of indiscipline.

According to Shri G.D. Sondhi: "Indiscipline is merely a species of the genus expression. The protests, strikes, demonstrations, picketing, window breaking, furniture smashing and defiance of not only the educational authorities but also of the authorities of law and order, are fundamentally the forms of expression. No doubt the forms of expression are all chosen and often destructive but they are, nevertheless, forms of expression."

Give them societies and clubs to organise and conduct, and they will be fully employed in constructive work. The introduction of N.C.C., A.C. C., the National Discipline Scheme, and Youth Against Dirt and Disease can also go a long way in curing this malady of indiscipline.

There must be ample provision of playgrounds, gymnasium, and 'akharas.' If educational institutions cannot provide these, let there be civic provision for them. Swimming pools must also be built by the institutions or by the municipal authorities. Sports tournaments can also prove very useful.

Dramatics, school, and college magazine, excursions, exhibitions, clubs, workshops, leaderships, projects, mass excursions, mass prayers, all these can keep the students gainfully occupied. Children must be engaged in constructive, recreational, and playful activities.

10) *Neglect of religion:* Problem of discipline in education is linked with the large problem of religion. Neglect of religious instruction is to a great extent responsible for lack of restraint among students who do not appreciate virtuous habits.

Orientation of the youth towards religious values can do a lot of good. It will make students God-fearing and pure. They will learn to lead peaceful and pure lives.

11) *Role of student unions:* The experience has shown that student unions are repugnant to the academic atmosphere of educational institutions and destructive of their liberal corporate life. This is the reason that even Shri C.D. Deshmukh expresses the view that student unions should be dissolved in their present form.

12) *Role of persons managing educational institutions:* Student discontent and its development into the dangerous forms of indiscipline is often due to the absence of reasonably minimum facilities in most educational institutions. There is overcrowding in school; buildings are insufficient, and badly equipped. There has been a mushroom growth of institutions without even the provision of bare necessities.

Low quality teachers are a common feature in most schools. Schools are generally under-staffed. The number of students in the schools is unwieldy. Every management is interested to admit more students so that its income from fees may go up. Educational institutions have become business centres; all these have led to indiscipline among the students.

It is necessary that sufficient funds are available for starting an educational institution. For the good of the cause of education, management should confine them to purely administrative matter and leave all academic affairs to principals and teachers.

27.26 Handling Problems of Individual Indiscipline

There are all sorts of anti-social acts committed by children. Students have been found guilty of a number of offences such as truancy, stealing, cheating, in tests and examinations, disobedience and rudeness, damage to school property, sex offences.

It is presumptuous to assume that there are answers to all such school problems. But the school has a big responsibility towards all these offenders – it cannot sweep this social crisis under the rug. It must understand the problems and attempt to deal with them within the limitations of its facilities since its basic mission is to provide education for all its students.

Each case of indiscipline deserves to be treated on its own merits. A few typical cases of misbehaviour in the school are treated below:

1. ***Truancy:*** A child is said to be truant if he is a wandering maniac and if he avoids school. Truancy is a disturbing symptom. Its causes are many. It may be due to rivalry between siblings or some physical defect. It may be due to poor scholastic achievement of fear of the teacher. The school failure is highly correlated with the incidence of delinquency. The mentally dull child finding school work beyond his power of assimilation, cuts classes, runs away from the school. Inconsistent handling of the child, alternating between strict control or too much leniency, would thwart the psychological needs of security and affection. This can also result in truancy. Punishment will not serve the purpose here. The conditions responsible for truancy must be eliminated.
2. ***Stealing:*** Behind every act of stealing, there is generally some unfulfilled needs of the individual. A child who steals must be studied carefully, his home and school environments must be studied. Some constructive solution must be found.
3. ***Cheating in tests and examinations:*** The faulty system of tests and examinations give rise to cheating. Pupils, being afraid of odious comparison or being degraded in the eyes of their peers, resort to cheating. Therefore, emphasis on tests and examinations should be reduced. Vigilance and good supervision should go a long way in checking the incidence of this offence. When an individual has actually been caught using foul means, he should be dealt with against his entire background.
4. ***Disobedience and rudeness:*** It may be an expression of rebellion against unreasonable attitude or demands of authority. The child may be feeling insecure and affection-starved. Punishments generally confirm the offender as that may give him false satisfaction of being a hero or martyr. This is substantially true, if the teacher is considered to be unfair. Such behaviour should serve as an eye-opener to the adults to change their methods of dealing with the children because most of the time adults are at fault.
5. ***Damage to school property:*** Sometimes students do a lot of damage to school property – break window panes, chairs, tables, desks, laboratory equipment, etc. They write on the walls. They try to wreak vengeance on the school authorities for imaginary or genuine grievances suffered by them. Certain harsh measures might succeed in getting the immediately desired result of conformity. But frequently the tension takes some form of expressions. For dealing with such problems a sentiment must be developed in the pupils that the school is their own and that they should treat the school and everything with proper care.

6. *Sex offences:* These are of quite a serious nature. They need very careful and skillful handling. Minor cases may be helped through proper sex education and sympathetic treatment. Serious cases may call for expert psychological or psychiatric treatment. The principal should try to get qualified assistance. Provision of rigorous athletic programme and other inter-sex activities can help a lot in properly channelising the libido of the child.

The principal should not lose his head; he should not be swayed by orthodox sentimentalism. He should tackle such cases through an objective and scientific approach. He should be conversant with the need of adolescence. He should be humane and intelligent in his approach. In such cases, commonsense should be his watchword, sympathy his guiding star – understanding his aim, and encouragement his method. The individual, who has been led astray due to certain psychological and social reasons, has to be brought on socially approved lines. The individual, whose potentialities have been developed to wrong channels, is in need of more help than others. More than anything else he needs security. Let him be giving love, recognition and the joy of success. Only a constructive, creative, and positive approach can cut at the root of individual indiscipline.

27.27 An analysis of the cause of Indiscipline made by the Indian Education Commission

The Commission enumerated a number of causes for these ugly expressions of uncivilised behaviour, e.g.

(a) Uncertain future facing educated young men leading to a sense of frustration which breeds irresponsibility, the mechanical and unsatisfactory nature of many curricular programmes;

(b) The totally inadequate facilities for teaching and learning in the large bulk of institutions;

(c) The poor student-teacher contact;

(d) The inefficiency and lack of scholarship on the part of many teachers and their failures to interest themselves in the students' problems;

(e) The absence of imagination and tact combined with firmness on the part of heads of institution;

(f) The prevalence of what has come to be known as teacher policies;

(g) The attempt of political parties to interfere in their work; and by no means the least;

(h) The impact of the conditions of public life in the country, the falling standards of discipline among the adults and their weakening civic consciousness and integrity.

27.28 Remedies suggested by the Indian Education Commission

The Commission felt that urgent steps were needed to curb the recent trends of indiscipline and unrest, and emphasised that the responsibility is not unilateral but multilateral – devolving on parents, teachers, educational authorities, State Governments and political parties, all together. These educational institutions can take two major steps:

(a) remove the educational deficiencies that contribute to it; and

(b) set up adequate consultative and administrative machinery to prevent the occurrence of such incidents.

The Commission emphasised time and again throughout the Report that standards in institutions at all stages of education, including colleges and universities should be improved and a better standard of student services should be provided. The Commission also recommended the appointment of joint committees of teachers and students, establishment of Central Committees under the chairmanship of the Vice-Chancellor or principal consisting of students and the teachers, and where advisable with the

Academic Council and the Court. This can generate a spirit of comradeship between teachers and students and help in the solution of so many problems.

Objective Type Questions

Multiple Choice Questions (Tick ✓ the right option)

(1) A disciplined person is of good character and pious by
(a) Mind
(b) Words
(c) Action
(d) All of the above

(2) Punishment should be
(a) Corrective
(b) Therapeutic
(c) 'a' and 'b' both
(d) None of the above

Fill in the blanks

(1) ____________ sometimes are used as a discipline device to make the right conduct and hard work [Rewards]

(2) ____________ indiscipline is indicated by mere unwillingness [Negative]

Important Questions

1. What do you understand by true discipline and social discipline? How can a teacher promote good discipline amongst pupils?
2. What is creative discipline? What steps will you take to achieve it in your school?
3. "Spare the rod and spoil the child." Does this dictum hold good in maintaining good discipline? If not, suggest a better alternative.
4. "Good discipline is self-discipline." Discuss.
5. "Remove hope and fear and that is the end of discipline." Do you agree? Say how proper discipline can be maintained in a school.
6. "A government could do everything with bayonets except sit on them." What steps will you take to introduce democratic atmosphere in a school?
7. Concept of discipline in a modern school based on new moral and social values is entirely different from that of traditional schools. Give your own views about the nature of discipline which you would like to be practiced in a modern school and state how you would plan to achieve it.
8. Discuss the case for and against corporal punishment.
9. What are the causes of present day student indiscipline? Suggest remedies.
10. "Indiscipline amongst students is a malady which can be cured by teachers alone." Discuss the statement with reference to the role of the teacher in maintaining discipline in school.

28

Student Government in School

The association of students in the management of the school as one of the positive disciplinary devices is gaining wide popularity in democratic countries. It is argued that so far as practicable the students should be allowed to participate in their own control. It is being realised that if a disciplinary programme is to be successful, it must have the support of the majority of students. Latest slogan in education is – *to obtain discipline, give freedom.*

28.1 Meaning of Student's Government

By Student Government in schools is meant participation of pupils in matters concerning organisation, administration, functions, and control through delegation of powers and responsibilities to the student body.

In a democratic country, one of the important functions of the schools is to give training to the future citizens through subjects, opportunities, settings, and activities that will fit them for successful adult life. The school has to provide practice to the children in the democratic mode of life. It has to enable the pupils to become 'fit to live' as well as 'fit to live with others.' Such type of morality grows, like flesh and blood, by what it feeds on; therefore, the only substantial method of cultivating desirable qualities is a regime of activities which give repeated exercise of virtue we desire to develop.

28.2 Specific Objectives of Student Participation

For the successful working of student government in any particular school, it is necessary that the principal as well as the teachers should have a clear picture of the objectives that the school has in adopting this system.

In a democracy, good citizenship is the major objective of education. Good citizenship is composed of elements which must be produced and articulated. Among the most important of these are:

(1) A knowledge of the theory of democracy;
(2) Sentiments of law and order;
(3) Intelligent respect for authority;
(4) Increasing self-direction and self-dependence;
(5) Prudent leadership and intelligent followership;
(6) Cooperation;
(7) Morale.

(1) ***Knowledge of the theory of Democracy:*** The student, through the practice of democratic procedures – as participating in an election campaign, evaluating the qualification of candidate, voting, representing a group, discussing proposed policies, serving on committees, discharging assigned responsibilities will learn in a practical and first hand way the theory of democracy. Important knowledge of democracy can be made meaningful and colourful and vital through the student council. Most of the time, the information regarding democracy is left academic and bookish because it concerns the interest and activities of adulthood. If pupils are to be informed about the democratic procedures they have to be "taught" in 'their own way' not in an "adult way." Student participation is thus, absolutely essential for imparting knowledge of the theory of democracy.

(2) ***Sentiments of Law and Order:*** For obtaining effective discipline in a school, it is extremely important that sentiments of law and order are developed among the students. Students should be helped to set the goal of efficient self-discipline and make serious attempts to achieve it. Students' participation without student self-discipline is impossible. The students have a clear conception of the laws needed, they help to set them, and because they have had a voice in making them, they are vitally interested in seeing them observed.

The promotion of good order in the assembly and at gates, safety on the playground and about the school, as well as promotion of neatness and the proper use of school materials and equipment, to mention a few possibilities, all represents fields of council activity in which thoughtful respect for law and order can be functionally developed.

(3) ***Intelligent Respect for Authority:*** One of the conditions for the successful working of a democracy is intelligent citizenry. Citizens should not be just blind followers. So is the case with democracy in a school. When, for example, a student finds assemblies programmes become more interesting, recreation schedules become better organised, and financing becomes more successful through the efforts of his elected representatives in the central organisation, he can not only understand and appreciate the part played by the council, but also gets a thrill from helping to elect it and to support its policies. Because he recognises himself as a part of the school's democracy instead of an isolated individual, his obedience to the rules of his governing body, even in those matters in which he may personally disagree will tend to be all the more complete, because he appreciates the necessity for such rules for the good of the school as a whole. It would not be too much to expect that because of this direct and personal interest, his own observance will be pretty sincere and conscious. This is really the most intelligent respect for authority.

(4) ***Increasing Self-direction and Self-dependence:*** For equipping the children for adult life, child's training for effective social living is imparted. This training for effective social living may come very naturally and easily through a miniature society in which the student learns the pertinent knowledge, accepts the worthy ideas, and actually practices the habits necessary for successful membership. Through student participation, the student becomes increasingly self-directive, in the matter of individual interests and abilities. One student has an interest and some initiative, ability in originating, another in executing, and in expressing, another in cultivating and the discovery and development of these potentialities are basic responsibilities of successful student cooperation because successful student cooperation depends upon them.

(5) ***Prudent Leadership and Intelligent Followership:*** Successful democracy depends upon skilled leadership, and this in turn, must rest upon intelligent followership. Intelligent leadership and followership, like all other characteristics of good citizenship, must be developed; they do not spring unprompted into being. Because the school enrolls all the children of all the people, it is only logical that it should accept a considerable share of this responsibility. The various subjects of the curriculum help to provide the bases of knowledge and ideals to some extent but in the general area of democratic participation little is scheduled or accomplished through this curriculum.

The actual participation of students in school administration provides natural settings for training in both leadership and followership. For instance, an elected leader who is autocratic in his methods, arbitrary in his decisions, careless in his commitments and erratic in his judgements will soon discover that he must improve or he will be replaced, and the follower whose class, activity or school suffers from his vote or his ineffectual attempts to allow good leadership will soon recognise that the fault is his own. Thus in both cases, it is almost inevitable that the student shall recognise the disastrous consequences of his unwise or careless efforts. He will learn valuable lessons to do something about it.

(6) ***Cooperation:*** This is another important element of democratic living which must be developed, because although in man's original nature there is a desire to associate with others, and share in their activities, there are no fully developed skills which result in effective co-operation. What is cooperation? Cooperation means combined efforts for the common good. The cooperative work will usually benefit from the united effort, but for the moment at least the immediate objective is a benefit for the group.

Now the question arises: Is the student taught cooperation through his academic courses? Hardly. In fact, cooperation in Mathematics, Humanities, Science, and other subjects is usually frowned upon, the emphasis being, "get it yourself." Even in those subjects in which cooperation is talked about and ideals set, such as Social Studies, very few get the opportunities in which actual practice is possible. It is obvious that as at present organised, the curriculum offers very few opportunities for the *functional teaching* cooperation.

Through the student-council organisation which represents all the co-curricular activities, there are hundreds of opportunities, large and small, for the practice of this important element of good citizenship. Student-student relations, student-teacher relations, teacher-teacher relations, and teacher-administrator relations should improve. All work together for the common good – the students furnishing the drive, the student contacts, and the execution, the teacher providing the experience, the administrative contacts, and the judgement.

(7) ***Morale:*** Morale is essential to any kind of organised effort. An army without morale would be little better than an unorganised mob, and a school in which each teacher and the student bustles around to his individual classes with little or no interest in his institution as a whole, not feeling himself as a vital part of the school, would not be a school worthy of the name. it would be as colourless as a factory in which the employees were war prisoners.

Two elements are basic to morale, something to be proud of or loyal to, and a feeling of personal responsibility. It is necessary, therefore, to develop and coordinate opportunities for many different kinds of participation in project meant for the common good as thrift in the use of materials and equipment, courtesy to visitors, friendly aid to new students, keeping the school plant neat and clean. These activities originated and promoted for the school as a whole represent a morale-developing setting.

Such participation, properly organised and supervised, offers the best of the opportunities for developing the elements given above. Students will realise that certain things ought not to be done by them because they are disliked by the entire student community and not merely because they are prohibited by the school authorities. School will thus become a motivated and functional miniature democracy, one which represents student interests and activities of all students, and a plan which more closely resembles adult democracy.

28.3 Scope of Student Government

The extent to which student participation in administration may be introduced in a particular school, depends upon the local circumstances and the amount of training individual pupils have received in leadership. It is not possible to switch over to a full-fledged student government system overnight. To be a success, it might take five to six years completely. The growth is to be processed. It should start with small beginnings, i.e. care of the notice board, study hall, school property, etc. Later on committees of students may be formed for the efficient working of the whole system. The scope of student government may be expanded on the basis of experience. Recognition of responsibility and preservation of authority rested in the teacher should never be lost sight of by the pupils. The teacher should be a guide and counsellor rather than a task master.

The plan of student participation must not be a sort of eye-wash to make pupils think that they are being consulted. In the words of H.G. Stead: "It is useless to institute self-government in name only, i.e. to call self-government a system whereby the head teacher impresses his or her views upon the teachers and they accept them and impress them on the pupils. Nor is it of any value to have a system of 'self-government' with a master or mistress always just round the corner to exercise authority." W.M. Ryburn also sounds the same note of warning. He says, "Where responsibility is handed over, it should be really handed over." The children will not be taken in by long if it is unreal. Pupil organisation should not be hedged about with many restrictions.

If student government is to be successful, teachers have to be prepared to help as much as they can. It is the spirit in which this help is given that makes the difference. When the youngsters have made a mistake, the teacher must be careful not to be irritated with, "I told you so." He can let them understand that no one's judgement is infallible and that the important thing is to learn from one's errors and rectify them as best as one can. If the consequences are too burdensome for a youngster, the teachers can, after a time help him out. But the student should experience enough discomfort or disappointment to learn that human beings must live with the unhappy results of faulty decisions. And when a youngster makes a disciplined decision, entailing self-control, hard work, or the postponement of immediate pleasure, he deserves to know that the teacher is proud of him. Success is often a more powerful teacher than failure.

A note of warning! The purpose of a school student council or any other self-government is not to make the problem of discipline easier. The teacher can, by no means, transfer responsibility for the conduct of pupils to the shoulders of any other person. The introduction of student-government means hardwork, constant vigilance, and occasional discouragement. Teachers must be prepared to tolerate the crudities, uncertainties, and perversities of the youth and sympathise and bear with them in their struggle to attain self-control and group mastery. Understanding, sympathy, kindly inspiration, and constant counsel must be supplied unobtrusively to keep pupil sentiment up to the level of effective action. No student government scheme will work itself without helpful guidance, supervision, and encouragement from the teachers.

That is the reason why the personality of the teacher who is associated with student government to guide and watch its functioning, matters a lot. This person must be chosen with great care. "He must be a leader, a teacher, a counsellor, a friend. The best educational and professional preparation, a pleasing personality, sympathy, unbounded enthusiasm, ability, vision, a sound knowledge of psychology, and a keen appreciation of human nature are requirements for this position."

28.4 Forms of Student Government

As some form of Student Council organisation is required for the operation of student government, it is necessary to know the forms of student-government which can be introduced in the secondary school.

For small schools, the most suitable organisation seems to be the class monitors or officers, whether nominated or elected – to form a single simple committee. As a general rule, the principle of election is preferable to the principle of nomination, although for special reasons and under certain circumstances, nomination may be resorted to.

In larger schools, any one of a number of forms of organisation may be attempted.

(a) The simplest form is the one in which the School Council consists of the members of the grade councils.

(b) A popular form of organisation is the one which copies the organisation of the national government.

(c) A variation of the form of national government can also prove useful. Here there will be three councils, one legislative, another judicial, and the third executive, and also some machinery to coordinate their efforts.

(d) Some schools may attempt an imitation of *Municipal Organisation* with Municipal President, Commissioners and heads of departments like health, recreation, and finance and so on.

What should be the guiding principles governing representation on the Social Council? The following principles should prove useful in constituting a Student Council:

(1) The Council should represent the school as a whole and not just a part of it. The practice of electing the Council from only the topmost class is not desirable.

(2) The average student should feel that he is represented. Council membership based on academic distinction fails to give this feeling.

(3) Both the student body and the teaching staff should be represented. The presence of teachers on the Council has the value of giving the students the moral support that they need in making decisions.

(4) The Council should not be too large. An unwieldy Council can often be a hindrance to the expeditious transaction of business.

Certain principles regarding the *powers* of a student need also be considered.

Firstly, the Council should have definite powers as well as responsibility. It is very necessary for the students to know exactly what their powers and responsibilities are lest they should overstep their limits.

Secondly, it is imperative that the head of the school should have the power of veto, as it is the head who is officially charged with the responsibility for the administration of the school. This fact should be clearly understood by the student body.

28.5 Some Cautions

For the successful working of student government in schools some cautions need to be guarded against:

(a) ***Student government in school should not be given any political colouring:*** Use of labels of the major political parties in the National Parliament can encourage outside influences to come in. This, as discussed in earlier pages, can be a cause of indiscipline. So even if the party system is favoured, the parties can be given non-political names. Citizenship training does not necessarily require the creation of school parliaments on a political basis. The emphasis in student government should be on the development of civic and social attitudes; knowledge of the actual machinery of government can be imparted in the classroom through civics.

(b) ***The objectives must be clearly and specifically defined:*** For example, if the parliamentary system of student government is adopted, is the objective confined to giving students an idea of the Indian Constitution and of the political parties, or it is wide enough to include training in effective citizenship also?

(c) ***There should be a real demand from the students for a student council:*** There is no point in imposing student government from above, if the students are not quite prepared for it.

(d) ***Student participation in school administration and school control should be introduced in gradual stages:*** Any form of government and administration is a difficult social activity, and student government is particularly difficult because of the immaturity of the students. Teachers

should be there to act as advisors to student councils and student committees.

28.6 Council Activities and Projects

"A student council without a schedule of suitable projects is as worthless as a car without gasoline, and a council with a schedule of unsuitable activities is as useless as a car with the wrong kind of fuel." The activities and projects in which students can participate must be clear – the only points to be remembered are:

(1) activities should be interesting and desirable;

(2) activities should enlarge the students' horizon;

(3) activities should develop responsibility and help to develop cooperation;

(4) activities should promote a worthy school citizenship.

Thus, one of the important parts of the councils' responsibility will be the selection of an activity or project. Now we proceed with the different types of activities and projects which could be possibly tried with effect. This list is by no means an exhaustive one. The resourcefulness of the teacher and the particular needs of the school will determine the selection of the activity. The student council can take up a number of service activities.

28.7 Service

Welcome new students, teachers and visitors, assume care of property of absentees, promote assistance for needy students, assist in community drives and campaigns, etc.

1. ***Public Functions:*** Assume and supervise general and special assembly programmes, promote music productions, concerts, and contents, organise patriotic programmes and celebrations, sponsor exhibitions, organise and conduct Flag Day, Children's Day. promote school-community day, picnics, etc.
2. ***Drives and Campaigns:*** Safety first, better health, punctuality, better speech, good sportsmanship, pictures for school, school beautification, etc.
3. ***Care of School and Personal Property:*** Organise and conduct lost and found; promote care of desks, walls, school equipment, grounds, promote care of personal property, clothing, materials equipment, encourage respect for all public property, promote proper care and use of bicycles, develop publicity – bulletin board, posters, cartoons, articles, etc.
4. ***Education:*** trips and tours, school citizen, parliamentary law, school orientation, what other schools are doing, etc.
5. ***School Equipment:*** Museum equipment and exhibits, athletic equipment and material, stage curtains and equipment, magazines, books, papers, pictures, etc. for library.
6. ***Courtesy and Conduct:*** Make and enforce general rules and regulations, encourage good behaviour about the school, promote proper behaviour at assembly and public events, encourage good conduct before and after school, establish and supervise a student court, develop appropriate assembly programmes, etc.
7. ***School Publications:*** Newspaper, school magazine, school history, school reports, bulletins and notices, etc.
8. ***Special Days:*** Birthdays of national heroes, festivals, Parent's Day, New Year's Day, etc.
9. ***Finance:*** Organise and adopt a financial system, develop budget for the entire extra-curricular programmes, develop and supervise money raising plans, issue activity, membership and admittance tickets, etc.
10. ***School Gardening and Landscaping:*** Organise and supervise a campus beautification project, beautify classrooms with flowers and plants, hold exhibits of flowers and vegetables, organise competitions in fruit, vegetables, and flower growing, etc.

11. *National Emergency:* Collection of funds and articles for the welfare of the jawans, promotion of relief drives, organising of cultural programmes in aid of defence, providing music and entertainment for the jawans, etc.

28.8 Advantages of Student Government

1. *Training in cooperation:* It gives training in cooperation. Self-government is a way of organising the community life of the school so that pupils themselves can take maximum possible shares in all matters pertaining to the life of school. Pupils can be helped to shoulder responsibility and to learn essential lessons necessary for successful living. It is a practical way of teaching 'civics' which includes much more than discipline.
2. *Training in right selection:* Pupils learn in a practical way the grievous and harmful results of electing wrong persons to fill positions of authority.
3. *Sense of responsibility:* It stimulates a sense of individual and group moral responsibility. Under autocratic method of discipline, the teacher must be holding himself accountable for all infractions of the established rules of order. Students feel free to violate any phase of purely school decorum, if they can escape punishment. Such an attitude tends to encourage dependence upon compulsion for right action both within and outside the school. It is the attitude of the subject rather than of the citizen, and cannot provide training for later assumption of democratic responsibilities. Neither does it cultivate a sense of individual moral accountability. Only by practice does one learn self-control for civic welfare.
4. *Development of initiative, judgement, and leadership:* It develops initiative, judgement, and leadership. These qualities must be developed through experience. Teaching instruction may give training in abstract processes or illuminate particular problems but it cannot inspire ingenuity in meeting social situations or give practice in personality leadership. On the other hand, student control of co-curricular activities does give democratic experience. It will carry over into life activities. But it should not lower school behaviour.
5. *Training in organisation:* It gives practice in administering social machinery. Public meetings must be held, committee work must be done, elections must be managed, leaders must be chosen, and policies must be obtained. Ability to discuss issues intelligently to control parliamentary procedure, to lead or to follow as the occasion demands and to take victory without unwanted pride and defeat without sulking, are qualities that do not come without effort. The student body should be used as a laboratory for training in democratic practices.
6. *Improved order:* It takes care of petty misdemeanours and reveals moral delinquencies, the teachers might not otherwise discover. In this way, it improves order in the assembly, the study rooms and about the building and grounds.
7. *Improved student-staff relations*: The duty of constantly watching for infractions of order is exacting and makes the teachers less-fitted to win the pupil's goodwill and esteem. The student's attitude of suspicion is removed. No individual likes to be "spied upon" but in case of teaching, policing, nevertheless, is at times necessary. The necessity of cooperation tends to develop mutual respect between teacher and pupils and convinces the pupils that the teacher is a safe-advisor rather than a mere taskmaster. The teacher thus freed from the petty worries of routine, has more time for simulating and inspiring and more vitality for good teaching.

8. ***Cultivates school spirit:*** Real student government is the flowering of a school spirit which takes years to grow. Pupils begin to love the school. They begin to sacrifice self-interests and interests of the group for the whole student body.
9. ***Value of discipline felt:*** Pupil learns to see the reason for rules and for obedience, and as a result, that obedience is far more real than when orders *trickle down from above*. A formal rigid discipline, which conditions children to the "military" type of discipline, is replaced by self-discipline which is rational and self-imposed.
10. ***Trial and error:*** Trial and error is the instrument through which life teaches us its most important lessons. It is better that these experiments of trial and error should occur in a sphere where error may not result in grave danger to society. Early experiences with small features and mistakes may save them from big ones with deeply injurious long range effects. If they are to know that actions have consequences, they must make choice and accept the bitter or sweet results. It will train them in the art of citizenship and self-governance so that in later life they may avoid mistakes.
11. ***Benefits to the school:*** So many benefits can accrue to the school through student government. In the first place, it enables the school to mobilise all its forces for a comprehensive programme of activities. It enlists the cooperation of both the students and the teachers much more effectively than would be possible if the programme were to be operated entirely 'from above.' Secondly, student government makes possible better articulation and conduct of co-curricular activities. It makes it easier to relate such activities not only to the actual needs and interest of students but also to one another. Thirdly, it provides better opportunities for teachers to gauge the special abilities of their pupils than is afforded by the curricular programme of the school. Finally, student government goes a long way in smoothening the administration of the school, as the responsibility for organising activities and for maintaining discipline, is in actuality, shared by students and teachers, even though the ultimate and official responsibility in these matters lie with the principal.

To conclude, we can say that student government builds up the morale of the students. They develop the loyalty and a sense of responsibility towards the school. They see a purpose and plan in school life. They learn to face difficulties and to love work for its own sake. School becomes a practice school of democracy, a laboratory of citizenship.

Objective Type Questions

Multiple Choice Questions (Tick ✔ the right option)

(1) Successful democracy depends upon
- (a) Skilled leadership
- (b) Dictatorship
- (c) 'a' and 'b' both
- (d) None of the above

(2) 'Trial and error' is the instruments through which life teaches us its most
- (a) Important chapter
- (b) Important lesson
- (c) 'a' and 'b' both
- (d) None of the above

Fill in the blanks

(1) ________________ reams combined efforts for the common good [Co-operation]

(2) ________________ membership based or academic distinction fails to give this feeling [Council membership]

Important Questions

1. "The introduction of student government means hard work, constant vigilance, and occasional discouragement. Teachers must be prepared to tolerate the crudities, uncertainties, and perversities of the youth." Discuss.
2. Discuss the arguments in favour and against the introduction of student government in schools.
3. "The practice of holding general elections and the present day disturbances by the students." Comment.
4. Describe and explain the type of organisation which can satisfy the demands of both freedom and discipline in a school. What part does the teacher play in such an organisation?
5. Explain the term 'student self-government.' Explain how it can work successfully for the High/Higher Secondary schools.

29

Guidance Programme in School

A good guidance programme is one of the essentials of a good school. If it is to make its impact felt on the growth and development of the child and improve the quantity and quality of the educational programme, it must be an organised service of the school. So long as it remains an incidental activity of the school and is left to the good sense of every teacher, much of its significance as an educative process is lost. It should be recognised as an integrating or unifying force by everybody in the school.

The extent of guidance and counseling setup will depend upon the resources of the school and the community. One school may be able to afford a separate room with enough space for staff and records of the entire school population. Another school may have to be content with a separate corner set aside for the purpose.

The nature and the size of the administrative setup also will vary with the size of the school because the guidance programme offered will depend upon the number of employees, educational offerings and facilities provided. In a big school, one qualified counsellor plus the guidance teacher with the active assistance of the head of the institution can run the guidance programme. In a small school, one part-time guidance master with the cooperation of the head and the members of the staff can handle the guidance programme. What is important to remember is that in each school students, teachers, and community are unique. Therefore, each professional guidance structure must be tailor-made.

29.1 Meaning of Guidance

If the literature relating to guidance is supervised, we would find its diversified meaning and scope and various opinions about it. Some writers grant it equivalent to education in its meaning. In these, John M. Brewer is worth to mention. He has explained it broadly in the following words: "The word guidance is frequently misconceived; it is best understood through the concept of self-guidance. Guidance is neither adjusting nor suggesting, neither conditioning nor controlling, neither directing nor taking responsibility for anybody ......Educate the coming generation, we must, and a true education, as we shall try to show, means guidance."

With this view Arthur J. Jones has explained guidance in these words:

"Guidance, as organised, is then concerned with crisis or with times of choice, with times when the ways diverge, with times of needed adjustment. It is clear that the help given may be direct or indirect, the one guided may be conscious of the help given or may be entirely unconscious of it. The guidance may be given at the time of crisis or long before it occurs. Indeed, the best guidance is usually that given long before the need for choice arises. It consists in assisting the individual in the gradual accumulation of facts and experiences that will, when the time comes, enable him to decide wisely."

It becomes clear by this definition that guidance is an individual help and it is an essential and fundamental part of education. Here a point is worthy to note, that aforesaid both definitions seeming different too, pay accent on one contemplative point – a person should be capable and prepared for solving his problems of present and future life.

S.A. Hamrin and E.C. Erickson have defined guidance in the following manner –

"Guidance in the secondary school refers to that aspect of educational programme which is concerned especially with helping the pupil to become adjusted to his present situation and to plan his future in line with interests, abilities, and social needs."

By observing the aforesaid definition it becomes clear that guidance is an individual service which is organised or planned for giving help in solving his problems. Guidance not only solves the problems of the individual, notwithstanding it also helps in solving them. Guidance is a process. Guidance to some individual is a process to provide help. Thus, this "process" gives help according to knowledge of real situation of the world around an individual, to make proper decisions in choices and adjustment. In form of service it gives information and help to children, teachers, guardians, and management for conducting processes properly.

29.2 Need of Guidance

The Secondary Education Commission felt this need and said that education authorities should pay more attention on educational guidance. There are several main causes which are being given below in short:

(1) In secondary schools, the number of children is increasing rapidly. The needs, interests and capacities of these children are different. If the capacities and powers of these are not moulded in proper direction, they would become useless persons both ways – personally and socially. Thus, this increase has made guidance programmes essential.

(2) Diversification of curriculum and establishment of multi-purpose schools have made necessity of guidance much more clear. These two facts placed this additional responsibility on administrators and teachers of schools that they should guide their pupils properly in the selection of curriculum and vocations.

(3) Today's society has become complex. The person would remain incapable in understanding it and establishing adaptation with it in want of proper guidance.

29.3 Types of Guidance

In its broad meaning, guidance is related to each sphere of life of the individual. But, for practical purpose, various aspects of life for which particular type of guidance is needed, recognition have been given. With this view, guidance can be divided in the following types:

1) **Educational Guidance:** It is related with appropriate adjustment of selection of school and choice of course, co-curricular activities, and educational programme. Besides it, educational guidance is also concerned with providing knowledge of the process of seeking admission of children, evaluation, and rules of timetable.

2) **Vocational Guidance:** It is related with giving help in the selection of some vocation, preparing persons for selected vocation, for achieving proper situation and progress. In this kind of guidance, people take more interest due to increase in the unemployment.

3) **Guidance of Leisure:** With the result of industrialisation one has to work for less number of working hours, people are getting attracted more and more towards this kind of guidance. It is concerned with the help of individual in proper utilisation of leisure. Therefore, the place of co-curricular activities of school is very important. Thus, it is most essential to make children acquainted with their activities and their programmes.

4) **Moral Guidance:** It is concerned with the character and ethical feeling and its development. Some learned persons are of the opinion that generally this kind of guidance has been neglected by public schools of America. When teachers and school authorities maintain discipline of children, they should feel this thing that the children need moral guidance.

5) **Civil Guidance:** Through this the individual is organised to become a useful member and an experienced citizen of community, province, nation, and the world.

29.4 Essential Requisites of a Good School Guidance Programme

The following requisites must be provided to develop and organise a good school guidance programme:

(a) *An effective guidance programme should be accepted as an essential function of secondary education by school administrators.* They should be convinced of its utility for promoting personality growth of the pupils. If the head of the institution fully believes in the concept of guidance programme, it will receive appreciation at the hands of the teachers and parents also.

(b) *Leadership by a trained guidance master must be provided in every school.* It may be his/her function to coordinate the efforts of several teachers in the school in the collection of pupil data, to initiate group guidance procedures and to do individual counseling.

(c) *The active cooperation of a band of teachers interested in guidance must be secured.* One guidance master will not be able to do full justice to such a multifaceted programme as of guidance. He must be assisted by teachers in the implementation of guidance activities. Teachers can contribute to the guidance programme by supplying data for Cumulative Records and also by assisting the guidance master in varied activities.

(d) *Arrangement should be made to enlist the support of parents and to introduce them to the idea of guidance.* No programme can function successfully in a school unless parents too feel convinced of its utility. It is truer of guidance. The parents should be made guidance-minded by bringing home to them the importance of a correct curriculum choice by their ward. It will really pay rich dividends if the school staff meets parents in conferences in the school session.

(e) *Provision for guidance programme must be made in school timetable as well as in the school budget.* Provision of guidance periods is tremendously needed for carrying on minimum guidance activities, such as maintaining of Cumulative Record Cards, arranging of career talks, educational talks and orientation talks, screening of films and arranging of plant tours, etc. If a whole-time counsellor's post does not exist in the school, the guidance master should be given a concession of 12 periods a week out of the teaching load for carrying on guidance activities. The provision of 6 periods should be made in the school timetable for class contacts, and other 6 periods should be utilised by the guidance master for other guidance activities such as arranging for experts for delivering talks, etc. filling up the Cumulative Record Cards, providing individual guidance to the students, maintaining the records, etc. Some budgetary provision must also be made to meet the additional expenditure, if necessary.

(f) *School administration should facilitate the implementation of guidance decisions.* If the counseling process indicates the need for a change in the student's programme, it should be administratively possible to make these changes. For instance, if instruction needs to be analysed and broken down into simple tests so that the less able members of the class can follow, the teacher should do this. If the student seems to need more participation in the recreational aspects of school life, additional avenues of participation should be provided. If these facilities are not made available, the attempt to counsel may increase the student's feeling of frustration on one hand and feeling of futility among the masters on the other.

(g) *A good guidance programme is dynamic, changing as needs change, undergoing continuous development in order to remain current.* Frequent evaluation is an essential programme development.

29.5 Guidance Personnel

"Guidance" in the words of Kelly, "is an all inclusive programme aiding pupils to achieve their optimum growth wherever they are. In such a programme, the total needs of students need to be met by a total staff. One cannot assign the learning relationship to the teacher, the counseling relationship to the counsellor, and the smooth functioning relationship to the principal. Each is involved in, and each should assume, all these relationships."

(a) The Principal

The principal occupies a key position in the school guidance programme. In the regular guidance programme, the principal has to play a great constructive role. His attitude towards guidance or pupil development may determine whether mere lip service is rendered to the programme or whether the guidance of pupil development is basic to the whole school programme. The principal has certain duties in respect of guidance programme:

(1) The principal should take the leadership in guidance by having the kind of relationship with the teachers which fosters a guidance approach to the pupils. The principal's pride in his teachers and their guidance efforts can give the public confidence in their schools.

(2) The principal should make himself thoroughly acquainted with the existing guidance programme through meetings and conferences.

(3) He should provide opportunities to teachers, pupils, and parents to discuss problems.

(4) He should encourage teachers to attend special guidance courses and seminars so that their knowledge remains up-to-date.

(5) He should adjust the teacher's work load to include their guidance duties.

(6) He should form a guidance committee to study the school's guidance needs. He can take the responsibility of carrying out the recommendations of the guidance committee.

(7) In consultation with the counsellor and the guidance master and other members of the staff, he should prepare an institutional plan in respect of the guidance programme; take general policy decisions regarding phasing of the guidance programme, provision of time and allocation of duties to the members of the staff.

(8) He should make sure that the entire staff has a part in the development of the guidance programme.

(b) The School Counsellor/Guidance Master

The Counsellor/Guidance Master is the nerve centre of the guidance programme. The person to function as the School Counsellor or Guidance Master should be a guidance-minded person with some specialised training in the field of guidance. He has the following duties:

(1) He should provide professional leadership to the other members of his team. He should stimulate, initiate, and organise the various guidance services and plan out the details.

(2) He, with the principal's guidance and in consultation with the members of the staff, should prepare a detailed plan of work for each year.

(3) He should help the teachers in carrying out various guidance functions.

(4) He, with the help of other members of the staff, should collect occupational material, arrange for its classification and filing.

(5) He should disseminate occupational information in groups. He should arrange career conferences, career exhibitions, career displays, films and film strips shows, etc.

(6) He should assume the responsibility for counseling all those pupils who need individual assistance.

(7) He should refer students, having the problems he cannot handle, to the experts.

(8) With the help of the District Employment Exchange he should help in the placement of pupils.

(9) He may give advice regarding matters of curricular and occupational choices and plans to the students and their parents.

(c) The Teachers

The teachers occupy the pivotal position in a school guidance programme. It is they who have the most frequent and the most extended contacts with the pupils in a natural situation. Without their cooperation, guidance service can never become an integral part of an educational programme. In fact, teachers remain the heart of the guidance programme. Guidance-aware teachers fulfill their functions as guidance workers in a variety of ways: -

(1) They should collect pupil information and maintain cumulative record cards.

(2) They should study the needs, interests, abilities, and problems of each child in the class.

(3) They should observe students in classroom and out of the class situations and watch for 'danger signals' in the pupil's normal developmental maturation, e.g. existence of disturbances, problems in getting along with classmates, marked withdrawal tendencies,over-aggressiveness, compulsive conduct, or persistence of a difficulty.

(4) They should contribute to the guidance programme by introducing the pupils to careers in their particular fields.

(5) They should use classroom situations to disseminate occupational information.

(6) They should get acquainted with the parents, invite them to the school and take an active part in the Parent-Teacher Associations.

(7) They should win the confidence of the pupils and help them in every way to evaluate their growth.

(8) They should help the counsellor and the guidance master in conducting various guidance programmes and in making necessary arrangements for them.

(9) They should exemplify a level of personal adjustment as students learn not only from what teachers say but also from what teachers are.

It is of primary importance that teachers assist the child conserve his native capacities and invest and use the same so as to bring the greatest satisfaction to him and benefit to society.

(d) The School Librarian

(1) He should help the counsellor and the guidance master in classification and filing of the occupational information material.

(2) He should display the material properly in the library.

(3) He should provide the right type of books to students of different age groups, classes, and tastes.

(4) He should circulate the latest information material among the students and the teachers.

(e) The Physical Education Teacher

The physical education teacher is another link in the chain of guidance personnel.

(1) He should conduct physical efficiency tests, games, sports, and recreational activities for students and enter the report in the columns of the Cumulative Record Card.

(2) He should arrange the activities in such a way that each student is able to participate in them according to his capacity and interest.

(f) The Art Teacher

(1) He should help the counsellor and the guidance teacher in the preparation of visual aids like charts, posters, etc. for popularising the guidance programme.
(2) He should help in the arrangement of career exhibitions and career conferences.

(g) The School Doctor

(1) He should conduct medical examination of the students from time to time and give his report in the columns of Cumulative Record Card to enable the counsellor to know the needs of the pupils and to give them medical or nutritive help.
(2) He should report physical limitations of the students to teachers and parents.
(3) He should develop a programme of helping children in physical hygiene.
(4) He should offer consultation to the students and their parents on the health problems of the students.

(h) Parents

Parents are an integral part of the guidance programme. They are, in fact, the child's principal counsellors. They must be made guidance-conscious if we are really interested in the welfare of the child. It is one of the important tasks of the school to get the help of the parents in the guidance programme to ensure optimum development of the students. It is very necessary that the school staff in general and the school guidance counsellor or guidance master in particular should help the parents to understand the child; to project themselves into the future so as to determine educational and vocational possibilities for their children in the decades ahead; to appreciate the school and the guidance department's objectives and practices; to utilise good principles of mental hygiene and right living in their families.

For achieving this object, Parents' clubs, Parents' Forums may be formed in the school. Parents' group conferences may be held from time to time. Parent Bulletins and Reports may be issued to keep them in touch with current happenings. Parents may be offered guidance in the individual capacity.

29.6 The Guidance Programme – Its Content

The desirable activities which should be taken up in the school by a counsellor or guidance master are:

(1) ***Educational Talks***: Talks on simple educational topics should be arranged by the counsellor or guidance master. He himself or the members of the guidance committee or some persons outside the school can deliver such talks. A minimum of two talks a month should be given.

(2) ***Orientation Talks***: These talks are meant to orientate the students with courses of studies of Matric/Higher Secondary and Indian School Certificate Examinations. As much information as possible should be provided to pupils concerning the importance of choosing this or that combination of subjects so that they make a wise choice of courses of study. A minimum of two such talks should be given.

(3) ***Career Talks***: Career talks mean a talk about the details of a particular job. Such talks are a must for a good guidance programme. Every career expert should be provided with an outline of the career talk at a much advanced date so that he/she knows what to prepare. As many of the career talks should be arranged, as possible.

(4) *Career Conferences*: Career conference is a group activity organised for the purpose of providing occupational information of a preliminary or supplementary nature to a large number of students together. In a Career Conference, several speakers belonging to different professions come and deliver talks about their own fields to students in groups. For example, a student journalist gives a talk on "Journalism as a Career" to a group of students interested in Journalism and a Nurse on "Nursing as a Career" to another group interested in the field of nursing and so on. It should be organised at least twice a year and may be arranged after the quarterly examinations of the schools.

(5) ***Plant Tours***: Visits to industries provide the students with direct experience of the work done and the physical and the social environment at which it is done. If the visit is to be of maximum value, the students should be prepared for it in advance so that they know what to observe, which questions to ask and how to behave during a visit. A visit is more useful when followed by a group discussion in which students talk about what they have seen and exchange ideas. As many plant tours may be arranged as possible depending upon the resources of the school and time available.

Screening of Films and Film Strips: Film shows followed by group discussions are a good means of disseminating information. Film strip shows accompanied by a suitable commentary can also prove useful. The films can be obtained on loan from the United States Information Service, New Delhi, High Commission for Canada, New Delhi, Central Film Library, Delhi, and State Audio-visual Education and Film Libraries, etc.

29.7 Essential Activities of a Good School Guidance Programme

A good school guidance programme does not appear suddenly. It develops gradually through various planned stages on the basis of needs and resources of the school. Below we list some of the major activities of a good guidance programme.

1. *Setting up of the School Guidance Committee*

The first step in initiating guidance programme in a school is to set up the School Guidance Committee. The Committee should consist of:

President	...	Head of the Institution
Secretary	...	School Counsellor or the Guidance Master.
Other Members	...	(a) Any five members of the staff- There can be different class incharges or different subject incharges.
		(b) President of the Parent-Teacher Association.
		(c) Student Secretaries of different classes.

It is the responsibility of the guidance-committee to plan out monthly and yearly programmes. It should prepare, so as to say, an institutional plan for the guidance programme to be taken up in the school. In its periodical meeting, the committee can also thrash out problems requiring group, solution, plan, and coordinate guidance activities and assess the work already done.

2. *The Guidance Centre*

The effectiveness of the educational and vocational information service in the school largely depends on the systematic organisation, proper maintenance, and regular use of the guidance centre.

What should be the proper place for the centre? Ideally, the centre should be a large room equipped with almirahs, filing cabinets, display racks, bulletin boards, tables, and chairs, etc. where the materials can be maintained and displayed. The room can also be used for holding talks, showing films and filmstrips, for holding parent-teacher meetings, etc. A part of it could be partitioned and used by the guidance master for individual discussion with pupils and their parents.

However, most schools are so over-crowded that it may not be possible to secure independent accommodation. In such cases the guidance teacher has to rely on getting a corner in the school library or in the reading room or in the passage and if this too is not available, he may have to use his own classroom after school hours.

Whatever be the housing facilities, the information material should easily be accessible to those who come to seek guidance.

A *Remark Register* should be placed near the entrance to the centre in which the visitor can record their impressions.

The information received from the various sources should be filed properly. To facilitate the use of information material, some sort of filing system should be used by the guidance master. The first thing for him to remember is that he should classify and file the material as soon as he receives it. He may also do this work during his guidance periods or before or after the school hours. This will not consume much of his time. Care should be taken to place the files back at their proper places after use. Some specific methods of filing are:

(a) Alphabetical system.
(b) National Classification of Occupations.
(c) Filing on the basis of school subjects.

The guidance master should adopt any one method which suits his purpose best.

Students should be encouraged to prepare *scrap books* on different careers. These can also be displayed in the centre.

Another activity which a guidance master can try with profit is the development of a job folder. In this *job folder* can be put together all relevant information about a particular job. A good job folder describes the activities, duties, and responsibilities of the job, the personal qualities and educational requirements for the job, details about special training requirements, if any, prospects for advancement, salary, etc.

The information material should be displayed neatly and artistically. Posters, charts, leaflets, monographs, newsletters, notifications of jobs and training courses, advertisement of scholarships, etc. have got to be displayed if they have to serve their purpose well. Walls, bulletin boards, display racks, display windows etc. may be sued for this purpose. Posters and charts can be pasted on cardboards and hung in the guidance centre, if there is one. Otherwise, they may be displayed in the reading room or in the classroom of the guidance teacher or in the verandah where a large number of pupils are likely to see them.

Displays should be given an attractive title or headline. The arrangement of the material should be changed every now and then to maintain continued interest on the part of the pupils.

It is essential to maintain a *Stock Register*. Guidance literature as soon as it is received, should be entered in the stock register by the Guidance master.

It is also important to maintain a *Proceedings Register* to record all the activities concerning guidance programme regularly.

The centre should function throughout the year to fulfill the aims of guidance. If pamphlets, brochures, etc. are not to be issued for reading at home because of their limited number, facilities should be provided for pupils to read them at the centre under the guidance of the guidance master.

Right at the beginning of the year, the guidance master should invite pupils to the guidance centre for acquainting them with his work and information materials available. He should invite the parents of the pupils also to visit the centre.

The utility of the guidance centre depends on how enthusiastic, enterprising and resourceful a guidance master is. He can either make the Guidance Centre a storeroom or turn it into a centre of all guidance activities.

3. Maintenance of Cumulative Record Card

An effective guidance programme pre-supposes information about the individual which is reliable, and valid and also comprehensive. This is possible when the work of collecting information is done on systematic basis and over a period of years. Maintenance of Cumulative Record Card is one of the most important activities of a good guidance programme. It is so designed that various types of information about the pupils such as identifying data, schools attended so far, health record, achievement records, etc. are added to it year after year. It as a matter of fact, can give a cross-sectional and longitudinal picture of a pupil and is thus of great importance in the guidance programme.

The Cumulative Record Cards should be maintained from the 6th class onwards by the teachers and the counsellor or guidance master working in cooperation. The class teacher generally fills in the information available to him about the pupil or from the pupil. The Counsellor or guidance master is responsible for filling in data about a pupil's abilities, interests, etc. Health record is to be given by the school doctor or nurse.

If the records are to be of maximum value, they must be maintained regularly and kept up-to-date. Cards of all pupils should be kept together at a place either in the principal's or in the counsellor's office. Since some of the information is of a confidential nature, the records should be made available to only those persons who are likely to use the information for assisting the pupil in making adjustments and in educational or vocational plans.

When the pupil leaves the school, his Cumulative Record Card should be sent to the next institution he enters, so that the teachers and counsellors in that institution easily understand the new entrant – his abilities, his shortcomings, his aspirations and resources, etc.

4. Testing

To make the assessment of an individual's skills and traits, standardised psychological tests can be used by the counsellor or guidance master. A note of caution here! The use of such tests should be made only by a trained counsellor or guidance master and testing techniques should never be used in isolation.

5. Counselling

Counselling is said to be the core of the entire guidance programme. It is a process in which the pupil is helped to form a decision, make a choice or find a direction at some important fork in the road such as that of planning a programme in the institution, or deciding a life career.

Counselling is a way of helping the individual to learn those things which facilitate adjustment, both immediate and remote and also assist him to remove obstacles to his learning.

Counselling is very essential when-

(i) the student needs not only reliable information but an interested interpretation of such information as meets his own personal difficulties;

(ii) the student needs a wise listener with broader experience than his own, to whom he can recount his difficulties, and from whom he may gain suggestions regarding his own proposed plan of action;

(iii) the student is aware of a problem and of the strain and difficulty it is causing but is unable to define and understand it;

(iv) the student is aware of the presence and nature of a problem but, because of a temporary strain and distraction, is unable to cope with it intelligently;

(v) the student is suffering from a major maladjustment of handicap which is more than a temporary one, which demands careful diagnosis by a specialist and help over a long period of time. Only a trained guidance worker should use counseling as a technique of guidance.

6. *Formation and Guidance Clubs*

To make the students actively participate in the guidance programme, they should be divided in different guidance clubs on the basis of their educational and vocational interests. Clubs such as Medical club, Engineering club, Home Science club, Photography club, Hiking club, etc. can be formed. Students in the different clubs should be encouraged to collect information and to prepare scrap-books and folders on different careers. They can be taken out on plant tours, to film shows, etc. club-wise so that they can make the best use of the guidance services available to them.

7. *Liaison with the District Education Officer, District Counsellor and State Bureau*

Report of the progress made should be submitted every month both to the Director, Staff Guidance Bureau, and District Education Offices. The report should be duly countersigned by the head of the institution. In the report, details to be given are bulletin board displays, literature collected in the month, the number and details of career talks, orientation talks, and educational talks arranged, details of films and filmstrips screened, details of plant tours arranged, cumulative record cards, guidance clubs, career days, and conferences, etc. Plans for the next month drawn out in the guidance committee's meeting and details about individual counselling provided to pupils also should be given accurately and neatly. Care should be taken to get the report dispatched in the first week of every month. This will help in establishing a much needed liaison of the school with the District and the State and spreading the good practices followed in a school to other schools as well as check the loopholes.

Education and guidance are the two sides of the same coin and must be treated as such in organising the school for the most effective education of the child. Good guidance means good education and good education is what we need the most. No educational programme can be completed without a well-planned, systematic, scientific, and comprehensive student guidance service. If every child has to be in school, it is every child which must be guided for optimum adjustment and optimum development. This will only be possible if the programme is well organised, well-conducted, and well-supervised.

29.8 Views of Education Commission About Guidance Programme

The Education Commission is of the opinion that, "Guidance and Counselling" should be regarded as an integral part of education. It should not be for problematic children only, notwithstanding, it should be for all children. Its aim should be helping them from time to time in determining their decisions and adaptations. The Education Commission has given suggestions at various levels of school education as below:

(A) *Guidance at the Primary Level*

(1) Guidance should be begun with the lowest class of primary school.

(2) In primary schools, it is difficult to appoint separate counsellors because their number is more. This arrangement would be very expensive. Therefore, with the practical viewpoint, their teachers should be imparted knowledge of the guidance in the training period, so that they may conduct this activity successfully. They, in their period should be acquainted adequately with easy diagnostic tests and individual diversities.

(3) In training school, guidance service should be conducted.

(4) For primary teachers in service courses should be arranged.

(5) In regional languages vocational literature should be prepared.

(6) At the completion of primary education, students and their guardians should be given help.

(B) Guidance at the Secondary Level

(1) At the secondary level, guidance should be helping in development of interests and abilities of students.

(2) Minimum guidance programme should be prepared for all secondary schools.

(3) For 19 secondary schools one counsellor should be appointed. But, other teachers of the school should provide the necessary cooperation to counsellor in guidance work.

(4) In each district, at least in one school detailed programme of guidance should be conducted, which should become an ideal for all schools.

(5) All the teachers of the secondary schools should be imparted knowledge of facts regarding guidance in the training period or in service period.

(6) In Indian conditions, on problems related with guidance research work and literature related with it should be prepared.

The aforesaid suggestions of the Education Commission are very important. The Commission realised the need of guidance. Due to this reason, it emphasised right from primary level about its arrangement.

Objective Type Questions

Multiple Choice Questions (Tick ✓ the right option)

(1) Health record is to be given by the

(a) School doctor

(b) School Nurse

(c) 'a' and 'b' both

(d) None of the above

(2) Guidance Should be begun with the

(a) Lowest class of primary school

(b) Upper class

(c) School level

(d) College level

Fill in the blanks

(1) ______________ is related to each sphere of life of the individual [Guidance].

(2) The Counsellor/Guidance master is the ______________ of guidance programme [Nerve centre].

Important Questions

1. Why do you think guidance service must be available in schools?
2. How will you organise a school for minimum guidance programme? What are the essential requisites of a good school guidance programme?

3. Discuss the role of principal, teachers, and guidance master/counsellor in the guidance programme.
4. What activities can be included in a comprehensive guidance programme? Suggest how will you organise them effectively.
5. Suggest the steps you would take up to start a good guidance programme in a school.
6. Discuss the part which a teacher can play in making guidance programme successful in a school.
7. How will you organise the guidance centre in your school? What steps will you take to ensure the regular use of the centre by the students?

30

Evaluation

Evaluation is more comprehensive and includes the testing of both tangible and intangible qualities. It relates to the child as a whole individual and in his total environment. In evaluation, one has to know where the pupils were at the beginning of the teaching-learning process, get a record of the changes brought in them, and judge how good those changes are in relation to previously established objectives.

This evaluation is the process of assessing the attainment of the pre-determined objectives of the teaching-learning process. It "signifies describing something in terms of selected attributes and judging the degree of acceptability or suitability of that which has been accepted." It is the appraisal of outcomes of a course of action. Hence, educational evaluation can be considered as the process of determining-

(i) the extent and how well an educational objective is being attained, and

(ii) the effectiveness of the teaching-learning experiences provided in the classroom.

Let us discuss the meaning of evaluation.

30.1 Meaning of Evaluation

Education is intended to bring about changes in knowing, feeling, and action. Through the different subjects in the school curriculum, the child is supposed to develop increasingly more understanding, acquire more knowledge, develop varied skills and abilities, imbibe wholesome values, possess healthy attitudes, develop broad and varied interests and achieve better adjustment. Evaluation is the latest medium evolved to assess measure and appraise such growths, changes, and developments. Not only does it measure change, it also judges the desirability and adequacy of those changes. It is an inclusive concept; it indicates all kinds of efforts and all kinds of means to ascertain the quality, value, and effectiveness of the desired outcomes.

Evaluation involves three steps:

(a) Identification and formulation of objectives;

(b) Their definition in terms of pupil behaviour – that is what changes do we expect in the child by each one of those objectives; and

(c) Construction of valid, reliable, and practical instruments for observing the specific phases of pupil behaviour such as knowledge, information, skills, attitudes, appreciations, personal social adaptability, interests and work habits.

Thus evaluation is concerned with all the goals of an educational programme, the degree of success in reaching the goals and suggestions for changes in the programme, so that the goals may be achieved more completely. Evaluation thus cannot be separated from the two fundamental aspects of the curriculum (i) Educational objectives, and (ii) Learning experiences. Its greatest merit, perhaps, is that it brings about an internal relationship between the education trinity, namely *objectives, learning experiences* and *evaluation techniques* in such a way that one influences and strengthens the other.

30.2 Definitions of Evaluation

Regarding meaning of evaluation, it can be said in the words of **J.M. Wright Stone**, "Evaluation is relatively a new technical term, use of which has been done for traditional tests of notion of measurement and for expressing more widely than examination. In evaluation stress is put at the main objective of educational programme and changes regarding personality. In it lies not only achievement of subject matter, notwithstanding also lies tendencies, interests, ideal, mode of thinking, working habit, personal and social adaptation, etc."

According to **James M. Bredfield**, "Evaluation is the assignment of symbols to phenomena in order to characterise the worth of value of a phenomenon usually with reference to some social, cultural, or scientific standard."

According to **Quillen and Hanna**, "Evaluation is the process of gathering and interpreting evidence on changes in the behaviour of the student as he progresses through school."

According to a magazine of DEPSE, "Evaluation is a term which has overtones that distinguish it from mere measurement. The latter implies only a precise quantitative assessment of outcomes of instruction, whereas evaluation signifies a wider, more comprehensive, and sustained process of assessing student progress."

According to this approach, evaluation is integral with the whole task of education and its purpose is to improve instruction and not merely to measure its achievements.

By watching the above definitions, the following points become clear:

(1) Evaluation is a wide term under which all aspects of children – physical, mental, and ethical, etc. come for evaluation.

(2) Its scope is wide in which lie both – measurement and appraisal.

(3) Evaluation is a process which goes on continuously.

(4) Its objective is not only to measure achievements of study or instructions, notwithstanding also to improve that.

30.3 Purpose of Evaluation

(a) The main purpose of evaluation is to test that the children have acquired prudence, attitudes, interests, skills, qualities, and abilities, etc. to what extent.

(b) It helps in knowing the weaknesses and goodnesses of students.

(c) Through evaluation, necessary knowledge is imparted for the classification and promotion of pupils.

(d) Through evaluation help is sought in providing proper educational and vocational guidance to students.

(e) Another purpose of evaluation is also to measure skill and success of teachers.

In short, it can be said that the important purpose of evaluation is to keep the maximum dynamic for the all round development of children.

30.4 Evaluation Devices

To accomplish the total purpose of evaluation, teachers, administrators, and counsellors can make use of the following devices:

1. Tests

(a) Achievement Test:

(i) Informal teacher-made, oral, essay type, short answer type, and objective tests.

(ii) Standardised objective type tests.

(b) Psychological Test

(i) Intelligence

(ii) Interest

(iii) Aptitude

(iv) Personality

1. Observation

2. Interviews

3. Rating Scales

4. Questionnaires, checklists, inventories

5. Records and Reports

(i) Diaries

(ii) Anecdotal Records

(iii) Cumulative Records

6. Socio-metry

7. Socio-drama
8. Case Studies and Case Conferences.
9. Student projects
   (i) Notebooks
   (ii) Assignments
   (iii) Autobiographies

Selection of a technique or techniques of evaluation depends on the nature of the objective to be appraised. Objectives such as acquisition of knowledge, application of knowledge, critical thinking, comprehension, and expression can be conveniently tested by means of written and oral tests. Practical tests will be useful in assessing the pupils' achievement in relation to certain experimental and constructional skills. Objectives of interests, attitudes, and appreciations are rather difficult to assess with a high degree of confidence; hence a number of techniques such as inventories, checklists, rating scales, interviews, observations, sociometric devices, role-playing, anecdotal recordings, and reportings are used. We may at times adopt more than one technique simultaneously to assess the pupils progress in relation to the rather intangible objectives.

30.5 Functions of Evaluation

What is an evaluation for? What is it supposed to do? The most obvious answer according to Troyer and Pace is that it is our means of measuring or evaluating the products of the educational system. We want to evaluate "because we are not now, never have been, and never will be satisfied with our efforts, and because by analysing them we hope to find ways of improving." By knowing its strength and weaknesses, we are enabled to plan more intelligently for its improvement. By analysing our experience, resources, and programmes, we help to clarify them and bring our efforts more directly in line with our purposes.

30.6 Principles of Good Evaluation

There are certain principles which can help us in making a good programme of evaluation:

(i) *Evaluation must be done in terms of the purpose of the programme – all of them.* All outcomes – emotional, social, intellectual, and physical should be properly evaluated.

(ii) *Evaluation must be carried on as a continuing process.* Effective evaluation is one which is going on all the time. This means that throughout the day, from day to day, from week to week, throughout the year, constant and continuous appraisal must be made, both by the teacher and the pupils.

(iii) *Evaluation should be carried on as an integral part of instruction.* If evaluation is deferred until the unit is completed, there is not much the teacher can do to bring about an improvement in learning.

(iv) *Evaluation should be viewed as a continuous process, definitely related to the total learning situation.* We must consider the growth of the child as a whole individual and in his total environment.

(v) *Evaluation should be carried on as a cooperative process.* It is not a one-man or a one-way job. It must be done in co-operation with other teachers – the children, parents, principals because all have a stake in the programme. The teachers and the pupils being the co-partners, share in the clarification of purposes and in the use of various techniques of evaluation. Parents should become involved in the discussion of goals – the clarification of goals in terms of the hopes they have for the children. Principals must cooperate in the programming in order to give it a balanced direction and systematic consideration. Unless a programme is cooperatively planned and co-operatively operated, it will not yield maximum returns.

(vi) *A variety of devices and techniques should be used to get a complete picture of the progress towards goals and purposes to be*

had. The evaluative instruments selected for use should be valid, reliable, objective, practical, useful, appropriate, and descriptive.

(vii) *The information collected through various devices should be used to help the child.* Let the mark obtained by a particular pupil be compared with his previous marks, let the strong and weak points be discussed to effect improvement in the future.

(viii) It cannot be denied that a pupil's performance in tests is much influenced by factors other than study – by his health and physical growth, by his native intelligence and range of experience and by his social and economic background. *Thus it becomes essential to bear in mind these background factors to evaluate properly the achievements of a child.*

(ix) *Evaluation should be sufficiently challenging and must encourage the pupil to put in his best efforts.* Let evaluation techniques create interest and fun so that the pupils do the hardest things in a playful manner. Matching, completion, and arrangement items can all be play and excitement for the pupil to test his memory.

30.7 A Complete Programme of Evaluation

A complete programme of evaluation will include the following steps:

(a) Finding out the various objectives to be achieved through an educational activity.

(b) Defining the objectives in terms of the behaviour of the pupil, i.e. what changes we want to introduce in the behaviour pattern of the pupils through the activity or course of studies.

(c) Identifying the situation which will provide the desired learning experiences to achieve the objectives.

(d) Choose the suitable evaluating device to evaluate the achievement in the light of objectives as well as the learning experience.

(e) Construct the test or plan the device.

(f) Administer the test and record the evidence.

(g) Interpret the evidence very cautiously.

30.8 Evaluating Different Facets of Pupil's Growth

(1) Internal Assessment

It has been thought necessary that the work of assessment should be spread evenly over the academic year, and that some credit must be given for daily classwork in all the subjects. This practice will be conducive for efficiency both in teaching and learning.

Methods suggested by the I. E. Commission, 1964-66 to overcome the shortcomings of the Internal Assessment

The Commission suggested the following methods to overcome the shortcomings of the Internal Assessment.

(i) The result of the internal assessment and the external examination should not be combined because the purposes and techniques of the two evaluations are different and because the results of the internal assessment of the different institutions are not strictly comparable. The results of the external and internal assessment should, therefore, be shown separately in the certificate given at the end of the course.

(ii) It should be an important point in the inspection of schools to review the internal assessment made to examine the correlation between the internal and external assessments. Persistence in over assessment should be regarded as a weakness in the school programmes. It should be taken due note of while classifying the schools and should also be related to grants-in-aid so that institutions which tend to over-stress their students persistently would stand to lose in status and finance. The grants-in-aid rules should also authorise the Education Departments to withdraw recognition for persistent irresponsible assessment.

(2) Evaluation of Physical Growth

If development of physique is one of the most important objectives of education, evaluation of this development is a very important part of the programme. It is through medical checkups that physical disabilities, which might be hampering the progress of the pupils in other areas can be diagnosed and remedial measures adopted. To check up physical growth –

(i) a physical medical test of each pupil should be held every term and at least annually;

(ii) a record of the physical disabilities is maintained, remedial measures adopted and progress observed;

(iii) a regular record of participation in games and athletics by each pupil is kept.

(iv) a rating scale of physical efficiency is used for each pupil; and

(v) a student is guided in terms of his needs by an expert.

Testing, Acquisition of Knowledge, Application of Knowledge, Critical Thinking, Comprehension and Expression

(3) Achievement Tests

The formal and informal teats are most commonly used for assessment by teachers, administrators, and guidance counsellors. An achievement test which measures the pupil's learning ability may be general and survey type or specific like diagnostic and prognostic tests may be for individual or group administration. The individual tests may also be a performance or non-verbal test. Generally, the tests used by teachers, are of the verbal group type.

(4) Oral Tests

These tests can be used to evaluate the pupil's abilities – such as power of oral expression, promptness in arguing, spontaneity of responses, etc. Even objectives such as knowledge and application of knowledge can be covered by oral tests which will consume much time in such cases.

This technique is quite valuable in case the questions are serially arranged to throw full light upon a particular unit of study. If the pupil gives an incomplete answer, that can be got completed by another question; and thus instantaneous and at the spot correction is possible.

This technique has certain drawbacks, some of which are: -

(a) It cannot be used effectively with recessive children.

(b) The questions often asked differ from individual to individual.

(c) There is usually no record kept of the pupils responses; hence, the valuation is likely to be subjective.

(5) Paper and Pencil Tests

(a) Essay Type Tests

In this type, the examinees are called upon to write an essay on each of the four or five questions, set in the form of a printed paper or dictated to them by the teacher. These tests help in securing evidence on attitudes and controversial issues. They test the student's abilities to interpret data; organise and summarise ideas; apply principles; describe events, persons, and places, think creatively and critically. Bean says, "Perhaps the most important reason for retaining essay items in appropriate setting or context, in school or in personnel examinations is that no substitute has been found that will evaluate the qualitative aspects of verbal expression of thought. To overlook the way in which a person communicates, or attempts to communicate ideas would result in a very incomplete education."

Shortcomings of Essay Type Tests

The essay type of test lacks most of the qualities of a good measuring instrument. The chief shortcomings are:

1. A test that is confined to a few questions can gauge but a few of the important areas in which pupil's activities should be tested. Rusk produced evidence to show that the essay called forth less than half the knowledge the average pupil actually possessed on the subjects, as determined by objective tests and required twice the time to do it.
2. The essay test includes many irrelevant factors, such as, the quality of the spelling, handwriting, and language used as well as bluffing. "The man who makes an examination paper in Geography is willy-nilly, marking English as well as Geography. He thinks that he is estimating the candidates' knowledge in Geography, whereas he is all the while being unconsciously influenced by extraneous things such as handwriting, neatness, spelling, grammar, correctness of the wording, the thousand and one things that go to make a series of written answer." For correcting such type of irrelevant factors, no corrective formulae exist.
3. Accurate marking of essay is an eternal problem. Essays are both vague and difficult to score, and the standards are likely to deviate to the widest degree because the answers given by the examinees are of all degrees of correctness. As essay is an intricate mental product which can be analysed in a variety of ways and yet can never be analysed completely. Each examiner, consciously or unconsciously, makes his own analysis, measures each element by his rods, weighs each factor in accordance with his own scale of values. The element of subjectivity plays such a cardinal role in the scoring procedure that teachers dare not see eye to eye with one another on a second series of values, assigned independently to the same papers. Sometimes, examiners have been found to reverse their judgement almost completely when asked to mark the same papers they had scored a year before.

   K.S. Acharlu conducted an investigation in which each one of the twenty seven examiners (who were all experienced and graduate teachers) valued twenty-seven essays written by school final pupils. He discovered a wide disparity, so much so that in the case of one pupil four examiners failed him, twelve gave him just pass marks, eight put him in the second division, while three gave him first class marks.
4. Comparatively much time is spent on answering the essay type of paper and evaluating the answers. If the examiner wants to be fair to all the examinees in an essay type of paper, he must be armed with elaborate checklists and with every answer paper; he must tick off the points in the list. This is impracticable.

The University Education Commission summarily expressed its verdict on the essay type of examination thus: "It has usually no clearly defined purpose; it is, invalid. Its sampling is very arbitrary and limited, it is inadequate. Its scoring is subjective and, therefore, not reliable."

It is thus a futile attempt to establish uniform standards of achievement for all teachers. The real remedy lies in supplementing essay type tests with objective tests.

(6) Objective Type Tests

A thorough and precise exploration of the mind of each particular child is the central purpose of objective type tests. Statistical methods have a cardinal role to play; the chances of reckoning upon gross guess work are scrupulously set at naught.

While the setter of essay type tests sets a small number of large questions, the objective test examiner sets a large number of small questions. It is quite evident that the new examiner atomises his tests; discarding the single bullet, he charges his gun with buck shot.

Objective type tests are needed for several purposes, e.g. measurement of achievement, intelligence, prognosis, diagnosis, etc. To a certain extent, they are also of value for unravelling interests and aptitudes.

The Radha Krishnan Commission (1948) recommended that the Central Government should appoint a number of experts to offer valuable advice and direction in the matter of the designing, standardisation and developing of objective tests for the Higher Secondary classes.

Advantages of Objective Tests

1. ***Extensive Sampling:*** The objective type test by its nature samples so widely that the results obtained from its use closely approximate those that would be obtained if pupil's performance in the subject in question could be measured completely. The comprehensiveness of the new test makes room for the inclusion of a wider range of questions. This eliminates the element of luck or chance. The phrases "chance of good scores" and "chance of poor scores" is unheard of in the fields of objective testing.

   Further, sample number of items provides the examiner with an opportunity to have them spread more evenly over the topics to be covered. The inclusion of a large number of items in the test tends to increase its reliability. It has been proved by many statistical studies that an increase in the number of items in a test is accompanied by a corresponding increase in the reliability of the test as a whole.

2. ***Objectivity of Scoring:*** The items are so framed that the answers are brief and usually admit of only one correct response. Subsequent scoring of a highly objective test by one person, or its scoring by different persons will result in practically no disagreement in the scores assigned. The award is sure to be the same, whosoever, the examiner may be. Such factors as personal likes or dislikes, moods of moment or widely varying standards of expectancy among the examiners are put to an end. In short, the mode of marking at which the new examiner aims, is out and out objective.

3. ***Economy of Time:*** This new type of tests takes less time. Since the responses are definite and brief, the examinees are in a position to answer a fair number of questions within a short interval. Examiners can also make available the scores of thousands of students within a couple of days with the aid of a scoring key or a scoring stencil.

4. ***Elimination of Bluffing:*** Fluency or expression and mastery over the language are the two factors, commonly put to proof in essay type examinations. In essay type, a fluent writer gains ascendancy over a slow writer and thus tends to score high. Further, an examinee, by the use of high sounding and bombastic words, is most likely to deceive the examiner into the false idea that his knowledge is very wide. There can be no such misunderstanding.

Instead of probing the mind at a dozen points, through objective tests probe it at a hundred different points. It affords the candidate a greater feeling of satisfaction; a feeling that at any rate he or she has got his or her deserts, and that the examiner was vigilant enough to lay a finger on his or her strong and weak points.

They do not lend themselves to cramming; skipping over certain portions of the course of studies and the pouring out of mugged up information verbatim. Capacity to deliver dead products of past thinking is of no avail in an achievement test.

These new type of tests are a more efficient means of measuring the educational outcomes, not only because of their objectivity, comprehensiveness, and ease of administration but also because of the scientific methods that the new movement has developed.

The various commissions and committees appointed by the Government of India fall in line with the view that objective type tests need to be adopted without any loss of time to avoid further deterioration in our education.

Limitations of Objective Type Tests

Objective type tests are by no means a panacea for ills connected with education, though such a mistaken notion prevails in certain quarters. They represent one line of reform in the whole scheme of educational reconstruction.

Dr. Salamat Ullah observes: "It is sheer naivety to think that the objective test by itself will lead to the educational salvation of our country. This can at best serve as a reliable means of evaluation and can in no way be the end. Any improvement in examinations cannot be effected unless the quality of education is improved."

Objective type tests lack many qualities and merits which essay tests have. Authorities in the field of mental measurement today recognise that there are certain aspects of learning and thinking that these tools do not measure adequately.

(a) They fail to evaluate such intangible outcomes as students' attitudes towards problems and subjects considered in the class, appreciations, interests, and ideals, though from the educational point of view the evaluation of such a segment of behaviour is very important.

(b) They touch but lightly upon reasoning, analysing, and ability to express ideas in a coherent and organised way. In other words, they cannot, as the essay type examinations, evaluate the examinee's general understanding of the subject or his interpretation of facts, his capacity for organising and formulating his knowledge nor his initiative and originality.

Types of objective tests

(1) Completion.

(2) True-False or Yes-or-No or Alternating Response.

(3) Multiple Choice Test.

(4) Matching Test.

(5) Arrangement Test.

(6) Definitions Test.

(7) Relationship Test.

(8) Classification Test.

(9) Distinction Test.

(10) Recall or Questions and Answer Test.

1. *Completion Test:* The objective in setting a completion test is to test the pupil's information on matters of general interest. Questions involve only the filling in of a proper name, date, or quality. It tests the recall.

Examples:

(1) Underline the most suitable one to complete the statement:

(i) The chief food of Bengal is.....
Wheat, maize, rice, potato, sugar.

(ii) Calcutta gets its sugar supply from Assam.

(iii) The Sunderbans, U.P., Bengal, Bihar, Bangladesh.

(2) Fill each of the blank spaces:

(i) The Aryans first of all settled in..........

(ii) Government for the people, of the people, by the people is known as..............

Some of the pitfalls to be avoided in a completion test

(1) Don't have the blank at the beginning as in ".....is the President of India." Encouraging the child to guess even before he knows the problem is not right on psychological considerations.

(2) Another common fault is ambiguity present in the part the child is to complete, e.g.

"The President of the U.S.A. ......" There are many ways of completion here. As a result, reliability and validity are adversely affected.

(3) Again, the teacher takes a sentence from a textbook and creates a blank by dropping off a word. Taken out of its context, a sentence has no specific meaning. The other bad effect of this is that children are encouraged to memorise the study material.

(4) Leaving too many blanks results in mutilated sentence, e.g. "The.....of.....is the.....of India. "Here the possible alternatives increase by permutations and combinations.

We should generally be sure that it is really important for the child to know or to learn what we have asked.

2. *True-False or Yes-or-No or Alternating Response*: In the test, a number of statements are given and the pupil is required to write T and F or Y and N against them.

(i) Origin of Buddhism is to be found in Hinduism.

(ii) Only Buddhist kings preach the doctrine of non-violence.

(iii) Dharamsala receives the heaviest rainfall in India.

(iv) Christ was born before Buddha.

(v) The extent of Mauryan Empire was greater than the Gupta Empire.

These tests are extremely poor testing devices, so it is advisable to avoid them as far as possible. If some of these are to be used the teacher must be sure that he has made an absolutely false statement.

One of the unfortunate effects of this type is that the best children in the group generally score low because they have a richer store of knowledge and experience and decision is proportionately more difficult for them than to the dullards. This type of test is also criticised under the plea that the idea of false things should not be given to the pupils because once the false notions are formed they remain stuck in the minds for a long time and it is very difficult to erase them.

3. *Multiple Choice Test*. This is the best testing instrument for most objectives which can be measured with paper and pencil. It gives the highest amount of validity and reliability, is easy to score, and yields results that are easy to analyse. In this test, importance is given to recognition of knowledge rather than recall. It is very useful both in assessing the understanding of concepts and in testing their factual knowledge.

Instruction: - Put a mark against the most suitable answers to the following questions:

Example:

1. In Aryan society the place of woman was:
(i) High
(ii) Low
(iii) Restricted

2. Who was the President of India?
(i) Stevenson.
(ii) Shri Fakhruddin Ali Ahmad.
(iii) Dulles.

3. Mehmood of Ghazni invaded India bcause:
(i) He wanted to get more wealth.
(ii) He wanted to establish Muslim rule.
(iii) He wanted to defeat Hindu rulers.

4. Hiuen Tsang was:
(i) a Hindu who wrote on Kalidas.
(ii) a Rajput who visited holy places.
(iii) a Chinese who wrote on Harsha.

5. What would you do to check spitting in the school compound?
(i) Request the principal to issue notice to that effect.
(ii) Boycott the spitters.
(iii) Place spittoons.

Some hints on the construction of multiple choice items

1. The number of choices must not be less than four. This will minimise guessing. More than five choices, however, will tax the child too much in reading.
2. In one and the same test, non-parallel or non-homogeneous opinions must not be given, as in the following:
   The American ambassador to India:
   (a) is named Bunker.
   (b) is elected by the people of U. S. A.
   (c) is appointed for 10 years.
3. The correct choices must occupy different answer positions in the different items. Each person is found to have a predilection for a certain position known as a favourite spot.
4. Expression like "What do you think....." must not be used since these ushers in the element of opinion which is not to be tested.
5. The test must be as concise as possible. The item should not be weighted with unnecessary material.
6. Be sure of the correct answer and be clear that there is no alternative answer. An item which has more than one correct answer is seriously defective.
7. Right and wrong answers must be roughly of the same length; otherwise the mere physical appearance of questions will afford clues to the child.

4. *Matching Type:* Two lists are given without any order or arrangement of their items. The pupils have to match items from one list with appropriate items of the other list.

Examples:

Instruction: - In group I, is a list of some important projects for the people of India. In group II, is a list of some purposes that they serve. Connect each project with its exact purpose:

I.

	Group I		Group II
(a)	The Central Tractor Organisation	(a)	It is to serve as a pilot project in increasing food production and improving rural life in all respects.
(b)	The Programme of Community Projects	(b)	It is to promote the speedy development of industries by giving financial assistance.
(c)	The Sindri Fertilizer Factory	(c)	It is to meet the people's need for irrigation and electricity.
(d)	The Industrial Finance Corporation	(d)	It is to meet the people's requirement in chemical manures.
(e)	The Bhakra Nangal Project	(e)	It is to meet the need for expansion of railways.
(f)	The Chittaranjan Locomotive Works	(f)	It is to carry out reclamation operations.

II. *Here are some causes (Group A) and their possible effects (Group B). Match them appropriately.*

Examples

	Group A		Group B
(a)	Absence of proper marketing facilities and good houses.	(a)	Has created the problem of sub-division and uneconomic holdings.
(b)	Lack of proper irrigation facilities like canals, wells, and tank.	(b)	Leads to an aversion to new and scientific methods of civilisation.
(c)	Lack of supplementary occupations.	(c)	Discourages permanent improvements in the land.
(d)	The uncertainty of land tenure.	(d)	Leads to forced unemployment of the farmers over a part of the year.
(e)	The illiteracy and conservative outlook of the peasants.	(e)	Considerably reduces the fertility of soil and increases the frequency and seriousness of famines.

III. *Here in the first list are given discoverers and in the second discoveries. Match them appropriately:*

Columbus	Australia
Vasco da gama	America
Magellan	South Pole
Captain Cook	The Pacific
Amundsen	India

IV. Here you are given some events with their era or years. You have to put the right year with the right event:

Event	Date
1. First Battle of Panipat	1556 A.D.
2. Buddha's Birth	261 B.C.
3. War of Kalinga	563 B.C.
4. Alexander's Invasion	326 B.C.
5. Guru Nanak's Birth	1398 A.D.
6. Akbar's Accession	1526 A.D.
7. Third Battle of Panipat	570 A.D.
8. Chandragupta Maurya's Period Starts	273 B.C.
9. Ashoka's Accession to the throne	322 B.C.
10. Battle of Haldi Ghati	1627 A.D.
11. Taimur's Invasion	1469 A.D.
12. Hazrat Mohammad's Birth	1761 A.D.
13. Deccan Campaigns of Aurangzeb	1682 A.D.
14. Invasion of Saleucus	1576 A.D.
15. Shivaji's Birth	305 B.C.

Some precautions to be taken in constructing Matching Test items:

(i) The questions must not be too long.

(ii) Homogeneous things must be mentioned in a column of a single set, e.g. all dates, all events. Avoid, for example, a hotchpotch of names of books and names of authors in the same column. The things mentioned must be in a rational order intelligible to the child like chronologically if dates, alphabetically if authors. This facilitates easy answering.

5. ***Arrangement Type: Some items are given to be arranged chronologically, according to size, location, or importance.***

Example: *Arrange the following in chronological order:*

(i) Coming of Aryans

(ii) Buddha's birth

(iii) Chandragupta Maurya's reign

(iv) Sher Shah Suri's reign

(v) Babar's Death

(vi) Hazrat Mohammad's Birth

(vii) Prithvi Raj Chauhan

(viii) Fahien's visit to India

(ix) Permanent Settlement of Bengal

(x) Kanishka.

6. ***Definitions: Knowledge of definitions can be tested in two ways. We can straightaway ask the definitions or give 3 or 4 definitions and ask the pupil to select the correct one.***

(i) Define Jezia, Electorate, Vote.

(ii) Which is the correct definition of democracy?

(a) It is a government by the nobles.
(b) It is a government by the dictators.
(c) It means President's rule.
(d) It is a government of the people, by the people, and for the people.

7. ***Relationship Test: In this test, relationship between two things is asked. For example, relationship between two items, e.g. crops and rain, crops and soil, etc. might be asked or pupils may be asked to establish relationship between two events.***

Example:

Suppose Rani were a high caste Brahmin lady living through the following period of Indian History.

(a) Late Vedic age (L.V.A.)
(b) Gupta Age (G.A.)
(c) Medieval Age (M.A.)
(d) Post Independence India (P.I.I.)

A few statements describing some aspects of her life are given below in a tabular form. Read each statement in relation to the condition of social life, prevailing in all the four periods of Indian History and put a tick mark within the brackets under the period wherein the condition is true.

Statements	**L.V.A.**	**G.A.**	**M.A.**	**P.I.I.**
1. She could move about in the streets without purdah.	( )	( )	( )	( )
2. She could get high education.	( )	( )	( )	( )
3. She had equal political rights as men.	( )	( )	( )	( )
4. She could embrace any religion.	( )	( )	( )	( )
5. She could marry her husband	( )	( )	( )	( )
6. She could divorce her husband.	( )	( )	( )	( )
7. She had to do sati in the event of her husband's death.	( )	( )	( )	( )
8. She had equal property rights with men.	( )	( )	( )	( )

Examples:

(i) What does Bengal not export?

Wheat, Cotton, Jute, Rice, Barley.

(ii) What functions do not belong to Vidhan Sabha of the State?

Executive, Financial, Judicial, Legislative.

9. *Distinction Type: Simple and clear distinctions are asked.*

Examples

(i) Distinguish between Jezia and tax.

(ii) Distinguish between direct and indirect taxes.

10. *Recall or question and answer Type: A question is asked to which simple and small answers have to be given.*

Examples:

(i) Which Mughal Emperors were fond of art and buildings?

(ii) Who is the brave and beautiful Rajput Rani who burnt herself?

(iii) Who was the founder of Maratha revolt against the Mughals?

(iv) Name the four Vedas.

(v) Who made the Grand Trunk Road?

(vi) Name two functionaries of the village.

(vii) Who is the originator of the Bhoodan movement?

(viii) Which period in Ancient Indian History is called the "Golden Age?"

Recognition Form of Tests

Chemistry:

Tick off which is correct.

1. Colour of oxygen gas is
   (a) Pale blue.
   (b) Colourless.
   (c) Yellow.
2. Carbondioxide
   (a) is odorless.
   (b) gives pungent smell.
   (c) smells like rotten eggs.
3. Which of the gases is combustible?
   (a) Sulphurdioxide.
   (b) Nitrogen.
   (c) Hydrogen.

Physics:

Tick off which is correct.

1. Who discovered the laws of gravitation?
   (a) Galileo.
   (b) Pascal.
   (c) Newton.
2. Albert Einstein is known for:
   (a) The manufacture of hydrogen bomb.
   (b) Theory of relativity.
   (c) Invention of television.

Mathematics:

(1) When the two sides of a rectangle are a and b and the area is represented by A. Underline the correct expression from the following, which represents the area.

(i) $A=2(a+b)$ (iii) $A=a \times b$

(ii) $A=\frac{a+b}{2}$ (iv) $A=\frac{a \times b}{2}$

(2) Choose the appropriate item from column B and match with the item in column A.

A	B
(a) The circumference of a circle of diameter 'd' is	πd^2 $\pi d^2 h$ πd
(b) The surface area of a cylinder of height h and diameter 'd' is	$\pi a\left(h+\frac{d}{2}\right)$ $\frac{\pi d^2}{4}$
(c) Area of a circle of diameter 'd' is	$\frac{\pi d^2}{6}$

Short questions requiring pointed answers

Short questions are set to which pointed answers have to be given. (1) The main purpose is to test a large amount of knowledge within a short time. (2) A greater number of questions can be given

3. What are the basic needs of man?
4. Explain two important factors responsible for the backwardness of India.
5. What are the fundamental rights of a citizen in a democracy?
6. Why did India advocate U.N. membership for China despite her strained relations with her over the border question?

(7) Testing Reasoning

Some test items could be prepared in the form of problems – a problem situation may be given which the pupil may study and suggest a solution. Some problems are:

(i) Himachal Pradesh was depending for food partly on its own resources and partly on Punjab. Now the Pradesh is facing a crisis. How is it caused? What is the remedy?

(ii) A state of famine has been declared in Bihar. Due to lack of rain, crops failed. Tube wells were not available in adequate number. How should the people in that state be helped? How to prevent the recurrence of such conditions in other states also?

Some statements can be given to the pupils for locating the error of reasoning.

(i) When a man works as a Chief Minister for five years, he is made a Prime Minister.

(ii) Punjab became a separate state because all the Punjabis wanted to stay in one state.

(8) Testing Skills:

For testing skills in reading, interpreting, and making maps, some test items are suggested below:

(1) Give the symbols for the following:
   (i) Battlefield
   (ii) Contours
   (iii) Forts
   (iv) Telegraph lines
   (v) Mines

(2) Compare a map showing population of India with one showing topography and explain the reasons of density of population in the areas shown.

(3) In a map of India show the areas of conflict between India and Pakistan during 1871. Show the movement of forces of both countries with different symbols.

(4) Find out the distance in kilometers between Calcutta and Bombay with the help of a scale given on the map.

(5) Conduct a socio-economic survey of your community and prepare a scrap book.

(9) Testing Attitudes, Interests and Appreciations

The attitudes developed in an area of learning and some hint of children's probable behaviour is suggested by items in which pupils are asked to indicate agreement or disagreement. Items like the following are appropriate in a study of intercultural understanding.

(1) Below are some statements about people. Place a check mark after each statement in the column that most nearly shows your feeling about the statement. Put a check under A if you agree, O if you disagree, question mark if you are not sure.

   (a) Some racial groups in our country are more intelligent than others.

   (b) It is important to know people well in order to understand them.

   (c) People who are different from us are probably not as intelligent as we are.

   (d) People behave in certain ways because of customs and environment.

   (e) If people in our country worked hard, they could have the things America or Russia have.

   (f) All children in our country have the right to education.

(2) *Situation tests* that describe some possible action to be taken can be used to evaluate

children's attitudes and skills. Although teachers recognise that such tests reveal only what children say, they would do, nevertheless problem-situation approach has many merits. Situation tests attempt to test both attitudes and skills in several content areas.

Select the sentence that best tells what should be done in each situation.

Ruby finds a ten rupee note in the school compound

What should she do?

- **(a)** She should buy sweets and other articles for herself.
- **(b)** She should put in her bag and take it home.
- **(c)** She should deposit it with the school principal.
- **(d)** She should enjoy the money with her friends.

Gagan is a new girl in the school. She looks a bit different from others and seems somewhat shy. What should other children do?

- **(a)** Leave her alone for a few weeks until she stops being shy.
- **(b)** Tell her she can stand on the side-lines and watch the game.
- **(c)** Stay away from her until they know more about her.
- **(d)** Show her around the school and invite her to play with her.

You get an off from school. How would you spend the day?

- **(a)** Seeing a picture.
- **(b)** Revising the previous day's work.
- **(c)** Seeing some friends and relatives.
- **(d)** Sitting quietly at home.

(3) *True False Type.* True False Type Tests may also be used to judge attitudes and the pupils' response may be 'Agree,' 'Disagree,' or 'Uncertain.'

1. They never fail who die fighting for a noble cause.
2. If all citizens could get education in India, India will become the largest democracy in the world.
3. To make democracy successful, minimum academic qualifications for legislators should be an M.A. degree.
4. *Pupils' comments* on slogans and common saying can go a long way in revealing their attitudes and interests.
   - **(i)** Jai Jawan, Jai Kisan.
   - **(ii)** Men must choose to be governed by God or they will be governed by tyrants.
   - **(iii)** Ignorance is a prison with invisible chains.
   - **(iv)** Man everywhere must become free by breaking all the chains.
   - **(v)** It is only the constructive use of science which can bring about a millennium.

(10) Testing through Assignments

Sometimes children may be given an assignment and asked to prepare the same at home. If the assignment is challenging, the pupils will be compelled to use a variety of sources to prepare the assignment. He will learn to collect and organise the facts. If the assignments are properly checked, different types of achievement can be appraised.

(11) Testing Interests

The pupil's interest in inventories can prove useful in identifying particular likes or dislikes of children, types of learning they feel most satisfying, activities they would like to repeat, out of school activities, clubs, hobbies, etc. The technique used to obtain this information may take a variety of forms. When the teacher is simply interested in obtaining facts related to the life of the child, he may prepare a series of direct questions and the child responds to them in yes or no.

(12) Evaluating Achievement in Crafts

Crafts are being introduced in all institutions. It is very imperative to have a detailed achievement scale at different class levels for every craft – spinning, agriculture, woodwork, leather work, etc. One such scale has been formulated by the Hindustani Talimi Sangh, Wardha. But that is merely a list of targets expected to be achieved by children of different classes than a scale of rating for an individual child *vis-à-vis* other children. According to the framers of that scale, a child of grade V, for example, must at the end of the year attain the standard of measuring 5 tolas in an hour, and be able to spin on an ordinary charkha in 2 hours 649 rounds of the count of 16 to 20 without any wastage.

Detailed rating scales are required for all the crafts. For example, in the case of spinning, the prior process of cotton cleaning, ginning, carding and silver making are all important and have to be considered in evaluation. Similarly, in the case of woodwork the pupil must be rated, among other things, on his ability to saw, to plane and to chisel – these being the essential processes in this craft.

While evaluating craft work, the teacher should also be careful about the concomitant abilities that pupils are expected to develop in the course of their craftwork. In connection with weaving, the pupils are expected to develop the ability to judge the quality of the implements, to take proper care of them and to repair and mend them; the ability to judge the quality of the yarn – its count, evenness, and strength; the ability to cut down wastage of materials to the minimum. Moreover, it is necessary for the teacher to look out for and to record the attitudes and habits of work developed by the pupils. Progress of the students in craftwork can also be checked through records maintained both by the teachers and the pupils daily and monthly. The actual products made by children provide another useful way of getting evidence of behaviour. The paintings of a student can give evidence of his skill and interest in paintings. Final assessment of achievement in craftwork should be based on these records and on the tests given to children monthly, quarterly, half yearly or annually.

(13) Testing Attitudes, Interests and Appreciations

Testing Attitudes

Oral questioning, essay type tests, objective type tests may give some indications of the attitudes of the pupils. In addition to these, various techniques can be tried.

Examples

1. Have you been to the museum during the past year?
2. Do you play a musical instrument?
3. Do you help your mother in the kitchen?
4. Do you have a radio-set in your home?

Similarly direct questions can be asked to have children indicate whether they like or dislike various situations, activities or things. Instruction: - Write down "L" if you like the activity, "D" if you dislike it.

1. Reading a book.
2. Going to the library.
3. Playing a musical instrument.
4. Helping in the kitchen.

30.9 Some more Techniques of Evaluation

The following devices of evaluation may also be tried profitably:

1. ***Observations:*** Observation is one of the best techniques available to the teacher in learning about children, appraising their growth, and diagnosing their trends. Observation can be (a) current as when we watch a person actually engaged in activity which may be 'natural' or staged, (b) retrospective observation is used when one has to look back upon past experience and pass a judgement on the child. The teacher can observe the child in various situations; note his comments, relationships with classmates and playmates, attitudes, feelings and new interests and the changes in the behaviour pattern of the pupils.

The teacher must systematise his observation in some manner and attempt to objectify the data. The teacher should be definite as to what he is looking for. He should select certain pupils for intensive observation and study.

2. ***Check-lists:*** Checklists can be used either by the teacher or by the children themselves in evaluating progress. They may be used as an overall guide in many situations or they may be applied specifically to the child's behaviour in planning, discussion, plan research, or construction. The specific points to be checked would be the behaviour characteristics. Checklists should be specific, descriptive of desirable behaviour, and easy to use.
3. ***Group discussions:*** Group discussion is an effective device for appraising growth, as all members of the group participate. Specific instances of behaviour can be noted. This provides opportunities for the teacher to note children's behaviour. Creativeness of contributions, sharing of ideas, respect for the opinions of others, considerations of differing point of view, boldness, etc. can be observed. Thus, a fair estimate of the children's needs and potentialities can be formed.
4. ***Anecdotal Records:*** "Anecdotal record is........a record of some significant item of conduct, a record of an episode in the life of a student, a word picture of the student in action; the teacher's best efforts, at taking a word snap shot at the moment of the incident; any narrative of events in which the student takes such a part as to reveal something which may be significant about his personality." A collection of specific instances of behaviour can provide the teacher with a documentary account of changes of behaviour which have occurred or which are in progress.

   While preparing an anecdotal record the teacher should indicate the date and time of the incident, the circumstances under which it occurred and an objective description of the situation. He should write the general comments or traits as, "Mohan cooperated with Sohan" or "Bobby was unkind in her manner." Word and phrases that have strong emotional connotations, i.e. love, hate, insolent, courteous, loyal, dishonest should be avoided.
5. ***The Daily Diary:*** In the daily diary, pupils can keep a record of time, what they do, think and feel at different times. If the student-teacher relations are sound and strong and if the students have found that the teacher is able to accept the facts of student life undisturbed, that he does not always feel compelled to point a moral plan, then they may report correctly how they spend their days and what they think and feel with respect to the activities that occupy their time. The information thus obtained can bring new facts to light.
6. ***Socio-metric devices:*** Socio-metric devices can prove useful for evaluating growth in social relations and observing changes in the social structure of a group. These devices are helpful in determining cliques, most popular children, least popular children, leaders, and isolates. These techniques are thus helpful in knowing about the individuals with their peers.

   Socio-metric devices help in appraising the extent to which leadership roles have shifted or to which preferences of children for one another have changed. If the teacher knows the changes which are most desirable and beneficial in terms of human relationships in the class, he is able to evaluate the progress of the class in this respect over a period of time.
7. ***Rating Scale:*** This technique is used to know the degree of development of a number of descriptions showing degrees of development. Usually a five-point scale is used, such as, Very High-Above Average-Average-Low-Very Low.

It requires sufficient training and insight to make unbiased and objective ratings. The rater should be in constant touch with the ratee and should have a clear conception of the trait being rated. Unless the rating is based on frequent observations of a certain trend in a variety of situations, it is likely to be unreliable.

The tendency of a rater is to converge towards the middle degree, omitting the extremes. To avoid this difficulty, the five-point scale may be stretched to seven or nine points to obtain a sufficient scatter.

30.10 School Records

"School records are to public examination what a patient's case-history is to a doctor. How well they are maintained will determine how effective our educational programme is. Records will yield generous dividends."

It is expected of educational agencies that they will develop all aspects of the pupil's personality. In addition to catering to the intellectual needs of the pupil, a good school will also attempt to develop in these social and personal traits such as leadership, resourcefulness, industry, emotional stability, courtesy, and persistence. Schools are also expected to provide an adequate programme of extra-curricular activities catering to their interest and abilities. A record of academic abilities is not enough. There must be a comprehensive and systematic method of assessing and recording the pupil's progress in all these aspects. Proper records should be maintained for every pupil indicating the work done by him in the school from day to day, month to month, term to term and year to year. Diaries of pupil, anecdotal and cumulative records maintained by teachers are very good evaluation devices. Even the literary record of a pupil's reading can indicate his interests.

Cumulative Records

The Secondary Education Commission has recommended the maintenance of cumulative records of each pupil by the class teachers which will include not only the personal data of the pupil but also his school-attainments, health report, personality traits and participation in activities.

The Indian Education Commission 1964-66 places a great emphasis on the cumulative records. "Cumulative record cards play a vital role in indicating the growth and development of the pupil at each stage, his academic and emotional stage, his academic and emotional problems, and his difficulties of adjustment if any, and the directions in which remedial action are to be taken to solve his problems or difficulties."

"When a school accepts the philosophy that it has the duty to meet the needs of its students in their growth towards proper development, it would provide for *gathering, recording,* and *using* cumulative factual evidence of each pupil's *growth, adjustment* and *potential.*" The cumulative record is a systematic accumulation of significant factual information about an individual which when progressively developed and maintained over a sufficient period of time, gives a summarised "growth record" indicating the direction and rate of development.

Cumulative record shifts the emphasis from a one time or once-a-year performance in a few academic subjects to the full development in practically all the important aspects of education and general, physical, social, and mental development over a longer period of time. It is this shift of emphasis which is necessary before examination reform can be complete.

Cumulative records serve a number of purposes:

1. They give us the "comparative" achievement of pupils. A pupil's achievement is compared with that of his classmates. This comparative function is helpful in selection, promotion, and classification of students for various jobs in the school and later life.

2. They have interpretative functions. The cumulative information and data over a continuous period regarding a pupil helps us to understand his progress or lack of it; and his behaviour is interpreted. Proper educational and other kinds of guidance can then be given.

Cumulative record is a record which preserves the results of four to ten independent and objective studies brought together on one card. It is based on the belief that such assessment are more informative than one, and that guidance may be more effectively given in the light of such a series of measurements than in terms of the results of one selective examination.

It should give a full view of the student; should show his interests, preferences, achievements, leisure time activities, his reading interest, his special traits, his attitudes, his special aptitudes. It should give both a clear cross-sectional and a clear longitudinal view of the student. It should sow the current status of the student in different areas of the growth and disclose developmental trends by showing his status in these areas at different times in the past. The record should tell a story of the child's growth and development in relation to the goals and objectives of the school's educational programme. But cumulative records should never become so unwieldy and complex that they are a burden rather than an asset in guiding pupils. They should be so planned that there is a minimum of clerical work which can be simply and readily done.

Designs of the Cumulative Record

Three designs which may be adopted for cumulative records are listed below:

(a) ***Folder type:*** It is broad card which can be folded into many parts - say eight parts having sixteen pages. The first four parts will be used for permanent record and the next four for periodical records. Some pages will be kept blank for annual entries.

(b) ***File type:*** For each pupil a file may be maintained. The permanent record will be written on the printed columns of the cover. The periodical data of achievement and activities may be entered on separate leaves of paper for each period or year, to be inserted and added year after year.

(c) ***Envelope type:*** The file type when closed on three sides and kept open on one side will form an envelope. The permanent record may be entered on the front and back cover. The periodic record may be entered on separate leaves tagged together and inserted into the envelope.

Characteristics of a Cumulative Record System

The specific items desired may vary from one school to another but there are certain essential characteristics of this system:

1. A cumulative record is started for each child at the time of his entrance to school.
2. The record is transferred as the child progresses from lower to higher school or moves to another school.
3. Cumulative records present as comprehensive a picture as is feasible for the child's growth and development.
4. The forms used are simple and easy to understand. The maintenance does not require too much of clerical work.
5. The cumulative record system is flexible, requiring a minimum data for all pupils but permitting great latitude in the types of additional data which may be accumulated for individual pupils.
6. The cumulative record system is so designed that it reveals trends of growth over a period of years. The record forms are so designed that data which are cumulative can be presented in chronological sequence. All entries are dated. Informal data are summarised at the end of each year to reveal evidence of pupil growth, as well as his special needs and problems.
7. Cumulative records are readily accessible to teachers. However, the confidential nature of data must be respected and the

records always kept in a secure place.

8. In the recording of date every attempt is made to distinguish facts from personal opinions. Teachers must distinguish between objective facts and subjective impressions.
9. A good cumulative record enables teachers to think more about what happens to the pupil in all his areas of development.

It is to be admitted that the introduction of cumulative records would increase the responsibilities, and work of the teachers; but the advantage would outweigh the disadvantage to teachers. The teacher will become an experimenter with human development and find the maintenance of the cards not a burden or a load, but a process of making his work more meaningful to him and more useful to the pupils. It is necessary that the teacher is given clear directions, encouragement, and sympathy for the proper maintenance of these records.

30.11 Maintenance of Cumulative Record

The Secondary Education Commission is of the opinion that this record would be maintained by the class teacher. The base of this record would be decisions of the class teacher regarding the child. But, whenever it is needed and possible, it should be supplemented by objectivity of their decisions, measurement, credible examinations, and decisions of other teachers.

Specimen of Cumulative Record

The Secondary Education Commission has produced the specimen of cumulative record as following:

General Data:

1. Name of Pupil ....
2. Date of Birth ....
3. Name of Parents ....
4. Address of Parents or Guardian ....
5. Occupation of Parents or Guardian ....
6. Education of Mother ....
7. History of School:

Name of Schools	Year	Causes of Migration
(i)	....	....
(ii)	....	....
(iii)	....	....

8. History of Family:
   (i) Situation of the Child in the Family..............................
   (ii) Family Discipline..............................
   (iii) Condition of Family (Economic, Social, and Religious, etc.)
   (iv) Opinions of Parents regarding Occupation..............................
9. Aspiration of the Pupil..............................
10. Aspirations of the Parents..............................

A. SCHOLASTIC ATTAINMENT

Subjects	Grade	19......... Remarks	Grade	19......... Remarks	Grade	19......... Remarks
1. Hindi I						
2. Hindi II						
3. English						
4. Mathematics						
5. Science						
6. Social Studies						
7. Optional						
(i)						
(ii)						
(iii)						

B. PRACTICAL ACTIVITIES

Subjects	Grade	19......... Remarks	Grade	19......... Remarks	Grade	19......... Remarks
1. Craft						
(a) Turn over						
(b) Craftsmanship						
(c) Application						
Total Grading						
2. Social and Citizenship Activities						
(a) Collections						
(b) Expression						
(c) Service						
(d) Proficiency Badges						
(e) Team Feeling						
Total Grading						
3. Physical Education						
(a) Physical Activeness						
(b) Participation in Games.						
Total Grading.						
4. Drawing and Painting						
(a) Technical						
(b) Expression						
(c) Originality						
Total Grading						
5. Music						
6. Dance						

C. HEALTH REPORT

(i) Height	19....................	19....................	19....................	19....................
(ii) Weight	....	....	....	....
(iii) Chest	....	....	....	....
(a) General	....	....	....	....
(b) Expanded	....	....	....	....
(iv) Sight (Eye)	....	....	....	....
(v) Hearing (Ear), etc.	....	....	....	....
Medical Report	....	....	....	....

D. PERSONALITY TRAITS

Traits	19...............	19...............	19...............	19...............	19...............
(i) Initiative	....	....	....	....	....
(ii) Integrity	....	....	....	....	....
(iii) Industrious	....	....	....	....	....
(iv) Leadership	....	....	....	....	....
(v) Self-confidence	....	....	....	....	....
(vi) Emotional Control	....	....	....	....	....
(vii) Social Viewpoint	....	....	....	....	....

Note: As far as possible attainments regarding each trait can be done in the following manner:

LEADERSHIP

(i) Games and Sports	Grade
(ii) Social Activities	Grade
(iii) Intellectual	Grade

E. GENERAL REMARKS

	19....	19....	19....
(i) Status of Child in taking Responsibility.			
(ii) Special Remarks.			
(iii) Signature of Class Teacher.			
(iv) Signature of Headmaster/Principal			

The class teacher should complete this record by the end of the year with the consultation of other teachers. He should seek opinion of those teachers necessarily who have been in the contact of the pupils of that class. The evaluation should be done according to the successive order of the five points. Along with this, literal explanation should also be given at places as per requirement.

In 1962, DEPSE invited some specialists for the study of current cumulative records, who found great diversities in cumulative records under use. Besides, they saw great difference among these methods of maintaining accounts of facts regarding achievements and development of children. The specialists felt that there are two main difficulties in maintaining cumulative records. Firstly, the current records are too widespread, with the result that quantum of work increases too much on teachers. Secondly, most of the teachers are not imparted training for maintaining records of this kind. Keeping these difficulties in view, the specialists have produced a specimen of records easy and brief and for its maintenance necessary instructions have also been given.

The specimen of this cumulative record has been given in appendix No. 4.

30.12 Some Problems regarding the Maintenance of Records

There are some serious problems regarding the maintenance of records which need consideration, for instance, who should maintain the record cards? Where to keep them and when to fill up these cards? How to check the maintenance? Below are listed some suggestions to tackle these problems:

(1) **Who should maintain the record cards?** The teachers in charge of various subjects should maintain records. Their duty is to evaluate the child's achievements from time to time and to record the same.

It is also the duty of the class teacher to maintain a file containing the record cards of all the students in his class. He should be responsible for getting the necessary entries made by the subject teacher or the class teacher or teacher in charge of various activities. The responsibility of the class teacher is very great as he has to act as a liaison between the pupil and the subject matter and between the pupil and the parents.

(2) **Where to keep them?** The record should remain with the class teacher, but should be easily accessible to the other teachers. Whenever they want to make entries, the best place is the principal's room or the staff room where it can be seen that these remain confidential.

(3) **When to fill up these cards?** Record of written work may be kept by the teacher and entries made fortnightly and monthly. Other entries may be made at the time of a particular event or tests. It is advisable that each teacher should have a small note-book in which he records his observation at the time of the incident about a particular pupil and then makes entries in the card at some convenient time.

(4) **How to check the maintenance of the cumulative record?** The principal or one of the teachers who is a specialist in this field should keep a proper check to see whether the entries are being made regularly by each teacher. The principal should sign the records and arrange to send report of the pupils' achievement to their parents at regular intervals.

30.13 Characteristics of a Good Cumulative Record

A good cumulative record should have the following essential characteristics:

(1) ***Validity:*** The record must be true, exact, and authentic. Nothing should find a place in it which is based on rumour or second hand information.

(2) ***Objectivity and reliability:*** Personal opinions and judgements should be avoided. It is essential that the teacher maintains an objective outlook.

(3) ***Usability:*** The record must be usable – it must be readily accessible and the arrangement of date must facilitate ready interpretations.

(4) ***Comprehensiveness:*** The information recorded should be so comprehensive as to give a complete picture of the child both horizontal as well as vertical.

30.14 Recommendations of the Indian Education Commission (1964-66)

The Commission has pointed out that evaluation is a continuous process and forms an integral part of the total system of education and is intimately related to educational objectives. It exercises a great influence on the pupil's study habits and the teacher's methods of instruction and thus helps not only to measure the educational achievements but also to improve it.

The Commission has given the following recommendations:

1. **The new approach to Evaluation** will attempt to improve the written examination so that it becomes a valid and reliable measure of educational achievement and to devise techniques for measuring those important aspects of the student's growth that cannot be measured by written examinations.
2. **Evaluation at the Lower Primary Stage**. Evaluation at this stage should help pupils to improve their achievement in the basic skills and development of right habits and attitudes.
3. **It would be desirable to treat classes I to IV** as an ungraded unit to enable children to advance at their own pace. When this is not feasible classes I and II may be treated as one block divided into two groups – one for slow and the other for fast learners. Teachers' should be appropriately trained for the ungraded system.
4. **Evaluation at the Higher Primary Stage.** In addition to written examinations, weightage should be given at this stage to oral tests as a part of internal assessment. Diagnostic testing should be through simple teacher-made tests. Cumulative record cards are important in indicating the pupil's growth and development but should be very simple and should be introduced in a phased manner.
5. **External Examination at the end of Primary Stage.** Although the first national standard of attainment is to be set at the end of the primary stage, it is not considered necessary or desirable to prescribe a rigid and uniform level of attainment through a compulsory external examination. However, for the proper maintenance of standards, periodic surveys of this level of achievement of primary schools should be conducted by district school authorities through refined tests prepared by the State Evaluation Organisations.
6. **A Common External Examination for Inter-School Comparability.** The district educational authority may arrange for a common examination at the end of the primary stage for schools in the district using standardised and refined tests. This examination will have greater validity and reliability of levels of performance.
7. **The Certificate at the end of the Primary Course** should be given by the school and should be accompanied by the cumulative record card and the statement of results of the common examination, if any.
8. **In addition to the common examinations, Special Tests** may be held at the end of the primary course for the award of scholarship, certificate of merit, and for the purpose of identifying talent.
9. **Improvement in External Examination.** External examinations should be improved by raising the technical competence of paper setters, orienting question-papers to objectives other than the acquisition of knowledge, improving the nature of questions, adopting scientific scoring procedures, and mechanising the scoring of scripts and the processing of results.
10. **Certificate given by the Board and School.** The certificate issued by the State Board of School Education on the basis of the results of the external

examination should give the candidate's performance in different subjects for which he has appeared and there should be no remark to the effect that he has passed or failed in the whole examination. The candidate should be permitted to appear again, if he so desires, for the entire examination or separate subjects in order to improve his performance.

11. **The Student should receive a Certificate** also from the school, giving the record of his internal assessment as contained in his cumulative record card and this should be attached to that given by the board.

12. **Establishment of Experimental School.** A few selected schools should be given the right of assessing their students themselves and holding their own final examination at the end of the class X which will be regarded as equivalent to the external examination of the State Board of School Education. The State Board of School Education will issue the certificates of these schools on the recommendations of the schools. A committee set up by the State Board of School Education should develop carefully worked out criteria for the selection of such schools. The schools should be permitted to form their own curricula, prescribe their own restrictions, and conduct their educational activities without external restrictions.

13. **Methods of Internal Assessment.** Internal assessment by the school should be comprehensive and evaluate all aspects of student growth including those not measured by the external examination. It should be descriptive as well as qualified. Written examination conducted by schools should be improved and teachers trained appropriately. The internal assessment should be shown separately from the external examination marks.

14. **Higher Secondary Examination.** During the transition period, higher secondary students will have to appear for two successive external examination at the end of classes X and XI within one year. Where, however, the courses in classes IX and XI are integrated the examination at the end of class X need not be insisted upon.

30.15 National Education Policy 1986 [POA]

Under the new 10+2 pattern of education, the examination has to be a part of the educational process. It has to serve as a reliable tool of measurement. What is more important is the feedback. The results have to be utilised to provide remedial teaching for the weak students. For the bright and the gifted, more challenging programmes have to be provided. The examination should also be utilised by teachers to improve their teaching methods. Under this system, the scheme of assessment aims at rationalisation.

The following are its important features:

(a) Internal assessment along with external examination.

(b) System of grading instead of marks.

(c) Standardization of raw scores.

(d) Question banks.

(e) Improving quality of paper setter.

(f) Improving evaluation process or procedures.

In accordance with the spirit of the new scheme, the system of evaluation and assessment has been modernized and simplified with the dual purpose in mind i.e. to improve both the quality of testing and the standards of teaching. The pattern of examination envisages the following improvements.

(i) Continuous evaluation

Continuous evaluation of the student's growth by the teachers themselves in certain areas.

(ii) Internal assessment

Internal assessment in respect of the third language, work, experience, community service, health and physical education.

(iii) Five point scale

The result shall be declared in terms of grades on five point scale instead of marks and divisions as in the past as under.

Grade 1. Outstanding Grade 2. Very good
Grade 3. Good Grade 4. Fair
Grade 5. Poor

(iv) No overall grade

No overall grade by adding up marks of different subjects shall be given. Subject wise grades will be awarded

(v) Provision improvement of grade

The new scheme provides for the permission to reppear at the next examination for the purpose of improvement grade.

(vi) Special provision for bright students

A bright pupil may be allowed to sit for the Board's examination, if he so wishes, a year earlier than when he should normally take the examination. His outstanding progress must be certified by the head of the institute.

Objective Type Questions

Multiple Choice Questions (Tick ✓ the right option)

(1) Education is intended to bring about changes in
(a) Knowing
(b) Feeling
(c) Action
(d) All of the above

(2) The formal and informal tests are most commonly used for assessment by
(a) Teachers
(b) Administrators
(c) Guidance counsellors
(d) All of the above

Fill in the blanks

(1) The __________ must be true exact and authentic [Record]
(2) __________ is concerned with all the goals of an educational programme [Evaluation]

Important Questions

1. Illustrate how objectives, teaching procedures, and evaluation procedures are related. Under what circumstances would one be changed in terms of the other two?
2. Discuss the advantages and limitations of various objective type test items – multiple choice, alternate response, simple recall, completion, etc.
3. How will you assess the achievement of the pupils in crafts?
4. What do you understand by Cumulative Records? Discuss some problems in the maintenance and use of Cumulative Records.
5. In what ways does the evaluation which comes near the close of a unit or topic differ from the evaluation which may come near the end of the school year?
6. Discuss the various techniques of evaluation which can be used for testing attitudes, interests, and appreciations.
7. Discuss different types of tests that can be used for testing acquisition of knowledge, application of knowledge, critical thinking, comprehension, and expression.

8. "Ill-equipped pupil, weakness of examining bodies, raising of the percentage of passes to required level are some of the present-day evils, which if combated can bring about the rise in standards, discipline, and less wastage in education." Elucidate.
9. "Examinations, subjective and objective only assess a segment of human personality - the cognition side - the intellectual or academic aspect. A cumulative record chronicles the development of human personality in all its aspect." Discuss.
10. What is the evaluation techniques used in your schools these days? Comment upon these and indicate how they can be improved upon.
11. Discuss the following statements:
    (a) "Evaluation must be conceived as "a continuous process of enquiry, based upon criteria developed cooperatively in the school, community, and conceived with the study, interpretation, and guidance of socially desirable changes in the behaviour of children."
    (b) "Examinations fulfill a double function - they are a mobilizing force in education, and they provide a means of testing its results. To ignore either of these aspects is to get a distorted view of the whole subject."

31

Accountability in School Education

The principal or head of an institution has the major roles and responsibilities; therefore, they are great authorities. The functioning of an institution depends on the roles of teachers and the principal. The principal's roles and authorities are shared by the teacher. He assigns responsibilities to teachers and hands over the authorities as well, but the ultimate accountability of the principal for higher authorities' discipline of the school, is conducting examinations. It is essential to understand the accountability and commitment in school education to know the roles and responsibilities of teachers and principal of an institution. This topic of accountability and commitment in school is related to pedagogical beliefs and attitudes.

31.1 Accountability in School Education

The term accountability in school education is given by pedagogy beliefs not the educational technology. An affective aspect plays a significant role and responsibility in school education. It includes emotions, feelings, beliefs, attitudes, and values of teachers and the principal.

31.2 Meaning and Definition of Accountability

The word "accountability" is a concrete and matter of fact expression for what the schools owe as duties and responsibilities to their establishing/employing organisation, to the student community and the society at large, with the utimate aim of doing good by their performance. The idea of accountability should not appear as objectionable or foreign to the institutions and teachers if they could open mindedly look at their own everyday activities and programmes. As explained by Prof. Ramesh K. Srivastava (university news, Vol. 38, 2000), "Most of us as customers, go to the market, have a definite idea of our requirements, select the best item in a particular category to suit our taste and pursue, scrutinise our merchandise and then bargain to get the best in the price range. But when the bought item does not come to our expectations, or when we visit a government office, a ration shop, or a court, and on finding that the concerned person is absent or on casual leave, we tear our hair and our blood boils. In all these cases, we have some expectations. Some codes or norms within ourselves and when the things or services don't correspond to them, we are disappointed.

Unfortunately no such set codes or norms exist in the academic world. There are no fixed qualitative targets, to achieve, no tangible yardsticks against which the academic excellence could be measured. Fixing of accountability, i.e., one such step in the right direction."

Definitions of Accountability

According to **Good's Dictionary of Education (1973),** "Educational accountability is the theory that teachers and school systems may be held responsible for actual improvement in public achievement and that such improvement is measurable through tests of teachers' effectiveness, constructed by outside agencies."

The International Dictionary of Management (1980) by Hano Johannsen and G. Terry Page (1980) defines accountability as, "Accountability for action carried out and performance achieved to other, e.g. by a manager to his superior or by the board of directors to its shareholders, also used more loosely to describe responsibility."

The Concise Dictionary of Education (1982) gives the following meaning of accountability. "Educational accountability is a concept in which the school system and especially teachers are held responsible for the learning and academic progress of students."

The Blackwell Encyclopedia Dictionary of Organisation Behaviour (1995) edited by Nigel Nicholson explains the term 'accountability' as, "The term denotes responsibility for particular activities, results or outcomes specification of the person(s) or group(s) who hold such responsibility in an organisation."

31.3 Dimensions of Accountability

Accountability may be viewed from several aspects:

- Moral Accountability to those affected by one's actions; pupils, parents, colleagues.
- Contractual Accountability to one's employer, which in the case of teachers may be the school board, the school district, regional or state government, supervisors, and superintendents.
- Professional Accountability to the standards one sets for oneself and one's professional aims, beliefs, and mission.
- Financial Accountability to the standards set by appropriate authorities.
- Social Accountability to the society/ community which has set up the school.
- Administrative Accountability to the administrative standards set up by persons concerned or authorities.

31.4 Components of Accountability

The above characteristics employ some components to indicate the nature of accountability. The following are the main components of accountability:

(1) Commitment to his profession or his job.

(2) Performing his duties sincerely and honestly.

(3) Completing his responsibilities with devotion.

(4) Review the performance of teacher or principal.

(5) Quality of work or quality of his profession.

(6) Involvement in his work or duties.

(7) Positive attitude towards his profession.

(8) Has the interest and belief in roles.

(9) Exercises his authority and rights properly.

31.5 Responsibility of School Education

After independence the *Secondary Education Commission (1952-53)* was established. It is also known as the *Mudaliar Commission*. The Commission has given recommendations for the reform of secondary education. Some of the recommendations are given in the following paragraphs.

According to the Secondary Education Commission (1952-53) secondary school has to provide vocational efficiency and character development among students. They should take to self-accountability. They can contribute to national life. Thus the school is a formal agency which helps in developing good cultural and social values and norms. Social efficiency should be developed among students. The managers, principals, teachers, and other school staff should be conscious enough for their irresponsibility and accountability. They should accomplish their responsibilities with devotion.

According to **T.P. Nunn**, "The schools are the main organs of a nation. The major tasks of the school is to integrate the spiritual powers, continue the success on the basis of past and ensure the success of the nation. The school should be conscious about its permanent sources which have encouraged during the past. The school functioning should be reviewed in this regard as their accountability. The ideals should accomplish their responsibilities and accountability."

Zakir Hussain had expressed, the scope or field of our schools is the whole community. The students should be provided all the necessary facilities for their education, because they are the national human manpower. They should be prepared to be healthy citizen in all respect then they should form a healthly community. The opportunities should be provided for the development of self-discipline, self-experience, and feeling of cooperation with self-confidence among the students. Thus, all the citizens of the nation will be committed to their profession and duties.

According to the Secondary Education Commission (1952-53), **"Life is an art of living."** It is a broad concept which should be the basis of secondary education. It involves the following qualities:

1. Social efficiency of life.
2. Working efficiency or commitment to the profession.
3. Impartial behaviour of teacher.
4. Good habits in tune with social norms.
5. Simple living with cooperative feeling.
6. Accountability and commitment to their responsibilities.
7. Proper guidance for the problems of their students.

In school education, principal, teachers and other staff have to play several roles and accomplish various responsibilities. Therefore, commitment and accountability are the essential qualities in school education. The quality of education is governed by the commitment and accountability of school workers.

31.6 Headmaster or Principal: Accountability in School Education

A principal is a pivot of school education. He has various roles, responsibilities, and duties in school administration. Sometimes he delegates his authority to his senior teachers in controlling the school programmes. He has to deal with different types of persons and authorities as follows:

1. Students and their parents or guardians.
2. Teaching staff members.
3. Clerical staff and other workers.
4. Management authorities.
5. District educational authorities or Regional authority.
6. State educational authorities.
7. Board of examinations.

The task of a principal is to develop the student and organise various programmes for student welfare, for example, guidance and counselling, NCC, and scouting, etc. He has to seek the cooperation for accomplishing his school responsibilities. If the school result is poor, it is the accountability of the principal but it is the responsibility of the teachers. The standard of a school education is evaluated in terms of final or board examination results. Thus teachers and principal are responsible for the school education. The school climate is formed by the working style of teachers and principal which is generated by the subject-teacher or his commitment to the teaching process and teacher-taught interaction.

The school education also includes social and cultural references. Culture is a particular way of a life of a society or life of a specific society. The society is the formation of men and culture. The child behaviour depends on these factors. Both these factors are complementary to each other; therefore the sociologists have used the term 'special culture.' Every society has its own way of life values, norms, roles, and responsibilities. A child culture comes from his society, therefore, different ways for assessing the social norms and values.

The social change influences the culture of a society, therefore, culture is not stable. It changes at a slow rate. The economic change is very rapid. The term modernisation is used in this context.

The school curriculum is developed in the view of social needs and requirements; therefore, school curriculum is not permanent. The teacher-education programme has the responsibilities to provide pedagogical knowledge of beliefs, attitudes and values to pupils, and teachers. It should also include social programmes. The curriculum should be flexible and practical in view of the social and cultural needs of a nation.

31.7 Teacher's Professional Commitment and Enthusiasm

Teachers should have the professional commitment and enthusiasm for accomplishing their responsibilities as well as their duties.

1. Teachers should give priority to their professional commitment and development.
2. Teachers should be enthusiastic towards their teaching and teaching programmes.
3. Teachers should have emotional tie with their students. They should provide educational guidance to their students.
4. Teachers should have a positive outlook and sympathetic attitude toward their students.
5. Teachers should try to understand their students with regard to their abilities, capacities, needs, aims, weakness, and their level of aspirations.

It is not essential for each and every teacher to follow the above ideals and beliefs because there is a great variation among students, knowledge explosion, and rapid change in the society. In an era of technology a teacher cannot ignore his pedagogical beliefs. Teachers have to develop a cognitive, psychomotor, and affective aspects of his students. It is the need of the day that the teachers have to develop their professional ethics for understanding their accountability.

31.8 Issues Involved in Accountability

Important issues involved in accountability are:

(1) Who is accountable to whom in our country?

(2) How can an institution be made accountable?

(3) How can teachers be made accountable?

(4) When different teachers in an institution are involved in teaching and evaluation, how can a particular teacher be held accountable?

These issues raise further issues when we consider accountability in school education.

(1) Are other social institutions accountable?

(2) School education is conducted by a number of agencies. Are these agencies accountable?

(3) How can an institution be made accountable when it has little or no control in the preparation of the curriculum, in the prescription of textbooks, in the admission of students, in setting question papers, etc.

(4) To what extent each section of personnel engaged in education, i.e. administrators, supervisors, teachers, etc., is accountable?

(5) Are students accountable for their performance?

(6) Are parents accountable for the performance of their children in studies?

A host of such issues arise. The situation seems to be very complex and does not permit any ready-made answer.

While discussing accountability in school education, the aspect of accountability of the Department of Education which formulates educational policies and also sometimes runs and manages its own institutions grants aid to private schools and recognises schools without grants, is hardly taken into consideration. There seems to be no mechanism to fix-up its responsibility.

Likewise, the Examination Boards/ Affiliating Boards seem to enjoy so much autonomy that their work seldom comes under scrutiny.

It is generally observed that only the heads and the teachers are made accountable for poor results at the Board's examination. Others associated with school education is not held accountable. This is a serious lacuna which needs to be removed urgently if worthwhile improvements on school education are to be brought about.

31.9 Assessment of Accountability in School Education

The school education accountability is assessed at various levels. The following are the main levels of assessing the accountability in school education:

(1) The community and local level bodies, the parents, and guardians select the school for the admission of their ward. The admission is on the basis of final results and discipline of the institution.

(2) At the district level school accountability is assessed and gradation is done on the basis of final results, administration, and commitment of the school teachers in their profession.

(3) At the state level school accountability is evaluated and gradation is done as, A grade, B grade, C grade, and also on the basis of principles and teachers commitment, discipline and final results.

(4) At the national level CBSE schools and central schools are assessed on the basis of the above criteria and the best school is selected as the model for other schools. The following are the criteria and basis for assessing schools. The accountability in school education is the main criterion.

(a) The responsibility and role performance of school management, its consciousness, and readiness in performing the duties.

(b) The responsibilities, commitments, and role performance of the principal in school administration, organisation, supervising, and controlling. His readiness and consciousness in performing his duties.

(c) The commitment of teachers for the following ethics of teaching profession. The responsibilities and role performance of teachers in teaching subjects and guiding students.

(d) The responsibilities and role performance of other workers and clerical staff are assessed for the accountability in school duties.

31.10 Accountability of State and Central Authorities in School Education

The accountability of school education is not only the school management, principal and teachers but also the higher authorities of state and Nation. The schools have to follow the rules, regulations, course curriculum, and other educational programmes. There is an hierarchy of school education authorities.

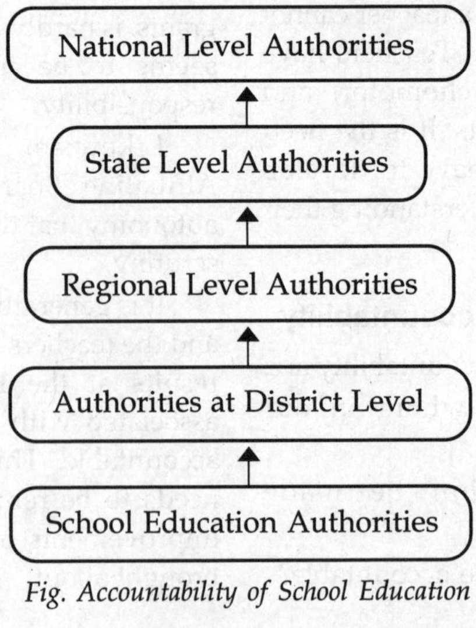

Fig. Accountability of School Education

As we have discussed that accountability is the review by the superior authority of his subordinates or assistances or lower authorities for accomplishing the responsibilities and duties.

Education is the state subject, therefore, every state has the freedom for organising state education, but major policies are framed by the Nation or the Minister of Education. The state has to follow the guide suggested by the Nation. The Education Commission and Committees are formed by the Nation for educational reform. Their recommendations are implemented in the state.

Therefore, the accountability of school education is of the state and central authorities. In a democracy the public or people of a nation can review the responsibilities of national authorities.

The state responsibilities are reviewed by the central authorities. The state reviews the responsibilities of its subordinate-regional authorities and district authorities. The district authorities are supposed to review the responsibilities of school teachers and principals. Therefore, it is not the principal or school management but also the state and central authorities that have the responsibility of school education.

31.11 Broad Parameters Determining Accountability of an Institution

The following are the nine parameters on which the accountability of an educational institution may be assessed:

Parameter I: Institutional Mission and Objectives

Criterion I. The objectives and mission of the institution are clearly stated, periodically reviewed, and communicated systematically to all its constituencies.

Criterion II. The objectives and mission of the institution reflect contemporary educational needs and are relevant to the region it serves.

Parameter II: Curriculum Design and Review

Criterion 1. The programme of teaching and learning are consistent with the objective and mission of the institution.

Criterion 2. The process of course/programme approval is designed to make the objective, content, expected outcomes, and weighting of different segments explicit.

Criterion 3. Feedback from students, employers, and external peers is used by the institution in the review and re-designing of course/ programme.

Parameter III. Quality of Teaching and Learning

Criterion 1. The programmes of teaching and learning offer a wide range of academic disciplines to train students to fulfill personal, societal, and national needs.

Criterion 2. The programmes of teaching and learning harness advances in technology to encourage student initiative in learning.

Criterion 3. The evaluation procedures in the educational programmes are rigorous and fair.

Criterion 4. The evaluation methods test the knowledge and skills that specific programmes are designed to impart.

Criterion 5. The regularity and the confidentiality of examinations are maintained and results are announced within reasonable time.

Criterion 6. The institution has open and participative mechanisms for evaluation of teaching and work satisfaction.

Criterion 7. The faculty has opportunity for continued academic progress and professional advancement.

Parameter IV: Publications, Consultancy, and Extension Activities

Criterion 1. The institution has a vigorous and well-scrutinised publication programme and actively encourages faculty and students to publish in academic form.

Criterion 2. The faculty of the institution participates in and contributes to advances in knowledge through research and consultancy.

Criterion 3. The institution is responsive to community needs and conducts relevant extension and awareness programmes.

Parameter V: Organisation and Governance

Criterion 1. The administrative organisation of the institution is such that powers and responsibilities are clearly assigned to designated bodies and individuals.

Criterion 2. The organisation is designed to facilitate tasks related to every aspect of the institution's goals and every segment of its constituencies.

Criterion 3. The institution has a realistic academic calendar which is generally followed meticulously.

Criterion 4. The institution's offices and departments are governed on the principles of participation and transparency.

Criterion 5. Management techniques and technologies are used, to the extent possible, for efficient running of every administrative and academic task.

Criterion 6. The administrative and academic units of the institution make optimal and innovative use of available facilities.

Criterion 7. Academic and administrative planning in the institution, move hand in hand.

Criterion 8. The institution has effective mechanism to monitor the functioning and progress of its academic and administrative units.

Criterion 9. All affected constituencies of the institution have access to relevant information pertaining functions and welfare.

Parameter VI: Infrastructural Facilities

Criterion 1. The institution has adequate infrastructural facilities to run the educational programmes and administrative functions efficiently.

Criterion 2. The growth and maintenance of the infrastructural keep pace with the academic growth of the institution.

Criterion 3. The infrastructure ensures a clean and efficient environment.

Parameter VII: Support Systems

*Criterion 1.*The institution has sufficient and well-run support systems to ensure the physical and intellectual health of all its constituencies.

Criterion 2. The allocation of facilities is based on principles of fairness and encourages creative and optimal use.

Criterion 3. There are fair and expeditious grievance redress mechanism at all levels of the institution's functioning.

Parameter VIII: Student Services

Criterion 1. The institution's prospectus gives a clear guidance to students about admission and completion requirements for all course, the fee structure and refund policies, and student support services.

Criterion 2. Financial aids to students are well-publicised and fairly distributed.

Criterion 3. The students of the institution have access to competent counselling and placement services.

Criterion 4. The students of institution have adequate and equitable access to learning support systems and to the records of their performance.

Parameter IX: Sources, Adequacy, and Management of Financial Resources

Criterion 1. The finances of the institution are judiciously allocated and effectively utilised to make its programmes and functioning cost effective.

Criterion 2. The budgeting and auditing procedures are regular and standardised.

Criterion 3. The institution has imaginative and effective resource mobilisation and management strategies.

The parameters are self-explanatory and relate directly to the effective functioning and development of an institution.

31.12 Tools and Techniques Used

1. Survey method.
2. Interview method.
3. Research on various issues relating to school education.
4. Performance of school levellers in various fields.
5. Examination results.
6. Rating of institutions.

In assessing accountability of school education, different sections may be involved. Views of students, parents, teachers, and media may also be obtained.

Objective Type Questions

Multiple Choice Questions (Tick ✔ the right option)

(1) The society is the formation of

(a) Men

(b) Culture

(c) 'a' and 'b' both

(d) None of the above

(2) "The School are the main organs of a nation." This definition is given by

(a) Ross

(b) T.P. Nunn

(c) Dewey

(d) Skinner

Fill in the blanks

(1) The school is a ____________ agency [Formal]

(2) The school education __________ is assessed at various levels [Accountability]

Important Questions

1. Give the meaning and definition of accountability. What are its various dimensions?
2. Mention any four dimensions or aspects of accountability.
3. List any three objectives of accountability.
4. Give any two methods of assessing accountability.
5. Mention any four areas of school life in which delegation of authority be done.

Unit V

Social Aspects of School

32

School and Home

The utility of the school depends to a great extent on the home and its relations with it. In early days there was no need for schools as home was the means of educating children. Home was the school and the father and the mother were teachers. Family life was the curriculum. In those days the child used to learn by following his elders or through their directions. But as the society became more and more cultured and complex, population increased, needs of life multiplied, vocations became specialised, the necessity for a more systematic and organised means of imparting education to children was felt and thus the school came into being and an important aim of the school was determined to be an all round development of the child.

32.1 Role of School and Home in the Education of a Child

Though schools try their very best to achieve their aim, but they cannot fully succeed unless and until they obtain full and active cooperation of the home. The child gets his first lessons at home and even when he is admitted in the school, he does not remain there for more than six hours. He passes most of his time in the home under the supervision of his parents. These eighteen hours outside the school have, therefore, a vital effect on his habits and development. This makes it clear that the school has a limited responsibility for the child's education, while the home plays a greater part in his training. The home is, in fact, a child's first school. He learns to a considerable extent at home before starting formal education in an organised school. He learns the language, the manner of talking, orderly living, healthy habits, and general behaviour towards his elders and youngsters. The foundation is laid down for those habits, thoughts, and ideals on which his future life is built. He imbibes the culture of the family in the home and takes it to the school. He thus influences others and is in turn influenced by the culture of others. In short, it may be said that his physical, mental, cultural, and moral development takes place to a considerable extent in the home and to a lesser extent in the school.

32.2 Need of Cooperation Between the School and the Home

For the all round development of the child, it is essential for the teachers to obtain knowledge of his interests, habits, attitudes and abilities. It is impossible to obtain full and correct information about the child unless and until the home establishes such an effective relationship with the parents that they may be ready to confine knowledge of their wards' shortcomings and behaviour problems and difficulties. On the other hand, if a child often comes late to school or is absent at times, is weak in certain subjects or has some behaviour abnormalities with his classmates, teachers should have a heart to heart talk with the parents, who should try to find out the cause of those problems and help the school in solving them.

Briefly, it can be said that cooperation between the school and the home is a two-way process. Communication between the home and schools is necessary for the parents to know the lines on which work is carried on in the school and how the child is being educated. On the other hand, teachers would know under what circumstances a child is living at home and whether conditions at homes are appropriate for the proper development of the child and also to what extent it is possible to adjust or alter them. Such active and close contact between the home and the school can enable both of them to perform their duty towards the child satisfactorily.

32.3 Methods of Obtaining Cooperation from Home

The question arises as to how the school and the home should be brought closer, how opportunities should be created for greater personal contact between the teachers and the guardians and how understanding, sympathy and mutual confidence can be developed between the two of them. Some of the ways and means to foster a spirit of cooperation in them are given below:

(a) Exchange of Essential Information related to Students

The school should send reports of the child's performance to the guardians periodically, so that they may know about the progress of their children. In cases of special circumstances, class teacher or the head may even write a letter to the parents. If possible teacher should occasionally meet the parents of his students and talk to them about their problems, e.g. the child's habits of missing classes, his bad health, poor progress in studies or misbehaving with his classmates. Action in such cases should be taken only after full discussion and exchange of ideas with the parents who can throw considerable light on the causes of such behaviour. A decision so taken is bound to be more effective in curing the child of his aberrations.

(b) Good Behaviour with the Guardians

School authorities should behave with courtesy and respect when meeting the guardians to ensure their goodwill for the school. In this way, teachers can get essential information about the child and his family background. The interest of the parents in school where the child is receiving education is only natural but it can be multiplied if they get proper treatment from the school authorities. Considerate behaviour towards the guardians of students is, therefore, a very important duty of the teacher.

(c) Teacher-Parent Association

In every school a teacher-parent association should be established to bring school and home closer. This association should meet quite often to provide opportunities to the parents to participate in important decisions and activities of the school. Thus parents' cooperation will be fully available to the school authorities. They may even consider themselves partly responsible for the success or failure of the school or the child. Through this association the school and the community can come closer to each other.

Aims of Teacher-Parent Association

(1) To promote mutual understanding and sympathy by closer relations between them.

(2) To make education imparted in the school more complete and effective by the cooperation of the parents in the school programmes.

(3) With the cooperation and active participation of teachers in the children's welfare programmes, family life generally and children in particular will improve immensely.

Functions of the Teacher-Parent Association

(1) To help the parents to understand and appreciate the school activities, school authorities' efforts, and the children's needs in relation to school.

(2) To organise meetings in which guardians and teachers can discuss the general problems related to students and the school, e.g. juvenile delinquency, indiscipline, to minimise the parents expense in the education of their children, students' coming to school late or missing classes.

(3) To think about new methods of teaching and jointly take proper decision in regard to school programmes.

(4) To conduct activities through which close ties may be formed between the school and the community, e.g. organising parents' day, cultural programmes and fetes, etc.

By adopting the ways and means mentioned above, the home and the school may be brought nearer to each other to join hands for improving the effectiveness of the education of the children.

Objective Type Questions

Multiple Choice Questions (Tick ✓ the right option)

(1) The child gels his first lesson at
- (a) Home
- (b) School
- (c) Gurukulas
- (d) None of the above

(2) For the all round development of the pupil it is essential for the teachers to obtain knowledge of his
- (a) Interest and habits
- (b) Attitudes
- (c) Abilities
- (d) All of the above

Fill in the blanks

(1) Cooperation between the school and the home is a ________ process [Two way]

(2) In every school a ________ should be established to bring school and home closer [Teacher-parent association]

Important Questions

1. Explain the role of school and home in the education of a child.

2. What is the need of cooperation between school and home?

3. What are the aims and functions of the teacher-parent association?

33

School and Society

The human society keeps itself alive by passing on its ideals, emotions, and activities to the coming generations. As the traditions, trend of thinking, ideals, and values are considered to be outmoded and no longer useful, it discards them and replaces them with new ideals and thoughts. This is accomplished through education. Different types of educational institutions are established so as to cultivate the new ideas and to transmit them from generation to generation. In this context Franklin says, "Society maintains educational institutions to preserve and disseminate among its members such knowledge, skills, ideals and traditions as are essential to its perpetuation and its constant development." Therefore, it is expected that these educational institutions will develop such qualities in children as would prepare them for participating successfully in the different activities of the society. Society in its turn tries to protect them and promote their development and expects from them that they would impart stability to the social life. It would thus be clear that the most important responsibility of the school is to make boys and girls aware of the ideals, thoughts, and traditions of the society and motivate them to make the society prosperous.

On the basis of the above views, it can be asserted that neither can a society remain alive without making adequate arrangement for education nor can educational institutions remain useful and therefore, stable without fulfilling the demands of the society. A society which has stable institutions naturally influences them socially, culturally, and even politically. The citizens who bear the financial responsibility of the school control the extent and type of education imparted therein. To achieve the objectives for which it has been setup, the school tries to purify the evils of the social environment. The school aims to prepare citizens who will be able to reform the society. Thus the school and the society are mutually dependent on each other. C.M. Cambell has in this connection emphasised the following points:

(1) There being a close relationship between the following of the school programme and the economic, political, and cultural life of the society, the curriculum of the school should be determined keeping in mind the needs of the society.

(2) It is essential for society to provide all available resources to the school in order to help it in accomplishing its programmes.

(3) The school fulfills its responsibility by participating actively in the plans for the development of the society and by providing proper leadership in regard to them.

It is thus clear that school and society cannot function without the cooperation of each other. It is the function of the school to make the children familiar with different aspects of social life so that they may understand the different factors involved in the social environment and imbibe good qualities of its culture. They may thus actively contribute towards social progress.

33.1 Schools as a Social Institution

In the opinion of Dewey, as food and reproduction are essential to maintain the body so education is essential for the experience of the society. Education starts when the child consciously starts taking part in the life of the society (family in this case) in which he finds himself. The school which is a social institution embodies the social consciousness of the race. Here children learn to respect rights, thoughts, and views of each other and to fulfill duties faithfully. School trains children in those social activities which are prevalent in actual life. Thus the school is a replica of the larger society, where living is learnt by living. Dewey says education being a social process, schools are generally a form of community life in which all those means are concentrated which prepare a child to share the heritage of the race and utilise his aptitudes and abilities for the benefit of the society.

Education is essentially a social activity. Society hands over this responsibility to the school to train the children in a way that they may participate successfully in the life of the community. The school is a community centre from this point of view. S. Balkrishna Joshi says, "*School is a dynamic community centre, which stimulates life and power all around.*"

School is a social institution which is established by the society for attaining its objectives. We are proving this fact through the words of T. P. Nunn, "School of Nation are those parts of its life whose particular work is to make firm of its spiritual power, to keep its historical continuity, to keep safe its past successes, and to provide guarantee to its future." In the form of social institution, the following functions have been determined for schools of today-

(1) Function of today's school is related with 7R instead of 3R:

(i) Reading,
(ii) Writing,
(iii) Arithmetic,
(iv) Recreation,
(v) Rights,
(vi) Responsibilities, and
(vii) Relationship.

(2) To provide training for democracy.

(3) Protection of culture.

(4) To work in the form of means of establishment of social justice.

(5) To work in the form of means of social reform.

(6) To develop scientific temper.

(7) To develop the value of interdependence (to depend on each other), so that, child may learn social and cooperative livelihood.

33.2 Schools as a Miniature Society

A school was supposed to be a place, till very recently, where instruction was given in some subjects of the curriculum. Thus, the work of the school was limited to teaching subjects in a traditional way. Textbooks were prepared from the point of view of imparting information and education was limited to this end only. It is true that information is an essential part of education, but it is also true that knowledge is higher than information and knowledge is not an end in itself, nor is it the ultimate aim of education. This realisation by educationists in the present times has compelled them to discard the traditional concepts and start looking at the school in the new perspective in which it is regarded as a "Miniature Society." In western countries this new point of view is getting momentum and an effort is constantly being made to change traditional schools according to the new concept of education.

In the opinion of the Secondary Education Commission, there is no doubt that school will be a society, but it will be a miniature society within a bigger society and its success and life will depend on a continuous and healthy interaction between the school and the larger society. What we want to ensure is that the school should take cognizance of the experiences and the problems which arise in the family and the society in general so that a close contact may be established between the school and the realities of social life. Similarly, whatever new knowledge, skills, attitudes, and values are acquired by the child in the school should be available for solving social problems and for raising the standard of social life.

In this connection, the Secondary Education Commission not only felt the necessity of increasing the utility of the school and society to each other but to achieve this end, it suggested that the school should be given a shape of a miniature society. The trends, the activities and different conditions of the society should be reflected in the school so that students may gain practical and direct experience of the life they will have to live as future citizens. School life is a part of social life, therefore, boys and girls should be provided such opportunities in the school that benefitting by their experience, they may have the ability to participate effectively in the life and activities of the society after leaving the school. For this purpose, during school life, opportunities for such activities and experiences, in a simple, true and balanced form, should be presented to the students so that they get familiar with the beliefs, aspirations and problems of the larger society. Thus only, the school can function as a true miniature society.

Our social setup functions on democratic principles. In order to make the school function as a miniature society, it is essential the democratic principles be adopted in the organisation of school programme and activities. This will give the students opportunity of gaining practical experience in the art of self-government, democratic functioning, and exercise of their opinions, privileges, and votes in a responsible manner.

Leadership is an essential feature of a democratic society. Children, therefore, should be given opportunities of gaining practical training and experience of leadership by handing over to them the school. To inculcate in them the desire to promote human welfare, different social service societies may be established in the school. For example, first aid.

It would be desirable to introduce a family atmosphere in the school administration so that the children may develop a cooperative interest in the welfare of each other and be prepared to serve and sacrifice for each other. Thus they will develop attitude of tolerance for others. Such atmosphere will create in them a habit of respect for elders and of kindness towards youngsters. They will also learn to love their teachers.

To acquaint the children with the economic affairs of the society, they should be familiarised with the local industries and agricultural productivity. The application of cooperative principles is acquiring momentum as a means of organising business and industry. In order to familiarize children with this concept, a cooperative store, a cooperative canteen, or a cooperative children's bank may be organised in the school to develop frugality in them.

Another feature of economic life in society is the act of purchasing and selling in a market. Children's fetes may be arranged so that they get practical experience of selling and buying, as the children will have their own stalls and shall arrange for procuring commodities themselves. The organisation of a cooperative bank for children further helps them in learning to manage money. They will learn to deposit their pocket money in the bank and to withdraw it by cheque when needed.

'Students' parliaments' can be arranged to teach the children how the government functions. They should also be educated in regard to the electoral system of choosing their representatives by establishing a miniature system in the school.

In order to make the school a miniature society, only those experiences of the society should be given to the children which will have a healthy effect in their future life, as responsible and active citizens.

Objective Type Questions

Multiple Choice Questions (Tick ✔ the right option)

(1) According to Dewey education is essential for the experience of the

(a) Culture

(b) Society

(c) 'a' and 'b' both

(d) None of the above

(2) "School is a dynamic community centre which stimulates life and power all around." This definition is given by

(a) S. Balkrishna Joshi

(b) S. Radhakrishnan

(c) John Dewey

(d) T.P. Nunn

Fill in the blanks

(1) ____________ is an essential feature of a democratic society [Leadership]

(2) ____________ is essentially a social activity [Education]

Important Questions

1. Why does society establish school?
2. "School is initially a social institution." Explain.
3. Why should school be made a miniature form of society?
4. What steps would you take for making the school a miniature society?

34

School and Community

Community in layman's language is a group of individuals who live together in a definite place for attaining common objectives and to lead a common life. Development of community needs a common interest, definite place to live, common level of normal life, and a feeling of togetherness. As a matter of fact, community is a very broad term. It refers to different types of social groups, e.g. family, religious group and local civic group and the city. The progress of science, technology, and culture has brought the human beings of the world nearer to each other. That is why today the concept of community has become broader. Today, the world is trying to give a practical shape to the concept of community. Thus the boundary of a community may be within a square mile or extend to the whole world. This boundary depends on the cultural and political similarity of its members. Specifying the meaning of community, Brownall has written, *"By a community I mean a small, diversified group of people, young or old, male or female, with different skills and abilities, living together as kin neighbours. It is a primary group, in which many of the major functions of life are carried on cooperatively within the group itself."*

> "School community cooperation is really something more basic than the parent, teacher, or student community relationship. The objectives and purposes of the school, its methods of teaching, the shape of its curriculum, the techniques of teaching and discipline are all ultimately desired from the community in which it functions. If there is no living, dynamic relationship between the two, education will be anemic, unreal, and unable to make any abiding impact on the mind and character of children. As social purposes change, as the techniques of production develop, as knowledge advances, as the meaning of culture deepens the life of community is powerfully influenced by all these factors. If the school is not able to keep pace with these changes and adjust its programmes to them, it becomes an outdated, backward-looking agency, an institution only interested in the teaching of certain prescribed courses and textbooks which may be no longer matter in any significant sense for the contemporary world."
>
> **- *K. G. Sayidain***

34.1 School as an Agency of Education

Education is a life-long process that begins at the cradle and ends at the grave. There are a number of educative agencies - the home, the school, the neighbourhood, the community, and the state which affect the educative process. The school is specially charged with the responsibility of providing the scheme of education. For the proper discharge of this 'special responsibility' assigned to the school, it is obligatory for all agencies affecting child growth and development, to join hands, have a common outlook and design a comprehensive programme for the physical, mental, moral, emotional, social, and spiritual growth of children. We are living in a dynamic society. This dynamic culture must be reflected in the school programmes. This will be possible only if there is an effective coordination among various agencies affecting the child.

34.2 School-Home Partnership

(1) Why teacher-parent cooperation?

It is almost a truism to say that unless the parents of 70 million students who are attending various types of educational institutions, and about two millions teachers who are staffing the different types of educational institutions, are brought together and enter into an intimate dialogue, no educational endeavour will succeed.

(a) For complete education of the child

They say that a pupil gets a fourth of education from his teacher, another fourth by his own efforts and the rest from his parents. If the teacher alone makes his contribution and the parents do not play their part, the education will be incomplete. The relations of a teacher and a parent with a child and their views about him are obviously different. For the teacher, a child is one of a large number of students in his class. To the parents, however, the child is a part of their own self and their future hope. The estimates of a child's ability, faults, and behaviour by teachers and parents often differ widely. It is only when the two come together and there is a perfect understanding between the parents and the teachers that the educational development of the child can be understood in the correct perspective. Parent-teacher cooperation is thus based on a bilateral understanding of a triangular relationship. The parties concerned are the parent, the teacher, and the child. The understanding is to centre round the growing personality of the child. A wise parent and a wise teacher should try to understand each other's efforts, so that the child's education may form an organic whole. The teacher on his side should understand how immensely his own immediate aims are furthered by the wholehearted sympathy of parents; the parents on their side should try to understand the limitations of the school. Chronologically and psychologically home starts the child off into life and its experiences. It is original and a basic source of informal and incidental learning which subsequently limits and slants the individual's content, quality, and rate of progress on different chosen fronts. In well-adjusted families, a child easily finds opportunities for full expression of his talents and development of his personality, but when family life is not harmonious it has an unhealthy effect on his development. The results of several studies have indicated that the progress of a child in the school is more closely co-related with factors in the home environment than with his intelligence. Parents in fact, are not only the first companions but also the first teachers of the children. The success of any educational programme stipulates healthy home influence in the early life of the student. The whole of the educational effort will be set at naught, if the parents pollute the early springs of life.

(b) For the improvement of education

Parental cooperation in the educational efforts is a valuable force in education. In the words of Bray: "It is hardly possible to overestimate the value of strong, sympathetic link between the home and the school." Promotion of talent and quality is one of the main goals of any system of education. In order to develop fully the gifts or talents a child has, it is necessary not only to have a closer understanding of the child himself but also of his home. Without such understanding a great deal of effort in school may be just wasted. A clever child may often not do well in school because of unhealthy and unwholesome home influences and surroundings. If the educational authorities are vigilant and have good contacts with the home, they would easily understand the various handicaps of a child who is lagging behind in the class and apply corrective measures well in time.

(c) For making homes helpful in the education

Parents can make their homes good nurseries instead of burial grounds for the noble sentiments inspired within the precincts of the classroom and the spirit of humanity and brotherhood cultivated in the school playgrounds. Parents should take a constructive interest in the education of their children. Indifference of parents towards the education of the children is a danger signal, because when the children sees the indifferent attitude of their parents towards their education, towards their institutions and towards their teachers, they cease to give importance to anything concerning education. Consequently, they become undisciplined. It is essential that guardians take proper interest in their wards.

(d) For the achievement of goals of education

The principal and the staff can get the cooperation of parents by keeping them informed regarding the aims of the school, the curriculum, methods of discipline, quality of teaching, administrative devices, and nature of the school plant and the needs of the school for improvement and development. For the preparation of institutional plans, their help and cooperation can be sought. The school can meet high standards usually associated with good homes. The school machinery may be geared entirely to the needs of the various age-groups of the students. The school can be a home away from home - a place where the sentimental love of the mother is supplemented by the thinking love of the teacher. A very happy stage in the education of the child will be reached when the teacher becomes the only true parent of the child and the parent the only true teacher of his children.

For successful education, parents must take positive steps to learn about the school and what it is trying to do for their children; in return the school must take into account how the child lives at home. At all stages, parents and teachers should help to make the children confident and secure.

(2) Area where parental cooperation is needed

The school needs parental cooperation in several fields:

- **(i)** Home work,
- **(ii)** Medical welfare,
- **(iii)** Lunch programme,
- **(iv)** Disciplinary problems,
- **(v)** Sex education,
- **(vi)** Moral and religious education,
- **(vii)** Curricular and co-curricular programmes,
- **(viii)** School's improvement projects,
- **(ix)** School's developmental projects.

(3) Goals of home-school relations

Home-School Relations have two broad goals:

- **(i)** To bring about a better understanding between teachers and parents, of what children are alike.
- **(ii)** To bring about a better understanding between teachers of good education.

(4) Values of home-school cooperation

When the above goals are achieved, youngsters gain in two ways:

- **(i)** They have a richer, fuller, more nourishing life in a school and out, than would otherwise be open to them.
- **(ii)** They get more consistent guidance in school and out; they stand a better chance of living up to the peak of their powers.

(5) Measures for securing cooperation

(i) Teacher's visits to the homes of the children: - If the teacher regards the parents of his pupils as friends and partners, frequent conferences to foster such relationships will be necessary. There is no better way to set about it than by making visits to the homes. These may be either *social or professional,* but they should always be *friendly.* Many teachers visit the homes of their children only when some child is in trouble or there is a problem to discuss. Consequently, home visits for both parents and teachers are often associated with unpleasant incidents. It should be ideal if the teacher visited parents only when relationships were pleasant. Children or parents should arrange these visits by a casual invitation to call or to attend some school occasion; but if such invitations are not forthcoming, the teacher should ask if he may call and make an appointment for the visit. Visits should be made as the need for them arises, but they should be unhurried and made at a time, if possible, when both parents are present. Teachers and parents are to be mutually interested in the childs development.

(ii) Parent's visits to the school: - If visiting the home of a child is good for the teacher, visiting the school should be good for the parents. Many schools fix regular visiting days. Some plan is better than none. But the practice is questionable because it fails to accomplish the purpose for which it is instituted. The primary purpose of the visitation of school by parents is that they may, in general, become acquainted with the educational goals of the school and specifically with application to their own children. This purpose is almost impossible for accomplishment of individual parents when the school is crowded with visitors. A better plan is to encourage parents to visits, one by one or in couples, to observe the normal, everyday work of the school and to remain there as long as they wish. Such visits should be unhurried.

(iii) Participation by parents in the educational process of the school:- One of the interesting developments in modern education is the practice of having parents' participation in the life of the school. Traditionally, the role of the parents was to observe the work of the school under carefully controlled conditions. The modern teacher, on the other hand, welcomes all help that a parent is willing and able to give. When the children are studying a topic favourite with the community, a specialist should be invited to act as a resource person on that subject.

(iv) *Participation of teachers in parents' groups:* - Whereas individual work with parents is essential for the welfare of children, group work with parents is also valuable. These groups may take many forms, Some teachers prefer what they call "Mothers Clubs," the nature of which is indicated by the name. A group of mothers having a common interest in children easily finds topics for group discussions. Such a club has its advantages. But if the educational process is a cooperative affair, fathers also must participate in it. Mothers, Club tends to exclude this important member of the educational partnership. Both father and mother must be invited to such clubs.

(v) Interest groups: - When the community is large enough to afford it, the sponsoring of interest groups is an effective way to work constructively with parents. These groups offer a wide variety of possibilities. Some schools sponsor nutrition groups, photography clubs for adults as well as for children, reading circles, first-aid, and home-nursing classes, etc. These interest groups offer not only to parent the opportunity to acquire new skills but also to the teacher the chance to know the parents of his children.

(vi) Personal notes to parents: - At regular intervals during the school year, teacher may send personal notes to all the parents. The notes should give a review or a bird's eye view of the school programme and the experiences the children are having. It may suggest the areas in which the parents can assist the teacher. This method of keeping in touch with parents is highly recommended. These notes may be sent along with the report cards at the close of the first and third quarters, and whenever the occasion warrants such a note.

(vii) Reporting to the parents: - The teacher has the full responsibility for the daytime care of children approximately for nine or ten months out of each year. Important and significant experiences take place during this time. Parents ought to be informed about them quantitatively and qualitatively. School Reports should not only report the childs's progress but also assist in establishing cordial parent-teacher relationships.

Reports that are sent to the parents regarding the progress of their ward after terminal and annual examinations should be elaborate showing the marks he secured in several subjects, his average daily conduct and perseverance, his achievements or otherwise in co-curricular work, his general attitude, cooperative spirit and the teacher's own opinion, if any, about his problems. The communication should be a two-way affair. The parents should be required to write back to the teacher about the child's peculiar problems in studies at home, his attitude towards school, the way in which he stands his leisure, and his hobbies. The school should then try to plan a programme for each individual child. It is expected that if this programme is adhered to, the best qualities in the child will be inculcated.

But the teachers should resist any unreasonable parental requests to give preferential treatment to their wards. Parents exaggerate the abilities or difficulties of their children. Teachers should take a balanced view and act accordingly.

Moreover, the School Report should contribute directly to the pupils growth. If the reporting system does not meet these three requirements, it needs overhauling. On the whole, there are four commonly used methods of reporting to parents:

- (i) The report card.
- (ii) The personal and informal letter.
- (iii) The evaluation of progress by the pupil with comments by the teacher and parents.
- (iv) Teacher-parent conferences.

(i) ***The Report Card:*** A good Report card should (a) place equal emphasis on the mental, social, and physical development of children, (b) eliminate comparison of the individual pupil with the achievement of the other pupils in the class, (c) indicate the aims of the school and the general objectives of education, (d) report the achievement of pupil in relation to the specific aim of each subject, (e) diagnose the pupil's difficulties and also make suggestions for the improvement, (f) provide for self-analysis, (g) consist of a personalised message to the pupil and parent, (h) indicate the relation of the pupil's present status in terms of requirement for graduation, (i) provide supplementary notice to parents of failing or unsatisfactory work, (j) be attractive in composition, appearance of printing and quality of paper.

(ii) ***Personal and informal letter:*** Many modern teachers are employing the use of personal letter as a substitute for the traditional monthly Report Card. This type of report has obvious advantages, provided it meets certain desirable criteria. One of the purposes of the report to parents is the establishment of a happy relationship with the teacher. Consequently, the letter should be *cordial, friendly, informal, and informing*. It should reveal the interest of the teacher in, and his knowledge of, each individual child. It should also suggest how the school and the home can cooperate in the promotion of the child's development. The letters should be in a language that parents can understand.

(iii) ***Letters to parent written by the pupils:*** The letters by pupil's can supplement other report forms and sometimes, substitute them. Children's letters, without the proper guidance of the teacher, will become meaningless. It is wise to use this record once or twice a year to supplement the usual reports adopted and used by the school. A pupil

can write on (a) What is the state of the unit of work current at the time of the report? (b) What type of boy or girl am I? (c) What kind of work do I do? (d) My comments, (e) Teacher's comment, etc.

(iv) ***Parent-teacher conferences:*** - Teachers should keep a cumulative folder for each individual pupil. Its contents can be used for pupil guidance. If progress reports of children are made to parents through conferences, many of the evils of the traditional report cards can be eliminated. The conferences should be informal, friendly, and cordial in nature. They should be held under conditions that are not hurried or strained. Both parents should participate in them. At its close, the teacher should prepare a written statement of what took place. Relevant portions of the statement should be copied in the child's record folder. Each conference should be carefully planned and fixed according to the parents' convenience.

(6) Parent-teacher associations

The chief instrument of bringing the school and the community in vital rapport with each other is the formation of parent-teacher associations. In meeting and talking with the parents, the teachers may learn many things that will help them to understand the student coming from that home. They may learn the economic condition of the home, the religious tendencies, and such facts concerning the home life of the students as possibilities of study at home, necessity for the student to work in the evenings to help support the family and opportunities for play and recreational activities. In return, the parents may see the necessity of prompt and regular attendance at school. They may acquire an understanding of the objectives of classroom instruction that will fit them to help and encourage the students. It is useful to the teacher. The knowledge that the work of a teacher is being appreciated by the parents of the children in his charge, gives him much solace and comfort and inspires him towards better and greater efforts. Thus parent-teacher associations may serve as an important two-way channel of communication between school and the community.

In progressive countries, this media of public relations has been fairly successful and they are proving a potent force in solving the problems and in furthering the interests of the school. In our country, the effectiveness of P. T. A.'s has been doubted and it has been held that whenever they have been started they have not met with an encouraging response. There appears to be lack of faith in both the partners – teachers and parents. Some positive steps should be taken by the teachers to make parents feel that the school belongs to them. The opinion of the parents should be welcomed and implanted within the resources of the school. The parents should have the feeling that they have their voice in the running of the school. Teachers should encourage wide participation on the part of the parents in the school activities on the level of responsibility. Let them share the school problems, and they will certainly start caring for them.

34.3 School's Partnership with the Community

The school's relationship to the home and to the community can be compared to the two concentric circles – the first and the smaller circle is the home; second and the larger circle is the community. One of the major tasks before the school today is to establish a two-way traffic between the school and the community. We can never shut out a school from the life of a community. School's report with life outside the school is a must for good education otherwise education will be anaemic, unreal, and unable to make any abiding impact on the mind and character of children. As social purposes change, as the techniques of production develop, as knowledge advances, as the meaning of culture deepens, the life of community is powerfully influenced by all these factors. If the school is not able to keep pace with these changes and does not adjust its programmes to them, it becomes an outdated, backward looking agency. In the present set-up, the school cannot be an island in the midst of the community. It has to be a 'watch tower' not an 'ivory tower.' The school must enrich the community and the community must support the school. Let us build up bridges between the two so that the two-way traffic is not only possible but pleasant and useful also.

The latest slogan in education in all the progressive countries is "Let us *study* the community, *use* the community, *serve* the community, and *involve* the community in the educational process." Let educational reform start with the re-linking of the school to life and the resorting of the intimate relationship between them.

No one can deny that the immediate community is a wonderful curriculum laboratory which can provide an extremely dynamic, interesting and real life opportunities for learning. Every community has, in his historical records, the stories of people and resources woven into the pattern of our national development. Basic social processes and problems operate in every community and these can be observed in action, as well as worked with for or against. The government can be understood in local, state and regional terms through people who are familiar to students. Social problems become concrete as we investigate them in our own communities. Thus the community provides concrete data on cultural, industrial, political, and geographic facts and relationships. These data are *tangible, seeable,* and *describable.* This is the reason that the school should take itself to the community, regard it as a laboratory, discover its resources, understand its culture, appreciate its problems, and also suggest solutions to these problems. It should open doors for experience through the use of resource people, field trips, community surveys, service projects, etc. It is not enough for a child to have the knowledge about the factories, the farms, social agencies and museums, council sessions and union meetings – he must have the 'acquaintance with' all these.

(A) Why the Teacher should Study the Community?

We can list the following reasons why the teacher needs to study the community.

(1) To understand the background of the pupils who come to the school and help them according to their needs.

(2) To utilise the community as a resource for the school curriculum.

(3) To utilise community leadership as a help in the development of the school's programme.

(4) To provide leadership to the school for community betterment and for the adult education of the out of school population.

1) *Studying the community in order to understand the background of the pupils:* The school has control over the "education" of the child for only a small part of his working hours – 8 months a year, five days a week and six hours a day. During the two months of vacation the school's influence over the child is practically nil. If the faculty of a school is to know and understand adequately their pupils, it needs to know the nature of the community from which the child comes, because it determines very largely the kind of a child he is. The teachers also need to know the educational influences which are operating simultaneously with the work of the school to enable him to develop in school educational experiences in consideration of and sometimes starting with those experiences the child has had elsewhere.

To approach two sets of students in the same class level in the same course with exactly the same teaching methods is to overlook what is known about the psychology of the learning process and about individual differences. It is inappropriate to use the same curriculum content for persons of widely differing socio-economic levels and varying amounts of experience outside of their own community. The attitude, desires and general value systems of the people of a given community are important in working with the motivation of the child in his school work. In some communities, the children are strongly motivated towards school achievement. In other communities, the child feels that school achievement makes very little difference in his life. A teacher who ignores the kinds of backgrounds from which his pupils come may find himself completely lacking in understanding of them. He may erroneously consider that they also come from the same type of background and have, in general, the same attitudes and other characteristics. Frequently, he assumes that they are all similar to those persons coming from his own background.

Teachers who are interested in making a study of the community may study the same under the following heads:

(a) The people
- i. Racial and national backgrounds
- ii. Birth rate
- iii. Size of community
- iv. Social structure
- v. Pressure groups

(b) Homes
- i. Physical condition
- ii. Ownership
- iii. Intra-family relationship

(c)
- (i) Business and professional opportunities.
- (ii) Basic industries
- (iii) Character of occupation
- (iv) Job opportunities
- (v) Wages and salaries

(d) Geographical and historical backgrounds
- (i) Location of community
- (ii) Local history

(e) Government
- (i) Political organisation
- (ii) Services
- (iii) Protection

(f) Health
- (i) Hospital and medical facilities
- (ii) Public health conditions
- (iii) Mental health

(g) Recreational facilities and needs
- (i) Adequacy of facilities
- (ii) Relationship to youth problems
- (iii) Relationship to homes

(h) Welfare needs
- (i) Agencies and provisions
- (ii) Attitudes
- (iii) Types needed

(i) Religious agencies
- (i) Activities
- (ii) Professional organisations – *satsangs*, etc.
- (iii) Civil groups such as Rotary's Association and political parties.
- (iv) Cultural groups such as clubs for the promotion of enjoyment of art, music, drama, literature, etc.
- (v) Welfare and charitable organisations, etc.

2) *Utilising the community as a part of the curriculum:* One of the important principles of teaching is to make learning experiences as concrete and realistic as possible. It is often possible to utilise things found in a community as a basis for learning. Museums, educational institutions, historic sites, places of geographical and scientific interests and other places can help the boys and girls

understand better something already included in the curriculum. Citizens in the community often can be brought into the schools as resource persons in order to enrich the explanations of the particular topic or idea.

3) *Utilising community leadership for advice to the school programme:* Often there are persons in the community who can be of great help in formulating proposals with respect to school policy within the broad framework of that already drawn by the department. A word of caution here! The school should remain to be the true representative of the community and must not become a tool in the hands of some groups to utilise education for their own ends,

4) *Providing leadership in community change:* The schools educational obligations are not limited exclusively to boys and girls of school age. Many times there are educational, cultural, and social needs of adults which can be met by the school better than by other agencies. The schools can take up some service projects, e.g. social service among the backward population of the town such as cleanliness, anti-mosquito campaigns, attending on the sick. School labour service may be organised on special occasions such as Republic Day, Independence Day, Gandhi Jayanti, and Gandhi's Death Anniversary, etc. Activities like planting of trees, road repair, and erection of platforms, cleaning of lanes, digging of manure pits, making of drains may also prove useful. Beautification of village through planting of trees, laying out of avenues, clearing up the public places like streets, temples, drains, etc. can help in bringing about an effective community change. Such community service projects lift education from the dull routine of leading each generation in the footsteps of its predecessor, to earnest yet joyous adventures in cooperative welfare. They help in raising the status of the pupils as they become participators in programmes of community development.

(B) School as a Community Centre

The modern approach to school-community relations is to regard the school as the 'capital' of the community. With tons of money invested in school buildings and equipments it is not enough to restrict its use to a few hours each day, five and a half days a week, or for only a few months in the year. It is, indeed unjust to keep the buildings open for only a thousand or at most twelve hundred hours a year for that is the exact situation. Most of the schools have been built, equipped, maintained, and financed by the public. Admissions is open to all, regardless of creed or political affiliations. Hence, all should be able to meet on an equal footing in the school which would become a natural community centre. Failure to use the school plant as a social community centre is poor economics as well as bad educational philosophy. It has now been recognised in our country that the starting point of education reform must be the re-linking of the school to life and restoring of the intimate relationship between them. Schools today must be a community centre – the 'capital' of the community. "It is to be an idealized epitome of life, reflecting within it the elements of all the major activities that make up the work of society. The idea of making the community the best of the school and the school best of the community represents a fruitful and essential extension of accepted educational thinking and practice. If we want to nourish and invigorate democracy, community study and service through school, education must be made essential. This movement is the most significant single development of its kind in our generation and it seems destined to teaching fields, with all types of students and in all community areas – local, regional, national, and international."

34.4 How to Make the School a Community Centre?

The following steps are recommended for making the school a community centre:

(i) Plan the programme of the school with reference to the needs of its community and its pupil. "The basic responsibility of any school," says the Secondary Education Commission on Teacher Education, "is two-fold: partly to the society that supports it, a society whose needs and demands reflect basic ideals, past experiences and immediate and prospective circumstances, and partly to the children and young people it serves." It may sound practically impossible in India, since the curricula of secondary schools are prescribed by the State Department of Education and the schools cannot attempt beyond the rigid limits. It may be remarked here that curriculum should be such as is 'capable of adaptation to local needs and situations." Craft is one of the compulsory subjects in the middle school. So a school should select a local craft. Similarly, the courses of study of a vocational school, should suit its peculiar geographical setting.

Community resources can go a long way in vitalizing class room instruction. The teacher can transform academic symbols into realities, by connecting them with conditions in the community about which the child is gaining first-hand knowledge from day to day. It would be tragic if a child in the third grade can point to a river on the map and give a definition of the river in terms of his geography textbook, but does not know that the stream flowing through his village is also the 'river' described in his geography book.

Similarly a child has read a whole lesson on cotton and its various uses. He is asked to state where cotton comes from. Is it not deplorable if he replies that it comes from the backs of some animals like sheep? It is the duty of the teacher to make his teaching as realistic as possible. He must make it clear, for example, that geography is nothing but a systematic account of the facts and phenomena of animal, plant, and human life; that composition is one of the ways of communicating experiences, ideas and feelings; that Arithmetic is but an epitomized and symbolic representation of the business life or the farm which they can observe for themselves outside the school. This method of presentation will preserve the unity and continuity of child's experience and bring about an interplay of influences between the school and the outside world. This method will enrich the school's educational programme by making it more concrete and vivid. The students will become automatically interested, more spontaneous. Out-of-school life of the child will benefit by the refining and enlarging influence of school ideas which will be carried over from the classroom to the child's home life. Thus the *child will find in the community an enlargement of the home, a play-field, and a summer club-room.*

Resources vary from community to community. The opportunities, which the teacher in an open rural area has, are only slightly related to those of a teacher in an urban area. But community study opportunities are available to every school and should be explored, especially those which lie within 'walking distance.' Evidently, the local factory, retail shop, business office is *real*, school children can *see* them, *hear* them, *ask* questions about them, and *examine* them minutely. If the teacher is resourceful and the class enthusiastic and clever, there should be no difficulty in listing available resources for proper and detailed study. Field trips, community surveys, and school camps should be organised for this purpose.

Field trips may be undertaken for securing information, changing attitudes, awakening interests, developing appreciations, promoting ideas, enjoying new experiences. They may be used to initiate a unit of study or serve as its core or give it the finishing touch. They impart first-hand knowledge, confirm, and supplement second-hand knowledge. They sharpen observation and evaluate principles.

Community surveys can provide excellent educational experiences to senior pupils. Surveys foster comprehensive understanding of community structure and processes in their everyday operation, interaction, and complexity. They are extremely useful in stimulating depth of insight into vital community problems and trends as these have been influenced by past conditions and present developments. They disclose problems which need solution.

Sharing in community improvements can prove useful for the pupils and the community. Involving individual activity of an integrated mental, physical emotional, spiritual nature, service projects are of genuine educational value to the pupils and of significant social value to society. If there is a regular and intelligent scheme of social service by students at public functions, and the school can anyway assure the community of its spontaneous help in adverse times, the school will automatically attract notice and sympathy.

Some other projects are education weeks, clean-up weeks, and youth projects in public safety, civic beauty, health, agricultural and industrial improvement, local history, and protection of resources. Teachers with foresight and patience can exploit projects for providing functional, realistic, and democratic education.

School camping is also a very useful activity. It encourages direct learning experiences. It has potential life situations. It is conducive to teaching by doing, seeing, hearing, testing, smelling, and feeling by the students. Teachers and other resource persons have to do the least talking.

(ii) The school can serve as the centre of adult activities. The school can be made the centre of social education. Bulletin boards may be set up to display new and other useful information about the local community in particular and the country in general. The school furniture-rooms, playgrounds, hall, gymnasium, and audio-visual aids may be freely lent to the adult community for purposes of education and recreation. Books from the school library may be issued to the adults in the community. But if, for dearth of books, this facility cannot be extended, at least the use of library reading room must be allowed.

Several adult organisations, such as literary societies and cooperative societies, may be allowed to hold their committee meetings in the classrooms. They may be invited to use the school hall for lectures, radio talks, and such religious discourses, as will not produce any adverse effects.

Schools can work on all days of the year and thus provide part-time courses to meet the needs of many older children who leave the school to earn a livelihood or to assist their parents in making both ends meet.

The teachers should be available for talks and discussions on various aspects of life. Schools can arrange various programmes – musical, dramatic, and cultural, and those relating to national and international affairs. The members of the community may be cordially invited to attend and even participate in them.

The school as a community centre should take steps to educate its members. It should organise classes in agriculture, domestic science, music, handicrafts and literature.

The school should not only be a mirror of the society but also its critic. *It should, therefore, launch campaigns against evils such as drinking, gambling, borrowing, etc.* The times call for measure to revitalise the community and to improve the school simultaneously.

The idea of making the community the best of the school and the school the best of the community represents a fruitful and essential extension of accepted educational thinking and practice. If it is wanted to foster democracy, community study, and service through the school, education must be made compulsory. The school must be made the social, intellectual, and cultural nerve centre of the community. It must become the educational dispensary of its community. School community relations will have to be made practical. Here is a challenge to the principal!

(C) Coordinating Community Forces for Action

For properly coordinating different community forces for action, two important tasks should be done:-

The first is to define the roles of school and community as precisely as possible. In meeting the needs of the school – in formulating educational policy, in planning the curriculum, in developing the methodology of teaching, in financing public education – what functions belong to the community? And similarly, in meeting the needs of the community, what exactly are the functions and capacities of the schools?

The second is to define the respective responsibilities of the school and community for developing effective means of communication.

The policies, directions, and goals of education should be set in consultation with the community. Methods of teaching are clearly in the professional domain, but the school owes an obligation to explain its methods to the community.

To conclude about what the schools can teach effectively the following points must be first decided. Which activities are clearly within the special competence of the school, which activities must be shared with community organisations; and which activities are clearly outside the school's domain?

Some components of the present day curriculum, such as home and family living, mental health, sex education, are clearly of special interest to various social agencies, public and private, where these agencies exist; there seem no reasons why the schools should assume primary responsibility. Instead, it would be far better for all concerned to work out a plan of *shared* responsibilities. In that case, the school should assume only those responsibilities which outside groups are not competent to handle.

There seems to be a tendency among the people to expect the school to assume more and more responsibility for individual welfare of the child. There is no absolute limit as to how far it can go. But the schools should investigate to determine just what their role is. Perhaps the schools would be wise to be the mobilizers in this case, rather than the mobilised. The school must serve the community, but they should be discreet in what they assume and not get involved in functions that could be better handled elsewhere. Schools should complement and strengthen the family, not usurp its responsibilities.

Again, the school curriculum is not the responsibility of the educators alone. It is the concern of the whole community. It is desirable to have a cross-sectional, fully representative committee of an advisory nature to advise the educators on the problems of curriculum.

(D) Measures for Winning Community Support

There are various ways in which the school can make its policy broad-based and develop itself into a real centre from which will radiate different activities and ideas that will envelop social and community life.

Here are some measures that may be adopted by the principal to win the support of the parents and the community at large:

(*i*) *Maintain a warm, welcoming school atmosphere.* Always be hospitable even to illiterate parents, however demanding they may be. If you want respect from the community, win its confidence, conduct yourself in a way that will make you trustworthy. You cannot demand respect simply because you are a teacher. You must earn it as a friendly "down to earth" human being who only happens to be a teacher.

(ii) Begin with real immediate problems right at hand. For best results there will be problems which (1) are of actual or potential concern to both parents and children, (2) are not controversial in terms of objectives, however much disagreement there may be on methods, (3) it can be solved, (4) require direct community participation by children and adults, (5) in their solution use varied resources which are readily available.

(iii) Get people working as teams – including, if possible, both children and adults on committees. In team work each individual shall accept responsibility for a part of the whole. Each may learn from the other how better to set up criteria, get facts, plan, execute, and judge project. Each can find stimulus and encouragement in the progress of the whole as he identifies psychologically with the larger enterprise. Never fail to give the lay people all possible credit for successes achieved.

(iv) "Plan big," but in order to assure initial success "begin small" and then expand as rapidly as possible. No growing programme can stand long on any plateau. It is always necessary to go ahead, or interest will rapidly dwindle. Do not stop too long to admire your achievements; instead move on to develop larger projects and to involve more participators in them. Remember that it is not enough merely to get people interested and concerned; they must also be moved to work actively in the project. Satisfying personal involvement is the key to developing interest and widening effort.

(v) Arrange for appropriate self-appraisal by the group itself. When all share in diagnosing a cooperative projects' effectiveness, they can grow together in both – insight and interest. Continued effective action is not possible without some kind of "how are we doing?" evaluation sessions at frequent intervals.

(vi) As the programme expands, develop appropriate structure and organisation. Sometimes cooperative community projects fail because expanding programmes outgrow their structural supports. So, having begun informally, with a minimum of organisation, you should go on to develop careful plans to find recognised leadership.

(vii) Responsibility for a community school does not lie solely with school people. Teachers may often need to take the lead in promoting community cooperation of this kind, but the community school is by no means "their show." Often school people do their best work when they follow community leadership.

(viii) Teachers should not be disheartened if progress is slow. A real community school cannot be developed in three days or 30 days or even in three years. There are long, hard traditions and much inertia to be overcome within school as in the community to achieve the end.

(ix) The vital importance of the individual teacher should never be forgotten or ignored. No school, however, well-equipped, is ever better than its teachers. A child is better off in a one-room rural school under an intelligent, imaginative, and dedicated teacher than in a multi-room city school, staffed by dull unimaginative and time serving bell-watchers. The community school is a recognised pattern for educational progress. Devoted educational leaders are needed to give the pattern a practical shape.

Objective Type Questions

Multiple Choice Questions (Tick ✓ the right option)

(1) School camping is very useful
- (a) Function
- (b) Activity
- (c) 'a' and 'b' both
- (d) None of the above

(2) Development of community needs a
- (a) Common interest
- (b) Activity
- (c) 'a' and 'b'both
- (d) None of the above

Fill in the blanks

(1) ____________ cooperation in the educational efforts is a valuable force in education [Parental]

(2) The ____________ should contribute directly to the pupils growth [School Report]

Important Questions

1. In what way in your opinion can parents be associated with the life of the school? Assess the educative value of such association.

2. "Education will thrive if schools become homes and homes become schools." (Vinoba Bhave) Comment.

3. Discuss the measures of reform which can be introduced in a school with the support of the community.

4. Discuss the relationship of a progressive school to the local community. How can a school function as an agency of community service?

5. As the head of a secondary school in a rural area what measures will you take to make your school a real community centre for the local population?

6. Suggest measures for winning parental cooperation for school programmes.

7. Suggest the guidelines for winning community support.

8. "The school teacher can best educate and influence the community by the work he does in or outside the school." Discuss and show what scope the school teacher in India has for educating or influencing the adults of his community.

9. How can a high school be developed into a community school?

10. Explain the importance of good school-home-community relationships. What can the teacher do in this regard?

11. "The school cannot be an island in the midst of the community. It should be a 'Watch Tower' not an 'Ivory Tower' institution." *H.S. Lawrence.* Comment.

12. "The school must lead in coordinating community effort for better education and must practice and promote democracy." Suggest ways how the school can play this role.

Unit VI

Health Education

35

The School Health Programme

"Health," according to the World Health Organization of the United Nations, "is a state of complete physical, mental, and social well-being and not merely the absence of disease or infirmity." Health thus defined cannot be attained through the efforts of medicine and pubic health alone, for where medicine and public health are things for people, the great need is to inform and motivate the young and old to bring to situations and decisions in life, the very best which they are capable in mind, body and spirit for the good of others as well as themselves.

The present concern in India regarding the lack of fitness of our children is persistent in drawing attention to the importance of education for total health. It is a happy augury for the future of education that we are becoming increasingly conscious of somatic factors in determining personality traits and attitudes as also the scholastic achievements of the scholars. Good health is a pre-condition for good education. The truth in the statement – a sound mind in a sound body, can hardly be disputed.

Health depends upon a reasoned awareness of the value of mental and physical fitness and of the means by which it may be developed and maintained. Fitness is not merely a function of living and acting, it requires that the individual understands the connection among health, nutrition, activity, and environment, and that he takes action to improve his mental and physical condition.

In its widest sense, health education is the very foundation of a successful public health programme. A great deal of ill health is the result of ignorance of simple rules of hygiene or of indifference to their practical application, and no single measure is likely to give a greater return in proportion to the outlay than health education.

35.1 Meaning and Definitions of Health

English word "Health" was used for condition of being "hale". The general meaning of health is attached to that healthy state through which all functions of the body and mind are accomplished properly and actively. Some definitions are being given below for giving a more clearer meaning of health.

(1) J. F. Williams- "Health is the quality of life that enables the individual to live most and to serve best."

(2) W.H.O. - "Health is a state of complete physical, mental, and social well-being and not merely the absence of disease or infirmity."

(3) Webster Collegiate Dictionary: - "Health is a state of being hale and sound in body, mind, or soul especially from physical disease or pain."

On the basis of the above mentioned definitions we can say this, that in health is included physical power in adequate quality, activeness or alertness and tolerance. Along with this, mental health is also included, by which needs of daily life may be fulfilled. With this view a healthy person should possess the following qualities:

(1) Sense of well-being.

(2) Self confidence.

(3) Self control.

(4) Cheerfulness.

(5) Absence of disease.
(6) Wholesome mental attitude.
(7) Free from anxiety.
(8) Courage.
(9) Ability to work with others.

Perfect health is a fine concept which cannot be attained by any means. Optimum health is that highest state of healthiness which can be achieved by individual. For achieving this objective, individual should be always ready.

The health of an individual is determined partly by parenthood and mainly by those elements which influence the health. The main elements affecting the health of individual are the following:

(1) Whole food.
(2) Physical activity- outdoor games, exercise, etc.
(3) Sleep.
(4) Proper vocation.
(5) Use of leisure.
(6) Healthy mental views towards life.
(7) Proper care of feet.
(8) Doctors' services as per needs.

35.2 The Important Role of the School in Health Education

The home and the family carry the primary responsibility for providing the total health of the child, but the school has a unique opportunity and role to play in contributing to the healthy development and total health education of each child. The school must recognise and assume its responsibility for providing an environment and experiences planned with the needs of growing, and developing, children. The school must accept its responsibility to foster understanding of the role of health in living and learning to live.

The school is in a unique position for promoting and constructing values, setting examples, and teaching children and youth the skills which will enable them to enjoy by obtaining and maintaining optimum fitness for living in today's and tomorrow's world.

That the responsibility is not that of the doctor alone is a new concept which must be understood and supported by society as a whole in order that medicine may exercise its full influence on human lives and play its part in building a better world. That is where education is involved. The improvement in the health of the nation will have to be recognised. It is more a matter of education and less a matter of legislation and sanitary engineering. The school will have to shoulder this big responsibility now. Health education will have to be conducted through teaching in the schools – elementary, secondary, and higher.

Health education as a purposeful programme in the institution of training, is a recent development full of vast potentialities.

There are solid reasons for making school play a major role in health education:

(i) *To learn effectively, a child or youth needs good health.* In the final analysis, health is a basic goal of all education, for the student can hardly achieve any other goal without having good health.

(ii) *Children and youth tend to respond better than do older people to health education in the development of desirable health attitudes and desirable health practices.* It is more difficult to change the ways of adults. The earlier, that an individual learns the elements of healthful living, the more likely it is that they will be applied.

(iii) *Children and youth can receive correct instruction from the qualified teachers in the school instead of relying only on the information obtained from the home and from their peers.* It is generally found that the information which the child picks up from these persons is often inaccurate and at times even dangerous.

(iv) *Now-a-days, with the increased scientific knowledge, the rules of healthful living have become more complicated and require, therefore, a greater amount of learning.* The schools are in the best position to provide time for this.

THE SCHOOL HEALTH PROGRAMME

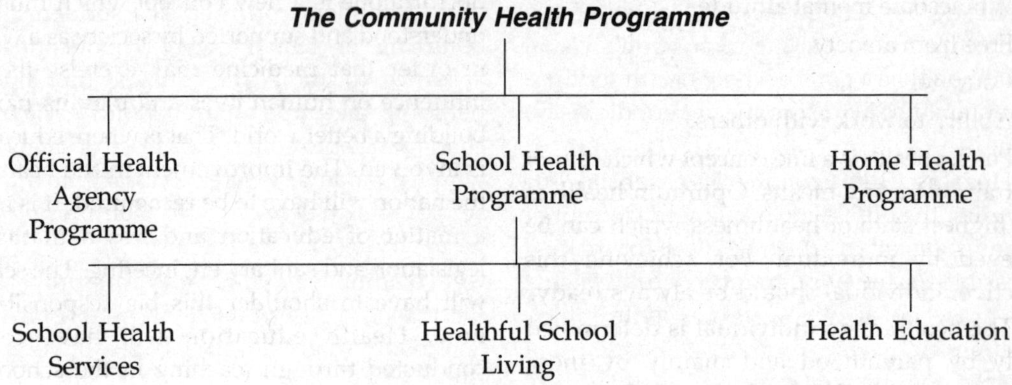

Fig. 24

(v) *The school reaches all individuals of the community from eleven or twelve years.* The face-to-face methods of classroom teaching can prove much more effective.

(vi) *The more the school has done before an individual reaches adulthood, the easier it will be for officials and voluntary health agencies to carry on from there since they will be dealing with more informed and sympathetic adults.*

(vii) *Parents too can be informed on health principles as some health education will be brought home to the parents by children receiving health instruction in the schools.*

35.3 What do we mean by the School Health Programme?

The school health programme is defined as "the school procedures that contribute to the maintenance and improvement of the health of pupils and school personnel, including health services, healthful living and health education." The school health programme is closely related to two other programmes of the school, physical education, and education of the handicapped child.

(1) School Health Services

There are certain specific reasons for providing school health services. These reasons include:

(a) They contribute to the realisation of educational aims.

(b) They are necessary to minimise the hazards of school attendance.

(c) They are important in adapting school programmes to individual capacities and needs.

There are six major phases of the school health service, (i) Health Appraisal, (ii) Health Counselling and Follow up, (iii) Emergency Care in Schools, (iv) Communicable Disease Control, (v) Identification and Education of Handicapped Children, (vi) Health of School Personnel.

Health Appraisal

Health appraisal is the process of determining the total health status of a child through such means as health histories, teacher and nurse observations, medical examinations.

Health appraisal is a cooperative process in which the responsibility is shared by the physician, nurse, school psychologist, teacher and others. Teachers are in the best position to reveal evidence of a health problem – their observation need to be followed by a medical examination by the physician. Cumulative health records are used in the school for maintaining information about each pupil as he progresses from his first year at school until he leaves at the end of his high school years.

Two phases of the appraisal programme – vision and hearing testing – both are especially important to improve the pupil's ability to benefit by his attendance at school. So a programme for appraising each pupil's visual status should be a part of school health services. There should be a programme of periodic vision testing.

Hearing, like vision, is essential for providing the pupil with a balanced concept of the environment in which he lives, for making it possible for the pupil to receive full benefits from his school activities, and for contributing, to his physical safety. It is recommended that children be tested annually during the elementary school years starting in kindergarten, since this is a period where hearing impairments may begin, and less frequently during the secondary school years.

Health Counselling and Follow-up

Health counselling is a procedure for helping pupils and parents to gain insight into the nature and significance of conditions revealed by various appraisal techniques.

The specific aims of health counselling are:

(i) To give pupils the information about their health status, revealed by appraisal procedures which they can use to good advantage.

(ii) To interpret to parents the significance of health problems and to encourage them to obtain needed care for their children.

(iii) To motivate pupils to want and accept needed treatment.

(iv) To promote each pupil's acceptance of responsibility for his own health in keeping with his stage of maturity.

Actual improvement in the health of children depends more on counselling and follow-up than on any other school activity. Teachers, Principals, Nurses, Physicians, all have important roles to play in this phase of the school health service.

Emergency Care in schools

The first aid or emergency care programme of a school is a part of the school health service. The school has five distinct responsibilities in case of accidents or in case of sudden illness occurring in school or in school-connected activities, (i) immediate care and first aid, (ii) notifying the pupil's parents, (iii) getting the child home or to some other place of safety, (iv) guiding parents, where necessary, to further sources of treatment, (v) completing the necessary records and reports.

To administer emergency care properly in the school, it is desirable that suitable facilities and appropriate supplies be available at all times. Each school should have a room designated as the "health room" where children can be sent when sick or injured, and where other school health activities can be conducted. It should contain a cabinet with appropriate fist-aid supplies. First-aid should be readily available when needed. All school personnel should be trained in first-aid.

Communicable Disease Control

Communicable diseases are a big menace to the community. So in addition to the health departments and the schools, everybody has to work to maintain control of these diseases.

The school responsibility arises principally from two factors:

(a) During the time that children are in school, the school is expected to protect their health.

(b) The congregating of children in a classroom increases the possibility of communicating many diseases.

The programme, in this direction, includes the education of parents and pupils, the encouragement of immunization during infancy, and continuous efforts to have sick children stay at home.

Identification and Education of Handicapped Children

It is generally observed that among the school population there are children having physical handicaps. This indicates a need for special school adjustments or adaptations. It is essential that these children be identified through the health appraisal programme of the school health services so that appropriate educational adjustments can be made for them.

Health of School Personnel

Teaching is hard work. One of the qualities which every teacher must have is good health. A healthy teacher has abundant energy, buoyancy, and ability to think clearly and plan carefully.

The appraisal, maintenance, and improvement of teacher health is an important responsibility of the health service programme of the school. Teachers' health must be preserved and amount of illness among teachers must be reduced.

The teacher must be free from handicap conditions. He must have a periodic check to discover his health status.

(2) Healthful School Living

Healthful School Living comprises the second major area of school health programme. It is "the provision of a safe and healthful environment, the organisation of a healthful school day, and the establishment of interpersonal relationships favourable to emotional, social, and physical health."

When we consider that millions of children and youth spend approximately five hours each day for about 180 days annually in school buildings or under school supervision, one can understand why the way they live in school is important not only from the educational point of view but also from that of its bearing upon their health.

Healthful living is a goal of school health education. It contributes to the pupils' understanding and appreciation of health.

It is the responsibility of school authorities to provide facilities which are conducive to learning and to health. The school should provide an environment that encourages good teaching, protects health, and fosters appreciation of beauty in form and colour.

Let us discuss major phases of healthful school living.

(3) Healthful Arrangement of School Day

Of the several factors of the school administration that affect the health of pupils, the most important are: (i) the length of the school day as well as the school year, (ii) the problem of getting to and from school, (iii) pupil grouping, (iv) the way in which pupil behaviour is handled, (v) the procedures for reporting pupil's progress, and (vi) school rules and regulations.

Children may become fatigued when school sessions are too long or when there is insufficient provision for alternating mental and physical types of experiences. The requirements concerning homework may have a bearing upon the health of pupils. So, all these factors need to be considered.

Emotional Aspects: The teacher has a great bearing upon the emotional health of his pupils. It is the teacher who largely sets the emotional tone of the classroom. A well-adjusted teacher can readily convey to his pupil attitudes of cheerfulness, enthusiasm, friendliness, and fairness when he practices them himself.

Teaching methods, which respect the personality of the pupils, should be used. Cooperative work of the pupils and teacher are desirable. The authoritarian approach to teaching tends to contribute to emotional problems.

Adequate Physical Facilities: The school has the responsibility for providing an environment that is conducive to safe living at school, and the school should help to teach every pupil to live safely in this environment. It is necessary; safety is promoted in classrooms, playgrounds and science laboratories, etc.

The school building, classrooms, the playgrounds, etc. should be kept clean and attractive. Dustbins may be placed at suitable corners. Toilet facilities may be provided, floors and walls should be properly cared for, and various classes may be given in turn duty of seeing that the school compound is clean.

It is important that schools give sufficient attention to lighting, heating, and ventilation, water supply, and waste disposal.

School Sanitation: In every school, sufficient care should be taken so that the sanitary arrangements are up to the mark. A sanitary committee, consisting of a representative from each class, can inspect the classrooms and the school surroundings from time to time.

In the residential schools, the dining rooms and kitchen should be often checked. The draining and washing places should be cleaned well.

Health Instruction: It is the responsibility of the school to acquaint every pupil with the need for maintaining excellent health. It is necessary that pupil knows about his own physical condition, what good health is and how to acquire it; how to avoid illness and accidents and how to protect the health of others. It is equally essential that he knows about sex, value of good nutritious food, safety, sanitation, mental and emotional health, etc.

In the lower grades, health teaching should be primarily integrated with other subjects. In higher classes, separate class periods may begin to be labeled "Health." Health instruction may be given the same recognition as other subjects in regard to placement in the curriculum. Direct health instruction in physiology and hygiene classes may be taken up. Instructions regarding traffic and street safety may be given. Extension lectures to the whole school may be given by the physicians. Health instructions may be imparted through subjects like biology, general science, physical education, home economics, and social studies.

35.4 Scope of Health Instruction

In developing a programme in health instruction, some of the factors that must be considered are the needs of the children as revealed by a medical examination, knowledge tests, and a study of their home life; the expressed interests of the children; the opinion needs of children in these grades; and a study of many other programmes of health instruction in order to compare the material and methods that have been in other places.

The course should include the following topics:-

Food – it's physiological importance, its source, its contamination, its preparation, its digestion, its assimilation, and its excretion.

Water, air, rest, exercise, recreation, sleep. The influence of abnormal conditions, and the bad habits on health; the causes of diseases and our defence against them; and special hygiene such as domestic hygiene, community hygiene, sex hygiene, mental hygiene, first aid, etc.

Junior teachers must begin hygiene lessons by practical methods carried out perseveringly; since no other way can be successful. He must not ask the child to write out all the reason why his hands ought to be clean before he has insisted on washing them. Every single child on every single morning of the school year must be examined to see if he is fit to join in school life, i.e. his hands and face clean, hair brushed, nails short, clothes tidy and as clean as possible. Every tooth drill can be made a game, and children can be given badges for neatness. So, first the practice and secondly, the theory.

The simplest rules of health can be taught in an interesting fashion by the use of attractive pictures on the walls illustrating washing of bodies and teeth and so forth, so that the children realise the beauty of a clean and healthy childhood. Scrap books can be kept by the children and similar pictures pasted in them with simple sentences written alongside. Health rules can be made into a rhyme and learnt by heart or into a code like the Scout Law. Stories can bring out the moral that cleanliness is next to godliness. The point is that *instruction in health should be made as interesting as possible: it should not be a drudgery of mere memory work.* Instruction in health should not invariably use fear as a motive, for conduct controlled by fear is the conduct of a slave.

Health education can begin with anything – opening a window, dusting a cupboard, covering a milk jug, taking a duster out doors to shake it. There is no school so defective that in it health education is impossible.

So many opportunities for linking theory and practice arises from the daily school routine. Arrangements for preventing the spread of communicable diseases among pupils, for coping with minor accidents, for changing clothes and washing hands and brushing hair, all can reinforce what is taught in the classroom, as can well-conducted milk distribution and school meals. School lunches, incidentally, might be of greater educational value were they to give choice of dishes, possibly on the cafeteria system. The provision of an ideal dietary by the school caterer may provide material for a useful object lesson on nutrition and may, more importantly habituate children to the tastes of desirable foods.

Contact with society at larger may be established by the introduction of doctors, nurses, and other health workers as occasional visitors to the classroom, and by discussion of local health services and health committee reports. All this, however, will fail if it is conceived as something which can be just "added" to formal lessons in order to make them less abstract. Practice must not be merely laid on as a veneer to theory; theory and practice must be welded into an indissoluble whole.

In the senior school, hygiene should be taken as a serious study along with Biology and Botany and so forth. A textbook for the pupils is always desirable. Again, the first emphasis should be on the practical side. Teachers themselves should appear neat clean and in the classroom, and insist on daily cleanliness in their classroom. They must take a parental interest in the physical fitness of their class and see that any child suffering from bad eyes, dull ears, etc. receives immediate attention.

Instruction with regard to hours of sleep, daily excretion, teeth cleaning, suitable clothing, etc. should be given. The drill instruction can work hard at making feeble backs strong and straight, shoulders square, walking brisk and active, chest developed by special exercises, and the general bearing of his pupils fearless and vigorous. Above all, activity should be the keynote of our education.

The syllabus of the high school should also include simple physiology and personal hygiene, care of drains, refuse, ventilation, care of drinking water and food with some facts about vitamins and a balanced diet, exercise, cleanliness of house and compound and information about the most prevalent disease and their treatment.

Teachers should also see that children are not overworked with home work. If the class teaching is efficient and the home task sensibly set, children should not need to spend more than one hour in the evenings from the 8th class downwards, and younger children should have nothing strenuous than a little writing practice to do.

How to Impart Health Education? The days when health education was regarded as synonymous with the delivery of public lectures are gone for good. Educators now have at their disposal a whole battery of visual and auditory aids with which to vary and enliven their teaching. It needs to be pointed out here that there is nothing unique about the methods of health education. Health education is merely one strand of the total educational weave. It must provide assumptions about the way life is lived, inculcate habits conducive to health, impart information which will provide a rational basis for habits already and yet to be acquired, encourage healthy attitudes and develop appreciations.

All aspects of health education must be carried on at all stages of the educational process although certain aspects are of greater importance and more easily dealt with at particular periods.

(i) The Environment: - The most potent of all educational media is, of course, the

environment. It is the type of house into which a child is born and the type of parents and siblings in its family which provide the material upon which the infant, long before it can speak or understand speech, bases its assumptions about the way life is lived. It is the type of school building and the type of school teacher which mould later assumptions about desirable ways of life. Any scheme of health education must, therefore, give high priority to the improvement of the physical and human environment; for in so far as environment negates teaching, we cannot go far.

(ii) *The Spoken Words:-* Though learning by doing is making some headway, the more usually recognised teaching medium is still the spoken word.

Fine variations of teen and emotional loading render possible not merely factual instruction but the reorientation of listener's attitude. Speech as a medium of factual instruction must be delicately adjusted to the particular audience. Simplicity, specificity, and varied repetition are the keys to successful oral instruction.

Discussions and lectures should be arranged in the schools which not only will instruct the pupils but also amuse them.

(iii) *Printed Material:* - Leaflets, booklets, and pamphlets can also serve as the medium of giving health education. These should be made available within the easy reach of children. Posters and charts are another form of printed material which can promote health education. If they are to be of real value, great care must be exercised in deciding just how and when they are to be used.

The popular press as a medium of health education is also gaining importance. Frequent letters to the editor on topical health matters which have become a common feature of modern newspapers can exert wide influence. The provision of short news paragraphs about the activities of the local clinic, the local school medical service, etc. can prove most effective.

(iv) *Film and Film Strip:* - The film is the latest method of imparting health education. It has the unique ability to portray motion and speed. Some of the films produced by the Ministry are of a really high standard of excellence. Films have importance because they directly appeal to the eye. So well-made film strips are invaluable, especially with topics that require repeated or detailed exposition.

(v) *Radio:* - It is unnecessary to emphasise the enormous possibilities of radio in health education, for most homes have a radio set. Health education by radio must not, however, be too "serious" if it is to reach those who most need it. In recent years, we have seen the development of some excellent discussion programmes bearing on various aspects of health, while dramatic presentation of health material has also produced some good programmes. Health educationists can make manifold the value of such programmes by a simple device of obtaining advance plans of programme and drawing the attention of pupils to what is forthcoming.

It is a great mistake to look upon radio as primarily a "mass" medium of education, for in one way it is the most intimate medium. By no other means, except occasionally by personal visits, is it possible for the health educator to obtain entry into the private family circle. Radio has, therefore, a peculiar intimacy which is often overlooked. Children's programmes might include occasional health rhymes, health plans etc. , but they must be very brief, very simple and technically excellent – for it would be a folly to destroy what might be good entertainment by ill-prepared health-material.

With rapid spread of television, new problems and new opportunities face us. The addition of visual to auditory power makes it clear that, used with responsibility and imagination; television could be a most potent instrument in raising the general level of health knowledge and health behaviour of the whole community.

(vi) *Mechanical Aids and Exhibitions:* - Certain mechanical aids can be exploited for giving health education. These can show what happens when a child is inoculated against diphtheria. It would not be difficult to devise a "quiz cabinet" which lights up when the button showing the correct answer to some health query is pressed. One can imagine the enthusiasm with which children would visit a "health arcade" planned on such lines.

Travelling vans for rural and suburban areas, railway coaches for large town stations, shop windows in busy streets each present their special opportunities and pose their special problems.

Whatever the media available, careful consideration must be given to their utilisation. Proper tool should be used properly, for we cannot tolerate blundering efforts at health education. Our approach must be that of the enthusiastic yet discriminating craftsman.

Right methods and right programmes alone can ensure the health of our children. A nation cannot afford to allow the major parts of its children and future citizens to grow up defective, under nourished and ill-developed in mind, body and spirit. Keeping a child continuously on the right load through all the periods of development is real achievement and it should result in a well developed, physically fit adult. "Here then is a golden opportunity" writes May Benjamin, "For the state to lay the foundation of a strong and healthy nation, for the children of today should be the promise of a better world, for are they not the citizens of tomorrow?"

35.5 Mental Health

(1) Importance of Mental Health

In recent years, psychological literature has borne testimony to the loss of manpower that has resulted from illness produced by mental causes. Accident proneness, absenteeism, and truancy are evidence of this sort of ill-health. There are many cases of delinquency. Helping the child fighting the illness in some way or the other and resolving the internal conflicts is thus an important task of the school. Schools are legitimately concerned about the mental health of student. They should be able to help their students avoid mental breakdown and achieve healthy personality growth. These are legitimate concerns of education.

It is said that a sound mind can only be found in a sound body. Physical fitness is not an end in itself, but is a "means" of promoting the mental and moral health of a child. Mental fitness makes children more useful persons in the world and better able to help others. It equips them to undertake work and pursue occupations which are suited to their taste. When we speak of mental health, we mean the health of the personality as a whole, considered from the physical point of view.

There are two great enemies of mental health, which are commonly found. These are the *feeling of insecurity* and the *feeling of inferiority*. These two perhaps more than any thing else prevent the child from exercising his powers and abilities in a normal way, and to the fullest extent. The small child, as he sets out on his journey, has a feeling of insecurity; in the face of his environment, physical and social, he feels helpless. This feeling should gradually pass away as he grows up. But if it does not do so, if fear persists and gains control of his life then he will remain uncertain of himself and incapable of constructive and courageous action. He will lack confidence in himself. He will be imitative rather than creative. He will be unable to use his powers as he should use them, and result will be a personality that is stunted and ineffective. Similarly a feeling of inferiority will have the same negative effects. If the child grows up with an increasing feeling that he is not as good as others that whatever efforts he makes are doomed to ineffectiveness, that failure is his portion and that success can never come his way, then the dynamism which is necessary for a healthy personality either disappears or refuses to develop. The feeling of inferiority is endangered and it results in repressions and inhibitions or in exaggerated reactions which cut at the very root of harmonious development and of mental health.

Healthmindedness is essential to productivity and enjoyment in nearly every wholesome enterprise, and its cultivation is one of the important tasks of the educator. The first task of the teacher is that it should give to children all possible chances of exercising their instinctive powers and should use the instinctive powers for a high and worthy purpose by sublimating them. Again, it is said that health and physical strength are responsible very largely for the saneness of our thinking. Healthy thought is the great panacea in the world, so it will be wise for the teacher to give good thoughts to the pupils. Further, mind is the healthy sculptor and cannot surpass the mental health pattern. If there is a weakness in the thinking model, there must be corresponding deficiencies in health stature. There should be little worries although there may be a lot of work for work kills no one, but worry has killed multitudes. Worry is a chisel which cuts cruel furrows in the face; on the other hand, cheerfulness works miracles. Laughter is a remedy which removes all maladies and rescues men from the gloomy thoughts which make their life miserable. The teacher from the very beginning should help his pupils to use their powers in healthy ways, should seek to interest them in worthy objects – objects which will form centres of positive sentiment. He should help them to integrate their personalities as they develop so that harmony is achieved and conflict is avoided as far as possible.

(2) *Measures to Secure Mental Health*

(i) The teacher should develop an attitude of friendship towards the pupil. He will feel that someone is interested in him and is ready to help him. Affection and friendship are positive forces which will help to bring out all the best that is there in the child.

(ii) Ample freedom should be given to the child to exercise all his powers of choice and judgement.

(iii) By the encouragement of confidence, honesty, cheerfulness, generosity, self-discipline, cooperativeness, persistence, ingenuity, vigilance, and a sense of social responsibility.

(iv) By the development of a home and school routine which provides opportunity for free choice within a supporting frame-work of accepted behaviour.

(v) Individual attention may go a long way to nip in the bud tendencies, which left to themselves, result in disaster.

(vi) Sex instinct should be properly sublimated. If the children are helped to use this power in different kinds of creative work, we shall have gone a long way on the road towards helping them to achieve mental health. It should, therefore, be the aim of the teacher to strive to give an education which will give full scope to the creative powers of his pupils.

(3)*Functions and Responsibilities of Teachers*

The teacher has a very important role to play in the School Health Service programme. He comes into contact with the children so often – that he is likely to be the first person to notice *functional signs* of diseases, which appears before *physical signs*. He finds that certain pupil cannot see from a distance what is written on the blackboard, some pupils are sleepy, some pupils have running nose, some pupil remain absent from the school quite often. Such defects may be pointed to the school physician as early as possible because these have a positive correlation with the scholastic achievement of the child.

The teacher should know the signs of different diseases, incubation period after exposure, the duration of communicability, and the means of transmission. Children suffering from communicable diseases should not be allowed to attend class. In this respect, cooperation of the parents must be obtained.

The teacher has added responsibility of reflecting health teaching in a positive way. Both the physical and mental health of the teacher must be good for both have a strong effect upon the developing personalities with whom the teacher comes into extended contact. The health practices and attitudes acquired by the pupils, the quality of the human relationships, and the "emotional climate," that exists in the room are almost without exception reflections of the behaviour and example of the teacher. The teacher, consequently, owes it to himself as well also to his pupils to assume responsibility for maintaining his best physical condition.

35.6 The Major Health Area

(a) Nutrition

Nutrition may be defined simply as the science providing the body with the nourishment which it needs for growth, maintenance and repair. Recent researches in nutrition problems have shown that very complex, chemical substances known as vitamins are absolutely indispensable to normal growth and development. These substances are contained especially in fresh, green vegetables, milk, butter, eggs, cord liver oil and in the outside coating of most grains. The lack of these vitamins leads to so many diseases. Malnutrition is the prime factor in the erosion of health. The malnourished children are generally under-developed, they are either too short or too light for their age, lacking in vigour and poise with a strained and worried facial expression. They fall a prey to so many chronic diseases. In the period of adolescence, malnutrition causes grave harm. The Indian Council of Medical Research and World Health Organisation recently surveyed several states in south India and found that 2 percent of the children belonging to the poor socio-economic groups suffered from 'frank' signs of deficiency. If it is assumed that for every case of 'frank' signs there are probably 10 children on the border line of malnutrition the magnitude of the problem becomes colossal. A survey carried out in Calcutta in 1954 showed that 75 percent of the children had some defect; and nutritional disorders constituted the biggest deficiency (40 percent). Surveys carried out in various schools in 16 districts of Uttar Pradesh in 1949-51 showed that, out of 6,400 boys examined, more than 3,700 had one or more defects. The results of other surveys tell the same story and it may, therefore, be concluded that the existence of disease is very high among Indian children and one of the most important contributory causes is under-nutrition or malnutrition. Report of the Secondary Education Commission points out: "At no period of life does malnutrition play such a large part in causing ill-health, or in promoting defects of growth as in the period of adolescence."

It is a universally recognised fact that an ill-nourished or under-nourished child cannot be taught properly. To try to educate under-fed children, is not only wasteful of the teacher's energy but is also cruel to the child because deterioration of physique is promoted by exhausting the nervous system. At the same time, the School Health Committee which submitted its interim report about 3 years ago pointed out, that the incidence of sickness and disease among school children due to malnutrition is extremely high. For the proper education of the child, he must be fed properly. The working efficiency of a child depends to a considerable extent upon the daily intake of certain nutrients and daily eating habits. It is of utmost importance that nutrition education is imparted to the pupil in school.

The primary aims of nutrition education should be to establish good habits and attitudes which will result in intelligent selection and consumption of nutritious food throughout life. Children cannot be depended upon to select by instinct a diet that meets nutritive values. Some sort of formal instruction is necessary.

Objectives of Nutrition Education

The following objectives may prove useful in planning nutrition education programmes for schools: -

(1) To understand what constitutes an adequate, balanced diet.

(2) To recognise that good nutrition is essential to good health and good diet is not possible without good eating habits.

(3) To know the nutritive values of individual foods and the supplemental values of a variety of foods.

The emphasis on teaching in the early grades should be on the development of correct food habits and attitudes. Some factual material can be introduced early. This knowledge should be progressively increased until, by the end of the middle school, children at that age have learned the basic facts of nutrition. In the higher secondary school, the information needed is that of wide application to food buying, meal planning and such factors as preparing the students for eating away from home and looking forward to the responsibilities of marriage and feeding the family.

Schools can help in another way also. If the home from which the child comes cannot or will not give him the food that is necessary for his growth, the school must step in and give the required food. It is now being realised in progressive countries that to make up the deficiencies of malnutrition is also the responsibility of the school. A very important programme that has grown up in recent years in India is that of mid-day meals for children in primary school. At present, about 40,000 schools provide mid-day meals to about 24.61 lakhs of children. With the help of UNICEF, which gives milk power free of charge, milk is distributed to about 6 lakhs of primary school children. In the third plan, the programme has been extended still further.

It is further suggested that in residential school and hostels, balanced diets suited to different ages should be prescribed by nutrition experts and managements be advised about proper standards for children's diet.

The Indian Council of Medical Research after many years of study, has standardised the dietary requirements of children from birth to 21 years. These will be of great use in providing supplementary school meals to children as a part of the school feeding programme. It has also been found by a comparative study of the prevailing diet with the standard requirements, that major types of malnutrition encountered among children are attributable to deficiencies of proteins, vitamin A and B complex and calcium. Besides, there is evidence of gross caloric under-nutrition. It has also been found that the nutritional deficiencies vary from region to region. Considerable research work has, therefore, been done by the Nutrition Research Laboratories of the Indian Council of Medical Research on the preparation of menus for school meals suited to different regions of the country. These menus take into consideration the common dietary deficiencies in that region and also the locally available food materials and are so designed that a nutritional meal according to standard requirements could be provided at low cost which varies, at the present day prices, from 8 paise to 12 paise per meal per day. As many as 52 such menus have been designed so far and the work is in progress.

The Central Food Technological Research Institute at Mysore has prepared a multipurpose food of a very good quality consisting of defeated groundnut flour. One ounce of multipurpose food yields about 12 grams of proteins and a substantial amount of calcium, vitamin A, and riboflavin.

35.7 School Meals

In the wake of under-nutrition and malnutrition of most of the Indian children, the significance of a school meal becomes obvious. It will assist in improving the health and physical development of the child. It will also play an important role in education because children who are healthier will make quicker and sounder progress in their studies. It is essential that we develop a universal programme of the school meals as an integral part of its programme of universal, free, and compulsory primary education.

School meals may be of three types: - the food served in the school by the school, the food brought to the school by the pupils, and the food purchased by the pupils outside the school from the vendors and *rehriwalas.*

Special problems which must be considered by the school head, in addition to the serving of nutritious, well-prepared food, include maintenance of sanitary standards to reduce the possibility of spread of disease through food, the health of the food service personnel, and the unwise practice of selling the articles on 'rehris', etc.

It is necessary that proper arrangements are made for the pupils to take lunch. There should be a lunch room, with washing and drinking, facilities so that those who bring their meals can eat conveniently and in good and healthy surroundings.

Children should not be allowed to purchase the things from 'vendors' and 'rehriwalas' as the food stuff often laden with dust is harmful to their health. The school cafeteria should be carefully supervised.

The school meal programme has been taken up in standard cities of India. In Madras, with the assistance of local donors the state and CARE, it is expected that the number of children served by the school meal programme would rise to about 1.7 million. *Kerala* has organised a school meal programme with the assistance of CARE, which has now almost 100 percent coverage at the elementary stage and provides school meals to about 1.8 millions children everyday. Andhra Pradesh provides school meals to about one million children and Mysore has recently started a programme for feeding 5, 00,000 children. School milk is provided to one million children in Rajasthan and the figure 5,00,000 has been proposed to be increased to one million very shortly, in Punjab. Smaller programmes are in operation in Madhya Pradesh and Maharashtra.

In order to assist the development of the programme still further, the Government of India has approved since 1962-63, a centrally-sponsored scheme of grants-in-aid to State Governments. Under this scheme, assistance is offered to State Governments to the extent of one-third of the total expenditure incurred by them on school feeding programmes. It is estimated that by the end of the *Third Plan* about 10 to 12 million children might have been covered by the school meal programme.

35.8 Right Posture

One of the common defects to be seen among our pupils is that they generally do not have the right posture. It is not uncommon that we meet with cramped chests, abnormal spine curvatures and so on. The teaching of correct posture is an important thing. Incorrect posture causes fatigue, fatigue in its turn leads to incorrect posture - a vicious circle. With right posture, the body is in a position of greatest efficiency, capable of greater activity, with a minimum expenditure of effort. Kruger says that it is evident that the body, being a jointed structure, can be held erect with a minimum of energy expenditure only if all its parts are in proper alignment. It follows that efficient use can be made of the body only when its parts are properly balanced; the muscles then serve their normal functions, i.e. to move bones that are in balanced relationship. When the parts of the body are in equilibrium, the weights of the head and trunk are balanced upon the vertebral column and transferred through pelvic girdle and legs to the feet. If any part of the body is out of its natural alignment, more muscular energy needs to be expanded to maintain the position of the body. Body energy used in this way is wasted energy. The weight of the body should be born by the bones, not by the muscles.

So, very earnest attempts should be made by all teachers to correct the posture of the pupils. There should be a daily lesson by the physical teacher for this purpose. Individual corrective exercises can help a lot in correcting lightly uneven shoulder levels and slight lateral curvatures. The teacher should make the pupils know that good posture is that accustomed position which enables the body to function efficiently. Of course, this definition includes the hygienic, aesthetic and psychological factors as the body would not be a thoroughly efficient unit unless it were also graceful in movement, and organically effective. For this purpose all the teachers, the physical education teacher and the medical officer must cooperate in order to achieve the best results.

35.9 Recreation

Recreation is a fundamental human need. It is a broader term than physical education, and includes, in addition to sports, games and rhythmic, any activity in which an individual participates for the pleasure of participation. A recreational activity is one in which participation is voluntary and spontaneous and does not require stimulation or reward outside the activity itself.

"Leisure" may be regarded as the genus of which 'Recreation' is a species. C.O. Burns has defined leisure so aptly as the "seed plot of civilisation" and as "the germinate time for art and philosophy." He claims that "Civilisation" may depend for its roots upon the way in which work is done but it depends for its finest flower upon the use of leisure.

The primary purpose of recreation is to "recreate" oneself in body, mind, and spirit; and it is with that object in view that we should judge the use to which a person puts his leisure. Even a cursory study of the present day classroom work would indicate the need for the rest so that the tired body, the jaded nerves, and the dulled spirits can be restored their original self and revitalised.

Thus, recreation is no longer considered to be one of the superficialities of life but is one of the most essential for the development of health, well-rounded and balanced personalities. It is a way of enriching one's leisure time with educational and cultural contents. It is not an escape from the toil of education into the emptiness of a vocation, but vitalizing elements in the process of education itself.

Recreation, by its very nature, is a sphere of freedom and free choice. It is an essential antidote to the compulsions, restrictions, and dullness and of monotony, so characteristic of the present day school life. "Recreation" as Slavson writes "is not a matter of motion, but rather of emotion, it is a personal response, a psychological reaction, an attitude, an approach, a way of life."

The significance of education and its immense possibilities to the youths are best understood when education and recreation are united and not when separated. In the words of L. P. Jacks, "the education which is not also recreation is maimed, incomplete, half done thing. The recreation which is not also education has no recreational value."

A good recreational school programme may consist of the following:

(1) The developing of life-long hobbies and interests.

(2) The cultivation of the habit and the pleasure of reading good books.

(3) The pursuit of the joys of outdoors living through camping, hiking, gardening, etc.

(4) The exposure to rhythm in all its forms – music, folk, and classical dancing, singing, poetry.
(5) The development of an appreciation of the arts.
(6) The development of skill that gives satisfaction in crafts.
(7) The pleasure of social recreation.
(8) The enjoyment of sports.
(9) The pleasures that come through water activities.
(10) The acquiring of the habit of rest, relaxation, and meditation.

Dr. Edgren comprises the entire programme of recreational activities in four significant phrases as "Doing things," "Making things," "Acquiring thing," and "Learning things." Choice of any of the recreational activities – either active or passive, may depend on the interest, sex, age, race, intelligence, and individual aptitude.

A programme of recreation is necessary for the health of the individual. It can promote the health of the individual because it is all the year round, it is for everyone, it includes everything, it is operated everywhere. Education and recreation must go side by side.

35.10 Safety Education

"Accidents are like chronic diseases in that they cause death, may require hospitalisation, may result in invalidation, and may give rise to loss of time from work." That is the reason why some sort of safety education should be imparted in the school. It is believed that accident rates can be reduced – whether it be in the home, in the school, in industry or in other areas of activity – provided the children are taught in the school on these lines. Safety education should form a part of the courses of study in health education.

Accidents occur in four kinds of environments – on the job, in public places including schools, at home, and in motor vehicles.

(a) Causes of accidents: **-** There are a number of causes responsible for most of the accidents:

(1) Most accidents occur because people fail to take the necessary precautions to protect themselves.
(2) Accidents may result from a lack of knowledge about the use of machines and gadgets that may be potentially dangerous. People may lack sufficient skill in some physical activity such as athletic sport or in the use of some piece of machinery.
(3) Many accidents are caused by physical factors that affect our skills such as faulty vision, poor hearing, fatigue, and muscular weakness; emotional strain, also becomes responsible for accidents.
(4) Poor attitudes account for a large percentage of accidents. People disregard safety regulations, they take chances, they believe that luck is with them. Or they do not care to practice the 'golden rule' – 'safety first.'
(5) Accidents result from violations of rules, regulations, and procedures. They do not "just happen."

In short, lack of information, poor skills, and faulty attitudes contribute to the behaviours and practices that cause accidents. This fact makes it necessary that we should depend considerably on education and training in order to improve behaviour.

(b) Basic Principles of Safety Education: **-** The following principles may serve as a guide for the development of a safety education programme:

(1) Safety education should be the responsibility of society and should be consistent with our best understanding of human growth and the development of society.
(2) The school should provide leadership in promoting safe living.
(3) Safety instruction should be an integral part of the school programme and

should further develop understanding attitudes, values, skills, habits, and appreciations which will assist the learner in meeting the responsibility of safe-living in today's world.

(4) Safety education should develop a continuous awareness of the value of human life and the physical well-being of individuals.

(5) Safety education should be continuous and contribute to the enrichment of all areas of living.

(c) The Programme of Safety Education: **-** In middle and higher secondary school, safety education should be taught as an important unit in health education. Children at this age are increasingly interested in adventure. They participate in various youth organisations such as Boy Scouts, Girl Guiding and other athletics. They need to be given greater understanding about the causes of accidents and how to prevent them.

Safety education can be correlated and integrated with a number of school subjects like sciences, social studies, crafts, etc.

(d) Methods of Teaching Safety: **-** The following methods for imparting safety education may prove useful:

(1) Safety discussion directly related to the use of equipment and material in certain courses such as science laboratories, crafts, and workshop.

(2) Films on safety may be shown.

(3) Lectures by non-school people, e.g. firemen, policemen, traffic engineers may be arranged.

(4) Safety school patrols inside and outside the school building can help.

(5) Bulletin board displays of posters and pictures on safety can attract attention.

(6) Dramatisation of safety lessons and of safety plays.

(7) Library and leisure-time reading of pamphlets and booklets on safety.

Objective Type Questions

Multiple Choice Questions (Tick ✓ the right option)

(1) English word "Health" was used for condition of being

(a) Hale

(b) Hil

(c) Hili

(d) Hala

(2) The primary purpose of recreation is to "recreate" oneself in

(a) Body

(b) Mind

(c) Spirit

(d) All of the above

Fill in the blanks

(1) __________ Should be continues and contribute to the enrichment of al areas of living [Safety Education]

(2) __________ health is that highest state of healthiness which can be achieved by individual [Optimum]

Important Questions

1. Discuss the responsibility and role of the school in health education.

2. What do you mean by school health programme? Elaborate in detail.
3. State the main aspects of health education. How can the school promote healthful living?
4. Discuss the various aspects of health education.
5. Study the methods of imparting health education in your area. Suggest improvements.
6. Discuss the functions and responsibilities of teaching regarding health education.
7. Write an essay on nutrition.
8. Suggest the measures for developing right posture among school children.
9. Suggest a good programme of recreation for a secondary school.
   "A sound mind can only be there in a sound body." Comment.

36

The School Physical Education Programme

History of the human race reveals that all human societies had arranged physical training or physical education in some way or the other. This education might be arranged or in sudden form. In that time, the arranged physical education was related with hunting and/or learning art of battle. The physical education which was to be provided was related with games and works. For the first time the Greeks felt the need of proper programmes of physical education and they provided important physical education in the educational programmes. In the 19th century, when German, Sweden, and other European nations developed their educational systems, then they worked as the background for need of organised physical education. Since this time, the demand of organised physical education increased day-by-day. But this demand was supported by two facts as given below:-

(1) In the context of self-development as it is human nature.

(2) Changed situations of human existence in machine age.

36.1 Meaning of Physical Education

Generally, the meaning of physical education is taken from development of physical organs (parts of body). But this view is very narrow. In it physical education is limited to "Construction of Body" only. But, physical education is not limited to "Body Building." It is source of good citizenship or promotion of health. Here the meaning of health is the physical and mental, both kinds of health. In fact, "Physical education is that phase of the whole process of education which is concerned with vigorous muscular activities and related responses, and with the modification of the individual resultant from these responses." Thus, we can say that physical education is the process or that part of plan of developing an individual wholly.

36.2 Importance of Physical Education

Physical education is closely related to the school health programme because health is not merely freedom from disease. Health must be positive. It must help one to *live best and serve most*. Physical aspect cannot be separated from the intellectual and moral aspects of education. The physical education has important potentials for helping children learn to communicate, to develop, and maintain a state of fitness, to acquire physical skills which will last. To educate a man, you must get round him in his entirety, mind, and body. Soul and character are to be regarded as an inseparable unit; it is only by the equal and continuous development of every part of the body that the battle of life will be fought with success. Spencer has also said: "To be a good animal is the first requisite to success in life, and to be a nation of good animals is the first condition to national prosperity." The oft-quoted precept - a sound mind in a sound body - is as true today as it was two millenniums ago. Man, in fact, is one being and cannot be educated in artificial segments.

His mental and moral nature is interlocked with his physical well-being.

Physical education contributes not only to physical fitness but also to physical efficiency, mental alertness, and the development of certain qualities like perseverance, team spirit, leadership, and obedience to rules, moderation in victory and balance in defeat.

36.3 The Background

The culture of any given country has always been reflected in the physical activities of its people. The activities of early cavemen were throwing stones, using clubs, and hunting and fishing; their primary object was *survival*. The Greeks participated in activities which later led to the Olympic Games. They extolled the philosophy of "a sound mind in a sound body." In Rome, spectator sports were conducted in which men versus beasts and chariot races entertained the crowds.

India is old in thought and deed. Throughout her long history she has stressed the harmonious development of soul, mind, and body. The Vedic and the Epic age gave considerable prominence to physical culture. Kalidas prescribed a sound body as a pre-requisite for a 'dharmic' life. In the Universities of Nalanda, Vikramashila, and Vallabhi, swimming and wrestling, shooting arrows, swordsmanship and breathing exercises were considered as essential.

Physical education was not in a satisfactory condition at the advent of the Europeans in the country. No systematic instruction was given.

In 1875, MacLaren's system of gymnastics was introduced in the school curriculum in Madras. Some forms of drill, physical training, and games were prescribed in some schools. Well-trained teachers were not available, so the work was entrusted to ex-army personnel or gymnasts. The most deplorable fact was that these drills were unrelated to school curriculum and were carried out outside the school hours and that too when convenience permitted it and facilities could be had without much trouble.

Things slowly began to change when educationalists realised the value of team games and the emphasis shifted from formal drill to games like football, cricket, hockey, tennis, track and field athletics. As the British population increased in India, games like golf, boating, swimming, etc. gained ground amongst the public; but the situation in the schools remained unchanged till the year 1920.

Scientific and physical education in India started with the beginning of a training centre in Madras under the auspices of the Y.M.C.A. With the increasing attention given to physical fitness, the need for qualified teachers increased. Several colleges for the purpose were started. A National College of Physical Education was established at Gwalior in 1957 to impart a three-year course in the subject leading to a Bachelor's degree and later on, to provide facilities for advanced study and research.

In 1959-60, an important programme – National Physical Efficiency Drive was started to activate interest in physical fitness throughout the country and to arouse the enthusiasm of the people for high standards of physical efficiency and achievement.

To promote the cause of physical education certain programmes have been started by the Centre: (1) Scholarship for specialisation in indigenous physical education activities; (2) grants-in-aid to *Vyaymashalas* and *Akharas* for purchase of equipment and library books at 75 percent of the approved expenditure; (3) assistance to the promotion of yogic exercises; and (4) preparation of model syllabuses for physical education programmes for boys and girls from the primary to the higher secondary stage.

A significant step has been taken for improving games and sports. National Institute of Sports was set up at Patiala with the primary object of producing first class coaches. These coaches, on completion of their training at the institute, would work at the national and state level, and coach young athletes and sportsmen in schools and colleges.

Sports activities in India are controlled by the national sports federations constituted for different games. Grants are given to national sports federations and national associations to encourage them to participate in international events, to invite foreign teams to play in India, to hold competitions for championships and to arrange coaching camps for talented players.

36.4 Present Position of Physical Education in India

The present position of physical education is not at all satisfactory. Our performances in international sports competitions is, as we are all aware, rather disappointing. The overall calculations indicate that either our standards are going or those of the other countries have improved. In 1954, during the second Asian Games at Manila, India's positions dropped down from 2nd to 4th. In the third Asian Games held at Tokyo, we were 7th. Since 1920, the year of our participation in the World Olympics, we have secured only one individual medal and that too, a bronze one in wrestling. We maintained supremacy in hockey in the Olympics consecutively for 32 years but in 1960 we lost that place too.

Most of the players, who have represented India in international competitions, have, however, been from services, police, railways, and other organisations. One may well ask what has been the role of students - our youth - in such competitions.

There is a growing awareness of our low standards in sports at both the school and college level. Some of the causes responsible for this state of affairs are:

(1) ***Low economic level:*** - Since the economic level of our people is still very low, the majority of our students are under-nourished and, therefore, physically not strong enough to withstand the strain of physical activity. So they do not participate in sports.

(2) ***Lack of financial and technical resources:*** - The financial resources in schools are very much limited. Most of our rural and urban schools do not have any playgrounds at all. Games are still considered to be and are practiced as an out-of-school activity in a haphazard and ill-organised way. Up-to-date adequate equipment for games and sports is not available.

(3) ***No provision in the time-table:*** - The time-tables of school do not have proper provision for games and sports. Indeed, in some cases none whatsoever it is still considered an optional co-curricular activity. It is not generally realised that games and sports have a vital contributing value towards the general organisation of the curriculum, aiming at the total development of the personality of the student. Quite recently games and sports have become highly specialised activities. They have assumed a scientific character and sportsmen are no longer products of a natural growth. It is the responsibility of educational institutions to contribute towards his pre-planned development of sports by making ample provision for training.

(4) ***General apathy of the teacher towards sports:*** - It is a sad fact that teachers have a positively negative attitude towards sports. Leave aside taking keen interest in sports, most of the teachers are quite unconcerned about what happens in this sphere. They still maintain that a good sportsman cannot be a good student. A few students are encouraged - that too in order to win distinctions in competitions. There is a complete absence of mass participation in games and sports.

(5) ***Lack of proper facilities for sportsmen:*** - Sportsmen are not given the same place of prestige and dignity, which the academically bright students get. With the result many students do not come in the field.

(6) ***Lack of encouragement for girls:*** - In our country we do not seem to realise that a

girl, who participates in sports today will be an interested mother of tomorrow. In Western countries, girls have equal opportunities of participation with the boys. But so far enough opportunities are not given to girls in our country.

The present position has been summarised in the University Education Commission's Report, which states, "We may say there are insufficient trained personnel, dearth of playgrounds and equipment, poverty of students, absence of organisation, poor types of programme, small variety of games conflict with academic work, and inconvenience of time."

36.5 Aims of Physical Education

The aim of physical education is not to produce those who are masses of brawn and muscle, but little else. Nor it is to produce experts in various branches of sports and athletics. The aim of this part of education which is concerned with the body is to devote its share in producing an integrated and harmoniously developed personality. The aim is to ensure that the body is given its due share of attention which it needs so that it can play a *positive part* in the life of the individual, a part without which life would be dwarfed, and comparatively restricted and ineffective.

Jackson R. Sharman states:

"The aim of physical education is to influence the experiences of persons to the extent that each individual within the limits of his capacity may be helped to adjust successfully to society, to increase and improve his wants and to develop the ability to satisfy his wants, of course only those wants that can be satisfied without annoying or trespassing the rights of others."

Physical activities harden the body and steel the soul against hardships.

The physical education is not only a health insurance but a valuable aid to health also. It not only develops physique but promotes fine adjustment between physical and mental health. It gives children training for good citizenship.

36.6 The Objectives of Physical Education

The objectives of physical education, particularly suited for India, are:

1. Development of organic fitness;
2. Development of neuro-muscular skills and
3. Development of character and personality.

1. ***Development of organic fitness:*** This is dependent upon a wide selection of activities arising out of the inherent interest of the participants, and so conducted that the normal functions of the body are developed and improved.
2. ***Development of neuro-muscular skills:*** The development of skills in a large variety of physical activities makes it possible for individuals and groups to obtain satisfaction and happiness in a variety of ways during leisure time. Many people are unhappy and maladjusted because they are physically illiterate and do not know how to enjoy their free time. Possession of skills in naturalized forms of individual and group play activities enables people to give wholesome expression to innate desires and interests.
3. ***Development of character and personality:*** Physical activities that give opportunity for self-expression and self-improvement are useful in developing character and personality. The relationships and experience of cooperation and competition on the athletic field call for decisions very similar to those which have to be made in everyday life. Leaders with moral purpose will make it possible for their athletics to act and decide in the light of values and consequence, and will relate the idea of sportsmanship as practiced on the laying field with the desirability of carrying it over into all relationships with their fellow-men.

Should Physical Education and Games be Compulsory?

It appears quite strange that play should be made compulsory. But in our country, it is only *compulsory that works*. We want our young men and women to take an intelligent personal interest in their physical welfare. At present, they have no knowledge of how to take care of their body, neither are they in the daily habit of exercising their body because this habit has not been ingrained in them by constant enforced practice in their earlier years. Consequently they have no interest in their physical development, health, and welfare. All young men and women should leave the university physically well-equipped for their leisure. Nothing but compulsion will give them this equipment. Punjab has made physical education and games a compulsory part of the school curriculum.

36.7 Guiding Principles for Designing a Satisfactory Programme of Physical Education

The Indian Education Commission 1964-66 outlined the following principles for designing a satisfactory programme of physical education.

1) The physical education programme should be planned for desirable outcomes keeping in mind the interests and capacity of the participants.
2) The traditional forms of play and physical activities that have developed in our country should receive due emphasis in the programme.
3) The activities promoted should develop in each child a sense of personal worth and pride.
4) A sense of sharing responsibility in a spirit of democratic cooperation should grow from experience on play ground and also in the gymnasium.
5) The programme offered should supplement other programmes of education and not duplicate them.
6) The programme should be within our financial means.
7) The programme should reach all rather than a selected few.
8) Special instruction and coaching should be provided for students with talent and special aptitude.

36.8 Physical Education in Secondary Schools

The Secondary School programme should provide activities that make for organic and structural development, provide opportunity for self-expression, and are meaningful, are enjoyed by the participants, and provide situations that encourage social development

The adolescent in the Secondary School desires to intimate the activities of the adults and he should be given sports, games, and athletics in their standard form. Skills learnt earlier should be perfected through guidance and practice. It is an age when boys and girls desire excellence and the physical education syllabus must include techniques for good performance.

The following items can constitute the scope of Secondary School Physical Education:

(i) Free Play.
(ii) Organised Games.
(iii) Self-testing Activities.
(iv) Dancing and Music.
(v) Basic Skills.
(vi) Athletics.
(vii) Individual Corrective Exerçises.

(i) ***Free Play:*** Free play at the Secondary School level is mostly based on skill and technique rather than random running, jumping and climbing activities of the primary group.

(ii) ***Organised Games:*** Organised games for the Secondary School may include tag games, relay games, basket ball, football, hockey, tennis and volleyball. These games, when under wise guidance and

leadership, act as one of the best citizenship laboratories we possess.

(iii) ***Self-testing Activities:*** Self-testing activities are those that allow for a self-assessment to be made in terms of win or lose, pass or fail, success or failure, or time and distance standards. Activities like diving, track and field athletics are self-testing activities.

(iv) ***Dancing and Music:*** Dancing and music are also very effective forms of exercise. Dancing especially promotes organic fitness, suppleness, and neuro-muscular coordination. It fosters desirable social attitudes. It is not competitive but cooperative. It affords to be highly recreational. Dancing is one of the best expressions of the activity needs of youth. Exercise for exercise's sake is generally rather meaningless and futile, but when such movements are incorporated into the pattern of a dance, they become meaningful and worthwhile.

It is really a very happy sign that music is being given an important place in the recent syllabus for primary schools. All activity is rhythm, while music can be depicted, expressed, and portrayed in action. If the motion is made in an aimless way it is relatively useless. So music can make dancing meaningful. Music has a vital place in physical education apart from the usual rhythmic activities. It can be used to give rhythm to pyramid building, spring-board, vaulting, tumbling, fencing drill, etc. It has its place where it only gives "atmosphere" to an activity in demonstrations. Music at all times must be appropriate to the activity.

(v) ***Basic Skills:*** Basic skills are developed not in one day or in one year. These are developed by continuous efforts and guidance.

(vi) ***Athletics:*** Athletics occupy an important place in the Secondary School Physical Education programme. Some sort of instruction in theory is also essential.

(vii) ***Individual Corrective Exercises:*** Individual corrective exercises are necessary for the correction of postural defects.

36.9 The Various Aspects of a Physical Education Programme

There are four aspects of a physical education programme: classroom programme, the adapted programme, the intra-mural programme, and the inter-scholastic athletic programme.

Classroom Programme Physical Education: This phase of the educational programmes is instructional in nature and is usually required of all students. It includes a variety of activities such as team games, individual games, dance, and gymnastics.

The Adapted Physical Education Programme: There are certain pupils in a school who have special needs and limitations. Such pupils include those with faulty body mechanics, nutrition disturbances such as over and underweight, weak and flat feet, menstrual disorders, nervous instability, poor physical fitness, and crippling conditions. With the cooperation of the medical staff, provision can be made for instruction through both regular physical education classwork and through special classes.

Secondary School Physical Education Programme

Classroom Programme	The Adapted Physical Education Programme	Intra-Mural Athletics Programme	Inter-Scholastic Athletics Programme

Intra-Mural Athletics Programme: This phase of the school physical education programme comprises competitive tournaments and sports days. Included is a wide variety of activities based on the needs and interests of students. It is usually conducted during out-of-class hours. It may be either voluntary in nature as required by all students; ideally, it should be *available* at the secondary level and above.

Inter-Scholastic Athletics Programme: This phase of the physical education programme is voluntary in nature and is conducted during out-of-school hours. It should be organised with the needs and interests of students in mind. A wide variety of activities are included for both boys and girls of which the more common ones are football, basket ball, base ball, track, hockey, swimming, and tennis.

In an ideal physical education programme, the required programme develops skills and interests that can be further utilised in the intra-mural programme. The latter in turn can be a source of the students who are found to be specially qualified for intra-scholastic athletics.

A programme of physical education must have three features: (1) It should be educative. (2) It should be protective. (3) It should be developed. The protective side of the programme envisages restricted activities, corrective and remedial classes for those who need them. The restricted and reconstructive work cannot possibly be undertaken by physical educationists without the use of formal exercise. This, of course, has to be undertaken in consultation with a medical expert. Restricted programme is intended for students who are physically handicapped either permanently or temporarily. Dr. W.L. Hughes is of the opinion that students having the following type of defects require the restricted programme.

Digestive disturbances,
Fatigue, particularly chronic fatigue,
Glandular disturbances,
Heart conditions, functional and organic disturbances,
Hernia cases,
Infantile paralysis,
Injuries – amputations and other permanent injuries and convalescent accident cases,
Kidney disorders,
Malnutrition,
Menstrual disturbances of a severe nature,
Nervous disorders of a serious type,
Post-operation cases,
Postural deformities of a serious nature.

The work has to be on the basis of the physical and medical examination of the student and it has to be individual, restricted, corrective, therapeutic, medical or a combination of all these.

36.10 Activities in a Programme of Physical Education

Physical education necessarily uses bodily activities for its programme and includes the following:

1. Activities which use the big muscles and further the development for the fundamental racial skills of walking, running, jumping, throwing, climbing, hanging, etc. Among these are:
   (a) Activities in which individuals alone can take part such as athletics, games like tennis hand ball, etc.
   (b) Activities both indigenous and foreign in which groups alone can take part such as simple relays, major games like cricket, hockey, football, kho-kho, etc.
2. Activities, which though not exactly of the racial type, contribute to growth and development and have an appeal because of their intrinsic values. Among these are:
   (a) Water activities like swimming, boating, obtaining, water games, etc.
   (b) Stunts and self-testing activities such as tumbling, pyramid building, exercises on gymnastic apparatus, etc.
3. Rhythmic activities such as folk dances, classical dances, gymnastic dances, etc.

4. Combative and defensive activities like wrestling, boxing, etc.
5. Outing activities like hiking and camping.

The overriding factor in the selection of activities must be their educational possibilities in an integrated scheme of General Education to create a national vitality based on character value and not mere physical stamina that comes out of exercise and perspiration.

36.11 Essentials of a Physical Education Programme

For any programme of physical education to go on smoothly, certain essentials must be provided:

1. *Playground facilities:* The Central Advisory Board of Physical Education for Secondary Schools has recommended the following standard of space requirements for playgrounds.
   - (i) 160 pupils – 2 to 3 acres;
   - (ii) 320 pupils – 3 to 4 acres; and
   - (iii) 480 pupils – 6 to 7 acres.

   The ground should be even and level, and should be well-laid out with various play fields, pitching and courts. The boundary lines and fixtures should be kept in good shape.
2. *Gymnasium:* Every secondary school should have a gymnasium attached to it. This should be located conveniently near the school building and the playground. The building should have a hall of about 60 ft. by 30 ft. with a 15 to 20 ft. high ceiling. The floor should be wooden. There should also be attached rooms for storing equipment, medical inspection, first-aid service, and corrective work, the physical education office. Water supply and sanitary facilities should be conveniently available.

   The hall can be used in all seasons. It will ensure the regularity of games throughout the year.
3. *Equipment:* Equipment – adequate and good – is another essential of a good programme of physical education. Available grounds and funds will determine the quantity of equipment needed. There should be sufficient equipment for simultaneous practice by a large group of children. In certain games, individual equipment is required, such as clubs, wands, dumbbells, hockey sticks, etc. It is necessary that sufficient numbers of pieces are available to engage all pupils of a class simultaneously.
4. *Teachers:* It is recognised that good leadership is the most important ingredient in teaching physical education. There should be qualified men and women teachers to give instruction in games. In addition to these physical education teachers, it is necessary that all teachers should share this burden. All teachers or at least those below the age of 40 should actively participate in many of the activities of physical education and thus make it a living part of the total school programme instead of being a side issue entrusted to an isolated member of the staff.

   For the successful functioning of these activities, it is necessary that a few selected students are given special training in leadership. They can prove very useful in demonstrating the activities for their fellow students.
5. *Time:* Programme of physical education is to be arranged in such a manner that every student in the school does get some time, some space, and some equipment for playing. The programme schedule should be clear and known to every one so that every one is in his place.

36.12 The Organisation of Physical Education and Health Education

Schools are the furnaces where the future manhood is moulded. They can play a vital role provided the programmes are well-planned and well-organised.

In planning the organisation for an institution, the education significance should never be lost sight of. Universal education is the order of the day and the criteria for physical education must necessarily be on the pattern of general education.

Buck's Guiding Principles for Organising Physical Education

(1) Physical activity is a biological necessity for everybody. Therefore, there must be such a scheme for organisation as will permit 100 % of pupils to participate.

(2) Physical activity is a daily necessity. The time-table should be so organised that *all* may have physical education periods *daily*.

(3) People do not have the same strength, endurance, or skill. Physical education must be organised to cater to physical capacities and needs.

(4) People do not have the same interests. Physical education must be organised to cater to various wholesome interests.

(5) There are various characteristics that must be kept in mind when organising various groups.

(6) Institutions do not have the same facilities, equipment, play-areas, or budget.

(7) The natural activities are the ones to which persons most readily respond.

(8) Physical education can influence or educate the whole man. It should be so organised and administered that this is possible.

(9) People demand physical recreation after they have finished with school or college. The organisation and administration must, therefore, plan for training in activities which have carry-over values.

(10) Participants desire satisfaction and benefit from physical activities when the time allotment is proper.

(11) The human race evolved through a great variety of activities. Programmes must contain a great variety, must be comprehensive to satisfy and to preserve and develop skills.

(12) All persons require and are deserving of equal attention. Organise so that a sound foundation is laid by means of a good general programme for all so that the representative teams and star athletes, do not receive all the attention, but only their share.

(13) If pupils are to perform skillfully and gracefully in games. There must be periods for teaching or coaching in the fundamental skills of the game and in the team work and ethics of the game.

(14) Proper organisation and administration of physical education requires also careful attention to all hygiene and sanitary measures.

(15) An integration of Physical Education, Health Education, and Recreation under one administrative head is essential.

36.13 Improving Physical Education

1. ***Schools are the preparation grounds for the future world athletes:*** We need to start with children in schools to lay the foundations of building world champions. By the time the child leaves the school he should be proficient in the fundamental skills of some games, which should improve and further develop during his university years.
2. ***Provision of proper play fields and equipment:*** The states and the public bodies should take steps to provide every school with a playground. School without a playground has no right to exist. Enough equipment must be available to the schools.
3. ***Provision of trained coaches:*** A trained coach is the heart and soul of any programme of physical education and,

therefore, should be made available to schools. Coaching camps should be held by the National Sports Federations. All these coaching schemes should realise that their potential champions are hidden in schools.

4. ***Provision of funds:*** The sports funds in schools should be strictly utilised for the organisation and improvement of games and sports. Liberal *ad hoc* recurring grants should be given by the States and the Central Government.
5. ***Provision of proper nourishment:*** Proper nourishment should be provided to the athletes. Some athletes are very keen and promising but poor. It is essential that some arrangement to supply the extra nourishing food is made at least to a few of these.
6. ***Theoretical instruction:*** Instruction in regard to scientific-basis for every sport may be given through theoretical lectures on diet, technique, and exercises with the help of audio-visual aids, like films and film strips.
7. ***Provision of competitions:*** Competitions help to improve standards in sports. School should organise Inter-Class, Inter-Group, Inter-State and National competitions. Sports and sports festivals can also help.
8. ***Better interpretation to parents,*** administrators, teachers, and community leaders of the contributions physical education can make to the lives of boys and girls as they grow towards maturity.
9. ***Employment of more qualified specialists in*** physical education either to work with classroom teachers or to do the day by day teaching of physical education.
10. ***Allocation of adequate time for physical education:*** There is agreement that the minimum daily instructional period should be at least thirty minutes in length. Two periods of 15-20 minutes are recommended for primary grades. In addition, there should be periods of free or supervised play as well as integration of physical education activities with other phases of the curriculum. Children who are in normal physical condition need two to four hours of vigorous activity each day.
11. ***Designing of a scientific programme of physical education:*** A number of schemes like the National Plan of Physical Education, the National Discipline Scheme, and the Auxiliary Cadet Corps are going on at present. A special committee appointed by the Ministry of Education under the chairmanship of Dr. H. N. Kunzru recommended that an integrated scheme with a syllabus selecting the best features of each should be evolved. The committee tried to bring about a compromise between the claims made by the enthusiasts of different schemes and the result is a mixed programme of physical education called the National Fitness Corps. This compromise scheme has provoked a good deal of criticism. The Indian Education Commission-1964-66, suggested that the matter should be re-examined and a satisfactory programme should be designed.
12. ***There should be specialised staff in Physical Education at the district level to stimulus, help and guide the instructors in physical education in schools.***
13. There should be special inspectorates for physical education manned by experts who can make their expertise available to field officers, teachers, and principles.

Objective Type Questions

Multiple Choice Questions (Tick ✔ the right option)

(1) Physical education is closely related to the
- (a) School health Programme
- (b) School work
- (c) Human Needs
- (d) Self development

(2) A National College of physical education was established at Gwalior in
- (a) 1952
- (b) 1957
- (c) 1960
- (d) 1962

Fill in the blanks

(1) ______________ activity is a biological necessity for everybody [Physical]

(2) ______________ help to improve standards in sports [Competitions]

Important Questions

1. Discuss the objectives of physical education. How far are those objectives the same as those of general education?

2. What are the guiding factors in planning a programme of physical education?

3. What facilities are required to make physical education successful in India?

4. Discuss the aims and objectives of physical education programme. Should physical education be made compulsory?

5. What are the different aspects of a physical education programme? What place would you give to Intra-mural and Inter-scholastic athletics programme in it?

6. Suggest a list of activities in a programme of physical education.

7. What are the essentials of physical education programme?

8. Give some suggestions for improving physical education programme in your state.

9. Discuss the principles of organisation of physical education programme in a secondary school.

37

Yoga for Educational Institutions

Before I deal with yoga and its Need in Educational Institutions, let me define Yoga and education as I feel it.

For me yoga is character building. Each one of us develop habits and behaviors without giving a thought to them whether. They integrate or disintegrate. Yoga is the reconditioning of the behaviour pattern in each of us ensuring unity and harmony in each and every cell of our body, poise and calmness in the mind and serenity in the self. This is the best personality one likes to possess wherein, he not only lives within himself in perfect maturity, clarity and peace but also with society.

37.1 What is Education?

This word 'education' is derived from the Latin 'educate' meaning 'to educe', 'draw forth' or 'unfold' the latent or potential, i.e. to develop the talents and gifts of an individual. In short it is the drawing out of the best qualities of a person. Though the approaches of both are identical, education views objectively and Yoga subjectively, hence, the need of Yoga in educational Institutions.

We are all endowed, in our individual ways, with innate capacities which need to be unfolded. Some of us have a keen sense of truth or justice, of beauty of loyalty. Some of us on the other hand may be extremely intelligent but lazy, indifferent, or pleasure loving; other may lie, cheat and remain selfish.

It is the task of good educationist to help his students to realize their strength as well as their weaknesses; to contribute to their growth and development on the one hand and to help them to eradicate their weakness on the other. Yogic discipline is on excellent aid in such an education for it attempts to remedy the defects and to cultivate the good in oneself. It brings discipline into the life of the student, be it at the level of the physical the mental or the spiritual, and makes him aware of his strength as well as his weakness.

Unfortunately nowadays, instructions given in educational institutions to enable a student to pass an examination are often confused with the term "education", which is also mistaken for a license to obtain employment and to earn one's livelihood. Of course, one cannot underestimate the need to earn a living, but does man live by bread alone? Is it not his duty to cultivate his own personality too? He must learn to understand his own physical and mental well-being so as to be perfectly conscious of his words, thoughts and actions.

37.2 Does Yoga help one to build up such qualities?

With my vast experience in daily practice and teaching of Yoga. I say without the slightest hesitation that yoga plays a positive role in the development of an individual as an integrated person. The daily practice of Yoga helps one to achieve a perfect understaning of the intellect of the body, for the body has its own intellect. This knowledge of the working of one's own body is based on direct experience.

For example: The brain may be sure of being able to perform Shirshasana (head balance). By this I mean that we may know the technique of doing Shirshasana to such on extent that we feel confident that we will be able to do it. But when it comes to the actual performance of the asana, one realizes that one has to understand the use of the arms, the neck, the correct position of the spine and how it supports the legs, how the legs are to be stretched, where exactly the weight should be and how one should balance by distributing the weight on to the various parts of the body and without putting a strain on the arms or the neck. In this way one gradually masters the art of keeping the body energy in a "zero" position, i.e. observing that the energy of the body is not dissipated but is adjusted and retained within the body.

By this training one learns what the body intellect is and what direct perception means. This is the factual knowledge or knowledge based on fact, as the body brings to the attention of the brain a new light, a new experience of the intellect of the body and teaches it to adjust or adapt itself.

This pliability of the intellect and its capacity to learn from new experience leads one to true-education as distinct from an education which depends upon information gleaned from books and lecture notes.

37.3 Importance of Yoga

(1) Yoga is a subject that has to be practiced and experienced, not merely discussed or argued about. Even if one wants to discuss it or argue about it, one has to experience it. What one experiences is direct knowledge which makes discussion possible. If the experience does not co-ordinate with the mental image (the thinking about of the experience), then either the experience is insufficient or the thinking over of the experience is not practiced. When both tally, that is factual or direct knowledge that is yoga.

(2) Through the practice of yoga one attains not only physical well-being or "toning" of the body, but emotional stability and clarity in the intellect also. Hence Yoga is an art which disciplines and develops the body, the emotions and the intellectual faculties, its purpose being to revive man.

(3) It is a science, since it is a systematic study based on the principles so pithily expressed in the aphorisms of patanjali, and also in other books on yoga such as the Yoga Upanishads.

(4) It is a philosophy, as it studies the principles of right conduct and shows thereby the road to right living which has a backing of centuries of experience.

Eight Steps of Yoga: The path of right living is paved with eight steps.

(a) Yama
(b) Niyama
(c) Asana
(d) Pranayama
(e) Pratyahara
(f) Dharana
(g) Dhyana and,
(h) Samadhi

I shall attempt to describe each of these very briefly.

(a) Yama: Yama or social ethics is made up of the five commandments of harmlessness, truthfulness to all beings abstention from theft, from unchastity and from avarice. This is meant to bring under control the karmendriyas or the organs of action.

(b) Niyama: Niyama or persona ethics comprises the five rules of internal and external purity, contentment, fiery aspiration, spiritual reading and devotion to God. Thus an individual's daily activities with regards to personal hygiene, cleanliness not only in body but in thought and speech, were emphasized long ago in Indian philosophy.

Niyama is the art of disciplining the Jnanendriyas or the organs of perception. Constant striving for self improvement by study and devotion to one's duty and vocation were insisted upon. These principles which are termed as universal principles, are worthy of emulation by one and all, whether one is rich or poor, a man or a woman, old or young, and irrespective of time, place or circumstances.

(c) Asana: Then comes Asana or posture, tersely described by Patanjali as "Right poise, right attitude, right position" These Asanas were devised to develop the physical-psychological stability, good health, lightness and agility of body and mind. A perfect body is the only fit instrument for God to dwell in while performing the Asanas, one should use the body as a bow, Asana as the arrows and the self as target to experience the state of just being, without the dualities of body, mind and self but all three as one.

Nature has provided us with an excellent capital the body to build up vast resources. The moment the body is neglected, education suffers. When the student's health is impaired, he lags behind in his studies. The state pays the price in terms of the drop outs and the consequent waste of time, money and energy.

(d) Pranayama: Pranayama or breath control is the right control of the life force which consists mainly of the regulation and control of the breath. Combined with the practice of asanas, it keeps the body and the mind fit, Regular asana and Pranayama practice are essential to maintain the body system, the masculine system, the respiratory system, the circulatory system, the digestive system, the excretory system, the reproductive system and the glandular system in healthy state.

(e) Pratyahara: Pratyahara is concerned with the restraint of the senses. It is in fact an education of the senses. In Yoga there are techniques by which the senses are drawn to their source and thereby made free from desires. This gives mental stability which is essential for intellectual clarity, alertness, sharpness and agility. An alert and agile mind is free from tensions and can deal with a day's work with ease.

(f) Dharana, Dhyana and Samadhi: Only when the body and mind are strengthened and refined by the practice of the first five limbs of Yoga, is one considered ready for the remaining three steps.

(i) Dharana
(ii) Dhyana and
(iii) Samadhi

These, however, need not be introduced at school or college level, but an aspirant may pursue them for his own self enlightenment just as a graduate proceeds for post graduate studies in a subject of his choice. Just as special care is needed to enable a young sapling grow into a healthy great tree which can give fragrant fruits and flowers, so meticulous care is needed for moulding a young aspirant so that he can be an example and a guide to others.

The first five steps of yoga if cultivated with devotion will prepare the body, the mind and the intellect to serve as fit vehicles for spiritual growth which has to end with final absorption into the Infinite our true purpose and natural end.

As the tree roots, trunk, branches, leaves, bark, sapflower and fruit so yoga represents a tree with Yama as roots, Niyama as trunk, Asanas as branches and leaves. Does not Pranayama aerate the body with the breath of life? Pratyahara which prevents the energy of the senses from flowing outwards and turns it within enabling him to find true happiness as the bark prevents the twigs not be eaten by worms or insects. The sap is the Dharana in the form of intelligence which flows throughout the body. Dhyana is the flower which in turn ripens into fruit as Samadhi. As the natural termination of the tree is in the fragrance of fruits so also the sadhana of yoga starts with the roots, the body and leads to spiritual realization trhough the senses, the mind, the intellect, the consciousness and the conscience. As the tree cannot be separated from the root to the fruit, the various aspects of yoga cannot be separated from Yama to Samadhi. This is integral Yoga.

Our bodies and minds are like follow lands, lying untilled and unsowed. As a wise farmer (the kestrajna) ploughs the land, (the field) provides water and fertilizer, plants the best of seeds, carefully tends the crops and at the end reaps the best of harvest; for a student of yoga his body and mind are the field. With Yama and Niyama he ploughs the body; removes the weeds in the form of impurities and diseases by asana; waters it with energy through Pranayama and practices Pratyahara as fertilizer for right thinking and right action; tends the self as a crop to reach Samadhi, the harvest of peace and harmony. Thus he becomes a true owner of his sacred body.

I wish to emphasize yoga is a harmonious all round development of the student in body, mind and spirit, a well rounded personality with strong character. Only such students can build a healthy, just, honest, self reliant independent and therefore a healthy and happy world.

Objective Type Questions

Multiple Choice Questions (Tick ✓ the right option)

(1) Yoga is ____________ building

(a) character
(b) nature
(c) habits
(d) behaviour

(2) The word 'education' is derived from the ____________ word.

(a) English
(b) Hindi
(c) Latin
(d) Greek

Fill in the blanks

(1) The brain may be sure of being able to perform ____________ (Shirshasana)

(2) The path of right living is paved with ____________ steps (eight)

Important Questions

1. What do you understand by education?
2. What do you understand by Yoga?
3. Give the importance of Yoga?
4. Explain the five steps of Yoga?